IRONY AND MEANING
IN THE
HEBREW BIBLE

Indiana Studies in Biblical Literature
Herbert Marks, editor

IRONY AND MEANING IN THE HEBREW BIBLE

CAROLYN J. SHARP

INDIANA UNIVERSITY PRESS
Bloomington and Indianapolis

This book is a publication of

Indiana University Press
601 North Morton Street
Bloomington, IN 47404-3797 USA

http://iupress.indiana.edu

Telephone orders	800-842-6796
Fax orders	812-855-7931
Orders by e-mail	iuporder@indiana.edu

© 2009 by Carolyn J. Sharp

The paper used in this publication meets the minimum requirements
of American National Standard for Information Sciences—Permanence of
Paper for Printed Library Materials, ANSI Z39.48-1984.

Manufactured in the United States of America

Library of Congress Cataloging-in-Publication Data

Sharp, Carolyn J.
Irony and meaning in the Hebrew Bible / Carolyn J. Sharp.
p. cm.
Includes bibliographical references and index.
ISBN 978-0-253-35244-6 (cloth : alk. paper) 1. Irony in the Bible. 2. Bible.
O.T.—Criticism, interpretation, etc. I. Title.
BS1199.I7S53 2008
221.6'6—dc22
2008026280

1 2 3 4 5 14 13 12 11 10 09

for Leo

A man that looks on glass,
On it may stay his eye;
Or if he pleaseth, through it pass,
And then the heaven espy.
George Herbert

The kingfisher rises out of the black wave
like a blue flower, in his beak
he carries a silver leaf. I think this is
the prettiest world—so long as you don't mind
a little dying, how could there be a day in your whole life
that doesn't have its splash of happiness?
Mary Oliver

CONTENTS

6. Conclusion   240

PREFACE AND ACKNOWLEDGMENTS

Analyzing the ways in which ironic texts signify can be challenging in biblical studies, where an assumption persists in some influential quarters that one can "just read the text" without the annoying encumbrances of theory. All exegesis is based on assumptions arising from the reader's experience and from cultural influences mediated by the history of biblical interpretation, the academy with its epistemological hierarchies, hermeneutical strictures and paradigms operative in communities to which the reader feels accountable, and other sources. Interpretation is a complex matter that requires attentiveness to various claims about words, syntax, and genres, the historical contexts of events and language, the bedeviled yet still important notion of authorial intent, and competing methodological priorities. Persuasive framing of textual signifying, intertextual relationships, and metatextual reading processes—in a word, theory—can be elusive. Yet theory is indispensable. It is not an artificial step that happens in a derivative way after one has already read a text. Theory is rigorous and precise thinking about what we are already doing when we read and what other readers may choose to do differently.[1] Because texts and reading processes constitute sites of power within cultures, I consider it an ethical imperative to reflect on what happens when we read. We can neither dispense with theory nor afford to ignore it.

Theorizing irony is not an easy thing, and I have been grateful for some excellent guides to that daunting process. The classic work of Wayne Booth has been an inspiration. While his notion of stable irony is based on a conviction about the determinacy of texts with which many have disagreed, I nevertheless have found his arguments eloquent and his thinking about irony profound. I have found valuable the nuanced theoretical musings of Linda Hutcheon as well.

Many have assisted me in the execution of this project. Julie Faith Parker and Linn Tonstad offered feedback and invaluable research assistance. Ashley N. Bradford and Paul K.-K. Cho offered helpful comments on two chapters. In the classroom, I learned much from Allan McFarlane's paper "The Sign of Ruth: An Absence of Self" and Niels T. Dahl's paper "The Book of ~~Esther~~ Mordecai." Warmest thanks to Noel Collier for building me a study in the summer of 2004. My gratitude is due to David M. Carr, Baruch A. Levine, and David Marcus for their comments on a version of the Balaam treatment in chapter 4 that I presented to the Columbia Seminar on the Hebrew Bible, and to Chip Dobbs-Allsopp and other members of the Lenox Colloquium for their responses to a version of the Esther material in chapter 2. Roy L. Heller and Jaime Clark-Soles, David and Sally McAlpin, Libby and Bill Tilghman, and Sandra Sharp offered continual encouragement. I am grateful to my Hebrew Bible colleagues at Yale Divinity School, Robert R. Wilson, John J. Collins, and Christl M. Maier (now of the University of Marburg) for a collegial and intellectually lively environment in which to complete this book. Special thanks to Dean Harold W. Attridge for his generous support of faculty research. Grant support came from the Griswold Research Fund of the Whitney Humanities Center at Yale and the Wabash Center for Teaching and Learning in Theology and Religion. I am very grateful to the superb staff at Indiana University Press, including Dee Mortensen, senior sponsoring editor for African studies, philosophy, and religion, and Herbert Marks, editor of the Indiana Studies in Biblical Literature series. Mark Minster has my profound gratitude for his erudite and enlivening comments on the manuscript.

Thanks finally to our children, Dinah and Jacob, who continually show me the delights of irony in all its forms. I dedicate this book to my husband, Leo A. Lensing, whose enduring support has meant more to me than words can say.

IRONY AND MEANING
IN THE
HEBREW BIBLE

INTRODUCTION

Ambiguity, paradox, and misdirection play through all literature. This is true to a certain degree even in those kinds of writing whose genres seem to preclude indirection or opacity (lists of addresses, say, or commands in the training manual for a Labrador retriever). The unspoken suffuses and lends force to signification on many levels in texts, by turns charming and frustrating the reader and giving impetus to our efforts to grasp what may remain artistically elusive. Irony is a particularly powerful means of signaling by means of the unspoken. Robert Alter has put it well: "The *not saying* of something (or the pretending not to say it) is an ancient rhetorical device. . . . Often enough the reticence is intended to increase the impact of what it purports to conceal while making it inevitable that a properly informed reader will at once, and with the added emotion attendant on discovery, recognize what is really meant."[1] Irony persuades by misdirecting in a complex way. Ironic texts require a specific kind of reader competence in order for the communication to have taken place at all: the audience needs to perceive that the communication is unreliable in some crucial respect. If one reads the stories of Jonathan Swift "straight," as an earnest catalogue of the unusual places to which Gulliver travels, one completely misses the satirical act of communication about English society, theology, and politics that Swift intended.

The vexed matter of authorial intention lies at the heart of current debates about reading. Many interpreters consider the "author" to be long dead and rightly unmourned. But for many others—myself among them—a nuanced notion of author remains essential, even as our view of textual meaning becomes enlivened by an increasingly sophisticated understanding of contextual factors that shape interpretation. True, the inevitability of textual decoding toward which Alter gestured can no longer be taken for granted. These days we see more clearly the unconstrainable nature of intertextuality and cultural bricolage, the dynamic roles played by readers and reading communities in every act of interpretation, and the ways in which texts contradict and erase their own claims even as they are making them. Notions of authority and intention are inevitably functions of discursive strategies and power relations.[2] Yet the question of author cannot be ignored when irony is seen to be involved, however complex our idea of author may become, even if "author" is broadened to include readers' interactions with texts and communities rather than being strictly identified with the intentions of a single historical person.

Consider the question of ironic authorial intention in the following letter written by a Yale student in October 1902 to temperance activist Carry Nation:[3]

> Dear Mrs. Nation:—Although it pains me deeply, I feel it my duty to inform you that after your soul-stirring address of warning and reproof, the Devil still grins at Yale Dining Hall. The enclosed menus tell the story. The hateful practice of serving intoxicating liquors has not ceased. Capt. Smoke holds open wide the gates of hell. Oh, this is terrible! Satan loves to shoot at brightest marks. Here are eight hundred shining young souls, the cream of the nation's manhood, on the broad road which leadeth to destruction. God Help us. Assist us, Mrs. Nation; aid us; pray for us. Let the world know of this awful condition and rouse the public indignation until it has ceased. Publicity will do it. Let the world know that Yale is being made a training school for drunkards, and Capt. Smoke will never dare to serve liquors again. [*Signed,*] Alone, But a Friend of the Temperance Cause

Is the student's letter intended earnestly or ironically? Grunwald and Adler are of the opinion that the letter is "almost certainly sincere." Carry Nation describes this and several other letters she received from Yale students as earnest pleas for help, which she subsequently provided, traveling to New Haven. As she tells it,

> I spoke to the students at the entrance of their dining hall. They spoke up and told me that "Champagne" was served on their ham three times a week. They gave me the menus, and on them were: "Claret Wine Punch," "Cherry Wine Sauce," "Apple Dumpling and Brandy Sauce," "Roast Ham and Champagne Sauce," and "Wine jelly." While I was talking to the young men, many were smoking cigarettes in the entrance of the dining hall, which was contrary to rules, but Capt. Smoke only laughed at this practice of vice. There should be an investigation and that quick. Students are crying for it. Faculties should demand of students a high standard. At Yale the students are pleading for a moral faculty.[4]

The letter may well have been intended earnestly. But perhaps it was not. Might there have been a young ironist watching quietly among the undergraduates who gathered to hear Carry Nation fulminate against the moral degradation of Yale? Certainly the letter's overwrought prose about alcohol-laced comestibles was possible as earnest communication at that time in American letters. One need only consult the cookbook writing of Harriet Beecher Stowe to see how serious she was about whether a butter was well made.[5] But affecting a tone of devastating irony was also possible, especially in the callow youths of the day, as anyone will acknowledge who has read *The Lawrenceville Stories,*[6] the tales of P. G. Wodehouse, or other works representing privileged young Anglo-American males at the turn of the last century. Did the Yale student mean to present himself as a Dink Stover or Bertie Wooster, or was his outrage sincere?

One might argue for irony in the case of this Yale student's letter according to the following points. Peculiarly overstated is the suggestion that the "Devil still grins" not just at Yale University, which might have been a more plausible reference given the concerns of some religious traditions historically regarding higher education, but a bit too specifically at "Yale Dining Hall." The assertion that "the enclosed menus tell the story" might seem unlikely to be earnest on two counts. First, the student would probably have understood that alcohol used in reductions in cooking does not survive the cooking process in amounts sufficient to intoxicate. Even if proving a conceptual temptation to an alcoholic (as temperance groups worried), alcohol used in cooking would not have been potent enough to affect the metabolisms of those at table. Thus the charge of putting a stumbling block before an active or recovering alcoholic might be made in earnest, but the suggestion that one might become drunk from eating roast ham with champagne sauce probably would not be. Second, it was well known that among temperance groups of the time there were varied positions regarding the use of alcohol in recipes, so to suggest that the menus alone could mutely relay all that needed to be said could be argued to be an overstatement.[7] Further hyperbole abounds in the letter. The fourfold use of names for the Tempter seems to drive home the dire nature of the spiritual emergency with rather too much verve. The reference to the Yale student body as "shining young souls" might be permitted as a flourish of earnest encomium, but surely the writer goes a step too far with the smug designation, "the cream of the nation's manhood," given that he must number himself among them. Ironic understatement may be present as well: the brevity of the sentence, "Publicity will do it," is suspect, for how could mere "publicity" solve the problem if Satan himself is holding wide the gates of hell? And finally, the reduction of Yale's nationally esteemed pedagogy and curricular opportunities to the risible phrase "a training school for drunkards" would seem unlikely as a serious charge even for one opposed to the dining hall policy.

Nevertheless, it is possible that the Yale student was earnestly overwrought and evangelical on this subject. If so, he could have anticipated a favorable hearing from Nation, a woman notorious for smashing saloons with a hatchet in her zeal for the temperance cause. But the letter makes a more interesting piece of literature as irony than it does as straightforward supplication. Now, objections have been raised regularly in literary criticism to the idea that since the imputation of irony makes a work "better" (more sophisticated, more subtle), therefore it is to be favored whenever possible. Works of art or literature just might not be that interesting, goes the objection, and it is not the place of theory to improve upon artists' original creations. All true. I would not argue that because the Yale student's letter is more interesting to me if it is read ironically, therefore it should be considered ironic. But I will argue, explicitly and implicitly throughout this book, that when a theory of irony can account well for significant aspects of a text's cultural references and diction, then that theory should be considered viable, even if it can never be deemed determinative because of the elusive nature of communication generally and irony in particular.

Is the Book of Jonah ironic? Very many readers have found it so, but there are readers who remain unconvinced. Is Samson to be taken as a model for pious heroism? Some readers assent to that possibility despite the narrative inconcinnities that have prompted Alter to describe the Samson story as a "satire of muscle-bound concupiscent male gullibility."[8] It is far easier to dismiss the argument for irony in a text, no matter how brilliantly constructed that argument may be, than it is to prove to a skeptic that a proposal of irony is the best reading of a text. After reading pages of rigorous historical-critical and literary argumentation for irony, the reader can simply shrug, "Well, I still don't see it," and that is the end of the conversation. Of course, any argument can fail to persuade on any topic under the sun. But arguments for irony are particularly vulnerable to the airy dismissal. There remain intelligent readers who are not comfortable with the slipperiness and obliqueness of irony, who prefer their textual cues direct and unvarnished. This raises the question of the controls that one might bring to a reading of a text as ironic. I will address that issue in detail in the next chapter, which sets out my methodological approach.

I regret that the present volume cannot treat all aspects of irony in every text in the Hebrew Bible that may be said to be ironic. Even as I restrict the scope of this book for pragmatic reasons, I feel other biblical ironies tugging at my hermeneutical sleeve, clamoring for attention. In my concluding chapter, I will point to some ironic texts, characters, and concepts within the Hebrew Scriptures to which I cannot attend in detail in these pages. I hope that other interpreters seduced by the lures and delights of irony will travel farther into those territories where I cannot now tread.

1

INTERPRETING IRONY: RHETORICAL, HERMENEUTICAL, AND THEOLOGICAL POSSIBILITIES

Universes hang in the balance with every act of reading an ironic sacred text. This apparently extravagant statement might be perceived as ironic by those who do not believe that reading matters deeply, those who do not see cultural constructions of the sacred as important, and those who may not be sure how to assess the claim. It might also be suspected of irony by those who think that however true the claim might be, its author is probably not pressing it earnestly in this particular context. Yet I, the author, do claim earnestly that reading sacred texts is profoundly important for all who are involved in creating written cultures and for every creature and aspect of creation with which culture-making beings interact. Notions of the holy that readers discover and construct from sacred texts have relevance for their treatment of other living creatures and the natural world, their view of the possibilities and constraints of community and culture, and their posture toward remembered pasts and imagined futures. Acts of reading do matter for all creation. Thus one critic's ironizing hyperbole may be another critic's passionate truth claim.[1]

Sacred texts deal with matters belonging to the gritty stuff of experience and matters belonging to the soaring heights of the spiritual imagination. They catalyze convergences and clashes of culture within and among communities. Sacred texts invite their readers to interpret suffering, to seek healing and enlightenment, and to make sense of the intersections between holy and profane. Discerning appropriate language to mediate the dialogue between holy and profane is no easy task for any writer, ancient or contemporary. Deciphering meaning in Israel's sacred texts is no easier for the reader. Within the Hebrew Bible we see a wealth of genres and styles and tones employed by biblical writers from many different subcultures and historical periods within ancient Israel, across a broad spectrum of epistemologies and theological perspectives. Crucial components of their understandings and practices are lost to us or remain poorly understood, rendering the task of interpretation challenging.

The power of the unspoken adds to Hebrew Bible texts much "fraught" background and implicit foreground.[2] Attentiveness to silence—to the importance of what is not said—is a significant part of the enterprise of reading, for, as A. J. Mandt has said, "meaningful discourse is a mixture of articulation and silence."[3] Biblical poetry is elliptical: psalms and prophetic oracles leave much to the reader's constructive skills, and the gaps in poetry are essential to poetic expression. Narrative, too, can draw the reader into its silences. Consider these observations of Alan J. Hauser about narrative poetics:

> [I]n the narrative poetry of Judges 5, which never once directly *curses* the Canaanites, the writer, through succinct characterization, heavily laden but terse dialogue, and a series of skillfully constructed vignettes which have a cumulative effect, devastatingly excoriates the Canaanites. In Genesis 22 the writer argues effectively that Abraham is a man of great faith without ever saying so explicitly, choosing instead to use sharply honed dialogue, pregnant silence, a sparse but precisely articulated story line, suspense, carefully focused development of characters, and phrases laden with implication to concentrate the reader's attention on the enormous sacrifice which Abraham is prepared to make. What is unspoken can be as important as what is said openly in moving the writer's argument forward.[4]

What, then, if the unspoken is at odds with what is articulated? Irony is a cultural phenomenon whose very possibility blurs the lines among the multitudinous possibilities for how to speak, how to hear, and how to understand. Language can represent naïvely and pragmatically, can describe clearly, can make its points directly. But language can also obfuscate, misname, and subvert what it seems to be saying. In the Bible, we have countless sophisticated ways in which language is used to express understanding of the mysteries of human nature (elusive enough in itself) and the nature of God (far beyond human understanding; that much, the friends of Job get right). What Carl Raschke says of a postmodern view of textuality generally may be applied with particular force to the interpretation of ironic texts: "Texts are no longer bare runes to be puzzled over. They are at once an intricate braid of the latent and the manifest, of form and function, of intimation and opacity, of word and image, of grapheme and difference."[5] Ironic texts are constituted precisely by that braid of the latent and the manifest, by the interplay between intimation and opacity.

Opportunities for misunderstanding are rife. We risk misreading, mishearing emphasis, even entirely missing the point. Negotiations of meaning and authority in Scripture are rendered almost infinitely complicated by the presence of irony. Irony complicates narratological constructions of the relationship between God and Israel and the representation of outsiders as foils and mediators for that relationship. Irony is essential to prophetic paraenesis in the Bible, both in the mode and content of its textual signification and in its rhetorical effect on its audiences. Those audiences are indicted again and again for not understanding their sacred traditions, yet the prophets' use of irony surely makes their communication that much harder to grasp. In what ways might a sacred text be understood as authoritative when the meaning of the text is located not in what it says but in the shadowy, sharp-edged realm of what it does not say? No hermeneutics of sacred texts can proceed effectively without taking account of the dynamics of resistance and misdirection enacted by irony.

Our hermeneutical task is rendered even more daunting by problems of temporal and cultural distance presented by these ancient texts, produced in social groups so different from the modern Western cultures that, so far, have tended to dominate in scholarly biblical criticism. How can the contemporary interpreter understand ironic plays on biblical tropes, ideas, terms, characters, and storylines without familiarity with the varieties of usage of ancient Hebrew language and culture over time? Reading is difficult when apparently simple statements may be fraught with ironic reversals or encoded with allusions whose significance has long since disappeared from the cultural record.[6]

Not only is the historical dimension of the endeavor problematic. The literary side of things is complicated as well. Scholars of the Hebrew Bible have, with some exceptions, contented themselves simply with identifying and commenting on local ironies of one sort or another in biblical stories. Those who identify themselves as literary critics often permit themselves to relish biblical ironies a little more, delighting at more length in the artistry and evocative force of ironic twists. But even in university English and comparative literature departments, where hermeneutical inventiveness is tolerated more readily than in some divinity school and seminary cultures, skilled decoders of irony often rest content with rather basic explorations of ironies of plot and characterization in biblical literature. And it is rare for a Hebrew Bible scholar to note that the detection of irony in a text might have larger implications for method—for example, for understanding the literary unity or composition history of that text.[7]

My study of irony in the Hebrew Bible will address itself to two arenas in which the presence of textual irony will be seen to have import for the act of reading: rhetoric and theological hermeneutics. As regards rhetoric, my interest has to do with the ways in which the spoken ironic word manages deftly to undercut its stated position and open up possibilities for new understandings that enjoy relatively greater freedom from the threat of critique. Ironic biblical texts invite their audiences to "overcome a naïvely realistic reading" of their plots and characters and rhetorics;[8] those invitations have often gone unheeded by interpreters whose hermeneutical predilections privilege the realistic as the predominant or only way that a biblical text can signify. I hope in this book to call attention to the invitation extended by ironic biblical texts themselves that we not read naïvely. On the hermeneutical side, I want to wrestle with two notions that interrogate each other in current methodological debates: that of authorial intention, which is especially elusive in ironic texts and may be perceived, as it were, only in the negative; and that of reader agency in constructing meaning through the act of reading, something that is both enhanced and complicated by irony.

I hope to illuminate a wide variety of instances of irony in texts in the Hebrew Bible, not only yielding particular exegetical insights but also bringing a more rigorous study of the phenomenon of ironic rhetoric into the scholarly discourse on these biblical passages than has been available heretofore. Irony has been noticed, sometimes reliably, in some of these texts, but complex ironies in less familiar narratives have often been missed or noted only glancingly. I hope also to use the study of irony in its many forms and modes as a way into some important hermeneutical debates about authorial intention, the possibilities of reading and misreading, and the importance of real and implied audiences in the construction of meaning. The notion of "author" is not dead. It continues to thrive, albeit in a more complicated existence lately, for those who understand all texts, sacred and otherwise, to address the reader from a position outside the reader's limited self-understanding. The notion of "irony" itself is not dead either, the pronouncements of some cultural critics notwithstanding. Irony remains a powerful weapon against idolatries of all kinds, against smugness, ignorance, and the self-absorption of individuals and communities. My study will explore the hermeneutical problems and potentials of biblical irony, then, as a quality and texture of communication in a way that aims to be responsive to important contemporary theoretical shifts that have taken place in literary and rhetorical criticism.

Helpful at the outset of our methodological discussion will be a look at ways in which theories about irony engage contemporary hermeneutical issues.

Irony and Contemporary Methodological Debates

Reading is not a simple act of recognizing codes and cues inked onto parchment or engraved in stone. Apprehension of human communications through written texts, especially across time and across cultural boundaries, can be so complex as to defy description. Relevant is Ilona N. Rashkow's observation about the dynamic and fluid nature of the reading process:

> For the reader in/of the text, interpretation does not proceed from partial to definitive meaning and then come to rest, but instead is an ongoing process. Elements of narrative cohesion constantly shift, blurring the distinctions between provisional and "fulfilled" meanings, between shadows and truth. Reading, like analysis, becomes an activity of repressing and reconstructing, of forgetting and remembering, and that activity, by its very nature, resists completion.[9]

Rashkow's observation highlights the complexity of reader construal. And what of the text? Do texts control the production of meaning in any way that may be discerned and discussed apart from the influence of the ideologies of individual readers, reading communities, and reading traditions over time? This is not an arcane issue of theory important only to denizens of ivory towers who venture, blinking, infrequently into the sunlight of the real world. Rather, this question arises whenever an act of reading is challenged by another reader, whenever one person finds another's explanation of a text unsatisfying or persuasive, whenever a reader confronted by an obscure or disturbing verse shuts the Bible and never opens it again. The question arises in university and seminary classrooms wherever students argue over contemporary ecclesial applications of prophetic oracles of judgment or Pauline exhortations against homosexuality. The question arises in every homiletical move a preacher makes—in every *d'var Torah* or Christian sermon preached well or poorly, as the preacher struggles successfully or unsuccessfully with the claims and silences of the biblical text.

What biblical texts communicate is bound up with how they are perceived to communicate. Readers and texts alike respond to the assumptions and priorities of multiple communities, ancient and modern, that gather silently around us as we read. These diverse communities have their own understandings of what constitutes text and truth. My suggestion that biblical texts may be ironic constitutes a claim about the inadequacy of codes of reading that presuppose earnestness, transparency, and reliability in the Bible. For some readers, the claim that there is irony in the Bible may go without saying, but for others, it may constitute a transgressive assertion. For irony does not simply ironize a character here and a way of thinking there. The presence of irony subverts the act of communication itself, in every idiom in which it operates. What L. Gregory Bloomquist says about the apocalyptic treatment of the Jewish Temple in the Gospel of Luke may be applied, *mutatis mutandis,* to irony in biblical discourse: "[I]it seeks to dismantle not first a building but rather the code by which the building has meaning: it is thus revolutionist at the level of the code, not just at the level of the visual or physical."[10] Richard Cooper notes of postmodern architecture that "traditional decorative details are added on to—and hence problematize—the simple, clear structures of modernist buildings. Conflicting codes are juxtaposed with the result that the systems they mediate are ironically relativized."[11] A similar relativizing effect may be postulated of biblical irony: its impact may be felt throughout the entire system of the biblical text and throughout the reader's hermeneutics.

The destabilizing operations of irony do not make communication impossible, as anyone who delights in irony knows. Notwithstanding the anxiety of every new generation of historicist readers confronted with theories of textual indeterminacy, communication does continue pragmatically as we continue to read. Meaning continues to be signified and construed not only despite but through the acts of deconstruction and reconstruction that shape rhetoric.[12] But irony does problematize hermeneutical naïveté about the ways in which words reflect that which they are signifying.

How does irony work in the dynamic engagements among readers, ironic texts, and interpretive communities? Irony as a literary phenomenon was of interest in the academy particularly in the 1960s and '70s, and there has been a resurgence of interest in theorizing irony in the last decade or so. The literature is so vast that reviewing it comprehensively would be impossible here, especially if one were to cover theories of irony in the discipline of philosophy. I will instead address some central points from major theorists briefly without, I hope, too much loss of nuance. I will highlight key insights of Søren Kierkegaard, Edwin M. Good, D. C. Muecke, Wayne C. Booth, Paul de Man, and Linda Hutcheon.

Kierkegaard is interested in the subjective freedom enacted by irony for the ironist and for those readers who participate through understanding the ironic viewpoint. Irony points toward that which is possible by categorically rejecting the inadequate actual reality. This rejection of what is inadequate is one sign of the integrity of a life well lived. Kierkegaard speaks of irony as an indispensable moral guide: "There is an impatience that would reap before it has sown. By all means let irony chasten it. There is in every personal life so much that must be repudiated, so many wild shoots that must be sheared away. Here again irony is an excellent surgeon. For when irony has been mastered . . . its function is then of the utmost importance in order for the personal life to acquire health and truth."[13] Thus for Kierkegaard, as Andrew Cross observes, irony is a mode of being, not just a literary trope one may employ: "'[I]rony' indicates a particular way of engaging in public (interpersonal) activity in general. . . . He [Kierkegaard] examines what it is to speak ironically, in short, in order to determine what [it is] to *live* ironically—to manifest in one's life, unqualifiedly, the attitudes and type of orientation toward the world that constitute irony."[14]

The persuasive force of irony works through its construction of community, a construction that remains powerful rhetorically even though it is frequently thwarted in praxis by the ironist's being misunderstood. Important for our purposes here is Kierkegaard's recognition of the tension that obtains between isolation and community building in the work of irony. Irony both delights and alarms the reader who would stand with the ironist, for the ironist beckons seductively and dismisses brutally at the same time. Kierkegaard is eloquent in his description of the dynamic force of irony: "The disguise and mysteriousness which it entails, the telegraphic communication which it initiates, inasmuch as the ironist must always be understood at a distance, the infinite sympathy it assumes, the elusive and ineffable moment of understanding immediately displaced by the anxiety of misunderstanding—all this captivates with indissoluble bonds."[15] The ironist stands alone in the subtle, scathing rejection of the obvious. Of the isolation of the ironist, Kierkegaard writes, "His searching eye looks in vain for a kindred spirit, and were not his golden age still a fresh memory for some, the play of his countenance would remain a mysterious hieroglyph for his contemporaries, among whom he lives as a stranger and alien."[16] Yet the act of communicating ironically not only posits but begs for the discerning ear—and in written irony, begs for the ideal reader.[17] The ironist requires the witness afforded by a hermeneutically competent communal response. Irony seeks expression within community, though its rhetorical construction of community remains fragile. Kierkegaard again: "It is merely an inconsistency which irony has in common with every negative standpoint that while according to its concept it is isolation, it nevertheless seeks to constitute a society. . . . But there is as little social unity in a coterie of ironists as there is truly honesty among a band of thieves."[18]

In addition to enacting the implicit construction of community, irony also deconstructs community through its performance of negation and through its fomenting of division within the implied audience. Glenn Holland notes that irony creates multiple divisions, since there will be those who understand it and those who do not, and also those who agree versus those who disagree with the ironist's point once they have understood it.[19] In addition, there may be those who might agree with the point of a particular irony but reject the mode or means of irony. Irony has been considered morally suspect from the time of classical Greek rhetoric to the present day, for at least two reasons. First, irony is based on a kind of dissembling that some deem morally unacceptable as being equivalent to—or treading perilously close to—outright deception. Second, irony enacts a form of rhetorical power that seems to claim for the ironist a kind of objective distance, an evasion of full engagement in community life that some may find objectionable. Thus the ways in which irony constructs and destabilizes the notion of community are complex as well.

Edwin M. Good's book *Irony in the Old Testament*[20] provides an essential starting point for interpreters of irony in the Hebrew Bible. Good underlines the importance of what is at stake in biblical ironizing, saying that irony "clarifies with extreme sharpness the incongruity involved in a matter of great moment."[21] That biblical irony may be light or comic is something that Good would surely acknowledge, but he is more interested in the momentous, as his chapter subtitles indicate: in Jonah we learn about "The Absurdity of God"; with Saul, "The Tragedy of Greatness"; in Genesis, "The Irony of Israel"; in Isaiah, "Faith on the Brink"; with Qoheleth, "The Limits of Wisdom"; and in Job, "The Irony of Reconciliation." Good finds theologically important the critique implicit in all scriptural ironizing, which he sees as grounded in the biblical authors' "stance in truth": "[I]rony is criticism, implicit or explicit, which perceives in things as they are an incongruity. . . . The ironist's criticism comes from a more or less explicit 'ought,' or a more transcendent 'is,' which, if it is not an integral part of the ironic discourse, is an implicit background to it."[22] Good's exegetical studies address ironies as rhetorical tropes intended by the biblical authors to drive their audiences toward "Old Testament faith," by which Good means commitment to the covenant of Israel with God. Good's epilogue, "Faith and the Ironic Vision," has the merit of taking seriously the theological purposes of the biblical texts he treats. He writes, "Liberating faith is the condition of the true irony that fears neither to perceive nor to state the ironic incongruities of which human life is so full."[23] He explains, "That the problem of human alienation from God is solved for faith by the reconciling divine action sheds the light of irony upon the solemn pro- grams by which [humans] would manipulate either alienation or recon- ciliation for their own partial ends. . . . The irony of faith is finally its radi- cal sense of redemption, its freedom in God."[24]

Some readers might object to Good's harmonization of all ironic He- brew Bible texts as leading toward the "imperative" of covenant. Others might take issue with his way of reading through an unacknowledged Protestant theological lens. Still others might find his exegesis to be a bit too innocent of engagement with the literary theory of his day. Never- theless, his work remains valuable as the first attempt at a full-scale eval- uation of irony in the Hebrew Bible. Good's emphasis on irony's move- ment toward freedom coheres with Kierkegaard's understanding, and his readings brim with persuasive insights about local textual ironies.

D. C. Muecke provides an extensive taxonomy of the different grades, modes, and types of irony, with a focus on verbal irony.[25] Muecke offers a thoroughly modernist assertion of the importance of intention and communicability in irony. In this, he gets at the central definitional problem: can something be considered ironic if no one perceives the irony?[26] There are ironic biblical texts that will not be discussed in the pages of this book only because I have not yet discerned their ironies. There are also texts to be discussed here concerning which my claims for irony will be contested by readers who take those texts as earnest or who see them as ironic in a way other than that which I propose. Both irony and the analysis of irony involve the construction of an implied audience. In fact, as George B. Caird notes, irony constructs "a double audience, the first understanding nothing beyond the face value of the words, the second seeing both the deeper meaning and the incompre- hension of the first."[27] Now, how well ironic texts mark their dissembling is another question. An author may try to be ironic but not succeed well, or an author's text may be suffused with ironies of which the author is only half-aware. But the issue of communicability is central to any analy- sis that is interested in rhetoric, and so it is here.

Muecke rightly names the signaling of irony as a kind of multidimen- sional communication: irony by definition communicates on more than one level simultaneously. He asserts that a number of elements should be present in most forms of verbal irony: what he calls "innocence or confi- dent unawareness," contrast between reality and appearance, elements of the comic and detachment, and an "aesthetic quality."[28] This multidimen- sional communication will be the better analyzed to the extent that a variety of rhetorical levels have been "marked" by the ironist and are then recognized by the interpreter.[29] That pragmatic observation holds even if one concedes that both marking and the perception of marking are subjective, culturally construed, and provisional, and thus that the processes of "marking" and decoding apparent markers can never be wholly determinative for meaning. This leads to one of the problems of the postmodern age: we have come to understand that all signifying is "other" than what it seems. Muecke anticipates the problem, for he deplores what he perceives as a tendency in literary criticism to consider all ambiguity as ironic. He notes further, "[S]ince all literature says more than it seems to be saying . . . practically all literature can be called ironical."[30] He contents himself with naming the issue and implying that practical-minded thinkers must nevertheless hew to the distinction between true irony and mere ambiguity: "[I]f we regard all discourse as ironical, what word do we use for distinguishing 'Holy Willie's Prayer' from the General Confession of the Anglican prayer-book?"[31] The postmodernist would not, in fact, distinguish between those two texts on a priori or categorical grounds, insisting rather that construals of both will inevitably rely on interpretive agency and cultural cues as understood by the reader. But Muecke's taxonomic question—what makes irony different?—has had an important role in the ongoing theoretical discussion.

Wayne C. Booth, another who is interested in irony marking, offers a response. He argues that ironic meaning wholly rejects that which is expressly stated. Irony is flagged for the reader by "absurdity or impossibility in what is said," such that the reader can continue reading only by seeking something that can substitute for the stated claims of the text: "[A]lthough the reader of metaphor usually comes to a point at which he must say, 'No—this far and no farther,' in irony the negatives press in on him from the beginning. . . . [T]he first step in reading it is a resounding 'No' and a pulling back to discover one possible way of making sense that can replace the rejected nonsense."[32] Booth notes that the persuasiveness of irony relies on the tacitness of what is being ironically affirmed. Irony allows latitude in the degree to which various readers will reject the unacceptable meaning. Because the flexibility of the unspoken allows for multiple responses, an ironic statement may be more effective rhetorically than would be a strongly formulated positive statement with which some readers might be loath to agree.[33] Irony does coerce, but more lightly than does dogmatic assertion. Booth sees the connection established between author and reader by means of irony to be an invitation accepted. To understand irony is to "perform an intricate intellectual dance together."[34] Booth underlines the inclusive community-building aspect of ironic signification: "the building of amiable communities is often far more important than the exclusion of naïve victims" in an ironic text.[35] His location of the impulse to community less in the anxiety of misunderstanding, as with Kierkegaard, and more in the relational choice not to believe something unacceptable, has significant implications for irony's function in establishing group identity: "I do not reject the printed statement because of any literal untruth. I reject it because I refuse to dwell with anyone who holds this whole *set* of beliefs."[36]

Booth's notion of stable irony as yielding determinate textual cues has come under heavy fire from critics of a more postmodern bent, including Stanley Fish.[37] Fish refutes Booth's position about determinate irony on one main count, articulated from a number of different angles. He observes that the existence of markers of stable irony can be contested by a reader who does not see irony where Booth does.[38] Fish argues, "the registering of an incongruity cannot be the basis of an interpretation, since it is the product of one," so one may not fairly appeal a priori to incongruities as markers. Readers' constructions of the historical context are based on assumptions that may or may not be true; readings of irony take shape in reading communities that operate according to particular assumptions and interpretive priorities. Fish's objections are cogent. One can hardly disagree with his concluding point that as regards detecting irony, "you always know, but what you know . . . is subject to challenge or revision, as a result of which you will still always know, even though what you know will be different."[39]

Yet this does not mean that one need surrender one's criteria for evaluating readings (including one's own prior readings) as more or less interesting, useful, or perspicacious for particular communities. Fish himself speaks of the conventions of the scholarly community as if there were only one such community and as if its conventions were monolithic, experienced in a single consistent way by all scholars and wholly determinate for the efforts of those scholars. His amusing series of remarks on the politics of scholarship has the effect of subtly inscribing a new kind of determinacy, contesting the notion of scholarly agency in composing arguments and reader agency in assessing those arguments in ways that do not fully persuade. He takes as his example the arguments mustered by Barry Slepian in 1963 for a wholly ironic reading of Jonathan Swift's poem "Verses on the Death of Dr. Swift," as opposed to the only partially ironic readings that had prevailed in Swiftian scholarship to that point. Fish notes, "[T]he establishing of a perspective proceeds according to quite regular rules, rules that Slepian followed, even though he may have been unaware of them"; these include demolishing the consensus view and "invoking [a] . . . powerful institutional formula," namely, that the poem may be divided into three parts. Fish goes on with evident sarcasm, "[O]nce you are told that a poem has three parts, and you know too that one of those parts has always been considered an excrescence, you know, with all the certainty that attends membership in the literary community, that the third part is about to be brought into a harmonious relationship with the other two and so contribute to the making of an 'organic whole.'"[40] Fish says of Slepian, "He succeeds neither because he alone is uniquely in touch with the work itself nor because he has created the work out of whole cloth, but because, in accordance with procedures authorized by the institution [of literary criticism], he has altered the conditions of seeing."[41]

But Fish then confuses that unduly determinative creation of his own—the monolithic reading community—with the text itself: "In ten years we have gone from Slepian's all-ironic poem (itself put in place of a poem that was only two-thirds ironic) to a poem that is only fitfully ironic, if it is ironic at all."[42] Clearly, we simply have contrasting readings of the existing poem, as we have always had—readings that may be responding to changing communal expectations about scholarship or irony or Swift as author, but readings that also take shape under pressure from a number of other catalysts, including, at least potentially, the reader's genius and growing awareness of new contextual factors. Fish's essay underlines the point that irony can be endlessly debated and that the criteria for determining what is ironic lie both within and beyond the hermeneutical endeavor proper. Nevertheless, if one may suggest that Slepian has "authored" a new, wholly ironic poem in place of the older understanding, and that subsequent scholars have "authored" yet newer versions of Swift's poem, surely one may still suggest that Swift himself authored a version of the poem—whether his intentions are retrievable or not. Fish's point about interpretations "changing the conditions of seeing" applies also to Swift himself as one understands him upon first encountering the poem, to Swift upon one's rereading the poem after Barry Slepian's argument has been made, and so on.

Reader response plays an inevitable role in constructing and perceiving ironies, but it is both intellectually unsound and unethical to argue that the testimony of authors and texts is fully and only constructed by the reader. Further, it is amusing but disingenuous to suggest that the scholarly interpreter is no more than a witless pawn of whatever literary-critical conventions happen to be current. Every reading constructs the voice of the author, and thus in practice every reading will, to a certain degree, erase or revoice that author according to the critic's own goals and cultural assumptions. But it is still meaningful to say that in various kinds of interpretation and at the hands of various interpreters, there are lesser and greater degrees of attentiveness to the "Otherness" of textual voices. This attentiveness is not entirely molded by whatever expectations of the academy happen to be fashionable. Thus a nuanced and theoretically sophisticated way of approaching the historical materiality of texts and textual witnesses remains a desideratum.[43] The radical-constructionist position renders ancient and contemporary authors voiceless not only to a certain degree in practice, as every reading does, but intentionally and fully in theory as well, which in my view is ethically untenable.

The appreciation of irony may provide a way forward here. Irony insists on the possibility of resistant reading while undermining any claim to definitive interpretation, including complete authorial control or wholly determinative reader agency. The heuristic category of irony suggests that there is such a thing as textual voicing and that some sort of "unspoken" presses upon the constraints of language in meaningful ways. Yet textual voicing can never be fully defined or domesticated, whether by the original author or by readers, whether according to the rubrics of naïve historicist reconstruction or those of a hypertextualized literary formalism. With irony, nothing is unequivocal—except for the point that the "said" is somehow misleading. Even the voice of the author is not unequivocal.[44] Claire Colebrook says in her discussion of German Romanticism:

> [T]he ironic response acknowledges the limited nature of any definition. The process of poetic creation will always be other than any created poem. Subjectivity can *never* be typified or exemplified in any literary character. There can be no ideal self precisely because subjectivity is the process that produces character and is always other than any presented persona. The self that lies behind masks and personae can only be known as different from what is presented, never presented "itself."[45]

So long as we move away from the notion of a stable self "lying behind" authorial and other cultural performances, we may appreciate the power of this insight for postmodern explorations of irony. The key is the elusiveness of irony itself, its rendering tenuous all constructions of subject and meaning while insisting with charm and subtlety that the meaning-making process remains important as a witness to Otherness. This elusiveness challenges the extremes of positivist historicist representationalism and radical-constructivist narcissism alike, while urging in the most persuasive terms that the hermeneutical endeavor not be given up.

De Man's work on irony encourages us to think further about semantic processes at work in the elusiveness and deconstructive power of irony. De Man's 1977 lecture, "The Concept of Irony," has long been cited in literary circles as a groundbreaking attempt to move the study of irony away from a focus on its embodiment in literary tropes to reflection on the broader epistemology of irony. De Man finds untenable

Booth's insistence that interpretive attentiveness to authorial cues can control textual irony from degenerating into a potentially endless cycle of negations. Booth had written, "Irony in itself opens up doubts as soon as its possibility enters our heads, and there is no inherent reason for discontinuing the process of doubt at any point short of infinity. . . . [P]ursued to the end, an ironic temper can dissolve everything, in an infinite chain of solvents. It is not irony but the desire to understand irony that brings such a chain to a stop."[46]

De Man appeals to Friedrich Schlegel's "Über die Unverständlichkeit," saying, "If indeed irony is tied with the impossibility of understanding, then Wayne Booth's project of understanding irony is doomed from the start because, if irony is of understanding, no understanding of irony will ever be able to control irony and stop it."[47] De Man's point is that if irony is conceded to exist at all, then it can never definitively be proven that irony is not subject to further irony. De Man suggests that irony finally destabilizes any attempts at enduring narrative coherence,[48] an observation that has relevance for readers' appreciations of ideological and narratological coherence of Hebrew Bible traditions. If Amos or the epilogist in Qohelet can ironize the use of language and tradition in Israel's self-understanding in their respective texts, then all Hebrew Bible traditions and linguistic representations are theoretically open to ironizing. If this is so, then modes of ancient Israelite storytelling and preservation of tradition become destabilized—perhaps also opened to dissent in a salutary way, but certainly destabilized. De Man helps us to see that the importance of ironizing in the Hebrew Bible goes far beyond the appreciation of this or that local irony as an artistic trope in a particular biblical text.

Another relevant work of de Man, "The Rhetoric of Temporality," argues that irony troubles the notion of consciousness of history, because it requires the fragmentation of the idea of self. For de Man, irony relies on "a discontinuity and a plurality of levels within a subject that comes to know itself by an increasing differentiation from what it is not."[49] By that logic, "human existence [is] a succession of isolated moments lived by a divided self."[50] The ironist's self-awareness of this problematized subjectivity renders the use of language problematic as well: "The ironic language splits the subject into an empirical self that exists in a state of inauthenticity and a self that exists only in the form of a language that asserts the knowledge of this inauthenticity."[51] This presents an insurmountable problem for history, according to de Man, because the experience of the ironist can be only a particular experience of Otherness and never an expression of a universal truth that transcends time: "Irony divides the flow of temporal experience into a past that is pure mystification and a future that remains harassed forever by a relapse within the inauthentic. It can know this inauthenticity but never overcome it. It can only restate and repeat it on an increasingly conscious level, but it remains endlessly caught in the impossibility of making this knowledge applicable to the empirical world."[52] For our present purposes, I find salutary de Man's insistence that the way in which irony problematizes authenticity—authenticity of the notion of self, of self acting as an agent in history, and of language representing the self and subjectivity embodied in history—is a matter of fundamental epistemological importance. After the work of de Man, it is not only difficult to be satisfied with reflections on biblical irony that treat it simply as a limited trope within literary artistry. It is also difficult to see "Israel" as a subject in biblical history without becoming immediately aware of the deeply problematic nature of that subjectivity, because it has been formed so completely by the dictions and ideologies of texts in its sacred corpus that are ironic. Scholars have long seen that "ancient Israel" is a fluid, multilayered construction that was continually shaped by challenges and competing views from without and within its culture. This idea is reinforced regularly by historical inquiry into archaeological evidence, ideological-critical interpretation of biblical texts, and research into the sociologies and cultures of groups that make up what we now term "ancient Israel." But engaging the thought of de Man, one becomes even more aware of the aporetic nature of biblical language, the biblical subject (whether individual believer or ancient Israel writ large), and representations of biblical history.

Aporia lies at the heart of irony. Irony resists definitions, including second-order definitional substitutions. This had been emphasized already by Muecke and others—many scholars of irony state somewhere in their treatments that irony cannot really be defined. But it may at least be noted that irony signifies more than just a sort of "opposite" of what is said, as Linda Hutcheon recognizes. Hutcheon moves away from the theoretical understanding of irony as a clearly defined logical opposition between the false literal meaning of what is said and the true tacit meaning of what is left unsaid. She argues that irony functions in a relational and additive way much as metaphor does, with an important distinction: where metaphor signifies and establishes connection chiefly through the construction of similarity, irony signifies and establishes connection chiefly through the construction of difference. The dialectical relationship between the said and the unsaid creates a "third" meaning; it is this third meaning, which is not simply the implied opposite of the false literal meaning, that is properly understood as the ironic meaning.[53] Thus in Hutcheon's model, the dynamics of interaction between the said and the unsaid are crucial for the signifying of irony.[54] Particularly pertinent is Hutcheon's observation that hyperbole works by signaling "excess, not opposition."[55] What is true of hyperbolic rhetoric generally, that it signifies not merely the opposite of what it says but something that stands in a complex kind of tension with what it says, is also true of modes of ironic expression.

The said and the unsaid are present together and signify together, creating a multidimensional act of communication that has its own internal dynamics as well as its charming call to the reader. Muecke suggests that irony is pleasing because of the sophistication with which that dynamic is crafted by the ironist: "[I]rony is more than a riddle or a message in code; it is something to be savoured, not merely solved. And what is savoured is the skill with which both the apparent and the real meaning are made to coexist, the apparent meaning plausibly maintained by the dissimulation, the opposed real meaning continually hinted at."[56] Textual irony signifies "more than": more than what it says, more than what the reader expects, and more than could be guessed from a superficial analysis of its syntagmatic relationships. Irony performs a complicated rhetorics of negation of the spoken and implicit affirmation of the unspoken, and the fluid relationship of those two things—negation and affirmation—is essential to its meaning.

Here I find helpful Mary Scoggin's exploration of Chinese terms that can be used to describe irony in Chinese verbal art:

> *Fan-hua,* "counter" or "back-speech," is a common modern suggestion for a term to translate the English word "irony." . . . "Counter-speech" might imply that one means the opposite of what one says, but we might also think of it [as] something said or done in response, like a counterquestion, a countermove in a game of chess, or a "counter-essay," a written response. Still better . . . I think Mu Hui's musical term "counter-tone" is a fitting candidate to catch the deeper sense of ironic paradox and simultaneously carry a resonance of Chinese poetic writing practices.[57]

Ironic expression partakes of all of the characteristics to which Scoggin points: a dynamic of "countering" (resisting both the position being ironized and potential misunderstandings of its own meaning), an ethos of responsiveness, and a subtle evocation of larger harmonies and dissonances within cultural practices. Irony invites the reader into an imaginative territory much larger than the overt markers in its own landscape would seem to allow.[58] Or, to shift metaphors, irony hosts its own Otherness, showing that the said and the unsaid require each other for the complex cultural organism of ironic communication to thrive.[59]

Illuminating here is Carol A. Newsom's observation about the inherently dialogical character of discourse and plot in the book of Job. Job presents a variety of perspectives on suffering and the nature of God, each viewpoint argued via elaborate poetic expression at considerable length. Newsom is unwilling to allow one perspective to trump the others in a way that silences their contributions to the discursive dialogism of the book. She comments:

> One is faced with the elusiveness of the divine speeches, the semantic ambiguity of Job's reply, the disconcerting segue to the prose in which God explicitly repudiates what the friends have said and affirms what Job has said; and yet in the narrative conclusion God acts, and events unfold, just as the friends had promised. The apparent monologic resolution is an illusion, and the conversation is projected beyond the bounds of the book. The shape of the book grants a measure of truth to each of the perspectives and so directs one's attention to the point of intersection of these unmerged voices.[60]

Newsom does not name as ironic the way in which the metadiscourse of Job "undermines any monologizing tendencies" by means of its multiple voices that continually talk past each other—in monologues. Nor does she name as ironic the way in which the unfolding of the plot covertly destabilizes the apparently legitimated perspective of Job himself, a point she makes persuasively. But these rhetorical features of the text are certainly ironic. One may read the significance of the clash of perspectives and narratological trajectory in Job in at least two ways. Is the monologic resolution of the plot an illusion, or is it rather the apparent dialogism that turns out to be illusory? Both readings are possible, because ironic texts allow for significant freedom in the reader's (re)construction of potential unspoken meanings. Much depends on the context within which each ironic text is construed. Muecke stresses the crucial "use of a context to supplement, modify, or even reverse the meaning of a text" and notes the breadth of possibilities available to the ironist: "The context that an ironist relies upon may vary from a single fact to a whole socio-cultural environment, from what is known to or felt by addressor and addressee alone to what is universally accepted."[61] The adept interpreter will reconstruct many aspects affecting the act of ironic communication: a sense of linguistics and literary forms; knowledge of potential political and social settings and their possibilities for influence on the production of texts; familiarity with ancient literary genres and traditions; a feeling for the artistic style, the theological temperament, and the rhetorical voicing of the biblical text.

Indeed, the very fact that one passage or line or trope in a text may be clearly ironic can alert the reader to the textual context itself as ironic in more subtle ways as well.[62] The employment of irony presents multidimensional contours for the reader's evaluation and underlines the subjectivity of interpretation. Irony does nevertheless place a constraint on unbridled hermeneutical relativism in one important regard. Hegemonic, flat construals of the "said" are preemptively and definitively deconstructed. Stephen H. Webb's reflection on hyperbole is applicable also to irony. He writes, "Hyperbole, then, marks the irresponsibility of language, that moment when by means of profusion and exuberance, language is no longer bound to instrumentality and utility. Hyperbole can be defined in functional terms as an inherent temptation within language, the original sin, we could say, against the structures that make communication reasonable, ordered, and trustworthy."[63] Irony, too, works against the implication that language is reasonable and trustworthy, as we have seen with de Man. Irony subverts its own communication, demonstrating that it cannot be relied on to communicate reliably. Whether by means of exuberant excess, devastating understatement, or some other form of incongruity, irony does make one thing clear: that its own communication is not reasonable. With irony, one may not know exactly what is being proposed as more trustworthy than the "said," but one does know that the surface meaning is not trustworthy.

When irony negates meanings, it does so by creating its own precise and sharp contextualization in a particular landscape that is shown to be deceitful and illusory. Yet the contours of that landscape, in the negative, remain the only visible landmarks that guide the interpreter in the negotiation of the new meaning to which the irony points. For the reader to remain competent while interpreting an ironic text, the reader is compelled to reorient her understanding to these deceitful landmarks while attempting to remain cognizant of their treachery. This reorientation is necessary, even if the reader allows it only temporarily or grudgingly as a heuristic concession that makes the interpretive journey through the ironic landscape possible. Because, as Booth says, "irony dramatizes each moment by heightening the consequences of going astray,"[64] the danger of misreading an ironic text compels the reader to practice a temporary assent—often actually a deferral of dissent—prior to the yielding of a full and earnest assent proper to the unspoken, however the reader may construct that.[65] The rhetoric of irony effects a change in the praxis of the reader prior to any affirmation of the ironic sense that the reader might eventually choose to bestow.

Textual irony moves fluidly between the aggressive or coercive and the evocative or playful, signifying through the reader's apprehension of charged semantic transactions among three elements: what is stated, what is tacitly affirmed by means of rejection of the stated, and what is made visible by means of the interaction between what is stated and what is unsaid. Irony operates in a rhetorically dramatized communal space negotiated continually by the author, the (real or implied) competent reader, and the implied incompetent reader.[66] Irony invites the reader's complicity in the rejection of the surface meaning of the matter being communicated and invites participation in the creation of a new meaning that simultaneously relies on and moves beyond that which has been stated. And whether ominously or teasingly, irony threatens the interpretive disenfranchisement of any unperspicacious reader who fails properly to decipher the text's invitation.

Irony is extraordinarily complex in its rhetorical functions of signaling, negating, and pointing beyond its own apparent limitations. This complexity of rhetorical dynamics notwithstanding, and despite my conviction that irony resists definition, it may be helpful to propose a working definition to help orient the reader to the theoretical grounding of my own readings of ironic texts. Here I am interested only in discursive ironies—verbal and literary ironies that take shape within human discourse. I am not here analyzing so-called cosmic ironies that do not find expression in creaturely acts of communication.

The pastiche-like nature of my definition below will be immediately apparent. It is eclectic because I have found elements of value in the work of all of the theorists of irony discussed above. I decline to choose one hermeneutical "system" over another when diverse elements may be held together, even if (ironic) tensions may result. My working definition, then, is this:

> *Irony is a performance of misdirection that generates aporetic interactions between an unreliable "said" and a truer "unsaid" so as to persuade us of something that is subtler, more complex, or more profound than the apparent meaning. Irony disrupts cultural assumptions about the narrative coherence that seems to ground tropological and epistemological transactions, inviting us into an experience of alterity that moves us toward new insight by problematizing false understandings.*

My focus on irony as aporetic, culturally disruptive, and invitational should indicate that I find irony to create not static definitional substitutions or propositions but fluid, irresolvable engagements with the cultural and semantic expectations of both ironists and audiences.

The specter of anachronism might seem to loom in this discussion when we consider applying contemporary literary-critical insights to Hebrew Bible texts. In order to forestall an objection that ancient Semitic texts likely did not engage in such complicated rhetorical transactions, I offer here a pertinent insight of Stephen A. Geller. Geller is interested to underline the literary character of biblical religion rather than the religious character of biblical literature. Musing on unsolvable questions raised by the story of Jacob wrestling at the Jabbok, Geller writes:

> Jacob's defeating God is blasphemous; his defeating a man is meaningless. One naturally tries to posit some intermediary, but still supernatural being: an angel. But why is the term *mal'āk*, "angel," then avoided, especially since it already forms one of the leading words, and angels play prominent roles elsewhere in the Jacob saga? . . . The only reasonable answer is that it is not the author's intention that we resolve this issue, that is, the ambiguity is precisely his aim. . . . That meaning is a dialectic that the mind forms out of relations, emerging in this case from oppositions of themes, contexts, and levels of significance, is a particularly modernist viewpoint. [But] I do not think that it is being forced on this biblical passage as something foreign to the way of thinking of ancient [writers].[67]

Geller expresses well the multidimensionality of ancient Semitic textual signifying by means of relationships established between the spoken and the unspoken. The use of ambiguity was an essential part of ancient biblical writers' artistry.

I concede, with Hutcheon and others, that the choice to infer or attribute irony lies ultimately with the reader. Evaluations of the appropriateness, significance, and meanings of irony will differ from reader to reader according to various understandings of text, political and ideological contexts, construction of implied audiences, and other variables affecting the reading process.[68] An example may illustrate the point. A 1989 article by Arlene N. Okerlund opens with this sentence: "We hardly need, one would think, yet another discussion of the differences between the Elizabethan sonnet and the metaphysical lyric."[69] Who is her audience? Who is this "we" that would not benefit from another discussion of this apparently exhaustively belabored topic? I am not a member of her implied audience if she has meant that statement literally, because, to my regret, I do need instruction in the difference between the Elizabethan sonnet and the metaphysical lyric. I am not a competent reader of Elizabethan poetry, nor, then, of Okerlund's article. Does she mean me? I dare say she does not. Put more subtly, she likely understands that the uninitiated may be reading but chooses to imply that her discourse is not primarily for them.[70] She writes to cognoscenti in her field. That her opening gambit is ironic is clear: she has feinted toward suggesting the redundancy of her article, but then takes a full ten pages to demonstrate precisely why her analysis is, in fact, needed. But more than that, the question of audience is crucial for determining intention. Her implied audience is composed of experts in Elizabethan poetry and poetics who in her view have, despite extensive exposure to conversations on related topics, not yet adequately comprehended the points she wishes to make. Understanding the implied audience is crucial for the apprehension of nuances in a piece of literature. Yet the implied audience is elusive—even for contemporary texts, and much more so for ancient writings.

Even conceding the elusiveness of implied audiences and textual determinacy as such, the rhetorical forcefulness of irony's negative constraints should be acknowledged as a crucial dynamic that shapes any responsive reading praxis. Ironic texts may be open theoretically to an unlimited number of readings, but not all of those readings will be able to claim persuasively that they are responsive to the text.[71] There are discernible flags of irony, notably incongruity and exaggeration in presentation, whether in content or in tone. By means of these signals, ironic texts do attempt to close off the interpretive arena to non-ironic readings, while yet relying on those false literal readings to construct the deceitful landscape through which interpretation must journey. The precise contours of an originary meaning in any ironic text cannot necessarily be definitively discerned even by a reading praxis that is responsive to the invitations and deferrals of irony. But the pressure of ironic representation does, at least, coerce the reader away from a naïve fixation on literalist construals of the said.[72] Irony brings considerable force to bear against the specter of idiosyncratic, uncontrolled relativism. Definitive understanding of a thoroughly ironic text is virtually never possible, but definitive misunderstanding is quite possible.

The notion of authorial voice, then, may helpfully be reconceived as an ironic dynamic process itself rather than a static, content-bound identification of an individual or individuals. Authorship is a claim to speak, a claim that any listener or reader may find ironic because of the duplicity and elusiveness of words and significance being communicated. For example, Kenneth M. Craig has argued that the very use of characters in narrative requires an authorially constructed distance that can ironize the claims of those characters.[73] Yet, ironic though the activity of authoring may be, it persists in practices of writing, editing, reading, and response. The author can never be effaced so long as any practice of communication continues, even though the possibilities for both understanding and misunderstanding may be virtually infinite. So to erase the claim that authorship is meaningful—that is, to "author" the claim that authorship is meaningless—would be a theory-driven error that is itself deeply ironic. Authorship circumscribes some alternatives for the operation of reading and opens possibilities for other alternatives, and irony is especially helpful in pointing out that there are profound stabilities and coherences to be found even in the most unreliable communication. Positing an author is thus both ironic and necessary.

Those who generate works of art and literature dare to speak into the void, risking tremendous vulnerability through the naked offering of their creativity to implied communities of those who will respond. To appropriate a text or work of art while saying one cannot ever hear the voice of the author is to exploit, to commodify. Anthropologist Johannes Fabian has said, "[T]he Other is never simply given, never just found or encountered, but *made*."[74] Our perceptions of alterity are constructed rather than "found," as postcolonial criticism shows. But equally important to the postcolonialist perspective is the point that the Other exists beyond what we make of him or her. If this is so, then the speech of the Other must be acknowledged.

It remains to lay out, briefly, some guideposts for method in the interpretation of irony. According to what criteria may we plausibly argue that irony is present? If irony can be plausibly argued to be present, how can we get at what it signifies? Any methodology for analysis of irony may rest on a few relatively secure theoretical observations—for example, irony often depends on hyperbole or understatement, always exploits some sort of disjuncture, usually plays on culturally conditioned differences between audience expectations and results. But ultimately, method in the interpretation of irony may not be able to avoid charges of being mercurial in its practice, of relying at crucial points on idiosyncrasies of reader perception or on special pleading in particular contexts. Method in the interpretation of irony risks appearing tautological to any who do not happen to agree with the outcome of the analysis.

Granted, the interpretation of irony is always something of an art. Nevertheless, for the sake of more precise scholarly discourse about biblical ironies, needed is the articulation of a rigorous, context-responsive, multidimensional methodology by means of which to argue for ironic meanings in biblical texts. Such a methodology will need to take into account the presence of textual cues, themselves constructed by readers in part but not entirely. It will need, then, to map the unspoken and freighted spaces that remain around the unreliable communications of irony, that signify through the absence of misdirection and thus are left as possible areas of meaning. Method is intended throughout this book to be the thoughtful articulation of prior experience with reading. Method does not, when properly applied, coerce the text, but rather responds to it in a way that can communicate persuasively what may already be happening in the practice of reading. It is therefore most fruitfully understood as a mapping of the terrain that already lies beneath the feet of the interpreter, yielding cleared pathways and unanticipated obstacles, anticipating potential points of reference while allowing the text and the reader, together, to create the hermeneutical journey. Below is my attempt to articulate such a method.

Method: Multiaxial Cartography

Instances of ironic communication are so diverse in form, authorial intent, and rhetorical effect that it would be impossible to construct a monolithic methodology adequate to the task of interpreting all ironic texts. Genre analysis is often needed, particularly to understand ways in which the medium of a communication may be being subverted by content inappropriate to that medium, based on expectations about what the genre is normally intended to signal. (This is so whether genre expectations are identified with historical usage of form in similar literatures contemporaneous with the time of composition of the biblical text, with our reader responses two and a half millennia later, or at any point in the shifting continuum that lies between those points.) The apprehension of tone, without which irony is inevitably missed, requires literary analysis of plot, characterization, and tropes such as hyperbole and understatement. An understanding of implied audience(s) in any text is vital to grasp the power and point of the rhetoric, and there, contextual historical information may often be useful, even though the definition of audience is in part constructed by the reader heuristically as she reads. So there are some diverse but reasonably predictable features that may be sought as points of reference in the interpretation of ironic texts.

But because irony subverts expectations by the falsifying representation of different kinds of unreliable communications, the discernment of irony—and more difficult still, the interpretation of what may be meant by the unspoken—will in every case depend on assessment of a host of contextual particulars. These contextual particulars cannot be anticipated ahead of time, except in the broadest and most general sense, by a methodology asking one prescribed set of questions or probing for only one kind of evidence. Irony by its nature thwarts attempts at comprehensive systematization,[75] and thus the methodology I suggest here must necessarily incorporate many planes of approach as a structural feature of its hermeneutic.[76] It must be multiaxial not only because a variety of hermeneutical approaches will likely prove fruitful for the interpreter, but also because textual irony draws dialogically on many kinds of provisional, context-dependent communication and thus requires an integrative, multifaceted response.[77]

A number of creative metaphors have been proposed by scholars thinking about the multidimensional process of reading and analysis. Peter D. Miscall suggests that the concept of "labyrinth" is helpful for thinking about reading. He writes of the polyvalent images he has explored in Isaiah:

> Attempts to unravel these threads and to find our way out of or to the center of the Labyrinth of Isaiah result in the construction of an ever more elaborate or complicated maze. . . . [A] Labyrinth of images . . . has multiple entrances and centers and, therefore, no entrance or center. A Labyrinth is a book fashioned from a reading that traverses a text by picking up and following certain threads, whether words, images or themes; by putting some of them down and picking up others; and by leaving others lying on the floor to be picked up by others in the future.[78]

I would like to build on Miscall's metaphor of labyrinth, especially to underline the important notion that complex texts have multiple entrances and centers. The metaphor of labyrinth-walking speaks well to the activity of reading in that it preserves the mysterious quality of traveling along formally structured yet nevertheless delightful and surprising paths. One may travel a new route even in a labyrinth with which one is familiar; similarly, one may reread a text and find new insights therein. Gaps exist (I am thinking here of labyrinths that are made of living materials such as boxwood), and breaches can be forced by the traveler without too much effort, so walking the labyrinth is indeed an ever-changing and potentially deconstructive activity. While there are strong cues to the traveler to traverse preordained paths, the traveler need not comply. The labyrinth metaphor implies a reader-directed creativity: the traveler may follow trails without a determinate goal or choose a path other than that intended by the labyrinth's creator. It is noteworthy, too, that the metaphor has classically involved the valence of risk (does a minotaur lurk in the center? will one ever be able to find the way out?). But the metaphor does signal, albeit subtly, the coercion of the labyrinth creator. Although existing paths may be taken in a number of combinations when one is walking a labyrinth, and new paths may be trodden where none existed before, labyrinths are not, in fact, wholly constructed by those who travel them. To my mind, this is relevant to the reading process as well. Labyrinths have been constructed in a prior meaning-making activity by an author according to an intentional artistic plan, which may be appreciated, ignored, or actively resisted in any number of ways by the interpreter. The resonances of "labyrinth," then, are helpful for hermeneutics whether the analogy is to constructing one or traveling through one.

Mark Cameron Love reflects on Miscall's metaphor of "labyrinth building" and comes up with his own metaphor—that of "creating a matrix" that continually shifts and reorders itself—to try to capture the constructive, deconstructive, intertextual, dynamic, and elusive aspects of the reading process.[79] Love's analogy of "matrix" usefully expands the conceptual range, adding the notion of depth and thus multidimensionality. His metaphor takes intertextuality more fully into account, because it allows for "sub-matrices" and for the continual readjustment, new creation, and reshaping of the whole or of particular parts, and it gets at the interaction of multiple levels of signification in ever-changing relationships of meaning. "Matrix" thus is a powerful metaphor for reading as well; yet it does not convey the sense of journeying that is so important for Miscall's idea and, in my view, for the act of reading. The metaphor that I want to describe my own method as a reader of irony needs to involve both the sense of journeying and the sense of multidimensionality.

What I have come up with is the idea of a multidimensional map, or more precisely, multiaxial cartography. This metaphor holds together the idea of a real anterior landscape (the text) and readers' productions (map-making), without being reductionist about either one in the activity of reading.[80] When one reads, landscapes unfold before one in the foreground, middle distance, and distant horizon—and even, as it were, behind one and far out of sight. One records where one has traveled, whether purposefully in a journal or an annotated map (analogous to the writing of articles, books, reflection pieces, or other writing) or implicitly in the remembrance of places encountered (evoking cultural intertextuality writ large). To talk about those landscapes, one may use a map. To revisit those places, one may use a map even though one finds that the landscapes are never "the same" since the journeyer and the topography inevitably change. To understand landscapes better, one can consult a variety of maps before, during, or after one's journey. It goes without saying that maps themselves are skewed to their cartographers' cultural biases—to see this, one need only consult an early medieval map that shows dragons at the edge of the world or a colonialist map that positions the imperial power at the center of its cartographic representation.[81] The use of numerous kinds of maps is helpful for the fullest picture geographically and culturally. One might ponder a political map of boundaries and governmental authority, a topographical map, climate-oriented cartographic data, a map oriented to cultural monuments and places of special historical significance, a map generated by satellite imagery, and novels and poems about the place to which one will be going. Multiple dimensions give the traveler the fullest and most complete construction of those land-scapes. Thus diverse viewpoints into the landscapes themselves and into the cartographic process are needed.

Are maps absolutely necessary for traveling? No. Here I concede a point to those who object to the dominance of theory in contemporary literary discourse.[82] One may travel without (material) maps, without consciously theorizing one's experience of the landscape, without taking into account others' journeys and the ways in which different sets of questions bring into relief different areas of interest in the landscape and history. But one's jour-ney is always directed by overt and implicit assumptions. Anyone who trav-els has some sort of map of information or rough spatial relations in their imagination, however incomplete, erroneous, or fanciful that map might be. Just so, reading always involves assumptions. Theory—done well—should help articulate those assumptions gracefully. Good theory is like an elegant, precise, and colorful map. It does not replace the journeying itself, but judicious use of theory can enrich the experience, make the experi-ence communicable to others, and suggest perspectives from which to view what one is experiencing as one moves through the landscape.

My cartography metaphor has significant points of contact with a model proposed by Susan Niditch, which she calls her "overlay map tech-nique." Drawing on insights from structuralist analysis and folklore stud-ies, Niditch turns her attention to various levels of signification suggested when traditional motifs are deployed in biblical literature. Levels of detail regarding basic plot, cultural assumptions, development of literary themes, and so on can be explored on a given niveau (as it were, on a par-ticular leaf of the overlay map) or looked at multidimensionally, through a number of the leaves, since their transparency allows for depth as well as horizontal detail.[83] My "multiaxial cartography" differs from Niditch's helpful metaphor in two respects. First, I aim with this model to imply a high degree of reader agency. The noun "map" as the central figure of the metaphor might imply a fixed document gazed upon by a decoder, who will simply examine various levels of overlays. By contrast, with "cartogra-phy" I focus more on the activity of mapmaking as evocative for both au-thors and readers. Cartographers work from preexisting maps, from sto-ries, and from encounters with the landscape, but they also draw and measure and construct relationships among topographical features, rep-resenting what they see and what they imagine according to the cultural mores, religious beliefs, and analytical practices of their time. This cre-ative action of cartography supplies a crucial metaphorical dimension for the act of interpreting ironic texts. Second, I intend with "multiaxial" to get at vectors of meaning both within texts and in acts of construing mean-ing. "Axial" is meant to imply motion and activity rather than static levels of meaning there to be observed. In mathematics, axes move toward infinity. They are plotted using specific coordinates, to be sure, but those coordinates are only heuristic aids for the signifying of motion toward values that are not constrained by what is visible in the axial diagram. The multi-axial quality of this cartographic process involves a kind of interdisciplinarity that not only puts diverse questions to the text but informs the way in which the analysis itself is being carried out. More than simply the collaborative or sequential use of complementary methods, the cartography I have in mind seeks to demonstrate through integrative queries the rhetorical ways in which texts are signifying across a variety of planes of communication simultaneously.[84] While an interpreter may ply a variety of single methods in sequence for heuristic purposes, the integrative process of working to understand the rhetorical space and action of a text in its wholeness is essential if the text is not to be left as an unconnected group of pieces of itself, fragmented and never fully "heard" rhetorically.

Such work of the imagination involves constructing a view of potentially reliable terrain in the spaces in between the spoken and the unspoken. Failing the positive identification of reliable terrain, the hermeneut may at least make a provisional identification of plausibly less unreliable terrain. This may involve a revisiting of the question of audience(s) and appropriate expectations. If the implied audience of a certain ironic text has been rendered unreliable, how might one discern a truer implied audience in the text, behind the irony? If the implied author of an ironic text is shown to have an unreliable voice, how might one then get at a truer authorial voice behind the facade? These things are difficult to discuss, but it is essential that we try, lest the points—or better, the counterpoints—of ironic texts continue to elude us. While misreadings can be fruitful,[85] there are also risks that attend the misreading of texts in community, with consequences that range from the mildly regrettable missed literary opportunity to the disastrously harmful ideological misreading.

Semantic multivalence is possible even with an ostensibly simple declarative sentence. How much more, then, do ironic texts yield multiple possibilities for the unspoken rhetorical aims and goals invisibly shaping every ironic utterance. The cartography for which I am arguing will require rigorous contextualization for every persuasive explication of irony. But there will remain that element of the artistic, the intuitive, the shared grasp of elusive brilliance that marks the construction of the ironic "community" of those who understand an ironist's point, or at least who understand what the ironist's point cannot be.

Must every interpretation of irony be idiosyncratic and persuasive only to the degree that its proponent happens to be eloquent? Perhaps, because irony is always both contextual and perceptual. But some readings of ironic texts will be more persuasive than others to a wider audience. I suggest that the following criteria might be useful for assessing ironic readings of texts.

(a) A reading will be more persuasive to the degree that it can account for multiple axes along which the unreliable "said" may be seen to signal incongruity.
(b) A reading will be more persuasive to the degree that it takes seriously the particulars of the "said" in its construction of the "unsaid" and its relationship to the "said."
(c) A reading will be more persuasive to the degree that it acknowledges constitutive aspects of the reader's own reading process as an essential component of the competent reading of irony. Whatever one's reading strategy may be, consistency between articulated goals of reading and the kind of map that is produced will be crucial for the persuasiveness of the reading generated by the map in question.

The quality of persuasiveness as such is not the only or necessarily the most desirable quality in a reading. What about liveliness, theological sensitivity, political boldness? What one looks for in a reading depends entirely on its appropriateness for a particular context and one's own desires. "Imaginative" or "subversive" or "evangelistic" may count for more in some interpretive contexts than "persuasive" does. I, however, am interested in clear and compelling lines of argumentation, hence the criteria that I have spelled out above have to do with persuasiveness. Persuasiveness is a readerly experience (whether one is reading a text or reading theory) fully as much as it is a byproduct of the elegance of one's method. The interpretation of irony is not fundamentally a theory-driven enterprise, notwithstanding the objections of readers who find it perverse to quantify irony, humor, and so on. Those who content themselves with genial claims that they "know irony when they see it" and find theory to be unnecessary for their own purportedly transparent methods of reading simply are not attending closely to the methodological assumptions they are already bringing to their reading. Theory gives words to a reader's experience of mounting suspicion, or of delighted disjuncture, of charming invitation to play or alarming alienation from the hitherto reassuring voice of the text. Theory simply attempts to articulate that experience and understand its features in terms that can be communicated to another.

This book will unfold as follows. In each chapter some biblical material will be read: a story or group of related stories, or in some cases a discourse or a variety of types of discourse, will be heard and responded to.

The possibilities for irony will be explored in the process of interpretation. The cartographic method described above has been applied along multiple axes that I have deemed responsive to cues from the text itself, the commitments of other scholars whose readings I find persuasive, and my own interests. My conclusions about ways in which irony shapes meaning in these diverse passages will constitute one set of mappings of the operations of biblical irony across biblical discourse and, in some cases, scholarly reception history. Taken together, I hope, these mappings will demonstrate the power of the unspoken in ironic sacred texts: power for deconstruction and for building, for affirmation and subversion, for liberation and for scathing indictment. I hope to show how much more challenging and more demanding of our active participation the biblical text can be when we appreciate the sophistication of its ironies.

It is my hope that these provisional maps of ironic terrain will prove themselves the sort of maps that, once unfolded, can never be folded neatly back up again by any reader who has considered the ironies presented here for consideration. The unpredictable and bewildering terrain of the Hebrew Bible resists attempts to control it according to methodological goals—theory ever chasing after practice,[86] trying to articulate what has happened as elegantly as possible while not missing the next surprising turn, the next complicated reading experience, the next ironic moment of textual resistance. My attempt to craft a multiaxial methodology is born of a desire to honor and affirm any possible resistance offered by the texts I am reading. It is my hope that the biblical texts in this study will not be coerced by theory, but rather that they will be illuminated even as the theory itself is shaped and rearticulated by reader engagement (mine and others') with the biblical texts. Mieke Bal describes beautifully the dynamic between texts and theory in her remarks about narratology. She speaks of theory as itself a subtext in relation to the texts it interrogates and illumines:

> I will assess . . . the theory's capacity to raise problems rather than solve them, to make it [viz., the text] more interesting, make it speak more excitingly, than it used to do without the theory. It is to be challenged on its own terms. But the text, in response to that challenge, will challenge the theory, point out its limits, and force it to go beyond itself. As a result, the very dialogue between narrative theory and a body of biblical texts leads to a transgression of disciplinary boundaries.[87]

A multiaxial methodology that takes account of the unspoken will make room for resonant spaces within which biblical voices may challenge and ironize not only the "said" of their own utterances but our own reading practices as we attend to them.

It is time to leave the relative safety of theory in the abstract for the dangers and delights of its dialogical practice with actual texts. We shall now muse on the story of the Garden of Eden as preparation for our expulsion into the wild, ironic world of the Hebrew Bible.

Leaving the Garden: The Wisdom of Irony

We begin at the beginning of biblically articulated consciousness of humanness, with Genesis 1–3. Some of the ironies inscribed in the story of the Garden of Eden have long been noticed by interpreters sensitive to the exquisite dilemma posed by God for the newly created human beings in the constraint placed on them not to eat fruit from the tree of knowledge. Choose to know truth? In choosing to know, Eve and Adam must disobey the Creator of all truth. Choose to remain ignorant? In choosing not to know, Eve and Adam would forfeit the capacity to understand what it means to obey. Sexual maturation seems to unfold from the choice to disobey, and in that maturation lies the only possibility for Eve and Adam to fulfill the Creator's command to be fruitful and multiply. Yet shame seems to lie therein as well—shame and curse. Anomalies lie everywhere just below the surface in this tale of origins and death. These are not just minor quirks in the picture of creation. These anomalies are deeply tensive fractures in a text that tells the story of who humans are in the world and in relationship to God.

Ironies abound in this story on multiple levels. The four axes along which our inquiry will probe are: semantic study of wordplay as it works within the narratological trajectory of Genesis 1–3; comparative study of ancient Near Eastern motifs of serpent and tree that may be seen to influence the tropes used here; ideological critique of desire and sexuality and their ironic connection to knowing and knowledge; and redaction-critical study of ways in which Genesis 2–3 may be responding, in a diachronic dialogue, to Genesis 1.

First, we listen for the semantics of language here in this story of humans coming to speak for the first time. How does language operate in the chaos of the cosmos as God works in stages to structure it? How does language operate in the Garden before there is human culture to freight it and define its meanings, before there are humans to speak truth and to misdirect? In the beginning, language signifies the identity of birds and fish and animals and humans. It also bespeaks the creative power of God. God speaks cosmos and life into being in Genesis 1: "Let there be!" It is not only the divine word that is powerful, it is language itself that expresses identity, of the many and of the self, of one and of incalculable others. God speaks blessing, and multiplicity teems forth over the mountains and through the valleys, bounding into seas and splashing into rivers, swarming up the trunks of trees and soaring into the clouds, digging down into dark earthy holes and undulating into cool subterranean caverns. Language sings the manifold possibilities of the future into the present moment: "Be fruitful and multiply!" It asserts unity—a unity that is rich in diversity and yet remains connected nonetheless—over against otherness.

But ironically, the semantic performance of unity is subverted in the epitome of its naming. God's last creative utterance in the sequence creates the possibility of boundaries that can be transgressed. The human beings are made in God's image, but there is threat in that unity, a threat that requires constraints (Gen 1:26). The 'ādām is named as being of the ground ('ădāmâ), and the woman ('iššâ) is named as being of the man ('îš). But otherness—distinction and boundedness and desire for that which is apart—permeates the unity that is claimed, and so power must be exercised. The curses unfold, not only as spoken "speech act" but as story, as narrative, to show us Who gets to curse whom. As it turns out, humans are not the same as God, and man is not the same as the ground, and woman is not the same as man. There is much irony here. The creator God speaks all things into their existence—not just into existence, but into their particular existence, speaks all things into the ways that they are. But further on, the act of pronouncing the nature of things inevitably obscures the simultaneous creation of differences between them. God's speech (and the speech of the biblical narrator, when God is not being quoted directly)[88] is holy and true, and yet unreliable. The divine word is powerful, yet we must perceive also the tremendous power of the unspoken in the moment of creation, in the very moment of assertion. Life itself is spoken, and obedience to the divine command is part of the very act of speaking. Yet in this seamless unity, we see the inevitable development of alienation (the humans hide) and the exercise of power across distinctions (God curses).

Our second axis of inquiry explores ancient Near Eastern motifs of serpent and tree. The voluble serpent as ancient Near Eastern figure of wisdom surprises the reader here. This narrative focuses in on this particular creature in a way that makes perfect sense for the plot of a folk tale. But it accords well neither with the cosmic scope of Genesis 1 nor with the central role of the humans as alluded to previously in both Genesis 1 (made in God's image, as the narratological culmination of the creative words God speaks) and Genesis 2 (as seen in the human's meaningful work of tilling the soil and naming the animals). Does the serpent guard the tree of knowledge or invite its plundering? The serpent is characterized as the savviest of all creatures (Hebrew ʿārûm), but is its wisdom to be understood as beneficial or malevolent? Both are possible. Serpent symbology in the ancient Near East associated snakes with youth, wisdom, magic, chaos, and chthonic forces.[89] Less than entirely useful is the older, theologically anxious view in biblical studies that the serpent is there to be "demythologized," robbed of the power it enjoyed in other ancient Near Eastern religions.[90] To the contrary, this serpent is extraordinarily powerful, successfully affecting the future of the entire human race against the express wishes of the Creator of the universe. George Savran writes:

> The snake speaks of its own accord. . . . In a world-view in which words are charged with creative power, this capability may point to a source of power outside of God, whether it be a whittled-down representation of those forces which oppose God in creation, or an allegorical representation of the independence of the human mind in confrontation with God. The very fact that the snake has the capacity for articulate speech, together with the subversive use to which it has been put, challenges the hierarchical order of the universe as it has been created.[91]

The serpent is the ultimate transgressor and model of all future transgression. It is wise without, apparently, having eaten of the fruit of the tree, and it knows things of great importance without, apparently, having obeyed God.[92] How are these things possible, unless either the serpent is functioning as God's representative[93] or God has not said all that could be said about wisdom, death, and power? The serpent may be demythologized in the sense that it is not technically divine, but it offers hope for all who would storm the gates of heaven and wrest power from the realm of divinity. Threat abounds: not only threat to human welfare but threat to the idea of God's power and God's framing of the pertinent questions for human life. Indeed, David M. Carr has argued persuasively in a diachronic study that the "Fall"-related aspect of the Garden of Eden story is precisely, and polemically, responding to the threat posed by a literarily prior tradition that prized wisdom and human autonomy.[94]

The serpent guards the tree in the center of the Garden, and by scripting that boundary, the serpent subtly invites transgression. The tree, itself an ancient Near Eastern figure for wisdom,[95] ironically connects wisdom and not-life—not exactly death, but mortality and challenging existence as qualities of life for the two primal humans— through the allure of its fruit. The syllogism simultaneously traps Eve and invites her to escape: life is wisdom, but wisdom is death. Death is wisdom, but wisdom is life. Paradoxically, embracing death is the path to fuller life, life in the image of God, life lived through being "like" God. Eat of this fruit, Eve hears, and you will be able to live even in the face of the death that you will have brought upon yourself. As Sam Dragga has noted, the serpent may understand immortality in a different way than does God. The serpent in fact revoices what immortality can mean. The individual may die, but if sexual procreation becomes possible through the expanded knowledge enjoyed by Adam and Eve, then they become immortal through their multiplying offspring in a way that can never again be constrained by the bounds of the Garden.[96] The serpent is perhaps being represented ironically as promising more (or other) than what it can deliver. Indeed, its symbology may well be intended to clash with the narrative, problematizing audience expectations on several levels. Reuven Kimelman observes:

> Those who see the serpent as a symbol of fertility or immortality should be surprised to find it associated first with the tree of knowledge of good and evil as opposed to the tree of life, and then with pangs of childbirth, expulsion from the life-giving waters of Eden, and ultimately death. Those who find in it a symbol of healing, as associated with the likes of Aesclepius, should be struck at its capacity for precipitating the sicknesses of humanity. Those who perceive in it a symbol of wisdom should find it hard to believe that such a sapiential figure could induce such folly.[97]

The serpent is the first ironist we encounter in Scripture. Its ironic double voicing speaks truth precisely despite its unreliability.[98]

Our third axis of inquiry probes on ideological-critical grounds the relationships represented in the Garden of Eden story between knowledge and desire. In this world that God has just created, differentiation is required in order for the divine creativity to reach its apex, to be fulfilled beyond God's wildest dreams. As Genesis 2 opens, myriad creaturely and botanical species have already been formed, have sprung up and branched out, each according to its winged or furry or gelatinous or leafy or prickly or iridescent or feathery or spongy kind. Already, the fullness of creation is represented in this story by breathtaking variety, by difference that matters deeply. But there must be further differentiation in order for the ground to bring forth its most abundant fruit. Humans are needed to till the earth. There is implied a much more important dimension to that function than simply digging in dirt and planting seeds, something wrestled with and commanded in multifarious forms throughout the Hebrew Bible. God requires the earth to give forth the magnificent abundance of cultural differentiation, because it is only in diverse expressions of human imagination, human spirit, and human longing that obedience to God and worship of God have any meaning.

The interplay between sweeping paradigmatic types and particular stories within Genesis 1–4 yields an ironic insight: the desire for knowledge is what creates the necessary differentiation that shapes human culture, including human responses to the divine, for good and for ill. Adam and Eve do not procreate until they have eaten of the fruit of the tree of knowledge and gain the wisdom to perceive their differences. Commentators have long suggested that humankind would not have spread over the whole earth, according to the requirements of the narrative, if the fruit of the tree had not opened Adam's and Eve's eyes to the difference of the Other, a difference that compelled touch, exploration, response, gasps of delight.[99] And Cain, the result of their first coupling, generates out of his sexual desire for his own nameless wife the possibility of new life, ironically enough, in the midst of his exile for the murder of Abel. Desire and otherness thus irrepressibly bring forth life in the midst of alienation and death. Genesis 4 claims the desire to own and encompass otherness, to see and touch what is unattainable. God's favor, so inscrutably withheld, is ever the primal object of desire, even more than sexual fulfillment. It may be that unity with God was ironically lost in the grasping for it.[100] But put another way, the narrative shows how the human search for God can go forward only because of the disobedience—the choice for autonomy and knowledge—that began with Eve in the Garden. Cain, his wife, and their offspring build cities: the birth of Enoch makes possible human life in community. They initiate agriculture: Jabal leads humankind into herding and tilling as means of life, enabling subsistence and offerings to God. They create music: Jubal's lyre and pipe sing humankind into the rich possibilities of celebration and worship, of dance and love song and psalm. They forge bronze and iron tools: Tubal-cain works into concrete and touchable forms the instruments humans need to manipulate the earth into bearing more fruit, to coax clay into shapes that allow for storage and writing and transport, to wrestle wood and metal into shapes that can be used to kill. In all this, he generates the possibility for change itself in human life. And this human culture, the inexhaustible differentiation and Babel of it, drives toward a defining moment in the narratological trajectory of the final form of Genesis: Abram comes from Ur. Abram the Chaldean strides into the horizon of the biblical tradition, proleptically gathers about himself the identity of an entire people, and journeys into and out of exile—to Egypt and back, to Gerar and back, to the terrifying brink of extinction (with the near-sacrifice of his son Isaac) and back.

Finally, diachronic inquiry into possible redactional purposes underlying the present composition of Genesis 1–3 yields not just polyva-

lence (a God who is distant and omnipotent in one account but change-
able and vulnerable in the other) but, rather, a dialogical connection
that highlights certain elements in both stories and ironizes others.
Those who read for signs of complexity in the historical growth of biblical literature—tradition historians and redaction critics—notice an
edginess running through Genesis 1–3, a responsiveness that is at times
complementary and at times confrontational in this story of God and
the first humans. Which voice is responding to which? Perhaps the story
in Genesis 1, with its interest in power and the controlling of chaos
through structure,[101] is a countering of the muddiness and unpredictable relationships we see in Genesis 2–3. Or perhaps the relationship
works diachronically the other way around: the cold transcendence of
the Priestly theology is warmed by the lively anthropomorphisms of the
non-Priestly story that follows.[102] Is Genesis 1 being ironized by Genesis
2–3, or does the ironic commenting work in the reverse?

The redaction-critical question is more complex than the assertions of
older source-critical scholarship would imply. The position that the
Priestly writing in the Pentateuch is later than the non-Priestly material
must still account for growth within traditions over time, possible use of
additional ancient traditions by a later editor, potential diversity of viewpoints within a single source, and overlapping concerns or shared language used in different sources, all of which may be expected of the creative process of any writer or group of writers. Further, as Joseph
Blenkinsopp has argued, linguistic and thematic characteristics of the
Garden of Eden story may suggest a relatively late provenance in wisdom
circles.[103] It does matter how one reads the direction of the dialogue between Genesis 1 and Genesis 2–3. Does the Priestly emphasis on the om-
nipotence and cosmic remove of God counter the portrayal of the God of
the Garden story, or does the God of the Garden elaborate on what the
God of Genesis 1 has proclaimed and done? The Garden of Eden story
goes to great lengths to explain the deficits of the world of its narrative,
which contrasts sharply with the abounding good world of Genesis 1.
Adam and Eve walk the Garden in a time before the earth bursts with lush
vegetation for animals and humans to eat. Irony appears here, precisely in
the careful attempts of the redactors to relate these two traditions about
primeval existence. What God says is true (all of creation is good; humans
are made in God's image; all vegetation is given to humans and animals
for food); and yet, in a crucial way that has to do with understanding the
world and life in it, what God has said is not true. Because these two creation stories have been placed in dialogue with one another, the unspoken now suffuses both Genesis 1 and Genesis 2–3. Neither discourse can
stand independently and still be as true as both stories are together.

The Garden story, read in dialogue with Genesis 1, shows that eating of the forbidden fruit of wisdom is the only way to live in a world that is lush, bursting with sustenance for all living beings, yet that to the pre-wise human seems to be just a dusty field. "Be fruitful and multiply!" is a divine command that can be fulfilled only in the eating of the fruit. God has authorized, indeed required, human discernment of the unsaid in the divine word of remonstrance and in the divine word of promise. The snake that God has made is wise and speaks truly, however undesirable its act of speaking may be. The snake invites Adam and Eve to equip themselves for life that must be lived, endured, in a world that is forever not quite bursting with blessings and sustenance in the way that its Creator made it to be. Their heeding of the snake's invitation allows them to go into a world that desperately needs both their toil and their progeny: that is, their fruitfulness and their multiplying, as God of Genesis 1 commanded and still commands, obliquely, through much of the Hebrew Bible.[104]

Reading the results of the above four avenues of inquiry multiaxially requires that the different sets of questions posed above be allowed to interrogate one another toward the fullest reading possible, a reading that maps different contours of the Garden story and thereby creates interpretive space in which freighted silences can be allowed to signify. Herewith, then, our first attempt to hear word and silence together, to hear different aspects of the text into a fuller interpretation. The semantic tensions in the story between identity of the whole and particularity of the parts are spoken into the very stuff of creation by a God whose word is all-powerful, a speech-act that cannot be resisted or reinterpreted by the chaos into which it comes. As humanity is made in the image of this God, humanity too has the capacity for powerful speech, seen in Adam's naming of animals and in his and Eve's speech before God after the fruit has been eaten, where they name their own words of truth in an attempt to misdirect God and avoid responsibility. Words become unreliable, but they remain nonetheless powerful. This is nowhere more clear than in the figure of the "demythologized" snake whose words change everything in the story of human life. Meanwhile, silence has become very powerful indeed in this story. The fruit of the tree is life and also death, but no one will acknowledge both at the same time. "Hiding" becomes a possibility for humans faced with the displeasure of the divine. Desire makes possible humans' recognition of their differences—nakedness, which constitutes both vulnerability and wisdom—and this in turn makes possible sexual delight and procreation in fulfillment of the divine command in Genesis 1, "Be fruitful and multiply!" Human culture and the possibility for change are generated through the energized gaps between powerful word and powerful silence, between majestic pronouncements of sameness and gleeful shouts of difference. God speaks us into being in Genesis 1, and we re-spond in Genesis 2–3, "Watch us live!" These are fundamental ironies of human culture: language being used simultaneously to confirm and deny, traditions being used to shape a story that undermines their power while yet confirming it, human yearning for sexual union depending on vulner-ability in order to ensure survival. And these ironies all are mapped in the Garden of Eden story as the key to understanding God's image in the lived life of created beings. This is the fruit of the tree of knowledge: God has made us for irony, because anything less would be limiting of human ca-pacities for creation, and we have been made in God's image.

Irony itself must, then, be seen as a fundamental texture of human existence outside the Garden, which is to say, out in the real world that Scripture "reads" through its stories and genealogies, its songs and prayers, its laws and speeches. The Garden story serves to authorize the ironic mode of knowing for all those human beings who must live in a world of thorns, resistant soil, pain, and domination. This world of theirs—of ours—is no Eden. Therefore we can strive to obey God precisely by dis-obeying the divine command not to know.[105] This may mean, then, that the pursuit of clarity as regards ironies and ironic perspectives within the sacred biblical texts themselves constitutes a transgressive inquiry into God's way of framing the dilemma of mortal existence (and, to be sure, an inquiry into humans' often ludicrous attempts to gain power or control). God cannot be right if we are alive and creating culture. And yet, if noth-ing is as it seems, God may be right after all. The best way Scripture can show this may be to contest it—to contest everything—through over-ear-nest assertions, hyperbolic characterizations, subtle understatements, sar-donic observations, and unreliable narrators.

2

FOREIGN RULERS AND
THE FEAR OF GOD

In her book *Irony/Humor,* Candace Lang finds Roland Barthes musing on the "single-voiced dogmatism of ironic discourse,"[1] a notion grounded in his idea that "irony is a meta-citation, the quotation of other codes *as quotations.* . . . The function of the ironic code is to put the stereotypes it repeats in quotation marks, explicitly attributing them to the Other."[2] This is a view of irony with which I am in sympathy. Barthes rightly underlines the "othering"—the rendering as different—not only of the content of the unreliable "said" but of the constructed speaker or thinker who could hold such a flawed notion. Irony puts in quotation marks the very dynamics of alterity and falsehood that it purports to claim. Competent interpretation of irony thus requires a strong objection to the said, a refusal of the aporetic pseudo-quoting that constitutes ironic communication. Interpreting irony requires a reconstructive listening that combines oblique disbelief with an imagination focused on what is not being said outright. Attending to clues of incongruence in an ironic text, the reader of irony responds by both heeding and disbelieving the text's tone, rhetorical style, or argument, its characterization of plot or narratorial persona, its manipulation of tradition, or its apparent construal of its own larger context.

What Barthes has said of texts generally is acutely true of ironic texts, namely, that they do not constitute a "group of closed signs, endowed with a meaning to be rediscovered" but are rather constituted by "traces in displacement."[3] The displacement that is the *sine qua non* of irony is a displacement generated not by the reader alone but by the ironist's self-conscious enactment of the authorial deferrals and distortions that create the ironic text. Paradoxes abound here. For one, the "discontinuities of readability"[4] in an ironic text do not hide the ironist but, in fact, make the ironist all the more visible and stubbornly resilient as a quality of the text's elliptical signifying. For another, the reader is subjected to the control of the ironist but is invited to break free at every moment. That invitation, however ironic it may seem, should be taken seriously, for the control of the ironist is actually a parody of control. The ironic authorial voice offers an imitation of control that purposefully undermines its own authority even as it asserts it.

Over against the notion of irony as hegemonic control of an only apparent multivocality, Lang suggests that the "inaugural gesture of postmodernism is the renunciation of all pretensions to a singular voice, by simultaneously [ensuring] a multiplicity of discourses (without quotation marks)."[5] Has postmodernity rightly been called the "age of irony," or do the intentionalist manipulations of irony identify it as just another discursive form of foundationalism? Perhaps we need not choose between those two views, namely, that irony constitutes a sort of dogmatic master discourse or else that irony is constitutive of the postmodern fragmentation of the coherent signifying subject. Both may be true. Linda Hutcheon, for one, affirms the role of the reader in interpreting irony but allows for textual intention as well, saying that "there exist multiple 'levels' of masked intention in ironic utterances, from absent to ambiguous to (paradoxically) clear."[6] Her emphasis on the maskings of irony can help us to see the interpretation of irony as a continually renegotiated analysis of numerous deferrals enacted in local, intertextual, and metatextual sites. Underlying the simulation of multiple discourses is the ironist's parody of control, which effectively ironizes both the ironist as controlling subject and the apparent fragmentation of the ironic utterance.

Irony frames the terms of discourse in a way that invites collaboration from the sophisticated implied audience, which is to say, the audience wise enough to understand that misdirection is going on. But the aporetic invitation of irony also undermines the ability of the reader to read. The reader remains necessary but is, at least in the initial gesture of irony, radically disempowered. Ironizing as a signifying practice would seem to put the astute reader—the reader who understands the unspoken invitation of the ironist—on a pedestal. But there are fissures at the base of this pedestal, and the pedestal shakes whenever the reader shifts position. The reader who has been so elevated is keenly aware of the treachery of the text and its ironist-author—for to be aware of this is the only way to have attained the pedestal in the first place. So the sophisticated reader may smile down from the heights of fuller understanding, but his smile is tense around the edges, and there is a hint of fear in his eyes. With Kierkegaard, we realize that the intimacy that irony builds is problematized by the veiled threat wielded by the ironist. What Ted Cohen says of metaphor's ability to form community is true also of irony: "Intimacy sounds like a good thing. . . . It is not, however, an invariably friendly thing, nor is it intended to be. Sometimes one draws near another in order to deal a penetrating thrust. When the device is a hostile metaphor or a cruel joke requiring much background and effort to understand, it is all the more painful because the victim has been made a complicitor in his own demise."[7] If the pedestal is an unstable place, so too is the community created by ironizing. The risk is always there for the unexpected blow, the "penetrating thrust" delivered by a deceptively friendly Brutus to the Caesar who trusts irony's dynamics.

If irony is implicated in operations of power, it follows that the notion of power itself is a peculiarly appropriate subject for an inquiry into irony. The focus of the present chapter has to do with political power in ancient Israelite literary representations of foreign rulers and of native rulers whose identity is marked by foreignness. Some background on monarchy in the Hebrew Bible will help to lay the groundwork for these explorations. The Deuteronomistic historiography offers a narration of political leadership shot through with ironies. Ironizing plays throughout the complex biblical representations of Israel's first three rulers, Saul, David, and Solomon. Saul, the original chosen one, has to watch as his chosenness is erased. He is a tragic figure whose exemplary intimacy with God shades over into alienation and madness as God turns his favor to the usurper David. Moments of local irony within the Saul traditions are many. Edwin Good notes the pejorative irony of the question "Is Saul too among the prophets?" and he finds ironic the fact that David's rise from obscurity to increasing leaderly initiative unfolds precisely while God's favor upon Saul is tracing an inverse trajectory.[8]

Sophisticated ironies color the passage that describes David's slaying of Goliath and subsequent reactions by Abner, Saul, Jonathan, and the women of "all the towns of Israel" who celebrate David's victory. Notably ironic—and not merely a by-product of the juxtaposition of different literary sources—is the fact that God's anointed king, Saul, and the commander of his armies, Abner, do not know who David is, given that

David is represented as knowing God quite well. David says of Goliath, "For who is this uncircumcised Philistine that he should defy the armies of the living God?" (1 Sam 17:26), and he plans to fight Goliath "so that all the earth may know that there is a God in Israel" (1 Sam 17:46). David shows himself not only glorious in battle but also devoted to the God of Israel. But the proleptic hints are lost on Saul and Abner. They ask the same kind of question that David had asked, "Who is this?" but in a way that shows their lack of connection to God's unfolding purposes. In 1 Samuel 17:55–58, Saul says, "Whose son is this youth?" and Abner replies, "As your soul lives, O king, I do not know." The king orders that inquiry be made about David, but the inquiry is clearly unsuccessful because Saul must resort to asking David directly as David stands before him "with the head of the Philistine in his hand." (That narrative detail heightens—perhaps comedically—the inept "so who are you, again?" sense of Saul's role in the scene.)

That God's anointed king and the commander of his armies are at a loss about the identity of this warrior who has dispatched a major military threat for them is ironic enough. But in the larger sweep of the narrative, the irony becomes sharper still, for David will turn his prodigious military strategizing and battle skills against Saul and Abner themselves. David, who had once been unknown to Abner and who keeps his motivations veiled throughout his career, accepts Abner's renewed offer of loyalty late in the day, but then may give covert approval for his own commander to assassinate Abner shortly thereafter (2 Samuel 3).[9] The ironies at the beginning of Saul's acquaintance with David intensify when the victorious Israelites are greeted by rejoicing women. The refrain that the women sing after David has killed Goliath, "Saul has killed his thousands, and David his ten thousands" (1 Sam 18:7) irks Saul, and, indeed, it does point to his being overshadowed by the mightier David. But we may probe further: who exactly will lie among the additional myriads killed, directly or obliquely, by David? Almost everyone allied with the House of Saul, for one thing. We may even add Saul and Jonathan themselves to David's death toll, if we consider the time David spent strengthening the Philistine army by amassing plunder and weakening local opposition (1 Samuel 27–30) as having played a significant role in the eventual defeat of Israel by the Philistines, Saul and Jonathan falling in that battle.

The ironies that characterize Saul cast their shadow over greater tracts of Hebrew Bible narrative than simply Saul's own story or even the Israelite monarchy writ larger. When we encounter the fall of Saul because of his transgression in the matter of the Amalekites (1 Samuel 15), as too with the exclusion of Moses from the Promised Land for a single infraction, we are drawn into a metanarrative that subtly destabilizes all other claims to enduring confidence in God's favor. By means of the Davidic superscriptions in the Psalms and other key texts such as Isaiah 55, Israel is invited to understand itself as David. But in the broader sweep of Israel's ancient history, given its domination by Assyria and Egypt, its crushing defeat by Babylon, and its domestication by the iron hand of Persia, biblical Israel's hope for the rejuvenation of the Davidic line appears no more than a chimera. In the shadow of its military defeats, post-Saulide Israel surely must fear the loss of its intimacy with God, anxiously glancing at the ironic possibility that instead of being the embodiment of Davidic promise, it might turn out to be Saul.[10]

Ironic fissures run deep in the biblical portrayals of David.[11] He is simultaneously pious Israelite shepherd and brutal military pragmatist who aids the Philistines against God's own people. He is at once the devoted lover of Jonathan and a schemer who ruthlessly brings down the Saulide monarchy, virginal youth and adulterous predator who gains sexual partners at the cost of at least three lives (viz., Nabal, Uriah, and his first child with Bathsheba). One can hardly avoid ironies in a literature that asserts the indomitable sovereignty of God over the affairs of the faithful while also carefully chronicling the manipulations, deceits, and betrayals of its paradigmatic faithful leader. The brash claim of the young David that "the battle is the LORD's" (1 Sam 17:47) cannot overcome the combined weight of the many narratives that detail his later employment of methods that the Deuteronomistic Historian could not possibly have condoned. A few of these ironies may have been created by the juxtaposition of different sources within the Succession Narrative, true. But the complex texture of the literature about David—his character, his hidden motivations, his actions—suggests that ironies were perceived and emphasized early on in the traditions about this king.

These ironies may be highlighted all the more in silences about David, which points up the inadequacy of any reading that suggests that a narrative is "not about" something simply because it does not directly address it. This will be relevant in the so-called matriarch-in-danger stories treated below. The suggestion persists in scholarship on these stories that they do not concern issues of morality and covenant faithfulness because there is no overt explication of those issues in the narratives. Meir Sternberg provides an antidote to such reasoning in the chapter of his *The Poetics of Biblical Narrative* entitled "Gaps, Ambiguity, and the Reading Process,"[12] wherein he probes dimensions of narrative suppression, silence, and ambiguation. Of particular significance for our discussion of royal power is his note regarding the thunderous narratological silences in David's betrayal of Uriah:

The suppression of essentials, the narrator's pseudo-objectivity, and the tone rendering the horror as if it were an everyday matter: all these create an extreme ironic discordance between the tale's mode of presentation and the action itself. . . . And the system of gaps, developed primarily to direct attention to what has *not* been communicated, becomes the central device whereby the narrator gradually establishes his ironic framework.[13]

David is a study in contradictions. As such, this iconic king's multivalent representations within Hebrew Bible literature serve as the basis for an ironizing view of Israelite identity itself.

And what shall we say of Solomon, that paragon of wisdom who is granted the inestimable blessing of building the LORD's own house? He shows himself a true heir of the ironized David, fatally foolish in his marriages with hundreds of foreign wives and concubines. What seems to be a prudent policy of alliance building becomes (in the Deuteronomistic view) a choice disastrous for the fate of his country. Solomon's indulgent attitude toward apostasy hurries Israel down the path to political division, military disaster, and spiritual ruin. The insight of David Gunn regarding Solomon is relevant here:

> "Solomon," we are told in 1 Kgs 3.3, "loved the Lord, walking in the statutes of David his father; only he sacrificed and burnt incense at the high places." But when we view the closing phase of his story, contemplate the multiplication of his foreign brides and calculate some seven hundred (and more) altars set up to foreign gods . . . then we may choose to read that apparently innocuous "only" (*raq*) as packing quite a punch. An ironic reading of the "only" clause can turn the narrator's evaluation from laudatory to condemnatory in a stroke.[14]

Solomon is certainly undermined in the Deuteronomistic History for his permissiveness regarding idolatry. He may be being ironized in the Book of Qohelet as well for his self-aggrandizement and hedonism, if we read the traditionally discerned oblique allusiveness to Solomon in that book as critique.[15]

Ironies abound, then, in Israel's traditions of its three founding monarchs. The biblical narratives of Saul, David, and Solomon sketch out the unseemly strengths, excesses, and confusions of the royal court. Fatal flaws in kingly personae depict, in miniature, the potent possibilities for cultural criticism that were actualized within the ancient writings of Israel's sociopolitical history. Early and late within the scribal traditions that represent Israel's royal court, incongruities and aporias unmask Israel's claims to power.

Royal power wielded by foreign kings is a rich site of ironizing in Hebrew Bible traditions as well. Ironies slice through the tale of Hezekiah in discursive combat with the Rabshakeh of the invading Assyrian forces (Isaiah 36). The Rabshakeh, no mean ironist himself, mocks Israel's faith through his claim that he is the LORD's appointed instrument and his devastating observation about the earnest but foiled hopes of other subjugated peoples. The insulting message sent by Sennacherib to Hezekiah, "Do not let your god on whom you rely deceive you by promising that Jerusalem will not be given into the hand of the king of Assyria" (Isa 37:10), locates the threat against Judah in a larger historical landscape of the devastations wrought by former Assyrian kings (37:12). But this wider lens of (misread) history is shattered in an instant when, as the narrative moves from Hezekiah's behind-the-scenes prayer and the LORD's answer back to the public view, Assyria's scathing sarcasm is itself brought to naught. The Rabshakeh's discourse and Sennacherib's missive are erased, their seductive words ironized decisively—in silence—by the action of the angel of the LORD in the dark of night: "Then the angel of the LORD set out and struck down one hundred eighty-five thousand in the camp of the Assyrians; when morning dawned, they were all dead bodies" (37:36). Ironic words in the mouths of foreign rulers may sound true, and may even be technically accurate, at least in part. (Where, indeed, were the gods of Hamath, Arpad, Sepharvaim, Gozan, Haran, Rezeph, Hena, Ivvah, and the people of Eden who were in Telassar?) But the apparent power of foreigners' irony is eviscerated by the power of divine intervention working in death-dealing silence.

In what follows, I will explore the intersections of irony and royal power in Hebrew Bible texts that betray an intense interest in foreign rulers. My thesis is twofold. First, I will attempt to show that irony in these texts about foreign rulers works as a distancing mechanism by means of which biblical authors could satirize dangerous systems of power—whether political systems of foreign nations that dominated Israel militarily or discursive systems of Israelite identity emerging from within the Israelite community. Second, I will attempt to show that the agile ironizing demonstrated in these stories has as a constitutive feature an attentiveness to biblical intertextuality, something that may be a hallmark of late traditioning processes in the Hebrew Bible responding to experiences of diaspora. Ilona Rashkow suggests that literary intertextuality and psychoanalytic transference, as processes, have much in common. She notes, "Intertextuality and transference work effectively to divide the text against itself, creating both a need for response and a response to the need."[16] This notion of division against oneself is central to classical understandings of irony and, I think, is helpful for understanding post-exilic traditioning processes of the Hebrew Bible.

Foreign rulers are figured in the Hebrew Bible as sources of considerable threat, not only militarily but culturally. Concern about the lure of the foreign court and the seductive power of the foreign ruler is palpable in the three so-called wife-sister or matriarch-in-danger stories in Genesis. Concern about the threat posed to those who refuse assimilation suffuses the dramatic stories about Daniel in the Persian court. Concern about the lure of the foreign and its implications for Israelite constructions of power can be read in the deeply ambivalent ironies of Esther. That irony textures these biblical stories about foreign power is no coincidence. Ironic rhetoric is an important tool in the politics of lived social relationships, as Michael Herzfeld argues in his cultural-anthropological study of political processes in Greece. More important for our purposes here, irony is indispensable for the politics of writing and rewriting the theopolitical traditions of a community. Herzfeld observes, "[I]rony—the trope most directly associated with critical reflection—threatens absolute power through its evocation of the absurdity of all claims to total transparency, certainty, and referentiality."[17] I will consider the implications of this claim through an exploration of the ironizing of foreign power and hegemonic discourse in the Hebrew Bible.

Any interpretation of an ironic text that attempts to integrate—and thereby master—the multiple levels on which irony performs may find itself repeatedly destabilized, its own authority continually deferred and challenged. Thus the readings of irony that I will offer here can be only provisional, maps whose borders and landmarks may show signs of erasure and redrawing, or, to return to Niditch's "overleaf map," transparent maps through which one can see yet other maps, other possibilities. Every text eludes the definitive integrative moment, but some can seem more elusive than others. In this chapter, it is particularly the Book of Esther that slips from my grasp each time I try to pin it down. The first three sections below, on the matriarch-in-danger stories in Genesis, the Joseph material, and writing in Daniel, in some ways constitute attempts to prepare to think about the mercurial Book of Esther, which hosts many brilliant interpretations and yet resists every one.

Below, I will consider four foreign rulers (Pharaoh, Abimelech, Belshazzar, and Darius) and two indigenous Israelite rulers whose characters express complex relationships to foreignness: Joseph as an assimilated "Egyptian" ruler and Esther as a ruler who undergoes a series of transformations from assimilated Persian queen to savvy Jewish resistance fighter to re-assimilated "Persian" ruler once again. First, we turn our attention to patriarchal and matriarchal difficulties strategically located at the beginning of the narration of Israelite identity.

Pharaoh and Abimelech as Innocents Ensnared

We pause here at the beginning of Israel's history, in that first freighted moment when an Israelite considers the power and danger of the foreign court. Abram has been called from Ur of the Chaldeans and promised by God that he will have offspring and land in a new place. He leaves his father's house, arrives in Canaan, and sets up an altar to the LORD. But then Abram keeps moving, with an alacrity that surprises the reader. He makes for the Negev and ultimately for Egypt. In Egyptian territory, the danger posed to Sarai's honor and Abram's life is clear, at least in Abram's mind and perhaps in the minds of some commentators as well, including Jon Levenson, who notes, "Although Abram is sometimes chastised for passing his beautiful wife off as his sister, it is hard to see how Sarai . . . would have fared better if he died at the hands of the lecherous and adulterous Egyptians."[18] Levenson's phrase "the lecherous and adulterous Egyptians" assumes that Abram's representation of Egypt is to be taken at face value as the narrator's position. The Egyptian officials recognize Sarai's beauty and commend her to their king, and Pharaoh does take Sarai into his court. But whether we can assume that he exploits her is another question, as is the "lecherous and adulterous" nature of the Egyptians generally in this story. In fact, the text underlines Pharaoh's outrage at the harm he and his people have experienced because of Abram's deception regarding Sarai's marriageability. Notwithstanding the tendency of readers to lionize Abra(ha)m in the history of interpretation,[19] one may more easily read this story as underlining Pharaoh's moral uprightness and generosity to a manipulative and deceitful sojourner. Unresolvable gaps and ambiguities remain, but there are some things we do know. Chief among them is the narrative fact that Abram perpetrated deception because he anticipated a reality that turned out not to be true (he was not, in fact, killed by the Egyptians once they learned he was Sarai's husband). His misperception of the Egyptian threat and his deceit stand out all the more clearly against the indeterminacies that otherwise govern the narrative.

In the second resonance of this motif of sexualized risk in foreign courts, in Genesis 20, we see Abraham's manipulative narcissism being shown up in no uncertain terms by King Abimelech of Gerar, one recognized as blameless by none other than the God of Israel. Abimelech has to muster a huge bribe (sheep, oxen, slaves, right of settlement anywhere on Abimelech's land, and a thousand pieces of silver) for Abraham to agree to intercede on his behalf. Abraham's anxiety that there would be no "fear of God" in the foreign court is even more heavily ironized here than it was in Genesis 12.[20] The "spoken" here is that the faithful sojourner will encounter godless, sexually predatory, bloodthirsty heathen who will assault the honor of the sojourner and his people. But this is unreliable: the narrator shows us a reality that is quite otherwise. Once again, the events that unfold do not bear out Abraham's fear.[21] The literary disjuncture is becoming more insistent: Abimelech is vindicated by God himself, and Abraham this time persists in an erroneous view of the foreign court that the reader knows to have been disproven once already in Abraham's experience.

In the third resonance of this cultural reflection on foreignness and power, in Genesis 26, the ironies are sharpened still further. Here, Abimelech is even more extravagantly moral than in the second story. He would not have approached Rebekah himself but worries that "one of the people" might have taken that misstep (26:10), a prophylactic anxiety that rivals the scrupulosity of Job regarding his children (Job 1:5). Mark E. Biddle has shown that Abimelech is concerned about bringing *'āšām* (cultic guilt) on himself and his people for any trespass against Israel as *sancta,* as a holy people set apart for the LORD.[22] The irony here is striking: this foreigner is scrupulous about not transgressing Israel's cultic boundaries. In this, Isaac—and his father, by implication—are being shown up by the foreign court for the unlikely covenant partners that they are. The divine promise of progeny to Israel is disregarded by the patriarchs to whom it has been vouchsafed but is guarded conscientiously by foreigners who have no stake in ensuring Israel's prosperity.[23]

We see in these tales three increasingly edgy portrayals of the patriarchs' being driven by an ungrounded fear of immorality and death-dealing in the foreign arena, followed by the subsequent revealing of their lack of discernment, parochialism, and failure to trust in God's promises, to say nothing of their apparent indifference to the physical integrity and social honor of their wives.[24] The stakes are high in these stories: the entire history of the covenant identity of Israel and the Israelites' social integrity is made to hang in the balance in these early negotiations with foreign rulers. The argument that these stories relate to the covenant is supported by the literary datum that the series of matriarch-in-danger stories is bracketed by passages involving the first articulation and a reiteration of God's covenantal promise to Abra(ha)m, in 12:1–3 and 26:23–24. Also significant is the revoicing of the covenantal promise in the Isaac story itself (26:2–5), which emphasizes that the obedience of Abraham is precisely what has been at issue: God will bless Isaac and his descendants "because Abraham obeyed my voice and kept my charge, my commandments, my statutes, and my laws." One may press the point still further: consider that the foreign rulers have shown themselves responsive to divine punishment (Genesis 12), receptive to dreams as a means of divine communication (Genesis 20), and astute in the use of the faculty of discernment that is central to the wisdom tradition (Genesis 26). This point is made by Robert Polzin, who argues that the narrative structuring of these stories reflects the structure of the Hebrew Bible itself, in that the Torah concerns itself with God's interventions in history, the Prophets address revelation in visions, and the Writings emphasize the importance of human wisdom.[25] Thus in the three essential modes of revelation in the Hebrew Bible, foreign rulers have shown themselves to be more adept than Israel's own founding fathers.

The connection to morality has been disputed in the scholarship on these three stories. But the position that morality is not at issue here can be maintained only if we insist on reading these stories as somehow removed from the unspoken matrix of social mores that relate women's sexuality to honor and shame in the ancient Near East. Just as the horrendous offense against morality perpetrated by King David against Uriah need not be spelled out but still is powerfully present in that narrative, so too the offense against the social integrity of Sarah, Rebekah, and the entire Israelite community need not be spelled out here in order for the ancient audience to perceive the sexual risk to the women and the threat of shame for their kinship group. Pertinent here is Ken Stone's analysis of anthropological theory about gendered sexuality and honor/shame dynamics in biblical literature. Stone observes, "In ethnographic accounts from various parts of the Mediterranean and the Middle East, one finds that women's sexuality is treated by indigenous men as a resource which, like other limited resources, can become the object of conflict. The point around which this conflict coalesces is the chastity of women, which male kinsmen are compelled to guard with vigilance."[26] The exchange of women among competitive males, whether happening by mutual agreement or by coercion, has as much to do with the honor and social status of the males as it does with the women's physical and social integrity. Stone continues, "[I]t is masculinity itself, within a certain economy of gender, that is at stake. Both the kinsman and the potential sexual partner can demonstrate their ability to embody a particular sort of manhood by their actions in preventing or accomplishing sexual contact with the woman."[27] By these lights, Abraham and Isaac have been shown up not only as weak covenant partners but as emasculated and shamed males who cannot effectively guard their women. That conclusion is virtually inescapable, unless one wants to argue that the androcentric norms of honor and shame that governed female sexuality in ancient Near Eastern and Mediterranean societies were not operative in the world of the narrator(s) who composed the Genesis stories—a case that would be highly implausible.

Because the patriarchs have threatened so much of value at the heart
of Israel's covenant identity and social integrity, I find unpersuasive
those readings that find the text chiefly to be lauding the patriarchs as
successful tricksters.[28] Abraham and Isaac may have survived each crisis
and done well in material terms, but this is not the central point of the
stories. Even if the motif of a trickster taking loot away from a conflictual situation lies in the folkloristic background of this kind of storytelling more generally, it would be difficult to argue that the plundering of
Egypt and Gerar is the point of the narratological arc here. The potentially staggering costs of the patriarchs' mistrust of God are only barely
avoided, and therein lies the drama. Foreign power, misconstrued as
ruthless by the anxious patriarchs, each time surprises the implied audience with its moral sense and cultic sensibility. Pharaoh and Abimelech
are innocents ensnared, their communities gravely endangered by the
unsavory machinations of needlessly fearful Israelite outsiders. Thus we
see an ironically inverted view of Israel's covenant with God. It is the
care taken by powerful foreigners, rather than trust or obedience on the
part of the Israelite forebears, that ensures that Israel remains socially
honorable and blessed by the God who has called them into covenant.

"Am I in the Place of God?": Joseph the Pretender

Sternberg has suggested a thematic connection between the matriarch-
in-danger stories and the Joseph material. He spies a shared subtext having to do with Egyptian imperial power:

> [I]ts earliest victims are Hebrews, always caught at the local inter-
> section of power and sex unrestrained. The matriarch's abduc-
> tion into the royal harem opens the theme (the wife-sister imbro-
> glio perhaps wryly glancing at Pharaonic marital license); next,
> Joseph gets sold into bondage and seduction. This completes the
> travesty of Noah's two-way linkage, whereby (Hamite) illicit sexu-
> ality should go with subservience, as if for control, (Shemite) pu-
> rity with power over the vile and violent. Turned upside down
> now, such an ideal world is at best a thing of the future, certainly
> unrealizable by the elect on the long way from Hebrewness to the
> promised territorial nationhood.[29]

Sternberg's literary instincts here are brilliant even if one may disagree
with some of his conclusions. "Turned upside down" is absolutely right.
But I would argue that this "ideal world"—the pure and faithful Israel-

ite culture conquering the impure and violent foreign culture—is not gestured toward proleptically, but instead is wholly ironized in the Genesis narratives.

A powerful ambiguity textures Hebrew Bible traditions about Egypt. Egypt lures as well as coerces. Israelites do persist in going down to Egypt, the stern warnings of God notwithstanding and textual traces of earlier disasters notwithstanding. The ghost of Abram stands—as sentinel or as host?—on the cultural threshold as Judahites flee to Egypt after the fall of Jerusalem (Jeremiah 43). But even more alarming for Israelite notions of identity, Egyptians insinuate themselves into Hebrewness, and hybridity is the result. We see the lure of cultural hybridity most clearly represented in the body of Hagar the Egyptian, who is carefully positioned between the bodies of Abraham and Sarah (Genesis 16) and from that position generates not only conflict but new life. This agonistic hybridity, dangerous but potentially fruitful, is hinted at also in the representation of the body and the political power of Joseph. We turn now to the story of this patriarch who journeys deepest into the dangerous territory of Egyptian culture.

In Joseph, we meet the patriarch with the most vividly etched character in the most richly ironic cycle of material in Genesis. The Joseph narratives brim with ambiguities and ironic reversals concerning wisdom and power figured in the setting of the foreign royal court. Multiple ironies in the Joseph story advance the implication that foreign power is used as a foil for the ironizing of Israelite parochialism. As many scholars have noticed, the Joseph material shows a keen interest in insider/outsider boundaries and assimilation, the investiture and divestiture of political power,[30] and the masking and unmasking of identity as it relates to power. As a youth, Joseph is uniquely wise, yet he is also lacking in discernment. His dreams are portents of his significance from God that he understands just fine, but he trumpets his own power in a brash and immature way that incites his brothers to strip him of his robe—that signifier of special status—and leave him for dead in a pit. Sold as a slave, the gifted Joseph is reinvested with power in the house of the Egyptian officer Potiphar. But Joseph's charisma threatens to be his undoing. His charm draws the attention of Potiphar's wife, and when Joseph resists her advances, she adversarially emphasizes his "Hebrewness," his Otherness. Divested again of his actual robe and stripped of the political power it represents, Joseph is thrown into prison.

Again Joseph thrives and after some time is reinvested once more with power. This time, the text underlines the marks of Joseph's adopted "Egyptianness" rather than the Hebrewness that had been named as problematic by Potiphar's wife. Joseph wears the pharaoh's own signet ring, robes of fine Egyptian linen, a golden chain around his neck. His identity is reconfigured via a new Egyptian name, Zaphenath-paʿneaḥ, which may mean "God speaks and lives."[31] Sternberg's observation that "an alien divinity may well lurk in his . . . Pharaonic nomination"[32] is of significance for our present purposes since, as I shall argue below, Joseph does inhabit a divinized identity in interactions with his family. Finally he gains an Egyptian wife, and at this point Joseph's cultural status has been fully transformed. He is second in authority only to Pharaoh himself: Joseph has become culturally marked in every way as a powerful Egyptian. How powerful? As powerful as God—at least to those who are duped by the exquisite ironies that unfold.

Famine threatens the people of Israel once again. The reader, hearing resonances with the impetus for Abram's initial descent into Egypt and Isaac's journey to Gerar, is invited to remember the dangers and surprises posed by the foreign court in those stories. Here, though, is a striking difference: the story unfolds with a crypto-Israelite in a position of power. The desperate Israelite brothers come to Zaphenath-paʿneaḥ and are manipulated by him into being completely at his mercy. He secretly returns their money to them when they had paid for grain, and later plants a silver cup in Benjamin's bag to implicate the brothers further. Each time, the brothers give voice to their fear that God has intervened in their lives to their harm. In the matter of the grain money, they cry out in terror, "What is this that God has done to us?" (Gen 42:28). The literary tension is palpable, for the implied audience knows full well that it is not the hand of God but the unseen hand of Zaphenath-paʿneaḥ that had planted the money. Heightening the irony, Zaphenath-paʿneaḥ's steward reinforces their lack of discernment with his assurance, "Your God, the God of your father, must have put treasure in your bags for you" (43:23). And in the matter of the planted silver cup, the ironized identification of Zaphenath-paʿneaḥ with God is intensified. He berates them for purportedly having tried to deceive him: "What deed is this that you have done? Do you not know that one such as I can practice divination?" (44:15). The point is that Zaphenath-paʿneaḥ can see all, and Judah concurs that Zaphenath-papaʿneaḥ is quasi-divine in his response that indeed, "God has found out the guilt of your servants" (44:16). From the viewpoint of the destitute Israelites at Joseph's mercy, Joseph and God perpetrate a single ruthless practice of divine manipulation.

Finally, the point is stated outright. Zaphenath-paʿneaḥ asks them rhetorically, "Am I in the place of God?" With this, he ostensibly puts to rest their fear that they will be enslaved or die at his all-powerful hand—but their fear actually increases. The question technically expects no answer, yet dread lies heavy on the brothers and on the implied audience, for misunderstanding the question or giving the wrong answer might mean death. This ironic question suggests that Joseph cannot be understood as God, and there is truth to that, on the face of it.[33] Yet he has been acting precisely like God, the only one with full knowledge of the identity of all of the players, manipulating their experience with a hidden hand, judging them for past sins hidden from the light of day these many years, holding their lives and the lives of their people firmly in his control.[34] There are subtle hints of *deus ex machina* working throughout the narrative, to be sure. But there are stronger and more overt narratological clues about *Josephus ex machina* as well. Is Joseph in the place of God? Of course not— and yet, it is he whose wisdom and power have ensured the survival of the Israelites, with those requisite moments of raw terror in which their earlier faithless abandonment of him could potentially have invited a response of merciless and inescapable judgment.

Hearing Joseph's question, our imagination is drawn back to our first encounter with Joseph. The seventeen-year-old Joseph had shared his two dreams that those in his family would make obeisance to him. The dramatic irony proleptically signaled by Joseph's dreams is noticed by Hugh C. White:

> On the one hand, they [the dreams] serve as genuine revelations of the future; but on the other, they mirror Joseph's conscious-ness of infinite superiority. The brothers, not seeing the larger purpose which will be served by Joseph's ascension to power over them, interpret the dream[s] altogether in terms of . . . the emo-tional system of sibling rivalry in the family. . . . The supreme irony of this [narrative] strategy is that by inciting the brothers to take action against the "dreamer" and his dreams, the familial system of jealous hatred is made to serve the very end of Joseph's ascendancy which it seeks to defeat.[35]

Indeed—and we may say more. The symbolism of the dreams, grain of the earth and luminaries of the heavens bending low to Joseph, becomes more richly ambiguous now that the reader has absorbed the whole story of Joseph's rise to power. James C. Nohrnberg remarks, "The first set of dreams seems to go back to the Creation and to suggest homage to the Creator."[36] The tamer possibility at the beginning of the story, that Joseph is dreaming of obeisance to himself simply as one with political power or social status, expands into something more momentous. Per-haps those dreams had always been a sign of the Israelites' forced obei-sance to something divine.

The dramatic ironies unfold to reveal a startling truth: Joseph has indeed become God to them. But his "divinity" has not been performed in a reliable way. Joseph is no transparent window through which the purposes of God are refracted. His divinity is in fact unreliable, because Joseph deceives and manipulates and because the reader knows that Joseph is not God. The text in Genesis 37 does not say God appeared to Joseph in a dream, as God had spoken to Abram in a dream (Gen 16:12–16) and had appeared to Jacob (28:11–17), not to mention Abimelech (20:3). No, here the text says only, "Joseph had a dream" and "he had another dream" (37:5, 9). White offers a fascinating observation here that underlines Joseph's agency over against divine intervention in the dreams: "[T]he dreams are not attributed to God as their source, but exert influence on events as they become speech acts. It is the response to the *report* of the dreams which shapes the course of events and leads eventually to their fulfillment."[37] So we may be right to worry about a subtle disjuncture between true divine revelation in dreams and what Joseph has revealed. Perhaps Joseph has overstepped his bounds. It is also possible that the unpredictability of Joseph's actions *qua* God provides a sardonic reflection on the actions of the deity with Israel.

This final episode in Genesis may be read as an ironic elaboration on the Garden of Eden story, in which Eve's direct and unvarnished attempt to grasp wisdom is depicted as illegitimate. As he matures, Joseph learns to employ wisdom more discreetly and successfully through misdirection, dissembling, and evasiveness. Adam and Eve tried to hide, but they were not very good at it. Joseph is far more skilled. His example demonstrates that wisdom is still the quality by virtue of which human beings are most like God. But if that is so, then the shrewd manipulation and ruthless omniscience that Joseph shows in his dealings with his brothers mirror aspects of the deity that ancient Israel has experienced to its terror. Joseph, beloved by many (although not all) in the narrative of Genesis and praised by many (although not all) in the history of interpretation, may not be so attractive when studied up close.[38] While he may prosper when God lets him, he is not being represented as a flawless exemplar of pragmatic wisdom that diaspora Jews should emulate.[39] The ironist unmasks him as a charming but capricious manipulator, by turns tender and ruthless. At the heart of this ironic portrait may lie an ambivalent experience of the unpredictability of God's power.

If Eden is being evoked in the figuring of Egypt here, perhaps we see also a gesture toward the expulsion from Eden. We see, by means of a double irony, that Joseph's God-like power to increase the blessing and fecundity enjoyed by the Israelites leads once again to their banishment from a place revered in the communal memory (in the so-called murmuring stories twice)[40] as a place of overflowing abundance. For the Joseph story does not end with abundance in Egypt. Joseph dies, and the temporary hybridity of Joseph's foreign power, precisely that which ironizes Israelite parochialism, dissolves back into polarized Otherness in Exodus. The numerous Israelites offend, by their very teeming and abundant presence, a new pharaoh who "does not know Joseph." Joseph's policy of exploiting the native Egyptians during the famine may have left the populace agitating against him. The ironic reversal is palpable. As Daniel R. Shevitz puts it, "Joseph despoils Egypt and delivers to Pharaoh the land and very bodies of the Egyptians. Should we be surprised, then, when a new Pharaoh uses this same method to enslave Joseph's descendants?"[41] One may, of course, read the disjuncture there not in synchronic terms as part of a single coherent narrative but in diachronic terms. Attacks on the beleaguered Documentary Hypothesis have been pressed, on one flank of that vast battle front, by scholars' claims that the "gap" between the Joseph material and the beginning of Exodus reveals originally separate blocks of tradition joined only at a late pre-Priestly or Priestly stage of redaction.[42] So for those reading diachronically, ironies perceived in the disjuncture between Genesis and Exodus may be generated by reader response and ought not be attributed to original intent in either of the two blocks of material. But even so, the redactional linkages to Joseph articulated in Exodus 1:1–8 in the final form of the text do authorize our retrospection on the ironic plight of the Israelites.

A pharaoh arose who did not know Joseph: thanks to Joseph's absence—to the words that Joseph could no longer speak—the protection of the Israelites evaporates. Egypt now brutalizes the Israelites and drives them out of the land. The Israelites flee into the wilderness to receive the Law, given to aid them in the construction of ethnic and theological boundaries for their community, which had become fatally permeable under Joseph's assimilatory strategy. Joseph may be powerful, but in a flawed way. Joseph is no Moses.[43]

There are, then, four distinct ironies that may be perceived in the Joseph story. First, Joseph's powerlessness as an Israelite is reversed when he achieves a hyperbolic level of authority as an Egyptian and becomes someone whom the Israelites completely fail to recognize. Ostensibly the source of his difficulties, Joseph's "Otherness" turns out to be the source of his power. It is Joseph's Otherness as an Egyptian official that makes him most valuable in the eyes of the Israelites. Yet his Otherness is only apparent, for deep down, Joseph is still his father's son and the brother of his brothers. So it may be more felicitous to say that his nativeness includes and incorporates Otherness, ironically hybridizing the portrayal of power we see here.

A second irony has been highlighted in the exchange between Joseph and his brothers in his rhetorical question, "Am I in the place of God?" (50:19). The implicit claim is that Joseph is not in the place of God, yet the audience knows that he has functioned in a quasi-divine role, omniscient and able to manipulate life-and-death matters unseen. One result is that the relationship between Joseph's pharaonic power and the power of Israel's God is left tensive and problematic.

A third irony in this material is etched deeply into the larger literary structure of the Book of Genesis. This irony is that wisdom may be pressed into service apart from halakhic obedience. Joseph has been living among Egyptians under an Egyptian name, eating Egyptian food, wearing Egyptian clothes, enjoying a hyperbolic helping of Egyptian political status, and in every other respect he has been assimilated into Egyptian culture so that he is unrecognizable to his own family. Yet God uses this hyper-assimilation of Joseph for the good of Israel, and it would seem that Joseph is not blamed for it. This may be seen to counter the implication in the Garden of Eden story that wisdom should not be sought apart from obedience to the dictates of God. The narratological anachronism (that the Law had not yet been given to Moses) need not detain us. Wherever the patriarchal material can be said to reflect an exilic or post-exilic provenance, the Law stands, mammoth and not quite silenced, in the unspoken background of these ironic texts. Joseph seems to have been successful where Eve failed. He has preserved life in the very heart of forbidden territory. On one level, then, we see the Joseph story ironizing the kind of blind parochialism of his xenophobic brothers, who resent difference even among their own and wield their power precisely to obliterate difference. An unspoken point of all of these ironies is that the brothers are threatening their own chances of survival by attempting to obliterate difference in this way.

Yet a fourth irony emerges as we consider the unsavory aspects of Joseph's character. His ruthlessness in dealing with his brothers may have been contained, but his subjugation of the Egyptians has far-reaching consequences for the Israelites living uneasily among them. Joseph's preservation of life in the short term, while viable for survival, nevertheless leads inevitably to the trauma of enslavement and the necessity of fleeing into diaspora in the wilderness. Thus as the plot moves into Exodus, the ironies move toward a further level of narratological complexity, writing and overwriting each other in an increasing density of silences. Even the flourishing of the Israelites in diaspora, their very strength and fecundity, turns out not to be enough. As the murmuring stories and conquest narratives show us, only the Otherness conferred by the Law can remedy the threat to Israelite integrity posed by memories of Egypt on the one hand and the lures of assimilation into Canaan-

ite culture on the other. Thus aporia remains. Joseph's original dislocation and assimilation become multilayered almost beyond reckoning,
for diaspora is a place and a metaphor of unresolvable contradictions.

Foreign rulers have shown up Israelite parochialism thoroughly, in
the wife-sister stories and, by means of an ironic double twist, in the hybridized Joseph. It may be only in becoming more like the foreign rulers
in the Genesis traditions—that is, earnestly moral and obedient to
God—that the Israelites have a chance of surviving life in the post-586
diaspora, that experience of cultural famine and political powerlessness
in the shadow of which the wife-sister stories, the Joseph material, and
the Garden of Eden story were likely composed.

Belshazzar, Darius, and Hermeneutical Risk-Taking

We turn now to the Book of Daniel, another late composition with an interest in the lures and dangers of assimilation in the foreign court. The
royal figures of Belshazzar and Darius are deployed in a constellation of
ironies that use the cultural act of writing to problematize the ephemeral
nature of political rule and to inscribe the lasting power of God's rule.

First, consider Daniel 5. The drunken Belshazzar's disrespect for the
looted Jerusalem Temple vessels receives its comeuppance: at the feast, a
sentence of judgment is written by the fingers of a disembodied hand. This
image provides marvelous fodder for those culture wars, perhaps more or
less over in English departments but still raging in biblical studies, over
whether seeking authorial intent may be considered a viable interpretive
endeavor—whether one can listen to a text, as Moshe Greenberg has suggested,[44] or whether the text's meaning is instead fully created and inevitably commodified by the reader. The fingers of the disembodied hand are
unquestionably there, in the perspective of the text, but they are not fully
material, and what they write is inexplicable and, at first, indecipherable.
They have produced a text that defies the competence of almost every
reader within the story, underlining the anxiety of readers outside the narrative world who know that we cannot ever truly master the text.

Yet what the inscribed text "intends" is crucial to understand, for very
real political reasons. This is not simply an exercise in semantics. As Donald C. Polaski has pointed out in his article on Daniel 5 and 6, even the
surface meaning of the text—an enumeration of weights that serve as coinage—is politically charged: "[A] list of coins is itself an example of royal
power. If the text's status as an inscription foregrounds its 'monumental
and symbolic role,' the text's content leads us to the treasury. . . . The hand
sent by God may be recording the seemingly banal—preparing an inven-

tory, perhaps—but it is also performing an act essential to the organization of imperial economic power."[45] This mysterious writing hand is impossible, yet there it is, challenging the power of the Persian empire to make decrees, promulgate certain kinds of readings, and control dissenting readings. This is mimesis, parody, and rewriting in a single act of subversion. And it is an act that needs a reader. To those readers who do not understand, the vanishing author may be an evanescent ghost to be exorcised, but its presence and the enduring presence of the writing it generates cannot be banished. The otherworldly power of the hand gestures toward a power that may be stronger than the imperium.[46] May be—there is no way to know for sure until its text can be "mastered." Thus the deciphering of the terrifying inscription is urgently needed but desperately feared.

Many readers fail, and the implied audience fails too, at least on its first reading. But Daniel the courageous hermeneut steps forward. He makes his decoding of the writing an indictment of Belshazzar's fatal ignorance of the true God of heaven. There is an Author, and his text is overflowing with deadly power far beyond the power of any reader to constrain. An intertext with the Joseph story is generated in Daniel 5 by the reference to the royal signet ring, whose removal serves to destabilize the authority of Belshazzar and underline the authority of Daniel as a resistant, non-assimilatory hermeneut. Here an observation by Mieke Bal about a similar transference in the Book of Esther is applicable. She writes, "The shifting of signet ring from body to body is the narrative representation of the subjective instability that writing promotes."[47] The royal power that Joseph had gained by assimilation is reinscribed in Daniel as the power of (re)interpretation of authoritative texts, shifting in this case from the native king to the displaced reader. After the transfer of power, the Persian king is promptly killed in what may be best read as an ironic narratological response to his hermeneutical risk taking. Here, the risks of reading are starkly illustrated: texts can kill. Misreadings are dangerous enough, but readings that get at the heart of what a text intends may thereby allow the text to enact the death of the reader himself.

The evanescent and unstable nature of the disembodied writing in Daniel 5 stands in sharp contrast to the ironized fixity and perdurability of Darius's writing in Daniel 6. Good King Darius "the Mede"[48] is unhappily constrained by his own writing of an interdict concerning Daniel. Court officials convince Darius of the need for an immutable ordinance commanding prayer solely to him. Daniel resists this written word, a show of power. Ironically, Darius's reluctant obsession with rigidity has caused him to write himself into impotence, compelled by the authority of his own writing to throw Daniel to the lions even though he would rather not. Upon Daniel's emergence unscathed from the lion's den, the delighted Darius writes again, placing the force and unchangeability of his own earlier written word under erasure. Darius's rewriting is presented as an earnest word of metatextual power addressed to people of every language throughout the whole world, an implied audience of everyone who will ever read or hear. Darius inscribes the narratologically endorsed truth that the God of Daniel is the living God whose dominion has no end and who delivers with signs and wonders (Dan 6:27–28).

Here the elusiveness of the unspoken frustrates attempts at hermeneutical closure. Polaski reads the significance of the irony one way: "In Darius's now authoritative and immutable law, written by his hand, God's enduring dominion looks ever so much like the law of the Medes and Persians. . . . Darius may be made to give voice to the subversive notion that his power is evanescent, but he does so only in the context of a robust exercise of his own power."[49] Perhaps. But one could switch the order of clauses in Polaski's last sentence—rewrite it—and the force of the irony would be entirely different: "Darius's robust exercise of his own power is fatally subverted by the notion that his power is evanescent." I would suggest that the tale undermines the authority of the Persian king as writer (Darius cannot resist his own word, but the faithful and wise Daniel can), while ironically manipulating that displaced and effaced authority to bind earthly listeners to Darius's textual claims on behalf of Daniel's God. Or again, Polaski suggests that the God of Daniel is in fact co-opted by the power of empire even as his writing ostensibly undermines that power:

> If Daniel is a subversive, then he is a subversive whose actions in fact buttress the authority of the empire. . . . To make God and writing close allies is to create the potential for destructive divine edicts. But this alliance so involves God in imperial power as to set a limit on God's ability to destroy the empire. The writers of the book of Daniel inhabit this contradictory space: its audience watches emperors be confounded through writing while the imperial mode of writing is celebrated.[50]

Polaski's insight that writing is being represented as an imperial activity is helpful. But here is precisely where the question of the identity and intention of the author is crucial. The Book of Daniel is powerfully focused on the identity of the one whom Daniel worships. The stories betray a fascination with the risks and possibilities of writing as an act of power, so it may be inescapable that writing is enacted in an "imperial mode." But the book's fascination has to do not just with writing and hermeneutics, but with who is doing the writing. The law of the Medes and Persians attempts to control the behavior of subjects who might otherwise challenge the imperial right to rule. Thus what Darius writes for himself are laws that direct ritual practice—first, that all must pray to him, and later, that all should tremble before the God of Daniel. So it was with Nebuchadnezzar before him, who decreed that upon the appropriate liturgical cue, all peoples were to fall down and worship before the golden statue of Nebuchadnezzar and, later, that any people who utter blasphemy against the God of Shadrach, Meshach, and Abednego should be torn limb from limb (Daniel 3). But what is written under the influence of Daniel and his God has to do more with who that God is.

In the stories of both Nebuchadnezzar and Darius, divine intervention changes the way that the emperors write. Once God's power becomes known, the Persian rulers still enforce imperial control regarding the behavior of their subjects, simply with reference to a different autocrat, God. In this, Polaski is right. But the diction of the decrees changes at the end of their texts, when they write words that identify the power and glory of God. God gradually "masters" their way of writing and changes the kind of texts they produce. Nebuchadnezzar shows this change briefly at the end of Daniel 3 with his last clause, "for there is no other god who is able to deliver in this way" (3:29) and at more length in Daniel 4, where he not only narrates his own story of dreaming, madness, and restoration, but puts into writing eloquent doxologies to the God who has mastered him (4:3, 17, 34–35, 37). So, too, Darius does not simply write another decree with the God of Daniel written in as the new imperial power. He starts to do that: "I make a decree that in all my royal dominion people should tremble before and fear the God of Daniel" (6:26) sounds quite like what Darius would have been capable of writing about himself earlier. But then he breaks out of the imperial signifying practice of decreeing constraints on the behavior of human subjects. The imperial mode of writing for mastery yields to rhapsodic praise of the living God whose kingdom will endure forever and who is capable of working signs and wonders.

This is not simply the imperial mode of writing now being dictated by a heavenly emperor. This is a new diction entirely, one that praises the God of Israel and teaches all the people who that God is. The disembodied hand had the semblance of human fingers—an ironic feint—but could not possibly be what it seemed. So too the writing inspired by Daniel's God may seem initially to mimic decrees of earthly emperors, but it is not what it seems. Where the hyperbolically fixed power of Persian laws constrains both subjects and the emperor himself, the ineffable power of the God of Heaven writes itself not through threat and imprisonment but through deliverance and rescue (6:27). Thus texts can kill, but texts can also preserve life. Writing can confine or writing can liberate. It all depends on who the author is.

The Ending of Esther and Narratological Excess

Another text concerned with the power of writing and rewriting is the Book of Esther. The plot of Esther may be lauded as the pinnacle of dramatic irony within the literature of the Hebrew Bible. Its complex dramatic ironies and deftly drawn plot reversals undermine the plans and expectations of characters within the book with surgical precision. This story offers some of the most subtly dramatic dialogue, masterful plot turns, and artfully sketched characters in all of biblical literature. Kenneth Craig has argued persuasively that the book's genre is "carnivalesque," a designation based on characteristic elements of farce, unexpected sharp reversals of power relationships, and implicit and explicit challenges to authority structures.[51] Carnivalesque relies on hyperbolic ironic renderings, that is, on hyper-sexualized, hyper-comic, and hyper-politicized representation of things that are not what they seem. Carnivalesque signifies by means of outrageous satirizing of cultural expectations regarding power, identity, and boundaries.

The ironies in the carnivalesque Book of Esther rely on excessiveness as the primary "key" or tonality of the narrative. William T. McBride puts it well:

> Esther does not merely [inhabit] Vashti's throne; she transforms that previously passive office into a vehicle for legislative action. . . . Mordecai does not simply replace Haman, matching his extreme personal favor with the king, but gains the acceptance of and promised wealth and peace for "all his seed" (10:3). . . . The formerly repressed (Semitic) elements now erupt and graft onto the previously privileged (Persian) ones, thereby exceeding those original values.[52]

Not only these but many other points of characterization and plot development in Esther are represented by means of hyperbole, overstatement, extravagance, or outsized reversal.[53] As many commentators have noticed, everything represented about the Persian court is hilariously overdone. Ahasuerus's ostentatious royal feast lasts an overblown 180 days for a crowd that is unthinkably huge: all of the royal officials, the entire Persian and Median army, and the nobles and governors of 127 provinces are there, eating and drinking themselves into a stupor "without restraint" (Esth 1:8).[54] Memucan laughably overreacts to Vashti's decision not to obey the king's command, sponsoring an edict that will attempt to legislate the sovereignty of every man over his own wife: the implied audience is not meant to take seriously his hyperbolic fear that Vashti's decision will catalyze the rebellion of the women of Persia and Media against their husbands' authority such that "there will be no end of contempt and wrath" (1:18). Ahasuerus's search for a new queen requires that all comely young virgins in the 127 provinces be sought (the number of provinces is already inflated). The women are beautified for an absurdly long twelve-month period before being brought to the king *seriatim*. Esther 3 narrates Mordecai's refusal to make obeisance to Haman; commentators have seen exaggeration here as well, arguing that Mordecai's piety is overstated since the acknowledgement of a highly placed public official would not have been seen as idolatry by Jews of the time. Even more excessive is Haman's response to Mordecai's insolence. He swiftly issues a decree not just to punish Mordecai for his insolence but to execute him, and to execute in fact not just Mordecai but all the Jews in Persia; further, he decides to choose a particular day for the genocide by casting lots, decisions that are morally outrageous and pragmatically ludicrous. In Esther 4–8, the drama moves by means of excessive turns of plot. Suspense is built through the progression of meetings Esther has with the king, in which time alternately slows to an excruciating crawl and moves with ruthless swiftness. Tension surges through the book because of the hyperbolically high stakes involved in instances of feasting, which normally are times of celebration but here mark times of betrayal, the unmasking of plots, death, and even the potential for averting genocide.[55] Esther 9 raises disturbing flags of excess in that the heroine who had asked for her people to be able to defend their lives now requests an extra day of slaughter. The Persian king is happy to oblige, and the Jews press on to execute huge numbers of people, celebrating merrily afterward amid the carnage. Excess marks the Book of Esther from its beginning feast saturated in alcohol to its concluding feast saturated in blood.

This diaspora story does not address the dangers of assimilation in the same way that the Book of Daniel does. Esther hides her Jewish identity at first. She does eventually identify openly with her people and save them. But she also uses her connections within the foreign court to distinct advantage in a way that, for other biblical authors, would have disastrously compromised her integrity and her Jewish identity. Esther has sex with a non-Jew (Ahasuerus), and there is no concern in the text to indicate that Esther kept kosher, two aspects of the story that troubled ancient rabbinic commentators.[56] A crucial question for interpretation of the book is the problem of how we are to understand Esther's Jewishness. Is she Jewish-as-Other or Persian-as-Other to the implied audience, or perhaps both? Does she hide her Jewish identity initially but live heroically into it by the end, as many commentators would have it? Or does she identify superficially with her people, struggling to save them because her own identity as constructed by Persians would have her killed along with them, but in the end remain as Persian as before, perhaps becoming even more deeply implicated in the cultural assimilation that had been central to her identity all along? Michael V. Fox argues that Esther is fully and unchangeably Jewish; indeed, he makes that case as well as it can be made.[57] But in what follows, I will suggest that Fox has articulated—beautifully—only the "straight" meaning of the text, which is not the final site of meaning as that is being signified through larger-scale ironies. The narrative's hyperbolic representation of Esther's choices not to guard the sexual and dietary boundaries of her Jewish body,[58] taken together with the narrative's ironizing of misreadings of Jewish tradition in the Book of Esther, fatally ironizes Esther's Jewishness, leaving it far more unstable than Fox's elegant position allows.[59] The gains are real, to be sure: the Jewish people are not slaughtered, and Mordecai is elevated to a position of political power. Yet in the final analysis, the losses can be argued to overshadow the gains and, in fact, to ironize them. The "said" in the Book of Esther is by no means entirely false, but it is ultimately not the most important thing for the implied audience to know.

While diverse aspects of excess could be profitably studied toward the larger goal of articulating one persuasive meaning—one out of many[60]—in the Book of Esther, it is the victorious ending of the Book of Esther that shall be probed here. In keeping with its excessive rhetoric and excessive plot twists, the Book of Esther (in the MT tradition) offers an excess of victorious endings in its own corpus. The narratological closure achieved by the slaughter of the Persians is followed by another closure fixing the celebration of Purim in writing for all generations to come. In this latter ending, social praxis and memory are mandated. And finally comes a third ending, the brief verses in chapter 10 regarding the royal record of King Ahasuerus and his elevation of the hero Mordecai to the position of second in the kingdom.

The Hebrew Bible offers a number of complicated "happy endings" that give pause to the reader alert to irony. As we have seen, the ending of the Joseph story in Genesis describes the flourishing of Israel in Egypt, but it is that very flourishing that causes the Egyptian overlords to become threatened by the growing power of the Israelites and to respond by intensifying the harshness of their working conditions. Thus what serves as narrative closure in Genesis 37–50 becomes the catalyst for new complications and agonistic drama in Exodus 1. The ending of the Book of Job has intrigued commentators who are dissatisfied with a narratological closure that can replace a man's ten dead children with ten new ones; readers have imagined the clench-jawed Job moving uneasily through the rest of his life, uncertain as to when this capricious God he worships might decide to allow the Adversary to test him again.

Walter B. Crouch has done insightful work on the faux closure of the Book of Jonah at the end of Jonah 3 and the reopening of the narrative structure in the conflictual engagement of Jonah with God in Jonah 4. In that case, a story that had seemed well and truly closed finally "ends" on an unexpectedly open note—the famous rhetorical question about whether God may not be concerned about Nineveh—that satirizes the earlier experience of closure the reader had experienced. But the most impressive and potentially disturbing closural "happy" ending within the Hebrew Bible is offered by the Book of Esther. Is the two-day slaughter inflicted by the Jews on the Persians meant to be read as justifiable, or as an overreaction that is not defensible even given the threat posed to the Jews? The history of interpretation of the Book of Esther shows that different reading communities have understood that ending in drastically different ways. Introductions to the book invariably note that some readers have found the slaughter ethically abhorrent while others defend it as necessary and entirely justifiable.[61]

It has long been noticed that the Jews end up acting in much the same manner as the Persians had been planning to act: they engage in unbridled genocidal slaughter that may look on the first day like simple self-defense—although even that is debatable—but on the second day looks more like premeditated genocide. There are some significant differences, of course: the Jews are facing an edict of their own annihilation and, at the time the decree was written that they might defend their lives, had not been in control of the government's power. (The power dynamics have shifted significantly by the time the days of slaughter arrive. By then, all of the Persian officials are allied with the Jews out of sheer terror.) Some commentators suggest that since the slaughter was carried out in self-defense, it must be considered morally acceptable. Levenson cites with approval the opinion of André LaCocque that the Jews' massacre of the Persians would be morally equivalent to a theoretical uprising in World War II in the Warsaw ghetto in which 75,000 German S. S. troops were killed.[62]

But other commentators are less sure that the narrator is presenting the Jewish slaughter as justifiable. While the narrator does use the phrase "to defend their lives" to describe what it is that the Jews are planning to do, we may ask whether that phrase in retrospect may be understood to have been being used ironically, for other narrative elements underline the nature of the slaughter as atrocity. First, there is the fact that the Persians are terrified of the Jews long ahead of time, such that all of those with political power (and thus authority over the Persian army) embrace a sort of prophylactic Jewish identity to save their lives.[63] Esther 9:3 takes care that the point not be missed: "All of the officials of the provinces, the satraps and the governors, and the royal officials were supporting the

Jews, because fear of Mordecai had fallen upon them." For all intents and purposes, the Jews and their allies constitute the imperial power at the time of the pogrom they enact. Second, quite noticeable is the heaping up of verbs for the killing that the Jews do, a kind of semantic excess that underlines the extreme nature of the violence being represented: "So the Jews struck down all their enemies with the sword, slaughtering and destroying them," which Fox translates as "a smiting by the sword and killing and destruction," 9:5.[64] Third, as David Clines has noted, the text's note that the Jews did "as they pleased" to the Persians employs a phrase, "as they pleased," that in Daniel constitutes "the sign of godless licence," (*kirṣōnō* in Daniel 8:4 and *kirṣōnām* in Esther 9:5; even more important, this phrase occurs in Esther 1:8 to characterize the unrestrained license of the Persian officials at Ahasuerus's drinking party).[65] Fourth, the fact that the Persians are not said to offer any resistance at all would seem to move the representation of the struggle out of the realm of self-defense proper.[66] Excess in the Jews' initial military response is mirrored in subsequent events: an extra day of killing is added for no stated reason. Far from the slaughter being presented as a morally appropriate and justified comeuppance for planned Persian violence, the narrative is signaling that this particular role reversal constitutes an atrocity that is not to be approved of by the implied audience.

The debate on this issue has grown sharp in contemporary scholarship, which is understandable in a post-Shoah world riven by horrific examples of ethnically motivated violence in eastern Europe, Rwanda, the Sudan, and elsewhere. Some interpreters take a tone of personal outrage at the suggestion that the Jews in the Book of Esther lose the moral high ground in the perspective of the narrative by butchering Persians for two days straight. Other interpreters are incensed that wholesale ethnic destruction on any grounds would be defended by contemporary readers as ethically viable. For some interpreters, the fact that the Jews take no plunder when they slaughter the Persians is a clear narratorial sign of their noble restraint, perhaps even their rewriting of the story of Saul and Agag so that the Israelites end up doing the right thing this time according to the holy-war code. But against this view, it may be argued that the holy-war ethos is not applicable here. The Persians are not being devoted to the ban, because the battle is not marked as the LORD's.[67] Indeed, it is fear of the dreaded Mordecai that falls upon the Persians (9:3) rather than a supernatural fear of the Divine Warrior in keeping with holy-war texts. Some, in fact, have seen an ironic incongruity in the Jews' scrupulousness about not taking plunder after savagely executing over 75,000 Persians, including women and children. Leslie Brisman writes:

In having their will with their enemies they go at it too vigorously; in refraining from plunder, they do the reverse. From both
directions, as it were, the text may challenge not just the *lex talio-
nis* but the chosenness of this scrupulous people. The scruple
that they took no plunder is repeated twice more: on the following day, the Jews of Shushan massacre another three hundred
and take no plunder (9:15); and in the provinces, they kill sev-
enty-five thousand and take no plunder (9:16). The narrator doth
protest too much, methinks.[68]

These factors, taken together, would suggest that the narrator is ironizing the holy-war mentality here.

The Book of Esther has been structured with attention to ironic reversals at multiple levels, as well as dramatic irony (the implied audience knows
much, at various turns of the tale, that characters within the story do not
know). How does the reversal in the ending of the narrative fit in with other
reversals? Is the same dynamic going on in all of the reversals, or does the
final "twist" destabilize earlier ironies of plot and characterization, thus
ironizing earlier ironies? On a straight reading, the Jews' taking charge
and slaughtering 75,810 Persians is a heroic act of self-defense that is to be
celebrated and commemorated without failure for all generations to come.
But on that reading, this would be the only role reversal in the book that is
not to be understood as ironic in some way. If the ending of Esther seems,
instead, to be similar in function to the other ironic role reversals and their
purposes, then we need to inquire into what is being ironized.

A way forward is offered by Stan Goldman. Goldman acknowledges
the ironic nature of the role reversal and slaughter, and he reads the
irony as signaling that the potential ethical offense presented by these
final plot twists is subverted. In his view, although the Jewish victory is
problematized by the story, the ironic force of the narrative itself provides a necessary critique of the role of the Jews:

> [W]hat seems to be a positive reversal of Jewish fortunes is under-
> cut ethically. But . . . there is still another reversal to come. . . .
> The author has not done the Jewish name a disservice because
> the narrative of the Jewish attack on the Persians is an example of
> Jewish self-criticism, a bold questioning of the Jewish self-image.
> Generative irony is an irony of an irony—in this case a negative
> portrayal of the Jews for a positive purpose. Irony here produces
> a levelling effect: Jews behave like Persians, and Persians behave
> like Jews. . . . Irony, like comedy, "mixes and confounds all rigid
> categories and fixed identities." . . . The massacre itself is unethi-

cal, but the reader's realization that first perceptions can be false to the multiple ironic levels of the narrative is ethical.[69]

Irony does carry an element of salutary self-critique within it, and Goldman's is an attractive proposal. What would be the unspoken meaning of this ironizing of brutality that Goldman sees as Jewish self-criticism? One might suggest that while the diaspora Jews proved themselves just as brutal and xenophobic as the Persians—albeit under duress of a sort that the Persians did not experience—at least they can ironize their own coercive agency and thus are not foolish in the same way as the gullible and hapless Persians are. It is important to be clear that this is a metanarratological perspective on the effect of irony in the Book of Esther rather than an ironic perspective evidenced within the book itself.

The landscape at the end of Esther remains soaked in the blood of 75,810 Persians as the Jews inaugurate their Purim festival. The slaughter is tied directly to a tension in the festival calendar such that the ritual will always invoke the story of massacre: Purim is celebrated on the fourteenth or fifteenth day of Adar, depending on where one lives, and any question raised about that issue must be answered in terms of which Jews stopped killing first and which Jews continued to kill for a second day (9:18–19). Fox notes, "In spite of the martial fantasies that animate the author, the festival is not said to commemorate the victories but rather the respite that followed the victories."[70] This is a telling observation: the festivities commemorate the silence after the slaughter. Irony would speak particularly forcefully in this narrative silence if it is not the actual victory as such that motivates the celebration but the cessation of massacre.

Esther is a book of paradoxes. Because this is so, it may be advisable to construct a reading that neither indulges in an earnest "straight" reading of the ending nor completely rejects the ending as not being consonant with the cues of the ironic narrative as a whole. If Esther 8–9 ironizes key unspoken conceptions about Jewish identity, holy war, and the risks of assimilation, we should remember with Hutcheon that it is a "third meaning" that emerges from the interaction of the said and the unsaid that is the point of irony here. The slaughter of the Persians should be read neither straight, as a wholly appropriate and justifiable action on the part of the Jews that should be celebrated without any moral compunctions, nor as if it constituted an ethically repugnant sign that the Jews had become no better than their bloodthirsty, xenophobic enemies.[71] Those two options would seem to represent the "said" and the "unsaid," and the goal here, as is the case throughout this book, is to tease out the deeper dimension of ironic signification created by the interplay between the said and the unsaid.

To interpret the ending in this book of ironic chiasms, we may profitably turn back to the beginning. (We are re-readers, as every reader attentive to irony must be.) We note with interest, in this narrative brimming with excess, the curiously understated representation of the choice made by Queen Vashti. The narrative feints toward her taking her place as a similarly extravagant royal: while Ahasuerus is giving his overblown feast, she holds her own feast for the women guests. But the spareness of the single sentence about her feast (1:9) contrasts markedly with the elaborate description of her husband's feast immediately preceding in the narrative. Looking in on Ahasuerus's feast, we see golden goblets lifted high in the garden court amid white curtains and blue hangings tied with cords of fine linen, marble pillars, and couches of gold and silver on a mosaic pavement of marble, mother-of-pearl, and colored stones. The reader, waiting to hear about the decorative trappings of the rooms in which the women gather and the lavish amounts of food and wine they enjoy, hears . . . nothing at all.[72] Likewise, little is said of Queen Vashti herself: we learn only that she is "lovely to behold" (1:11). Regarding her decision to decline to appear before the king, the officials, and the peoples, we learn only that she "refused to come at the king's command" (1:12). Vashti is a woman pointedly unmarked by excess, not affected by the extravagance and opulence of her narrative surroundings. She held a feast; she was lovely; she refused to obey the king. Simple integrity: that is what we know of Vashti. It is possible to read Vashti as silenced and disempowered, as a woman objectified by the male gaze and swiftly manipulated into narrative absence in the story because of her recalcitrance. A number of feminist scholars have expressed their disappointment in the characterization of Vashti. But given that the signs of power in the beginning of the story—the courtly excess and the kingly overreaction—are rendered risible, the character of Vashti is better read as remarkably powerful.[73] Spare in word and deed, she shows hospitality to her guests but allows nothing to compromise her integrity. Her refusal to be humiliated makes visible both her character and her impressive power of resistance.[74] She is neither coerced nor seduced by the excesses all around her.

Vashti's action sets the entire plot of the book in motion. In one sense, all of the Persian males in the story are responding to Vashti and her power: they are (over)reacting against the unexpected power of this woman to defy the stated command of the most powerful man in the land. What does the power of the Persian court power actually mean, if a single woman can quietly defy the express command of the mighty King Ahasuerus? Vashti's example makes clear at the beginning of the carnivalesque excesses of the Book of Esther one crucial point: it is possible to maintain one's integrity, defy the king openly, and avoid execution while not taking part in the florid overreacting that surges all about one. It is possible to resist royal coercion without engaging in hyperbolic countermeasures.

The reader might ask: but is Vashti's refusal painted narratologically as ineffectual? After all, she is summarily removed from a position that had presumably enjoyed significant court power and benefits. But there is one narrative clue that Vashti is not being drawn as ineffectual or powerless. Her refusal to come before the king is "punished" by a mandate that she do precisely what she has already chosen to do. That she may never again come before this offensive king presumably will be fine with her.[75] She no longer needs to make herself available (sexually or in any other way) to an insensitive boor whose appetite for wine, women, and status has been portrayed as insatiable. Ahasuerus is not purely comic in his excess. He is dangerous. His grandiose appetites and paranoid fears have significant and sometimes fatal consequences for those around him. So it is not just that Vashti is impatient with her annoying buffoon of a husband. She understands the very real danger to herself—to her integrity and possibly to her physical safety—posed by the king's demand that she subject herself to the gaze of his drunken male guests.

In her decision not to comply, Vashti models for every other character in the Book of Esther the possibility of refusing to play along in the terms that have been proposed. Vashti's recusal of herself from the exaggerated dynamics of excess at the beginning of this story serves as a model of dignity: she declines to allow the reactionary terms of the royal court to stand as her only options. Further, because she absents herself (and only secondarily, then, is her absence "mandated" by the thwarted king), in a paradoxical way Vashti cannot be annihilated. She has refused to step within the bounds of the circle within which destructive power is exercised. The erasing of Vashti from the royal context seems like a lame afterthought of the king designed to preserve the illusion of royal control, for she has already left his presence. Thus even as Vashti becomes absent, she remains present as a model of resistance to the misuse of power. Beal notes the irony of her erasure serving all the more to underline her presence: "[P]recisely in this process of marking off for oblivion, Vashti and her refusal are also indelibly *written into* the story in a way that will be difficult to forget. . . . [T]his text demonstrates the ironic impossibility of marking for oblivion."[76]

Hyperbolic slaughter has been hinted at in the earlier part of the story. As commentators have noticed, the gallows which Haman built for Mordecai and upon which he himself ends up impaled is ridiculously tall. Thus an oversized means of neutralizing the perceived threat of Mordecai ends up serving as the oversized means of neutralizing the real threat of Haman. Also on this second day of slaughter, the sons of Haman are executed for a second time, as it were: already killed by the sword, their bodies are then

impaled for good measure.[77] Could excesses in this narrative be interpreted as pleasing or worthy of celebration rather than as evidence of narratorial disdain? Yes. Jack Sasson sees the hyperbole of Esther as evidence
of the artistry of the storyteller.[78] Other interpreters have suggested that it
is because the stakes are so high that the characters and plot turns are so
exaggerated in this book.[79] It is certainly the case that hyperbole and extravagance are wielded brilliantly as part of the storytelling art in the Book
of Esther. But the presence of Vashti reminds us that there are moral consequences here. Because of Vashti, we can see that the storyteller uses excess carefully, not just as an expected element of plot or characterization
but as a weapon of satire marking hubris, overreaching, and paranoia.
Excess abounds in this story not just as a droll texture to an amusing tale
but as a serious matter of profligacy, overzealousness, and misuse of power.
Instances of excess in the Book of Esther are not intended to be valorized,
nor should they be taken lightly.

In my view, there is no example of excessiveness that should be read
as innocent in this story. The repeated representation of unfortunate
excess in this narrative may lead the reader to suspect even the most apparently excellent types of excess: Esther's beauty, the legally mandated
celebration of Purim, and Mordecai's political elevation. These instances of excess mark the beginning of Esther's story, the end of Esther's story, and the end of Mordecai's story, respectively. Esther's extravagant beauty is implicitly undermined by the ridiculously elaborate
processes of beautification that all of the king's virgins undergo. Her
desirability as the most gorgeous virgin in the land is compromised for
at least two reasons. First, she is taken into the harem of a king whose
apparently discriminating eye for female beauty cannot be taken seriously since he sleeps with a new woman literally every night of the year.[80]
Second, it would be difficult to see as morally upright within Hebrew
Bible tradition the representation of an Israelite virgin's sexuality being
effective in luring a foreign man into coitus. In the intertestamental
story of Susanna, the protagonist is a beautiful virgin who, it is carefully
underlined, "feared the LORD" and had been trained "according to the
law of Moses" (Sus 2–3). She uses oils and ointments as part of a beautification process too (v 17), but there the similarity with Esther ends. Susanna steadfastly resists sexual assault and is vindicated by the heroic
Daniel. In other diaspora stories as well, resistance is valorized (as noted,
Joseph resists the advances of Potiphar's wife and Daniel resists nonkosher food). By contrast, Esther is never said to fear the LORD, and she
does not resist the attentions of the king but instead actively competes
for the position of favored concubine. Through her frank sexual availability, not just her romanticized desirability, she gains access to the

royal court. One may see hints here of the dangerous sexuality of the Foreign Woman, especially if one is inclined to read Esther's "heroism" in the two-day slaughter as excessive.[81]

Even the legislation of Purim and the empowerment of Mordecai can be seen as a little too elaborate in ways that are significant for the ironic tenor of the book. First, consider the way in which the legislation of Purim is inscribed at the end of Esther 9. Never has any law been more strictly or carefully codified than this law, which is legislated in language that would seem to place it higher than the Shema in importance. But this law was based on the throwing of lots rather than divine decree, ratified by a Jew in exile who was not a priest, and intended to celebrate a deliverance that had nothing to do with God's actions on behalf of God's people in antiquity (God being notoriously absent in the MT of Esther). This law was ordered by an assimilated Jewish woman in diaspora who compromised her sexual integrity in order to gain access to the ear of a foolish and despotic foreign ruler and who achieved success through political machinations and the slaughter of over 75,000 people. Further, the after-the-fact nature of this holiday and its secular ordination is made quite clear: "The Jews adopted as a custom what they had (already) begun to do, as Mordecai had written to them" (Esth 9:23). Most significant for our reflection on excess, the requirement for keeping Purim is spoken and reiterated with so much verbiage, with every possible contingency of its celebration noted and named and re-emphasized, that a strong case can be made for ironic hyperbole:

> Thus because of all that was written in this letter, and of what they had faced in this matter, and of what had happened to them, the Jews established and accepted as a custom for themselves and their descendants and all who joined them, that without fail they would continue to observe these two days every year, as it was written and at the time appointed. These days should be remembered and kept throughout every generation, in every family, province, and city; and these days of Purim should never fall into disuse among the Jews, nor should the commemoration of these days cease among their descendants. (9:28)

As if to ensure that the implied audience not miss the irony, the author uses a specifically scriptural term to denote something that is not Scripture, "as it is written." That the matter should be understood as hyperbole is further underlined by resonances with Esther 1 in the reiteration of the word "province" in this verbose commendation of the holiday and the subsequent taking up of the erroneous and unquestionably excessive claim of there being

127 provinces under Ahasuerus's control. If it had been a sign of comic excess in Esther 1 that there were supposed to be 127 Persian provinces when all knew that in reality there were far fewer, on what grounds should the reader take as earnest in Esth 9:30 the mention of those same 127 provinces as the territory across which Purim is to be promulgated?

The fixity and enduring importance of the holiday and its human origin are once again stressed in an authorial move that piles hyperbole upon an already excessive idea:

> Letters were sent wishing peace and security to all the Jews, to the 127 provinces of the kingdom of Ahasuerus, and giving orders that these days of Purim should be observed at their appointed seasons, as the Jew Mordecai and Queen Esther enjoined on the Jews, just as they had laid down for themselves and for their descendants regulations concerning their fasts and their lamentations. The command of Queen Esther fixed these practices of Purim, and it was recorded in writing. (9:30–32)

The finger of God had inscribed the ritual practices of Israelite religion on Sinai. What can it mean that the author of Esther says that the Jews had "laid down for themselves" regulations concerning their fasts and lamentations? Beal notes that a number of scholars "have argued that the story of deliverance and the festival established to commemorate that deliverance in the book of Esther are presented in ways that closely parallel the Exodus story, the initial institution of Passover, and the giving of the law at Sinai."[82] Indeed; but we may say more about the silences that envelop these apparent congruences. Surely there is a staggering difference between the events of Sinai and the events of Susa. I read these parallels as most certainly intended—and as ironic. The Purim decree seems to be scripture, but it is not. It is a flawed imitation with none of the authority given the real Scripture by its divine source.

This "scripture" is a simulation of Torah. It is mimicry, the best that assimilated Jews in diaspora can come up with. And its permanence? Fox, following Clines, urges that we understand this "inscripturation" as conveying the permanence and importance of the words of Esther.[83] But is this how writing is understood in the book? By now we have seen that writing in the Book of Esther gives only the illusory appearance of enduring authority, as was the case in the other Israelite diaspora novella fascinated by the idea of writing placed under erasure, the Book of Daniel. When one looks closely at what Clines argues, one can see a tension here that points to the ironizing of the fixity of writing. Clines says, "What the story has shown us, though it has never said so *expressis verbis,* is that Persian law, for all its professed irrevocability, is immensely malleable. . . . The Esther story is . . . a reflection of Persian bureaucratic practice. But it is more than that: it has adopted the Persian perspective on this issue as its own."[84] Exactly—with all that such adoption implies. The final comment that the command of Queen Esther about Purim "was recorded in writing" may elicit knowing smiles from the implied audience that has seen what Beal calls "overwriting," contested writing being subtly overturned by more writing. If we take seriously the undermining of writing in this book, we see that the narrator may be communicating a skeptical view of the authority of this particular holiday over against the festivals and practices legislated on Sinai by the Holy One of Israel.

The last instance of apparently glorious excess that we may find suspect is the elevation of Mordecai in the final verses of the book. As has often been noticed, the way in which both Ahasuerus and Mordecai are spoken of in chapter 10 resonates with the regnal formulas employed liberally in Kings and Chronicles. Such formulas note key elements of a particular king's reign (whether for good or ill) and sometimes direct the reader to another book for a full account of the deeds of the king (e.g., "are they not written in the Book of the Acts of Solomon?," 1 Kgs 11:41; "they are written in the Book of the Annals of the Kings of Israel," 1 Kgs 14:19; cf. 1 Kgs 14:29; 15:7, 23, 31). We see a sly nod to that genre expectation in Esther 10:1–2. What is mentioned about Ahasuerus? That he "laid tribute on the land and on the islands of the sea," this notice following immediately after the fixing of Purim in 9:32. He imposed a heavy burden of taxation on his own country, which had just been devastated by the Jews' slaughter of 75,810 of its citizens? That would make little sense, some commentators' praise of Ahasuerus's fiscal policy notwithstanding; but then, much of what this foolish and manipulable king has done has made little sense. This may be a gesture toward the narratological "loose end" of the plunder that the Jews had refrained from taking: the Persian king himself now secures for the royal coffers the plunder of his devastated people. Ahasuerus's power continues unchecked. This king is a dangerous man subjugating his own people (whoever may be left of them), likely at the advice and counsel of Mordecai, his second-in-command, precisely as had happened with Joseph in Egypt.[85] Shevitz argues that the Book of Esther

> is a farcical commentary on the Joseph tradition. . . . [T]he authors of the Book of Esther have pronounced sentence on Joseph and his version of civil religion: It is a joke! In denuding the entire Esther story of reference to God, the text shows what is left of the sacred history of Israel when politics is substituted for piety: a Purim spiel,

a Bacchanalian orgy of mockery, and a masquerade. It is not for nothing that on Purim Jews disguise themselves as non-Jews.[86]

This narratological move reinforces the ongoing power of the Persian regime—and possibly Persian colonization, if the "islands" signify territories outside the boundaries of Persia proper—at the expense of any who are not Persians and even those who are.

What do we see in this imitation of Israelite royal historiography, which certainly cannot be taken at face value? We have the power of a foolish and dangerous foreign king immediately followed by the honoring of Mordecai the Jew as one implicated in the appraisal of this king's reign. In a word: Mordecai has become a Persian official. In the character of Esther we have seen the inscribing of hybridity. As Beal writes, "The one and the other are endlessly entangled, irreducible to either a single whole or an opposition."[87] Esther's identity as a Jew, masked at the beginning of the book, is occluded in an ironic way at the end of the book as well, when she has revealed herself as an ally of her people yet becomes fully "Persianized."[88] This hybridity, then, is driven to its fullest possible conclusion in the induction of Mordecai into the court of the kings of Media and Persia. Mordecai is next in rank to Ahasuerus, just as Joseph was second-in-command to the Egyptian pharaoh. Mordecai is praised for his good deeds on behalf of his people, and that is surely a good thing. But unless one forgets all that we have learned about Ahasuerus in the Book of Esther, one cannot fail to gain the impression that Mordecai has been co-opted into the blundering reign of a dangerous foreign despot whose judgment has shown itself, in virtually every matter, to be seriously impaired. Beal writes, "Carnivals like Purim and carnivalized literature like Esther are expressions of festive outbreak against the structures and norms of moral, economic, ethnic, and sexual hierarchies which structure relationships between individuals and groups in a society."[89] If this is true, then it must surely trouble the implied audience—brought up short in their delighted laughter at the comeuppance of the Persians—that in a final ironic twist, Mordecai becomes one of "Them," absorbed into the same Persian economic and political hierarchy that the Book of Esther has worked so hard to mock and destabilize.[90]

It is deeply ironic that what will be recorded in the annals of history is the manipulation of Ahasuerus and the resulting elevation of a foreigner (a once-despised Jew who had been marked for obliteration at the king's own behest) to the position of second-in-command. But more: note that these are not the annals of Israel's and Judah's kings. These are the annals of the kings of Media and Persia, of boastful, sexually insatiable, narcissistic, easily manipulable foreign rulers. Comedy may be intended, in part.

The implied audience is perhaps expected to find amusing the idea that the tricking of the Persian king is recorded in the Persians' own historical records. But what is left unspoken? The authority that Mordecai enjoys is a lesser authority accorded him in diaspora, far from his homeland and from the glorious (and inglorious) reigns of the kings of his own people. Mordecai's power is exiled through these verses. The dislocation of Mordecai's authority is emphasized; with this narratological stroke, the co-optation of Mordecai is complete. He has become Other to his own people even in his deliverance of them, just as happened with Joseph. So: What will happen when a Persian ruler comes to power who "knows not Mordecai"? Will there be another enslavement and time of oppression, another exodus, and a renewed need for the Law in the wilderness of diaspora?[91]

I have argued that the ending of Esther presents three kinds of moral and political excess that should not be read as if they were narratologically appropriate in a simple way. Those three excesses are the slaughter of Persians, the promulgation of Purim as if were handed down from Sinai, and the elevation of Mordecai in the annals of foreign kings. Whether one sees the slaughter enacted by the Jews as being presented as a laudatory defensive action, as morally repugnant "overkill," or as something in between, there can be no doubt that the story narrates a fullness of action that is far more than the implied audience has been led to expect. The comeuppance of the Persians is comic in the classical sense: the ending arrives at a satisfying closure that, on the face of it, seems appropriate to the crime committed by the highest Persian officials. The implied audience is invited to laugh in triumph. But given the many reversals in the book, the audience must laugh warily, for there is something uneasy at the heart of the celebration. The end of the book throws all into doubt once again, just as the end of Jonah throws into doubt all that preceded it. As Craig notes, "[Carnival] laughter is ambivalent. . . . Those who laugh are merry and exultant and simultaneously mocking and ridiculing. Such laughter is therefore an *attitude* which answers to the experience of ambivalence while allowing humankind a vehicle by which to overcome paralyzing fear."[92] The celebratory laughter of Esther is a laughter of ironic mockery that aims in a number of different directions: at the Persians, who have been shown to be less than powerful; at the Jews, whose cowering in fear at the prospect of their own annihilation has been transformed by a simple edict into a merciless killing spree twice as long as the original edict specified; at the implied audience, whose expectations have been reversed again and again by the plot turns of this book. The implied audience that has perceived the irony understands that much has been left unspoken, and the lots may yet fall another way in a new round of reversals.

The excesses at the end of Esther should be read, in my view, as signaling that survival in diaspora is indeed possible without the Temple and without observance of the Law, but that survival will then become virtually indistinguishable from the cultural pressures surrounding the Jews in diaspora. The Jews may survive by assimilating, but at an extravagant and perhaps not entirely necessary cost of human life and cultural identity. Assimilation will require that they survive by substituting human strategizing and new "scriptures," new decrees, for the plans of God from of old and the Torah. And they risk gravely misunderstanding their own identity in the process.

What might it mean that the presence of Vashti remains, never fully erased, watchful from the sidelines in the Book of Esther?[93] Vashti is the only character in the book whose actions may be interpreted as revealing measured integrity. She refuses to participate in excess—and she does not die. She survives and simply relocates her identity away from the blandishments and threats of royal power and status. Vashti's refusal reveals the king's weakness: this king is indeed powerless to harm those who disobey him. Esther's timorousness at the beginning, and her careful plotting and strategizing to overturn Haman's influence and reverse his genocidal intentions: all of this is shown to constitute yet another overreaction. We know this because Vashti has succeeded in defying the king, at his most drunken (and hence uncontrollable), in front of the most important officials of his realm and all of the people (and hence with his status most clearly at stake). She does not even get thrown into prison; the king simply finds another beautiful woman who will take her place and do his bidding. If the Jews had resisted the royal power inscribed in Haman's decree, might the king simply have sent them away and found more appropriately abject "Others"? What is most deeply ironic about the Book of Esther is that its heroine is a fully assimilated Jew who ends up recreating Jewish identity in the image of the Persians. The native Persian woman, Vashti, is the heroic figure of resistance.

Assimilated Jews may survive in diaspora without God, but only at the cost of their moral integrity, and at the cost of rewriting the Torah, and at the cost of inducting their own leaders into the annals of despicable foreign rulers. Diaspora dilutes identity. Assimilation renders one and one's people unrecognizable. In the absence of Law—in the impossibility of the full observance of the Mosaic Torah in actual cultic praxis and in ethos in Persia—the Jews in the Book of Esther have created another writing, a new "second writing" or neo-Deuteronomy that is dangerous, for it is not the word of God. Much has been made of the absence of God in the MT of Esther, commentators debating for many centuries whether the lack of explicit mention of God means that God's agency may be assumed to underlie the events of the book or, rather, that God was understood not to be present. Just as the fearful Israelites made for themselves a golden calf when Moses delayed coming down from Mount Sinai, so too—per the author of the Book of Esther—the absence of halakhic guidance in diaspora life in Persia has required the fashioning of a new kind of guidance. Emerging from the terror of genocidal threat comes not the Torah proper, but a new edict, the second writing of something that must be observed from generation to generation. And what must be observed is a carnivalesque festival: nothing is what it seems.

The narrative overtly celebrates this carnivalesque holiday of reversals and subversion of foreign power, true. As with all ironies, there is some truth to the "said." But it is only a partial truth, a truth rendered incongruous by its context, a truth the more important parts of which are belied. Here, the story shows what Purim is not: it is not Torah. The slaughter of the Persians is no divinely commanded holy war. Just as Joseph was no Moses, so Esther is no Daniel. Rather, she may be read as a fully assimilated, sexually compromised female ruler whose foreignness is inscribed insistently in the powerful silences between the lines of this overwritten book. After the Jews are saved and Jewish identity need no longer be hidden, there is still no mention of Esther beginning to keep kosher in diaspora, as Daniel was so careful to do. Nothing is said to have changed regarding her Jewish identity. Torah remains unproclaimed and unobeyed in this book. God remains unmentioned. Esther remains a foreign queen still in regular sexual congress with a foolish and dangerous non-Jew. In saving her people, Esther has simultaneously consolidated her political power and moved irrevocably into a diaspora from which there is no return. She has become fully vested as Queen of Persia and queen of paradox.

* * *

In the Genesis matriarch-in-danger narratives and the stories of Joseph, Belshazzar, Darius, and Esther, we have encountered a highly self-conscious textuality that ironizes notions of power. We have overheard an intertextual conversation that variously promotes, ironizes, and rejects assimilatory strategies in diaspora. The matriarch-in-danger stories build on each other: the silences of the Genesis 12 version are filled in by details in Genesis 20 and hyperbolic anxieties in Genesis 26, leaving the audience acutely aware of the fragile nature of covenant and the irony that Israelite identity may be guarded more ably by foreigners than by the patriarchs themselves. The Joseph story shows the wise youth growing in savvy, becoming a ruthlessly powerful God-like figure to the undiscerning Israelites in a way that responds to the Garden of Eden story's disavowal of secular wisdom. But the ironies increase in complexity as Joseph's own brutality with the native Egyptian population creates a dangerous circumstance for the Israelites' flourishing in Egypt. In Daniel, the motif of the wise youth prospering in a foreign court nods intertextually to the Joseph material, and then uses the transfer of power with Belshazzar's signet ring to signal its own effacement of both Belshazzar and the valorization of cultural assimilation that the Joseph material ostensibly represents. With Esther we see hybridity only superficially valorized. The hyperbolic narration of Jewish assimilation is taken as far as it possibly can go, with the Jews overdoing "Persian" plans for slaughter and creating a festival that celebrates it as if it had been handed down on Sinai. In Esther, hybridity eventually means death—or more accurately, massacre. The last word in the book may be read as an ironic gesture that hearkens back to Genesis 12: the hero Mordecai is "elevated" into the ranks of those foreign rulers who have problematized Israel's identity from the very beginning, when Abram first heard the siren call of Egypt.

All of these stories are concerned with discernment and resistance in a foreign landscape. We see in them a series of complex metanarratological perspectives on the ironies involved in Israelites' alternately assimilating, becoming hybridized, and resisting foreignness. Thus we have in these narratives what may be characterized as mutually interrogatory claims. The continuous clashing and revoicing of these claims yields an ironic hermeneutics that relativizes hegemonic construals of power in diaspora. Textual fixity and the notion of immutable authorial intent are skewered through the intertextual interplay. Yet the disembodied author—the ironist who writes and rewrites—remains insistently present. Like Vashti, the ironist is unforgettable precisely because of his habit of vanishing. Authorial self-effacement is a highly self-conscious and effective strategy in ironic writing: because the ironic author inscribes unspoken meanings that are elusive and speaks in voices that are not his own, the ironic author can never be fully effaced.

Taking into account the late provenance of the Joseph material, the Book of Esther, and the Book of Daniel, we may venture a diachronic observation. The ironic character of this attentiveness to textuality—that is, to writtenness—as well as to intertextuality and its paradoxes may be said to be constitutive of late traditioning processes in the Hebrew Bible. In the inner-biblical reception of Israelite traditions over time, later traditionists show their keen awareness of multiple possibilities for interpretation. These writers have found brilliant ways to acknowledge aporias that, given the impossibility of full resolution, begged for elaboration, rewriting, and ironic commentary. We see that the power of rewriting brings with it ironies all its own. Here, I would note in passing, exists an opportunity for scholars of postmodern pastiche, narrative disjuncture, and the poetics of ellipsis to theorize anew a method of historical criticism that has been hitherto somewhat disrespected by literary critics: redaction criticism. Redaction criticism in a postmodern key—reading that incorporates attentiveness to the ironies and aporias generated by rewriting and overwriting—could yet yield some fascinating fruit in biblical studies. The rewriter, that is, the late traditionist in the Hebrew Bible, must acknowledge the power of prior written traditions. Yet the rewriter may also ironize these traditions in order to free up spaces within the tradition for what yet remains to be spoken. The cultural power enacted by this ironizing, which both speaks earlier traditions and revoices them, is potentially immense. When we read these late texts closely, we may be startled to find that it is not Joseph, not Daniel, not Esther, but the ironist who is wearing the signet ring on his evanescent hand.

At stake in all of these narratives is the question of maintaining Israelite integrity when faced with the threat of foreign power. We turn now to study of a related issue: ways in which gendered and sexualized power may be used by ancient Israelite ironists to explore the question of preserving Israelite integrity. Our focus will be on the alluring and dangerous figure of the prostitute.

3

THE PROSTITUTE AS ICON OF THE IRONIC GAZE

The figure of the prostitute is prominent in several striking narratives in the Hebrew Bible, and metaphorical constructions of female sexuality in terms having to do with prostitution animate the diction of the biblical prophets. Ironic reversals abound in the prose stories and prophetic oracles that deal with the figure of the prostitute directly. Irony also suffuses texts that hint more obliquely at gendered dynamics of power and economic bartering for sex, whether explicit or implicit, narratologically "actual" or metaphorical. Cultural reference to prostitutes offered biblical authors rich possibilities for exploring the charged and paradoxical relationships between anonymity and intimacy, power and vulnerability. The prostitute as dramatic character provides an important metaphor for biblical writers interested in telling stories of risk, sin, exposure, the transgression of social boundaries, and accountability.

This chapter will analyze the intricate ironies at play in biblical stories of five women who are characterized—three openly, two more subtly—as prostitutes: Tamar, Rahab, Jael, Gomer, and Ruth. All of these ironies involve metadiscursive reflection on points of intersection between cultures or ethnic groups. In every biblical story considered here, the figure of the prostitute (or pseudo-prostitute) carries in her body and in the implied risks and pleasures of her sexuality the boundaries being scripted or transgressed for the Israelite community in the narrative. To look closely at the figures of these prostitutes is to read a multivalent symbol-text in which story and counter-story unfold in the same moment. The constructed figure of the prostitute is a powerful icon for the ironic gazes of authors and hermeneuts alike.

Before engaging the stories of these biblical women, it will be important to lay some groundwork with an exploration of key theoretical notions concerning the ways in which biblical texts rely on constructions of women's sexuality for their meaning-making. In this, I will attend to sexuality theorist Elizabeth Grosz and gender theorist Judith Butler as I engage leading Hebrew Bible scholars who have analyzed issues of women and sexuality in antiquity.[1]

Gender roles, understandings of corporeality, and norms for sexual behavior are constructed socially by individuals and groups (most visibly by those who produce literature, art, and laws), according to social and political criteria that have to do with the authorizing of power relationships in interpersonal, domestic, and public spheres. Understanding how women's and men's bodies and agency are constructed is of crucial importance for appreciating the narratives of body and sexuality that we find in biblical texts treating prostitution.[2] In literature that represents communal or individual identity by means of appeal to the erotic, the possibilities for reinforcing, nuancing, or subverting audience expectations regarding sexual agency constitute rich sources of narratological power. The play of the constructed body through many different levels of signification is articulated well by Elizabeth Grosz:

> The body must be regarded as a site of social, political, cultural, and geographical inscriptions, production, or constitution. The body is not opposed to culture, a resistant throwback to a natural past; it is itself a cultural, *the* cultural product. . . . The body is neither—while also being both—the private or the public, self or other, natural or cultural, psychical or social, instinctive or learned, genetically or environmentally determined. In the face of social constructivism, the body's tangibility, its matter, its (quasi) nature may be invoked; but in opposition to essentialism, biologism, and naturalism it is the body as cultural product that must be stressed. This indeterminable position enables it to be used as a particularly powerful strategic term to upset the frameworks by which these binary pairs are considered.[3]

The presence of women's bodies in biblical narrative and poetry is freighted indeed, for all of the reasons cited above concerning social boundaries and sources of power in identity construction. Embodied women characters stand out as implicit sources of conflict with masculine notions of self, community, and God. One simple but potent reason is that women are rare in biblical literature. The protagonists in biblical stories and the speakers in biblical poetic discourse are constructed as almost all male, at least in those texts in which gender identity can be determined as a feature of characterization or narratorial voice. As Alice Bach writes:

> [B]iblical narratives are written by men with an ideal audience of men. . . . [O]n the level of story the gaze of the male characters directs the narrative, making women objects of their gaze, and on the level of the fabula the powerful male gaze is represented in the look of the author, ideal audience, and traditional interpreter: men looking, telling, explaining. . . . Except for brief moments of female focalization in biblical narratives . . . the gaze is owned by male characters, authors, and spectators. Indeed this perspective seems natural and unchangeable. The male gaze is assumed.[4]

The dominance of male voices and their implied normative male gaze renders the female as a charged and virtually marked "Other" even in those biblical texts in which women act as heroines. Femaleness can be marginalized even in texts in which particular women are valorized as strong, clever, or obedient in whatever ways the androcentric norms of that particular context require.

Paradoxically, sexualized otherness both promotes and destabilizes the sociopolitical systems that promulgate it. Textual representations of those systems are vulnerable to destabilization as well. Judith Butler argues regarding patriarchal systems of meaning: "On the one hand, women are excluded and erased from such a system, and on the other hand, they are everywhere recirculated *within* that system as fetishized objects, phantasmatic sites of erotic investment. . . . As a commodity that must be exchanged between male owners in order to consolidate masculine authority, women are essential to the very economy from which they are (perpetually) excluded."[5] One might remark the importance of sexualized violence in texts as the most aggressive defense of the economy of phallocentric identity, whether of individuals or of cultures. As Regina M. Schwartz has said in her study of the conflicting stories of David in the Hebrew Bible, "Israel is threatened from without and from within and in the very midst are acts of adultery, rape, and incest. This is no accident: Israel's war with the sons of Ammon is a war of definition, the sexual violations are tests of definition, for in both, Israel's borders—who constitutes Israel and who does not—are at stake."[6] Even heroines who resist male-led or male-sponsored violence can be co-opted into the foundational assumptions of systems of violence, as happens in the Book of Esther.[7]

Audiences and readers are complicit in this often violent phallocentric economy to the degree that their own values and their own gazes are circumscribed and directed by androcentric norms shaping the texts they encounter.[8] The presence of irony in texts about women and sexuality offers a tool with which resistant readers can deconstruct the androcentric gaze within those texts. The question as to whom the ironic text constructs as a responsive or disobedient reader, then, becomes both undecidable and marvelously evocative.[9]

Phyllis Bird has written on the polyvalent ways in which sexuality and gender figure in stories of prostitutes in the Hebrew Bible. Her work provides support for Butler's contention that commodification, with its attendant valorizing (or fetishizing) and exclusionary dynamics, lies at the heart of patriarchal portrayals of prostitution.[10] Bird notes that prostitution

> is a product and sign of the unequal distribution of status and power between the sexes in patriarchal societies. . . . Female prostitution is an accommodation to the conflicting demands of men for exclusive control of their wives' sexuality and for sexual access to other women. The greater the inaccessibility of women in the society due to restrictions on the wife and the unmarried nubile woman, the greater the need for an institutionally legitimized "other" woman.[11]

Bird argues that a profound cultural ambivalence lies at the heart of many figurings of the prostitute in the Hebrew Bible. Ostensibly untrustworthy, self-interested, and socially marginalized, the prostitute nevertheless can serve as a strategic ally for other characters in these stories, providing crucial access to information through her relatively unrestricted connections to males in power. The potential for dramatic reversals of power relationships is great when prostitutes figure as characters in Hebrew Bible narrative, precisely because the social and political ambivalences inscribed in the body of the prostitute can destabilize other cultural constructions that are brought into intercourse with her.[12] The figuring of women's sexual autonomy and attendant social marginalization within patriarchal social systems bespeaks deep anxieties and overcompensatory denial about power dynamics that are virtually by definition out of the control of the male narrator. Again, even heroines are a locus of risk for male subjectivity, especially if they are sexual initiators. Alice Bach notes that the same danger constructed in the male characterization of "wicked" women such as Delilah can also be seen to imbue representations of valorous women, albeit more subtly:

> Esther and Judith are the women who are communally useful (indeed essential) and therefore heroines. But the mechanisms through which they accomplish their heroism are potentially as dangerous and murderous (to the individual masculine subject, if not the community) as their usefulness whenever the manipulation of a threatening, powerful, and potentially excessive, uncontrollable female sexuality is glimpsed in their narratives.[13]

We will need to remain mindful of the multiple aspects and changeability of figures of the prostitute within Hebrew Bible traditions, not only because of the variety of ways in which the trope is used in the literature, but because of the undecidability of key issues of sex and power in these stories and in readers' appropriations of them. Yvonne Sherwood notes of Hosea's prostitute-wife, "there are potentially many different texts and many different Gomers to be made" by reader responses to the overt claims and subtle fractures in the biblical text.[14] Bach, too, stresses the "endless conflict and negotiation that goes on within the mind of the reader, a matter of drawing lines, contesting boundaries, reinterpreting symbols, and rearranging experience into constantly shifting categories."[15] Where irony textures biblical narrative and prophetic discourse, it adds unstable tectonics and mercurial boundaries all its own. Irony demands attention to cues and clues that originate from the text, yet its very presence deconstructs any simplistic construal of intent. In this chapter focused on issues of gender and sex, irony will be seen as a powerful tool for the unmasking and destabilizing of all interpretive discourses, not just phallocentric ones.

Irony is a means of double voicing whereby androcentric cultural norms are mouthed, perhaps earnestly, and are yet subverted by figures that both embody and reframe those norms. Whereas the creation of a truly woman-centered discourse may have been pragmatically impossible for ancient biblical writers (male or female) writing about women,[16] nevertheless irony provides a powerful way to approximate such a new discourse, because it simultaneously mimics and undermines the expectations of the dominant paradigm. In the readings that follow, I will analyze ways in which biblical texts may inadvertently destabilize their own assumptions about gender, sex, and power.

A final note is in order before commencing with the exploration of stories about Israelite and Canaanite prostitutes. There are several women characterized as prostitutes in the Hebrew Bible whose stories cannot be taken up in detail here, and in each of these stories, important ironies may be discerned. There is the prostitute with whom Samson has sex in Gaza (Judg 16:1–3). Samson uproots the gates of the city and walks away with them, literally displacing crucial boundaries in a postcoital act of sabotage upon which an interpreter of irony might muse at some length. There are the two prostitute-mothers whose dispute over a surviving neonate gives King Solomon an opportunity to exercise his famous "wisdom" in 1 Kings 3. Here, justice is rendered through the imitation of cruel injustice in the threat of dismemberment of the living infant before the eyes of his mother. These stories, already ironic as seen through the gaze of traditional commentators and even more ironic when metacommentated by interpreters who do not subscribe to phallocentric social norms, would alone provide enough material for a book-length study of gendered ironies of sexual control and autonomy.

And there is another woman character whose story can be touched on only briefly here. She stands, forlorn and voiceless, figured obliquely as a prostitute by the rhetoric of her brothers in order to serve the purposes of ideological violence enacted against outsider males by the insiders of Genesis. She is Dinah. The story of Dinah in Genesis 34 is a complex indicator of how much is at stake in the imputation of whoredom, in the figuring of women's sexuality in ambiguous circumstances as prostitute behavior, for ancient Israel and for other phallocentric cultures.

In Genesis 34, Dinah is raped by a Hivite prince. Later, she is avenged by the bloody mutilation and execution of the men of Shechem by two of her brothers. The story has troubled readers from intertestamental times to the present day.[17] Feminists and others have long struggled with this story, proposing readings that condemn or rehabilitate Shechem, condemn the brothers for hyperbolic violence or laud them for heroic redemption of Dinah's honor, and craft for Dinah herself a role and a voice that have been arguably suppressed or ignored in the biblical account.[18] In contemporary scholarship, particularly lively has been the polemical argument between Meir Sternberg, on the one hand, and Danna Nolan Fewell and David Gunn, on the other.[19] For our purposes here, it is noteworthy that the biblical story of Dinah and Shechem is left open-ended, concluding with a powerfully ambiguous rhetorical question: Simeon and Levi respond to Jacob's rebuke with the retort, "Should our sister be treated like a prostitute?" The question seems to expect a negative answer, but the matter is more complex. It is by no means certain that the narrator's view is coterminous with the perspective of Simeon and Levi. Dinah herself is left voiceless, and the woman's body and the Israelite social body are left in a state of aporia. Communal boundaries are figured in the sexualizing of women's autonomous choices even here. The figure of the prostitute, or even the perception of the veiled outline of a potential prostitute, is so fraught with risk for Israelite communal identity that wholesale slaughter of "Others" is required to balance the scales. Yet such hyperbolic excess is also condemned. In stories involving women, sex, and power, the perspectives of biblical traditionists are ironic and often ambivalent, anticipating and inviting ambivalent reactions in readers.

The first prostitute story on which we will dwell in detail is the story of the "prostitute" Tamar, a story that presents deception named as righteousness and righteousness named as deception.

Tamar the Righteous

Genesis 38 is positioned awkwardly in the midst of the translucent narrative artistry of the Joseph account. Here we encounter a strange story of fertility thwarted, sexual desire exploited, and the masking of identity. Tamar is figured as a wronged woman who loses her husband because of his wickedness, who is given no chance to bear children because of her brother-in-law's illegitimate interest in safeguarding the inheritance of his own progeny, who is ignored by the patriarch Judah when his promise of redemption comes due, and who must take matters into her own hands in order to become pregnant and secure standing for herself once more in her community. How are the identities of the characters in this story shaped by means of their engagements with Tamar's sexuality?

Ironic readings may interpret Genesis 38 as reflecting patriarchal Israelite traditions or as subverting the same. As Jan William Tarlin mischievously notes, "Genesis 38 can appear as an elegantly ironic tale in which a canny and courageous woman risks dishonor and death to uphold the value system of Israelite patriarchy when the patriarchs most concerned have proved incapable of doing so," or Genesis 38 may be read "as an elegantly ironic tale in which a canny and courageous woman risks death and dishonor to expose the foolishness and fragility of Israelite patriarchy even while appearing to perpetuate it."[20] Tamar sits veiled at the city gate whose name means "Opening of the Eyes"—and we may ask, whose eyes are closed? The shifting spaces and elusive meanings of irony are resistant to closure, intriguingly oppositional without obvious resolution. But there are ways in which one can adjudicate the possibilities, mapping the ironic landscape along more than one axis at a time.

First, a glance at the larger literary context. What we know of Judah is that he has just sold his brother Joseph into slavery for economic gain. Whether that detail is intended to ameliorate Judah's role in the brothers' fratricidal rage, as some commentators would have it, is not clear. Reuben's compassion for Joseph completely overshadows the mercenary instinct of Judah, and it seems to me just as likely that the narrative detail about Judah is intended to show Judah's calculating nature in an unflattering light. Esther M. Menn argues that the character of Judah is represented as uncharitable and ineffectual on a number of counts within Genesis 38 and in the larger literary environment as well. Tying Judah's journey (38:1) to the forced descent of Joseph into slavery and the imagined descent of Jacob into Sheol mourning, Menn writes, "With the extended play on the verb 'to go down' . . . that provides linguistic and thematic cohesion between Genesis 37, 38, and 39, the description of Judah's journey as a descent implies a moral judgment on this character and hints at a loss of status due to his flawed leadership of his brothers."[21] So even at the very beginning of the story, there may be subtle narrative indications that Judah is not reliable.

What we know of Tamar, by contrast, is precisely nothing at all. While it may be considered likely that she is a Canaanite, the narrative does not say that outright.[22] Thus that sons Er and Onan are wicked and displease the LORD is narratologically more likely due to their father's influence than their mother's, at least in the case of Onan, who, commentators agree, is presumably motivated by greed to ignore the levirate duty just as his father was motivated by greed to sell Joseph. Where details in these narratives are spare but strongly articulated, they must be brought to the forefront for interpretations that seek to probe the unspoken. And there are other grounds as well for trusting Tamar more than Judah. Diane M. Sharon argues that the narrator represents negatively Judah's willingness to visit a prostitute: "Judah patronizes a prostitute during the potentially tumultuous days of sheep-shearing instead of marrying to provide an opportunity for continuity. Judah, too, has the potential for progeny, an opportunity that he would waste, as surely as Onan does."[23] Richard J. Clifford offers this: "Judah is a one-man show. . . . Even the divine slaying of his children does not slow him down. The rapid pace and terse tone of the narrative suggest Judah's brusque and imperious style. . . . Judah is not just impetuous, he is a sinner. He sinned in marrying a Canaanite, in visiting a prostitute, and in peremptorily ordering the burning of his daughter-in-law. He sinned [also] by failing to ensure that the levirate law was observed."[24] Moving through the story of Genesis 38, the reader has been strongly encouraged to be neutral or sympathetic to Tamar and suspicious of Judah.

Tamar is a woman whose powerlessness has been inscribed in three different ways in this story. She is a widow (twice over, for hyperbolic good measure), she has been sent back to her father's house and thus has lost her claim to any status in the house of her father-in-law, and she has identified herself through dress and behavior as a prostitute. Her apparent powerlessness, however, changes dramatically as the plot unfolds.[25] Tamar veils her identity in garments readily recognizable to the male gaze, mimicking the sexual availability of the prostitute in order to achieve a goal that would not normally be associated with prostitution. In her sartorial masking, she proleptically ironizes the simplistic hermeneutic that Judah will use to (mis)identify her purpose: she knows exactly how he will misread her.[26] He expects, naïvely, that the commodifying transaction will work in a single direction and to his benefit. She garbs herself to meet his expectation, knowing that her signifying as prostitute is only part of what is being represented in their interaction, and not even the most important part. Tamar is an ironist, veiled literally by garments and figuratively by what she does not say.

Later, she uses the signs of male identity and social power—the pledge, the signet, and the staff that Judah has given her—to name and ironize the authority claimed by Judah. The character of Judah has already been ironized in some local moments of dramatic irony. Judah does not realize that God has taken his two sons while the reader is well aware of that fact; he does not recognize his own daughter-in-law at the place named Opening of the Eyes, even after speaking with her.[27] In the final moment of reckoning, when she confronts Judah, Tamar undermines not only the authority of the male speaker who has tried to command her execution by burning, but the authority of the male who would control woman's social viability through patrilineal levirate norms. Tamar's ironic double voicing seems to acknowledge Judah's claim to authority but actually eviscerates it. The observation of Butler about feminine discourse applies here:

> If the feminine is that which cannot be accommodated by the masculinist production of subjects, then the feminine is, strictly speaking, not an identity, but a *difference from* that which counts as identity, the wild and untamable, the specter, the sign of that power regime's fundamental limitation, that which exceeds its control. . . . The discourse that emerges from the site of that difference will constitute a rival and contestatory configuration of power; it will mime and dislocate the master's words, rework his discourse, work his discourse against him to compel his defeat.[28]

Tamar's speech, as indeed her veiled silence earlier, constitutes a "rival and contestatory configuration of power." She speaks aloud the signifying represented by Judah's having given her his identifying possessions—

"Take note," she says, "whose these are, the signet and the cord and the staff" (38:25)—and in so doing, Tamar mimes and dislocates her master's words.

Tamar's ironic double voicing of the stentorian tones of patriarchal privilege flags for the reader two levels of ironic meaning produced by the interplay between the unreliable said and the unsaid. First, she underscores the patent plot ironies, the events that transpired with full knowledge of the reader and Tamar herself but with no discernment on the part of the clueless Judah. Second, there is ideological irony in Tamar's feigned naïve reading of Israelite tradition as an outsider, a delicious moment of comeuppance in which she reveals that she has both the moral right and the tangible proof of same even though she may be no Israelite and in any case has been repeatedly rejected by Israelite males. Judah, by contrast, appears willfully illiterate in the traditions of his people.[29] Seeing Tamar perform her "reading," we witness the victory of the untutored outsider hermeneut over the credentialed insider who cannot understand his own text.

In her revoicing of Judah's powerful claiming of the insignia and her own more powerful fruitfulness, Tamar speaks a profound irony that plays out in multiple ways across the patriarchal landscape of Genesis and into the David story. In the literary context of Genesis 37–50, Judah has ruthlessly attempted the commodification of others and has been bested at his own game. Judah's refusal to compel Shelah's fulfillment of the levirate obligation underlines the fraternal strife that seethes throughout the Book of Genesis and especially in the Joseph material in which Genesis 38 is embedded. The levirate ideal of fraternal solicitousness may be being ironized in passing here,[30] but in any case, Tamar's claiming of the tradition undermines the discomfort of the eponymous ancestor of all of Judah with the continuation of his own lineage. In the larger context of Genesis, Judah has attempted to control and thwart the continuation of patriarchal heirs, not only by selling his brother Joseph but also by separating from his own kinship group to sojourn with Adullamites and blocking the continuation of his own family line through Shelah. Yet ironically, in what was to have been an anonymous encounter with a roadside prostitute, he has unwittingly fathered a line that will culminate in David himself.

The story attributes a lean kind of literal-minded "righteousness" to Tamar, who comes off better than Judah, according to Judah himself. How are we to read this confession? Is it safe to assume that Judah's viewpoint is coterminous with the viewpoint of the narrator? No. Judah is a misguided man who believes Tamar to be the cause of the deaths of Er and Onan when the narrator makes clear that it was their own wickedness—possibly even following his example, if we consider Judah to have been motivated by greed too—that caused Judah's God (not Tamar herself and not her god) to smite them. This same Judah cannot discern that a woman with whom he is having sex is a woman he has known for years in his own household, even when she speaks with him at some length beforehand about terms of payment. This Judah has sold his own brother Joseph into slavery, profiting from the commodification of family. Judah is indeed right when he names Tamar as more righteous than he. But, as is so often the case with ironic narratives, he is only partially right, and he is right for the wrong reasons. In his confession, he carefully focuses only on his error in not giving Shelah to Tamar, thus masking his own lack of discernment, his misguided rush to judgment, and his premature call for summary execution. There is much less to Judah the Patriarch than meets the eye.

Tamar, on the other hand, is excessive in every way. If we had been uncertain as to whether she was a Canaanite, our anxiety grows as she (possibly) becomes doubly, excessively Canaanite by virtue of leaving the Israelite household into which she had been taken and returning to live in her father's house after the death of Onan. Tamar redresses the wrong done to her not by appealing it through judicial processes but by exaggerating her sexuality, masking her identity as a widow and assuming the identity of a woman who has sex indiscriminately with men for economic security. And through a single sexual encounter, she becomes pregnant not only with a child, and not only with a male child (this matters for the disposition of future inheritance), but with twin boys. The story is saturated with the exaggerated excess of this "Other," a foreign woman who is doubly defined by her sexuality—not only by Israelite patrilineal tradition but by her own actions as well. The irony is heightened when this excessive Tamar is named as "more righteous" than Judah. If what we have here is a contest of commodification, deceptive sex against unjust social authority, then the threatening "seepage," in Grosz's term, of the outsider woman has flooded every boundary that the story has etched.

Why does the text mention that Judah did not have sex again with Tamar once he understood that she had been the "prostitute" with whom he had had sex earlier? This remark is so incongruous that reading it straight is virtually impossible. There is no narrative context in which it would make sense except as an unmasking, a sardonic twisting and ironizing of what has gone before. Tamar is no prostitute, nor is she in any way sexually available to Judah—of course he did not have sex with her again. Would Judah have had sex again with the prostitute had she not been Tamar? Perhaps, but there was no such prostitute—so of course he did not have sex with her again. Is the point that Tamar was so desirable or so sexually skilled that Judah would theoretically have wanted to have sex with her again, had all of the townspeople not now seen that she was his daughter-in-law? What desire is at play here, and how has it now been thwarted? Why is Judah's desire, written in the negative, the focal point at the end of the dramatic confrontation scene?

The unspoken answer here is thunderous: Judah the undiscerning, lustful patriarch did not again have sex with a veiled and possibly Canaanite woman in the midst of his culture and kinship group because of the excessive, overwhelming results. Two male children have been generated through this single encounter, and now a twin threat to Shelah's inheritance of Judah's line exists where none existed before. Here, we may have a hint at the alarm some streams of Israelite tradition felt toward King David the outsider and master commodifier, on which, more shortly.

Second, we may consider hermeneutical ironies within and beyond Genesis 38 when we reflect on who reads and who misreads Israelite tradition. The mocking critique of Judah (both the eponymous patriarch and the sociopolitically configured territory) and the valorization of the borderline-Canaanite Tamar can be read "straight" as either naïve or foreign. W. Sibley Towner considers the narrative to be early, as it seems to be innocent of the polemic against Canaanite people and practices that marks much of later Hebrew Bible tradition.[31] J. A. Emerton has gone so far as to suggest that the story was of Canaanite origin and circulated orally among a Canaanite audience before being taken into Israelite tradition due to its "inherent interest."[32] The vulnerabilities of this speculation do not detract from its important signal of a kind of double voicing going on in this text. This ostensibly Israelite tradition is narrated in a way that seems to laud its ethnically undefined heroine and to credit commendable agency to the Canaanite friend of Judah, Hirah the Adullamite. The story disconcerts its reader in a manner so matter-of-fact that the reader might indeed be misled into explaining its presentation of astonishing disjunctures by means of other historical contexts. But what of the context in which we find it, namely, squarely in the middle of familiar Israelite literary territory—the Joseph material— looking like something it's not? Tamar is not the only one who speaks through a veil here. Ideological masking is going on at the level of the text's discourse, as well.[33] The expectations of the implied audience—in my view most certainly not Canaanite—are being ironized.

Judah cannot, in fact, be the *levir* for Tamar: for a father-in-law to have sex with his daughter-in-law merits capital punishment according to Leviticus 20:12, and Tamar has not followed the prescribed practice (viz., going to the elders in the gate) in appealing for justice in the case of failed levirate obligation. To assume that the text is naïve as regards accepted practice, a historicist assumption for which no evidence can be adduced beyond simple speculation,[34] would be to fail to appreciate fully the artistry of the passage. If this story is decidedly not about levirate marriage, then the levirate issue is being used to mask another ideological concern. Here we may move to another level of ironic signification produced by reading the Tamar story as part of the larger story of the family of Jacob and the metanarrative of the history of Judah. Redaction critics and synchronic readers alike must wrestle with the difficulty of discerning how the perspectives of these narratives—Tamar's story and Joseph's story—overlap, displace, affirm, or contest one another. Juxtaposition is no simple textual phenomenon, as Carol Newsom has demonstrated in her work on polyphony in the Book of Job.[35] Juxtaposition enacts a tensive engagement that brings metanarratological questions of subordination, appropriation, and confirmation to the forefront of the reader's experience. The two issues of juxtaposition to be explored here are those of dual narrative trajectories and simultaneous character development.

All of what happens—from Judah's marriage and his fathering of Er, Onan, and Shelah to Tamar's marriage and bereavement, to her waiting in vain for levirate succor and finally deceiving Judah into impregnating her, to her giving birth to the twins Perez and Zerah—all of this takes place in the pregnant dramatic moment in the Joseph story in which Joseph has been sold to captors and is on his way to Egypt. There is much that is unspoken about Judah's character in the Tamar story that informs our reading of that larger context. Judah, the eponymous ancestor, becomes willfully estranged from his own people and does not know what is required to save his people. Judah is unable to recognize that which is right in front of him in the most intimate way.[36] The genealogical notice about the twins born to Tamar makes the point that David springs from Judah's stock. Reinforcing the interest in David are significant literary echoes between the story of Judah and Tamar and the story of David and Bathsheba.[37] While it is theoretically possible that the rhetorical motivations for such a story linking Tamar to David are supportive of the Davidide monarchy,[38] it seems more likely that this odd and embarrassing story yields devastating satirical implications. The unspoken here? A minor point may be that just like Judah, David foolishly risks everything for the fulfillment of his own sexual needs (with Bathsheba). Robert Alter's label of Genesis 38 as "a tale of exposure through sexual incontinence"[39] can certainly be applied to the Bathsheba affair as well. A more far-reaching ironic perspective might be sketched as follows. David is a disaster as a leader, illegitimate and ethnically an outsider (given that Tamar may be Canaanite and Ruth is Moabite). Centuries later, Ezekiel will disrespect Jerusalem with the formulation, "Your father was an Amorite and your mother a Hittite" (Ezek 16:3). The story of Judah and Tamar may trade on that same form: David's "father" was an undiscerning, sexually indiscreet, manipulative man who did not keep his word and who was willing summarily to execute family in order to hide his own sin, and his "mother" acted like a whore.

Here we glimpse irony as subtle as a smile behind a diaphanous veil and as radical as the subversion of a monarch's claim to belong to the country he rules. Through the gaze of the biblical ironist, we see what can unfold when a possibly Canaanite "prostitute" ensconces herself in the midst of an Israelite family. May it be considered a blessing, this birth of twin male children in David's line? Yes. But that is not the only thing to say here. This blessing is only part of the truth, and it is not the most important part, for the reader knows much more. The reader knows that an outsider subverts the claims to authority of an Israelite insider, and not just any insider but the eponymous ancestor of the territory over which David will rule. This story's mercurial play of betrayals (Onan's and Judah's) and deception (Tamar's) results in the conception of a morally compromised half-breed lineage, birthed precisely at the narrative moment when the brothers have sold Joseph into slavery. David was born, as it were, amid betrayal and lies. The narrative insertion of Genesis 38 makes clear that deception and false claims to righteousness attended the very conception of the Davidic line. The larger literary context establishes that the ancestors of David were themselves born into conflictual internecine dynamics. These stories seethe with protracted manipulations and threats of revenge. All of this is where David came from. It is no wonder that Israel will come to ask scornfully, "What share do we have in David?" (1 Kgs 12:16).

Rahab the Clever

Tamar now yields the "prostitute" veil to a woman accustomed to wearing it on a daily basis: Rahab of Jericho. The story of Rahab is fraught with triumph and tragedy that bleed into each other, the official silences of the narrative barely suppressing the mingled shouts of victory and screams of terror that cry out from between the lines of Joshua 2. Rahab the Canaanite prostitute, long seen in Jewish and Christian tradition as one of a select group of paradigmatic outsiders who convert to faith in the God of Israel, is also a woman who betrays her friends and townspeople in order to save her own life and the lives of her family. The gaps and unspoken horrors in this triumphalist narrative have put conflicting pressures on interpreters for many centuries.[40]

Joshua is about obedience. Here I mean to underline both the narrative's depiction of the obedience of the biblical hero Joshua and my reading of the Book of Joshua as a sustained rhetoric urging obedience. The

Book of Joshua has been seen by commentators to stand in some contrast to individual stories and the overarching narrative arc of the deeply
ironic Book of Judges. Where Joshua narrates a coherent and triumphant mission, Judges tells stories of failed missions, the ongoing apostasy of the Israelite people, the flaws and limitations of their charismatic
leaders, and Israel's repeated failure to observe holy-war regulations.
But the roots of such breaches are traceable to Joshua himself, for it was
Joshua's decision to save, out of the blood-soaked streets of an entire
community destroyed, not only an outsider, and not only a woman, but a
Canaanite prostitute and her family.

Is Rahab part of Israel? No. Yet she is in the midst of Israel, and herein
lie the powerful ironies of the story of Rahab the prostitute. Aaron Sherwood has pointed to some local ironies within the story of Rahab. For example, he notes that in Joshua 2:5 and 2:8, the Hebrew verbs *yādaʿ* ("to
know," often with a sexual connotation in contexts where sex or sexual violence may be expected) and *šākab* ("to lie down," often with a sexual connotation) are used without the expected sexual freight even though the
spies' host is a woman whose daily business is sex. This is surely an ironic
signal that Rahab as prostitute will not be what the reader might expect.
Joshua's anxiety regarding the strength of the Canaanite forces is assuaged
not by Deuteronomy 11:23–26, which Sherwood sees as an intertext for
Joshua 1–2, but by Rahab, and "the spies' lives are ironically safer in the
hands of a Jericho native than in Joshua's."[41]

Rahab's body is defined by the narrative as a site of forbidden intercourse with the enemy (that is, with numerous Canaanite males) and
thus arguably poses a great danger culturally to the Israelite spies. Foreign women are often construed in the Deuteronomistic History as se-
ductresses who invite Israelite males into apostasy. The spies' spending
the night with Rahab portrays the ultimate risk: that the vanguard of
the Israelite invasion might be corrupted by the enticements of an actual Canaanite. For the Deuteronomistic writers, the story of the spies
bedding down on Rahab's roof describes what might seem like an alluring sexual fantasy. (How would Joshua know what his men do? Under
cover of night, far from their commander, the spies do have several options spread before them.) But underneath its seductive surface, this
story throbs with the terror of ideological nightmare. Two Israelite males
alone at night with a Canaanite prostitute: might the whole conquest
end here, when the Israelites come into intimate contact with those
whom they have been told to slaughter without mercy? This is not an
unrealistic anxiety. Phinehas knew how much was at stake in the single
act of coitus of Zimri and Cozbi, urgently interrupted by his own righteous spear (Numbers 25). Each encounter with the Canaanite Other is

a moment fraught with danger for the entire rhetorical project of holy-war ideology and for the destiny of the people of Israel.[42]

Rahab yields to the Israelite spies and their God. But is the risk she represents mastered and controlled? Only apparently and for the short term. It is true that instead of corrupting the spies, Rahab serves as the crucial point of entry for the Israelite troops and the xenophobic ideology that accompanies them. Thus are penetrated both Jericho and the Canaanite body politic writ larger, this conquest of Jericho being the first in a long series of conquests narrated in Joshua. All would seem to go as Joshua has planned. Indeed, the loyalty of Rahab has been celebrated as heroic since New Testament times; the so-called confession of Rahab has long been accounted in Jewish and Christian tradition as one of the paradigmatic confessions of outsiders won over to Israel's faith.[43] Not only Rahab's body but her heart is penetrated by the ideology of the invaders, if we read her confession as earnest rather than coerced. Ancient interpretive traditions in line with the Deuteronomistic view of colonization in Joshua celebrated not only Rahab's loyalty but her beauty and virtue as well.[44] Discerning parallels between the fall of Jericho and biblical narratives of the Exodus, Tikva Frymer-Kensky goes so far as to claim that the rejuvenation of the entire nation of Israel is figured in the character of Rahab: "This resourceful outsider, Rahab the trickster, is a new Israel. . . . She is the quintessential downtrodden from whom Israel comes and with whom Israel identifies."[45]

Frymer-Kensky's claim underlines a foundational irony involved in colonization, namely, that domination of the colonized inevitably requires a shift in the identity of the colonizer. For Rahab also penetrates Israel. In the words of Susanne Gillmayr-Bucher, "Rahab successfully moves the border between herself and the spies, between self and other. She, the stranger, offers an identity narrative for the Israelites, and places herself with them."[46] Two distinct traditions represented in Joshua 6 wrestle with the significance of that breach of Israel's sexual, cultic, and communal boundaries. At the fall of Jericho, Rahab and her family are brought and left "outside the camp" of Israel (Josh 6:23). This technical terms signals the permanent distancing of the Rahabites from the Israelite community constituted around the holy-war camp (see Deut 23:15).[47] Colonized, marginalized, living a life of constant threat on the edge of the camp with thousands of xenophobic holy-war ideologues a mere stone's throw away,[48] Rahab and her family may have saved their lives only at the cost of everything else that made their lives humane and bearable.

Rahab and her descendants do not disappear but remain insistently present to Israel, their colonizers. Another tradition in Joshua asserts that the line of Rahab has lived "in the midst of Israel to this day" (Josh 6:25). How is the reader to understand that notice? Did Rahab's line survive triumphant despite the vast powers of the Israelite state arrayed against them, slowly increasing in strength and subtle influence until the kingship of Israel itself toppled into apostasy with the cultic practices of Jeroboam and all who followed in his ways?[49] Or did the Rahab group survive as a broken people haunted by cultural decimation, bearing traumatized witness to the power of Israel's God and Israel's culture much as a few exiles in Ezekiel's unyielding theology were to survive simply as loathsome, dehumanized testimony to the righteousness of God (Ezek 12:16)? A postcolonial reading could argue that the presence of Rahab in Israel does not subvert Deuteronomistic holy-war legislation in any liberating way: rather, coerced into an allegiance that required the wholesale slaughter of her friends and neighbors, Rahab is merely the exception that proves the xenophobic rule governing Deuteronomistic traditions of ethnic cleansing and colonization.[50] Or did Rahab's people survive as the underdog survives, against all odds, celebrated for unexpected heroism and lauded as a model of faith?

Ironies abound among these possibilities for triumph, trauma, and tricksterism. The figuring of Rahab sharpens the triumphalist narrative strands within the Book of Joshua. Yet it irrevocably complicates those strands by insisting on the gendered and "Othered" aspects of Israel's heritage. Danna Nolan Fewell writes of Achan and Rahab, "Fluid identity boundaries render nationalistic categories ambivalent and call into question the obsession with annihilating outsiders."[51] Also reading the stories of Rahab and Achan together is Lori Rowlett, who argues that the point of such stories is in fact to reinforce control over the Israelite audience:

> Comparison of Rahab's behavior and fare with Achan's reveals that the true organizing principle of the narrative is not ethnic identity, but voluntary submission to authority structures, including the patriarchal political arrangement as well as the central ruling establishment represented by Joshua. . . . The primary ideological purpose of the conquest narrative is to send a message to internal rivals, potential Achans, that they can make themselves into outsiders very easily.[52]

An ironic aporia lies at the heart of this ideological move in Joshua. A Canaanite, a sexually autonomous and politically uncontrollable foreign woman, has made possible Joshua's conquest of Jericho: this is an irresolvable problem. Rabbinic exegetes, anxious to silence the potential scandal, hurry to suggest that Rahab "the innkeeper" marries Joshua and becomes the ancestor to impeccably Israelite priests and prophets, among them Huldah, Jeremiah, and Ezekiel.[53] Rahab is figured in these interpretive traditions as a heroine whose righteousness has profound positive implications for Israel's history. Yet her stubborn presence at the margins of Israel's holy-war camp provides continual pressure on traditions of xenophobia, insistently unraveling the rhetorics of Israel's identity that demand purity, no mixing, no mercy. The Canaanites, as it turns out, are within the community of Israel—pushed to the margins all the more vehemently because this is an internal community dispute. Rahab's presence "in the midst of Israel to this day" turns the ancient Israelite ethnos, Israel's ethnic-cultural identity, inside out. She transforms not only the boundaries but the very center of what ancient Israel is and can be.

Assimilation of threatening elements from outside requires transformation of the center. Colonization is never the simple dominance of one culture over another. Exchange is mutual. Influence seeps across the nominally one-way boundaries, and hybridities result: anxious, creative mixings of cultures and loyalties and relationships and stories. Assimilation can ensure survival for both host and newcomer. But ironically, the choice to assimilate—as Rahab chooses—is also a choice to die, for survival under those conditions can mean cultural death. Much is at stake for those Canaanites and others who are coerced into allowing Israel to set the terms for the cultural conversation, Joshua's sword flashing overhead as incentive to talk. Falling victim in Jericho are Rahab's faith in her own culture and her own stories of origin, faith in her own deities, faith in the beauty and resilience of her people. Faith may have to give up its center and its convictions in order to assimilate successfully.

In the larger sweep of the Deuteronomistic History, Rahab's capitulation to Israelite coercion is tragic, not only for Rahab but for Israel. It is implicated as such, peripherally and subtly, in this narrative by the editors responsible for the notices in Joshua 6 that Rahab was set outside the camp yet remained "in the midst" of Israel "to this day." Rahab's faithfulness and cleverness, however heroically written, are editorialized by Joshua 6 as a tragic strategy of adaptation with huge potential to harm both the outsider and the dominant colonizing culture. The irony here is that this Israelite discourse that may have intended to dehumanize the Other also dehumanizes itself, sowing the seeds for its own future destruction as king after king chooses apostasy rather than purity.

Read multiaxially, the story of Rahab becomes a matrix of interpretive trajectories yielding a political rhetoric of penetration that fails in practice. This is a gendered story of the rape of Jericho that paradoxically highlights the impotence of Israel, an ostensibly aggressive literary overture that unwittingly reflects the moment of weakness in which the whole Deuteronomistic ideological project begins to unravel. The political rhetoric of the holy-war ideology requires that the Israelites take no prisoners. Yet interactions with outsiders are required from the very first moment in order to assess the risks—so negotiation, with its attendant dangers of cooperation and capitulation, is necessary. What is Israel to do when an outsider mouths words of faith and trust in the God of Israel? Rahab ironizes the whole martial project by "confessing" that Israel's God is unstoppable. Is this what the prophet Jeremiah would mean when he was to prophesy, "No longer shall they teach one another, or say to each other, 'Know the LORD,' for they shall all know me, from the least of them to the greatest" (Jer 31:34)?

The story of Rahab poses this question: Who is Israel once the Deuteronomistic project reaches its completion and all of Canaan has been conquered? The question is problematic where outsider women are concerned. Outsider males can be coerced into circumcision as proof of their loyalty, but what mark or mutilation shall be required of surviving outsider women? The political rhetoric of conversion-or-destruction cannot comprehend negotiation, cannot tolerate a politics of pragmatic collaboration. In the Rahab story the walls that come tumbling down are not only Jericho's but also the walls separating insider from outsider and uncompromising rhetoric from continually renegotiated praxis. And the gendered and sexual aspects of the story reinforce this blurring of boundaries and breaking down of walls. What does penetration mean when a single indigenous, unarmed woman can penetrate the conquering male military forces? Rahab is not valorized in the biblical narrative so much as co-opted. But Rahab's power as a sexually autonomous woman genders the narrative in new ways that destabilize the masculinized insistence on firm boundaries. Israel becomes impotent precisely at the moment of consummation, when Jericho has been invaded and its resistance broken down.

In the Deuteronomistic History, the story of conquest and purity that comprises the history of Israel in Canaan rolls forward with an unseen fatal flaw at its heart. Moses is dead, and the new hero, Joshua, has erred. The Canaanites are irrevocably ensconced in the midst of Israel from the very first military foray. How can this triumphant historical story be written when it has already been unwritten in the first chapter? It is not only the multiple-source question that introduces fractures into the grand historical metanarrative of ancient Israel. Certainly there is polyphony in the literary shaping of Joshua and Judges, in conflicting strands of tradition in the Books of Samuel, in the diverse historiographical sources underlying the Books of Kings. But more than that, we have here the ironizing and unraveling of plot by the very characters figured in it. Sex and negotiation are the downfall of every pure ideology, as Phinehas knew. Human desire for the Other and acknowledgement of the needs of the Other are more powerful even than the army of the invincible God who "reigns in heaven above and on earth below," the One whose name Rahab whispers with trembling lips. The Deuteronomistic narrative of domination cannot stand before the power of this prostitute whose character makes hearts melt and knees go weak and whose descendants will lead kings astray. Dread of the Israelites may have fallen on the inhabitants of Canaan. But how much more should Israel tremble before the mighty Rahab!

Jael the Bold

Next in Israel's metanarrative of prostitutes who both ensure and ironize Israel's glorious victory over outsiders, we meet Jael. Heroine or barbaric murderer? The history of interpretation of Jael is fractured by passionate ambivalence about her,[54] something we will see also in the reception of Balaam. Ironizing characters are often memorialized by the irony of an indeterminate legacy, as generations of readers argue about the play of said and unsaid in these stories. Married to a man who is allied with an enemy that has brutally oppressed Israel (Judg 4:3, 17), Jael surprises all who encounter her. She reverses the implicit expectations of her husband and the Israelite army, she reverses the expectations of the implied audience, and she reverses the expectations of the hapless Sisera, whom she invites into her tent with promises of succor and then butchers in his sleep.

The kinship relationships described here complicate any simple notion of insider/outsider boundaries. The Kenites are connected to Israel via Moses's father-in-law, as Judges 4:11 takes care to mention. Yet Heber, Jael's husband, had "separated from" the other Kenites, and there was peace between Heber and the Canaanite king Jabin, Israel's oppressor for twenty years. "Peace" may have involved active support. Commentators speculate that Heber may have been responsible for the iron-working needed for the Canaanite chariots; Baruch Margalit suggests that Heber may have been a mercenary who contracted with the Canaanite king to police the area locally, thus betraying his nomadic Israelite allies.[55] Given the conflicting ties and expectations that are expressly flagged in this short narrative, what does loyalty mean here? Is Jael an outsider or an insider to the Israelite community? Liminality and its dangers may in fact be the point of this narrative. No particular incentive or disincentive can reliably guarantee loyalty when multiple loyalties are put under pressure in a time of war.[56]

The sociology of gendered roles in ancient Israel allows us to interpret as sexually provocative Jael's invitation to a strange man to enter her tent when neither her husband nor anyone else is present.[57] A number of commentators have argued that Jael's treachery becomes a more explicitly sexualized treachery in the poetry of Judges 5, in the eroticized slow-motion scene in which Sisera sinks between Jael's feet as his temple is penetrated by the tent peg.[58] In her invitation to Sisera to join her in her tent, Jael participates, however obliquely and ironically, in the persona of the prostitute. The drama of this story suggests that this battle is fought decisively along sexual and cultural lines, not (only) on the battlefield.

The extravagant blessing of Jael in Judges 5 ratifies this seductive, fatal role played by outsider women who feel the force of the Israelite army and respond in a way that guarantees their own safety. In this, Jael stands in sisterhood with Rahab, coerced by fear into a newfound loyalty to Israel. There is no narrative motivation given for Jael's betrayal of her husband's clan except that the fearsome Israelite army and its God will destroy all those who stand in the way of the extermination of the Canaanites. This holy war—signaled as such in the prose tradition by the divine panic into which the Canaanites are thrown (4:15) and in the poetic tradition by the cosmic scope of the battle (5:20, 23)—is relentless in its momentum. Blessed Jael, as blessed Rahab before her, aids Israel in a fraught moment in which her only choices are loyalty to Israel or a violent death.

The power of Deborah as warrior leader in Judges 4 and as epic poet in Judges 5 underlines the ironizing of masculine strength here. Ironies abound in the emasculation of the male characters in the story. The unimpressive Barak whines and cringes when faced with the task of fighting the Canaanites. Deborah must command Barak in the name of the LORD, must assure the reluctant army commander of her presence, and must spur him on to victory at the appropriate moment. The helpless Sisera is penetrated in his sleep by a woman in a way that mocks male virility.[59] The courage and vision of Deborah far overshadow the mettle of the Israelite commander, and the courage and vision of Jael satirize the powerlessness and lack of discernment of the slumbering Canaanite commander.

The biting line with which Deborah ironizes Barak's dreams of glory tears at holy-war ideologies larger than Barak could understand. She says, "[T]he road on which you are going will not lead to your own glory, for it is into the hand of a (mere) woman that the LORD will sell Sisera" (4:9). This battle was indeed decisive, for after the victory of Deborah and Jael, the land had rest for forty years, a lengthy period that puts Deborah, as judge, in the company of the glorious Othniel, Ehud, and Gideon. The poetic cry of acclamation celebrating the death of Sisera names this as a defining victory for Israel: "Thus may all your enemies perish, O LORD!" (5:31).

Indeed? May all of Israel's enemies perish at the hand of an outsider, a woman who acts the prostitute and by sexual deception manages to do better than the top commanders of Israel's army? The emasculating death of the enemy commander may also signal the ineffectual and weak strategy of the Israelite army. The resistant reader may see the entire ideological structure of war-making being subverted here. Gale A.

Yee has articulated well the threat that the woman warrior poses in cultures in which the males normally are the military aggressors:

> [I]f warriorhood is defined as male, the woman [warrior] is accorded the same privileges, prestige, status, etc. that a man finds in this domain. To talk about a woman warrior, then, is to describe metaphorically a liminal figure in the human social order. The woman warrior is neither female nor male as these are customarily defined. . . . She is thus ultimately dangerous and not simply because of her alleged bellicosity. . . . [S]he occupies a structurally anomalous position within the human domain and is thus potentially and actually disruptive.[60]

The aggressive discourse of holy war begins to unravel in this quiet tent, where a woman has the power to destroy the top-ranking enemy leader with no mention of the Spirit of God coming upon her, but only her own wiles, persuasiveness, and strength to aid her.

Foreign women using the implicit promise of sex to control strangers: this is apostasy when Israelite males are involved. Moreover, it lies at the heart of the holy-war ban. Foreign women may not be kept as spoils of war because of the danger posed by their sexuality—and the concomitant risk of intimacy and influence—for the social and cultic identity of Israel. Yet here in the story of Jael, gendered sexuality is the means of victory. This irony reconfigures the power relations that underlie the cultic identity of the Israelite community. The story of Jael and Sisera undermines traditional kinship rules; it also skewers martial ideology generally and ideals of masculine heroism more particularly.

In fact, the ironies of this narrative unfold along several axes at once. The sociology of kinship represented in this story is complicated. Heber's group has separated from the other Kenites associated with Israel, yet his wife subverts the alliance with the Canaanite prince whose politics give Heber his livelihood. What does this say about the dangers and opportunities presented by kinship ties with Canaanites? Dangers abound, possibilities of intrigue and betrayal and surreptitious switching of allegiances. Did Jael win the military battle? One could argue that she did not, that the war had already been won; the fleeing Sisera was merely a loose end. But the outcome of the ancient Israelite/Canaanite culture wars is what is at stake here, and in that, Jael's action is certainly determinative. The complexities of kinship here ironize any naïve polarity of insider and outsider. Jael's unexpected actions ironize simplistic views of kinship and the political implications of family ties.[61]

That this story ironizes martial ideology generally, or Israelite holy-war ideology in particular, is a more difficult case to make, at least on the face of it. Ambiguities abound. Deborah's initial oracle claims that the LORD will give Sisera into Barak's power (4:7). But in her response to Barak's hesitancy, Deborah asserts that Sisera's capture will be effected not by Israel's commander but by the power of a woman. These are marked not as the words of God but as the words of Deborah. Why do they so directly countermand the earlier oracle?[62] God does rout the Canaanites by means of a divine panic, so the initial oracle is proven to have been true; but Sisera indeed falls to Jael, Barak arriving late and redundant on the scene. Much that is unspoken remains between these competing testimonies, brought into close engagement with each other by verbatim repetition of the language that Sisera will be "in the power of" either Barak or Jael.

Deborah revoices holy-war tradition in her gendered and ironic gloss on the original oracle. The number of warriors does not matter (Israelite forces being winnowed down expressly to make this point in several stories narrating holy-war battles, for example in the story of Gideon's battle against the Midianites in Judges 7). But here, it is also the case that traditional views of masculine power and battle roles do not matter. One might argue that Jael is "acting like a man" in her embrace of militaristic goals and her furthering of the holy-war agenda. But such a position would fail to take into account the intensely gendered (sexualized) ways in which the character of Jael operates in the narrative. For in fact, the battle itself lies far in the background. The drama at the foreground is in the tent of a woman who stands as a liminal figure on the threshold of alliance with Israel, on the threshold of death, on the threshold of unexpected greatness. This is a holy war that is no holy war—the battle lines keep shifting.

The larger literary context of Judges 5 provides a lens through which to see more clearly the ironies of Judges 4, which seems to be later than the poetry and to be responding to it.[63] The epic tradition in Judges 5 celebrates the vagaries of human choice among the Israelite tribes and limns the cosmic dimensions of the battle. The reader has the sense that with the endless marching to war and delaying on the part of many of the tribes, the stars may have had to fight from heaven because no one else was available. The poem finds its own deepest irony in the brutal comeuppance, exquisitely delayed at the end of the poem, of the Canaanite women who wait in vain to paw through the spoils. This battle has been pitched between those who mistakenly think that male military action is decisive, and those insiders—those who perceive the invitation of irony here—who understand that the sexual and kinship choices of women and men across cultural lines are what actually matter for the outcome.

Mieke Bal sees in the story of Jael a recalibrating of the Israelite imagination. She suggests that this story demonstrates the destruction of the "head of the hero" as "the Achilles heel of domination": "The confrontation of Jael with the enemy of her people unleashes in the mind the possibility of a reversal of roles. How to represent (to oneself) this (rare) situation in which a woman, for once, has absolute power over a man? It is important to see the image of 5:27 in this context: it is the liberation of an always limited imagination, as much in its experiences as in its means of expression."[64] Adrien Janis Bledstein reads Judges overall as a satire of "human (most often male) arrogance."[65] I would argue that the point of the irony is to satirize men's power to destroy. J. Cheryl Exum hints that such critique would be unlikely in biblical tradition: "If one wished to argue that the narrator is using Sisera's mother's speech to condemn rape, one would have to say he is also condemning plunder, and thus condemning war."[66] But indeed, I believe that is precisely the point of the ironies in Judges. Bledstein invites the reader to "hear a woman's [narratorial] voice as it varies from light mockery to lethal irony, using at times derision, burlesque and parody to convey serious criticism of one who does 'what is right in his own eyes'";[67] and always in Judges, we see that "what is right" involves apostasy and horrific violence. As Lillian R. Klein puts it, Judges is a "*tour de force*" of irony, touching on every level from non-ironic to multilayered irony," in an ironizing of "ever more extreme sins against Yahwist ethics and the separation between Yahweh and his people."[68]

The larger literary pattern in Judges points to spiraling moral decay and growing internecine strife as indicators of increasing social disintegration. Military brutality, masculinized power over others by means of the sword, becomes more and more exaggerated and less and less effective as the Book of Judges unfolds. As we move toward the end of the book, we encounter Samson's brute vengeance for petty reasons, the Danites' ruthless predations on hapless country dwellers, the Levite's condoning of horrific violence against his concubine and subsequent dismembering of her body as a means of mustering troops to battle. Every one of these stories ironizes male military aggression. Sexual coercion and objectification of women figure prominently in all of these stories. The heroism of Jael had been simply the first and least offensive case in this book of unraveling morality—the self-defense of a vulnerable "tent-dwelling" woman alone. Other ways of waging war lead to escalating violence that is less and less honorable.

The threat of Jael within the larger context of Judges is, finally, one that casts the shadow of terror over all male warriors (Israelites and non-Israelites alike) who see national identity in terms of the boundaries their troops can guard. It can all come undone in a moment of sexual indiscretion. The "prostitute" in the midst of a people can be the gateway to victory or defeat. What appears to be sexual refuge may be death.

What appears to be an opportunity for the exercise of male power over the female body (rape) may end up with the penetration of the male and the undoing of an entire people. This "prostitute," Jael, functions as an icon for the ironist who would relativize claims to power based on militaristic notions of community identity.

We turn now to another prostitute whose presence in the text seems to be debased and silenced through aggressive prophetic diction: Gomer. Victim of rhetorical battering, Gomer nevertheless stakes a claim for new ways of imagining God's agency. For a brilliant ironizing of violent discourse in the Book of Hosea connects Jael and Gomer as sister-warriors in the battle to undermine martial metaphors for the God of Israel.

Gomer the Beloved

What wife was more passionately beloved than Gomer? And what beloved wife ever faced from her spouse such dire threats of beating, sexual degradation, and dismemberment? Ironic questions, these, as anyone with a sophisticated understanding of the interconnections between sexual valuation and violence in patriarchal cultural systems will recognize. Gomer is constructed in hyperbolic terms in the rhetoric of Hosea, simultaneously cherished and despised with such vigor and depth of passion that the reader is made afraid, seeing her trauma and seeing the power of language to harm. Gomer's story is unreal. It is fabricated through the obsessive gaze of a character who seems to be a homicidal madman. Yet her story—the metaphor of her—has been embodied in the lives of countless real women over the centuries in many phallocentric cultures.[69]

The problems inherent in the uncritical reception of metaphorical signification have long been recognized. Violent discourse causes harm, both in its violent construction of the terms for understanding the subject and in its availability as justification for and incitement to embodied violent acts. Feminist scholarship in particular has been alert to the devastating consequences (both in rhetoric and in real-life applications) of readers' blurring the distinctions between metaphorical tenor and vehicle where the metaphor enacts sexual violence. Such an ostensibly cherished wife as Gomer, threatened and abused at every turn by the rhetoric of her husband-God and by the violent discourse of the Book of Hosea (not to mention by the history of interpretation),[70] becomes herself irony incarnate. As her character is spoken, it is also continually unspoken and revoiced by the pressures of the unstable and unreliable discourse of Hosea. Here I will explore two ways in which irony functions in the book of Hosea and in the characterization of Gomer in particular. First, I will attend to divisions and fractures within the personae of the speakers, Hosea and God. Second, I will probe the irony inherent in the dynamic of a coerced renewal of purity as a metaphor for the repentance of the people Israel.

First, we consider ways in which the rhetoric of Hosea and the speaking persona of God are divided against themselves. God as Husband and prophet as husband are in considerable inner conflict, if the surging currents of rage and love in the rhetoric of Hosea be read straight. But reading Hosea as a psychological Rorschach test—as the representation of historical emotions experienced by the historical prophet—may not be fruitful in the absence of evidence about the man Hosea. Hortatory rhetoric crafted to engage a large communal audience may or may not express the emotional state of the individual writer, who is not necessarily coterminous with the implied narrator in any case.[71] Better to focus on the dynamics of textual representation as rhetoric.

The conflicting attitudes shearing across the turbulent rhetoric of Hosea undermine each claim made by the text. Claims contradict one another: professed love and violence may not be contradictory in the actual practice of pathological obsession, but the ancient biblical author's apparent lack of awareness of the incongruity between love and torture may be named in contemporary terms as a literary site of cultural conflict and irony. These conflicts render radically unstable the authority of the speaker. God will punish, yet God will woo. God will rend and destroy, yet God cannot bring himself to punish. God will be like rot and maggots to Israel, yet God will be like dew, cedar, and vine to Israel. God will cause miscarriage, abortion, and infanticide, yet God will nurture Israel as a mother nurtures a child. God ruthlessly kills the mother, yet God will show mercy to the orphan.

How can we believe Hosea—that is, allow ourselves to be persuaded by this rhetoric, even just as a heuristic exercise—without being lacerated on sharp-edged ironies every step of the way? It is difficult to find the narrative's theological and ethical compass: each time the reader commits to one position, another presses alternative claims. Hosea the prophet stands for the aggrieved and rageful God-husband, protesting his love one moment and shouting threats of dismemberment the next. Gomer, the figure of faithless yet beloved Israel, survives the hyperbolic threats and promises of Hosea 2 only to be manipulated again in Hosea 3 in a bizarre economic transaction. The children Jezreel, Lo-Ruḥamah, and Lo-Ammi stare wide-eyed as they and their mother are threatened with unspeakable brutality one moment and rhetorically soothed the next. No point of view is safe. The reader is left with nowhere to stand.

Gomer's body is Israel. Gomer's children, the fruit of her body, are also Israel. Both of these equations are made by the prophet himself in Hosea

1 and identified as a key to understanding his oracles. The metaphor-laden discourse in Hosea 1–3 then goes on to establish associations of sex and apostasy, marital chastity and religious fidelity, trust and betrayal and violence, constructing a body of metaphors that is gendered as by turns female and childlike.[72] This body is at the mercy of the raging male voice that narrates her identity and her voice. The only words Gomer can speak in this text are words mouthed for her in scorn by the male speaker. As Francis Landy observes, "The sadistic fantasy relies on the pain of the woman, on imagining her consciousness; one notes the care with which God puts words in her mouth, projects himself into her speaking and acting."[73] Hosea creates trauma through words.

Ironic reversals suffuse the Book of Hosea, but these reversals are not located on the level of dramatic irony—narrations of the unexpected and the subversive in characters' motivations and in the unfolding of events. This prostitute story is quite different from those we have examined heretofore. Its devastating ironies operate on a level of rhetoric that is more complicated than plot. It is the discursive practices of the prophet Hosea—his choice of shocking words and images, his polyvalent symbol systems, his aggressive employment of rapidly shifting metaphors—that enact ferocious ironies on his audience. These discursive practices ultimately deconstruct Hosea's own prophesying in a way that may have been only partially intended by the book's author.[74]

That language has limitations is clear. That the use of metaphor can serve to mask dissimilarity is likewise clear. Perhaps less obvious is that the voice of the speaker in Hosea deconstructs itself through contradictions both overt and oblique. There is no easy way to avoid the staggering conflicts that surge through the poetry of this prophet. The reader is unable to plot judgment and salvation along a linear trajectory, with judgment finally yielding to salvation in a redemptive chronological progression. Hosea and his God declare love, and rage, and love again, followed by more rage. God threatens dire harm and humiliation, ranting on and on, then softens into compassionate declarations of mercy (11:8–9), then rages anew about bringing more horrific destruction, then gently coaxes the battered Israel to return (Hosea 14). The turbulence of this discourse resists any attempt to map it onto a linear progression for closure-oriented readers. This God simultaneously cherishes and rends. The unpredictability and instability of the male voices in Hosea undermine their own authority, divided against themselves in every moment of their speaking. This rhetorical confusion is significant not simply as a measure of compositional disarray but as an ironic way of representing the failure of consistency in Hosea and God as personae.

The resistant reader may have a place to stand after all: with Gomer.

Gomer does remain mute. But her muteness in this mercurial book may be constructed by the reader as having more enduring authority than the dissociative rantings of the prophet and his God. Gomer remains present in the text beyond Hosea 3, in the shadows cast by the text's unusual collocation of disturbing images for pregnancy, childbirth, nursing, mothering, and sexuality. Gomer, herself Israel and mother of children who are also Israel, is present in the ranting of Hosea that she (unnamed) is in labor with Ephraim, a child who does not come readily to the birth (13:13). Gomer and her children are present in Hosea's vicious rhetoric of Samaria's little children being dashed into pieces and pregnant women ripped open (13:16). Gomer's children are present when the prophet exhorts Israel to confess to God, "In you the orphan finds mercy" (14:3). Gomer lies dismembered, silenced by the muteness of death yet powerfully present as her orphaned children gather around her body and stare up at the God in whom they are supposed to find mercy.

Gomer is rhetorically battered. Yet it is not Gomer but the punitive prophetic voice—blurred with the divine voice—that breaks down throughout the discourse of Hosea, divided against itself. The uneven transitions from oracle to oracle, the overwrought hyperbole of this rhetoric, and the unpredictable changes in tone all unravel the integrity and authority of the speaker. The body of Hosea may remain chaste, unassaulted by God and no longer rendered impure through sexual contact with his prostitute wife (the abstinence in Hosea 3 anxiously tries to rescue the prophet's body and therefore the prophetic corpus of Hosea from irretrievable taint). But Hosea's words cannot be trusted, for they are barely intelligible, choking on violence and contradiction. Thus is male authority ironized through the fractured discourse of Hosea, even though the discourse is aimed as a weapon at the Israelites as a shamed and effeminized people. Relevant here is Jan William Tarlin's argument that male subjectivity (and not just the metaphorized female) is violently destroyed in the rhetoric of the Book of Ezekiel.[75] Tarlin asserts that political exile, Ezekiel's physical dislocation in the visions, and the violent nature of the prophetic sign acts all traumatize and emasculate Ezekiel as a representative of his people:

> Yahweh loses no opportunity to degrade, humiliate, and injure the prophet's priestly body. . . . The priestly ego is shattered (even, indeed, feminized) by being forced to embrace its own vulnerability, insufficiency, and lack—by being forced to incorporate castration. . . . Yahweh forces Ezekiel to undergo the fall of the southern kingdom in his own body. The all-sufficient priestly body is subjected to famine, shorn of its hair, and reduced to muteness and paralysis.[76]

Tarlin suggests that this violent emasculation serves to unite Ezekiel in solidarity with other human beings in an imaginative utopian space beyond the reach of abuse and violence, a proposal I do not find fully persuasive, although I wish it were so. But of great importance is Tarlin's insight that the male is threatened by fractures in discourse even as the male attempts to direct an overcompensatory punishing rage against an Other gendered as female. So too in the violent rhetoric of Hosea: the blows Hosea lands end up fracturing his own coherence as speaker.

Being an audience is not easy in the Book of Hosea. We see women and children being eviscerated by words, we watch metaphors surge out of control, we see the breakdown of the prophet. We are lured into voyeurism, shamed and compelled at the same time, disturbed by our unwilling complicity in this horrendous violence. That readers of the Book of Hosea and other sexually graphic discourses are put willy-nilly into the position of voyeurs has long been noticed. Landy hints at this in his reading of Hosea 2:

> The body, imagined as anarchic and subversive, is nevertheless passive, subject to the look of the surrounding males. Vision is a means of appropriation, of immense symbolic resonance, as the rhetoric of striptease and advertising shows. The underlying fantasy, then, is of gang-rape, the woman encircled by predators. The fantasy, however, is reversed; the sight turns back on the seers, and taunts them with their incapacity to claim her. The husband, in exhibiting his wife, simultaneously discards her and asserts his prerogative over her.[77]

But the ironic instability of the prophetic voice finally requires that the implied audience recognize something crucial: this God of violence cannot be the same one who "is God and no mortal" (11:9). Can it be that this God, the God whom Hosea has been portraying as ruthless and bent on dismembering his chosen people, is no true god but an idol to be repudiated?

To address that question, we turn to a second major irony in the figuration of Gomer. Articulated twice in Hosea 1–3 is a forced renewal of purity, a coerced revisiting of that innocence required of Gomer by the dominating male voice so that she may be worthy of his love. In Hosea 2, the unfaithful wife is humiliated and abandoned in the metaphorical wilderness. Her sources of sustenance removed, her clothing torn from her body, she wanders bruised and naked, unable to find her paths, at the mercy of wild animals. God bellows, "I will lay waste her vines and her fig trees," and we watch as Israel's land—Gomer's body—is violently unmade, re-created as a wilderness. Landy notes the fatal contradiction in the ways in which the violent deity promises renewed gentleness. Of Hosea 2:15ff, he writes:

> Her forgetfulness annuls her history as the domain of memory, as well as providing potential extenuation. God, in turn, revokes history, takes her back to the beginning. But is this possible? God supposes that through reversing time he can erase the memory of his violence, that he too can make a new beginning. However, in practice, return to the wilderness can only mean the end of Israel's political existence in the land, and hence the death and exile that the book portends. It is coterminous with the deadly wilderness that Israel becomes in v. 5; the place of devastation and thirst is the scene of romantic fulfillment.[78]

Finding herself invited into the wilderness of her own death ("I will now allure her, and bring her into the wilderness," 2:14), Gomer hears words of tenderness from the very husband who has savaged her. Their betrothal will be renewed "as in the days of her youth," and she will once again be safe and secure. "I will make you lie down in safety. And I will take you for my wife forever: I will take you for my wife in righteousness and in justice, in steadfast love and in mercy" (Hos 2:18–19). So Hosea says. That Gomer's body is gaunt from lack of food and slashed by the metaphorical thorns that had hedged up her way matters not, apparently, for the purification that this rhetoric would enact upon her. This is a pornographic renewal of purity:[79] that which is claimed as newly fresh, newly trustworthy, newly worthy of love, has ironically only reached that point of "repurification" by being coerced into the most degraded and violated state possible. And we see a strange rearticulation of this forced repurification in Hosea 3, wherein the prophet is commanded to take an adulterous woman and love her. He purchases her—of consensual covenant there can be no discussion, with such a baldly stated economic transaction—and requires of her that she be chaste with other men and with him. She is coerced into obedience, her "purity" purchased for fifteen silver shekels, some barley, and some wine.

These skewed narrations of repurification happen at the beginning of the Book of Hosea and are followed by many oracles of rageful indictment. The implied audience, drawn into ongoing dynamics of violence in this rhetoric, reaches an inescapable conclusion: coerced repentance clearly does not work. Being battered into obedience has nothing to do with true repentance. The fact that this sort of compulsive obeying is set in the context of a love story renders all the more sharply the incongruity here. Being bought for obedience substitutes commodification for willing faithfulness. Indeed, insidious hints of the woman's captivity in Hosea 3 ("You must remain as mine for many days," 3:3) render even more implausible the possibility of willing faithfulness.[80] This diction of coercion works against its claims for true purification and covenant faithfulness in Hosea, deconstructing its own semantic content and its speaker. Return to me, Israel, because I have thrashed you into wounded helplessness? Return to me, Israel, because I have purchased your freedom with money and now will confine you? The transparent irony of this forced renewal unmasks the inadequacy of the theology behind it.

The double-voicing of Israel's own attempts at repentance also undermines these attempts to return. "Come, let us return to the LORD, for it is he who has torn, and he will heal us." "My God, we—Israel—know you!"[81] The fragmented words of Hosea 6:1–3 and 8:2 stutter the audience's failed attempts to repent earnestly, to claim their knowledge of the LORD in the face of what Hosea sees as their overwhelming sinfulness and ignorance. Sin chokes the words of repentance in their mouths, renders their protestations of faithfulness into a mercurial vapor breathed by liars. Israel is not capable of obedience on its own, per Hosea. Yet the text undermines its own conceptions of obedience and faithfulness by its addiction to fantasies of return based on battering, humiliation, commodification, and evisceration.

At the end of the book, we find these words addressed to God: "In you the orphan finds mercy." There is no way to hear those words without perceiving the darkest of irony, given what has transpired rhetorically in the preceding thirteen chapters of violent diction. For it is Hosea and his God who have made Israel into orphans in the first place—Hosea 1–2 is quite clear about that. These words about the orphan finding mercy in God ironize the god of death to whom the earlier prophetic discourse had made obeisance. The audience of the Book of Hosea has been insulted, drawn into voyeurism, shamed, and attacked with some of the most vicious diction in the Hebrew Bible. Rhetorically broken, that audience is now prepared to listen. And now, Hosea 14 uses irony to present the true God, whom any clear-eyed prophet would proclaim. This is a God of mercy and compassion, a God who provides shade and coaxes forth fruitfulness from God's beloved people. The god of rape and dismemberment has been an idol—the idol constructed by the betrayed and vengeful narrator of the Book of Hosea, who himself desperately seeks to understand love and forgiveness but who is continually consumed with rage.

According to this reading, one may see the entire Book of Hosea as ironically destabilizing its own discourse. Indeterminacy and dangerous silences make any definitive reading impossible. Mercy destabilizes violence, but violence destabilizes mercy. On it goes, as the children of this ferocious text stare in terrified confusion. But the strong reader may choose to find a fulcrum, a piece of stable ground from which to assess the turbulent, self-destroying rhetoric of the prophet. If one reads Hosea 14 straight, with its surprising suggestions that God is like dew and a lush garden and a protective tree, one may see that the rhetoric of a violent god of war and evisceration is itself fatally wounded here. The idols of the implied audience are shattered. The deceptive fruitfulness of wrong ways of thinking is ripped open.[82] The implied audience is left as trembling, traumatized orphans staring at what Hosea's rhetoric has done to their "mother." As it turns out, their mother was not only Gomer but the God whom they thought they could manipulate.

This reading—that the unexpected botanical imagery and language of mercy in Hosea 14 are earnest and that the earlier violent images of God are thereby ironized—is not the only reading one could muster. The crosscurrents of rage and love that surge throughout the book may be seen here as well. Hosea 14 could be interpreted simply as another moment within the cycle of vicious battery and tender wooing that was voiced by the male speaker in Hosea 1–3. Another possibility, intriguing although not arguable on any basis other than reader response, might be that Hosea 14 is the tender speech of Gomer herself, that she finally whispers to her terrified children an alternative view of the God in whose name Hosea has been railing. But the ironies texturing the discourse of Hosea leave both speakers and audience broken and ready for repentance, for the rekindling of imagination and obedience in new ways. I think that however one reads, the god of death whom Hosea's brutal rhetoric has constructed cannot survive this re-imaging of divine love as fruitfulness, balm, shade. Ironically, the prophet's fractured and ambiguous discourse has left gaps in which a new spiritual imagination may flourish unexpectedly.

Hosea is not an easy book to read. In Hosea we perceive the importance of silence—of the unspoken—as a refuge from the pounding diction of judgment and death-dealing that animates much biblical tradition. The final sapiential word of the Book of Hosea (14:10; English, v 9) may be seen to suggest that the ironies here, these subtle deconstructions of an extraordinarily difficult discourse, may easily be missed by those who read without discernment.[83] This verse invites "those who are discerning" into wisdom with the ironist, so that this broken people can begin to build community once again. To be sure, this may not be the amiable community envisioned by Wayne Booth but instead a scarred and tentative community, trembling at "the elusive and ineffable moment of understanding immediately displaced by the anxiety of misunderstanding."[84] Orphans they may be. But these orphans are ready to understand, and they will no longer worship a violent god who is the work of their own hands.

Ruth the Loyal

Perhaps unexpected in our study of prostitutes in the Hebrew Bible is, finally, the character of Ruth. Ruth has been celebrated by readers since the first century for her steadfast loyalty to Naomi, a loyalty that incidentally secures Israel's future by means of the Davidide line, in which Ruth's son Obed serves as a crucial link. Ruth, a Moabite widow, might seem an unlikely sort to further the goals of the Israelite monarchical power structure, and we will address the ironies there. But our hermeneutical interest is primarily in probing the ways in which the body and desires and behaviors of Ruth, as a Moabite and as a sexually viable woman with no husband, are used in the figuring of (apparent) prostitution in order to advance the rhetorical purposes of the Book of Ruth. Surprisingly many commentaries laud the Book of Ruth as if it were a lovely, uncomplicated tale with little significance for the ethnic and sexual identity of Israel. Commentators do remark that Ruth is insistently named "the Moabite" in the text of the Book of Ruth, but often they do not press beyond the observation that this appellation might underscore her status as an outsider. In what follows, I will probe the social and political implications of Ruth's Moabite ethnicity, sexual viability as a widow, and prostitute behavior for the rhetoric of the book.

With the Book of Ruth, as with any ironic text, a straight reading is certainly possible. With Ruth, a straight reading is also stirring and beautiful. So I would like to underline, in passing, the value that straight readings can offer—a point I will make again in my treatment of Qohelet, who is more cantankerous than Ruth but who likewise has been cherished by many readers just as he is. Nevertheless, a strong case for irony can be made in both of those books. Is Ruth absorbed into Israel in a tale of valorized assimilation, or is Israel ironically opened up and made vulnerable by the presence of Ruth in its midst?[85] If reader response is any guide, the earnest celebration of Ruth's initiative, kindness, and valor is a persuasive way to read the text.[86] And indeed, that "straight" reading is entirely justifiable, as far as it goes. Ruth is a strong woman whose agency in a potentially conflictual situation may be read as admirable.

But there are flags of irony throughout the story: silences, narrative moments in which main characters do not know all that the reader has been given to know, and subtle cues that hidden agendas are at work in what characters do and say. Two ironic trajectories will be traced here. First, we will consider the ironic way in which traditional Israelite gender roles are subverted by the two main woman characters, and particularly the way in which sexuality is commodified by both Ruth and Naomi in order to gain security. Second, we will explore the ironic way in which Ruth reads Israelite tradition in order to secure a future that ultimately produces a master outsider who manipulates tradition to his advantage: David.

First, ironies of gender. Key males die off quickly in the story, leaving three women who need to renegotiate kinship bonds in the absence of those males. Orpah remains with her native Moabite culture and her gods, a choice that Naomi commends to the recalcitrant Ruth. But Ruth clings to Naomi. Jon L. Berquist has argued that there may be intimations of sexual and romantic fidelity here, as the occurrences of the verb *dbq* in the Hebrew Bible outside of Ruth all express the clinging of a man to a woman as wife or sexual partner.[87] There are no signs that Naomi welcomes Ruth's determined "loyalty." She gives up trying to dissuade her, but when the women enter Bethlehem, Naomi stresses how bitter and empty she is, pointedly making no mention of the woman at her side. The social and economic liability of supporting Ruth presumably would have been enormous for Naomi, already a destitute widow who had sojourned for years in Moab and now saddled with a widowed Moabite female relation.

The next plot turn is heavy with dramatic irony. Ruth plans to seduce a wealthy man, Naomi assists her, and after some initial resistance and reframing of the possibilities by Boaz, she succeeds. Berquist reads sexual intention even as early as Ruth 2, noting that "during a morning's gleaning, Ruth located the ranking man present and began her seduction" and suggesting that she then refocuses on Boaz and begins her sexual manipulation anew, finally succeeding on the threshing floor.[88] In fact, Ruth succeeds by acting like a prostitute, approaching a man on the threshing floor in the middle of the night (a time and place of notoriety, something conceded even by commentators who resist the idea that sexual activity took place in this erotically charged scene). Ruth uncovers Boaz's feet and lies down—the euphemism for a sexual overture is clear—and stays the night. She leaves surreptitiously at dawn with a payment of barley. These would seem to be the actions of a woman who has traded sex for economic security.

Praised in the biblical text for her fidelity to traditions and people she barely knows, Ruth may be better understood as insistently loyal to her own survival. Bonnie Honig has considered the interpersonal bonding initiatives of Ruth in light of immigration dynamics in contemporary culture. Honig highlights one aspect of immigrants' response to transition, what she calls a "furious and hyperbolic assimilationism," a "frenzied attachment in which the transitional object is fetishized."[89] The transitional object in the Book of Ruth is membership in the Israelite community, represented initially by Ruth's attachment to Naomi and later by her marriage to Boaz. Ruth's fetishizing of the security of communal belonging is sexualized, both in her initial clinging to Naomi (following the implications of Berquist's analysis) and in her seductive overtures to Boaz.

This fetishizing of security amounts to a commodification of Israelite identity at any cost, and it involves Ruth's manipulation and coercion of both Naomi and Boaz. Israel's anxiety about guarding its cultural borders makes good sense when we think about what transpires in Ruth. The foreign woman is a potent threat indeed if a widowed Moabite can easily seduce her way into a sizable inheritance in a community she has never seen before! The ironic blessing that results, the child Obed, is to make Boaz's house like the house of "Perez, whom Tamar bore to Judah" (4:12). It cannot be (literary) coincidence that the women of Bethlehem name in their analogy the house of another woman who conceived through playing the prostitute. Boaz has been used by Ruth just as Judah was used by Tamar. Survival gained through prostitute-like dissembling: apparently this ethos runs all through the heritage of the illustrious David.

The second irony worthy of attention has to do with the way in which Ruth reads Israelite tradition. In the Book of Ruth, the Torah is ironized when this Moabite is not excluded but allowed into the Israelite community: she makes use of the tradition of levirate marriage and has land redeemed by means of her kinship connections.[90] Further, the implied audience's notion of what counts as loyalty and integrity (*ḥesed* and *ḥayil*, two leitmotifs in the Book of Ruth) is ironized. Ruth as hermeneut brilliantly rereads Israel's own traditions regarding her acceptability in the community and regarding her right to press a legal claim, just as Tamar had renegotiated what levirate marriage might mean with the stubborn Judah. It would seem that outsiders—and more shocking: sexually viable, autonomous outsider women—consistently outperform Israelite insiders as interpreters of the Israelite codes of community life. Is this outsider tricksterism earnestly lauded as *ḥesed* and *ḥayil*, or are these signals of irony?

To respond to this question, we may turn to the genealogy at the end of the Book of Ruth. A number of readers, particularly those with feminist and womanist sensibilities, have noticed that Ruth is "erased" at the end of the book when Naomi whisks little Obed away from his mother. Has Ruth's labor—in the fields and in childbirth—been commodified by the Israelite community? The effacement of Ruth does not seem to be an artistic part of a peaceful denouement, with the smiling heroine slipping contentedly into the background. No, it is at the zenith of drama in the book that Ruth is pointedly left barren once again and silenced. She is commended, to be sure. The women of Bethlehem mention her, in their speech to Naomi, as "your daughter-in-law who loves you, who is more to you than seven sons" (4:15). But she is left unnamed, and her child—renamed as Naomi's child—is the focal point of the rest of the story. Is this what the Book of

Ruth has been planning through all of the scenes of bitterness and strained welcome? It is difficult to escape the sense that Ruth the Moabite has herself been used in a calculated way, her body and her initiative manipulated to produce security for Naomi and to secure a dead Israelite husband's inheritance (4:5). Roland Boer's Marxist reading argues that Ruth's labor is commodified to serve "the unfolding patriliny," and more, that Naomi's role involves effacement too, as Naomi disappears into the Israelite society that has required Ruth's labor to maintain itself. Boer writes:

> [T]he disparate identity of Israel and its patriliny is ensured through the appropriation of Ruth's labor and body. . . . [W]hat happens to Ruth is that she must both work the fields and produce a son, only to disappear when her tasks are done. . . . The indirect object—the woman—disappears and men give birth to men. Ruth's effacement is complete. As for Naomi, she becomes an honorary male, operating in the world of men, trading land and living off the surplus labour of Ruth. Like Ruth, she also disappears, although in a somewhat different direction.[91]

The male-dominated system of production has managed a Moabite woman's labor, sexuality, and the results of her sexuality, symbolically doing away with the agency and identity of the woman herself. It would seem that Ruth is not the point of the story at all.

If Ruth is not the point of the story, then we may move away from valorization of her to consider another reading. The genealogy revoices all that has gone before, including the power of the Israelite system of cultural production that has commodified Ruth in order to "produce" the monarchy. How might this story be told subversively? The Book of Ruth has been engaged for four chapters in telling a dramatic story of Otherness that has been fruitfully but manipulatively at work in the midst of Israel's collective "body." The story has narrated a nadir of desperation and deep bitterness, moments of great joy and consolation, and detailed plotting in between by Ruth and Naomi. One may hear the village women's blessing, "May your house be like the house of Perez, whom Tamar bore!" in 4:12 as pointed and knowledgeable—that is, as an irony intended as such by the women themselves—or as an innocent subtext stumbled upon inadvertently by the women of the village in what is being portrayed subtly as ironic. Our only other encounter with the Bethlehemite women highlights their supposed or real failure to understand who is before them. "Is this really Naomi?" (1:19) is an ambiguous line that could be read straight as, "Can we truly be sure that this is Naomi?" but it is perhaps better read ironically as, "We know this is Naomi, but we can hardly believe our eyes." The character of the women of Bethlehem cannot definitively be resolved. We could consider them naïve onlookers inadvertently commenting on audience expectations and unwittingly embodying audience gullibility. But they may also be a satirical chorus commenting on dramatic irony, and this is the reading I prefer. They are positioned in a location of metatextual evaluation, flagging for the reader at the beginning of the book that the character Naomi may be other than she seems, and at the end of the book drawing on Israel's ancient traditions about Leah, Rachel, and Tamar to signal to the reader that once more, veiled deception is afoot. Their assessments of the situation focus the audience's attention at the beginning and end of the book in crucial ways. First, they name the unrecognizable nature of once-insider Naomi in the company of a Moabite, and last, they name the hyperbolic blessings that should result from Ruth's sexual machinations with a man she barely knew on the threshing floor.

When we consider the last five verses of the Book of Ruth, we can see the wondrous potential for irony that is offered by the use of genre in simple literary juxtaposition. After everything that has gone on at the initiative of the Moabite Ruth and the once-insider Naomi, we come to a standard genealogy tracking patrilineal descent. It is possible to read these verses straight, as earnestly intended genealogy, but it would not be wise, for here, as with much sophisticated irony, what is said is not patently untrue but, rather, is markedly incongruous in its context. The genealogy has much more to say when we consider the incongruity of its spare and official diction in light of the drama that has just unfolded. These verses, placed just here, demonstrate with devastating irony that genealogies narrating communal identity according to official codes of male identity are woefully inadequate to the task of describing what has truly been going on in the background of the official narrative.[92] The gaps and interstices of this genealogy are filled with polemical detail that entirely changes our perception of the few official words of the genealogy proper. The detailed social machinations and sexual plotting that have unfolded in the Book of Ruth are so conspicuously gapped in the standard diction of the genealogy that the ironies leap out at the discerning audience. Moabite maternity is erased here.[93] The danger of Otherness is silenced and masked by official storytelling. And whose Otherness is at stake? That of David the usurper. As André LaCocque writes, "If one condemns Judah for his relations with Canaanites; Tamar's foreign origin and her recourse to incest; Perez as a mongrel; Rahab, ancestor of Boaz, for her 'professional' activities; and Ruth for reasons similar to those concerning Tamar—then one also rejects David."[94] The point could not have been made more clearly than by narrating this beautifully told, shocking story and then concluding it in a true and yet patently false way. "In the days when the judges ruled" (Ruth 1:1), in those desperate times when apostasy and brutality were the norm in Israel and heroes rapidly became anti-heroes, there, and there only, we find the roots of the Davidic line.[95] Irony runs all throughout the heritage of the supposedly glorious, supposedly Judahite David.[96]

*   *   *

A range of ironies plays through these stories of prostitute-women who trouble Israel's narratives of communal identity. "Otherness" and desire are powerfully joined here. The maleness of directed discourse reveals its longing for that which its words are trying to both penetrate and master. It is ironic indeed that women's sexuality as power is figured in many of these stories as penetration, as unexpected entrance through guarded gates into the center of a communal body that remains profoundly ambivalent about its own desire for contact. What might be the "third" meanings, the meanings that are generated by the interaction of the spoken and the true—or at least truer—unspoken meaning in these ironic narratives centering on the figure of the prostitute? Three possibilities will be articulated here.

First, the Hebrew Bible's preservation of the foundational Israelite rhetoric of holy war is fatally complicated by the stories of Jael and Rahab. The decisive action of foreign women at crucial junctures in Israel's narratives of its history subverts any simplistic understanding of holy-war rhetoric. Xenophobic construals of Israel's future will always be undermined by necessary interactions, even formative interactions, with those deemed outside the bounds of community. In the tensive engagement between the alluring whispers of Jael/Rahab and the enraged shouts of holy war, a third ironic meaning is generated: this hybrid and fragile community is who Israel has always been. There never was a pure, self-contained ethnos that struggled mightily against foreign influences in order to maintain its original unbesmirched state. Israel has always been a mixture, and the rigid promotion of cultic and ethnic boundaries must be understood ironically in light of this truth. Israel wages war against itself and its own heritage when it marches to battle under the banner of holy war. Israel tries to govern its own unruliness when it proclaims kingship as the means by which battles with the Other might be successfully fought.

Second, female sexuality and fecundity guarantee the birth of the heirs of patriarchal lineage: sons. In the stories of Tamar and Ruth, we see male offspring born who figure Israel itself and its leader David as metonym. Rich blessings and profound ambiguity attend an Israel considered, via David, to be the offspring of intercourse between the female outsider and Israelite regnal discourse.[97] That regnal discourse speaks its contemptuous rejection of the Other, of foreign women's ways that tempt true believers into apostasy. But the endings of Genesis 38 and Ruth 4 show that even though official diction tries to name the lives of Israelites, subversive women may nevertheless conceive and give birth to an Israel that understands itself differently. Tamar is named "more righteous than" Judah. Ruth is loyal beyond anyone's wildest expectations, a sister in spirit to Tamar. These women, eminently worthy of rejection according to the terms of patriarchal social and cultic discourse, are nevertheless acclaimed by reason of their unexpected righteousness and excessive loyalty. These textual markers of worthiness point, subtly but unmistakably, toward the figure whom Tamar and Ruth have in common but who is not, in fact, acclaimed for righteousness and loyalty: David himself. David is many things—mercenary, war chieftain, powerful administrator, psalmist—but he is not acclaimed in Hebrew Bible narrative for righteousness and loyalty to others. David extorts resources from surrounding estates and indirectly causes the death of Nabal, takes Abigail matter-of-factly as booty, commits adultery with Bathsheba and has Uriah treacherously killed, serves with the Philistines for over a year and maintains ties with the Philistines throughout his reign.[98] David comes off the worse in two ways: by virtue of the despicable Moabite blood running through his veins, and because he cannot live up to the examples of righteousness and loyalty that even his foreign female "prostitute" ancestors showed. King David, ethnically hybrid and morally compromised, is thoroughly ironized by these narratives of his symbolic birth-mothers in the tradition.

A final "third" meaning may emerge from the interplay of the spoken and the unspoken in these prostitute narratives. Israel's aggressive anxiety concerning mixing with Canaanite (or other outsider) traditions and peoples may itself be what precludes Israel from understanding the love and grace of Israel's God. Here we must attend closely to the story of Gomer, in some ways the most complicated of the prostitute "icons" that we have been reading through the gaze of the ironist. Gomer is beloved by God despite the raging rhetoric that threatens to dismember her. Gomer and her children endure despite the vicious diatribes of Hosea, despite the disbelief and mockery of the implied audience that hears her story misnarrated by a god of destruction and his terrifying prophet. If all that is idolatry—which is what I have proposed in my resistant reading—then Gomer need not be feared and raged at. For the anxiety Israel manifests in the presence of the Other may itself be recognized as sin. The rhetorical battery and threatened killing of Gomer present an insurmountable problem. The true God is other than the abusive god who would have killed her; hence, Israel must learn to cherish this woman who apparently represented apostasy but whose orphaned children are yet loved and protected by God. In reflecting on this mystery, the community of Israel learns to privilege not judgment but love and forgiveness in its theology.

The permeability of Israel's boundaries of communal identity is probed in several different ways in these five stories, valorizing the prostitute figure who serves as the locus of permeability, but also using the icon of the prostitute to undermine the claims of biblical patriarchal rhetorics of power and purity. The prostitute presides, fully in control of Israel's desires for potency and release, at the discomfiture of patriarch Judah and at the defeat of a Canaanite army through the execution of Sisera, at the deconstruction of shouts of holy war and the battering diction of a prophet, and at the subversive unmaking of the officially glorious King David. The ironist does not see as others see. Indeed, the normative male gaze of ancient Israelite literature is reversed in several of these prostitute stories, where the powerful gaze is rendered as female: Tamar gazes at Judah, who cannot recognize her because of her veil; Jael gazes at the sleeping Sisera before she butchers him; Ruth gazes at the sleeping Boaz before she awakens him and negotiates her deal. But the prostitute also cowers, coerced into betrayal of her people and living marginalized at the edges of the "camp" represented by Israel's martial discourse, browbeaten into acceptance of her own powerlessness at the sharp edges of Israel's marital metaphors. The prostitute may succeed at the game of economic manipulation by showing her excessive "heart of gold" only to find that her story of sisterhood, loyalty, and ingenuity is co-opted—or perhaps had always been written—as part of the genealogical metanarrative of one of Israel's most brutal kings.

The prostitute in the Hebrew Bible, heroine and seductress and manipulator, simultaneously insider and outsider, may be styled the ancestor of biblical irony itself. For she threatens to subvert every biblical community that guards its boundaries too aggressively and every biblical discourse that trumpets the purity of its own ideology without allowing space for the Other. Were the Hebrew Bible authors aware of and intent on elucidating all of these connections? Some of these subtleties, in my view, were certainly intended. Hyperbole, veilings and unexpected unmaskings, and other narrative clues signal intention and inventiveness in our texts. But other connections have emerged from counter-readings that take prostitutes as subjects of their narratives in ways for which the biblical authors may not have been prepared. Here, then, is a rhetorical function of ironizing that can never be entirely foreseen or controlled by the ironist who employs it: irony falsifies the entire semantic landscape, including the very place on which the ironist stands. Irony changes the timbre of all voicing in narrative, and this includes the narrator's own voice.

A narratological fabric woven with threads of irony may be at its strongest, at its most tensile and resistant, where irony is intended to govern the signifying. But those excessively strong threads may, in turn, pull at the places in the narrative fabric where they are attached to simpler threads, to those parts of storytelling and story that mean to be taken at face value. Fissures in the fabric threaten, at these points of rhetorically dangerous juncture. Minute gaps in the reliability of discourse are the result of indeterminacy generally, but perhaps they are especially due to the presence of irony in a fabric that weaves itself out of many stories, preserved and reshaped, as is the case with the Hebrew Bible. Intertextuality becomes the means by which ironic texts and originally non-ironic texts are joined in a single multifarious discourse, with new connections woven by readers who learn from the stories to hear other stories in these words. A wild, unstable, and unpredictable intertextuality is born once irony has been allowed to ironize the speaking of the text itself.

We turn in the next chapter to the discursive performance of prophets who serve as ironic guides in Israel's tangled story of self-definition. Balaam the foreign seer finds himself co-opted by the God of Israel, and ironies drench the Israel that is blessed by him. Amos deconstructs Israelite traditions with the deftness of a surgeon. Micah speaks a word so ambiguous that it may be made to serve as an oracle of doom or salvation, depending on his audience's hermeneutics. And finally we will consider Jonah, a prophet desperate to flee from the ironies inflicted on him by his God.

4

THE IRONY OF PROPHETIC PERFORMANCE

The phenomenon of biblical prophecy may be interpreted as inherently ironic even apart from particular ironies that are wielded by prophets as weapons in their rhetorical arsenals. Prophets are represented in the Hebrew Bible as speaking divinely authorized, powerfully performative words. The biblical prophet "double-voices" God. In doing so, he represents a perspective that he can never fully understand and that he may, at least in theory, misrepresent. Prophetic speech and prophetic sign acts are mimetic, and accurate mimesis of divine revelation is essential to the truth of the biblical prophetic message. The prophet reiterates what God has already said or enacts with his body and with props (a basket of figs, a tattered loincloth) something that God has already revealed. Translation is a life-or-death matter here: the authenticity of prophecy depends entirely on the reliability of the prophet's translation rather than on the prophet's originality. Yet there is a fundamental and inescapable discontinuity about the performance of prophecy. "Thus says the LORD," pronounces someone who is not, in fact, the LORD. Intermediation unavoidably destabilizes the subject, both the divine subject who must speak through another and the prophet who must speak words not his own. Further complicating matters for the interpreter, divine and human utterances are mixed together, sometimes without clear markers of the identity of the speaker, in the written prophetic books. It can be challenging for the reader to determine in some turbulent oracles whether the one lamenting is Jeremiah or God, whether an outraged reaction to the people's faithlessness is Ezekiel's or God's.

Prophetic speaking on behalf of the deity creates a conflictual site of theopolitical discourse within Israelite culture. The presence of the formula, "Thus says the LORD," at the beginning of some oracles may be read as implicitly problematizing the claim to divine authority of any oracle that does not bear those words. Even more alarming, that formula, "Thus says the LORD," can come from the mouth of a false prophet (as Hananiah in Jer 28:2). This throws the notion of human mediation of divine speech into a potentially irresolvable storm of indeterminacy, clearly a concern for biblical tradition, as Deuteronomy 18:15–22 shows. The prophets themselves knew how essential it was to understand the difference between God's word and human words. Their God thunders, "For it is God that I am, and no human; the Holy One in your midst" (Hos 11:9), and, "My thoughts are not your thoughts, nor are your ways my ways" (Isa 55:8). Yet prophetic intermediation troubles this binary even as it attempts valiantly to reinforce it. If this is indeed the voice of the "Holy One in your midst," it would be death to ignore it. But if this is a false word, an incomplete or deceptive or misguided word, one would transgress against God himself by heeding it as if it had been God's own utterance.

The anxiety about false prophecy visible in Deuteronomy 13 and 18 and in the drama of Jeremiah 28 is contending with the need for divinely inspired language over against the impossibility of speaking for God. Because the divine word can easily be commodified for human agendas, the problem of ascertaining which intermediary words were authentic is an urgent matter for Israelite communities and their leaders. Divine and human words in ancient Hebrew prophecy blend into a fluid, composite discourse, the authority of which is paradoxically both enhanced and threatened by the changeability of the speaker. Prophecy in its very utterance becomes an ironically changed word, elusive and "other" than either its human speaker or its divine source. Prophecies are given voice through the idiosyncrasies and flaws of the human prophet rather than spoken direct from the mouth of the One who is beyond all language.[1] Not surprisingly, the act of contesting prophetic authority is characterized by the prophets themselves as stubborn sinfulness. The Jeremiah traditions, in particular, are acutely aware of challenges to Jeremiah's authority and, in response, rain down God's punishment for Israel's generations-long failure to heed the prophets. Thus the discourse of biblical prophecy relies on the implied hostile audience and the notion of the unheard word. Intermediation may be represented in certain political contexts as a route of resistance less risky for marginalized groups than open dissent,[2] but there can be a cost for the prophet. Prophets may be held accountable for the divine word, a bitter truth on which the political prisoner Jeremiah had ample time to reflect at the bottom of his muddy cistern.

Ironies dance about the predictive and performative aspects of biblical prophecy. A prophet declares, say, that a king will not succeed in battle. That decisive word, finalized and unavoidable, becomes avoidable and thus wrong if the king heeds it and does not go to battle that day. 1 Kings 22 shows us that the king of Israel who consults Micaiah has a chance to cower in the royal palace and survive. Yet off he goes to his death just as Micaiah had predicted. Dramatic irony stalks this battlefield: the enemy troops mistake the king of Judah for the targeted king of Israel, and upon learning their mistake, they leave off pursuit, but meanwhile, a random enemy archer unwittingly deals a fatal blow to the king of Israel. So often in biblical narratives, the ironic plot unfolds inexorably despite the clear warnings that characters and readers alike have been given. The reader understands that Jezebel must die even before she does fall, inevitably, from her window. The ostensible surprise of some narrative developments is thoroughly ironized by the reader's foreknowledge that what God speaks through the mouths of "his servants the prophets" can never be undone.

When a prophet speaks a word or acts out a scenario, he creates a new and unavoidable future for those who hear and see it. Such death-dealing performance might encourage the audience to stay home from the theater. If the audience stopped their ears and closed their eyes, would they survive? If they never saw Ezekiel lying on his side doing that terrifying play-acting with his miniature model of the besieged Jerusalem, would the disaster still come? How tempting it would be simply not to look into the face of death—yet not heeding is precisely what has brought the disaster upon the people in the first place. The prophetic performance coerces assent from its audience whether they be willing or unwilling. Not to look, not to listen is the very definition of stubbornness that has brought God's wrath upon Israel. But to see is to understand and, at least provisionally, to assent to one's fate. To hear is to invite the awful truth of divine agency into one's world, however reluctantly or unwittingly, and to live and die with the consequences. With performative words of judgment searing their minds, the audience is forced to collaborate in its own destruction. Words and sign-acts surely cannot kill . . . and yet they do.

There is another ironic twist in the endless series of turns that constitutes the Möbius strip of prophetic performance. For to recognize the irony in prophetic indictment is possibly—just possibly—to escape its fatal grasp. The chance to repent and thereby avert disaster always lingers in the shadowy unspoken that envelops prophetic irony. Glenn Holland has argued that where the implied audience is able to perceive its own ironizing or the ironizing of its traditions, it will then feel shame, which may lead to a change of behavior just as the prophets hope (with the exception of Jonah, who is irked at that result).[3] If the prophetic word is heeded, it renders itself redundant. This is true not only of the orally delivered prophetic oracle that historians think was declaimed in the city gate—it is true of the textualized prophetic word as well. In the case of written prophecy, the ironies are all the sharper because the fixity of written words of judgment may be yet effaced if the people repent. In Daniel and Esther we have seen the importance of overwriting, the practice of adding new writings to apparently immutable decrees: the clash of conflicting pronouncements creates a space, an aporia, within which a godly believer or an entire people can escape destruction. In the case of written prophecy, we see that taking the written word seriously creates the possibility that its truth may be overwritten by a new word of promise. Mark Brummitt writes of Jeremiah's scroll:

> Paradoxically, the scroll's success will effectively erase its contents: the people's return from "their evil ways" will render its "plans" unfulfilled. There will be no need to justify events, no need to give account, nothing to account, and no need for theodicy at all. Conversely, the writing will hold only if its "plans" come to pass. . . . Those who hear, handle, and reject the scroll, at the same time confirm its charge of evil, and ink it in indelibly. And, as they unwittingly "write" the scroll, they are themselves unwittingly "written": marked down for the disasters listed within it.[4]

A chief rhetorical function of prophetic texts is the deconstruction and reconstruction of communal memory as a prophylactic against future sin. In many Hebrew Bible traditions, the possibility of relapse is constitutive of what it means to be human. Hence in the Israelite prophetic imagination, there will always be a need for scrolls inscribed with "lamentations and groaning and woe" (Ezek 2:10), and there will always be a need for prophets who consume them and speak them forth anew. Brummitt's focus on the way in which the audience is "written" by the scroll is instructive. In Jeremiah 36, the prophet's scroll is pared down, column by column, and burned by the king. The text is destructible, but it can be rewritten. In fact, like the monstrous hydra of Greek mythology, the words of the rewritten text come back stronger and more threatening than ever ("and many similar words were added to them," Jer 36:32). When an implied audience actually heeds the words of Jeremiah, what is destroyed—or better, transmuted—is the audience itself. It becomes a new people to whom the scroll's words of judgment no longer apply. The audience, too, can be rewritten.

The destabilization of the audience's sense of self and sense of community is the very thing that holds out promise in the performance of the prophetic word. What Gary J. Handwerk has said about ethical irony elucidates the function of irony in the rhetoric of the Israelite prophets: "Verbal incongruities set up and provoke a deeper interrogation of self-consciousness. For ethical irony, an incompatibility in discourse suspends the question of identity by frustrating any immediate coherence of the subject."[5] Handwerk says further, "The ironic subject is thus defined in and by the process of interrogation."[6] This, too, would seem to apply to the subject Israel as it is continually problematized and redefined by the interrogatory interventions of biblical prophecy. I would not want to suggest that the notion of subject—of an enduring, morally active, coherent agent—was problematic for ancient Israelite authors in the way that the subject has been problematized in late modernist and postmodern theory. But I do find relevant to ancient Israelite discursive strategies Handwerk's interest in the way in which irony interrogates and destabilizes the subject.

The metaphors, invective, and other discursive means employed by the biblical prophets all catalyze an interrogation of self-consciousness—best understood in ancient Israel as a consciousness of communal identity—and simultaneously frustrate the audience's impulse to counter that uncomfortable destabilization by means of idolatry. Israel comes to see that it cannot rely on its old discourses of identity, but its idols, too, have been left smashed in pieces by the prophet's rhetorical blows. Irony leaves the constructed subject, Israel, in an untenable position of incoherence such that turning to God seems more and more like the only possible response. Amos and Ezekiel, in particular, are brilliant at effecting this complex destabilization in their audiences. The audience of Amos gradually loses its grasp on its identity as the prophet destroys piece after piece of Israel's tradition history. But Amos also supplies them with the one thing that is needful: "Seek me," thunders the God of Amos, "and live!" (Amos 5:5). Ezekiel brutally destroys his audience's conception of itself as chosen and pure—his offensive hypersexual images of moral degradation are designed to leave his audience repulsed and in a state of shock. But he, too, supplies them with what they need to hear most: the God of Ezekiel whispers, "I have no delight in the death of anyone. Turn, then, and live!" (Ezek 18:32). Thus a profound theological irony lies at the heart of biblical prophecies of judgment. Those who choose not to heed the prophetic word will be destroyed, thus proving the power of the very word they considered irrelevant or inefficacious. Conversely, those who heed an authoritative and apparently inescapable prophetic word of judgment may, in fact, escape destruction, and this, too, demonstrates the power of the prophetic word.[7]

Readers have long appreciated local ironies in the rhetoric of the Israelite prophets. Easiest to spot are the savage ironies with which the prophets mock their enemies within and outside of the community of Israel. Amos eviscerates the indolent rich. His implied audience feels the sting no less for Amos's reliance on hyperbole and cliché as vehicles of his mockery; the flush of shame rises even if the couch on which one reclines is made not of inlaid ivory but of more modest material. As I argued in the preceding chapter, Hosea's rhetorics of negation ironize the people's understanding of God. Thomas Jemielity writes of the ironic play on Exodus 3:14 in Hosea 1:9, "The Yahweh who sears the text of Hosea proclaims himself as I AM NOT. . . . You are not my People; I am not your God. Hosea's is the irony of the void."[8] Hosea leads his audience into a rhetorical trap, gently mouthing for them just the words they need to express their repentance—"Come, let us return to the LORD, for he has torn and he will heal us"—only to have God turn on them with devastating sarcasm: "What shall I do with you, Ephraim? What shall I do with you, Judah? Your love is like the morning mist that goes away early. . . . Therefore I have hewn them by means of the prophets; I have slain them by means of the words of my mouth" (Hos 6:1–5). Here Hosea has voiced the people in a way that initially invites their grateful assent. Finally, the constructed audience sighs, we may have relief from the relentless attack of the violent diction of Hosea; finally we can speak of repentance and turn the wrath of this terrible God away from us. But the invitation to dialogue was only an illusion. The prophet tears the very breath out of their mouths as inadequate, as mere vapor.

Many other examples of irony in the prophets could be mentioned. The hilarious ironies in the Book of Jonah practically tumble over one another in their haste to undercut a straight reading of that story, and interpreters usually have seen that, although they continue to disagree about the precise point of the narrative and what exactly is being ironized. Brian C. Jones has noted that Isaiah and other biblical prophets use sarcastic imperatives summoning the people to battle or to defense that "not only ironically underline the inevitability of defeat and the pointlessness of resistance" but also "satirize the subject."[9] Martin Kessler finds deft uses of irony in the Jeremianic oracles against Babylon.[10] Unexpected and dramatic reversals of fortune are a major motif in the prophets. Israel is not invulnerable simply because of its covenant with God; enemies used to punish Israel will not have the upper hand forever; those who think they can domesticate God shall see how wrong they were; and so on. David Fishelov has pointed to devices of satire employed regularly in the biblical prophets, including contrasting the targets' confidence in their success with "the humiliating fall awaiting them," exhorting the targets to continue sinning, cataloguing aspects of material wealth or power that the targets currently enjoy but will lose, and using animal imagery to represent the targets.[11] Fishelov ably sums up "the satirical goals of the prophets: to expose and ridicule the materialistic, egoistic and hedonistic values of the sinners as ultimately chimerical and inherently disastrous."[12] These examples suggest that irony may be said to be not just a favorite trope of the prophets but a defining texture of prophetic discourse.

Further ironies are hinted at in representations of the personae of various prophets. Jemielity argues that Elijah bests those around him by using irony: "Frequent instances of quick wit, eiron-like triumph over the wealthy and powerful, and placing evildoers in ridiculous or demeaning situations run through [the] legends about Elijah. Often he achieves these victories in disguise, pretending to be something less than he is."[13] David Marcus argues convincingly that the story of 2 Kings 2:23–25, in which children who had ridiculed a prophet are mauled by bears, is intended as a satire against the prophet Elisha.[14] Marcus also sees irony in the story of the unnamed man of God and the prophet at Bethel in 1 Kings 13, which he reads as satirizing "the curious ways and petty concerns of some prophets."[15] Many have argued that Jonah's unreliability, moodiness, and argumentative nature serve to ironize the figure of the Israelite prophet,[16] although others insist that Jonah is being represented as a true and faithful prophet.

That readers continue to disagree about Jonah demonstrates once more the characteristic elusiveness of irony as a rhetorical art of the unspoken. Before turning to analyses of Balaam, Amos, Micah, and Jonah below, I would like to consider one other irony in the prophetic corpus that eludes definitive identification. The question of the tone of Ezekiel 34 raises the problem of literary ironizing that may be too subtle, or too veiled in cultural assumptions now no longer understood, for the contemporary reader to know whether irony was intended. We may glimpse a reverse irony in the way in which Ezekiel responds to the characterization of him by his adversaries. When the prophet's audience is said to consider him a "singer of love songs" in Ezekiel 33, that audience is being mocked for misunderstanding the import of the prophet's words and his divinely authorized vocation.[17] Quick upon the heels of their misguided characterization of him, in 34:12–16, Ezekiel launches into tender prose about God's restoration of Israel, perhaps not unlike what a "love song" might

sound like if it were sung by an Israelite prophet. These elaborate promises of restoration and nurture are unlike anything else in the Book of
Ezekiel. Is the passage to be read "straight"? Certainly the general thrust
of this material, that the LORD will take care of Israel since Israel's leaders
have abdicated their responsibility, is not directly contradictory to those
few other texts in Ezekiel that promise restoration. If the passage is sincere, it also follows beautifully from the stern indictment of Israel's leaders
in 34:1–11 for harming their own people.

Nevertheless, the tone of verses 12–16 is dramatically unusual for
Ezekiel. Elsewhere in the Book of Ezekiel, restoration will be effected
only in spite of Israel and only for the sake of God's holy name, not for
any divine solicitude for Israel as God's beloved people. Will Israel frolic
in bucolic joy upon being nurtured and protected by God? Far from it.
Normally in Ezekiel, survivors will come to loathe themselves after restoration when they understand more fully who God is and see more clearly
how sinful they had been (see, e.g., Ezek 20:40–44). A further clue that
the tender tone of Ezekiel 34:12–16 is not to be read "straight" is the
gradual shift from images of pastoral care to an image of judgment,
which I believe constitutes a brilliant strategy to entrap the audience. At
the end of the first section, God has promised to shepherd his sheep
himself, "but the fat and the strong I will destroy" (34:16). The audience
hears that destruction is to come upon the corrupt leaders who have
betrayed the people of Israel, so this judgment would seem to be in keeping with the images of care. But then the divine shepherd turns his attention to the flock itself, and his pastoral attentiveness starts to press
uncomfortably close. God starts to question the ethics of the sheep he
had been metaphorically nurturing just moments ago. What's this about
muddying the water with your hooves and thrusting aside the weaker
sheep? God asks. The sheep are not so hapless and helpless after all, as it
turns out. The divine attentiveness that had seemed so nurturing a few
verses earlier gradually becomes relentless in judgment. Finally Ezekiel
springs the trap: God the loving shepherd will judge mercilessly "between sheep and sheep" (34:17). This is as sweet a love song as Ezekiel is
capable of singing, apparently. Throughout the Book of Ezekiel, the
prophet's hyperbolic polemics of shame have served to ironize the implied audience's misperception of the purpose of the prophetic word.
Ezekiel performs sign-acts that signal the inevitability of punishment,
and he enacts shaming through his violent pornographic diatribes. In
the larger context of the discourse of Ezekiel, then, the atypically bucolic passage in Ezekiel 34 that promises God's pastoral care for Israel
as sheep may be heard as a scathing ironic evisceration of the metaphor
of God as loving shepherd (or of the people's reliance on that trope).

Those who have considered Ezekiel to be a mere "singer of love songs" are led down a deceptive path to the rhetorical slaughter.

The possibility of reading Ezekiel 34 as ironic does compel the readerly imagination, given all the earlier prophecies presenting Ezekiel as one who zealously employs a poetics of shaming as his chief rhetorical weapon. But the signals of irony here are muted enough that the case for irony likely could not be made to the satisfaction of a skeptic. I may be overreading Ezekiel 34; indeed, my own doubts remain strong enough that I have presented this example as a hermeneutical problem. The problem causes me to wonder how many ironic subtleties have been lost in ancient literature because the audience has grown less culturally competent over the centuries or because the text dares to attempt a subtlety greater than readers can grasp.

The case of Ezekiel points up another problem for reception of irony in written prophetic texts: since much biblical prophetic literature was delivered orally in its original context, readers are not privy to a host of aural cues. John Haiman has synthesized some important studies on verbal cues for irony across cultures.[18] Not only do readers of ancient prophecy miss facial cues (one imagines Amos subtly narrowing his eyes as he moves in for the ironic coup de grâce, Ezekiel mouthing his hyperbolic polemics with exaggerated expressions of alarm or with a chilling deadpan expression). We also miss essential cues provided by intonation. Per Haiman, irony and sarcasm are flagged by a number of predictable aural signals, including inverse pitch obtrusion (a stressed syllable is uttered at a lower pitch than would normally be expected in earnest communication), prolongation of vowels, a flattening of affect, and the employment of exaggerated emphasis, heavy pauses, monotone, singsong, or falsetto. Scholars of language have found many types of aural cues of irony to apply nearly universally, across linguistic cultures as diverse as English, Russian, Greek, Tagalog, Japanese, German, Mandarin, Spanish, and Ukrainian.[19] Not having access to aural information about Israelite prophecy, then, we are at a distinct disadvantage.

Nevertheless, literary-critical tools can help us see that ironies shape representations of prophecy in the Hebrew Bible in important ways. There is a common thread uniting the Balaam pericope, the Book of Amos, the Book of Micah, and the Book of Jonah: according to these biblical ironists, Israel's traditional piety is not what it has seemed to be or is not all that it should be. Israel's inadequate understanding of faithfulness, obedience, and trust in God are grist for the ironists' mill in all these texts. Despite the fact that these diverse texts likely come from a wide variety of settings and historical periods within ancient Israelite culture, these texts share a subversive stance regarding earlier tradition—or, better, regarding the inadequate way in which they perceive their implied audiences to have understood earlier traditions. We turn first to the literary representation of the foreign seer Balaam in the Book of Numbers.

Oracular Indeterminacy and Dramatic Irony
in the Story of Balaam

The Balaam material has received attention from scholars interested in the inner-biblical and post-biblical history of interpretation of the Balaam traditions and scholars interested in historical questions raised by the Deir ʿAlla inscription, fragments of a plaster slab with inked text datable to the eighth century BCE that describes a seer named Balaam son of Beor. Literary criticism of this material has focused on the story of Balaam and his donkey, which intrigues scholars of folkloristic narrative and those who appreciate biblical humor. A number of commentators suggest that this tale has been embedded in the larger narrative simply for the purpose of ridiculing Balaam.[20] This purpose may well have been among the reasons that the donkey story was brought into its present literary location. But one may inquire more deeply into the role of irony in the literary relationships that obtain throughout the Balaam pericope. I am not persuaded that the donkey tale provides the only negative satirical valence in a story that otherwise lionizes Balaam.

I will propose here a reading that attempts to take account of complex literary and rhetorical connections across Numbers 22–24 and between that corpus and Numbers 25. Pausing briefly on the early reception history of Balaam, we will consider perceptions of ambiguity in the Balaam story from a variety of ancient reading communities as one form of authorization for an ironic reading of the Balaam material. I will mount an argument for irony in the Balaam narrative, then, by adducing literary evidence having to do with the presentation of Balaam's voice as unreliable, textual ambiguities at crucial moments in the text's characterization of Balaam, and dramatic ironies within the plot. My analysis throughout responds to work done by Baruch A. Levine in his magisterial commentary on the Book of Numbers.[21]

The reception history of Balaam provides ample evidence that ancient audiences perceived radical incongruities in the Balaam material and attempted to resolve them. First up for consideration are intra-biblical representations of the Balaam tradition. Within biblical tradition is a notable divergence of views about whether Balaam was worthy of commendation—to the degree that he acknowledged Israel's God and acted on behalf of Israel, however inadvertently—or malicious, and if he was malicious, on what grounds that assessment should be made. Numbers 31 explicitly connects Balaam with the exogamous sexual mixing and idolatrous offerings in which Israel engaged at Baal-Peor, amplifying the literary connection in the narrative between Numbers 22–24 and Numbers 25. Numbers 31:8 has Balaam executed (cf. also Josh 13:22), tying up the worrisome loose end about Balaam as a foreign diviner having been allowed to live *contra* Deuteronomic prohibition (Deut 13:5). Deuteronomy 23, Joshua 24, and Nehemiah 13 view Balaam negatively for intending to curse Israel and for practicing divination. Micah 6:5 offers an elusive reference to Balaam that is ambiguous or perhaps positive; I will have more to say below about the complex larger point of that Micah passage.

Regarding the LXX translation of the Balaam material, John William Wevers has shown that there was a concerted effort by Septuagint translators to depict only Elohim (*theós*) speaking to Balaam, not the Lord (*kýrios*). Wevers interprets this fact as reflecting a negative appraisal of Balaam: "the notion that Balaam was actually a prophet of Yahweh, a seer with whom Yahweh had converse, was repulsive to the Alexandrian" and "Balak may attribute Balaam's oracles to Yahweh, but the Greek knew better."[22] The three New Testament references to Balaam are all negative. Each context, explicitly or indirectly, connects Balaam to sexual impropriety. The charge is "licentious desires of the flesh" in 2 Peter, "sexual immorality" in Jude, and "practicing fornication" in Revelation, all of which likely reflect a traditio-historical interpretation of Numbers 25.

In extra-biblical reception of the Balaam traditions, we see both hyperbolically negative and hyperbolically positive portrayals of Balaam. This bifurcated ancient readers' response may illustrate the ambivalence of reading communities regarding signals of irony in the biblical material. Allied with positive readings are the instances in which Balaam's oracles are quoted in Testimonia (4Q175), the Damascus Document (CD 7:18–19), and the War Scroll (1QM 11:6–7), each time with implicit confirmation of the oracles' integrity and no visible concern about Balaam's credentials or his motivations.[23] But in a fragmentary Qumran text, 4Q339, Balaam's name appears in a list of false prophets.[24] The Book of Enoch (1:2) may be borrowing on the description of the biblical Balaam in characterizing Enoch as "a righteous man whose eyes were opened by God."[25] For Josephus, Balaam was the greatest of the prophets in his day and did relay the word of the true God, but Balaam later counseled Balak to send Moabite women to tempt the Israelites.[26] As John Greene notes, Philo considers Balaam "nothing more than a wizard"; Origen recognizes that he had been a true prophet but was also a magician and hence "was made to serve both good and evil inclinations" in the spiritual battle between good and evil. Similarly, for

Clement of Alexandria, Balaam is both a true prophet and an illegitimate sorcerer.[27] Ancient rabbinic readings are of two minds as well. Balaam "as a prophet is said to have been superior to Moses [because] he,
and six others, were sent to the Gentiles"; Balaam is favorably compared
with Moses in *Sifre to Deuteronomy* 357, f. 150a, and *Numbers Rabbah* XIV,
20, because Balaam knew the deity with whom he was speaking whereas
Moses did not, Balaam knew in advance when God would come to him
but Moses did not, and Balaam was able to speak with God whenever he
wished but Moses was not.[28] But Balaam was also said in rabbinic tradition not to have a share in the life to come.

The points I want to make with this brief overview of reception history
are two. First, the divergent ways in which different ancient readers understood Balaam's authority and his motivations illustrate the contextual
needs (theological and political) of those interpretive communities in their
own historical moments, but they may also be responding to the dynamic
between the "said" and the "unsaid" in the story of Balaam. Second, the
marked ambivalence in Balaam's reception history shows a consistent
reader alertness to the possibility of significant disjuncture between the
character of Balaam and the truth of his words and self-representation.

We turn now to the Balaam story proper, a story rich with textual
cues for ironic reading. Again, the three issues to which I will attend are,
first, cues about the unreliability of Balaam's voice; second, textual ambiguities at key moments in the text's characterization of Balaam and
the God he represents; and third, dramatic ironies that become evident
in the way in which the plot unfolds.

The voice of Balaam surprises the reader for a number of reasons.
He speaks the name "YHWH" with familiarity although he is a foreigner,
and he avers that YHWH is the one who has directed him; yet the narrative consistently uses "Elohim" when speaking of the God who appears
to Balaam, varying this only when speaking of the "angel of the LORD"
in the donkey story and the way in which the LORD puts a word in Balaam's mouth before his first and second oracles. Scholars have long
mulled this variation and have concluded either that it renders the Balaam narrative supremely useful for classic source-critical analysis[29] or
that it renders the narrative useless for the same.[30] But the consistency of
the lack of consistency, as it were, may argue not for a text-critical cause
but for a rhetorical motivation for this precise variation in the divine
name that Balaam uses and the divine name that the narrator uses. It
may represent the flagging of a discrepancy, in the perspective of the
narrator, between what Balaam knows about God and what the narrator
knows about God. What Balaam says is not entirely false, else it would
not lure the reader. But its truth is only partial, and it is true to a degree

that is inappropriate for this context. Even when he is right, he is not entirely right; his authority is perhaps being subtly undermined.

Another question about the reliability of Balaam's voice is this: we notice that from the outset Balaam selectively reports only part of what God has said to him, namely, the part about him not being permitted to accompany the Moabite delegation (22:13). He hides the rest, namely, that Israel is blessed of God and thus cannot be harmed by the Moabites. This withholding, which is clearly telegraphed to the reader, constitutes a dramatic irony that not only manipulates Balak but renders all of what Balaam says suspect. Robert Alter writes of a related narrative technique in which subtle variations or omissions occur in reported dialogue: "[A] prominent, and, I think, distinctive convention of this body of classic Hebrew narrative [viz., Genesis to Kings], which has been analyzed by Meir Sternberg, George Savran, and by me, is the modification of dialogue in near-verbatim repetition in order to indicate the attitudinal angle, the changed audience, or even the downright mendacity of the speaker who repeats someone else's already cited words."[31] And more: it would seem that Balaam is stalling to ensure that he receives more compensation. After his initial refusal of the task, he receives the second Moabite delegation—officials "more numerous and more distinguished" than those in the first group—and hears Balak offer him, in essence, anything he wishes: "I will surely do you great honor, and whatever you say to me I will do" (22:16). He seems to demur again but actually offers signals about his expectations regarding enhanced compensation: "Even if Balak were to give me his house full of silver and gold, I could not go beyond the command of the LORD my God" (22:18). This faux protestation of Balaam has obliquely cued a heightened session of bargaining. One is reminded of the way in which Ephron the Hittite sets the price of the Cave of Machpelah for the burial of Sarah in Genesis 23:15. His speech, "A piece of land worth 400 shekels of silver—what is that between you and me? Bury your dead," seems to demur graciously but in fact serves as an unmistakable indicator of the amount required from Abraham, which Abraham then pays.[32] So, too, with Balaam: he underlines the level of the compensation required, while pretending to claim a nobler motivation theologically. This has been seen by readers for centuries: the negative appraisal of Balaam as greedy is an ancient one in rabbinic and Christian traditions.[33] The Moabite delegation does not object, and the next morning, Balaam goes with them, ostensibly despite his demurral, but in fact because of it. The visible outcome is that Balaam does accept the contract and the increased payment that the Moabite delegation has offered. The narrative here increases the dramatic suspense about how this story will unfold, since the audience knows that no cursing of Israel will succeed. And it presents Balaam again as one who tells only part of the truth, and precisely the part that serves his own interests.

Another strike against the character of Balaam as mercenary is delivered after Balak sees that Balaam has not cursed Israel. Balak says with scathing irony, "I was going to reward you richly, but 'the LORD' has denied you the reward."[34] Then, and only then, when Balaam understands that he is not going to get his money, he offers his own oracular cursing of Moab, Edom, Amalek, and the Kenites, slinging barbs at Assyria and Eber as well. There is no mention of the spirit of God coming on Balaam for this last bit of "oracle"-giving; there is no suggestion that the LORD manifested himself to Balaam and put a word in his mouth. This is Balaam mouthing off for spite because he has not received the money that has been his guiding motivation the entire time. While Balaam's greed has been excoriated by interpreters from early times in the reception of the Balaam traditions, the notion that his prophetic utterances might be compromised due to corruption from his mercenary motives has received less attention in contemporary scholarship.[35] This aspect of his characterization may be read as an ironic narrative signal that his discernment is wholly for hire for crass motives, and thus that his prophetic voice as such cannot be trusted.

Another signal that Balaam's voice is unreliable is the hyperbolic and narratively ungrounded way in which he makes claims regarding his relationship with the God of Israel. "I could not transgress the edict of YHWH my God," he proclaims (22:18). But his confidence is unsupported by the narrative itself, which has established no relationship between God and Balaam prior to that claim, as many interpreters have noticed. Balaam does not express awe when God appears to him, nor does he answer with an affirmation of obedience when God tells him not to curse Israel (22:12). To the contrary, a strong tradition within the history of interpretation has it that Balaam blesses Israel only reluctantly. "YHWH my God" indeed: Balaam's pragmatism here, his sangfroid in going about his business in an unexpected audience with the Creator of the universe, is as ridiculous here as it is in the episode with the talking donkey. Scholars have been quick to notice how ludicrous it is that Balaam simply chats with the donkey as if that were the most natural thing in the world. It may be that in the conceptual world of the donkey story as folk tale, talking animals are to be expected. But structural connections that run between the donkey story and the rest of the pericope are significant. The donkey turns aside from the angel three times in spaces of increasing narrowness, and its failure to proceed frustrates the goal of Balaam. Balaam builds an altar three times in spaces of increasing breadth (the first time and second times, he can see "a portion of the people"; the third time, he can see all of Israel's encampment), but his failure to achieve the desired result frustrates the goal of Balak. James Ackerman sees this "triadic pattern" also in the fact that Balaam's eyes are not opened in the donkey story until the third episode of recalcitrance, and Balaam does not call himself the one whose eye is "open" (*šĕtum*, on which, more below) until his third oracle for Balak.[36] Robert Alter describes the parallel between the donkey story and the interactions of Balaam and Balak as follows: "[T]he ass in this episode plays the role of Balaam . . . to Balaam's Balak. . . . In Balaam's poetic imagery, first Israel is spread out like the dust, then crouched like a lion, and finally rises like a star, so that the Moabite king, waiting for a first-class imprecation, is progressively reduced to impotent fury, quite in the manner of Balaam's blind rage against the wayward ass."[37] Thus a case can be made for substantial literary connections between the donkey story and the surrounding literary context. The reader is justified in seeing as analogous Balaam's unruffled chatting with the deity and his casual conversation with a donkey. Both narrative gestures underline Balaam's not understanding the momentousness of what is happening.

A third way in which the voice of Balaam is rendered unreliable is through the savage mockery of his abilities of discernment in the story with the donkey, something that many have seen. David Marcus has done an excellent job of describing ironies in the tale of Balaam and his donkey. Marcus notes the elements of satire, parody, and ridicule not only in Balaam's lack of discernment regarding the angel, but also in his having to concede that he who "obtains knowledge from the Most High" did not know something, that he has to use brute force on the donkey to try to teach it whereas the donkey simply uses words to teach him, that his foot gets ignominiously squeezed against the fence, and that Balaam "is shown to be ignorant of the conventions of proper discourse" because he stupidly volunteers concrete answers to his donkey's rhetorical questions.[38] R. W. Moberly has noticed the irony of Balaam's being unable to discern what his donkey is doing when she balks: "how can the man who cannot interpret the obvious actions of his ass interpret the more difficult actions of God?"[39] Additional points of irony are emphasized by Michael S. Moore's study of comparative ancient Near Eastern material on the functional roles of diviners, oneiromantics, and seers:

Will Balaam, the "oracle-reciter" so famous for conveying divine "answers" to divinatory requests in the past, have a "word" placed in his mouth? and/or . . . should these traditional avenues fail, will Balaam use some other means, like, say, a "magic wand," to get himself out of this predicament? . . . [T]he deity opens the

"mouth" of the she-ass, but not Balaam's mouth! A more humiliating indictment of an "oracle-reciter's" abilities would be hard to
imagine. . . . [And] three times Balaam beats his she-ass, using a
"rod" (*maqqēl*) as a riding crop, not as a magical source of power.
For this Israelite narrator, all power comes from Yahweh, and
Yahweh cannot be manipulated by any means.[40]

The story of Balaam and his donkey certainly renders Balaam as a ludicrously unaware person. But there may be a sharper edge to this satire.
The donkey perceives divine opposition to their journey—in the figure of
the angel standing in the road—and responds obediently by not going
further. By unflattering contrast, Balaam's inability to obey (because of
his lack of perception) may be at issue here. As George Savran notes, "The
ass is the exemplar of obedience and submission to divine authority, while
Balaam himself is initially reluctant to accept the dictates of God."[41] Balaam does not obey "the LORD his God" because he cannot perceive aright.
The donkey story does not just show Balaam to be stupid; much more importantly, it ironizes the foundational claim of Balaam to be obedient to
God. By virtue of his obtuse and manipulative nature and his lack of gifts,
Balaam is unable to obey the LORD. It is not only in the journeying as such
but in claiming to speak only what the LORD puts in his mouth that we see
Balaam is incapable of true obedience.[42]

Thus even if we continue to see the presence of the donkey story in the
larger Balaam narrative as the result of redaction, we may acknowledge
that the likely purposes of such redaction were substantially more complex than simply ridiculing Balaam. Instructive here is a point on narrative technique made by Geert Van Oyen regarding intercalation in the
Gospel of Mark.[43] As has long been noticed, Mark's Gospel frequently in-
serts a story into the middle of another ongoing narrative, resuming the
first narrative only after the inserted story has concluded.[44] This technique
Van Oyen considers (following Tom Shepherd)[45] to create a "dramatized
irony" among key characters in the stories, some of whom are not operating with all of the relevant information available to the reader. A related
point is made by Robert M. Fowler, who finds that the author of Mark uses
intercalary insertions to flag the importance of "perceiving and filling
gaps in narrative."[46] The donkey story in the Balaam pericope works hard
to fill the potential gap having to do with Balaam's abilities in discernment and his credibility: we learn that he is undiscerning and lacks credibility. This intercalation shapes the reader's understanding of what will
follow in the oracle-giving. Equally important, the reader is encouraged to
bring a retrospective skepticism to what has already transpired in the narrative, namely, Balaam's apparent obedience to God.

Thus in a synchronic reading of Numbers 22–24, the presence of the satirical donkey story suggests that there may be more going on in the oracles than Balaam's transparent rendering of exactly what God has put in his mouth. I will argue below that there are ample clues within the poetry, too, that support just such a skeptical reading of Balaam's prophesying. He says he can speak only what the LORD gives him and could not go beyond it "to do less or more" (22:18), but the narrator does not say this. It is essential to remain attentive to characterization in biblical narrative, and particularly to the differences in perspective and reliability of various characters and personae. The distinction between the narrator and Balaam is crucial. The implied reader is not supposed to mistake the narrator's voice for Balaam's. The reader has seen that Balaam manipulates others, in particular by withholding the whole truth and emphasizing only the part that serves his own interests. The reader also has been led to suspect that Balaam is motivated by a mercenary ethos. After the donkey story, the reader knows that Balaam could not see or obey the LORD if, as it were, the LORD were standing right in front of him and his life depended on it.

All of this has transpired narratologically before Balaam even begins to open his mouth to "bless" Israel. The reader attentive to narratological clues thus far has been prepared to be suspicious of Balaam's oracles themselves. We turn now to the four oracles of Balaam, our hermeneutical senses alert for potential false notes, misdirection, and manipulative use of ambiguity. This seer's pronouncements may, at least in part, be what God has put in his mouth. But we have learned that when Balaam is speaking, he may not know whereof he speaks, and more important matters may well be concealed in what he does not say.

The first oracle begins by narrating what has transpired (23:7–8). Balak has brought Balaam to curse and doom Israel. In rehashing earlier events, Balaam would seem to be stalling here, trying to figure out how to please Balak and thus not jeopardize his payment while submitting to the constraints that God has placed on him. Balaam comes up with a savvy rhetorical question: "How can I curse the one whom God has not cursed?" (Num 23:8), an artful dodge indeed. It leaves open the possibility that if the LORD becomes displeased with Israel, cursing could be the result. Balaam then offers an evasive and potentially polyvalent observation about the target of his attentions: Israel is "a people dwelling by itself, not reckoned among the nations" (23:9). Is Israel's a well-deserved state of majestic solitude signaling that Israel has been set apart by the LORD for great things, that Israel will not "share the fate of other nations," a Targumic interpretation?[47] Or is the reference to Israel's solitude meant to signal that other nations dare not approach too closely because the fighting force of Israel is insuperable? Perhaps that is what Balaam is hoping the

Lord will understand by his ambiguous remark. But Balaam's statement also highlights for Balak the fact that Israel is all alone, with no allies among the nations to come to its defense should the Moabites decide to attack. This is the reading of Levine, although he gives it a different valence than my argument does. Levine weighs a number of options and ends up translating the relevant verse, "It is truly a people encamped apart, and unallied with other nations," commenting, "The Israelite people was destined to conquer its land unsupported by allies."[48] Whether the oracle intends to suggest that Israel will conquer its land is not so clear to me. But "unsupported by allies" is clearly a cue that would be welcomed by Balak regarding the extent of Israel's defensive capabilities. Balaam is managing to say two things at once, meeting the requirements of the Lord while not yet jeopardizing his fee from the Moabites.

The other concrete thing Balaam ends up saying about Israel is that Israel is numerous. This too is ambiguous in a way that may be read as serving Balaam's interest in duplicity. "Who can count the dust of Jacob?" (22:10) may be understood as lauding the strength of Israel's army and the mighty dust cloud it kicks up as it marches. It may also be taken as an oblique reference to God's promise to make the offspring of Abram as the "dust of the earth" in Genesis 13:16. The obvious allusion to Genesis 12:3 in the third oracle of Balaam, "blessed are they who bless you, and cursed are they who curse you," would reinforce the notion that this is an intended play on that divine promise of offspring. But the comparison of Israel to "dust" is unusual in the patriarchal promises, coming up elsewhere only in the story of Jacob at Bethel (Gen 28:14). It should be noted that this promise to Abram comes immediately after, and is directly connected with, the separation of Lot from Abram because the land was not big enough to hold them both, such that Lot settled in Sodom, where a series of unfortunate events led to incest with his daughters and the resulting conception of Ammon and, more to the point, Moab! The implication may be that Israel's strength of numbers, ironically enough, led to the generation of Israel's enemies in the first place.

Balaam ends this first oracle with a suitably evasive proclamation, "That I might die the death of the upright! O that my end might be like theirs!" (22:10). Is Israel upright? We don't know. We haven't heard yet, and Balaam has not pronounced them so. Even if the meaning of the term *yĕšārîm* is "valiant" here, as Levine argues,[49] this is an ambiguous rhetorical flourish because the death of the valiant, presumably, is a death in (glorious) battle. So long as Israel does die, Balak would not object to the characterization of Israel as *yĕšārîm*. And God would surely be pleased to hear the suggestion that the Israelites are upright and/or valiant. So Balaam's carefully ambiguous declaration pleases everyone again, and again the seer deftly avoids committing himself. This polyvalent reading is underscored by dramatic irony as the narrative moves forward into the sin of Baal-Peor (Numbers 25). In that story, the reader learns two things: that Israel is far from upright, and that the Israelites do die (24,000 of them). There may be a further proleptic dramatic irony in Balaam's declaration that he wishes his death would be like that of the *yĕšārîm:* Balaam's own "end," narrated in Numbers 31:8 and Joshua 13:22, will be to be put to the sword along with a variety of Canaanite apostates. Balaam's death does turn out to be like that of the apostate Israelites in Numbers 25.

Balaam has brilliantly avoided committing himself so far, employing mercurial and ambiguous language in order to pander to the LORD and Balak simultaneously. A straightforward blessing this first oracle is not. If these are potentially dangerous ambiguities for Israel—and I think they are best read as exactly that—then we are beginning to glimpse the unsettling possibility that since the LORD put these words into Balaam's mouth, it may be the LORD's perspective on the "blessing" of Israel that is ambiguous. Here is an unspoken irony lurking in the shadows of this oracle: if Israel does indeed turn out to be cursed rather than blessed, it would be God himself who performs it, just as we have seen in Exodus 32 in the matter of the Golden Calf and as we are about to see in Numbers 25. On both of those occasions, God wreaks deadly havoc upon the Israelites for their apostasy.

What does Balaam say in his second oracle? "God is not a human being, that he should lie, or a mortal, that he should change his mind" (23:19). The reader's unease at God's obscure intentions is heightened. What is God's purpose, exactly? The reader may be expected to know that God did indeed change his mind, with results that were catastrophic for humankind (in the Flood narrative, Gen 6:6). And God has already changed his mind in the Balaam narrative, as well: "You shall not go with them" (22:12) becomes "get up and go with them" (22:20), with no narrative motivation supplied for this unexpected shift. So, is Balaam correct that God will not change his mind? We have good reason to doubt him. If he is wrong, he may be wrong because he is a non-Israelite seer and does not, in fact, know this God as well as he had implied with his blustering assertions about the "LORD my God." Another option is that God is the ironist here, toying with Balaam and with the Moabite audience. Our doubt grows stronger at the two rhetorical questions that follow: "Has he promised, and will he not do it? spoken, and will he not fulfill it?" (23:19). These rhetorical questions are unsettling, especially for the rereader who already knows what will happen in Numbers 25. God will protect and bless the Israelites unless they fall away in apostasy, in which case God will become their worst enemy and destroy them without mercy—precisely what happens at Baal-Peor. "Has he promised, and will he not do it?" becomes at once a real question rather than rhetorical—has God changed his mind about blessing us?—and a veiled threat: God has promised to destroy apostates from among Israel, and indeed he will do just that. Just below the surface of Balaam's rhetoric, ambiguities continue to percolate.

How are we to take Balaam's statement in this second oracle that God "has not looked on misfortune in Jacob nor has he seen trouble in Israel" (23:21)? Commentators have noticed that those verbs of seeing could yield at least two semantic senses. Is it that God has seen no *ʾāven* in Jacob and no *ʿāmāl* in Israel because Israel is so righteous? Or is it that God will not look upon, in the sense of countenance, *ʾāven* and *ʿāmāl* in Israel? The latter would imply that God's blessing and protection are available only so long as God finds no iniquity in Israel. For the rereader, this would be an obvious ironic warning, given that the incident at Baal-Peor is just over the narrative horizon of the story.

Consider now the potent ambiguities of a syntactically similar statement further on in this second oracle, in 23:22: "El, the one who brought them out of Egypt, is like the horns of a wild ox to them" because there is no augury or divination *bĕyiśrāʾēl*. The simplest reading is that no augury or divination could be effective against Israel, with the preposition *bêt* taken in the adversative sense.[50] But one could also read it as asserting that God protects Israel only because no illegitimate forms of intermediation are practiced within Israel. God may be like the horns of a wild ox to them indeed—an ambiguous metaphor, since a wild ox, untamable and capricious, could turn its horns on them in a moment.[51] What if augury or divination were to be found in Israel after all? One might even speculate, based on implied assonance, that the highly unusual term *tôʿapōt*, "horns," which occurs else only in Job 22:25 and Psalms 95:4 in very different meanings,[52] might be intended to evoke a subtle anxiety in the audience about *tôʿēbōt*, "abominations" in Israel, under which category fall two sins relevant to the Balaam story: using illegitimate means of divination[53] and precisely the sort of exogamous sexual mixing that happens in Numbers 25.

The savvy Balaam continues his purveying of ambiguities with two asseverations, "Now it shall be said of"—or, and this is important, *to*—"Jacob and Israel, 'See what 'El has done!'" (23:23). The next line of the poem is ambiguous: "Look, a people rising up like a lion . . . It does not lie down until it has eaten the prey and drunk the blood of the slain." Is Israel being figured as a lion?[54] Or is it Moab that is being so represented? The text is elliptical. Both Levine and Milgrom translate the line about a lion-like people rising up to drink the blood of the slain as being told not *of* Israel but *to* Israel.[55] Here Balaam may be cueing Moab that it can be victorious against Israel in battle. The point of this endeavor, the entire motivation for Balak to have brought Balaam here, has been for Moab to gain the upper hand so that it may slay Israel. How much more unambiguous it would have been if Balaam had said, "Look, the people Israel rising up like a lion!" A little clarity would have resolved everything. But Balaam does not want to resolve the ambiguity. He wants to play each side against the other, and ambiguity serves his purpose beautifully. These ambiguities serve also the purpose of the ironist behind the story, who may be intent on drawing the reader into constructing the powerful unspoken threats behind these "blessings" of Balaam.

The third and fourth oracles are of a different kind. The majority redaction-critical view is that they stem from a different source and are diachronically earlier, and the case could be made on literary grounds alone that we have a noticeable change in tenor here. In 24:1, we encounter the strange notice that Balaam "saw that it pleased the LORD to bless Israel, so he did not go, as at other times, to look for omens." One might ask what, then, Balaam had been seeking before. It was supposed to have been clear from the very beginning that the LORD would only bless Israel. This statement either ironizes Balaam's earlier alleged clarity regarding the LORD's purpose or his misunderstanding of what has actually transpired in the oracles to this point, namely, mixed blessings and ambiguity. This third oracle that Balaam delivers is hyperbolically lavish in its praise of Israel. Israel has fair encampments like flourishing palm groves, aloes, cedar trees; water shall flow abundantly from Israel's buckets; his kingdom shall be exalted. Beautiful—and beautifully hyperbolic, which is a classic flag for those looking for irony, because overstatement and understatement, which skew an utterance's relationship to its context, are the tools most essential to the ironist's art. But nevertheless, we have this lavish praise and no obvious clues within these terms of admiration themselves that irony is afoot. God is like a wild ox again, only here the straight meaning is laid out clearly—so clearly, one might note, that the unresolvable ambiguity of the other mention of God as being like a wild ox stands out all the more. Here, God's ox devours Israel's enemies and breaks all their bones. No signals of irony are here, if we can bring ourselves to overlook the hyperbole and the fact that the tenor of this oracle is quite unlike what has gone before.

Which, of course, I cannot. There is a clue that Balaam's prophesying in the third and fourth oracles is not as straightforward as it might seem. Consider the unusual term *šětum* used to describe Balaam's "eye," a metonym for his gift for discernment as a seer. This term is crucial for understanding whether Balaam is being represented literarily as reliable, whether he truly sees aright in the view of the narrator. And as may not be surprising by this point in our exploration of the Balaam material, the whole scholarly debate around the semantic range of the term is centered on its tremendous ambiguity. It can mean "open" or "shut" or "perfect/true," depending on how one derives it etymologically and whether one considers it to be straightforward or antiphrastic in sense. The play on semantic possibilities with *šětum* is intrinsically important to the characterization of Balaam overall. The word is extraordinarily rare—known in biblical Hebrew only in these two oracles—and it carries with it a heavy freight of semantic ambiguity.

The options for its derivation are three. One possibility, argued by William F. Albright in 1944, is that it comes from *t-m-m* used with the relative particle *še-> še tāmmâ ʿāyin*.[56] Thus Balaam is one whose eye would be "whole" or "perfect" or "true."[57] Another meaning, "shut," is possible if it is taken from *śîn-ṭēt-mēm* as a late byform of the well-attested *sāmek-ṭēt-mēm*, "to stop up, shut up, keep closed" (as can be seen in an occurrence in Lam 3:8). A third meaning, "open," is possible if the word is taken from *š-t-m*. As Milgrom and Levine note, the later meaning of the root *š-t-m* means "open" in Aramaic and in Rabbinic Hebrew, and it works well with the parallelism that comes up a verse later, where Balaam says he is *gělûy ʿēnāyim*, "with eyes uncovered" or "unveiled." The play of both possibilities may well have been intended. If *šětum* is an antiphrastic euphemism, as David Marcus has argued, with the literal meaning "shut" intended to convey its opposite, then its selection in these oracles might argue for potent ironizing based on wordplay in the semantics of this single word.[58] Marcus notes that "antiphrastic euphemism is a literary device closely related to irony and sarcasm" and discusses instances in which another such euphemism for blindness in Hebrew and Aramaic is used satirically to evoke double entendre.[59]

The ironic play on these two semantic senses would be both artful and highly appropriate to the ambivalent characterization of Balaam by other literary means in the material. Double entendre should not be ruled out given the parodic nature of the Balaam story generally, the rarity of the term *šětum*, and the appropriateness of both "open" and "shut" narratologically. "Shut" works beautifully as a designation for Balaam's eye precisely because of the donkey story. As Milgrom notes, one could read this as indicating "Balaam was heretofore blind to God's revelation or he was actually physically blind, which would account for God's having to open his eyes to see the angel."[60] But consider also the fascinating interpretation that Levine relates in his argument for the meaning "open," which he favors. A Mishnaic ruling in *ʿAbodâh Zārâh* 5:3 uses *štm* to address the problem of non-Jews transporting wine on behalf of a Jew and possibly stealing some of the wine for the illegitimate purpose of pagan libations. Levine explains: "So long as the non-Jew in question remained under supervision, the wine is permitted for use by Jews, but if the non-Jew was on his own sufficiently long, it must be acknowledged hypothetically that he could have siphoned off some of the wine for use in pagan rites."[61] Levine notes that Rashi connects that Mishnah passage with Numbers 24, saying that the meaning of *yiptaḥ*, "open," there is like *šĕtum hā῾ayin*, which also means "to open."[62] This is important for two reasons. Levine simply argues for the later meaning of "open" as the meaning of *šĕtum hā῾ayin* in the Balaam passage. But it is also relevant that we have the occurrence of this word and its explicit connection to Numbers 24 by Rashi in a context that is observably anxious about the possibility of a pagan tainting something that should be restricted to Israelite cultic praxis. This is the case in the biblical passage too, where we see anxiety in the biblical writers about the pagan Balaam tainting the Israelite cultic practice of intermediation with the God of Israel. The artfully ambiguous semantic range of *štm*, then, plus Rashi's "early reader response" that highlights anxiety about the blurring of boundaries of cultic practice with Jewish and pagan rites, provides substantial impetus for a reading of intentional ambiguity in the characterization of Balaam as *šĕtum hā῾ayin*. It is all the more brilliantly ironic that one sees Balaam characterizing himself thus and meaning only to boast about the clairvoyance of his vision, whereas the narrator and the reader know full well that there is also an inescapable blindness about Balaam's intermediation.

Finally, the fourth oracle may seem to prove a bona fide blessing for Israel after all—but it is a "blessing" only in ironic relief. In the fourth oracle, Balaam blesses no one, instead degenerating into venomous cursing of a variety of other groups, starting with Moab. Here, in this last oracle, precisely when there may be no ambiguity left because these are curses leveled against Israel's enemies and we hear of a star coming out of Jacob and a scepter rising out of Israel to crush Israel's foes, Balaam speaks unambiguously and in his own voice. Balaam has not sought omens as he did on the first three occasions. Nor is the LORD said to have put a word in his mouth, as he did on the first two occasions (23:5, 16). Nor is the spirit of God said to come upon him, as it did on the third occasion (24:2). This is Balaam, on his own initiative, angrily telling Balak that he will now "advise" him what Israel will do to Moab. Notably, the verb is *yā῾aṣ* in 24:14, rather than a technical term for prophesying. Given what we know of Balaam's character and the fact that the narrator does not have God involved in this last bit of spiteful "advising," the power of these curses may be considered suspect. Balaam has just spent considerable effort trying to curse Israel from three different locations, supported by elaborate sacrificial rituals at each of those locations, yet he was unable to perform what he wanted to perform. So these curses he spews at the end without God's intervention could well be taken as the choleric ravings of an impotent charlatan. The irony is sharp indeed: just when the implied audience might cling to these powerful curses on Israel's enemies as finally constituting an unambiguous blessing for God's people, they have to concede that they cannot rely on the unauthorized words of a powerless foreign diviner who has not, in this last instance, had any authorization by the God of Israel.

Thus on two different fronts, major ironies may be seen to pervade the entire story of Balaam and are not restricted to the satirical tale of Balaam and his donkey. First, the voice of Balaam is being represented narratologically as unreliable. Second, substantial ambiguities bedevil many key moments in the oracles that Balaam delivers. These ambiguities point to the way in which Balaam is trying to manipulate both God and Balak; more darkly, they may hint that God is in fact not blessing Israel in any straightforward way but rather warning Israel about the possibility of apostasy.

It remains now to touch briefly on the dramatic ironies of plot that infuse the broader storyline and characterization of Israel in Numbers. The implied audience has witnessed the drama of the potentially devastating cursing that Balak has so carefully arranged, with the intricate and tension-producing financial negotiations, three separate and massive sacrificial endeavors, and the emotional intensity of Balak's increasing frustration (24:10). But all of this drama goes completely unnoticed by the Israelites below. It is the definition of dramatic irony that some characters (and the audience) know more than do other characters, especially if the unaware characters are somehow at risk. This, then, is a major dramatic irony that skewers not Balak, and not Balaam, but the oblivious Israelites.

What might Israel's lack of discernment be meant to signify? The placement of the Balaam material immediately preceding Numbers 25 is an essential key to the larger plot. Consider the other thunderous dramatic irony that unfolds as the Israelites promptly proceed to have sex with Moabite women. The absence of any narratological bridge—there is no notice of time having passed or any journeying having been undertaken—underlines the close connection of Numbers 22–24 with Numbers 25 literarily. God has been working with a manipulative foreign diviner to protect Israel from Moab's aggression and to ensure that Israel becomes the most abundantly blessed of all nations. All of this has been going on, God's protection and blessing lavished upon the Israelites, and they simply ignore it, blundering on into the worst apostasy of their history besides the Golden Calf episode. This God who has so extravagantly blessed Israel and protected them from harm ends up having no choice but to slaughter 24,000 Israelites himself—or 24,001, if one counts the hapless Zimri, impaled in the act of intercourse by Phinehas, a man who apparently has no sense of irony at all.

A brief return to Micah 6:5 will support this reading. The prophet Micah is a master of artistic ambiguity, as I will argue in my study of

Micah 2:12–13 later in this chapter. Here, I would like to revisit the phrase "from Shittim to Gilgal" in Micah 6:5 as evidence that Micah sets up Balaam's blessing as positive precisely in order to highlight the irony of Israel's subsequent apostasy at Baal-Peor. According to many interpreters, the point of the place names in Micah 6:5 is that God led the Israelites "from Shittim to Gilgal," that is, across the Jordan River into the promised land of Canaan.[63] But I am not convinced that the "Shittim to Gilgal" allusion is a simple reference to a saving event in Israel's history with God. The clause is syntactically ambiguous—it states simply, "from Shittim to Gilgal," with no verb and no conjunction, leaving translators to supply context as best they can (hence "*what happened* from Shittim to Gilgal" in the New Revised Standard Version, with no annotation about having supplied this clarifying text; "*[Recall your passage]* from Shittim to Gilgal" in the Jewish Publication Society translation).

How does this reference fit in with what precedes it? The logic of the argument in Micah 6:3–4 would seem to run as follows. God has been unjustly ignored or disobeyed by Israel ("in what have I wearied you?"), given that God redeemed Israel from slavery in Egypt and provided Israel with leaders in Moses, Aaron, and Miriam; or perhaps the point is that they were intermediaries, prophetic and priestly. Balak wanted Balaam to curse Israel, but Balaam "answered him" that he could say only what the LORD put in his mouth. Thus this foreign seer had been obedient to God. The two place names that follow are notorious for Israelite apostasy. Shittim was the place at which the Israelites engaged in apostasy immediately following the Balaam story (Numbers 25). Gilgal was known to the prophet Hosea, a contemporary of Micah, as a site of abominable Israelite sinfulness: "every evil of theirs began at Gilgal; there I came to hate them," says God in Hosea 9:15 (the situation to which this alludes is uncertain). Also significant, Hosea 9:10–15 links Baal-Peor, and hence Shittim, with Gilgal in an artistic composition that begins with a poetic reference to God's deliverance of Israel but then moves to the ways in which Israel has spurned God's covenant.

Micah 6:3–5 offers precisely the same kind of rhetorical movement as we see in Hosea 9:10–15. Israel's failure to be obedient to the God who delivered them is, after all, the substance of the "controversy" that God is pressing against the people (Mic 6:2). Israel is to remember that despite all God has done for them, and despite the fact that even a foreign seer will bless Israel out of obedience to God, Israel has sinned again and again. The reference in Micah 6:5 to the *ṣidqôt* of the LORD may be translated either as "saving deeds" (cp. Judg 5:11, 1 Sam 12:7, Ps 103:6) or as the expectation of righteousness that the LORD has of his redeemed people (Ps 11:7, Isa 33:15). Both meanings may apply in this Micah passage: *ṣidqôt* may be evoking its full range, expressed in the relationship between God's deeds of salvation or vindication for Israel and Israel's appropriate covenantal response. In the next passage ("With what shall I come before the LORD?" . . . "He has told you, O mortal, what is good"), Israel is enjoined to do justice, to love mercy, and to walk humbly with God (Mic 6:6–8), underlining the human response required. For these reasons, it makes much better sense of the local context of Micah 6:3–5, as well as the larger literary context of the judgment that pervades all of Micah 6, to read "from Shittim to Gilgal" as a reference to sites where the people indulged in apostasy. Thus Micah connects the blessing of Balaam with the ironic disobedience of the people thereafter, in an inner-biblical reading that moves in the same direction as Numbers 22–25 does.

What is the ironic metanarrative of Numbers 22–25 that is created by the dynamic interplay among the hyperbolic "said"s and mercurial "unsaid"s here? One reading would go something like this. Israel is relying too smugly on the divine promise to Abram that the one who blesses Israel will be blessed and the one who curses Israel will be cursed (see the explicit allusion to Gen 12:3 in Balaam's third oracle, 24:9). God may allow himself to be manipulated by an avaricious, unreliable foreign seer in order to protect Israel from the enemies that threaten Israel all around—this even though Israel itself remains oblivious to the mortal danger that looms on all sides. But God is powerless to protect Israel *from himself* if the abundantly blessed Israel continues to pursue exogamous sex and idolatry.

Numbers 22–24 uses the heavily ironized figure of a foreign intermediary, a manipulated deity, and an oblivious Israel to underscore the point that Israel's blessings will not avail if Israel itself refuses to recognize what is at stake in Israelite relations with foreign nations, figured in sexualized terms as Israelite relations with Moabite women. This story should be lauded as an extraordinarily impressive product of ancient Israelite ironic art. We may be hereafter compelled to raise an eyebrow at asseverations that "nowhere else in the Old Testament is a non-Israelite seer viewed so favorably as in Numbers 22–24,"[64] that Balaam's oracles constitute "some of the most lofty prophetic utterances about Israel to be found in the Torah,"[65] and that "[t]hrough Balaam, God blesses Israel with accolades and promises unsurpassed in the entire Pentateuch."[66] Those readings are not entirely wrong. They are insightful and attentive to the text. But in my view, such readings are only partially right. They are attending only to the surface meaning, the "said," and what they miss in the silences and ambiguities of the text may be the most important point of all. The ironist responsible for the Balaam narrative has offered his audience extravagant hyperbole, razor-sharp satire, freighted silences, powerful ambiguities, and thunderous dramatic ironies toward the end of showing that Israel may be blessed and protected by God, but that is only the beginning of the truth about who Israel is and what Israel's destiny might be. Numbers 22–25 both obscures and reveals the veiled threat that faces an Israel unaware of the conditional nature of its own privileged status.[67]

The stakes are tremendously high. As Dennis T. Olson notes, the plague that kills the Israelites in Numbers 25 destroys the last remaining members of the original generation except for Caleb and Joshua (Num 26:63–65). The larger narrative of Numbers 22–25 can be seen to contain an artistically wrought and terrifying inclusio, with a concrete answer in Numbers 25 given to the rhetorical question back in Balaam's first oracle. "Who can count the dust of Jacob?" Apparently God can, literally as well as metaphorically, given the rendering of the precise figure of 24,000 Israelite dead after the divine plague. In the words of Olson, "the story of Balaam occupies a strategic position at the end of the first generation (chapter 25) and the genesis of a new generation (chapter 26.)"[68] The scribe who shaped Numbers 22–25 invites his audience to see that with abundant blessing comes inescapable accountability.

In diaspora, the threat of destruction from enemies without is more than matched by the community's proclivity for destruction from within. The hyperbolically blessed Israel ignores that ironic truth at its peril. Such is the conviction of the author of Numbers 22–25. A similar conviction is expressed in the discourse of the prophet to whom we turn next: a superb ironist, Amos of Tekoa.

Hermeneutics of De(con)struction: Amos as Samson *Redivivus*

Many interpreters have seen that the Book of Amos is brilliant at employing prophetic genres and conventional diction in unexpected ways that destabilize the confidence of his implied audience.[69] Amos opens with consummate irony, building momentum in a diatribe against foreign nations only to drive home an indictment of Judah and Israel (Amos 1–2) in what Alter has called a "rhetoric of entrapment."[70] Amos alternately lulls and confuses his audience with deceptively simple rhetorical questions ("Does a lion roar in the forest when it has no prey?" 3:4; "Does disaster befall a city if the LORD has not done it?" 3:6) that serve to ensnare and condemn the hearers.[71] Amos proffers a faux call to worship with biting sarcasm ("Come to Bethel—and transgress," 4:4),[72] and he skewers his audience with a proleptic ironic lament over a "dead" Israel whose doom is still approaching (5:1–3). According to Amos, the Day of the LORD will be a day of unexpected reversals that ironize its audience's hopes for redemption (5:18–20). Francis Landy finds irony in the timing of the locust plague at the start of the second growing season (7:1–2), irony in God's question "What do you see?" (7:8) to a prophet who can see only what God reveals, irony in Amaziah's accusation of corruption directed at the only one who in fact is free of such corruption (7:10), and irony in the vision of the basket of fruit that normally would represent thanksgiving for the produce of the land now symbolizing the land's destruction (8:1–3).[73] Scholars have noticed an abundance of ironies in the confrontation between Amos and Amaziah in Amos 7.[74] Paul R. Noble finds irony in Amaziah's forbidding Amos to prophesy in the royal sanctuary: "Amaziah offers what he considers to be a decisive reason why Amos cannot prophesy there, but in fact the double use of the root *mlk* to qualify the shrine at Bethel neatly encapsulates what, from the narrator's perspective, is fundamentally wrong with the place: because it is completely under the control of the monarchy, its affairs are conducted in accordance with the requirements of national politics rather than religious propriety."[75] The interjection "Silence!" in Amos 8:3 may be read ironically as a command of God to the corpses strewn about proleptically in the prophet's vision: since the people of Israel will be dead soon enough, they should keep silence now just as their corpses will be incapable of utterance.[76]

Other features of Amos's irony are worthy of mention as well. Especially noteworthy is Amos's use of ambiguity to increase suspense and entrap his audience. In one deft moment of ironic ambiguation, Amos presents a series of devastating events as the work of a God who had expected their ferocity to impel his people to return to him: "I gave you cleanness of teeth [i.e., famine] in all your cities . . . yet you did not return to me. . . . And I also withheld the rain from you. . . . I struck you with blight and mildew. . . . I sent among you a pestilence . . . yet you did not return to me," 4:6–11). These horrific signs of God's power were not sufficient to keep the Israelites sincere about obeying their God; but the sequence of narrated disasters is ironic in that the normal human response would be to flee from their cause, not submit to it. Because the Israelites did not return to God, God is now prepared to enact similar terrible punishments upon them. Thus because of their failure to reckon with God, the people will indeed be confronting their God after all: "Therefore thus I will (continue to) do to you, O Israel; consequently, it is indeed this that I will do to you: prepare to meet your God, O Israel!" (4:12).

There is yet another turn to this flashing blade. Amos here is reversing a Deuteronomistic tradition that suggests that God will hear the prayer of his people when they cry out in desperate straits of exactly this sort. The various punishments God has sent, per Amos 4 (famine, drought, blight, mildew, locust, pestilence, war), are named in almost the same order in Solomon's prayer in 1 Kings 8:35ff (drought, famine, pestilence, blight, mildew, locust, war).[77] Amos is likely drawing upon his audience's knowledge of (proto-)Deuteronomistic tradition here. But where the Deuteronomists insisted on the efficacy of repentance, Amos revoices the tradition ironically to make the point that the time for repentance is long gone.[78] As Shalom M. Paul notes, "Maledictions, whether in treaties, legal collections, boundary stones, or elsewhere, are always future oriented. . . . [Here,] the only results they may have had, ironically, was to lead the people to accelerate their [illegitimate] cultic activity. This series has been aptly and adeptly called both 'ein Parodie zur Heilsgeschichte' ('a parody on salvation history') . . . and an 'Unheilsgeschichte' (disaster history)."[79] Through its stubbornness, Israel has reaped more of these same devastating punishments, and the point of these punishments now will simply be Israel's destruction.

Or again, the Book of Amos positions three doxologies of praise to God the Creator (4:13, 5:8–9, 9:5–6) in a larger literary context in which the ironic intensity increases as the real purpose of the doxologies—heightening the imminence and inescapability of doom—becomes clearer.[80] Amos's implied audience is put in the untenable position of needing to acknowledge the praiseworthy power of a Creator who comes to destroy them. And finally, M. Daniel Carroll R., among others, notes Amos's ironizing of Israel's cult traditions: "Irony reigns, as cultic celebrations mask the harsh facts of national failures. . . . The rulers and the governed share the Yahwistic faith . . . as all move about in a world that claims YHWH but does not truly meet him at the sanctuaries."[81] The list of local ironies in Amos is lengthy indeed.

Central to Amos's hermeneutical strategy is a focus on the Exodus traditions as a primary cultural site for Amos's attack on the false confidence of his audience.[82] Amos subverts Exodus traditions in a variety of interrelated rhetorical moves that undermine any naïve sense of Israel's election. The ways in which Amos alludes to the ancient deliverance from Egypt are crafted to further the larger purpose of the Book of Amos: namely, to strike into the hearts of his audience a fear so compelling that they will be forced to repent, to "seek God and live" (5:4; cp. 5:14). When Amos cites the Exodus, his diction focuses not on the traditional images of God's love for Israel, his having delivered them from oppression, or his tender care for them in the wilderness, as so many inner-biblical allusions to the Exodus do. Amos focuses, first, on the strength of the Canaanite forces defeated by God as a way of underlining the indomitable power of God as divine warrior: "I destroyed the Amorite before them, whose height was like the height of cedars, and who was as strong as the oaks; I destroyed his fruit above and his roots

beneath" (2:9). Next, Amos alludes to the deliverance from Egypt as fo-
rensic evidence of Israel's greater accountability for sin: "Hear this word
that the LORD has spoken against you, O Israel, against the whole family
that I brought up out of the land of Egypt: You only have I known of all
the families of the earth; therefore I will punish you for all your iniqui-
ties" (3:1–2). Israel alone is accountable in this unique way—accountable to a deity whose power to destroy has just been made abundantly
clear. The foundational event that constituted Israel as the LORD's own
people has become a cause not for rejoicing but for sheer terror.

In 5:17 and 8:2, the LORD proclaims imminent judgment against Israel: "In all the vineyards there will be wailing, for I will pass through
the midst of them [to destroy]," and "The end has come upon my people
Israel; I will never again pass them by [in the sense of sparing them from
punishment]."[83] In both passages, the verb used is the same verb as that
employed in Exodus 12:12 to describe the LORD's passing through to
strike down the firstborn of Egypt. Here is a reversal of the security Israel enjoyed during the ancient first Passover of the angel of death in
Egypt. A few verses further on, Amos presses the point home, alluding
obliquely to two of the plagues that had been visited upon Egypt in the
time of the Exodus (the plague of darkness and the death of the firstborn males) as now looming for Israel (8:9–10).

Amos extends his ironizing of the Exodus to include the time of the
wilderness wandering. In Amos 8:11–12, the LORD says, "I will send a
famine on the land, not a famine of bread or a thirst for water, but of
hearing the words of the LORD. They shall wander from sea to sea and
from north to east; they shall run to and fro, seeking the word of the
LORD, but they shall not find it." This is deeply ironic coming from a supposed prophet, because the prophets are those who supply the people
with the word of the LORD in times of judgment. Since Amos declines
the mantle of prophet (7:14, on which, more below), he can deliver this
oracle with no self-consciousness and with a straight face. The people
will wander in search of the sustenance that they need: neither food nor
water, but the word of the LORD. Hans Walter Wolff points out that the
verb used for this wandering in 8:12, *šûṭ*, occurs also to describe the wandering of the ancient Israelites searching for manna in the wilderness of
Sinai (Num 11:8).[84] In that first wilderness journey, they found the word
of the LORD inscribed on stone tablets. In these latter days they have
disregarded God's word too often, so they will be left to wander. The
redemption Israel enjoyed in that first Exodus is over for good.

In his most devastating ironic twist, Amos finally refers to the Exodus itself as just one of a number of saving acts the LORD has performed
on behalf of various peoples: "Did I not bring Israel up from the land of

Egypt, and the Philistines from Caphtor, and the Arameans from Kir?" (9:7). This unthinkable statement is Amos's coup de grâce: even that first Exodus meant little. The glorious Exodus, the essential hallmark of identity for ancient Israel and the foundation of her story of redemption, is just another event in the history of the nations of the earth. The LORD delivers all and judges all. Divine deliverance implies no special status on the part of the rescued, all of Israel's ancient traditions to the contrary notwithstanding. With this, Amos destroys Israel's last shred of confidence in her enduring identity as God's chosen people.

Israel can have no answer to this final blow.[85] This last word of judgment deprivileging Israel among the nations creates an inclusio structure with the oracles against foreign nations at the beginning of the book, the rhetorical thrust of which was, similarly, to frame Israel's and Judah's indictments for sin in the larger context of the profane and sinful behavior of other nations. Israel languishes among the nations, in the view of God. Israel is judged just as they are, and they had been delivered from oppression as Israel once was. No privileged metanarrative is left. Israel must cower, terrified, in a position from which it can only seek God and live. Nothing else will save.

What kind of prophecy is this? Surely not the traditional prophecy that predictably calls Israel back to its touchstones of cultural security— but this will not surprise the reader who remembers that Amos is, after all, not a prophet. The degree to which Amos is *not* a prophet needs now to be explored. In what follows, I will analyze ways in which allusions to the Philistines, oblique attacks on the Davidic traditions, and the representation of Amos as a charismatic judge figure—specifically, as Samson *redivivus*—all work together semantically to contest Israel's self-understanding, reframing this people as a profane nation deserving of destruction. These three rhetorical aspects of the Book of Amos (allusiveness to the Philistines, critique of David traditions, and representation of Amos as a type of Samson) will be taken in turn.

First, consider that in Amos, the Philistines are mentioned in instances that seem marked for special notice. The initial oracle against Philistia (1:6–8) runs much as do Amos's other oracles against foreign nations. But shortly thereafter, a summons to Ashdod and Egypt as witnesses against Samaria shifts the rhetorical balance in an unexpected direction (3:9).[86] Why would these despised enemies, one of which has already been itself judged in Amos 1, be accorded the (rhetorical) power of judgment over Israel? Pragmatic explanations, while reasonable enough,[87] fail to satisfy the interpreter seeking to explain the surprise of this move. There is an ambiguity within the syntax of the call to witness that bears examination. The preposition ʿal used in the command, "Proclaim upon the ramparts of Ashdod and upon the ramparts of the land of Egypt,"[88] could be read as either "upon" (the translation I prefer) or "against." A declaration of judgment against Ashdod and Egypt would be expected by the implied audience. But Amos has set up an incisive irony in the earlier verses of Amos 3: Israel's chosenness renders it all the more accountable to divine judgment, and indeed, per Amos the word of the roaring Lion is so compelling that virtually anyone can and must prophesy when that word encounters them. The following verb in verse 9, "proclaim," is a plural imperative: the addressee cannot be Amos. It must be the denizens of fortified cities in Ashdod and Egypt, who are being mustered as the LORD's prophets against Israel itself. Rather than constituting the target of divine wrath as the audience would expect, Ashdod and Egypt are to testify to the rightness of God's judgment against the oppression happening in northern Israel. These two intractable enemies, perhaps evoking the martial spectrum from local hostilities to international warfare, are called to the LORD's side against Israel. The double-edged irony here is palpable. The sinfulness of these paradigmatic enemies renders them expertly capable of judging that quality in the LORD's own people; there could be no more apt judge of the excesses of Israel than these despised "Others" who have themselves just been indicted.[89]

The mustering of Philistia and Egypt against Israel is part of Amos's broader reversal of traditions of trust in David and the Exodus traditions.[90] Amos is blurring the line between insider and outsider. Even nations themselves worthy of obliteration can look with horror on the sinfulness of the northern kingdom of Israel. The pairing of Ashdod and Egypt functions as a word trap that begins to prepare the audience for Amos's larger-scale reversals. By the time the Book of Amos concludes, Amos will have attacked Israel's confidence in the Davidic line (see esp. 6:5, treated below), reversed the significance of the Exodus in his people's heritage, and, through his utterances, changed the implied audience into "Philistines" themselves. The unusual pairing of Ashdod and Egypt in this call to witness therefore should be taken seriously as dramatizing the major sites of ironic dislocation in Israel's self-understanding.

Amos's use of the Philistines as a foil for Israel continues in 6:2, where he mentions "Gath of the Philistines" in a sarcastic rhetorical question that suggests Israel has no status or power different from that of defeated enemy cities: "Are you better than these kingdoms?" Here the force of that blurring of identity is made explicit: Israel is no better than the Philistines. The fate suffered by those of Gath will be the fate of the indolent sinners sprawled on their couches in Zion and in Samaria. "Gath of the Philistines" is named as the culmination of a list of places whose identity—for purposes of escaping divine punishment—is virtually indistinguishable from that of Israel. And the final note of judgment struck in the Book of Amos provides the culmination of the stunning reversals worked by Amos throughout the book. A comparison of Israel with the Philistines and the Arameans as peoples whom the LORD has (also) delivered from oppression renders virtually meaningless Israel's own redemption from Egypt as any evidence of Israel's special status. These are not random foreign nations but, in fact, those whose comparison with Israel would have been the most offensive to Amos's implied audience.[91] If the beginning of the Book of Amos may be taken to govern the entire book, as some have suggested, then the chiastic inclusio with Aram + Philistia as the first two nations mentioned in Amos 1 and Philistia + Aram in 9:7 shows literary-structural intentionality about establishing a connection between the oracles against the nations at the beginning and the minimizing of the Exodus at the end.

Second, consider the sharp critique leveled by Amos against the ancient Davidic traditions. The Book of Amos signals its interest in David traditions directly in two places (6:5 and 9:11) and in a number of places more obliquely, particularly with subtle reference to a united Israel and Judah that harks back to the time of the united monarchy under David and Solomon. For example, it has been suggested by Andersen and Freedman that the seven nations indicted in the OAN in Amos 1–2 represent a united Israel at the height of its political power under David and Solomon, the territories either governed directly by those monarchs or under the sway of them.[92] One might consider the fact that in the oracle in Amos 6:11 about breaking the "little house" into "bits," the noun for "bits," *bĕqi'îm*, occurs elsewhere only at Isaiah 22:9 in a description of the breaches in the city of David. That scathing oracle of judgment may be targeting not just social power but dynastic arrogance. In addition to these potential references to Davidic traditions, there are two overt references to David. In 6:5, the elite of Zion and Samaria are indicted for their uncaring frivolity. In this context David is cited neither for his kingly power nor for his faithfulness to God, but as a musician whose lyrical improvisations show his callousness in the face of the disaster befalling his people. And in 9:11, an unexpected oracle of restoration begins with the image of the fallen "booth of David" being raised up by God. Here we have an apparent note of restoration that draws on the memory of David. But below, I will argue that this is in fact a feint toward restoration that is subverted in the next line, 9:12. It is important to note that even in a "straight" reading of 9:11, there is no reference to the restoration of a Davidic ruler as such. Even in these words of hope, the Book of Amos uses the "booth of David" image as a representation of defeat and abandonment. In the Book of Amos, then, "David" serves to evoke neither chosenness nor royal power but callousness and ignominious defeat. This David is not the hero who trusted in God and defeated the Philistines. The Book of Amos has taken away David as a source of cultural and theological confidence for the implied audience.

As our third window into the ironies of the Book of Amos, we turn to the book's representation of Amos himself. The use of irony in his oracular sayings exemplifies one facet of the persona of Amos as a speaker of judgment. But more than that, the role of Amos is itself portrayed in ironizing fashion, deconstructing the implied audience's expectations of what a prophet is supposed to do in calling Israel back to its own religio-cultural roots. Amos rereads formal tropes central to the cultural identity of his Israelite audience in order to enact his devastating message of judgment. Irony and sarcasm are consistently employed in Amos to undermine the foundational Israelite election traditions on which his implied audience relies in their understanding of their identity as a people chosen and protected by God. Even the notion of justice is not sacrosanct. Amos pries it out of the fingers of his audience and uses it against them: their abundance of festivals, solemn assemblies, offerings, and music will be met by God's own enduring torrent of justice and righteousness, a metaphorical flash flood of divine reckoning that will sweep away everything in its path (Amos 5:24).[93] That the figure of the prophet employs irony in so many different ways raises a crucial question about who Amos is in the book. How is his audience, misled and skewered by sarcasm and duped by irony, meant to understand the persona of the prophet himself?

Amos performs a scathing criticism of audience expectations generally on this point, firmly resisting domestication of his role as "prophet" by the implied audience. The Book of Amos offers an ironic portrayal of the prophet painted in terms reminiscent of one of Israel's early judges in the period of the monarchy, Samson. The persona of Amos is that of a hermeneut of Israel's own sacred traditions who has unexpectedly turned against Israel and who treats Israel as one of the foreign nations. The prophetic task in the Book of Amos becomes to divide the implied audience against itself and persuade it to choose a newly faithful identity over against its own history of misguided trust in tradition. For the Book of Amos, the question of intended audience is complicated. Those skewered by the prophet's irony—the "cows of Bashan," those who falsify trade balances, and so on—are the victims of the irony proper and are fated for complete and utter destruction. Who then is to learn from the ironic portrayal of their fate? The true audience: an implied audience constructed as more competent, those who can appreciate the sophistication of Amos's mockery and infer the appropriate lesson from it.[94] Building on the work of Hans Walter Wolff, Möller sees the construction of Amos's persona as "debating prophet" (one shown to be arguing with his audience to no avail) to be central to the rhetorical strategy of the Book of Amos.[95] This strategy comes into clearer focus when we consider that the persona of Amos as judge—and particularly, as Samson *redivivus*—is deployed in the book to bring to ruin the "Philistinized" implied audience, clearing a cultural space for new understandings of Israelite identity to emerge.

The Book of Amos invites its audience to understand Amos as a hermeneutical Samson *redivivus* by illustrating Amos's coherent deconstructive hermeneutic being applied to Israelite traditions and by showing Amos's refusal of the category of prophet as a descriptor of himself. The representation of Amos as deconstructive hermeneut, when read against the backdrop of prophetic vocations in the corpus of the Latter Prophets, is created by means of consistent moments of incongruity in the textual representation of Amos's vocation as (putative) prophet. Immediately as the book opens, Amos is identified not as a prophet but simply as one "among the shepherds" (1:1). There is no inaugural mention of the LORD speaking through or to Amos, as in Hosea (Hos 1:1). There is no mention of the word of the LORD coming to Amos, as in other prophetic books.[96] There is no naming of Amos as seer,[97] even though Amos has visions later in the book. In the beginning of the book we encounter none of the literary means of authorization of the prophetic role that we see, in one form or another, in every other book of the Latter Prophets. Indeed, one of the first indictments of the people of Israel in the Book of Amos is precisely that they have forbidden the prophets to prophesy (2:12). Amos cannot be a prophet for this people.

By what authority, then, does this shepherd (or pastoral overseer)[98] speak? The implied audience ventures further into the discourse of Amos uncertain of the speaker's legitimacy and wary of his claim on them. The audience is compelled to acknowledge, at least provisionally, the thunderous voice of the LORD roaring from Zion without understanding the credentials of the one who announces God and without knowing how to evaluate their own relationship to him.

The figure of Amos comes to the fore briefly in 5:1, in his sardonic invitation, "Hear this word that I take up over you in lamentation, O house of Israel," a line in which the Hebrew preposition "over" (*ʿal*) may also be read as "against." Amos's ambiguity here, as elsewhere, veils an adversarial irony: this prophet who seems to be mourning the destruction of his people is in fact pronouncing it with relish.

The disorientation of the audience regarding Amos's role continues in Amos 7. Amos refuses the intercessory role modeled by paradigmatic prophet Moses on behalf of Israel in the Exodus and in the wilderness. Amos sees visions of two catastrophic events looming as enactments of divine judgment (locusts and cosmic fire, 7:1–6), and in apparent good intercessory fashion, he pleads with God and successfully forestalls them. Are we to read those moments of effective intercession "straight," as earnest on the part of Amos himself? Scholars who read a bona fide progression in Amos's attitude from mercy to judgment do read them that way.[99] But irony beckons from the shadows of the unspoken, here as elsewhere in this thoroughly sarcastic book. In my view, the entire sequence is yet another rhetorical trap, another way station on Israel's journey to destruction. A major disjuncture is readily perceptible in what Amos says of Israel here and what he has said elsewhere in the book. His piteous query, "How can Jacob stand? For he is so small" (7:2, 5), stands in blatant contradiction to Amos's indictment of Israel for its vaunted strength (in sin), its callousness and indifference to others' vulnerability, and its pride (2:7, 13–16; 3:10–11; 4:1; 5:12; 6:4–8, 13). Particularly relevant is the pronouncement that the LORD "abhor(s) the pride of Jacob and hate(s) his strongholds" (6:8) and the instance in which Israel is condemned for arrogant boasting in its own strength (6:13), these coming immediately prior to the opening of the visions in Amos 7. Jacob is not small. Jacob has just been excoriated precisely for boasting in its power to oppress and to withstand retribution. But the lures of the false "said" are potent indeed: Amos can save us, the implied audience thinks, seduced into clinging to what seems like a traditional and reliable promise in this highly untraditional book. But a third time Amos is shown an image of imminent judgment: the LORD positioning himself in the midst of his people for judgment.[100] And this time, in a thunderous silence, Amos simply does not intercede. Israel has no intercessor in Amos after all. The rhetorical emptiness of the preceding intercessions becomes clear: Amos had never intended to save Israel from the wrath of its God.

The horror of that realization would be enough, but there is more. This material serves as narratological preparation for a more explicit reconfiguring of Amos's identity in the rest of the chapter. Amaziah characterizes Amos as a "seer" (7:12), but even though Amos has just seen three visions, he nevertheless contests the suggestion that his vocation may be understood in affiliation with that of formal prophets (7:14). Instead, Amos narrates a story of being taken by the LORD from caring for flocks of sheep in order to prophesy. Amos insists that he, as a non-prophet, will not be domesticated or constrained by one such as Amaziah: he will speak the word of the LORD, a word of wholesale judgment on the house of Jeroboam.

Amos's refusal of definitions here ("I am neither a prophet nor a prophet's son") has been read by some as indicating simply that he was not born into the professional guild of prophets or that he prefers not to be associated with the mercenary motives of prophets who work for hire. But in this refusal of identity we may detect further resonances of Amos's identity as Samson *redivivus*, for Samson's character is fractured and full of aporias as well. Dennis T. Olson has written that in Judges, "Ironies abound. . . . Characters shimmer with dissonant identities. . . . Samson is a judge who does not lead, a Nazirite who breaks all Nazirite vows, a lover of Philistines who kills them."[101] Samson was never what he seemed to be, and neither is Amos. Other textual "refusals" in the Book of Amos point further toward a purposeful rejection of what the label "prophet" might represent. Amos does not call Israel back to its ancient traditions but instead uses those traditions to indict Israel all the more (3:1–2; 9:7). Amos feints toward intercession but finally stands silent when Israel needs an intermediary to stave off disaster. Amos emphatically rejects identification as a prophet, yet he has given terrifying oracles concerning Israel and has uttered judgment against the reigning Israelite king. The incongruence between Amos's claim and Amos's performative utterances, if taken seriously, deconstructs the persona of Amos as traditional prophet.

This hermeneutical pattern of refusal opens up a rhetorical space in which emerge other possibilities for imagining Amos's agency.[102] If Amos is no prophet, what is it that the figure of Amos is doing qua (non) prophet? Amos pronounces judgment on Israel's own understanding of itself, battling his audience's misguided presuppositions and complacency as fiercely as any warrior might attack an enemy on the battlefield. An image closely following his refusal of prophetic identity in Amos 7 clarifies the matter. In Amos 9, Amos is commanded to shake the pillars of the Temple until they shatter on the heads of all the people. Interpreters have occasionally noticed that this image is evocative of Samson,[103] and this reading should be given more attention than it has received in Amos scholarship. Just as Samson brought down the temple of Dagon on the heads of the Philistines, killing more in his own death than he ever had in his lifetime of judgeship, so Amos is being commanded to bring down the rhetorical house on the heads of his own people—on the heads of the implied audience that has been too confident about its privileged status as God's people.[104]

In this regard, we may revisit the displacement of the oracles against foreign nations to the beginning of the Book of Amos. Israel—a constructed "Israel" that relies on a particular understanding of itself—is to be discomfited along with her local enemies. The Book of Amos opens with judgment pronounced on Israel's enemies, but as the logic of the book unfolds, it becomes clear that Israel has been her own worst enemy. This echoes with artistic precision the metanarratological plot that unfolds within the Book of Judges. Judges begins with the narration of Israel's defeat of various enemies, but the plot of the book spirals inexorably toward the moral implosion of Israel due to its own callousness and lack of care for the weak. In Judges, Israel is its own worst enemy as well, something that becomes obvious to the reader who reaches the atrocities of Judges 19–21. As a judge of old, a Samson *redivivus,* Amos is being raised up to defeat this inadequately conceived "Israel" precisely in order to save his people from destroying themselves.

Ehud Ben Zvi has argued that the ideal reader for prophetic works in the Hebrew Bible is a highly competent "rereader" who has pored over the biblical material and become steeped in its idioms and intertextual allusions.[105] We may assume that the implied audience of Amos is not meant to read the Book of Amos only once. The competent implied audience is to "reread" the Book of Amos knowing that Amos is no prophet, yet somehow he has been raised up by God to judge a faulty construction of "Israel." The location of the oracles against the nations at the beginning of the book is a decoy, an ironic gesture, just as the analogous move is a decoy in the Book of Judges. Defeat of external enemies is not the ultimate horizon of Amos's vision but, rather, leads inexorably to the defeat of Israel and Judah themselves.

What happens when we reread the book in light of the proposal that the persona of Amos is being figured as a hermeneutical Samson *redivivus?* A brief exercise in rereading will demonstrate that the perception of literary irony can often work backward from the decisive moment of recognition, the moment when the reader realizes that too many moments of incongruity have piled up, too many hyperbolic characterizations have been encountered, or too many inaccurate representations have come from the narrator for the reader to continue with a "straight" reading. As Booth says, the reader experiences a moment of resistance and will go "thus far, and no farther."[106] The reader of Amos encounters textual signals throughout the book that build their influence subtly until the moment when the reader encounters both the image of a man shattering a temple on the heads of people, and the word *caphtor* (9:1, 7), which is a homonym that can mean both "capital(s)" (in the sense of the tops of pillars or columns) and "Caphtor," the Philistine city. At this point, the incongruity and hyperbole of the image of destruction become clear in light of the larger web of allusions and overt references to the Philistines in the Book of Amos. The irony of Amos's positioning as de(con)structive hermeneut emerges. Israel is no different from the Philistines, and Amos, a new Samson, is wreaking destruction on their idolatrous and barbaric heads.

Rereading, we see more. Remember that at the very opening of the book, the reader is greeted by the image of God "roaring" from Zion, an image that some scholars have argued governs all of the oracles in the Book of Amos.[107] Alert to potential allusions to Samson, the rereader recalls that in the first story of the life of Samson, a young lion comes "roaring to meet" Samson (Judges 14) and he tears it apart with his bare hands. Now, the roaring God of Amos 1:2 is the same deity of whom Amos says in

4:12, "Prepare to meet your God, O Israel!" These two words find resonance in both books: Judges 14:5, "roaring to meet him," *šō'ēg liqrā'tô*,
echoes in the description of a God who from Zion "roars" (*yišʾāg*, Amos
1:2), and whom Israel must prepare to meet (*liqra't*, Amos 4:12). Who will
save Israel from this roaring lion? The intertextual suggestion is clear:
only a Samson could. Amos as Samson *redivivus* is the only one standing
between his people and the roaring God of judgment.

Continuing to reread with the traditional figure of Samson as intertext,
the reader remembers that the enemies of Samson, the Philistines, occupy
an unusually prominent place in the Book of Amos. In Amos 6, David is
depicted not as the warrior who killed Goliath, the Philistine giant from
Gath, but instead as one who sang "idle songs" and improvised on musical
instruments (6:5). That David tradition is mustered here in a context that
skews its valence, making the royal warrior seem useless at best and quite
possibly effeminized and ineffectual at worst. The ironic point is devastating: as the Philistines were destroyed, so Israel shall be destroyed.

The rereader may also notice an oblique allusiveness in the collocation
of sweetness and death in Amos 8, reminiscent of Samson's exploits with
the lion in Judges 14. The vision of summer fruit in Amos 8 brings into interpretive tension two incongruous images: sweet fruit and horrific death.[108]
Yvonne Sherwood has underlined the hermeneutical tensions generated
by the vision's metaphorical vehicle and its tenor, writing, "no discourse of
naturalness can ease the friction of the union between summer fruit and
mass carnage."[109] Indeed; and this collocation of edible sweetness and
death is highly anomalous for the Hebrew Bible. Sherwood suggests here a
reference to the Garden of Eden, with its death-signifying fruit,[110] and
given the significant number of ancient Israelite traditions to which Amos
alludes and which the book subverts, that story may belong on the list of
intertexts. But there is also a notable deep-structure similarity here with
Judges 14, within the semantic web of allusions to Samson. In that chapter,
Samson goes to the Philistines to seek a wife. He rips the roaring lion apart
with his bare hands, as we have said, and leaves the animal's carcass lying in
the road. Upon returning, Samson notices that bees have made a hive in
the carcass of the lion. Scooping honey out of the rotting carcass, he continues his journey, eating the honey dripping from his gory, defiled hands.
Sweetness out of death: Samson later alludes to this anomaly in his riddle at
his wedding feast. His riddle about something to eat coming from the eater
is a juxtaposition so incongruous that his Philistine audience cannot solve
it. Similarly, Amos, our hermeneutical Samson, sees his God, who is like a
roaring lion poised to devour his people, offer the illusion of a basket of
sweet fruit at a time of festivity (harvest).[111] But in reality the image signifies
carnage. Samson kills thirty men after the wedding feast (Judg 14:19). At

the LORD's "harvest" feast in Amos 8, too, comes the slaughter of people whose corpses will be left lying in the road (Amos 8:3).

Keeping the Philistines in mind and training the gaze on Amos 9, the rereader finds that the persona of Amos comes into full and terrifying focus. Amos is commanded to wield his rhetoric against the pillars of Israelite election traditions, concretized here in words and images that are explicitly evocative of Samson's pulling down the Philistine temple upon himself and his captors: "Strike the capitals until the thresholds shake, and shatter them on the heads of all of them" (9:1).[112] The final thrust of this rapier-sharp ironic posture toward Israel's old traditions comes in 9:7: even in its most defining moment of deliverance, Israel should be regarded as no better than the Philistines or the Arameans.

Is the rhetorical point of this allusiveness only that Israel will suffer destruction? I suggest that the irony works to undermine what is false in order to clear a space in the cultural imaginations of the implied readers for what is true. Amos is saving his people with this act of heroism. Here, the audience is required to deconstruct and reconstruct on two distinct levels. In the figure of Amos, the characterization of Samson as destroyer (of the Philistines) and the characterization of Samson as deliverer (of the Israelites) converge. What changes in the performance of this irony? Not Amos, but the audience. Israel has been required to rework its own understanding of its beliefs and identity in light of Amos's ruthless ironizing of their foundational traditions.

Israel is accorded a measure of grace in the last verses of the Book of Amos. The final interpretive task for the rereader alert to irony is to determine two things: first, where the bitterly sarcastic judgment material stops and the lyrical restoration material begins; and second, how to read these two possibilities, judgment and promise, together. Encountering the last eight verses of the book, the audience is left awash in ambiguity. Verse 8 suggests that the eyes of God are fixed upon a kingdom of miscreants for judgment and it shall be utterly destroyed. How, then, to read the parenthetical remark, "except that I will not utterly destroy the house of Jacob, says the LORD" (9:8)? By the lights of traditional redaction criticism, this phrase is an obvious later addition. But it may be read in literary terms as a recognition of the multiple implied audiences of the book. The Israel that was so sinful, so insensible of God's will, cannot escape the devastating scrutiny of a righteous God, but some will yet stand. The following verse specifies who will not escape: those who believe that no harm can possibly come to them. The only path toward survival is to acknowledge the power of God to destroy and to refrain from offering excuses by means of Israel's election traditions.

On that day of judgment, then (9:11), God will raise up the fallen "booth of David," that is, shamed and defeated Davidic tradition. But to what purpose? Verse 12 is wholly ambiguous syntactically. The plural verb, *yîrešû*, "they will (dis)possess," does require a plural subject, and there is none specified if we are looking to an antecedent "Israel" as the unexpressed subject. But there is a compound plural subject ready to hand in verse 12, if the reader sets aside the preconception that God's raising up of the booth of David is non-ironic, earnest restoration. The plural subject is "Edom and all the nations that are called by my name."[113] On this reading, the verse would be suggesting with brutal sarcasm that God will raise up the fallen booth of David as an ironic feint toward restoration, just so that Israel's enemies would have one final chance to attack and dispossess Israel. Such a proposal might surprise the reader accustomed to encountering earnest restoration material at the ends of prophetic books (cf. Ezekiel 40–48, Hosea 14, Joel 3:16–21, Obadiah 21, Mic 7:18–20, Hab 3:17–19, and Zeph 3:9–20). Indeed, it might be surprising not only for its subversion of this minor pattern of promise oracles concluding prophetic books, but also because of the implied good news that it constitutes for Edom and the rest of the nations "called by YHWH's name." But such a surprise would be entirely in keeping with the rhetorics of reversal that we have seen throughout the Book of Amos.

Linville suggests that the ambiguity of the repeated refrain "I will not cause it/him to return" in Amos 1–2 may sharpen the rhetorical trap sprung on the Israelite audience there, refusing the notion of a rapprochement between Israel and her God and suggesting that this could constitute a threat to reconstitute the foreign nations after their own punishment. Linville writes:

Having numerous options for what "it" might be (typically regarded as "the punishment" or the "decree of punishment") only leads to the trap of having ruled out any hope for the expression indicating a possible reconciliation between Israel and YHWH. For instance, one might read "Shall I not bring him (collective singular referring to the accused nations) back?" which in six cases might be a rather sarcastic question, but in the last two cases challenges the reader's sense of YHWH's ultimate reconciliation with his people predicted in Amos 9,11–15.[114]

Building on Linville's insight but taking it in a slightly different direction, I would argue that this possible reading ("Shall I not restore him/them?") in the intentionally ambiguous Amos 1–2 may confirm the reading of 9:12 as empowering Edom and all the nations that are called by the LORD's name. The elegance of the chiastic ironic structure would reveal a level of artistry beyond what has traditionally been appreciated in the structure of the Book of Amos. In Amos 1–2, devastating judgment against Israel's enemies is subverted by an ambiguous threat that turns out to be an ironic promise to Israel's enemies. Correspondingly, in Amos 9:11–12, a beautiful promise to Israel turns out to be subverted by an ambiguous threat that constitutes a promise of restoration for Israel's enemies.

This would be an unexpected move, for Amos to offer an oracle of restoration to Edom and other foreign nations. One might object that this borders on an unthinkable manipulation of Israelite prophetic tradition. But remember that this is the Book of Amos. Should such an interpretive move qualify as unexpected given the ruthless judgment material that immediately precedes it in all of Amos 9, and given that the point has been made in numerous different ways that there is no possible escape for any remnant, no safety for refugees of any sort? Further, the way in which Amos has structured 9:10 moves toward further comeuppance of those sinful rebels who have dared to continue to say, "Evil shall not overtake or meet us." Carroll R. has rightly characterized that "quote of proud defiance" in verse 10b as "absurd and destructive in context," indeed, as ironic in the extreme because their "ridiculousness" flies in the face of all the rhetoric of Amos aimed at persuading Israel of God's power for judgment.[115] Amos must respond to this brazen quotation. Although verse 10a already makes the point that those speakers will die by the sword, without further rhetorical rebuke these sinful speakers would be allowed to have the "last word." They would hear (rhetorically speaking) their sinful and misguided discourse met by beautiful words of restoration in 9:11–12, something that would in fact serve to confirm their misguided claims of security. Amos is far too skilled a rhetorician for that. He uses his audience's covert expectations once again to savage their hope. We have seen precisely this hermeneutic at work before, namely, in the way in which Israel's arrogant boasting, directly quoted in 6:13, is followed by a series of "faux promise" texts in 7:1–9. Just so, the arrogant quoted discourse of Israel in 9:10b sets up a response from Amos that is at first apparently irenic but soon becomes a shocking pronouncement of judgment. Amos as a deconstructive hermeneut is nothing if not consistent.

It is characteristic of Amos's discourse to note a special feature or aspect of Israel's election tradition precisely to take away its power, using it to undermine Israel's confidence and hold Israel all the more accountable to God's judgment. The reader is reminded of Amos's uncompromising position on the status of the "remnant" earlier in the book and immediately before this passage. In 3:12 we see Amos's savage attack on the notion that a remnant in Samaria will survive: theirs will be the sort of "rescue" in which a shepherd, powerless to save, can only retrieve mutilated body parts from the mouth of the avenging Lion. And in 9:8–10, we have just seen Amos toying with his audience's hope for a remnant as a predator might toy with prey before devouring it. "I will destroy the sinful kingdom from the face of the earth," says the God of Amos, "except"—(false) hope is kept alive for one last moment, with brutal ironic intent—"except that I will not utterly destroy." God goes on to confirm that he plans to shake the house of Israel as with a sieve, and no single person shall escape—telegraphing the true intent of his deceptive gesture toward saving a remnant. No one will escape. God will at first refrain from utterly destroying, but only so that destruction may finally be all the more complete. God will raise up the booth of David as an ironic gesture of faux compassion, precisely so that Israel's enemies may finally dispossess the remnant of Israel that had thought it could escape God's wrath.

The final three verses of the Book of Amos may be read as an earnest proclamation of restoration. While one may see ambiguity in the initial images, I do not see irony there. The elusive verse 13 begins on a distinctly ominous note, "The time is surely coming, says the LORD," a formula that may be read as an introduction to eschatological judgment, as Amos 8:11 makes abundantly clear. As the verse unfolds, the audience must ask whether it is a good thing that the one who plows will overtake the one who reaps and the treader of grapes will overtake the one who sows seed. Is this an image of abundance, of the crop being so bountiful that the harvesting of one will take a long time and run into the sowing time for the next crop? Another possibility would be that the one who plows will come from behind and plow under (i.e., ruin) the harvest, and the treader of grapes will stomp on the seed in the ground, denying it the necessary aerated soil. The implied audience of the Book of Amos has been rendered unable to trust any images of beauty and abundance so far, so the audience of Amos will be tense, braced for the sort of devastating reversal that has come in every other rhetorical move that has been made throughout the discourse of this deconstructive prophet. But the last part of the verse, about mountains and hills dripping with wine, seems to be a straightforward image of bounty, and the final two verses of the Book of Amos seem unambiguously to be full of promise. The traumatized audience that has survived Amos's rhetoric to this point may finally cling, trembling, to these words of hope. But these words could have come only here at the end, unlike in Jeremiah, where the Book of Consolation is located in the middle of the prophetic book, and unlike in Isaiah, where words of promise and words of threat are intermingled until the last terrifying words of the book. In Amos, hope must come last because the restoration of which these verses speak is

wholly dependent upon the prior deconstruction of Israel's sinful ways
and false reliance on her foundational traditions.

It is plausible that the many scholars are correct who attribute these
last verses to a later redactorial hand. Yet we may also read this last note of
hope as a final gesture fully consonant with Amos's methodology: destabilizing an audience that has learned not to trust its own safety in the presence of the God who roars from Zion. The disjuncture between 9:13–15
and the rest of the Book of Amos produces a "third meaning," an ironized
space in which the reader's anxiety about being misled is a necessary part
of the signifying relationship between audience and text. If the audience
has truly learned who the God of Amos is, the audience knows that even
its most powerful traditions of promise may be upended in a moment.
Amos's thoroughgoing irony and sarcasm in the preceding chapters have
heightened his audience's alertness to duplicity, to doublespeak that traps
them. Because this is so, even beautiful words of promise can no longer be
taken naïvely at face value in the rhetoric of Amos. This audience unease
is precisely what Amos has been trying to effect.

Those words of promise may surprise the reader, but has God changed?
Assuredly not. Again, it is the audience that has been changed through its
experience of Amos's ironies. The new age of restoration may dawn only
after this deconstructive work has been completed. A new audience struggles, stunned and traumatized, out of the ruins of their old hermeneutics,
prepared now to proclaim the God of the Book of Amos. In the words of
Amos 3:8, now the audience has finally understood what the roaring Lion
means, "who can but prophesy?"[116] Amos's devastating rhetoric has created a newly sophisticated audience that can stand in sympathy with the
ironist. This turn to the sophisticated audience is flagged directly—star-
tlingly—in the last three words of the book: "says the-LORD your-God."
The weight of Amos's turn toward his audience is conveyed through that
last, unexpected pronominal suffix: *your* God.[117] This is the God whom
the implied audience is urged to seek and thereby to live.

The juxtaposition of death-dealing words of judgment and earnest
words of promise creates a space within which the "third meaning" of the
Book of Amos as a whole can take shape. In Amos, irony constitutes not
simply the texture or tone of what is being said but a new plot in its own
right. Irony in Amos is a three-dimensional plot that re-narrates the audience's relationship to tradition. Irony is not simply a literary quality but a
force that changes the axis along which the reader's expectations are allowed to unfold. The climactic point of the new plot is this: that the God
who destroys and this people who dare not rely on their ancient election
traditions can encounter one another anew. This bruised and fragile Israel can stagger out into a new world of promise, its vision finally cleared.

The audience of the Book of Amos knows now to trust the promises of God, while never again taking those promises for granted.

Contested Hermeneutics and the Undecidability of Micah 2:12–13

From the ambiguities of Balaam's prophesying to the deconstruction of the implied audience in Amos, we have seen ways in which representations of prophecy work to destabilize the audience's perspective. A major issue in contemporary scholarship on the prophets has to do with the reader's construction of theological coherence in the prophetic books more generally.[118]

Form-critical work on prophetic books has proceeded by the light of one methodological assumption or another regarding the logical or theological integrity of smaller units of prophetic speech. Older positivist historical searches for the *ipsissima verba* of the prophets have yielded in more recent times to approaches that emphasize the multivalence and indeterminacy of prophetic books as written texts. But a grappling with the notion of coherence still underlies many diverse avenues of inquiry. Scholars of historical- and literary-critical stripe alike have explored connections among First Isaiah, Deutero-Isaiah, and the more shadowy Trito-Isaiah. Literary and rhetorical analyses have mapped concentric structures and catchword connections within and among books in the Minor Prophets. Significant scholarly energy has been expended in redaction-critical work by the present author and others laboring to honor competing voices in the prose of the Book of Jeremiah. Several scholars have addressed the issue of coherence in the Book of Micah.[119] Coherence as a hermeneutical construct matters in a number of crucial ways for many readers of prophetic literature. And incoherence matters too, for in the light of our rosy-fingered postmodern dawn, coherence has shown itself to be continuously unraveled by the problematizing of textual authority and by deconstructive strategies that promote the "interruption" of hegemonic textual discourse.

Here I will explore the possibility that Micah 2:12–13 is hermeneutically undecidable, and further, that its undecidability is neither regrettable or accidental but, in fact, important for configuring the theological space between readers and the text of Micah. My efforts here will build on the work of Erin Runions in her article entitled, "Playing It Again: Utopia, Contradiction, Hybrid Space and the Bright Future in Micah," which appeared in 1999.[120] Citing Homi Bhabha's theorizing of hybridity,[121] Runions says that the "play of contradictory elements creates what might be called a hybrid space that both disrupts the text's colonizing drive and challenges the reader's ideological position."[122] In what follows, I will explore the potential of Micah 2:12–13 to create a hybrid space in which the addressee is challenged to embrace both terror and hope. I will suggest that the polysemy of Micah 2:12–13 compels the reader to move forward with a hermeneutic that is capable of facing a dangerous but potentially fruitful encounter with the prophetic word.

The Hebrew of Micah 2:12–13 is problematic. Granted, aporias abound everywhere that there are texts and everywhere that there are readers. Every text participates in a virtually limitless semantic universe of cultural and linguistic codes, and every text has innumerable intertexts pulling on it, shaping and misshaping and reforming its possible meanings for particular situated readers. Every text is unresolvable. But Micah 2:12–13 constitutes a particularly acute case of unresolvability. It has generated diametrically opposed reader responses in the history of interpretation from early rabbinic commentary to the present day. Many commentators, including Rashi, read Micah 2:12–13 as a prophecy of hope: God will gather the dispersed of Israel and will lead them out of captivity. But other interpreters have suggested that verses 12–13 are a false prophecy of the sort uttered by the false prophet characterized in verse 11 ("if someone were to go about uttering empty falsehoods")—on this reading, verses 12–13 do constitute a prophecy of hope, but it is an untrustworthy prophecy of hope. And finally, a minority of commentators, including Abraham Ibn Ezra and David Kimḥi, have insisted that verses 12–13 constitute a prophecy of judgment: God will round up the Israelites for destruction, breaking through their defenses and leading them into captivity.[123] While the "hope" reading has enjoyed significant traction in the history of interpretation and approaches the status of a consensus view in current scholarship, the "false prophecy" interpretation and the "judgment" reading have demonstrated a tenacity that invites renewed attention. In what follows, I will lay out the semantic ambiguities of the Hebrew and then explore ways in which the "undecidability" of this text may be significant for the rhetorical strategy of the Book of Micah.

First, we consider the bona fide textual difficulties in Micah 2:12–13. Two formulations in verse 12 are problematic. The first question has to do with whether we should emend the Masoretic vocalization of *boṣrâ* (Bozrah) to *baṣṣîrâ*, based on Arabic usage, yielding a noun meaning "sheepfold" that stands in parallelism with the noun in the following clause, *dōber* ("pasture" or "pen"). One problem is that *ṣîrâ* is not attested otherwise in biblical Hebrew.[124] More important, Bozrah as a place name for an Edomite sheep-processing center makes good sense of the sheep imagery as well. Andersen and Freedman read the word as "Bozrah," with a positive valence. They say, "Its presence here [in Micah 2:12]

could be intended to evoke memories of the original divine shepherding of Israel from the land of Edom into Canaan after the Exodus."[125]
Perhaps, but as Delbert R. Hillers has noted, the image of a flock marching out of a pen is not without problems: "'Breaking out' of a fold is not
a desirable thing for sheep to do, certainly not something a shepherd
would do for a flock."[126] Alternatively, "Bozrah" might refer to a regional
slaughtering center where sheep are both shorn and butchered. Andersen and Freedman suggest Exodus as an intertext supporting this reading. I would choose Isaiah as a stronger intertext instead.

Specifically, the use of "Bozrah" in Isaiah 34:6 and 63:1 would support a reading of this image as one of judgment. Isaiah 34:6–7 reads,
"The LORD has a sword; it is sated with blood, it is gorged with fat, with
the blood of lambs and goats. . . . For the LORD has a sacrifice in Bozrah,
a great slaughter in the land of Edom. . . . Their land shall be soaked
with blood, and their soil made rich with fat." Brian Britt notes that Isaiah 53:7 "explicitly associates" sheep-shearing with sacrifice: the Servant
described as having been "like a lamb that is led to the slaughter, and
like a sheep that before its shearers is silent."[127] Isaiah 63:1 continues the
imagery of slaughter, with the LORD coming "from Bozrah in garments
stained crimson," having waded through blood.[128] The idea in Micah
2:12, then, would be that the Israelite survivors will be gathered like
sheep brought to Bozrah to await slaughter.

The second textual difficulty is the phrase at the end of verse 12,
tĕhîmenâ mē'âdâm, a formulation that is opaque. The root of the verb is
usually taken as *hē-wāw-mēm*, "to murmur, roar, discomfit," from which
derives the noun *mĕhûmâ*, "tumult, confusion, disquietude, panic," especially, the lexicons note, "due to divine judgment." The predicate in that
clause, *mē'âdâm*, is grammatically clear but semantically "utterly baf-
fling," in the words of Andersen and Freedman. Is the *min* causative, tumult "caused by human beings," or privative, "away from or isolated
from human beings"? Andersen and Freedman also register the possibility that it could be revocalized to *'ĕdōm*, "Edom," thus handily creating a geographical parallelistic pair with "Bozrah." A significant draw-
back to this suggestion, as they note, is that *'ĕdōm* is always written *plene*
in its other one hundred occurrences in the Hebrew Bible, so the defective spelling here would be anomalous.

But their instinct regarding the possibility of a place name may still be
pursued: *'âdâm* could be taken as a place name, as it seems to be in the
traditio-historical cartography of Hosea at Hosea 6:7. We do not know
much about Adam as a place, but in Hosea, in a literary context that de-
cries bloodshed, Hosea says, "at Adam they transgressed the covenant;
there they dealt faithlessly with me."[129] If one chooses not to emend the

MT, one may read Bozrah just as it is vocalized in the MT, as the place name, and to take Adam as a place name also. The gathered ones will make noise from as far away as Adam, or perhaps will groan from the kind of situation that characterized the bloodshed of Adam per Hosea.

Notable again is the polysemy that lies ready to hand. Many commentators take *tĕhîmenâ mē'ādām* to mean that the city or metaphorical sheepfold is noisy with the cheery hubbub of a large and thriving population. But negative valences of this image cannot be ruled out. Runions points to the undecidability of the image here, in service of her larger argument that repetition is employed in the Book of Micah to destabilize monolithic understandings. She writes of this text:

> The male shepherd king, *rescuing* his people from disaster, repeats differently to form a hybrid figure, so that the idea of rescue is not always clear. . . . The word used to describe the sheep's noise . . . does not, after all, generally connote well-being, but rather chaos and confusion. A similar ambiguity occurs in 4.1–7 where again Yahweh is the king and shepherd going up before his flock. . . . But here Yahweh says that he will gather up the lame, the ones *whom he has harmed* (4:6). Given these ambiguities, the image of the shepherd as caring leader, as is so commonly asserted, is at best equivocal. This could equally be an image of controlling sheep so that they could be made useful, or led to the slaughter.[130]

Absolutely right. The more Israel understands its own tradition history, the more chilling these ambiguities become. As with the place name Bozrah subtly evoking a secure place for sheep in their sheepfold that yields to a horrific image of slaughter once one goes deeper into the tradition history of Edom, so too here we may have a first impression of the bustle of a thriving city that yields to a terrifying connotation of bloodshed when the implied audience reflects on its ancient tradition (lost to us now) about the place Adam.

Additional semantic ambiguities beset Micah 2:12–13. Is the "gathering" that God will do in 12a beneficial or destructive? Is the "one who breaks through" in 13a breaking into a walled city to harm those huddled there and leading them into slavery, or is he breaking out of a besieged city and leading its trapped denizens to freedom? The procession may be a victory march imaged along the lines of the second exodus in Deutero-Isaiah. But it may also be an image of the filing away of captives into exile, as we see in Amos 6:7, wherein a similar procession is described with an ironic edge: the callous elite of Samaria will lead their people indeed, at the head of the line of folks being taken away into exile.

Cited sometimes is the suggestion of van der Woude that verse 12 represents the message of salvation spouted by the false prophets and that verse 13 offers the appropriate corrective judgment by Micah himself.[131] The least popular option has been the notion that verses 12–13 are spoken by Micah and are entirely negative in their sense. Yet it is that reading that, in my view, best renders the complex irony of Micah's prophetic voice, which I take as directly challenging the implied audience on their hermeneutics. Interpreting 2:12–13 as judgment allows the passage to connect beautifully both with the reference to false prophecy in 2:11 and with the terrifying judgment material that follows in Micah 3.

Micah 2:6–11 complains that the people would prefer a narcotic false message of security to a true prophetic word from God that holds them accountable. The people are represented in scathing terms as being eager to silence the prophetic voice: "'Do not preach'—thus *they* preach—'one should not preach of such things. Disgrace will not overtake us'" (2:6). Micah takes up their objection and caricatures it with brutal sarcasm: "if someone were to go about uttering empty falsehoods, saying, 'I will preach to you of wine and strong drink,' such a one would be the preacher for this people!" (2:11). It is their hermeneutics that Micah is contesting. They want the prophet to mediate a certain kind of message from God—a message of security—but their interpretive values are fatally skewed.

To drive home this point, in 2:12–13 Micah undertakes a heavily ironic mimesis of what they seek with their flawed hermeneutics. He launches into a prophetic performance of his own that on the surface seems to meet their hermeneutical requirements for a prophetic word of security. But the ambiguous images that Micah employs are much more dangerous than they might seem to his hermeneutically misguided audience. Micah's mimesis of false prophecy has a deadly edge to it: God will gather God's people, certainly, but not as a nurturing shepherd. No, Micah's God will gather God's people as sheep headed for the blade. The metaphorical "pasture" will be cacophonous from far away with the bleating of these sheep waiting for slaughter. The irony of the image is heightened because of sheep's lack of ability to understand what is going to happen to them. Sheep have no conception of whether they are being led to lush pastureland or to the slaughtering stone; they will trot to the altar for sacrifice as readily as to the sheepfold. The tenor of this metaphor, then, has to do with the slaughter of many who had wrongly assumed they were safe and who tried to manipulate the prophetic word into collaborating with their error. Micah continues in his devastating ambiguous performance: the LORD himself will go out at the head of these sheep. Is that a good thing? Are they safe in their enclosure? No. God is one who breaks through—through the walls of a fortified city,

and through the hermeneutical smugness of those who do not understand their own accountability.[132]

Consider now the signaling of Micah's own agency as speaker in 3:1,
entirely anomalous for the Book of Micah and unusual for the prophets
more generally. *Wā'ōmar,* "and I said," is the way many translations render
it, but it is better rendered contrastively, "but I said."[133] Micah's assertion of
his own identity as prophet draws a sharp distinction between the false
understanding of salvation he had ironically drawn for them in 2:12–13
and the true message of God for this corrupt people. That true message
unfolds in Micah 3: because the rulers have cannibalized their own people, metaphorically flaying them and breaking their bones and chopping
them up like meat in a cauldron, they may cry out to the LORD, but he will
not answer them. Just as the leaders should have been gently shepherding
the people but have in fact been slaughtering and eating them (Ezekiel 34
comes to mind), so too, with brilliant poetic justice, Micah purports to
offer hope, but in fact, his prophetic word will ravage them.

I would note in passing that a similar savage performativity is enacted
in Amos and in Hosea. In the preceding section of this chapter, I argued
that Amos uses sarcastic attacks on Israel's election tradition to destroy his
audience's smugness, portraying himself in Amos 9 as a Samson *redivivus*
pulling down the pillars of tradition on the heads of his audience. In chapter 3, I suggested that Hosea's diction of gendered violence, matricide,
and dismemberment makes his implied audience into orphans—into Lo-
Ammi, "Not-My-People," and Lo-Ruhama, "Not-Pitied"—so that the audience as traumatized orphans will turn back to the God in Hosea 14. As in
Amos and Hosea, so too in Micah 2: this prophecy is a form of entrapment
that eviscerates the implied audience's erroneous hermeneutics.

In 2:12–13, Micah has made a feint toward just the kind of oracular
performance that his audience, with their skewed hermeneutics, is seeking. The more dreadful aspects of its polysemy come home to the implied audience with increasing clarity once Micah asserts his own agency
and speaks plainly at the beginning of Micah 3. He underlines the distinctiveness of his prophetic identity again near the end of that chapter,
so that his audience will be crystal clear about his role as true prophet in
contradistinction to the false prophets who speak misleading words of
šālôm: "But as for me, I am filled with power, with the spirit of the LORD,
and with justice and might, to declare to Jacob his transgression." As
Micah 3 thunders to a close, 2:12–13 is finally understood to have been a
devastating oracle of judgment that gestured ironically toward the audience's misguided hopes, only to dash them.

My reading presses the case, then, for coherence in all of Micah 1–3
rather than seeing 2:12–13 as an awkward interpolation of an unexpected

word of salvation. But the consistency for which I argue in 2:12–13 does not "solve" the aporias that beset Micah 2:12–13. Even though I am persuaded of the plausibility of an ironic reading of 2:12–13, I must acknowledge that the positive connotations of 2:12–13 as a potential oracle of hope cannot be erased. They persist in the history of interpretation, and they persist textually in the hybrid space created by Micah's ironic prophesying. As with all ironic communication, the unreliable "said" can never be retrieved once it has been uttered. The meaning of 2:12–13 remains undecidable, whether the question is posed from a postmodern standpoint of textual indeterminacy or from a historicist standpoint that takes seriously the possibility of deciding between two viable options.

Illuminating here are observations from John D. Caputo's *More Radical Hermeneutics.*[134] Caputo explores the necessity of interpretation in a world in which no reading masters a text, but instead alternative readings continually contest and reformulate each other in a deconstructive dialectic. He suggests that apophatic biblical theology inhabits those places of aporia where the idol of determinacy has been dismantled. For Caputo, reading is a theologically formative experience. He notes that when readers bring their urgent needs to the text, "the words of God break off, silence rules, an unendurable absence, a tormenting caesura sets in, just when we need a saving word."[135] Just as Micah refuses his audience's demands for security, so too the aporetic nature of Scripture refuses its readers' demands for closure—something that is especially true of the ambiguous prophetic word. Salvation can lie only in the unsayable, far beyond any human commodification of God's revelation. What the implied audience needs to understand is precisely its lack of discursive mastery, a point that Micah forcefully drives home. In this, Micah stands again with Amos, who mercilessly mocks his audience's appropriations of their own traditions, and with Hosea, who sarcastically quotes the people (Hos 6:1–3; 8:2; 9:7; 10:3; 12:8; 13:2, 10) in order to eviscerate their discursive strategies. In all of these performances, undecidability challenges readers to give up commodifying the prophetic word if they want to live.

Caputo underlines the inevitability of engagement with textual aporias: it is necessary that we read rather than that we inhabit a passive or voyeuristic role in interpretation. No "staying on the sidelines," Caputo admonishes,[136] something that was surely true for ancient audiences horrified by Ezekiel or Hosea. Caputo is thinking about story here, about the compelling lures of narrative. But his observation is helpful regarding Hebrew Bible prophecy as well. The aporias in Micah 2:12–13 not only entrap the audience, they require that readers or hearers learn to accept responsibility for understanding the divine word with a hermeneutics appropriate to the truth of the God Micah proclaims.

The undecidability of Micah 2:12–13 thus invites two hermeneutical responses. First, this prophetic word refuses commodification, undermining idolatry and equipping the audience for theological accountability. Second, the aporetic nature of Micah 2:12–13 compels theological decision making on the part of those who encounter this oracle. The stakes are high no matter which reading comes to the fore. If this is a true promise of restoration, the community needs to learn to trust God even in the midst of trauma. If this is a false word of promise (as van der Woude argued), the community needs to learn to discern between true and false prophecy in order to live. If this is an ironic prophecy of doom that skewers the incompetent hermeneutics of those who are counting on restoration without accountability (my own reading), then the community needs to learn to read aright not only the surface content but their own deeper interaction, communally and historically, with the divine word.

Catherine Keller has noted that Caputo's hermeneutical project "[liberates] Biblical theology from its literalisms and its univocalisms."[137] So too does the biblical text itself. Micah affirms the proto-postmodern truth that God's syntax is not our own, God's word is not our own. What Caputo writes of biblical signifying generally is more acutely true of ironic biblical texts: "God's address to us is always accompanied by silence . . . the trace of God is invariably marked by undecidability. We are unsure of the difference between the word and the silence, between what is God's saying and what is God's silence, what is God's word and what is ours. That is the way undecidability hovers over sacred texts."[138] The divine word is in excess of and more powerful than the reader's commodification of it. The undecidability of Micah 2:12–13 creates a hybrid space in which coherent revelation becomes possible only because it continually refuses the audience's attempts at manipulation, refuses the fetishizing of the audience's misguided expectations. For those who have ears to hear, who come to understand this through Micah's ironic performance, then—and only then—Micah 2:12–13 may become a prophecy of hope.

Hope itself is ironized in the final prophetic text to be studied here: the Book of Jonah. This prophet (or anti-prophet) finds God's redemption to be a cause for sullenness and misery. My treatment will focus in particular on the complex role of the psalm in Jonah 2.

Irony as Emetic: Parody in the Book of Jonah

Irony plays irrepressibly throughout the Book of Jonah. Exaggerated twists and turns in the plot, incongruities and surprises, freighted silences and unexpected confessions in discourse all yield a text that is rich indeed in its many misdirections.[139] Although there are those throughout the history of interpretation and into contemporary times who have insisted that Jonah should be read "straight," a great many readers from diverse reading traditions have perceived an overtly satirical character to the Book of Jonah.[140] Many have argued that the figure of the disobedient and petulant Jonah is employed in the book to ironize the institution of prophecy generally. Even readers who argue for the meaning of the book as being what it seems to be on the surface—as with one recent interpretation, which claims that Jonah shows the Jewish people as having been insufficiently committed to their mission to the Gentiles[141]—nevertheless see that irony is used as a literary device. For example, Uriel Simon, who takes Jonah as a sympathetic character[142] and argues against reading harsh satire of the prophet, acknowledges that irony has an important role in the book, although in his view that role is kinder and gentler than many readers have supposed.[143]

Debates over the meanings of the ironies in the Book of Jonah tend to focus on the question of divine mercy or sovereignty as those notions are framed in postexilic traditions within the Hebrew Bible.[144] Many argue that the book's numerous local ironic touches are employed either in defense of a universalist divine mercy extended to the Gentiles or in defense of divine sovereignty conceived more broadly. But other plausible and intelligent readings have been proposed, each responding to one or several aspects of the ironizing that goes on in Jonah. No single view has commanded a consensus in the field.[145]

Well known are the ironies that characterize Jonah the failed and petty prophet as a grudging servant of God, that contrast Jonah's disobedience with the behavior of the morally exemplary idolatrous mariners, and that paint as ludicrously responsive the hyper-repentant Ninevites. These and other ironies have been constructed toward the end of rendering virtually every event in the book implausible for the implied audience.[146] Where interpreters have not seen irony, generally, has been in the discourse about God rendered in the text. Readers have noticed that the psalm in Jonah 2 sounds ludicrous in Jonah's mouth, although some do continue to take it as an earnest proclamation of biblical piety that shows Jonah's hard-won new maturity in difficult circumstances. But the rest of what Jonah says about God and what God says about himself are usually taken as a trustworthy representation of the narrator's point of view and thus as a reliable guide to the message of the book.

Those who read the psalm as awkward or unbelievable in its context tend to have difficulty integrating a theory of the rhetorical purpose of the psalm into their analyses. Some scholars suggest that the psalm seems to have been added redactionally to the text and has no intrinsic connec-

tion to its literary context. Even for those scholars who take the presence
of the psalm in its literary context seriously, its force has not been adequately accounted for in the larger narrative, beyond the remarks interpreters make about its hyperbolic and potentially nauseating quality
placed as high-flown piety in the mouth of the recalcitrant Jonah. In what
follows, I will attend to the question of the reliability of the voice of Jonah
as speaker of the psalm in Jonah 2 and move from there to consider the
question of the reliability of the theological claims made by Jonah and his
God in the book. I will argue that Jonah's "knowledge" that God is merciful (4:2) is rendered unreliable by means of the preemptive sabotaging of
his character in Jonah 2, as well as by the events of the plot that happen to
Jonah himself, who is not treated mercifully by God.[147] Finally, the remark
made by God at the end of the Book of Jonah will be analyzed to see what
it may contribute to our understanding of the character of God and our
construal of the implied relationship between God and Israel.

The awkwardness of the psalm in Jonah 2—its quality of being unexpected and markedly different from what surrounds it—has long drawn
the attention of interpreters.[148] Although it is possible to speculate about a
transformation of Jonah's character in the belly of the fish, the characterization of Jonah as pious stands transparently over against the behavior of
the prophet that we have seen in Jonah 1. More important, his piety seems
equally unexpected over against his behavior in the latter part of the book,
a point that is devastating for readings that postulate a significant spiritual
transformation for Jonah in Jonah 2. Both in terms of characterization of
the protagonist and in terms of plot development, the psalm seems drastically unlike the material surrounding it. The diction of Jonah 2 is notice-
ably different from that of the surrounding prose, as well. Further, it has
long been noticed that in the psalm Jonah says what is true, or what might
be true, in a way that is rendered absurd under the circumstances. Scholars have attended especially to two discursive features of Jonah 2. First, the
deliverance of which Jonah speaks as already accomplished has actually
not yet happened in the timeline of the plot.[149] Second, figures of speech
and images that ordinarily would be employed in metaphorical senses in
Israel's psalmody are here used in ways that are hyperbolically literalistic
in Jonah's actual briny circumstances.[150]

Adequate apprehension of the force of the irony in Jonah needs to take
account of both the pervasive ironizing that goes on throughout the book
and the unique qualities of what happens in the psalm. Required, more
precisely, is an inquiry into the relationship between the ironic texture of
the prose and the ironic texture of the psalm. This is a question that may
be posed simultaneously on redaction-critical and literary levels (that is, on
diachronic and synchronic levels), without those two hermeneutics being

seen as necessarily mutually antagonistic. Is the psalm original to the composition of the book (even if the author perhaps knew the psalm as an earlier source) and therefore presumably employed in a way—however complex or subtle—that supports and furthers the rhetorical goals of the prose? Or is the psalm a later addition that counters or tries to destabilize the patent ironizing of the prophet in Jonah 1, 3, and 4? The question matters greatly for whether one sees perceived narratological and semantic disjunctures between the psalm and the prose of Jonah as meaningful.

As some have argued, Jonah's praise in Chapter 2 might be construed as sincere thankfulness regarding God's appointment of the fish to save him from drowning. Interpreters ancient and contemporary have argued that Jonah finds the fish's belly a welcome refuge.[151] But Kenneth M. Craig has noted the point of James Ackerman that the verb "to swallow" used in Jonah 1:17 always has a negative meaning in the Hebrew Bible. Craig continues, "[I]f the interpretation that *Jonah* views the fish as a vehicle of divine rescue is correct, it appears the author has included this motif to highlight Jonah's *mis*understanding of the swallowing. The author seems to delight in creating discrepancy in awareness both among characters on the one hand and characters and the audience on the other."[152] This point is persuasive, in my view. If Jonah is giving earnest thanks here, he is misguided. The deliverance from drowning may be perceived as an "out of the frying pan, into the fire" kind of deliverance at best, so the psalmic utterance bears within it the seeds of its own ironizing. As with so many aspects of plot and characterization in Jonah, here the irony unfolds in slow motion, and what had seemed positive gradually comes to be adjudicated by the reader in another light. The "rescue" of the drowning Jonah by the fish is, on one level, what it seems. But on a deeper level, it constitutes an ironic feint toward a view of deliverance that becomes increasingly untenable as three days pass and the reader is given the opportunity to consider Jonah's fishy intragastric imprisonment at more length. Jonah's prayer for deliverance is heard not (only) as prayer asking deliverance from drowning but also and more finally, as prayer asking deliverance from his dark and pungent place of captivity.

The psalm, too, is not what it seems—or more precisely, it does not end up being what it had seemed to be at the beginning of our reading experience. Jonah's elaborate poetic utterance is cloaked in the garb of a prayer of lament.[153] But as its rhetoric unfolds, incongruous notes are struck; the psalm is gradually revealed as a calculated attempt on the part of the unregenerate prophet to manipulate God while remaining unaccountable himself. First, God is named as the agent responsible for Jonah's being cast into the deep (2:4). This is perhaps true but more importantly untrue. It is untrue both in pragmatic terms, for the sailors cast him into the ocean at his own suggestion, and in the larger theological sense, for Jonah's disobedient flight from God in the first place is what has occasioned God's resorting to threatening measures with the storm. The ocean waves and billows pass over Jonah quite literally: ironizing of the normally metaphorical language of the psalms is evident here, and one could argue that Jonah is a willful misreader of Scripture, misapplying tropes in his own biblical heritage that were intended to signify spiritual realities.[154] (Relevant here: Marcus underlines the irony that the sailors and the king of Nineveh seem to be better acquainted with the Hebrew Scriptures than is Jonah.[155]) Jonah reports that his response to God from the depths of the sea was "I have been driven away from your sight" (2:5a), an ironic claim since Jonah had chosen to flee from God's sight initially. This is Jonah's attempt to lay the blame for his current distance from God on God himself. Jonah nevertheless insists, "Surely I shall look again upon your holy temple" (2:5) with an unexpected assurance born of either his trust in God—which would be out of character for Jonah—or, more likely, confidence in his own power to manipulate God into resolving the situation.

According to the narration of the psalm, Jonah has thought all of this while sinking down through the ocean waters to hyperbolically mythical depths. His reported inner discourse serves to portray the action as a dramatized slow-motion fall into the briny deep. He then reports that he prayed, from this deep place of furthest possible alienation from God and farthest possible distance from the oxygen that his lungs desperately needed. The urgency of the situation in both spiritual and pragmatic terms is conveyed so well that the reader becomes anxious for God's answer: we hold our breath with Jonah at the foot of the undersea mountains, our cells clamoring for the oxygen of God's response. And Jonah supplies it, just in case God might not have been inclined to heed his prayer. Jonah asserts that his prayer was received ("I remembered the LORD, and my prayer came to you," 2:8). Jonah claims boldly that he will now fulfill "his vows," something that would require that he get back onto dry land in order to do. Thus Jonah's thanksgiving turns coercive and may be seen as manipulation, perhaps even as a subtle form of bribery of God.

The fish, spoken to by God, vomits Jonah onto terra firma.[156] What had God said to the obedient leviathan? The silence here in the narrative is so huge, it could engulf the entire city of Nineveh. It could have been simply a divine command to transport Jonah to dry land. But could God have delivered such a command to the fish without remarking on the incongruity of Jonah's words vis-à-vis Jonah's character (not pious) or the plot as it has unfolded (Jonah was not in a position to demand anything, and yet has managed to extort safe passage so that he can pay his vows)? Commentators have enjoyed suggesting that the fish vomits Jonah out because his newfound "piety" is nauseating in its hypocrisy. This is delightfully plausible.[157] There may be another thunderous silence around the divinely fishy answer to Jonah's prayer as well. Jonah expects to be saved so that he may pay his vows to the LORD in the Temple. But he finds himself disgorged and tasked again with making the laborious journey to Nineveh. No trip to the Temple is in Jonah's immediate future, as it turns out. The irony and humor of this are palpable. Jonah has expended considerable energy, initiative, and ingenuity to flee God's command, all to no avail. He undertakes a perilous sea journey in the Mediterranean that almost ends with his death and is carried hither and yon in the belly of a huge fish for three days, only to end up essentially where he started: on dry ground in (or relatively near) his homeland, with the long overland trek to Nineveh still required.[158] And we may note the ironic temporal contrast implied in the fact that the arduous journey to Nineveh goes so quickly, narratively speaking, that it passes in the blink of an eye. Not a single word is given to this journey that would have taken many long days of travel. The unspoken point may be this: run from God, and one can run for many days and get nowhere at all, not to mention almost die twice. Obey God, however reluctantly, and one's feet are sped as if with wings.

The multiple ironies that unfold during Jonah's time in Nineveh have been addressed in detail by many commentators. The city is extravagantly repentant: every single citizen and all of the animals show signs of regretting their previous life choices. Jonah sulks equally over matters large (the non-destruction of Nineveh) and small (the transience of physical comforts such as the shade provided by the plant God causes to spring up). Jonah is rebuked for his lack of compassion by a God who has shown no compassion at all to Jonah himself, so we may find doubly ironic the fact that Jonah has claimed that God is gracious and merciful, slow to anger, abounding in steadfast love, and ready to relent from punishing (4:2). Jonah himself is not in a position to know this about God, and the theological claim has not been borne out by events in Jonah's experience in any case.

Some have argued that the Book of Jonah was written so late that it would have been well known to the actual audience that Nineveh had been destroyed in 612. Does Nineveh's future destruction loom in the silence after God's last rhetorical question, thus rendering ironic the entire thrust of the book that Jonah's task is to induce Nineveh to repent? It is an excellent proposal, and one worthy of the compelling ironies that surge through the Book of Jonah. Such an irony would implicate not only the Ninevites, whose prompt and ready repentance in this story clearly will not avail them later in history, but also the God who sent Jonah on this mission. The question may ultimately be unanswerable. But we can press a more modest claim: that the repentance of Nineveh and its deliverance or unspoken future destruction are not, finally, the point here. The Ninevites are sketched so fleetingly and in such caricature that it would be unpersuasive to suggest that the central focus of the narrative is on them. As if to drive home the point of their superfluity, the humorous rhetorical question of God at the end of the book names the denizens of Nineveh and their animals in the same breath, indeed giving the presence of (mere) animals in Nineveh the "last word" in God's claim about caring for the city. No, this narrative is surely not about Nineveh in the final analysis.

The narrative urgency and the focus of much of the dialogue move toward the central dynamic of the book as concerning the relationship between Jonah and God. The audience is invited to consider who each one becomes to the other as the ironies of plot and character unfold. Jonah does turn out to be right, after all—God does show mercy to Nineveh, as Jonah had known he would—so Jonah is an unreliable speaker whose words nevertheless end up being true. Toward what insight does that impel the audience? Do we see here the incongruity of the prophetic word over against actual historical events unfolding? If so, Jonah is the only one who anticipates this incongruity and resents it. The reader may be intended to sympathize with Jonah despite his unappealing stubbornness, lack of charity, and pettiness. Here, then, I would agree with those scholars who find Jonah sympathetic, although I would contest the position that Jonah is supposed to be seen as heroic. The reader comes to appreciate Jonah's position despite Jonah's unsavory character, a narratological feat that shows the story effectively ironizing reader expectations of the prophet as well.

And what is said about God? The point that God is sovereign over the forces of nature and over all nations is rendered somewhat ridiculous through the implicit near-powerlessness that attends God's manipulation of those things in Jonah's case. Storm, fish, plant, and worm are mustered to force Jonah to embrace his task, but all of God's power is insufficient to effect a change of heart in the angry prophet. Jonah is a resistant reader of God's motivations and God's actions, and his resistance is never broken down. The book closes—or remains open, since narratological closure does not happen—without Jonah having changed his position. Also vulnerable is the most obvious expressed point of the book, that the "sovereign" God is merciful.[159] There are many unspoken meanings that one could construct in the silences of the Book of Jonah; the lively history of interpretation of the book testifies to that. I would focus our attention on the possibility of hearing a freighted silence around the portrayal of God that, far from supporting the characterization of divine mercy, strongly resists that characterization. The observation has already been made here (and by others) that God has not shown himself to be merciful to Jonah himself. Two additional lines of evidence present themselves as well.

Consider first that the language describing God as slow to anger and merciful (4:2) reflects a number of traditio-historical trajectories within the Bible that have close associations with God's power not to save but to destroy. This web of resonances includes Exodus 34:6, Nahum 1:3, and Joel 2:13. The Exodus reference comes after the story of the Golden Calf apostasy. The refrain about God being slow to anger and merciful follows two passages that demonstrate God's mercilessness. The first passage is the chilling pericope about the Levites, who answer Moses's call to stand with him "on the LORD's side," going back and forth repeatedly throughout the Israelite camp, slaughtering the idolaters among their kin, friends, and neighbors (Exod 32:25–29). The second one is a crisp notice that, for good measure, the LORD also sent a plague upon the Israelites for their apostasy (Exod 32:35). In Nahum 1:3 we find the refrain about God's being slow to anger transmuted into an ominous threat addressed to Nineveh: the LORD is "slow to anger but great in power; he will by no means clear the guilty." Here, the use of the refrain depends on a telling silence about God's mercy. Joel 2:13 offers an exhortation to return to this merciful God who has devastated the land of Israel, the claim of God's mercy belied by the terror with which the prophet and his people face the Day of the LORD and the onslaught of God's ferocious locust-warriors. Thus we see that the traditional refrain about God's mercy is sung chiefly in the ruins of ravaged landscapes littered with the bodies of those whom God has slain. The refrain deconstructs itself in its very utterance, both in Exodus and in the two Minor Prophets whose words place pressure on Jonah from both sides in the Scroll of the Twelve.

The second line of evidence that undermines the characterization of God as merciful has to do with the language of pitying/sparing (*ḥûs*) in Jonah 4. This diction may be read in light of the other occurrences of that unusual verb in the prophetic corpus, and particularly in view of the dense cluster of occurrences in the Book of Ezekiel.[160] Seven of the Ezekiel passages drive home the point, with virulent and uncompromising diction, that God will not spare Israel. God will not pity, God will not have mercy, for Israel's abominations have made her unworthy of redemption. The two remaining Ezekiel occurrences (16:5 and 20:17) employ *ḥûs* in an artful way to highlight the suspense of punishment initially deferred but still looming now: in Ezekiel 16, deferred while the metaphorical Israel grows up; and in Ezekiel 20, deferred repeatedly when Israel had stumbled rebelliously through the Exodus and wilderness wandering time under Moses's leadership. God will finally wreak vengeance with a furious intensity that is all the more devastating for its

having been delayed. The Jeremiah and Isaiah instances of *ḥûs* underline the impossibility of God's sparing the objects of his wrath. Whether
it is God acting (Jer 13:14), or enemies acting as instruments of the divine purpose (Nebuchadrezzar appointed against Judah, Jer 21:7; the
Medes appointed to destroy Babylon, Isa 13:18), the point is the same:
there shall be no escape, not even for children: "I will dash them against
one another, parents and children together, says the LORD. I will not pity
or spare or have compassion when I destroy them" (Jer 13:14).

This verb *ḥûs*, then, comes up only in the context of a thunderous divine negative: *lō' 'āḥûs*, "I will not spare." Most of the occurrences, indeed,
come up in a sequence of other verbs for pitying or having mercy that are
likewise negated in a growing crescendo of ruthlessness. The occurrence
in Ezekiel 24:14 sounds the impossibility of God sparing in a dynamic that
grows to *fortissimo:* "I will not refrain, I will not spare, I will not relent!"
That the verb is used in the prophetic corpus only in the negative is of utmost importance for understanding the irony of the rhetorical question at
the end of the Book of Jonah. This rhetorical question is unmarked—
there is no interrogative particle here. The absence of a direct flag of interrogation is not unusual in biblical Hebrew syntax, but here in this most
ironic of prophetic books, it is eminently worthy of interpretation. The
first three words in Jonah 4:11, assuming no interrogative inflection, may
be read as straightforward declaration: "But as for me, I will not spare"—
lō' 'āḥûs. Here in Jonah, as elsewhere in the prophetic corpus, we have,
quite literally, *lō' 'āḥûs* instead of an asseveration to the contrary. Readers
may postulate an unmarked interrogative here, but the semantic pressures from other prophetic usages render this a complicated utterance at
best. "No, no, NO!" thunder the intertextual resonances crowding around
this last moment of God's speech to Jonah. In the mouth of the God of the
prophets, the verb *ḥûs* has performed its powerful semantic function only
in the negative. This is something that Jonah, as both a literarily late book
and a tradition-history-savvy prophetic character (explicitly represented
as such in 4:2), would have known well. This verb of sparing describes precisely what God will not do—has not ever done—for Israel or for Israel's
enemies. God has never been a God of mercy. Jonah has cited traditions
about God being slow to anger that are overturned in literary traditions
before and all around him (Exodus, Nahum, Joel), the touted divine grace
belied by the horrific plagues and death that accompany every acclamation of this God who is allegedly "slow to anger." Throughout the prophetic corpus, this expression, *lō' 'āḥûs*, is coherent only in the implacable
negation of its possibility.

What are we to understand about God's so-called mercy, then? God
will not be merciful to Nineveh. Historically, the late Book of Jonah surely

was aware of the fall of Nineveh in 612. Literarily, the open-ended quality of that last exchange between Jonah and God leaves the narrative vulnerable to a variety of resolutions.[161] Further, the traditio-historical pressure of centuries of experience with *lō' 'āḥûs* has trained the implied audience to recognize that even if punishment is delayed (Ezek 16 and 20), it will inevitably come stalking in the death-triad of sword, famine, and pestilence. One "third meaning" of the ironies in the Book of Jonah, then, would be not that God is unexpectedly or undesirably merciful to the brutal Assyrians—that is merely the "said," the patently obvious meaning of this thoroughly ironic text. The more hidden point is that God has been irredeemably unmerciful to God's own people in exile.[162] God has always been unmerciful with all nations, including the nation called by God's name. God's people were named Lo-Ammi and Lo-Ruḥamah in Hosea. The Book of Jonah responds that God's true name is Lo-'Aḥus.

God never spares, and Jonah knows it. Jonah's excuse in the beginning of chapter 4 ("for I knew you were a God gracious and merciful, slow to anger") has, as it turns out—and we did not know for sure until the *lō' 'āḥûs* of 4:11—the manipulative, wheedling character of all of Jonah's self-serving utterances. By the end of the book, the implied audience attentive to the book's ironies knows that Jonah's psalmic expression of trust in God can be only foolishness at best and rank hypocrisy at worst. God is not merciful, and therefore, Jonah is not (only) a parody of the Israelite prophet; he is a parody of the psalmist. What Jonah claims about God cannot be trusted, even though he has vast swaths of Israelite tradition available to him that he can manipulate deftly. But God cannot be trusted either. The audience confirms the unspoken charge of divine caprice from what God himself does and says in the Book of Jonah and from attentiveness to intertextual resonances in Exodus, Joel, Nahum, and Ezekiel.

This God of Jonah's cannot be appealed to, whether in earnest trust or manipulatively, without grave risk and dire consequences. The Book of Jonah spews out of its artistic mouth those readers who would proclaim a "God of deliverance" straight, whether in songs of praise (Jon 2) or in despair (Jon 4). Uriel Simon has noted that when God questions Jonah about his ire concerning the plant's growth and destruction, Jonah shows himself "oblivious to the irony" and reads the question straight,[163] fatally undermining his heroic character. While in my view Jonah was never heroic to begin with, Simon's characterization of Jonah as oblivious to irony is helpful. The implied reader who identifies with Jonah earnestly is also being ironized. For God is no God of deliverance: Jonah knows only ruthlessness at his hand, and such, too, can the implied audience expect. Nineveh may seem to flourish for a moment, but it will be destroyed in the blink of an eye, in less than 150 years if one considers the reign of Jeroboam II and the actual destruction of Nineveh in 612 to have been dates intentionally linked by the traditionist who wrote the Book of Jonah.

The Book of Jonah does seem to parody the figure of the prophet. There is truth in that; the "spoken" in irony always bears traces of truth even as it places them under erasure. But that skewering of prophecy, while not untrue, turns out to have been only an ironic feint before the real movement of the book takes over. God's speaking the ambiguous and terrifying phrase *lōʾ ʾaḥûs* brings the ironies of Jonah 2 finally into focus as central to the entire book. The Book of Jonah ironizes beyond recovery the figure of the psalmist, one who offers earnest lament and praise to a God of deliverance who turns out to have been ruthless all along.

* * *

This chapter has argued for the performance of ironic themes and ironizing discursive postures early and late within Israelite prophetic tradition. The story of Balaam works through dramatic ironies and poetic ambiguities to show the seer as an unreliable mercenary attempting to manipulate both Balak and God, the encamped Israel as oblivious to the drama unfolding around it, and God as having expended every effort to protect the Israelites but finally unable to save them from their own worst enemy, namely, apostasy in their own ranks. The Book of Amos ironizes foundational traditions of Israel's election that were relied upon by the implied audience as guarantors of Israel's chosenness in the eyes of a redemptive and merciful God. The Exodus and the Davidic royal covenant are left in tatters as Amos takes on the persona of the mighty Samson, pulling down the pillars of Israel's false confidence in order to save Israel from itself. Micah 2:12–13 deconstructs the flawed hermeneutics of the Israelites, luring them to their doom with prophetic words that seem hopeful only until one ponders their ambiguities more deeply in light of Israel's tradition history. The glorious traditions of the Psalms, with their poignant supplication and stirring trust in God's mercy, are ironized through the figure of Jonah, who mouths all the right words in contexts that can only render his character and his discourse absurd, and through the figure of God himself, who turns out to be no God of deliverance after all.

Last, we turn to Israel's wisdom traditions. These texts have been given a provisional "last word" in my treatment of biblical irony for the reason that Israelite wisdom is the epitome of discourse that doubles back on itself. Israelite wisdom traditions show their authors to be capable of breathtakingly sophisticated metacognitive reversals. Wisdom in the Hebrew Scriptures self-consciously ironizes irony itself.

5

"HOW LONG WILL YOU LOVE BEING SIMPLE?" IRONY IN WISDOM TRADITIONS

Many diverse types of irony enliven Israel's wisdom literature. The rallying cry of biblical wisdom literature is, "How long, O simple ones, will you love being simple?" (Prov 1:22), itself ironic in its implication that it is the conscious choice of the ignorant to remain unenlightened. Local ironies are common in the collections of aphorisms we find in the Book of Proverbs. In sapiential maxims, fools are mocked by demonstrations of the incongruity between their behavior and their expectations; irony forms the subtext of such maxims. Ironies texture much of the dry wit in Proverbs more generally. Bruce K. Waltke notes two examples in his introduction to his Proverbs commentary: Solomon's command that his tutee cease listening to instructions to stray from wisdom (19:27) and the suggestion of King Lemuel's mother that he give strong drink to the poor rather than imbibing intoxicants himself (31:4–6).[1] Waltke underlines the risk of misreading the latter injunction. The command, he says, "means exactly the opposite. English translators, fearful that an unsophisticated reader will miss the irony, purge the text of the powerful figure by making it say the intended opposite."[2] The following verses, which urge King Lemuel to defend the rights of the needy, would indeed seem to contradict a "straight" reading of verse 6 that one should give strong drink to one who is perishing.

One may read Proverbs 30:29–31 not as a commendation of kingly grandeur but as an ironic slight on royal pretentiousness:

> Three things are stately in their stride;
>> four are stately in their gait:
> the lion, which is mightiest among wild animals,
>> and does not turn back before any;
> the strutting rooster, the he-goat,
>> and a king striding before his people.

Many more examples of local ironies in Proverbs could be offered. Ironies may be discerned also in the juxtaposition of aphorisms. The juxtaposition of two apparently contradictory proverbs in Proverbs 26:4–5 ironizes any absolutist understanding of the applicability of one or the other: "Do not answer fools according to their folly, or you will be a fool yourself" is immediately followed by, "Answer fools according to their folly, or they will be wise in their own eyes," yielding the implication that not only fools but the (ostensibly) wise will be foolish if they do not carefully assess the particulars of a situation, including the situation of interacting with fools.[3]

Another feature of Israelite wisdom tradition that may be evaluated as ironic in effect is wisdom's emphasis on dialogical means of ascertaining truth. Dialogue between sage and disciple, parent and child, or sufferer and interlocutor structures Proverbs and Job. One might consider the Book of Qohelet implicitly dialogical in its didactic soliloquy, too—Qohelet is clearly responding to the well-established propositions of orthodox wisdom teachers—even if one does not follow T. A. Perry's dialogical schema for identifying different voices in the text.[4] Biblical wisdom dialogues may be considered ironic for two reasons. First, the invitation to dialogue embodied in direct address and didactic instruction suggests that the implied audience has a voice and a role to play. Yet we do not hear the voice of the audience in Proverbs and in Qohelet, so the dialogical effect is, in a real sense, illusory. One may proceed from that conclusion, then, to the implication that the invitation to dialogue is extended only ironically. The sages writing in Proverbs and Qohelet are in fact enacting monologues in the Bakhtinian sense of closed systems of discourse, even if, in the case of Proverbs, parallel or juxtaposed monologues may be perceived within the different collections.

A second sense in which biblical wisdom dialogism may be seen as ironic has to do with a potential converse effect noticed by Carol A. Newsom. Newsom argues that the fact that Lady Folly is voiced in Proverbs (Folly's message is characterized and even quoted in numerous texts) means that the false teaching of Folly is, in fact, invited into the discourse of Proverbs and allowed to be heard. The reader may choose not to accept the discursive framework established by the text of Proverbs and may choose to align with the voice of Folly instead. Regarding a feminist resistant reading of Proverbs 1–9, Newsom puts it this way: "For the reader who does not take up the subject position offered by the text, Proverbs 1–9 ceases to be a simple text of initiation and becomes a text about the problematic nature of discourse itself. Not only the dazzling (and defensive) rhetoric of the father but also the pregnant silence of the son and the dissidence that speaks from the margin in the person of the strange woman become matters of significance."[5] Newsom does not name this as ironic as such. But I would argue that this phenomenon—the textual hosting of false voices whose integrity is undermined by the dominant discourse but which are nevertheless allowed to speak—may be seen to ironize the instructions of the sages not to heed Folly. For as Newsom notes, one possible reader response would be to find the seductive enticements of Folly, as they are represented in the Book of Proverbs, more enigmatic and interesting than the dominant curriculum presented in that book.[6]

Irony in biblical literature reaches its intellectual zenith in the nuanced thinking of Israelite scribes about processes of perception and understanding themselves. Wisdom literature preserves ancient Israel's metacognitive reflections on how Israel can know what it knows and can claim what it claims. Ironic awareness of metacognition is evident throughout the Hebrew Scriptures, but it is expressed nowhere so clearly and with such sophistication as in ancient Israel's wisdom traditions. The literary means by which ancient Israelite scribes demonstrated the subtlety of their thinking about thinking are many and varied. Where Qohelet and the speaker of Psalm 73 communicate directly their evaluations of their own epistemological processes, other biblical authors employ means that are more indirect. Juxtaposition, parataxis, and repetition in Hebrew narrative invite the reader to appreciate different emphases in parallel or contiguous stories; these differences engage each other and may, perhaps, ironize each other. Variations in the repetition of a tradition (as with the matriarch-in-danger stories in Genesis) or even within a single tale (as with the way in which Isaac's servant modifies what he has been told to say to Rebekah in Genesis)[7] cue the implied audience to construct an unspoken cultural context concerning ways in which particular narrative gestures build on and sometimes destabilize the audience's prior assumptions about the text. We do not encounter in the Hebrew Scriptures elaborate philosophical taxonomies of kinds of discourse and the epistemological and moral underpinnings on which such categories rest. But we do encounter sustained attention to ambiguity, aporia, and contradiction in wisdom texts that are self-conscious about serving a formative purpose for their audiences.

A few words on the majestic and daunting Book of Job are in order before we turn to Qohelet and Psalm 73. Job shows us, on a scale unprecedented in biblical literature, the rich ironic possibilities afforded by protracted dialogue among multiple perspectives, on the one hand, and by the interplay between prose framework and poetic body, on the other. Withering ironies cut through every poetic speech made by Job and his friends as they contest each other's points. Dramatic irony throbs beneath the poetry because the audience knows, as none of the human characters in the book do, that everything that has befallen Job has been the result of a capricious heavenly wager.[8] One scholar maintains that "the portrait of Job in the frame story is an ironic exaggeration of the concept of conventional piety," not a serious example of faith.[9] Another has suggested that the entire Book of Job is ironic because the text does not answer the question it pretends to consider.[10]

The Book of Job displays a remarkable attentiveness to voicing, and it is that attentiveness that makes Job such a multifaceted and fascinating figure. He is unequivocally commended above all others—the narrator in the prose framework makes this clear at the beginning and at the end of the book—yet his closest counselors continually challenge his moral authority and impugn his integrity. Job is a kingly figure in this narrative, but he is the king of irony, enthroned on the ash heap of the agonies and aporias of his life. He rules all that he surveys, yet he rules from a position of utter powerlessness. Job acknowledges his own (metaphorical) kingship as it is rent from him by the implacable hand of God: "He has stripped my glory from me, and taken the crown from my head" (19:9). The word "crown," used in the Hebrew Bible for actual crowns on the heads of rulers and statues of deities, may stand as a metaphorical figure for the well-being and moral adornment of the blessed more generally. But the semantic valence that Job had enjoyed prosperity equivalent to that of a ruler is worthy of attention. At the beginning of his trauma, Job had wished, with heavy irony, to have died at birth so that he might have enjoyed as much power as (dead) kings and princes: "Why did I not die at birth . . . then I would be at rest with kings and counselors of the earth who rebuild ruins for themselves, or with princes who have gold, who fill their houses with silver" (3:11–15). Later, Job again uses the image of royal power ironically when he complains bitterly about not knowing the charges against him: "O that I had the indictment written by my adversary! . . . I would bind it on me like a crown; I would give him an account of all my steps; like a prince I would approach him" (31:35–37). In his powerlessness, Job is ruler only of the ironic.

Myriad ironies, both local and metanarratological, abound in the Book of Job. In 1965, Edwin M. Good found in Job a dominant irony having to do with the rejection of the culture of magic, pervasive in religious and ritual forms throughout the ancient Near East, that suggests that humans can affect what a deity does. Job becomes reconciled to God only because Job finally understands that although God is inscrutable, Job can have no recourse other than to trust God.[11] Good highlights various ironies within the speeches of the friends, for example their sardonic point that the deeds of the wicked are the very things that condemn them to punishment. The larger irony there is that the friends are wrong in their assumption that Job may be numbered among those who have sinned. As Good puts it, "the poet's irony is at work throughout the speeches of the friends. They say much that is remarkably true. But the poet . . . sees their earnest exhortations with an irony of his own that renders doubly ironic the irony in their own mouths."[12] Reconciliation is possible at the end of the Book of Job only because all false assumptions have been thoroughly ironized from every conceivable angle. Good writes, "Had Job won his case, the poem would be a cynical satire on a God who is not God. Had Job been crushed under God, it would satirize a God who will not let [humanity] be [human]. But God finds [the human] guilty and acquits him. That is the fundamental irony of The Book of Job and of Biblical faith."[13] Good lays out well some of the salient dimensions of irony in Job. Another crucial irony, noted by James L. Crenshaw, may be considered to frame the entire Book of Job in terms that locate it sarcastically within the corpus of biblical wisdom tradition. That irony has to do with the question of who attends to humankind. In Proverbs, the answer is God; in Qohelet, the answer is no one at all; and in the Prologue to Job, the answer is the Adversary! Crenshaw writes, "[T]he Adversary is entrusted with the ironical task of *watching over* Job's life. The same verb was also used to connote the protection that God's statutes provided from the notorious loose woman in Proverbs."[14] Crenshaw proposes that an even more radical irony is perceptible in the character of God: "[T]he prologue depicts a God who permits wanton destruction of innocent victims just to prove a point. . . . Above all, this guilty Lord ties all loose ends together neatly, totally oblivious to the misery resulting from entering into dialogue with the Adversary."[15] Crenshaw rightly sees that the Book of Job resists resolution of this urgent theological problem, instead allowing to stand the aporia created by the "tension between profound questions and naïve theology"[16] that has been played out in the tortured life and broken body of Job.

Two recent readings of Job offer further compelling angles on irony in the book.[17] These are Carol A. Newsom's *The Book of Job: A Contest of Moral Imaginations*[18] and Catherine Keller's "'Recesses of the Deep': Job's

Comi-Cosmic Epiphany," a chapter in her book *Face of the Deep: A Theology of Becoming*.[19] Newsom's work will be treated in some detail below. Keller's will be mentioned briefly as an example of constructive theology that builds on the perception of ironies in the biblical text.

Newsom's thesis is that competing moral imaginations and dictions are brought into dialogical encounter in the Book of Job in order to render a truth about human piety more multidimensional and profound than any one discursive system could account for on its own. The dialogical dynamics of Job resist the subordinative processes of "monologization"—the coercive privileging of a single perspective as definitive—and resist finalization as well. Newsom explores the rhetorical strategies of the didactic tale in Job 1–2 + 42:7–17, arguing that elements of patterned repetition and other semantic redundancies work with plot and characterization to provide a powerful monological story that is reassuringly coherent, morally unambiguous, and "authoritarian."[20] Suggesting that the unitary force of the didactic story is subtly destabilized by the dynamism of the unfolding plot, Newsom argues for the moral necessity of "interruption" in the Levinasian sense of the "ethical imperative of the disruption of discourse,"[21] a breach that speaks the truth of an Other into the ostensibly closed system of monologic storytelling. The friends urge recognition of the intrinsic order of God's creation and the efficacy of spiritual "technique" (prayer, repentance) as a means of negotiating one's place in that order. Job employs biting sarcasm, violently parodic use of language, and the urgent existential "now" of his anguish to emphasize alterity—the unbridgeable difference between the human and the divine—and to bear stubborn witness to the injustice of his turmoil. Elihu muses on what has been left unsaid and models for Job the displacement of human egocentricity through the spiritual discipline of praise.

Job insistently refuses the viability of the friends' discourse and the traditions that lie behind it. As Newsom writes:

> His alienation from received language is reflected in his extensive use of irony, parody, and other means of subverting traditional speech. His repudiation of the language that the friends still speak so effortlessly is evident not only in his parodies but also, most paradoxically, in his act of literal appropriation of their speech in the last cycle (chaps. 24 and 27). That gesture raises to intolerable clarity the failure of the resources of their language to comprehend the realities of Job's torment and puts an end to the dialogue.[22]

But the final word has not been spoken. The voice of God goes on to affirm the sublimely incomprehensible nature of deity and refuses Job's dominant legal trope of answerability, choosing instead to reconfigure Job as a tragic subject whose existence is both limited and precious.

Building on Newsom's groundbreaking work, I would note further that while all of the voices in the Book of Job speak things that are true to one degree or another, each of these voices ironizes the others. And more: the dramatic irony that lies beneath the entire book renders ironic the entire dialogical enterprise. The matter may seem to concern the give-and-take of intellectual and spiritual debate, but in actuality it does not. Even the position of God is ironized, Newsom has argued, because God has acted in the end just as the friends had said he would: he rewards the righteous Job and threatens punishment of those who have done injustice with their words.

Two observations may be added about unspoken ironies in the characterization of Job, for the subjectivity of Job himself has been deeply ironized throughout this book, in the poetry and in the prose framework. First, in the poetry: Job cries out for answers from God—what is his guilt? what is the divine purpose behind this torture?—but receives no answers to the questions he has posed. Instead, the divine response from the whirlwind undermines the standing of Job even to pose questions at all. Job is silenced, his agency as a figure in dialogue with God completely undermined by the unanswerability of God's power. Job cedes his subjectivity to God's construction of it ("I recant and repent in dust and ashes,"[23] 42:6). The subject who has insisted so fiercely on his integrity and his right to lay charges against God has, finally, been required to relinquish that very subjectivity, which had been the only thing he had left. After the speech of God thunders to its close, Job is left utterly bereft and voiceless. The Adversary may have taken Job's wealth, security, social status, children, and physical well-being, but it is God who has stripped Job of his subjectivity. Job has cried out for dialogue as a means of honoring his subjectivity—acknowledge, Lord, that I deserve an answer!—but God responds in a way that savagely ironizes the right of Job to speak at all. So where dialogue had seemed to be the only avenue left to Job to preserve his subjectivity, it turns out that dialogue has finally robbed him of everything. This is irony indeed.

A second ironizing of Job's character occurs in the prose framework. Despite the resolution provided by the prose ending, the character of Job has undergone such trauma and loss that he will never be the same again. The reader cannot conceive of Job's faith and trust in his God being anything like it had been before the Adversary made his wager. All is restored to Job, but the extravagance of his recompense is suspect—Job is given twice as much wealth and ten new children at a stroke. Although it may be a feature of folk tales to tie such narrative "loose ends" up neatly, the replacement of children cannot be made to compensate for the agony of loss in this particular literary context, *pace* those who find readers' moral objections to the ending of Job out of place. The book's own attentiveness to Job's agony works against the theory that the ending was not supposed to be understood as problematic. It will not suffice to suggest that in folk tales such endings are commonplace and considered normative, for this "folk tale" self-consciously frames a literature that delves extraordinarily deeply into human emotional suffering. Thus one may suggest, with Newsom, that there is finally no true dialogue in the Book of Job and no closural ending either. The gestures toward dialogue and closure, in the poetry and prose respectively, in fact ironize each other. Job seems strangely isolated even amid the well-wishers who have flocked back to him to pay tribute. The "dialogue" with God has ironically silenced him. The "restoration" of what he had lost ironically renders his claims of injustice meaningless. Yet Job did suffer what he suffered—he went through unspeakable agonies of spirit and body. He will never forget, and most assuredly neither will the reader.[24]

Catherine Keller employs the notion of a "tehomic theology" in her interpretive project. She means here to promote a genesis-oriented, incarnational theology attentive to primal beginnings, uncontrollable becomings, and the dynamism of chaos. Keller's treatment of Job suggests irony in a crucial dimension of the Joban theology. She finds the allusions to chaos monsters (Sea, Dragon, and Rahab earlier in the poetry; Leviathan and Behemoth near the end) to "structure the entire drama" of the Book of Job as a "parodic reversal of the very sequence of creation."[25] Keller argues that the theological perspective of the Book of Job, "hybrid" because of the conflictual interaction between the prose and the poetry, constitutes a complex midrashic elaboration on Genesis 1. The Book of Job depicts "billowing life running wild within its ordered ecologies."[26] By means of that depiction, the book destabilizes human arrogance and the human desire for cognitive control. Keller writes:

> Through parody, I submit, the Joban poet resists a hardening theological anthropomorphism that in the combined context of an urban and exile-prone monotheism was already tending to reduce nonhuman nature to a background effect. . . . Did the Joban poet thus resist a double alienation: the loss of the wild integrities of creation and the loss of human justice in history? . . . [P]erhaps the whirlwind rhapsodizes astronomical bodies, weather and wild animals *because* these resist human dominance.[27]

Keller's and Newsom's readings, taken together, underline the untamable ironies of incarnational living and logocentric discourse in the

Book of Job. Ironies attend the desperate living of Job and the powerful living of wild creatures and their creator. Ironies attend human discourse as well, both within the voice of a single speaker and among the dialogic interventions of speakers with one another.

In the Book of Job, we encounter a paradox: experience teaches us about God, yet experience cannot teach us about God. For Job, it is true that God is both ruthlessly attentive and absent in his time of greatest need. God neither heeds Job's cries for justice nor gives him respite from the calamities that have befallen him and the agonies that continue to rack his body. So Job's experience of God as not being predictably benevolent to the righteous is represented as true. It is verified, beyond the shadow of a doubt, by what happens to Job as the book unfolds. Yet the life experience of a single believer cannot rightly be considered to yield all necessary information about God for a coherent theology, for God is much more than the human intellect can grasp. God's rebuke of Job in the whirlwind makes that abundantly clear. Thus Job has spoken wrongly about God, as the friends aver (e.g., he is attacked by Elihu in 35:16, "Job opens his mouth in empty talk; he multiplies words without knowledge," and the attack is pressed further by God in 38:2, "Who is this who darkens counsel by words without knowledge?"). Yet again, though, Job's wrongness is not the sort of wrongness they perceive. Paradoxically, Job's experience and his reflection on that experience are right—"he has spoken rightly" about God, as God says—but Job is also in the wrong (although not for the reason the friends have stated), and so it is appropriate that he repent or otherwise change his mind about his posture toward God heretofore (Job 42:6).

Ernest W. Nicholson suggests that the point of the divine speech from the whirlwind is to reinforce for Job the power of the creator over creation and thus "reawaken faith."[28] It is a theologically beautiful suggestion, but one may nevertheless interrogate it. Did Job need a reminder about the power of God over creation? One suspects not—and neither did his friends, for that matter. In fact, Job understood the "mastery" of God all too well. He balked at the way in which God wielded power, not helping the innocent and persecuting them with a relentless divine hand. Thus the paradox remains: life experience teaches us rightly about God, and yet we cannot rely on life experience to teach us (everything) about God. Since God is beyond human understanding, we can speak only out of our lived experience; nevertheless, we dare not speak out of that experience as if it were adequate grounds for theological understanding. The divine speech makes this clear, heaping irony upon irony in a barrage of sarcastic questions to which no mortal could possibly venture an answer. The irony of God deigning to speak to Job at all is signaled at the beginning of the creator's address: "I will question you, and you shall declare to me" is devastatingly ironic in light of what follows.

With these musings on ironies in Proverbs and Job in the background, I will now explore two instances of ironic voicing within ancient Israelite wisdom, in the Book of Qohelet and in Psalm 73. I will attend to the primary speaking voice constructed in each of these texts, probing in particular the dialogical engagement of the said and the unsaid and what that may imply for the authority of the speaker. Colebrook suggests that the appreciation of irony leads inevitably to a deeper understanding of the contradictions inherent in all speech:

> All speech is haunted by irony. Not only can we question whether what is said is really meant; any act of speech can be repeated and quoted in another context, generating unintended forces. Further, and more importantly, insofar as speaking creates some event of decision, force and difference, or makes a claim about what is other than itself, it must refer to what is not itself. One can only make a statement about the world, or really say something, if one recognises the force of contradiction.[29]

Biblical wisdom literature recognizes the force of contradiction in human experience and the need for a theology that responds to disjuncture. Qohelet and Psalm 73 are remarkable for the way in which they deploy self-conscious metacognitive strategies in order to underline and reflect on the contradictions of human life. Each of those texts deftly plays out the risks and possibilities of attempting to speak an authentic theological word to the contradictions of life. The varying lengths of these texts (12 chapters in Qohelet, a mere 28 verses in Psalm 73) demonstrate that the genius of ancient Israelite irony could be enacted on as expansive or as small a scale as the authors liked. The breadth of vision of Qohelet and the pathos-in-miniature of Psalm 73 perform their ironies with a sense of aesthetic proportion to their particular subject matter that is pitch-perfect.

Ironic Representation, Authorial Voice, and Meaning in Qohelet

Who authored the Book of Qohelet? The Book of Qohelet presents an optimal arena for the testing of modern and postmodern ways of reading, in two distinct senses: reading the text itself and reading the question of authorship.[30] Qohelet exploits a shifting and unstable constellation of freighted signifiers, structuring devices, and rhetorical tools to convey its message. Pressed into service are autobiographical, poetic, and sapiential

literary forms; profound philosophical speculation and mundane pragmatic observations; incisive aphorisms, didactic parables, and elliptical
metaphors. The deftness with which these diverse forms and literary styles
are woven together in service of a cohesive tone of skepticism raises a crucial question about another literary variation discernible in the material,
namely, the two distinct authorial voices. Are the vacillations between
first- and third-person voices used to speak of (the) "Qohelet" indicative of
redaction, or are they literary devices employed by a single author? The
composition-history question matters not only for historical-critical reconstruction of the development of the book; it matters for exegetical efforts
to understand the ways in which apparent tensions in the book may be
significant for the meaning of the text. Qohelet has been interpreted in
strikingly differing ways based on different historically and literarily con-
textualized evaluations of real or implied authorship and concomitant
expectations regarding real or implied audience(s). Scholars who argue
for one or more redactors explore the play between a prior radical skepticism and a later, more orthodox reshaping of the book's message.[31] Interpreters who favor the possibility that the book is the product of a single
author are more interested in "Qohelet" as a fictional persona, the construction of which serves larger rhetorical goals in the book.[32]

It is precisely regarding these sorts of issues of authorial intent and
the constructedness of authorial voice that the modern/postmodern debate continues to rage. Despite optimistic claims that the modern and
the postmodern need each other, that these kinds of reading modes
"interpenetrate each other and are not to be polarized,"[33] it remains
clear that modern and postmodern approaches disagree sharply about
the natures of text, authorship, and literary representation. Does original intent pose any prior hermeneutical claim, however negotiable that
claim may become in light of later interpretations? Or can any reading
claim persuasiveness if it evokes the consent of a particular audience?[34]
Put another way, is it the case that "each reading is ultimately as incor-
rect as every other one, although some may be more reasonable than
others in one reading context or another"?[35]

It goes without saying that authorial intent is a tricky thing to discern
and demonstrate; that texts are full of ambiguities, gaps, elusive references, and elements that may be used in their own deconstruction; and
that any historical-critical reading is necessarily provisional and partial,
shaped by the biases and ideological suppositions of its proponent. Any
honest historical critic will affirm the thoroughgoing provisionality of interpretation. But postmodernist readings have unquestionably posed a
formidable and appropriate challenge to naïve understandings of the
ways in which texts and language represent that to which they attempt to

refer. For postmodern readings influenced by deconstructionism, excava-
tive exegesis is both oppressively hegemonic and fundamentally misguided. Many postmodernists would consider the opening paragraph of
this section to be deeply flawed, not least because there is no "text" or "author" in Qohelet to "press into service" anything on behalf of a deposited
"message," some inherent meaning purportedly extant apart from each
reader's act of construction of text, author, and meaning. These objections are entertained by a reasonable number of biblicists working today,
and much creative work has been done in biblical studies by literary critics
of a poststructuralist bent. But many other exegetes have little patience
with the radical problematizing of text and signification that has been
central to postmodern lines of inquiry. What Stephen D. Moore observed
in 1992 is still true of much biblical scholarship: "As regards deconstruction, then, biblical exegesis is still in the 'before' stage. The sand repeatedly kicked in its face has so far had little effect."[36]

What constitutes competent reading? Any hegemonic requirement as
regards what constitutes viable interpretation could be contested.[37] The
hermeneutical challenge proves particularly acute in the case of the Book
of Qohelet, which has been perceived by many interpreters to be elusive
and riddled with contradictions. Graham Ogden highlights the interpretive crux writ large: "The two well-known views of Heine—that Qoheleth
is the quintessence of skepticism—and F. Delitzsch—that it is the quintessence of piety—make us immediately aware of the basic problem. The
contents of the book appear to be so confusing that two *opposite,* and not
just variant, interpretations seem possible."[38] One recent interpretation of
Qohelet finds the book unsettling, ephemeral, confusing, at times unin-
telligible, marked by anxiety and frustration on the part of its author and
evoking the same in its readers.[39] The apparently unstable nature of the
text and meaning(s) of Qohelet thus makes it a fertile terrain for exploration of divergent hermeneutical approaches.

My readings of ironic texts have pointed to pervasive ambiguities and
indeterminacies as highly significant and—in the case of Micah
2:12–13—even as the means, paradoxically, of a subtle coherence enacted
rhetorically. Here, too, I will argue for the possibility of an underlying coherence. My position is that a consistent and rhetorically purposeful irony
shapes the entire Book of Qohelet. On my reading of the ironic metanarrative here, the persona of "Qohelet" is being represented as complicated
and conflicted because his viewpoint is meant to be rejected by the reader
as an inappropriate way to approach life. This is not the definitive or the
only way to read the Book of Qohelet, of course. But I will make the strongest case that I can for an overarching irony that subverts the skeptical
perspective of "Qohelet," even though I know that the "said," the surface

meaning of the skeptical and quasi-Stoical sayings within the book, will nevertheless retain their authority and their appeal for many readers.

No biblical book is more thoroughly basted in reduction upon reduction of irony than is the Book of Qohelet. The multifaceted irony of Qohelet calls the reader into the intimacy of shared confidence one moment and mocks the reader from a great distance the next, painstakingly constructs a deceptive rhetorical edifice and then dismantles it in a stroke. Many moments of irony within the discourse of Qohelet have been appreciated by commentators, in particular with regard to apparent contradictions or reversals of discrete maxims.[40] Some interpreters have noted the ironic subversion of genre expectations and the general ironic tenor of the book.[41] Indeed, the pervasive presence of reversals and instabilities throughout the text of Qohelet has itself been argued to constitute the coherence of the book. Fox suggests that "Qohelet's persistent observation of contradictions is a powerful cohesive force" in the book, a consistent way of documenting and lamenting the incongruities of life.[42] Seow is certainly correct that Qohelet's argumentation is primarily about "the very fact of contradiction."[43] But the crucial governing irony mediated by the construction of the persona of "Qohelet" has not yet received adequate attention. The ironic metanarrative structure of the book enacted via the unreliability of its authorial voice seems to have been only glancingly noticed even by as skilled a reader as Harold Fisch.[44] For Fisch, Qohelet's aesthetics of negation serves ultimately to show up skepticism itself as *hevel*, as an emptiness that both constitutes Qohelet as ironist and causes him to stand divided against himself. Fisch argues, rightly, that the epilogue of Qohelet provides the sharpest irony of the book, that "this skeptical rejection of skepticism is the final twist of Qohelet's super-irony."[45] But the blurring of the essential line between the Book of Qohelet and the persona "Qohelet" requires a more focused hermeneutical response. The following will explore ways in which ironic representation and authorial voice shape the text of Qohelet toward a larger rhetorical goal, namely, the deeply ironic inscribing of the catastrophic effects of disobeying God in the persona of "Qohelet" and the corpus of the Book of Qohelet.

We turn first to the persona of "Qohelet" and the authority he commands in the text. The authorial voice of "Qohelet" is a remarkably self-conscious and self-revealing voice, the ostensible transparency of which is unique within biblical literature. "Qohelet" speaks openly and explicitly not only of his actions but also of his goals, his desires, and his affective states. There is much to interpret here, not only regarding what "Qohelet" says he has done and wanted and thought, but also on the metanarratological level regarding what it is that the author may be doing in the construction of the persona of "Qohelet."

Traditional historical-critical readings manifest a capricious bipolarity in their assumptions regarding the self-representation in the Book of Qohelet. Virtually all modern critical scholars show no hesitation in rejecting the ancient and modern-conservative identification of "Qohelet" with Solomon, and most seem prepared to treat with a degree of skepticism the claims in Qohelet 1 and 2 regarding the author's unparalleled royal power and lavish lifestyle. Yet many of the same interpreters seem to take at face value the different authorial voices in Qohelet as directly and transparently reflecting two different historical persons, usually conceived as a relatively radical skeptic and his more conservative editor. Within that framework, then, scholars debate the degree to which the positions of "Qohelet" and the epilogist may fairly be said to differ.

The possible rhetorical functions of the two "I"s in the Book of Qohelet have been considered by a number of scholars. T. A. Perry, Tremper Longman, Michael V. Fox, and Gary D. Salyer all have wrestled with the implications of the double voicing in Qohelet. Perry's view that the book has been constructed as a dialogical text has the merit of taking seriously the text's engagement of differing perspectives as an intentional rhetorical device. The force of the dialogue, for Perry, is more than the sum of its parts—the representation of "lived and live debate" renders in fuller dimensions the positions that are taken (and, as I would add following Hutcheon, a tacit but crucial third position that emerges from the engagement between the dialogic partners).[46] Perry's suggestion that the voice of "Qohelet" is presented as "limited and yet valid" is a significant advance over unsubtle redaction-critical approaches that assume the epilogist wholly trumps "Qohelet."[47] But Perry's finely calibrated division of the text into two distinct speakers throughout is not fully convincing, although it is fascinating to read and has helpfully sharpened the debate regarding multivocality in the book. His methodological criterion that the individual speakers must present a "consistency of argument" and hence that tensions are necessarily indicative of a change in speaker is vulnerable to the charge of tautology when pressed as far as it is in Perry's work. The dialogic markers that Perry musters to claim change of speaker are in some cases extremely subtle.[48] That would not constitute a flaw in Perry's argument if the language of Qohelet is as sophisticated and nuanced as Perry maintains. But more rigorous and detailed argumentation would be needed to adjudicate specific instances, as for example to define when *gam* is used adversatively to flag a change in speaker rather than denote emphasis in some other aspect of semantic signification; to determine when conjunctive *wāw* is employed as a signal of major disjuncture (and thus, for Perry, change in speaker) rather than minor disjuncture or connection; and to discern when causative *kî* is to be understood as introducing an ironic conclusion rather than a straightforward result.

Longman suggests that Qohelet may have been a real person rather than a literary persona, although he gives a nod to the latter possibility.[49] Of particular interest in Longman's analysis is his suggestion that the frame narrator is quoting the speech of "Qohelet" for didactic purposes, to warn against skepticism.[50] This nuanced hermeneutical move on Longman's part manages to safeguard some of the heuristic distance of a "persona" while not abandoning the evangelical affirmation of the literal sense of the text. That the speech of "Qohelet" is being used for a larger purpose is certainly correct. The present treatment will probe in more detail the significance of the ways in which "Qohelet" is being used as a foil. In my view, the rhetorical enactment of that move is more complicated than simply a caution regarding the dangers of skepticism, although Longman's argument seems correct to me as far as it goes.

Fox's frame narrator dominates what Fox sees as a hierarchy of "nested levels of perspective." The literary sophistication with which Fox credits the Book of Qohelet is, I think, exactly right. I am in agreement with Fox when he writes, "In my view, the words of Qohelet (1:3–12:7), the title (1:1), the motto (1:2; 12:8), and the epilogue proper (12:9–12) are all the creation of the same person, the author of the book, who is not to be identified with Qohelet, his persona. In other words, it is not that the epilogue is by Qohelet, but that Qohelet is 'by' the epilogist."[51] Fox asserts that while the views of the character "Qohelet" are not precisely coterminous with those of the frame narrator, the latter generally approves of Qohelet and is largely in sympathy with his perspective. This view does account for some areas of continuity between the epilogue and the rest of the Book of Qohelet and indeed constitutes the obvious "straight" reading of the epilogue. But I will argue that the epilogist in fact has created "Qohelet" with far sharper ironic intention, as a foil, and that the ironic intention continues right up until the earnest command to fear God and keep God's commandments.[52] More is at stake in the double voicing of this text than a simple framing of the skeptical voice or reorientation of priorities by a more traditionally pious frame narrator. Distance is built rhetorically into the text between the reader and "Qohelet" as well as between "Qohelet" and the frame narrator—and not only at the beginning and end of the book, although most certainly and dramatically there. For example, the intrusive mention of "Qohelet" in the third person in 7:27, along with an unexpected feminine singular form of the verb, flags in a self-conscious way the constructedness of "Qohelet" as persona and, I believe, reminds the reader to keep some distance from "Qohelet."

Gary D. Salyer has analyzed the "I" of Qohelet as well. He suggests that the author's rhetorical choice to use first-person narration yielded risks as well as compelling strengths of presentation,[53] for "it is the nature of all I-discourses to imply their own limitations and, therefore, to invite dialogic dissension with their major premises and conclusions."[54] Salyer helpfully underlines the centrality of irony, paradox, and ambiguity in the textual representation of Qohelet, which he sees as structuring a dialogue between public and private modes of knowledge. Per Salyer, the self-consciously fictive representation of "Qohelet" constitutes a device of masking that simultaneously reinforces the book's overall tenor of ambiguity and invites the reader into (the perception of) an intimate knowledge of the narrator.[55]

While the tensions and ambiguities within the Book of Qohelet cannot be definitively resolved and, indeed, should be read as significant in their very tensiveness and ambiguity, still more can be said about the relationship of "Qohelet" to the larger function of the book. To get at the ironic meaning of the persona of "Qohelet" in the multivocal Book of Qohelet, we will examine below three defining contours of authorial presence in the text: autobiographical voice, caricature, and the movement between particularity and ideal.

The Book of Qohelet presses the point that "Qohelet" was an exceptionally wise sage whose empirical observations of human existence constitute a reliable basis on which to construct his skeptical philosophy regarding epistemology, value, and purpose in human life. This overt statement is made again and again in the book. "Qohelet" grounds his authority to speak and to teach concretely in his personal identity and experience. He is a "son of David," a "king in Jerusalem," and has done all that a king can do, from constructing a magnificent court to amassing riches to indulging in pleasures of the flesh. In fact, he has done "more than all the kings who were before" him in Jerusalem (2:9). Ah—more than all one of them (or all two of them, if one allows Saul into the lineage, construing "in Jerusalem" more loosely)? Interpreters have noted the problems with this claim, which seems to posit a lengthy lineage of previous monarchs in Jerusalem and thus stands in obvious tension with the narratological fiction that Solomon is the speaker. Unease begins to stir in the reader. "Qohelet's" impeccable authority is being established quite explicitly, but his voice seems less than wholly reliable. Either he is being represented overtly as not Solomon, or he is being represented subtly as a Solomon who is wrong about something, namely, the length of the list of kings in Jerusalem before him. The first option, that "Qohelet" is being portrayed as a speaker other than Solomon, is an interesting possibility given the authority of earlier Israelite traditions regarding Solomon's unequalled wisdom. Is Qohelet then truly wiser than Solomon himself, or might he be a boaster like the *alazon* of classical Greek rhetoric, one who pretends to a greatness that he does not have? Stuart Weeks rightly worries about this issue, particularly because the speaker is called by a name other than Solomon while nevertheless trading on a Solomonic identity. Weeks writes, "However used ancient readers were to fictional attributions, there is no reason to think that they expected characters to change identity. Since Qoheleth is not apparently intended to be a name for Solomon, the author seems to be presenting us with a character who openly disguises himself as another character. . . . One consequence, of course, is that the reader knows Qoheleth's account of his kingship to be untrue."[56] The second option, that "Qohelet" is being represented subtly as a Solomon whose wisdom has failed late in life, is also interesting. Walter Brueggemann suggests that "Qohelet's" Solomonic life is intended to offer a lesson:

> [I]n royal fiction, the voice of the speaker is the old king who is belatedly able to see that the achievements on which he has spent his life add up to nothing. The text [1:12–2:26] thus constitutes a belated critique of concerns of self-aggrandizement for which Solomon is the primary example in Israel. The text is a refutation of ambitious, aggressive displays of self-achieving power. In this way, Solomon by inference is made a didactic example in Judaism for how *not* to live in the world.[57]

Quite right, and I would add only this: if the Solomon-like character of "Qohelet" is being ironized regarding the choices he had once made, then the narratological door has been opened, at least a crack, for the possibility that the reliability of his voice in the present time of the narrative is also being represented as compromised.

The text continues. Precisely because of his power and wealth, "Qohelet" considers that he has had the opportunity to explore all of the options for understanding and appreciating the good in life. His stature, as reflected in his accomplishments and possessions, is greater than any king who went before him (2:9). No one will be able to claim an authority, at least an authority based on experience, that supersedes that of "Qohelet," for "what can the one do who comes after the king? Only what has already been done" (2:12). Hyperbole here flags the distinct possibility that irony is afoot, but the uneasy reader must reserve judgment, lacking adequate information this early on in the discourse. Maybe he really was the richest and most powerful ruler ever—perhaps we should silence our nagging doubts. The comparativist reader may practice a kind of historicist credulity here, seeking refuge from text-induced anxiety in the knowledge that royal boasting has taken many forms throughout the ancient Near East. In royal inscriptions and other texts, emphasis is normally given to military victories, monumental building projects, impressive deeds of justice on behalf of subjects, cultic donations, and the like, a chief rhetorical goal being the political lionization of the king and promotion of his royal authority. With pseudonymous royal autobiography in Mesopotamia, the same effects are achieved obliquely on behalf of a later ancestor of the (fictional) Akkadian ruler, as Longman has shown, and the fact that such Akkadian texts employ standard literary tropes, well-worn folkloristic topoi, and hyperbole need not necessarily be seen as betraying the text's lack of historical accuracy.[58] So the presence of hyperbole alone is not enough for the reader to judge the text's earnestness or irony here, true. But the comparative method of genre analysis illumines best where the conventions of genre are in fact observed or else clearly subverted; and it seems that that is not the case with the textual representation of this authorial voice, which lacks accurate information about the putative referent. At most, we may say that the Book of Qohelet is structured loosely along the lines of a fictional autobiography with a didactic ending and that the author may have been familiar with Mesopotamian literature, including the Gilgamesh epic and the Cuthean legend of Naram-Sin.[59]

The abandonment of any pretense to restraint or accuracy in "Qohelet's" self-representation finally compels the reader beyond credulity. The depiction of Qohelet cannot be chalked up to expectations generated by the genre of royal autobiography. The strain in the voice of the speaker is too palpable: hyperbole and vagueness together have shaded over into ironic caricature. Here is relevant the argument of Crenshaw that in "Qohelet" we see flawed logic insufficiently masked: "The simple truth is that Qoheleth accepted an astonishing variety of transmitted teachings without submitting them to the test of experience. Occasionally, he uses emphatic language, e.g., 'I know,' when asserting something that none can confirm. . . . One suspects that rhetoric aims at obscuring faulty logic in such moments."[60] Crenshaw's astute recognition of the epistemological difficulties with many of "Qohelet's" claims would have been expected, I think, of the implied audience of the text as well. I agree with Crenshaw about the weaknesses of "Qohelet's" discourse, that "his attempt to forge philosophical concepts, while innovative and bold, never quite got off the ground."[61] Indeed, I would argue that the text invites us to recognize those epistemological flaws in the perspective of its protagonist. The implied ancient audience is encouraged to become increasingly uncomfortable with "Qohelet's" grandiose boasts and philosophical assertions.

Additional evidence that "Qohelet's" self-aggrandizing reflection on his past is intended ironically is not long in coming. The entire basis for "Qohelet's" authority is undermined by the concession that all is *hevel*, van-

ity or transience or worthlessness. All of the things that have just constituted "Qohelet" as authoritative speaker are, with one devastating stroke,
delegitimized. The crucial question for the reader becomes, on what authority, then, does this "Qohelet" speak to us? Either we are to take his
royal stature as still significant—in other words, resist his claim that it all
means nothing—or we must acknowledge that it does mean nothing and
he speaks to us not as a king but as a wretch, proclaiming his edicts not
from his opulent palace but from atop the ash heap of his illusions.

And finally, the contradictions and tensions that inhere in what "Qohelet" is teaching serve to destabilize the last remaining source of potential confidence in the sage: the content of his instruction. In the words
of Thomas Krüger:

> The expectations of readers awakened by the form of the book of
> Qoheleth as a work of instructive wisdom literature are, however,
> systematically disappointed by its content. The teaching author-
> ity of King Solomon is "deconstructed" and repudiated already
> in the first chapters of the book. In chapter 3, at the latest, the
> reader notices that regarding the tensions between the state-
> ments of the king in 1:12–2:26 and their "revision" in 3:10–4:12,
> the book conveys no clear teaching, but instead carries on a "de-
> bate" between different teachings.[62]

The self-representation of "Qohelet" is marked by pervasive ironies that
bid the discerning reader to stand with the book's covert rejection of
"Qohelet's" reliability and the trustworthiness of his conclusions.

Might "Qohelet" be considered an ideal author according to the canons of postmodernism, an ancient prototype of the postmodern hero who
is sensitive to the particularities of his sociopolitical location and his own
psychic idiosyncrasies, who not only names them but dares boldly to connect his experience of them to the construction of his ideology? The possibility intrigues but must finally be rejected. "Qohelet" extrapolates un-
abashedly from his particulars to universals, pronouncing hegemonic
epistemological claims and inflexible moral judgments that leave no room
for otherness, variant particularities, change, or a diversity of perspectives.
Herein may be discerned another thoroughgoing irony in the Book of
Qohelet: his particularity cannot underwrite his categorical, universalis-
tic claims in the way that he purports to find it to do. His experience is not
merely unusual. It is, by the text's own admission, unequivocally unattainable: it cannot be emulated by anyone else. Since that is so, his claims for
universal truth become, in fact, almost ludicrous. The authority based on
"Qohelet's" experience fails because it is based on caricature.

An objection might be raised to the notion that the voice of (almost) an entire biblical book is being represented ironically. I should like to cite two examples from more recent literature as evidence that an authorial voice intended from the start as wholly ironic was received later in a way that was completely at odds with its intended purpose. In diverse literatures of the world, the speaking voice of a main character or narrator has occasionally been conceived of as ironic but been regularly (mis)-read as "straight" by a consensus of later interpreters.

The first example of a case in which the speaking voice of a text has been argued to be wholly ironic is Jonathan Swift's poem, "Verses on the Death of Dr. Swift," mentioned briefly in chapter 1. Scholarship on the poem had seen irony only in the first two strophes, but once a scholar argued that the third strophe was entirely ironic, many interpreters came to see that possibility as viable. The weight of interpretive tradition may not be decisive if one is interested in "changing the conditions of seeing," as Stanley Fish said. Indeed, an author can even be self-conscious about the likelihood that one's writing may be misread by others—Swift certainly was.[63]

My second example is Bruce Zuckerman's treatment of a nineteenth-century Yiddish story by Y. L. Perets, "Bontsye Shvayg" ("Bontsye the Silent"). In the story, a desperately poor man dies, having lived his life quiet and unnoticed, "like a tiny grey particle of sand on the seashore, among millions of his ilk."[64] Abused, tormented, cheated, and ignored, Bontsye had suffered in silence for a lifetime. In heaven, Bontsye is offered extravagant rewards for his humility—"all of Heaven is yours!"—but all he requests, at the climactic moment of the narrative, is a hot buttered roll every morning. The hosts of heaven bow their heads in shame, and the heavenly prosecutor laughs, a laugh that Zuckerman interprets as triumphant because Bontsye has just shown himself to be not extraordinarily moral but merely an idiot, or, in Zuckerman's words, "the ultimate schlemiel."[65] Zuckerman argues that Perets's writing offers a hyperbolically sentimental representation of Bontsye's desperate straits in life, which are pathetic beyond any possible verisimilitude. There are clues throughout the story that Bontsye has been morally "good" mostly from a lack of backbone and lack of discernment of what is going on around him. More telling, Bontsye is surprised at the lengthy rendering of the details of his life in the heavenly court because "he, himself, had never given a thought about his whole life. In the other world he had forgotten each moment the previous."[66] Far from being a saintly man who chose to suffer in silence, Bontsye may better be understood to have been simply unaware as he stumbled through the various misfortunes of his life.

Zuckerman uses this story to illustrate the fact that in the history of interpretation, readers have come to assign to stories meanings that seem to be blatantly contradictory to what the original story says. His chief example is the cultural notion of the "patience of Job," which bears little relation to the evident impatience and despair of the biblical character Job. Zuckerman also cites the example of the Aqedah: the story of Genesis 22 clearly indicates that Isaac was spared, but a tradition persisted in rabbinic interpretation that Isaac had been slain by Abraham. Textual ambiguities in the biblical story can account for only part of the hermeneutical impetus behind this reading of the Aqedah. Also in play were other contextual forces, including the probability that the biblical account was being understood against the background of other versions of the story in Israelite and Canaanite traditions and in other ancient Near Eastern cultures.[67] In any case, Zuckerman finds unpersuasive the reading of "Bontsye Shvayg" as an earnest story of a hero who suffers and is rewarded. He argues, instead, that Perets has written a parody of the figure of the humble sufferer in Jewish tradition. Zuckerman's arguments for reading "Bontsye Shvayg" as a satire are compelling.

I suggest that an analogously subtle satire has been effected in the persona of "Qohelet" as he is represented in the Book of Qohelet. By means of the self-absorbed caricature and unreliable authorial voice that constitute the persona of "Qohelet," the unsaid message of this ironic text has been inscribed. What then is the unsaid, and what might be the "third" meaning that emerges from the tensive relationship between the said and the unsaid? We may approach the question by examining what the corpus of the Book of Qohelet might signify through its beginning and ending(s) about the body/persona of "Qohelet" and his own beginning and ending.

Beginnings matter for the rhetoric of the Book of Qohelet, and they matter in an ironic way, because for "Qohelet," beginnings are not true beginnings at all. The proem at the start of the book (1:1–11) establishes the dissonance that obtains throughout the book between apparent newness and the inescapable reality of sameness, tedium, and circularity. According to "Qohelet," there is nothing new under the sun; everything that exists or is done has all been before and will be again (3:15). No new act can surprise the wise person or change the course of things, for God has long ago approved what one does (9:7). Apparent boundaries between past, present, and future reflect more the limitations of the human mind than the reality created by God. Humans cannot know what God has done from beginning to end. Our vision hopelessly obfuscated, we muddle through life in epistemological semidarkness, blindly repeating patterns that have obtained since the beginning of creation. The inescapable shadow of death looms over all human endeavor, depriving it of ultimate significance or permanence. Hopeless circularity and death trump every human beginning, including not only all forms of human striving but birth itself (7:1). All things, all discourses are wearisome—the polyvalence of the Hebrew *kol haddĕvārîm* permits the sense that the discourse that follows 1:8 is itself nothing new. In fact, even speech itself is not possible (*lō' yûkal 'îš lĕdabbēr*). The earth remains forever; it has always been there and always will be there. The sun rises and sets over and over again. Nothing has ever changed. No creation ex nihilo here, no form wrested from formless chaos, and indeed, no engaged creator at all: just tedium, circularity, and sameness, reported by "Qohelet" to himself in soliloquy. A more impersonal, abstract, distanced beginning to a book of personal reflections would be hard to imagine.

Consider now the end of the corpus (in every sense) described in Qohelet 12. We encounter exhortation: "Remember your creator in the days of your youth!"[68] The freighted symbolic language that follows seems to figure both the apocalyptic end of the universe and the catastrophic end of the human body. Interpreters over many centuries have read as both cosmic and anthropomorphic the images of disintegration, fear, weakening, and rupture in 12:2–6.[69] The polysemous allegorizing resolves into a focus on the corpus of the human being by verse 6 (dust to dust) and returns to the Creator via the image of the breath of life returning to "God who gave it." The sage has learned, at the end of his discourse and at the end of his carefully constructed life, to remember the Creator before death comes. The writer dies, and with him dies the corpus of his work: the text itself. As Salyer notes, the text itself not only speaks of *hevel* but creates it:

> The narrator's choice of words often leaves the reader in a state of perplexity, confusion, or indecision. By doing so, the implied author has consciously constructed a text which would recreate the same sense of *hebel* at a literary level that one often experiences in real life. . . . In that regard, the type of vain rhetoric we encounter in the book of Ecclesiastes is a performative concept as well. It's [*sic*] chief effect is to provide the reader with a narrative experience of life's absurdity.[70]

He reflects on his own morbidity as all disintegrates around him.[71] We hear "Qohelet" gasping with his dying breath, "Vanity of vanities, all is vanity!" The rhetorical force of the connections between chapters 1 and 12 thus links the beginning and end of the corpus of Qohelet. In this beginning and end of the text, we are confronted with the genesis and apocalyptic end of the persona of the sage.[72] With him, unquestionably, dies the wisdom endeavor that this particular sage has embodied in the discourse of his book. What Ronald Paulson says of Jonathan Swift may be applied also to the brilliant "Qohelet":

The point is that Swift's body is completely gone, and his works as well. What survives is his memory. . . . The ironies thus demonstrate the instability of Swift's identity even here, or perhaps of all places here, in his "fame." . . . [H]is body has been destroyed and remade into something utilizable—an "example," no more real than the original, and indeed capable (as Swift's profoundest irony shows) of itself being turned into as much of an idol as the old broken one.[73]

Just so, "Qohelet" and his unreliable sapiential ways are being deconstructed as an idol. Important also is the point Paulson makes about memory. According to "Qohelet," no one is remembered, for nothing can withstand the ravages of time: "The people of long ago are not remembered, nor will there be any remembrance of people yet to come by those who come after them" (1:11). Yet ironically, "Qohelet" himself has indeed been remembered, not only because his writings have survived but because the epilogist performs the remembrance of "Qohelet" explicitly in his metanarratological conclusion (12:9–10). Thus the corpus of "Qohelet," in both senses, has not only been destroyed and made into something utilizable. It has also, in that last act of remembrance by the epilogist, been ironized one last time—because now, Qohelet 1:11 cannot stand either.

And a final point: the reader who has been lured in by the musings of "Qohelet" dies too. This brilliant last stroke dispatches, as it were, all those who choose not to stand with the ironist in resisting the persona of "Qohelet." Fox observes of 12:1–8, "We finally descry ourselves. We see our own death, and Qohelet will not let us turn away."[74] This is quite right. In the allegorizing of 12:1–8, all humans die, and thus all readers of the Book of Qohelet die. But I would suggest that it is the reader duped by the ironized persona of "Qohelet" who dies in a particularly telling way hermeneutically, brought to the point of disintegration by the aporias and contradictions that slice through the book. Only the reader who stands with the ironist can live to reflect on the death of Qohelet.

That the Book of Qohelet may be musing on what transpired in the Garden of Eden is an idea of ancient pedigree. Early rabbinic tradition explored in various ways the literary and theological links between the pronouncements of "Qohelet" and the story of the Garden.[75] Modern scholars, too, have noted possible literary connections between Genesis 2–3 and the discourse of Qohelet.[76] Language shared between the two corpora is not per se determinative for the argument—as indeed shared language alone rarely is, barring the pointed use of uncommon words or demonstrable verbatim quotation[77]—but it is suggestive: *'ādām* and *rûaḥ* figure prominently in Qohelet, and the several pointed references to humankind as created and God as Creator include apparent allusions to the

creation story in Genesis 2 (Qoh 3:20, "all are from the dust, and all return to the dust again"; and 12:6, mentioned above). Proceeding from the
warrant afforded by the language of dust, breath, and creator, one may
justify probing more deeply into the claims made in Genesis 3 by various
parties and the refutation of those claims in the Book of Qohelet.

In Genesis 2–3, God says that if the humans eat of the tree of the
knowledge of good and evil, they shall die; the snake counters that they
will not die but will become like God in that they will know good and evil.
The choice facing Eve and Adam about whether to obey God's stricture
regarding the tree is the determinative choice for the narratological shape
and rhetorical power of the story. What choices matter for Qohelet? In the
Book of Qohelet, no human choice matters in any durative way except for
the choice to fear God. "Qohelet" is irked by evil and by the prospering of
the wicked and the undeserving, but he has no investment in ethical
choice-making as such, and not much interest in pragmatic choice-making, either.[78] Not only do humans have no way of anticipating the results a
particular choice will yield ("you do not know which will prosper, this or
that," 11:6); there is no way of guaranteeing that a particular result will
obtain for long before being overturned or undone. That this is meant by
the author of the book as an ironic lesson about wisdom's inefficacy in the
matter of human ethical choice is clear from the remarkable statement in
7:16–18 that one should be neither too righteous and wise nor too wicked
and foolish, but rather "take hold of the one without letting go of the
other; for the one who fears God proceeds with both."[79] This paradox underlines the impotence of human choice in every arena but the fear of
God. This is where the snake lied, subtly and brutally: the humans have
not, in fact, become like God just because they can now discern good and
evil. The distinction between the divine and human realms is simply
brought into sharp relief. Despite their ill-gotten capacity for wisdom, humans can never discern the works and plans of God, they "can never find
out what God has done from beginning to end" (3:11), nor can they parse
"all the work of God, that no one can find out what is happening under
the sun," no matter how diligently they apply themselves (8:17).

The rhetorical distance obtaining between creator and created is so
vast, so unbridgeable, in the Book of Qohelet that one cannot postulate
any kind of meaningful dialogue between this skeptical Adam and his
God. Here is no startling intimacy, no insistent divine kiss of life on the
mouth of the dust-creature fashioned by God's own hands. This God
does not call to his creatures, seek them, yearn for their response. This
God is far, far away in heaven, while we are indescribably minute, im-
probable, and foolish here on earth (5:1). Everywhere in this book, God
is the distant creator whose choices at the beginning of creation have

already determined the peculiar shape of human misery millennia ago, today, and a thousand years hence. The rhetorical horizon of reference for Qohelet is invariably the past: not the retrievable past of human historical events, but the past almost beyond conception, the very dawn of time. His is a past prior to all of the tedious cycles of useless human toil. There is no future worth speaking of, and there is only barely a fleeting "now," a present moment made tangible and perceptible only in the enjoyment or suffering of it. Human becoming, human possibility, is weighted down by the unspeakably heavy burden of that most ancient time before historical time itself, the prelapsarian time in the Garden of Eden, the crystalline moment in which archetypal humans had the crucial choice before them and chose badly.

Here, the unsaid begins to emerge from behind the ironic mirror that is Qohelet's rhetoric. In the Garden, God assigned dire consequences for humans' impertinence in striving for wisdom against God's command. Those consequences were and are, first, desire that causes suffering, and second, unremitting, fruitless toil (Gen 3:16–19). Obedience would have been better, then and ever since. The misery so evident in the constructed life and mind of "Qohelet" is that truth, ironically embodied. What "Qohelet" says about life is perhaps technically correct, but it is not the most important thing to know. "Qohelet's" exhortations to delight in the moment, to embrace joy, cannot serve ironically to undermine the relentless cynicism and despair of the rest of his discourse, *pace* those interpreters who want to privilege the motif of joy in the book. "Qohelet's" rhetorical grasping for joy is a desperate, unconvincing paraenesis that serves only to highlight how distanced his (constructed) reality is from the desired fruits of his lifelong search for wisdom. His claim that the savoring of joy is paramount rings hollow, for in this one matter, he apparently has no experience! Is there anywhere in the Book of Qohelet, is there even a single phrase, wherein the reader has been induced to imagine "Qohelet" himself laughing with delight or ardently kissing the wife of his youth? Regarding joy, this speaker does not know whereof he speaks, not in the terms in which the narrative has presented him. What he does know, namely, hedonistic self-indulgence and bitter rationalization, cannot be spoken without irony. He is an unreliable sage, and he is not joyful. We believe what "Qohelet" says only at our peril.

How is "Qohelet" an ironic figure in the presentation of the Book of Qohelet? It is not the case that his persona is ironic because everything he says is supposed to be understood to be wrong—far from it. He is right; he sees that one must fear God (3:14, 5:6, 7:18, 8:12, 13). More than that, "Qohelet" is himself an ironist; this far, Fisch and others are correct. The reader may hear in the discourse of "Qohelet" that characteristic ironic lament regarding "the world's failure to meet the expectations of the ironist."[80] But "Qohelet's" whole endeavor of living by empirical wisdom is misguided. The authority and, indeed, the ironic tone of "Qohelet" have been represented as arising organically out of his lived experience and his rational extrapolation therefrom. But his experiences and his epistemological reflections on them have caused him only misery—not joy, not peace, not the confidence of righteousness, but misery. The reliability of his narrative voice has been undermined from the very beginning of the text. Now we see as "Qohelet" dies, as his persona disintegrates, that he has always lived wrongly. The persona of "Qohelet" embodies both the epitome of wisdom and the epitome of the misery caused by privileging the sapiential project over the fear of God. It is herein that the governing meta-irony of the book lies, inscribed from within the constructed persona of "Qohelet" and not simply imposed by a later redactional frame. "Qohelet" has been posted as the new scarecrow in the Garden of Eden.

The wisdom endeavor is thus skewered by the irony of the Book of Qohelet not via direct, polemical engagement, but in a way that is far more effective for its embodiment of the anti-hero and his own particular kind of unremitting toil. The book represents the sage as one who strives mightily but ultimately fails in the dystopian habitat constructed by his proud epistemological autonomy. Even in his radical skepticism and despite his acute mental suffering, "Qohelet" remains thoroughly committed to the traditional empirical method, ostensibly challenging but finally still embracing the conventional view of how the pursuit of wisdom can be lived in a flawed world. By this rhetorical move, the Book of Qohelet works brilliantly to contain and subdue any potential objection to its thesis that obedience to God is the only path that makes sense, that can truly be lived.[81] Humans have suffered death as a result of their pursuit of wisdom apart from obedience to God. What ostensibly confirms but finally negates the perspective of "Qohelet" is death.

The author of the Book of Qohelet obliquely makes reference to the literary trope of the death of the sage here to marvelous ironic effect. In Egyptian wisdom instruction, as well as Second Temple and later Jewish and Hellenistic literature, a sage's wisdom and moral authority are often enhanced via the formal narrative choice to render the sage's death as a calm and peaceful one, the kind of death that underscores the power of the sage's teachings to equip the wise for living and dying well in the face of potential calamity and loss.[82] Leo G. Perdue has argued that "[p]araenesis served as a nomos for future moral behavior, being issued during ritual occasions when the teacher 'dies' and the disciples, separated from their teacher, assume a new social identity. . . . The collapse of the worldview constructed by the teacher is a real and imminent possibility. . . .

[T]he teaching and the paradigm of the sage's life and ritual death . . . hold out the promise of experiencing a good death, i.e., facing the end without fear and regret."[83] But in Qohelet, the paraenesis of our sage drives toward the acknowledgement that joy is fleeting and death will be horrendous. Darkness, trembling, crookedness, dimness, anxiety and fear, failing libido, brokenness, mourning (12:1–6): all these await those who age and move toward death. Perdue says of the death of the sage generally, "This final rite of passage becomes the greatest test of the authenticity of the teacher's way of life."[84] What of "Qohelet," then? The teaching of this sage, as it turns out, cannot help with death, for "Qohelet" can only gasp, "Vanity!" as he dies. The persona of "Qohelet" disintegrates, along with the "wisdom" to which he laid such confident claim, under the ironic gaze of the author of the Book of Qohelet.

Zuckerman notes that, having reflected on the rereading of "Bontsye Shvayg" in Yiddish interpretive tradition, one may suggest that the reception of Qohelet in interpretive tradition may enshrine a similar misreading:

> If a Yiddish parody that unremittingly attacks the pietistic norms of its time can be rethought into a paragon of piety, perhaps a similar process can act upon an ancient parody and turn its antihero back into a symbol of patience par excellence. . . . [T]he editor of Ecclesiastes portrays a Wisdom of contraries, in which Qoheleth's radical "truth" is encapsulated by the larger, conservative "Truth." Both views are thus joined in a biblical counterpoint that must mean more than would the choosing of one to the exclusion of the other.[85]

Zuckerman is correct, I think, that this ancient parody has been turned into a symbol of wisdom par excellence. But I find strong hints of ironizing going on even in the epilogue. On my reading, the epilogue is not simply an attempt to bring the truth of "Qohelet" into lively contrapuntal relationship with traditional wisdom, although the reader may certainly construct the competing truths in that way. In the epilogue, a devastating ironic turn is administered via the author's reflection on the legacy of the constructed persona of "Qohelet" in 12:9–10. Perdue again: "On the social level, the paradigmatic death of the teacher is symbolically reexperienced, legitimation is achieved, and the threat of dissolution is overcome. And in the appropriation of the teaching and its transmission, the community achieves, as it were, its own victory over death."[86] May the audience understand that this sage's teaching, at least, would survive him and his evident despair? The question is only barely possible at this point, given the ways in which "Qohelet" has already been fatally ironized and his corpus disintegrated; but it must be posed. This unreliable "wise" man taught people not the fear of God, not the Torah, but just "knowledge" as such (*limmad daᶜat*), and the discerning reader knows by now how to interpret that observation.

Another thoroughly ironic observation follows in the epilogue: that "Qohelet" tried to find pleasing words. Which would those be? "Fools fold their hands and consume their own flesh" (4:5)? Or, "All their days they eat in darkness, in much vexation and sickness and resentment" (5:16, v 17 English)? Or perhaps, "Like fish taken in a cruel net, and like birds caught in a snare, so mortals are snared at a time of calamity" (9:12)? In many analyses of irony, one finds interpreters surprised that one or another ironic aspect of a piece of literature has escaped detection by the majority of readers. The verse that says "Qohelet" tried to find pleasing words is one such instance for me. The implied audience that reads verse 10 straight as an earnest commendation of "Qohelet" either lacks a sense of irony or has a masochistic sense of what "pleasing" could mean, for the words of "Qohelet" urge the reader on to the grimmest possible contemplation of the absurdity, injustice, and brutality of life, with no hope whatsoever of remediation or transcendence of those desperate truths. One might argue that the words of Qohelet are necessary: terrible, but at least honest.[87] This may be. But the words of Qohelet have never been pleasing or delightful. Interpreters who recognize this incongruity and appeal to the elegance of the disturbing formulations in the Book of Qohelet merely dodge what should be the inevitable recognition of crushing irony here. The well-known syntactical problem presented by the second half of the verse, *wĕkātûv yōṣer divrê 'emet*, may be resolved without repointing once one realizes it is meant contrastively: "but what has been written in righteousness [i.e., the Torah] comprises [real] words of truth."

The images in 12:11 further develop this contrast between the negative evaluation of the unreliable "Qohelet" and the unspoken true message of the text that it is the Torah that is reliable. The tightly linked language of 12:9 and 12:12, which share *yōtēr* and *harbēh*, establishes the point that the "many" proverbs of Qohelet and the "many" tedious examples of didactic literature are to be evaluated (negatively) together. Commentators usually consider "goads" and "nails firmly fixed" (presumably on the ends of prodding sticks) to be similes for the salutary if sometimes uncomfortable guidance provided by the wisdom tradition generally or by the sayings of "Qohelet" in particular. These goads would spur one on to wise reflection and moral behavior, as many commentators would have it. But consider the potential irony: goads are also catalysts of an ephemeral pain that causes a reactionary change of trajectory, instruments employed by shepherds to cause unthinking animals to move in whatever direction may be needed at the time. Remember that according to "Qohelet," there is little discernible difference between humans and animals (3:18–21). Krüger remarks the ambivalence of the comparison: "Like 'ox goads,' the 'words of the wise' can also incapacitate and injure hearers, and like 'nails,' 'collected proverbs' can also lead to 'dogmatic' hardening and inflexibility."[88] On that point, we see here an ironic reversal in the epilogue: "Qohelet" is right, yet as always, he has not understood why he is right or what is important about his rightness. On this ironic reading, the image of "goads" skewers both the wisdom tradition itself and those who blindly allow themselves to be herded hither and yon by it. Here, then, would be a simile for the shifting and capricious trajectories of the sapiential discourse of "Qohelet."

The meaning of the following clause, *wĕyōtēr mēhēmmāh bĕnî hizzāhēr,* seems ambiguous. It is possible to read 12:12a as saying that the students should be warned away from anything other than these didactic "goads," as so many interpreters do. But another reading makes much better sense of verse 12 as a whole: it is in what remains apart from these sapiential traditions that the discerning reader is to take warning. The disciple is to heed the caution signaled by what has gone unspoken, what remains different from the transient goads of "Qohelet's" many proverbs and skeptical ruminations. This would be the Torah, something that becomes explicit in verse 13 with the mention of the commandments of God. The ironic reading of verse 12a, "it is in what remains apart from these, my son, that you must take warning," makes by far the best sense out of what follows immediately after this "warning" clause: the making of many books is openly derided as endless and tedious (12:12b). These "many books" can only be wisdom books; the disdain here is certainly not directed toward some imagined proliferation of, say, prophetic writings or law codes. The book one needs, the book in which one must take warning and by which one can evaluate all of the other innumerable books produced in such tedious fashion, is the Torah. Where Paulson notes that Swift wanted to "replace the potential, the dead idol himself . . . with the living reality,"[89] we may say that the epilogist is urging his audience to replace the dead idol "Qohelet"—and all that he stands for—with the living reality of the Torah.

I have argued that the Book of Qohelet is not a straightforward collection of skeptical sapiential material that has been edited by someone betraying a more pious *Tendenz,* but is instead a unified, thoroughly ironic discourse that represents its anti-hero as an unwise Solomon and as a sinful Adam who strove for knowledge apart from obedience to God. The difference in rhetorical purpose and power between those two compositional models and the discourses they presume is significant. The tradi-

tional redaction-critical view postulates an earlier skeptical corpus that
was perceived as in need of correction (the older, usually pejorative scholarly view of redaction) or responsive reinterpretation (the newer, more
appreciative scholarly view of redaction influenced by canonical criticism)
by a later editor with different interests at heart. The traditional redaction-critical view thus enshrines an oppositional model of the voices within
the Book of Qohelet. However the sophisticated redaction critic might
seek for areas of thematic or ideological overlap, boldly set the two *Tenden-
zen* in dialogue with one another, and so forth, it remains the case that
according to the redactional model, the final form of Qohelet embraces
two distinct ideologies of diverse provenances with moderately or markedly different rhetorical goals. The redaction-critical bifurcation inevitably fragments the rhetorical act of communication assayed by the Book of
Qohelet, robbing the text of much of its power and rendering myopic the
binocular ironic vision of its author.

   An ironic reading of Qohelet, on the other hand, apprehends the
text's extraordinary power to convict and persuade all the better through
what is unsaid, through what is presented as unreliable, through what is
voiced in as convincing a way as possible and then is thoroughly delegitimized by the ironic metanarratological posture. An observation from
Connop Thirlwall's 1833 essay on irony provides us with apt language to
describe the rhetorical effect of the ironizing of "Qohelet":

> The writer effects his purpose by placing the opinion of his ad-
> versary in the foreground, and saluting it with every demonstra-
> tion of respect, while he is busied in withdrawing one by one all
> the supports on which it rests; and he never ceases to approach it
> with an air of deference until he has completely undermined it,
> when he leaves it to sink by the weight of its own absurdity. Ex-
> amples of this species are as rare as those of the other [viz., verbal
> irony] are common.[90]

Such kinds of irony may be rare, but they are brilliant when executed
with the virtuosity demonstrated by the author of Qohelet. Zuckerman
makes reference to the "Ozymandias effect" that irony has in the case of
Job. The famous 1818 sonnet by Percy Bysshe Shelley might well have
been uttered by the epilogist of the Book of Qohelet:

> I met a traveller from an antique land
> Who said:—Two vast and trunkless legs of stone
> Stand in the desert. Near them on the sand,
> Half sunk, a shatter'd visage lies, whose frown
> And wrinkled lip and sneer of cold command

Tell that its sculptor well those passions read
Which yet survive, stamp'd on these lifeless things,
The hand that mock'd them and the heart that fed.
And on the pedestal these words appear:
"My name is Ozymandias, king of kings:
Look on my works, ye mighty, and despair!"
Nothing beside remains: round the decay
Of that colossal wreck, boundless and bare,
The lone and level sands stretch far away.

The stunning irony of the quotation within Shelley's poem—"Look on my works, ye mighty, and despair!"—is the irony that I see in the shattered visage of the persona of "Qohelet." One is reminded of the assertion by Paul de Man that "the ironist invents a form of himself that is 'mad' but that does not know its own madness; he then proceeds to reflect on his madness thus objectified."[91] The book bears the name of "Qohelet," yes. But it is an ironic gesture, just as the wrecked works of Ozymandias are evoked ironically for those who gaze upon them now.

Booth notes that in ironic representation, "the movement is always toward an obscured point that is intended as wiser, wittier, more compassionate, subtler, truer, more moral, or at least less obviously vulnerable to further irony."[92] What is the goal, then, of Qohelet as unified ironic corpus? The rhetoric of the book drives toward the goal of rendering the command to obey God's commandments impervious to further irony. Consider the extraordinary success of this literary masterpiece on that score. The Book of Qohelet preempts further irony regarding obedience to God in a way that the Pentateuchal stories of the obedience and disobedience of Israel cannot begin to do. Non-ironic Hebrew Bible traditions regarding obedience to God clearly were far from impervious to the scathing sarcasm and deeply subversive ironies of Hosea, Amos, and Jonah. The achingly earnest paraenesis of Deuteronom(ist)ic tradition could not begin to defend itself from even a single withering observation about the vagaries of human life and fortune in the way that the Book of Qohelet has.[93] The Book of Qohelet thunders an irresistible "Hear, O Israel!" that is all the more powerful for the way in which its primary point and the name of Israel itself go unspoken.[94]

The way in which Qohelet conveys what is intended to be significant about its message must be appreciated as deeply ironic if the text is not to be misunderstood. The competent interpreter is coerced into resisting the urge to read naïvely. We can no longer read the maxims and the autobiographical material as if they constituted straightforward, unproblematized mimetic representation. The politics of ironic representation in Qohelet mocks both unsophisticated assumptions about authorial voice and narcissistic notions of authority. In this, the overzealous redaction critic and the overly self-referential postmodernist alike find themselves turning on the spit along with "Qohelet."

What, then, of the many interpretations of Qohelet that acclaim "Qohelet's" skepticism as a salutary way forward in an uncertain world? There is much of value in that position—as there doubtless was in the time of the author of the Book of Qohelet, otherwise the "said" would never have been compelling for the implied audience. Readers who argue that the skepticism of "Qohelet" is presented as an antidote to stale religious orthodoxy have attended closely to many truths spoken in the book even if they have misread the overarching purpose per the epilogist, just as one who agrees with a particularly keen argument of one of Job's friends has found something important there despite the overall judgment of the book that the friends spoke wrongly. The reader may still delight in "Qohelet's" refreshing candor and crankiness. But the epilogue invites the interpreter to understand that "Qohelet" has been drawn as a foil, and this should be understood in contemporary interpretations, even if one then chooses to make the foil a sympathetic vehicle for one's charmingly resistant interpretation. In this case, the epilogue invites the interpreter to stop short of saying that the Book of Qohelet is presenting the reliance on empirically based, skeptical wisdom as a viable alternative to the halakhic piety found in much of the rest of Scripture. It is not. The book is working as hard as it can, with rhetorical tools as sophisticated as those one might encounter in any work of literature ancient or contemporary, to make the point that "Qohelet's" reliance on wisdom alone is precisely *not* a viable way to live. As Berger says, "the book is itself an instantiation of the vapour, the [*hevel*], that Qohelet detects in the universe."[95] We are meant to look on the works of "Qohelet" and despair.

Yet, the text cannot but claim that which it ironically subverts, and this is part of the meaning of the text as well. What has been said by "Qohelet" has been said, however it may then be contained and negated.[96] If the ironic process produces meaning through the friction and disorientation created by the interaction of the said and the unsaid, what emerges from the tension between the said and the unsaid here? It is not only the primacy of Israel's covenant seen in concrete relational and historical terms, as Fisch would have it, although that is a key insight.[97] It is that obedience to God is the only human response that can prevent the (true) inescapable miseries of transient, unpredictable human life from defining the human person. Only obedience, not wisdom as such, can name the human person apart from the injustice, chaos, and disintegration that eternally constitute the cosmos. Wisdom and striving cannot free us, cannot enact justice in the life of the human person or in the eternal rounds of the universe. Obedience alone names us, defines and constitutes us, for that is all of who we are (*kî zeh kol-hā'ādām,* 12:13). The author of the Book of Qohelet has reinscribed human identity in a way that is decentered from the foundationalist narratives of Israel's historical formation but that yet points to halakhic obedience as the source of that identity.

The author of the Book of Qohelet has permitted himself, through the persona of "Qohelet," to express some dangerously heterodox sentiments about death, the futility of human endeavor in a single lifetime and in historical perspective, the inequity of the fortunes of the righteous and the wicked, and the triumph of chance and divine caprice over all. In this, the skill of the author as rhetor becomes transparent. He has rendered with remarkable depth of dimension a fictional context in which his own position, that obedience to God is essential for right living, emerges not only more clearly but more persuasively. His ironic landscape, with all of its deceitful hues and unstable, shifting contours, has both determined the map and made the map all the more necessary. By the end of the book, the implied audience is desperate to choose obedience. Here, we may add to Hutcheon's suggestion that "the power of the unsaid to challenge the said is the defining semantic condition of irony."[98] It is in resisting the profound pull of the said, and in being wounded by its razor-sharp ironic edges over and over until the lesson to withdraw is learned,[99] that the interpreter of Qohelet is compelled to work with the author of the book to create the power of the unsaid. The reader thereby shapes the truth of what emerges through the hermeneutical struggle. Thus the participation of the reader is essential, in praxis, to create the meaning of the Book of Qohelet; and yet the reader cannot function competently as reader of this text outside of the intimate community established by the ironist. It is still possible to mishear the unspoken in this text. The pressures of the unsaid in the Book of Qohelet are specific pressures generated by charged gaps and pregnant silences, not by limitless, empty silences open to potentially infinite meanings.

The ironist who composed the Book of Qohelet invites each reader into a new community constituted by freedom: the subjective freedom found in honoring the commandments of God. Here emerges the Israel that has remained unnamed. Kierkegaard's notion of the radical freedom enacted by irony's rejection of the said illumines, if only partially, the transaction that takes place between the text of Qohelet and its readers. In understanding the book aright—whether or not one then assents to its rhetoric—the competent reader is freed to acknowledge that agency, significance, and truth are found in obedience. However temporary and provisional such an acknowledgment might be for a particular reader at a particular time, this heuristic move is necessarily coerced by the ironic text. The irony of Qohelet hereby enacts community rhetorically, enacts the (re)constitution of Israel over against the faltering strains of traditional wisdom. Irony indeed "captivates with indissoluble bonds," as Kierkegaard has said.

The metanarratological message of the Book of Qohelet inscribes the results of the sin in the Garden of Eden on the body of "Qohelet," on the corpus of the text, and on any hapless interpreter who falls victim to its irony. The psychic wounds and physical disintegration of the despairing and cynical "Qohelet" represent the self-inflicted wounds of an(y) Adam who tries to reenter the Garden of Eden and grasp again wisdom apart from obedience. The same disintegration is acknowledged by the epilogist in the comments in 12:12 about the debilitating tediousness of books and study. He has no choice but to destroy his own text, using words that echo "Qohelet's" musings on circularity and tedium. The epilogist flags the end of sapiential discourse itself (*sôp dāvār,* 12:13) and thereby represents ironically that the Book of Qohelet ought never to be used as a didactic manual. By this final ironic rhetorical act, not only the voice of "Qohelet" but also the voice of the epilogist is silenced. Its final whisper carries across centuries of the debris of human endeavor: Fear God, and keep his commandments. Hear this: It is only obedience that defines you, you who are wise and you who are foolish, you who are powerful and you who are powerless, you who delight in life's pleasures and you who rage at life's miseries. Hear, O Israel, and obey.

Rereading Desire as Doublespeak in Psalm 73

> What is to be done with works of art that are small in scale, short in duration, or excessively modest in the claims they make on our attention? . . . Works that occupy very little time or space imprint themselves only lightly on the human sensorium, and their meanings decay rapidly; they often seem no more than harmless litter scattered across the cultural landscape. Even as they summon us to brief moments of rapture, their momentum drains away.[100]

With these words, Malcolm Bowie reflects on the cultural problematics of micro-works of art. His topic is the German *Lied,* but one may draw on his observations *mutatis mutandis* as we consider the wisdom dilemma presented in exquisite miniature in Psalm 73, one of the Psalms of Asaph.

Psalm 73 has been praised by many commentators as an artistic and powerful narration of one Israelite believer's "pilgrimage from doubt to faith."[101] But the psalm is plagued by a number of semantic problems, including a lack of clarity regarding the role of "Israel" (v 1) in the psalmist's rhetoric, the mystery surrounding some sort of revelatory experience that apparently has catalyzed a change of heart in the psalmist (v 17), syntactical obscurities related to key particles and prepositions, tensions in the literary flow from verse to verse, and a seemingly disjointed narratological line near the end of the psalm that has spurred some scholars to rearrange the order of verses. Further, scholars have not been able to agree on the genre of the psalm, something that may point to fundamental contradictions inscribed within the ethos of the psalm.

As I have read and reread Psalm 73, I have become convinced that its semantic incongruities, syntactical infelicities, and obscure concepts do not, in fact, resolve harmoniously into a coherent story of personal transformation. I have come to see Psalm 73 instead as an ironizing locus of intersection between the skepticism of the wisdom writings and a dialogical representation of Israel's story in the Psalms of Asaph. In what follows, I will argue that Psalm 73 ironizes both the narcissism of the individual worshipper and the failure of Israelite kingship, all toward the goal of driving the implied postexilic audience deeper into the tradition history supplied by the rest of the Psalms of Asaph. The audience is invited to embrace their own accountability and come to understand better who God has been to Israel in Israel's history. I will argue that far from affirming the speaker's perspective, Psalm 73 is about destabilizing and disrupting the confidence of the speaking subject so as to invite the implied audience into a better understanding.

Attentiveness to resonances with Job and Qohelet has been important for many scholars' readings of Psalm 73, and such attentiveness will be essential for my own argument as well. For two reasons, this reflection on Psalm 73 is positioned strategically after my introductory musings on ironies in Job and my exploration of the ironic voicing of Qohelet. First, I want to underline the point that the literary and theological pressures of both Job and Qohelet have rightly been felt in interpretation of Psalm 73. And second, Psalm 73 as a miniature wisdom work gives us an intense close look at the agony of another Job—not only in what the psalmist says but in how he utters his conflicted discourse—while also hinting at the bitter candor that is the dominant tone of Qohelet. The anguished struggle of the psalmist might seem to vanish by the end of Psalm 73. But the closure in Psalm 73 is a faux resolution, I will argue. Unfulfilled desire, envy, feelings of abandonment, aggressive overcompensation for psychic distress: all these are powerfully present in the psalm near the end no less than at the beginning, and they leave indelible traces in the "cultural landscape" of Israelite communal worship.

Wisdom motifs have long been seen in Psalm 73. Striking similarities between Psalm 73 and the diction of both Job and Qohelet have been discerned by many commentators. J. Luyten has outlined the evidence for wisdom concerns that Psalm 73 shares with Job and Qohelet. He addresses commonalities in linguistic usages, thematic connections, declaration of innocence without formulating accusations against any enemies (Job), and literary style as regards the autobiographical narration of an epistemological struggle (Qohelet).[102] Crenshaw even suggests that the *běhēmôt* in verse 22 is best translated not as "beast(s)" but as Behemoth, a reference that "may be a faint echo of the divine speeches in Job."[103] Broader thematic connections with Job and Qohelet are apparent as well. The psalmist laments the prospering of the wicked and his own being unjustly punished despite his innocence, which are the driving complaints of Job. The psalmist characterizes these epistemological contradictions and the spiritual struggle to understand them as *ʿāmāl*, laborious or wearisome work, which is a central complaint of Qohelet.[104] The psalmist's sophisticated articulation of metacognitive issues—his self-conscious reflection on his own thinking and its limitations—ties this text closely to the overall tenor of Job and Qohelet.

The rhetoric of the psalm is situated in the interstices between skeptical questioning and confident declaration of faith. It is most often read as the latter, that is, as an earnest narration of earlier spiritual wrestling that has been magnificently resolved. But the readings I find most persuasive on this psalm permit substantial aporias to remain in the final analysis or problematize its polished narration. Exemplary here are two treatments: J. Clinton McCann's 1987 article, "Psalm 73: A Microcosm of Old Testament Theology," and a 1991 study by Walter Brueggemann, "Bounded by Obedience and Praise: The Psalms as Canon."[105]

McCann notes that tensions between arguments for reading Psalm 73 as a wisdom psalm and arguments for reading it as a song of thanksgiving are grounded in the psalm itself. Borrowing terminology from another work of Brueggemann, McCann asserts that the psalm holds together within its form and rhetoric both the "legitimation of social structure" via traditional covenantal theology and the more subversive "embrace of pain" that characterizes real life lived in the presence of God. Hosting this tension between resolution and ongoing anguish makes Psalm 73, in the view of McCann, a "microcosm of Old Testament theology."[106] Brueggemann's view of rhetorical processes throughout the Psalter situates Psalm 73 within that corpus as a crucial "threshold from obedience to praise."[107] He notes that regarding royal ideology, Psalm 73 is "placed at the 'faultline' after Psalm 72, that is, the disruption of faith after the failure of Solomon."[108] Per Brueggemann, the psalm inhabits a kind of liminality that is essential to Israel's movement toward theological understanding, both in terms of the community's journey of faith generally and in terms of the community's view of kingship more specifically. Brueggemann finds Psalm 73 emblematic of the "larger move of the drama of the Psalms from innocent obedience to unencumbered doxology . . . by way of the suffering voiced in the complaints."[109]

Psalm 73 as "threshold" and as "fault-line": these images capture well the fragility of the space created by the psalmist and the risk that this rhetoric represents to the community. And more can be said about the disjunctures that are enshrined within the rhetoric of this psalm. The reader's ear may detect in the utterances of this psalmist a hyperbole that overcompensates for anxiety about his narrated story and the God who dominates it. But this anxiety is well masked: even scholars who confirm the significant influence of Job on this psalm have not usually found gaps and ambiguities in the psalmist's storytelling. Although the Book of Job does offer a kind of closure through its narrative framework that seems to tie up loose ends nicely, the book has left many readers dissatisfied by the imposed coherence of the prosaic narrative on the turbulent poetry. Job "repents" or somehow comes to understand that he has no standing to question the Almighty, yet we do not know exactly what he has perceived that catalyzed this change of heart. The divine rebuke of the friends stands in significant tension with the clear resolution of the story precisely along the lines of argument that the friends had put forth (namely, that if one is innocent, God will in fact restore one). The Book of Job, in short, is full of aporias, and its apparently closural ending invites resistance. As I read Psalm 73—with Qohelet whispering in one ear and Job in the other—I discern gaps in the psalm's narration of the storyline, as well. I suspect that just as the apparent closure of the Book of Job is destabilized by the wild poetry preceding it, so too the apparent closure of Psalm 73 may be being destabilized by what precedes it.

Although there are a number of difficult semantic formulations within Psalm 73, the structure and meaning of the psalm are seen by many commentators to be transparent. On structure, the opinion of Lawrence Boadt may be taken as representative: "The structure and its message are straightforward, and each section leads naturally to the next as though in a logical argument."[110] Valuable work to connect the two structural halves of the psalm has been done by Leslie C. Allen, who argues for a rhetorically structured closure on the basis of catchwords that play throughout the psalm. He writes:

> The poet appears to be deliberately ranging over earlier vocabulary and reversing its contexts. The grim end of the wicked . . . has as its counterpart a happy end for the psalmist. . . . H. Ringgren noted that . . . "to declare" in v. 28 is used as a contrast in v.

15. The refusal of the psalmist to narrate his lament is replaced by a resolve to narrate his new theme of joy and praise before the congregated community. . . . The slippery places reserved by God for the wicked are contrasted with a gracious portion from God for the psalmist. It may even be suggested that the negative associations of the comprehensive term . . . "all" in v. 14 are replaced by its triumphant usage in vv. 27, 28.[111]

Further regarding the interplay of structure and meaning, one may consider David C. Mitchell's thumbnail sketch of Psalm 73 as part of his larger analysis of an eschatological progression of thought in the Asaph Psalms. Mitchell sums up Psalm 73 as follows: "The wicked prosper. God will destroy them when he arises."[112] While all of these positions have merit, the reader alert for irony may find that there is more to be considered than the overt "said" of this psalm. To the reader attentive to disjuncture, there are a number of textual complexities and unexpected shifts in this poem that disrupt these structural schematics.

It is relevant to structural questions that the genre classification of Psalm 73 has proven to be a topic of ongoing debate. Thanksgiving song, lament, or didactic wisdom psalm? The poem has elements of all three, and it has been seen to partake of other genres as well.[113] The debate about genre is no mere formalist concern. Genres encode cultural expectations for the meaning of rhetoric, foreground creative points without having to elaborate on every aspect of relevant background, offer subtle persuasion regarding cultural values, and invite certain kinds of audience response. Newsom's analysis of genre in her book on Job is material to our discussion. She writes:

> [T]he shared horizon established by the invocation of a generic form allows an author important measures of economy. The intimacy among those who share expectations about an utterance allows certain things to go without saying. . . . [T]exts do not "belong" to genres so much as participate in them, invoke them, gesture to them, play in and out of them, and in so doing continually change them. . . . Through their capacity to define situations, control perspectives, and give them aesthetic shape, genres are forms of moral imagination.[114]

Thus the question of the genre of Psalm 73 is highly significant for interpretation, and not simply for taxonomic reasons. Not only are historical issues at stake regarding the development of genres in late Israelite literature. Psalm 73 participates in at least two genres whose assumptions seem to be contradictory. The interpreter may find significant, rather than just incidental, the dynamic interplay between divergent sets of cultural expectations and rhetorical cues. What Newsom says of Job (discussing the genre of the prose framework versus the genre of the poetic section) may be applied to Psalm 73 as well: "By means of generic markers the reader is invited initially to form one set of expectations, to respond according to those conventions, and to see the world from a particular nexus of values and perspectives. Then the reader is suddenly snatched away from those conventions into a radically different set, only to be as suddenly snatched back again."[115] The tensive interweaving of generic cues in Psalm 73 is different from that in Job in that it occurs in a holistic way, operating continually throughout the psalm rather than in discrete blocks of text. But just as in Job, the psalm's shifting among various expressions of genre does invite reader disorientation and encourage a subtle movement toward a more complicated worldview. By its participation in divergent genres, Psalm 73 guides the audience into an instructive experience of liminality.

A further complexity may be cited: the voice of the psalmist is polyphonous. Brueggemann puts it incisively: "This Psalmist, like all of us, is double-minded and double-tongued."[116] In form and in discursive affect, Psalm 73 seems to be saying two things at once. Its narrated epistemological journey underlines the importance of not being excessively concerned with the apparent prosperity of the wicked and the suffering of the innocent speaker. But the psalm in fact concerns itself with precisely those things and those things only, apart from a few exceptional moments in which the focus of the psalm is wrenched back onto God. I will probe the interpretive possibility that the double-voicing of the psalmist noticed by Brueggemann may fruitfully be understood as a kind of irony. What the psalmist is performing by means of his rhetoric is, in a hermeneutically meaningful way, not consonant with what the meaning of his words seems to be. This disjuncture invites the audience into discernment of the "unsaid" lying behind the incongruities of the psalm. A useful contemporary term for speech that intends to dissemble and mislead is "doublespeak." My thesis is that the psalmist misdirects his audience through ironic "doublespeak" about what he says he desires and what his words show him actually to desire—his discursive actions belie his words. I hope to show that the ambiguities, overstatements, and omissions within his own discourse may readily be construed to deconstruct what he is claiming. Further, I will argue that there is a didactic lesson to be had, in the best tradition of ironic biblical wisdom literature, for those who perceive the ironic incongruities that beset the rhetoric of this psalm.

The traditional reading of the psalm takes it as a story of spiritual rejuvenation or transformation. The psalmist tells of how his feet had almost

stumbled, that is, how he had come dangerously close to grave spiritual
error because of his envy of the prosperous wicked (vv 2–3). Other people
praise the wicked, and the wicked themselves suggest in their arrogance
that God is powerless to intervene regarding their immorality ("And they
say, 'How can God know? Is there knowledge in the Most High?'" v 11).
Verses 12–14 lay out the position that the psalmist says he has come to re-
pudiate, namely, the view that the wicked are "always at ease" and that the
speaker has maintained moral purity in vain since he has been "plagued"
and "punished" despite his rectitude. He reflects confidently, then, on
that erroneous position as one that he no longer maintains: "If I had said,
'I will speak in this way,' I would have betrayed the generation of your children" (v 15). Thus verse 15 draws a clear distinction between his present
view and the older view he had held. His reflections on the moral problem
had been laborious in a tedious or fruitless way (ʿāmāl), but then he experienced an epistemological breakthrough. Per the traditional reading, a
mysterious moment of revelation in "the sanctuary of God"[117] (v 16) showed
him that the flourishing of the wicked is but transient and insubstantial in
the face of the ruin that God will inflict upon them (vv 18–19). Their apparent strength and impregnability are mere illusions (v 20).

Thus far, the traditionally understood narrative seems entirely coherent. But the remaining verses of the psalm complicate and disturb the
psalmist's neat storytelling, particularly by blurring the line between the
older erroneous view and the speaker's current view. Hossfeld and Zenger
note the disjuncture: "In vv. 21–22 the petitioner looks back once again to
the time before the experience of God that changed him. The reposition-
ing of these verses undertaken by some commentators not only levels the
antithesis that governs the *whole* psalm but also dissolves the important
contrast between vv. 21–22 and vv. 23–26 (or the reverse)."[118] But do verses
21–22 present the psalmist as looking back? Another possibility is that the
"before" and "after" of the petitioner may not be as distinct as some readers would have it. A case can be made that there is no strong contrast between verses 21–22 and verses 23–26. A straightforward reading of the
syntax of these latter verses would suggest that the psalmist's bitterness
and need for help continue through verse 26—even after his experience
of God in the Temple. Three semantic ambiguities, taken together, allow
for a reading of the Hebrew that locates the psalmist's failure to understand not only in the past but also in the narrative present moment of the
psalm. Those three semantic ambiguities involve the unexpected cohortative form in verse 17b (which commentators tend to read as past tense),
the interrogative ʾêk in verse 19 (which commentators tend to read as an
exclamative), and the kî in verse 21 (which commentators tend to read as
temporal in sense). If one reaches for the most common and transparent

use of each of these words in Biblical Hebrew, we have instead a psalmist who remains desperate to understand, who continues to ask earnestly how God will dispatch the wicked, and who claims with great force that his soul still, in the present moment, is embittered. We will explore the semantics of each of those issues in turn.

The proposal that the psalmist suddenly saw all clearly in a single revelatory experience in the Temple is not impossible.[119] But he may instead have been assured that seeking God's presence throughout his epistemological and other travails is prudent—is not really fruitless *ʿāmāl*. In the Temple, he may have discovered new passion for the arduous task of wrestling with his God. He may have become recommitted to the epistemological task in light of the futility of other avenues of remediation. He may have been overwhelmed by the power of the Almighty, such that he knew that his spiritual trials were as nothing before the creator of the universe—the theology of the Book of Qohelet and the example of Job would support this possibility. We cannot know. But the aporia is itself significant; of that we can be more confident. First, then, the cohortative form *ʾābînâ*, "let me understand!/O that I might understand!": this may be taken seriously not as a past-tense indicator but in its more normal optative sense.[120] What the psalmist has understood, then, is that continuing to wrestle with the theodicy issue is important or appropriate, not just "a wearisome task" (v 16), and he begs anew for enlightenment.

Do the clauses in verses 18–19 spell out what the psalmist discerned in the Temple, namely, that the wicked will meet their comeuppance? Our second semantic ambiguity, regarding the clause beginning with the particle *ʾēk* in verse 19, renders that interpretive assumption problematic. Conceptually unlike anything in the Hebrew Bible is this suggestion that an abstract future reality was brought home to a petitioner in some kind of vision or revelatory encounter: "How they will become a desolation in an instant, swept away completely by terrors!" Two alternative readings are possible.

The first alternative: if *ʾēk* is an exclamative there, with the perfective aspect of the verbs it would work much better as a reminiscence of devastation already wrought on *Israelites:* "How they have become a desolation in an instant!" A semantic parallel can be seen in the famous lament of David over Saul and Jonathan, which uses *ʾēk* as exclamative with the perfect, "How the mighty have fallen!" (2 Sam 1:19, 25, 27). The fate of the wicked has not been cited in the psalm since verse 12. Closer to hand in terms of literary juxtaposition and intensity is the description of the suffering of the innocent speaker in verses 13–14, "In vain have I kept my heart clean . . . all day long I have been plagued, and I am punished every morning." Further supporting the reading that verses 17–18 have to do with the destruction of Israel rather than the wicked is the fact that the closest logical expressed plural referent for the suffix on *'aḥărîtām*, "their end," in verse 17b is "your children," that is, Israel, in verse 15b. Michael D. Goulder has suggested that a plausible historical provenance for the Psalms of Asaph is after the Assyrian crisis in the late eighth century BCE; he argues that these verses deal with the Assyrian onslaught that devastated Samaria and resulted in the deportation of many northern Israelites (see 2 Kgs 17). If this is so, one could read verses 18–20 as a lament over the destruction of the Israelites and an assertion (in v 20b only; note the imperfect aspect there, as one would expect) that the LORD will eventually "despise the image" that the Assyrian conquerors have set up in the capital city.[121] In the logic of this reading, then, the psalmist concedes that it had seemed wearisome to keep speaking bitterly about the prospering of the wicked, yet he cannot avoid the struggle when he sees what God has done not only to him, a single innocent sufferer, but to the entire nation of Israel. That is, he saw anew that these are urgent questions indeed.

A second alternative reading for *'êk* at the beginning of verse 19 is that it be taken as a true rhetorical question concerning the fate of Israel. If we assume the same historical context as above, again with Goulder, the anguished cry of the psalmist could be earnestly interrogative: "How can it be that they have become a desolation in a moment, swept away completely by terrors?" In support of this reading of *'êk* is the fact that this particular interrogative appears only twice else in the Psalter and four other times in the wisdom corpus of the Hebrew Bible, and in all but one of those six occurrences, *'êk* functions as a true interrogative rather than an exclamative.[122] It is worth noting that the Job occurrence of *'êk* as interrogative is not far from a use of *'ābînâ* as a true cohortative in a context wherein Job is seeking to understand why the innocent suffer (Job 23:5). In the case of Psalm 73, then, it seems more likely that the psalmist is reflecting on the terrible fate of Israel rather than describing some abstract conceptual content of a revelation to him from God concerning the eventual fate of the wicked.

Our third semantic ambiguity is the *kî* at the beginning of verse 21. Interpreters take it as temporal so as to keep what follows in the past tense of the narrated story: "When my heart was embittered . . . I was stupid and ignorant, I was like a brute beast toward you."[123] But the converted imperfective verb that gave us the past tense is at considerable remove from the imperfects in verse 21, with intervening perfective verbs that disrupt any implied ongoing narrative sequence. The sequence of verbs from verse 15 through verse 22 may be read instead with asseverative *kî* in verse 21, as follows:

If I had said, "I will speak in this way,"
 I would have betrayed the generation of your children.
But when I pondered so as to understand this,
 it was a wearisome task to me,
until I entered into the sanctuary of God.
 O let me understand their [viz., Israel's] end!
Truly you have set them in slippery places,
 you have made them fall to ruin.
How they have become a desolation in a moment,
 swept away completely by terrors!
Like a dream upon awakening, O Lord,
 In the city you will despise their image.
Indeed [asseverative *kî*], my heart is embittered and my gut
  perforated,
  I am brutish and do not understand; I have become (like
  the) beasts with you.

Thus the imperfective forms may be read in verse 21 as reflecting the ongoing state of the speaker. The past state of the speaker and the present moment of the speaker, in the narration of the psalm, are not so different from one another. The coherent story of his spiritual transformation begins to unravel.

One may read the psalmist's agonized reflection as enshrining an aporia rather than pointing to the neat resolution of a problem that other relevant biblical wisdom books—Job and Qohelet—have found intractable. But another image still needs to be addressed in this context: the image of God walking hand in hand with the psalmist in a relationship of trust or intimacy (as many commentators would have it). The psalmist says, "I have become (like the) beasts with you. And yet I am always with you! You have seized my right hand."[124] Building on the work of others, Hossfeld and Zenger have pressed the case that we have here an allusion to the ancient Near Eastern motif of a deity guiding a royal figure by the hand into the afterlife.[125] Goulder agrees with the suggestion that a royal persona is being evoked, but he suggests a more mundane environment for the king's guidance: "[A]s king, he has continual access to God's presence in the shrine. It was the kings' prerogative that God should hold . . . their hand, and they often took names with this root, Ahaz, Ahaziah, Jehoahaz. . . . God would *guide him with his counsel* in the diplomatic and perhaps military decisions that lay ahead; counsel was particularly associated with kings (Prov. 8.14; Isa. 9.5; 11.2)."[126] Per Kraus, the democratization of kingship seen in Deutero-Isaiah suggests that by the time of Psalm 73, "this symbolic conception from the area of the royal prerogatives has become an expression for a position of honor and of the immediate salvific communion between Yahweh

and the 'servant of God' (Isa. 42:6)—indeed, even between Yahweh and
Israel (Isa. 41:13)."[127] We may now revisit *lĕyiśrā'ēl* in the first line of Psalm
73: this is not just the journey of a single righteous individual. Via the royal
persona evoked in verse 23, and whether through so-called democratization or simply through royal representation on behalf of the people, this
may be understood as the experience of an entire worshipping community—that is, the people of Israel.[128] Hossfeld and Zenger describe the communal aspect beautifully: "The 'I' in Psalm 73 and Job do not do this [viz.,
insist on their innocence] out of individual self-righteousness, but as 'structural' agents of the problem: their 'life-crisis' is the expression and result of
a severe social and religious shock in their epoch."[129]

The order of clauses in what follows is important. If this were a narration of God's purpose in leading the kingly figure into the afterlife, we
would prefer something like, "You will seize my right hand, and afterwards
you will lead me to glory." But instead the psalm articulates the divine
gesture of seizing followed by a phrase that speaks of being guided in
God's counsel—something appropriate to politics in the world of the living, not after death. The trope of seizing by the hand likely does underline
the royal identity of the speaker. But the "seizing" in question may not be
the gentle divine guidance that commentators tend to read here. If the
psalmist continues to suffer in life, then the God whose hand holds him so
fast may instead be—here is the ironic twist on the tradition-historical
reference—the oppressive and inescapable God of Psalm 139, from whom
one cannot flee on earth or even in Sheol (Ps 139:8).[130]

Noteworthy for this line of argument is the shared vocabulary of
nāḥâ ("lead"), *'āḥaz* ("seize"), and *yāmîn* ("right hand") in Psalms
73:23–24 and Psalms 139:10, the latter in a rhetorical context in which
God's ubiquity and power are represented as fearful for a speaker who
realizes that flight will not avail. Job saw the truth of that as well. Job repeatedly laments the lack of escape from an oppressively attentive God,
in his famous satirical allusion to Psalm 8 and elsewhere:

> What are human beings that you make so much of them,
>   that you set your mind on them
> visit them every morning
>   test them every moment?
> Will you not look away from me for a while,
>   let me alone until I swallow my spittle? (Job 7:17–19)

Another relevant intertext presents itself in Job 16, where within the space
of two verses, Job speaks of being seized (*'āḥaz*) by God and his kidneys
(*kilyôtay*) being slashed open (Job 16:12–13), just as the psalmist in Psalm
73 speaks within the space of three verses about his kidneys (*kilyôtay*) being

pierced and being seized (*'āḥaz*) by God (Ps 73:21–23). Verse 24, then, should be read not as a strange prediction offered by a trusting believer: "You guide me with your counsel, and afterward you will receive me with honor" or "You will take me to glory," that latter phrase always having been difficult for commentators to explain adequately in the theological world of the Hebrew Bible in any case. It may be read instead as a precative gesture in the jussive mood: "In your counsel guide me! After such honor [ironic: the "honor" of being attended to relentlessly by God], take me up!"

In the following verse, the speaker points to the desperation of his plight, just as Job and Qohelet do. The NRSV translation, "Whom have I in heaven but you? And there is nothing on earth that I desire other than you," and other similar efforts are imprecise as regards the crucial prepositions. The line should be translated exactly as the Hebrew stands, with a Joban sense of bitter rhetorical question and complaint: "Who is on my side in the heavens? And with you, I cannot delight on the earth." Given the sense of ongoing spiritual trauma that the psalmist has expressed—not just earlier in the psalm but also immediately contiguous with this verse—one may understand this with straightforward syntax as a rhetorical *cri de coeur,* "Who advocates on my behalf in the heavens?" [expected answer: no one], followed by a bitter asseveration, "And given your [oppressive] presence, neither can I delight [in life] on earth."[131] The supposed narrative of transformation has by this point unraveled completely. We see instead a psalmist who understands, with Qohelet, that he has no advocate in the heavens. We see a psalmist who is utterly alone and bitter, as Job was, and cannot enjoy life on earth. Carrying this sense forward and reading the perfective verb in verse 26 in a straightforward way, we hear the psalmist moan, "My flesh and my heart have failed."

The surprise, then, finally comes in the next clause, which must be read as contrastive: "Yet God is the Rock of my heart and my portion forever." Through good and ill, for weal or woe, the psalmist claims God as his portion, a position that is fully consonant with the worldview represented by Job and Qohelet. Regardless of the suffering of his life, the apparent prospering of the wicked, and the inexplicable distance of God from him—none of which has been resolved for the psalmist—the psalmist seeks nearness to God and claims God as his only refuge. Why? Two reasons are articulated in the text, and I suggest that they be heard as uttered in Joban whispers of bone-weary resignation rather than as effervescent cries of joy. First, the psalmist knows that those who distance themselves from God ultimately perish (v 27a), for God brutally punishes the straying of apostates (v 27b). However miserable his daily existence may be, with unfair chastisements meted out and no apparent notice taken of his righteousness, and despite the horrific trauma that Israel as a nation has experienced, nevertheless the psalmist knows that nearness to God offers the only real chance of survival. It may not help the quality of daily life to walk in innocence, as the psalmist has done; but apostates have no hope at all. With Amos 9, Psalm 139, Qohelet, and Job as insistent intertexts pressing on this verse, we can discern irony indeed in the psalmist's claim. His pronouncement that nearness to God is "good" for him has been spoken after his excruciating epistemological struggle has gone unresolved and after the realization has dawned that there is no escape from God's grasp. This resolution, then, is strikingly like what happens in the Book of Job and the Book of Qohelet. Both stories of agony are "resolved" not by restoration or the healing of trauma (Job is restored only after he has acknowledged in utter despair that he cannot stand before God) but by the plaintiff's realization that God is inescapable and indomitable.

The second reason the psalmist gives for making God his refuge is so that he might recount all of God's works (v 28). Here is another crucial irony, for this speaker has not uttered a word about God's works in the traditional sense. Throughout the psalm, we have heard nothing of God as the mighty one who has wrought great deeds of redemption on behalf of Israel. What works might this psalmist recount? The same verb, *spr*, occurs in verse 15, where the psalmist had reflected on his own illegitimate way of speaking against God, complaining of his own mistreatment at the hands of the deity. The psalmist can tell of God letting the arrogant prosper and thrive without apparent accountability for their exploitative ways. He can tell of having been plagued and punished every morning without cause. He can tell of his insight that there is no escape from this God who seizes him and holds him fast. Verse 28 presents a brilliant aporia in the discursive practice of this psalm. This last clause is no mere denouement but, arguably, the entire rhetorical point of the psalm, the incipient action toward which all of the psalm's narratology has been driving. The psalmist may stay near God—because it is too dangerous to be far away from the deity—but we do not know what the psalmist plans to tell of God.

These questions and textual disjunctures support an ironizing rereading of Psalm 73. The voice of the psalmist may productively be heard with suspicion when the reader attends to disjunctures within the rhetoric of the psalm and, further, is alert to its relationship to the preceding Psalm 72 and a plausibly constructed intertextual conversation between Psalm 73 and Isaiah 58. We learn the royal identity of the speaker only late in the psalm, after we encounter the metaphor of God seizing the hand of the speaker (v 23). If a royal voice has been speaking, then this is the voice of a king who has not done what Israelite kings should, namely, attending to the needs of the powerless and righting injustice. On this, the implied audience would certainly know Psalm 72 with its extended catalogue of kingly duties. The audience might also be expected to know Isaiah 58, which can be argued to have specific intertextual connections with our psalm due to the occurrence of two extraordinarily rare words only in Isaiah 58 and Psalm 73.[132] In the Isaiah passage, God excoriates those in Israel who "seek me and delight to know my ways as if they were a nation that practiced righteousness" (Isa 58:2). Benjamin D. Sommer has argued that the Isaiah passage has drawn on Psalm 72, thus establishing a linkage among Psalm 72, Psalm 73, and Isaiah 58. If that is so, then we may find relevant to our interpretation of Psalm 73 the Deutero-Isaianic charge of hypocrisy in the Israelite community embodied in the figure of the king.

Of interest regarding the (un)reliability of the king is Luyten's note of the artistry with which the author of Psalm 73 works with elements from various genres to create a unique composition. Luyten writes:

> The lament over the enemy found in the traditional psalm of lament grows here into . . . the most extensive description of the wicked in the Book of Psalms. The self-pity that refers, in the individual psalms of complaint, to the danger of death, harassment, or guilt feelings has here as specific focal point the speaker's bitterness and lack of understanding. The prayer, the most essential element of a lament, is entirely absent; and the confidence motif is all the more emphatically developed. Ps. 73 has the past tense in common with the psalm of thanksgiving. . . . It is just these elements of selection, amplification, and transposition with relation to the traditional genres and motifs which Ps. 73 has in common with the wisdom literature, in particular with Job.[133]

Luyten is doubtless correct that expectations of the psalm's audience are subverted in a number of ways in this psalm. Expected elements from various genres are either gapped or hyperbolized in Psalm 73 in a way that may demonstrate that expected conventions in psalm composition are being subverted with an ironic sensibility. If the prayer, the "most essential element in a lament" per Luyten, is missing and the confidence motif is "all the more emphatically developed," then it is reasonable to discern a rhetorical effect that the speaker appears arrogant or confident for the wrong reasons. The perception of an unseemly arrogance in the speaker of Psalm 73 is a viable reader response.

An ironizing rereading may also problematize the psalmist's claim that nearness to God is good for him. The possibility of a coercive undertone to such "nearness," for which I have already argued above, is reinforced when one considers that the obligatory service of the levitical priesthood may lie behind the clause in verse 23, "I am continually with you." Perhaps this

Asaphite, undoubtedly a levitical priest if we take the superscription seriously, cannot avoid being near God in the Temple due to his regular clerical duties, even though he struggles spiritually with what his relationship of service to God means. This is suggested by Harry P. Nasuti's reading of verse 23a and specifically the word *tāmîd,* "continually," there:

> As opposed to its use in connection with the common seeking of the Lord in the psalms, the use of this term to indicate the continual presence of the speaker with his God has interesting ties to the levitical order. One may note the continual presence of the levites before the Lord in 1 Chr 23:31, and, even more interestingly, in 1 Chr 16:6, 37, where it is the Asaphites in particular (along with certain of the priests in 1 Chr 16:6) who are to minister continually before the ark. Such examples, especially in conjunction with the implied setting of the psalm in the sanctuary of God (v 17), argue for an almost literal interpretation of the psalmist's being "continually with God," as well as raising anew the possibility of some levitical connection.[134]

Yet another aporia is hereby constructed—this one regarding the speaker's identity. Is he king or levitical priest? Is he speaking in the persona of king to evoke the royal representation of the entire nation, or perhaps drawing on the motif of kings' being guided by the hand of God while not necessarily being, himself, an actual king? Or is he, as king, drawing on a motif of continual service to God that would resonate with the Asaphite tradition? There is no way to resolve these questions. Two provisional answers might suffice, one historical in nature and one literary-critical. Historically, one may agree with Nasuti that royal and cultic valences to the identity of the speaker need not be seen as mutually exclusive, "given the cultic activity of both Hezekiah and Josiah."[135] From a literary-critical perspective, one may affirm that the speaking personas in biblical texts are often constructed as complex and need not be understood to represent the historical *realia* of those who performed the texts.

In any event, the reading of Psalm 73 as the narration of an individual's faith journey has been problematized by the argument that the rhetoric of the psalm trades on the cultic position of an iconic Israelite king. It is relevant that the psalm occupies an important place in the larger theological trajectory discernible within Book III of the Psalter that moves from the portrayal of pious, Torah-grounded kingship to the destruction of the monarchy and the postexilic community's emerging articulation of reliance on the kingship of God in place of failed human kingship.[136] The complex rhetoric of the psalm in fact presents its audience with both of

these aspects of identity: the implied audience may hear both an individu-
alistic tone appropriate to the spiritual journey of a single person and a
later intimation that this person has a royal identity representing the
larger community.[137] Understanding these complex dynamics in the poem
is especially important for assessing its function within the Psalms of
Asaph (Psalms 50 + 73–83) and as the lead psalm for Book III of the Psalter, especially since, as many have argued, it seems likely that its position in
the Psalter is the result of intentional redaction.[138]

Consider, now, that this kingly persona has failed in his attempt to
resolve his complaint. His obsessive focus on the wicked continues even
after his narrated moment of revelation. On my ironizing reading, it was
always intended to be clear to the audience that he has failed. Any implication that this king has experienced transformation that has set the
theodicy dilemma to rest is unreliable. In fact, his narcissism constitutes
an invitation to the audience to construct a more adequate meaning in
the unspoken, in the gaps and aporias that remain in this complicated
liturgical poem. One construction of the unspoken is that this king has
been so consumed with pondering the epistemological dilemma that he
has neither recounted all of God's works (v 28) nor advocated for the
powerless in his society. In the literary structuring of the Psalter, the
elaborate description of kingly duties in Psalm 72 has prepared the implied audience to understand just how disastrously this king has de-
faulted in his royal leadership. According to Psalm 72, kings are to judge
with righteousness, defend the cause of the poor, give deliverance to the
needy, and redeem the weak from oppression and violence. But the royal
speaker of Psalm 73 simply fulminates ineffectually—and that not even
regarding the oppression of the poor and needy in his realm, but regarding the injustice of the general prospering of the wicked.[139]

Solomon and David are both explicitly invoked at the boundary between Psalm 72 and Psalm 73. Solomon is named in the Psalm 72 superscription, and the closing line, "The prayers of David son of Jesse are
ended" (Ps 72:20), draws a stark demarcation between the ethos of Psalm
72 as the end of Book II of the Psalter and the ethos of Psalm 73 as the
beginning of the failed monarchy of Book III of the Psalter.[140] When the
implied audience encounters Psalm 73 in the final form of the Psalter—
perhaps in liturgical performances of the psalm,[141] and certainly in its crucial redactional role within the final literary form of the Psalter—the audience finds that this royal speaker is no ideal king. He is no David, and he is
not even a Solomon, since he has failed at the epistemological task. This
king should have been attending to the needs of the powerless, but instead
he was by turns ruminating narcissistically and ranting. He should have
been telling the magnificent works of God on behalf of his community.

He admits as much himself, noting that if he had continued to obsess about the flourishing of the wicked and his own unjust fate he would have "betrayed the generation of your children" (v 15), and yet he continues to give himself over to such obsessing through most of the rest of the psalm. Has he truly made God his only refuge, "in order to recount all of your works" (v 28)? If so, why is it that he has not recounted a single attribute or saving deed of the Almighty here? The irony is palpable. One may thus read Psalm 73 as an ironic reflection on the failure of the Israelite monarchy that is as rhetorically complex, in miniature and in its own unique way, as are the books of Job and Qohelet.

The rest of the Psalms of Asaph do describe God's marvelous deeds on behalf of Israel, simultaneously affirming the point made by the psalmist in 73:28 and underlining his own failure to do so. Rich and detailed explorations of Israel's tradition history with God are characteristic of almost all of the rest of the Asaph psalms—Mitchell says that the "feature of historical review . . . is pursued almost obsessively in the Asaph and deutero-Asaph Psalms"[142]—and that should be taken as significant for our interpretation of Psalm 73. A number of readers have argued for meaningful coherence within the Asaph collection on literary, historical, and theological grounds.[143] Psalm 50, the Asaph psalm that stands separate from the others, is alone with Psalm 81 in representing God's voice rather than that of the psalmist or the praying community; virtually this entire psalm, with the exception of the introit, voices God's own holy speech. The rest of the Psalms of Asaph then invite the worshipping community to dialogue, and they model such dialogue in their own internal literary dynamics among the various psalms. The opening of speech belongs to the voice of the divine: "The mighty one, God the LORD, speaks and summons the earth" (Ps 50:1). The guild of Asaph knows that "our God comes and does not keep silence" (50:3). It might have seemed that God was absent or unknowing, but God has always attended to God's people and now challenges Israel to a dialogue. Israel has bankrupted the sacred speech entrusted to her: "What right have you to recite my statutes or take my covenant on your lips? . . . for you cast my words behind you" (50:16–17). The attentiveness to speech—to words and mouths and tongues uttering rightly or wrongly—is then taken up and performed in intricate ways in the remaining Psalms of Asaph. A dialogical ethos textures the doubts and hopes of the implied ancient worshipping community that is being formed by these texts. Within Psalms 73–83, psalms that speak of seeking God in absence or in contradiction alternate with psalms that extol God's deeds on behalf of Israel. Psalm 73 has a crucial role in this alternating sequence. It inaugurates a dialectic that moves between divine abandonment and divine presence, in which competing views of history clash.

Boadt's argument for didactic progression over the course of several Asaph psalms is worth considering:

> Together, Psalms 73 and 78 fittingly serve as bookends to this series of proclamations of God's cosmic rule over all nations, which ensures that divine justice will triumph. The series opens with the doubts of the psalmist whether God can save and maintain his cosmic rule; but it ends with the firm hope that the lessons of trust and fidelity are being learned . . . in meditation on the experience of covenant relationship with God.[144]

Boadt's insight into the dialogical connections among the Psalms of Asaph is certainly valuable. But God's rule is not, in fact, central to Psalm 73, nor does the narration of God's mighty power in Israel's history find resonances here. Psalm 73 feints toward such narration but, in fact, does not perform it. One may read the tone and discourses of this short collection in a rather more ambiguous light if Psalm 73 is taken as the introduction to all of them. The concluding words of Brueggemann and Miller's article are apropos here:

> If Psalm 73 is positioned where it is in the late canonizing process with the end of the dynasty to reflect on, Israel may here be reflecting upon and reconsidering a dynastic (and communal) career of bad choices that led to "perishing" and not to "prospering" (Ps. 1.3, 6; 73.27). The psalm imagines that in time to come, Israel may rechoose, and rechoose rightly. That choice will reject autonomy and prize obedient communion.[145]

My ironic reading is compatible with Brueggemann and Miller's position that Psalm 73 signals an acute awareness of Israel's disastrous mistakes in the past. But the literary dynamics of an ironic reading press urgently forward as well, across the boundary separating Book II from Book III and on into the rest of the Psalms of Asaph. I noted above that Psalm 73 ends with an aporia, because we do not know what the psalmist plans to recount about God. Two choices present themselves. The implied audience may inhabit the place of interpretive uncertainty, becoming one with the psalmist in his epistemological anguish and honoring the intractability of the questions he raises. Or the audience may read further in the Psalms of Asaph, seeking coherence and possibilities for resolution of the textual ambiguity in that larger corpus. And indeed, the forward movement of the last line of the psalm, with its infinitive "to recount," impels the reader on into further poetic musings. As one response to that perceived propulsion of the rhetoric of the psalm, I will pursue the theological question briefly into the other psalms of Asaph. Who is this God for the psalmist and for the Israel adduced in the first clause of the psalm?

The God of the (other) Psalms of Asaph is a God who promises to judge with equity (Ps 75:2) and exalt the righteous (75:10), a glorious warrior who destroyed Israel's enemies in the past (76:3) and led Israel through the wilderness (77:20), yet one who does not always answer believers when they call (77:7–9). This God is one who appointed the Torah for the people of Israel so that obedience might save them from rebellion and subsequent punishment (78:5–8), yet who can still seem deaf to the anguish of the people (79:9–11). This God is fully capable of planting a vine and abandoning it to destruction (Psalm 80), one who claims that his apparent absence or neglect has historically served to test the people (Ps 81:6–12) and whose dominion over Israel's enemies proves that he is "Most High over all the earth" (Ps 83:9–18). The Asaph psalms' complex theology moves fluidly from bold assertion of trust to bitter denial of God's presence, from joyful acclamation of God's power to anguished resistance to God's wrathful hand. These, indeed, are the divine qualities to which the psalmist of Psalm 73 can attest in his experience.

The unreliability of the psalmist's voice in Psalm 73 may be the point. Essential to the theological dynamic of the Psalms of Asaph as a whole is the profound unreliability of those who dare to praise God and appeal for God's help. The history of Israel recounted in the Psalms of Asaph makes this transparently clear: the Israelites and their leaders remember God one moment only to forget him the next. Thus the unreliability of the psalmist's voice in Psalm 73 may be seen as an indispensable hermeneutical key to the ironic theology grounding the Psalms of Asaph as a whole. Without this irony, there would be no lament. But without this irony, there could be no honest praise either.

*   *   *

Job, Qohelet, and Psalm 73 make skilled use of subtle ironies in the characterization and voicing of their speakers in order to gesture toward larger unspoken truths. In so doing, they problematize both the biblical subject who speaks and the interpreter whose hermeneutics would try to control biblical signifying. The Book of Job shows us that the dramatic agonies of human experience are not, finally, the central issue to be considered in theological inquiry. In the Book of Qohelet, humans' desperate striving for autonomy and epistemological control is roundly rejected in favor of halakhic obedience. Those complex metanarratological assertions are affirmed by Psalm 73, but the psalm goes even further. It names, in the heart of postexilic Israel's liturgical life, the essential irony involved in the human desire to know and obey God at all.

But the ironies in these texts double back upon themselves, for what has been said has been said and can never be fully erased. Thus we find that Scripture continually undoes itself in the very utterance of its sacred words, offering both silences and excesses of meaning that create unresolvable aporias. In biblical wisdom literature in particular, those aporias invite the reader on into further epistemological inquiry and sustained spiritual wrestling, taking as guides both life experience and other Scripture texts. Thus ironic Scripture invites us into more Scripture. The ironic divine word compels us to move once again into the texts that constituted the ancient Israelite community and that continue to constitute new communities of readers.

6

CONCLUSION

The unspoken is powerful in the Hebrew Bible. Irony in ancient Israelite literature serves as a many-edged tool for the destabilization of the overconfident subject, the problematizing of nationalistic rhetoric, and the subversion of ancient believers' misunderstandings of tradition. Irony underscores the inherent fragility of Israel's relationship with God and the impressive capacity of the Israelites, and all humans, for self-deception. Irony in the Hebrew Scriptures also invites its implied audience to something better, something more worthy of the God who calls Israel into covenant.

Ironic biblical texts construct community in ways that may be by turns alarming and enchanting but are always compelling. Biblical ironists dramatize what is at stake in encountering the word of God, offering an alluring invitation to insiders and enacting a polemics against those who do not understand, those who are not positioned rightly with regard to the complicated truths of Torah, Prophets, and Writings. Ironic texts parody and mock what is inadequate, yet they allow for flexibility in reconstructing the unspoken and thereby tolerate the development of diverse communal hermeneutics that are responsive to multiple aspects of scriptural signifying.

Ironic biblical texts construct the agency of the reader/hearer as morally significant. With ironic texts, we can see that reading—in its broadest sense of interpreting cultural signs—matters greatly for ancient Israel. Reading and rereading are formative activities for individuals and communities. Ironic biblical texts demonstrate the importance of reflecting on dialogism, alterity, and the "irresponsibility of language," to use again the formulation of Stephen H. Webb.[1] In this, they not only encourage a fuller and more complex appropriation of Scripture by its readers. They also refuse the limitations of bibliolatry and literalism, preferring instead to honor the unspoken and the unutterable as essential aspects of God's interactions with the world of human life and human language. Ironic texts resist monologic speech and monologic interpretation, instead welcoming the lively play of competing interpretations in the life of the reading community.

Irony and Scriptural Signifying

But is there truly so much irony in the Hebrew Bible? Perhaps this entire endeavor has been an exercise in overreading. Perhaps these stories simply mean what they seem to say on the surface. Perhaps juxtapositions of contradictory themes or ideas simply resulted from scribal carelessness or were allowed for pragmatic reasons having to do with aspects of scribal technique, lengths of scrolls, or other priorities that are now lost to us. Perhaps the ancient Hebrew mind was not capable of such subtlety in its forms of literary expression as this book has proposed.

I acknowledge cheerfully that irony lies in the eye of the beholder. Various reconstructions of intersecting aspects of historical and cultural contexts will yield varying results. One reader's irony is another reader's earnest assertion. To see that this is so, one need only consult the list of prizes given for "Oddest Book Title of the Year" by the British trade publication *The Bookseller.* Among the winners are the following volumes, entitled earnestly by their authors but easily construed as ironic by readers: *The Joy of Chickens* (Prentice Hall, 1980), *Versailles: The View from Sweden* (University of Chicago, 1988), and *How to Avoid Huge Ships* (Cornell Maritime Press, 1992).[2]

But even given scholars' divergent assessments of literary, social, theological, and political contexts within which Hebrew Bible literature was produced, I hope I have made my case well enough that no reader will be able to harrumph, "It is just not possible that so much irony exists in the Bible." One finds such a position in David Quammen's review of a book by Steven Johnson on the cholera epidemic in London in 1854. Quammen comments dyspeptically on what he sees as Johnson's overly frequent use of the word "ironically" and its variants: "The tragic irony of cholera" was one thing, "the dominant irony of the state of British public health" was something else, the "dark irony" of the miasma theory was this, the "sad irony" of Snow's argument was that—and I could cite many other instances. That's a little too much irony for one short book, and it seems to reflect Johnson's insistence that his insights, beyond being interesting and significant, are ingenious reversals of expectation.[3]

But is it difficult to imagine that there might be a discernible "tragic irony" in the cholera epidemic and also an irony worth noting about the state of British public health? Quammen says he sees this not simply as "careless wording" on the part of Johnson but, rather, revelatory of a flaw in Johnson's viewpoint. There may be readers of this volume who likewise reach the point of skepticism earlier than I do regarding the pervasiveness of irony in ancient Semitic literature. I would implore those readers to consider all of the ironies within the Hebrew Bible upon which this book has not touched. Many local and broader ironies within Scripture yet beckon to the interpreter alert to the hermeneutical possibilities.

In the introduction, I highlighted some texts whose ironies could not be analyzed in detail in these pages. Edwin Good's *Irony in the Old Testament* may always be consulted with profit, and a more recent volume, Ze'ev Weisman's *Political Satire in the Bible,* also brims with examples of irony in biblical literature.[4] Following are some brief gestures of my own toward shadowy figures, ambiguous words, and elusive plot dynamics that, in my view, perform ironizing within the Hebrew Bible but that cannot receive their full due here. I hope these musings will defend against a jaded skepticism about irony generally, and also that they may spur on other interpreters who wish to enter the deceptive landscapes of biblical irony.

Genesis is rife with ironies, from the creation stories through the patriarchal misadventures to the magnificent ironies of the Joseph saga. Edwin Good remarked a number of the ironies in Genesis with acuity. Deeanne Westbrook has seen in the choice placed before Eve "one of the greatest ironies in all literature, an irony every bit as bitter as that which mocks the life and career of Oedipus" in that "Eve, born without ethical knowledge, abides in a place in which she is forced to make not only for herself, but for all humankind, an ethical decision" of the greatest moment.[5] We might also note the irony of Eve being named as "mother of all living" while yet having ushered mortality into human experience and having given birth to the first murderer. Does the man know what he is saying when he bestows her name (if not, dramatic irony is afoot), and is what he means the same as what the narrator means?

The murder of Abel by Cain ignites a pervasive ironizing of the cultural practice of primogeniture in the several stories in Genesis wherein a younger son triumphs over the firstborn. Commentators do regularly note the reversal. But the full implications of that insistent ironizing pattern for Pentateuchal notions of kinship and authority have yet to be probed, to the best of my knowledge.

Juxtaposition often creates intended and unintended ironies, because the priorities of one source may distract from, undermine, or redirect the priorities of another. I touched in chapter 1 on the possibility that the sin of disobedience in the non-Priestly creation story ironically constitutes a necessary fulfillment of the command to be fruitful in the Priestly creation account. Thomas Jemielity finds the author of the J material to be a master of dramatic irony. He writes, "For the Yahwist, God is a supreme narrative or dramatic ironist . . . delivering scripts to a cast denied the whole play. . . . [T]he Yahwist gives us a divinity achieving its objectives despite the incomprehension, resistance, and scepticism of the human actors. The Yahwist's is a comic irony, close to romance. The individual stories and adventures come to happy endings despite complications, reversals, setbacks, and all the other familiar devices of comedy."[6] Many narrative moments within the non-Priestly material could be explored with an eye to local dramatic ironies. One could also probe the implications of a metanarratological dramatic irony having to do with the epic sweep of Israel's covenant history being not perceived, not trusted, or misunderstood by individual characters within the non-Priestly traditions.

Disturbing ironies are generated by the story of the Aqedah. Unthinkable death-dealing is asked of Abraham, but the sacrifice of his beloved son is then foiled by a God who appears satisfied with Abraham's unquestioning obedience. No human blood was spilled. Yet the death of Sarah follows virtually immediately in the narrative after this near-sacrifice (Gen 23:1–2). Further, a thunderous silence envelopes the traumatized Isaac, who will know God best thereafter by the divine epithet Terror (Gen 31:42). Isaac's subsequent lack of prominence in the stories of Genesis and elsewhere in the Hebrew Bible may be probed as an ironic response to the spoken, that he had been saved on Mount Moriah. Abraham and Jacob are towering figures in later biblical tradition, but Isaac is virtually absent. Was his death merely deferred, deflected, inscribed in Scripture in the silences between words?

One could highlight a number of ironies in the Book of Exodus. Moses's protestations of his inadequacy at the burning bush are overruled by God initially, yet his inadequacy is confirmed by his being barred from the Promised Land on grounds that will forever remain dubious. Had Moses been right all along? Glenn S. Holland points out the irony that when Pharaoh's heart is hardened by God, Pharaoh thinks himself free to ignore the God of Israel: "Who is the Lord that I should heed him and let Israel go?" Pharaoh snarls. "I do not know the Lord, and I will not let Israel go" (Exod 5:2). Holland writes, "But Pharaoh is completely under the power of the Lord he does not know; he unwittingly serves God's purposes by his obstinacy, and ultimately must capitulate to God's command. . . . Much like Oedipus, when Pharaoh believes himself to be most free he is in fact most fully a part of a divinely ordained series of events serving the purposes of the deity."[7]

Holy-war tradition is manipulated by the prophets to describe God fighting against Israel itself in instances of that nation's covenant faithlessness. That this is an innovative ironic usage of ancient tradition is clear, but more can be said. Are the seeds of ironic destruction contained within holy-war tradition itself? Faithless individuals are always rooted out of the community that lives according to the tenets of holy war—Achan reminds us of that. But if the whole community can be construed as faithless, then even in the instances when Israel and Israel's leaders show themselves most heroic, they risk destruction. Within biblical narratives of conquest and security, the characters' lack of awareness of the dangerous sword they wield is certainly ironic, even if the larger-scale dramatic irony does not unfold fully until the exilic and post-exilic periods in the metanarratological reflections of Ezekiel and Jeremiah. In fact, holy-war tradition may be considered not just a two-edged sword but a sword whose very handle is all sharpness and burnished blade: there is no way to wield it against an Other without lacerating oneself as well.

Many narrative ironies permeate the Book of Judges. Lillian R. Klein, Mieke Bal, J. Cheryl Exum, and others have done a fine job of elucidating those. Baruch Levine has noted the ironies inhering in the Gideon story even at the level of the names of the characters: "Here is Joash, bearing a Yahwistic name, and a scion of a noted Israelite clan, who names his son Jerubbaal, and, what is more, operates a Baal altar with an Asherah image (or other object) near his home."[8] The story of Jephthah and his daughter is built upon the most tragic of dramatic ironies: the hero, once a man of no account, makes a vow to God after military victory, but the fulfillment of his vow with integrity requires the sacrifice of his innocent daughter. Claudia Camp has provided an excellent view into ironies in the Samson narrative regarding Israelite identity, although she does not name them ironic as such. Connecting the symbology of the cutting of hair with the practice of circumcision, she writes:

> Both hair-cutting and circumcision are Janus-faced. Both can mean castration, but both also mean purification, and both are a sign of a vow made and renewed, in the latter case endlessly re-

newed. Circumcision is particularly powerfully freighted with double meaning; it symbolizes not only castration but also fruitfulness, the opening that allows the flow of the seed (Eilberg-Schwartz 1990: 141–76). . . . If, in the cutting of his hair, Samson is also symbolically circumcised, then the Strange Woman's is the hand by which he enters not just manhood, but *Israelite* manhood. Only now does he leave the ranks of the uncircumcised, the Philistines; only now is he truly separated, a Nazirite.[9]

Biblical representations of the kings of Israel and Judah offer manifold valences of understatement, overstatement, ironies of characterization, and dramatic irony. In chapter 2, I discussed ironies attending the representations of Saul, David, and Solomon, and in chapter 5, I noted that one may consider the oblique allusiveness to Solomon in the persona of "Qohelet" as ironizing the vaunted wisdom of Solomon. Brueggemann observes also that the naming of baby Solomon with a name that suggests peace (*šālôm*) may be mildly ironic since Solomon's aggressive economic policies "will establish a peaceableness for some at the expense of others."[10] Irony also may be seen where Solomon spares Abiathar from execution (1 Kgs 2:26–27). Brueggemann remarks that when Solomon banishes Abiathar to Anathoth, whence will come Jeremiah some centuries later, "Solomon has left alive the most abrasive voices of critique of the monarchy, an abrasion that comes to full voice in the tradition of Jeremiah."[11]

The complex characterization of David holds in ironic tension his potential for sublime devotion to God and his base commitment to personal gain. Numerous subtle touches throughout the David material highlight dramatic ironies, conceptual incongruities, and unexpected reversals. Uriah's stalwart refusal to sleep with his own wife may be read as a pathetic dramatic irony given that the one to whom he is protesting, David, has already committed adultery with her. Further, as Shimon Bar-Efrat has noted, "[t]he subtle irony reaches its zenith when Uriah swears by David's life, namely, by the life of the man who did just what he will not do. . . . It is also ironic that it is by his honesty and adherence to his principles, his lord and his comrades that Uriah brings about his own undoing. The fact that Uriah is the bearer of his own death-warrant is particularly poignant in its irony."[12] We see brilliant irony in the story of David unwittingly pronouncing judgment upon himself after hearing Nathan's parable of the ewe lamb (2 Samuel 12). Bar-Efrat notes a number of other ironic touches in the narration of Absalom's revolt against David, in which events unfold with unseen consequences, particular players do not have all of the relevant information, and what constitutes good and bad news may be understood variously by different characters within the story.[13]

Ironies texture even the more earnest material in Kings. For example, it has long been noticed that Huldah's prophecy that Josiah would die "in peace" (*běšālôm*) was wrong on the face of it, given that king's violent demise in conflict with an enemy ruler. Scholars have argued for at least two readings that would suggest an ironic double entendre regarding that event: that Josiah died at the hands of purported allies in peacetime, and that Josiah died in Jerusalem rather than on the battlefield.[14]

A biblical book that might not seem to have much use for irony is the passionately earnest Song of Songs. Yet even there, Francis Landy has observed a kind of rupture in its rhetoric that may be termed ironic. Landy finds that the urgent longing of the lovers for union is frustrated not only by the obstacles placed in their path by others but by the speech of the lovers themselves:

> Yet there is . . . an element of disunity in the Song, in the violence
> with which it dismembers the body, its total disregard for logical
> connection, the abruptness with which it embarks upon and
> abandons episodes in the lives of [the] lovers. The disunity is also
> that of the lovers, whose work of integration can never be completed. . . . [T]he discourse of the lovers separates them. It is a
> displacement of love, in which foreplay—seduction, sweet-talk—
> repeatedly defers fusion.[15]

Thus desire itself is ironized, ostensibly sought but repeatedly stalled. The dynamic in the Song's poetry of seeking and refusing integration is, we see, a dance not only of love but of irony. A deeper theological irony may suffuse the intertextual gestures that the Song makes to the Garden of Eden, something that Landy has noticed as well. He writes, "[T]he Song is a reflection on the story of the garden of Eden, using the same images of garden and tree, substituting for the traumatic dissociation of [humans] and animals their metaphoric integration. Through it we glimpse, belatedly, by the grace of poetry, the possibility of paradise."[16] If this is so, given that union is perpetually frustrated in the Song of Songs, we might also say that this glimpse of the Garden is itself ironic, for the Garden and all it represents remain forever unattainable.

A fundamental irony attends the presence of wisdom material within the larger corpus of the Hebrew Bible. The attribution of most of Proverbs to the agency of Israelites (Solomon and the scribes of King Hezekiah's court) and the fiction that most of the Book of Qohelet owes its composition to (one like) Solomon underline the relevance of these maxims for the life of Israel. Yet within the biblical wisdom literature, the absence of reflection on Israel's history and cultic practices might suggest that true wisdom requires moving away from the fetishizing of Israel's covenant status and the memorializing of the LORD's saving deeds on Israel's behalf. Here, though, the irony can be construed as running both ways. The iconoclastic proposal that Israel's history and cultic practices are irrelevant—which lingers at the shadowy margins of wisdom literature, never spoken outright and only hinted at in the proem of "Qohelet"—is arguably ironized by the critique of Solomon in Kings precisely for his infidelity in cultic matters, an infidelity with devastating consequences for Israel's history. It is ironized as well by the critique in the Book of Qohelet of the pursuit of wisdom apart from halakhic obedience. Israel is absent, for the most part, in the biblical wisdom literature. Yet Israel's covenant and Israel's fate are powerfully present in the silences that echo between the corpus of biblical wisdom literature and the rest of the Hebrew Bible.

The way in which judgment and promise continually displace each other in the rhetoric of Jeremiah has been noticed by A. R. Pete Diamond.[17] He argues that there are fundamental ironies in the way in which the Book of Jeremiah performs judgment as a means of hope and satirizes (false) hope as a cause of judgment. The people shrink from God's horrific punishment, but in the perspective of the prophet as represented in the prose of Jeremiah, some also long for God's violence as the means to power for a specific elite within diaspora Judaism.[18] As Diamond puts it, "In Jeremiah, doom and hope are subtexts of each other."[19] He notices that Israel is smug when it stands under judgment, but recalcitrant also in the face of God's promises of restoration ("Return, O virgin Israel, return to these your cities. How long will you waver, O faithless daughter?" Jer 31:21). Diamond interprets this textual dynamic as ironic:

> [T]he resistance to hope constitutes the compositions' anxiety. If this resistance succeeds, then the failure of YHWH is complete. Ironically, while the polarization and estrangement, the dispute between [G]od and Israel continues, their relative positions have shifted in emotional and psychological tenor! They have displaced each other and taken up each other's former postures. YHWH must now fight for hope where previously in the scroll he faced, in his view, intransigent, misplaced hope in communal security.[20]

Diamond also sees irony in the ways in which older traditions of Israel's election and divine favor, rejected before the fall of Jerusalem, are taken up again and reread toward particular political ends. His example is Jeremiah 33:23–26: "Have you not observed how these people say, 'The two families that the LORD chose have been rejected by him,' and how they hold my people in such contempt that they no longer regard them as a nation? Thus says the LORD: Only if I had not established my covenant with day and night . . . would I reject the offspring of Jacob." Diamond finds here an ironic self-interest that complicates the role of the prophet:

> Ironically, this very reliance upon the old election traditions had rendered the Judaean community impervious to Jeremiah's mission of doom. . . . Now on the other side of Jerusalem's collapse, revitalization interests repossess these disenfranchised traditions. With [them] the "colonial elite" can secure their own aspirations for cultural power, prevent the admission of divine failure, and localize Jeremiah's oracular destabilization of these traditions to the "generation of wrath." Ironically, the tradition wielded so effectively by Jeremiah's opponents . . . now in the composition of Jeremiah's restoration scroll supercedes Jeremiah once again! . . . One "Jeremiah" defeats another.[21]

It may be said that irony is the métier of prophecy, because prophecy powerfully undermines that which is not adequate and urges the reader to assist in constructing that which is more desirable, more moral, more truthful, more pleasing to God.[22] Apropos here is the observation of Stephen Geller about prophecy as a performance of "creative indeterminacy" that defies canonical attempts to reduce it to a single message. Reflecting on the turbulent and confusing Isaiah 6, Geller writes:

> The stump of the felled national tree is those disciples who see and hear God through the prophet, have total faith in God through him. In fact, once one has read those final words, the entire chapter begins to oscillate continuously in one's mind between its positive and negative poles, rapture-gloom, despair-hope, rejection-acceptance, destruction-new growth. . . . In no passage is the essential difference between the static canonical approach—which looks for stable truth in the text—and the fluid literary approach which values precisely what is unstable and moving in it, more perceptible and necessary to comprehend. This creative indeterminacy is clearly not accidental or incidental. Rather, it is intrinsic to the religious orientation of the New Prophecy, and through it, the whole of biblical religion.[23]

I would add only that the pronouncement of creative, indeterminate words in the name of the one true God is a rhetorical act performed by every ironic text in Scripture, and not only in prophecy. There is a fluidity and openness to ironic signification. Irony is matchless in its effectiveness as a means of persuasion precisely because it cannot be definitively named or constrained. Brueggemann interprets the doubleness of representations of Solomon in the Bible in a way that may apply to many kinds of scriptural ironizing. He says, "Ancient textual acts of imagination continue to be open to and generative of subsequent acts of interpretive imagination whereby ancient memories could be readily aligned with contemporary agendas. It is this tricky way in which the biblical memory of Solomon negotiates self-conscious covenantal faith while still accommodating lived reality that makes the tradition enormously supple and open to belated use."[24] While many aspects of textual performance might be described as open and generative of subsequent readings, the interplay between the spoken and the unspoken in ironic texts is particularly lively and welcoming of interpretive acts of creative imagination.

Leaving the Garden Again: New Beginnings

The apophatic way of irony directs us into the truth of negation. Reading irony, we encounter the powerful theological witness of the aporia. Across the Hebrew Scriptures, conversations begun through ironic comments on tradition allow for rereadings and fresh contextualizations of traditions that otherwise might have been bound to a few dominant perspectives. I find both literarily artistic and theologically rich the critique of ancient Israel's traditions offered by biblical ironists. What one scholar says about irony in the Gospel of Mark applies well, I think, to the ironies that animate the Hebrew Scriptures: "[I]ronic narratives disrupt the superficialities of ordinary experience, opening up new and richer possibilities of understanding. . . . [T]he possibilities of tensive language, of plurisignificance, and of narrative irony represent movements within living traditions which ultimately function to keep those traditions supple and healthy."[25] The interpreter of irony becomes accustomed to suspecting misdirection and rejoices to appreciate deeper levels of significance than may have been clear on the first foray into a text. Reading through the Hebrew Bible with an eye for irony seasons us as readers. It trains us to sustain our encounters—historical, literary, and theological—with the wildness and untamability of Scripture.

Having journeyed into the landscapes of the Hebrew Bible as intrepid explorers, we may wonder whether we can ever return, hermeneutically speaking, to the place of innocence. Is it possible to return, now that we know that words of God and words about God can misdirect us? As Cain was driven from place to place, so too the interpreter of biblical irony may feel like a wanderer on the earth, unable to rest safely in any one hermeneutical spot for long. A hermeneutics that accounts for irony is of necessity unsettled, open to textual alterity, not-being, and not-being-what-one-thought.

Interpreters of irony know that in textual misdirection, evasiveness, and the play of indeterminacy, the holy word can show itself as exceedingly powerful, impossible to domesticate or fetishize. Its silences and unspoken truths invite readers beyond the limits of our own hermeneutical myopia. Webb uses the word "conversion" to speak of this function of language: "Every trope models a conversion, demanding a change from one way of speaking (or living) to another . . . asking us to see what could not be seen before, underwritten with a promise that is pledged only to those who are willing to inhabit the newly imagined space."[26] The ironies in Scripture invite us to turn away from our misunderstandings and our idolatries of the written. They call us to reform and renew our imaginative views of what is possible. We left the Garden back at the end of chapter 1, when we began this journey into readings of the silences and whispered misrepresentations and veiled subversions of Scripture. If the readings in this book have been helpful, even where you have disagreed with them and have argued back as you read, then we can look up together and recognize the landscape better than we had seen it before. We have only just left the Garden, after all. This is just the beginning of our mapping of a scriptural world that is never exactly what it seems. We interpreters are urged to be fruitful and multiply, in hermeneutics as in life. Naïve no longer, we go.

NOTES

Preface and Acknowledgments

1. There is an important ethical dimension to Jonathan Culler's observation that "theory is the discourse that seeks the opening of the subject to the nonidentical, to alterity, the other, the indeterminate, or some other site or event beyond instrumental reason" ("The Literary in Theory," in *What's Left of Theory? New Work on the Politics of Literary Theory*, ed. Judith Butler, John Guillory, and Kendall Thomas [New York: Routledge, 2000], 287).

Introduction

1. Robert Alter, "Anteriority, Authority, and Secrecy: A General Comment," *Semeia* 43 (1988): 155–56; emphasis in original.

2. See Erika Mae Olbricht, "Constructing the Dead Author: Postmodernism's Rhetoric of Death," in *The Rhetorical Analysis of Scripture: Essays from the 1995 London Conference*, ed. Stanley E. Porter and Thomas H. Olbricht, 66–78, JSNT-Sup 146 (Sheffield, UK: Sheffield Academic Press, 1997). Reflecting on Roland Barthes's essay "The Death of the Author" (1968) and Michel Foucault's piece "What Is an Author?" (1979), Olbricht probes the functions of discourses about the author. She suggests that reader response criticism is not enough to mediate questions about subjectivity and textual indeterminacy. Instead, it will be useful for interpreters to consider the role of the "discursified" author in various literary theories. Olbricht finds it paradoxical that the author "exists beyond the page" as well as being constructed through literary discourses (77). The paradox can be resolved neither by views of meaning as entirely determinate nor by wholly constructionist views of textual meaning.

3. Reproduced in Lisa Grunwald and Stephen J. Adler, *Letters of the Century: America 1900–1999* (New York: Dial Press, 1999), 27. Their source for the letter was Herbert Asbury, *Carry Nation* (New York: Knopf, 1929), 267. The letter is quoted in its entirety in Nation's autobiographical work, *The Use and Need of the Life of Carry A. Nation* (Topeka, Kans.: F. M. Steves and Sons, 1905), 138. In that source, Nation says that she received the letter in 1904.

4. Nation, *Use and Need of the Life of Carry A. Nation*, 138.

5. Stowe and her sister, Catharine E. Beecher, communicate their dismay at unsavory butter in their 1869 volume, *The American Woman's Home* (reprint, New Brunswick, N.J.: Rutgers University Press, 2002): "A matter for despair as regards bad butter is, that at the tables where it is used it stands sentinel at the door to bar your way to every other kind of food. You turn from your dreadful half-slice of bread, which fills your mouth with bitterness, to your beef-steak, which proves virulent with the same poison. . . . Hungry and miserable, you think to solace yourself at the dessert; but the pastry is cursed, the cake is acrid with the same plague. You are ready to howl with despair. . . . Yet the process of making good butter is a very simple one . . . so simple, that one wonders at thou-

sands and millions of pounds of butter yearly manufactured which are merely a
hobgoblin bewitchment of cream into foul and loathsome poisons" (136).

6. Owen M. Johnson wrote *The Lawrenceville Stories* originally as three separate stories: "The Prodigious Hickey" (1908), "The Varmint" (1910), and "The
Tennessee Shad" (1911). An edition was printed by Simon and Schuster in 1987.

7. Catharine Beecher writes of three distinct positions held within the
temperance movement regarding use of alcohol in cooking. One group advocated abstinence with no exceptions; another forbade alcohol in beverages only,
yet abstained from using alcohol in cooking "to avoid the appearance of evil"; a
third group abstained from intoxicating beverages but allowed the use of spirits
in cooking. See *Miss Beecher's Domestic Receipt Book, Designed as a Supplement to Her
Treatise on Domestic Economy* (New York: Harper and Brothers, 1857), 183.

8. Robert Alter, *The Pleasures of Reading in an Ideological Age* (New York:
Simon and Schuster, 1989), 32.

1. Interpreting Irony

1. Consider the view of Glenn S. Holland: "[I]rony is necessarily a *subversive*
way of understanding meaning. . . . Although domesticated irony can be a diver-
sion and palliative for gentlemen, irony unhindered by established limits has the
potential to destroy worlds" (*Divine Irony* [Selinsgrove, Pa.: Susquehanna University Press, 2000], 33; emphasis in original). Or consider Regina M. Schwartz's
claim, "Every archaeologist's spade and every linguist's verb ending is deeply inscribed with politics." Ironic hyperbole or earnest assertion? Encountered in a
critique of ideological-critical over-reading, this statement would best be interpreted ironically. But read in Schwartz's analysis of the vulnerabilities of a historical positivism that pretends to hermeneutical neutrality, the sincerity of the assertion is clear. See Schwartz, "Adultery in the House of David: The Metanarrative of
Biblical Scholarship and the Narratives of the Bible," in *Women in the Hebrew Bible:
A Reader,* ed. Alice Bach (New York: Routledge, 1999), 336.

2. The famous description of literature in the Hebrew Bible as being
"fraught with background" comes from Erich Auerbach's discussion of differences between ancient Greek and Hebrew literatures in chapter 1, "Odysseus'
Scar," of his *Mimesis: The Representation of Reality in Western Literature* (Princeton,
N.J.: Princeton University Press, 1968).

3. A. J. Mandt, "The Domain of Silence in Humanistic Discourse," *Soundings* 65 (1982): 31.

4. Alan J. Hauser, "Should Ahab Go to Battle or Not? Ambiguity as a Rhetorical Device in 1 Kings 22," in *Rhetorical Argumentation in Biblical Texts: Essays
from the Lund 2000 Conference,* ed. Anders Eriksson, Thomas H. Olbricht, and
Walter Übelacker (Harrisburg, Pa.: Trinity Press International, 2002), 142.

5. Carl Raschke, "Fire and Roses, or the Problem of Postmodern Religious
Thinking," in *Shadow of Spirit: Postmodernism and Religion,* ed. Philippa Berry
and Andrew Wernick (London: Routledge, 1992), 101.

6. See Michael Herzfeld, "Irony and Power: Toward a Politics of Mockery in
Greece," in *Irony in Action: Anthropology, Practice, and the Moral Imagination,* ed.
James W. Fernandez and Mary Taylor Huber (Chicago: University of Chicago
Press, 2001), 63–64. Polemics and overstatement in Herzfeld's anthropological
work have been criticized by others in his field (see Zeba A. Crook, "Methods
and Models in New Testament Interpretations: A Critical Engagement with
Louise Lawrence's Literary Ethnography," *Religious Studies Review* 32 [2006]:

87–97), but his insights into ironizing cultural representations in Mediterranean societies remain helpful. Also illustrative is Baruch Halpern's reading of the David story (*David's Secret Demons: Messiah, Murderer, Traitor, King;* Grand Rapids, Mich.: Eerdmans, 2001). Halpern sees veiled allusions and double entendre everywhere in the Succession Narrative, hidden from all but those who pay excruciatingly close attention to details and convoluted connections in plot and narrated speech. Something Halpern says of Hushai's counsel to Absalom may be taken as applicable to the interpretive issue of reader competence generally with ironic texts: "[T]his bracketing with rumor indicates an understanding of the impact of news on the hearer, who overreacts, misinterprets the reality which the words reflect. In sum, words—even truthful words—can be and are deceptive; they have two sides. This is both an unusually honest (and virtuoso) exposure of the scribal ethic about composition and a key to understanding how an inner circle was meant to understand the text" (47).

7. Instructive here is the study of Brian C. Jones, *Howling over Moab: Irony and Rhetoric in Isaiah 15–16* (Atlanta, Ga.: Scholars Press, 1996). Many interpreters over the centuries have noticed that prophetic discourse relies heavily on sarcasm and ironizing of audience expectations. But Jones goes the requisite next step, asking whether marked changes in tone in a piece such as Isaiah's oracles against Moab necessarily constitute reliable indicators of redactional activity or, instead, may signal moves into ironic discourse within a unified literary composition. Thus redaction criticism is not a method with prior claims that should be plied before one considers more peripheral matters of ironic "style." Jones also makes the salutary observation that other traditions within the Hebrew Bible may be used judiciously to establish the larger context in which incongruities may be seen to signal irony in a particular text. Of his chosen text, he writes, "The principal clue that Isaiah 15–16 is intended ironically is the conflict between the negative attitude toward Moab expressed nearly everywhere in the H[ebrew] B[ible] and the deeply sympathetic attitude expressed in Isaiah 15–16" (137). Of course, where ancient Israelite traditions are less monolithic than the predominant attitude of contempt toward Moab, the task of the interpreter becomes more complex.

8. The phrase is Mieke Bal's, in her "Dealing/With/Women: Daughters in the Book of Judges," in *The Book and the Text: The Bible and Literary Theory,* ed. Regina M. Schwartz (Oxford: Blackwell, 1990), 18.

9. Ilona N. Rashkow, "Intertextuality, Transference, and the Reader In/Of Genesis 12 and 20," in *Reading between Texts: Intertextuality and the Hebrew Bible,* ed. Danna Nolan Fewell (Louisville, Ky.: Westminster/John Knox, 1992), 61.

10. L. Gregory Bloomquist, "The Role of the Audience in the Determination of Argumentation: The Gospel of Luke and the Acts of the Apostles," in *Rhetorical Argumentation in Biblical Texts,* ed. Anders Eriksson, Thomas H. Olbricht, and Walter Übelacker (Harrisburg, Pa.: Trinity Press International, 2002), 171.

11. Richard Cooper, "Textualizing Determinacy/Determining Textuality," *Semeia* 62 (1993): 4.

12. Jonathan Culler underlines the resilience of communication in a way that is helpful for understanding irony as a deconstructive force in texts: "The combination of context-bound meaning and boundless context on the one hand makes possible proclamations of the indeterminacy of meaning—though the smug iconoclasm of such proclamations may be irritating—but on the other hand urges that we continue to interpret texts, classify speech acts, and attempt to elucidate the conditions of signification. . . . The humanities . . . often seem touched with the belief that a theory which asserts the ultimate indeterminacy

of meaning makes all effort pointless. The fact that such assertions emerge from discussions that propose numerous particular determinations of meaning, specific interpretations of passages and texts, should cast doubts upon an impetuous nihilism. An opposition that is deconstructed is not destroyed or abandoned but reinscribed" (*On Deconstruction: Theory and Criticism After Structuralism* [Ithaca, N.Y.: Cornell University Press, 1982], 133).

13. Søren Kierkegaard, *The Concept of Irony, With Constant Reference to Socrates,* trans. Lee M. Capel (Bloomington: Indiana University Press, 1965), 340.

14. Andrew Cross, "Neither Either Nor Or: The Perils of Reflexive Irony," in *The Cambridge Companion to Kierkegaard,* ed. Alistair Hannay and Gordon D. Marino (Cambridge: Cambridge University Press, 1998), 126.

15. Kierkegaard, *Concept of Irony,* 85.

16. Ibid., 263.

17. Of course, the ideal reader of any particular text can turn out to look suspiciously like the scholar who is analyzing the text. William John Lyons has suggested that the ideal reader of the Gospel of John, per New Testament scholar J. L. Staley, would seem to be none other than "Staley himself, albeit with a few additional presuppositions which he believed made him into an ancient reader." See Lyons, "The Words of Gamaliel (Acts 5.38–39) and the Irony of Indeterminacy," *JSNT* 68 (1997): 24n5. There are unavoidable epistemological tautologies involved in speaking of the ideal reader. Nevertheless, it is important to underline that the author desires an understanding audience. Indeed, the contrast between the implied competent reader and incompetent reader is dramatized in ironic texts, because they lay out the falsity—the foolish misperception, the failure to grasp what is at stake, and so on—consequent to misreading.

18. Kierkegaard, *Concept of Irony,* 266.

19. Glenn Holland, "Paul's Use of Irony as a Rhetorical Technique," in *The Rhetorical Analysis of Scripture: Essays from the 1995 London Conference,* ed. Stanley E. Porter and Thomas H. Olbricht, 234–48 (Sheffield, UK: Sheffield Academic Press, 1997), 236–37.

20. Edwin M. Good, *Irony in the Old Testament* (Philadelphia: Westminster, 1965).

21. Ibid., 24.

22. Ibid., 30–31.

23. Ibid., 244.

24. Ibid., 246–47.

25. See D. C. Muecke, *The Compass of Irony* (London: Methuen, 1969) and *Irony,* The Critical Idiom (London: Methuen, 1970). For discussion of numerous examples of irony in English, American, French, Russian, Spanish, and German literature, see Leonard Feinberg, *Introduction to Satire* (Ames: Iowa State University Press, 1967), 157–75 and passim.

26. Clearly, Muecke's answer is yes. He notes drily, "Nor is it relevant to the question of the importance of irony that more people lack a sense of irony than have one" (*Irony,* 1–2).

27. George Bradford Caird, *The Language and Imagery of the Bible* (Philadelphia: Westminster, 1980), 104.

28. Muecke, *Irony,* 24–48. That the nature of each of these elements could itself be endlessly debated—by what criteria is something appropriately deemed "comedic" or "aesthetic"?—is something that Muecke does not address.

29. Muecke says concerning irony that "there must be grounds for guessing and these must be marked in the text or in its relationship to its con-

text. . . . 'Marking', in this sense, is a form of metacommunication; that is, along-side the ironic message there is a 'straight', though generally indirect, message intended as a fair hint of the real nature of the ironic message. In general terms, marking an ironical text means setting up, intuitively or with full consciousness, some form of perceptible contradiction, disparity, incongruity or anomaly which can then be naturalized or assimilated by the addressee's recognizing its metacommunicational function" ("Irony Markers," *Poetics* 7 [1978]: 365).

30. Muecke, *Irony*, 32.

31. Ibid. "Holy Willie's Prayer" is a poem that was written in 1785 by Robert Burns to satirize hypocrisy in the Scottish Church.

32. Wayne C. Booth, *A Rhetoric of Irony* (Chicago: University of Chicago Press, 1974), 24.

33. Ibid., *Rhetoric of Irony*, 29.

34. Ibid., *Rhetoric of Irony*, 31.

35. Ibid., *Rhetoric of Irony*, 28. Here he is responding to those who under-stand irony chiefly as a derogatory rhetorical operation in terms of its construc-tion of implied victims. But even the construction of the implied audience "in the know" can be framed in negative terms. What Feinberg says of satire can also be applied to any irony that parodies or mocks, namely, that it "appeals to a strong feeling of superiority" in its audience (*Introduction to Satire*, 10).

36. Booth, *Rhetoric of Irony*, 35; emphasis in original.

37. Another critic of Booth's work is Candace Lang; see her *Irony/Humor: Critical Paradigms* (Baltimore: Johns Hopkins University Press, 1988), esp. 40–47. Lang takes Booth to task for his underlying methodological assumption that irony represents the disjuncture between textual expression and anterior au-thorial intention. She criticizes him also for not taking adequately into account "the philosophical foundations of irony" (49). As a postmodernist, Lang faults Booth for his understanding of text. She is certainly correct that Booth's is a pre-postmodern understanding of textuality, although her representation of his view shades into caricature: "Thus [for Booth] the truly multivalent text is unthinkable: discrepancies or incoherencies can only be interpreted as errors, as attempts to communicate anxiety over life's contradictions, as despairing demonstrations of the inadequacy of language as a vehicle of self-expression, or as gratuitous wordplay with intent to mystify" (45).

38. Stanley Fish, "Short People Got No Reason to Live: Reading Irony," in *Doing What Comes Naturally: Change, Rhetoric, and the Practice of Theory in Literary and Legal Studies* (Durham, N.C.: Duke University Press, 1989), 180–96.

39. Ibid., 196.

40. Ibid., 189–90.

41. Ibid., 191. Fish is right that any persuasive interpretation will alter the con-ditions of seeing that subsequent readers/viewers bring to literature or art. But his dogmatism about Slepian neither having been uniquely perceptive nor having created the ironic Swift poem out of whole cloth is in fact not supportable by his own thesis. Persuasive readings are created through varying interactions among reader acuity, constraints and opportunities created by the real or imagined audi-ence, and features of the text. Slepian's perceptiveness and textual cues to Swift's ironic intentions will be assessed variously by different critics.

42. Ibid., 192.

43. See F. W. Dobbs-Allsopp, "Rethinking Historical Criticism," *Biblical Interpre-tation* 7 (1999): 235–71. Dobbs-Allsopp underscores the essentially literary nature of historicist engagement with texts and argues that the guild needs to "[reconcep-

tualize] historical criticism in such a way as to facilitate the integration of the full panoply of literary methods, theories, and strategies of reading currently employed by literary scholars, as well as rethinking and retheorizing the objectivist and foundationalist assumptions which have informed and motivated historical-critical practices in the past" (236). Another scholar committed to retrieving nuanced historical-critical inquiry in concert with other methods is Mark G. Brett. See his "Reading the Bible in the Context of Methodological Pluralism: The Undermining of Ethnic Exclusivism in Genesis," in *Rethinking Contexts, Rereading Texts: Contributions from the Social Sciences to Biblical Interpretation,* ed. M. Daniel Carroll R., 48–74 (Sheffield, UK: Sheffield Academic Press, 2000). Brett aims to "deconstruct the opposition between narratological analyses and the old historicism" (58).

44. Frank Stringfellow has paid attention to the psychology of verbal irony in his essay "Irony and Ideals in *Gulliver's Travels,*" in *Critical Essays on Jonathan Swift,* ed. Frank Palmeri, 91–103 (New York: G. K. Hall, 1992). Thinking about the fragility of unintended ironies and double ironies in Swift's work, Stringfellow observes, "The case of *Gulliver's Travels* suggests that the ironist, writing in the ironic mode, cannot give unequivocal assent to any ideal. . . . [W]hen the ironist repeats the words—the ideals and commands—of authority with the apparent intention of mocking them, the mockery may in fact conceal a measure of acceptance as well. We are used to saying that, in an ironic statement, the ironist can actually intend only one of the two more or less contradictory levels. But perhaps this is psychologically too simplistic; perhaps it is truer to say that both are intended, so that to speak ironically is necessarily to speak with unconscious ambivalence" (102).

45. Claire Colebrook, *Irony* (London: Routledge, 2004), 73.

46. Booth, *Rhetoric of Irony,* 59n14.

47. Paul de Man, "The Concept of Irony," lecture given at Ohio State University, transcribed in *Aesthetic Ideology,* ed. with introd. by Andrzej Warminski (Minneapolis: University of Minnesota Press, 1996), 166–67.

48. De Man argues, "[O]ne could say that any theory of irony is the undoing, the necessary undoing, of any theory of narrative, and it is ironic, as we saw, that irony always comes up in relation to theories of narrative, when irony is precisely what makes it impossible ever to achieve a theory of narrative that would be consistent. Which doesn't mean that we don't have to keep working on it, because that's all we can do, but it will always be interrupted, always be disrupted, always be undone by the ironic dimension which it will necessarily contain" ("Concept of Irony," 179). De Man here speaks of theories of literature. But the implications are significant for the implicit theories of narrative—that is, for notions of the reliability, representational quality, and veracity of storytelling—that play out in ancient Israel's self-understanding as a community, as well.

49. Paul de Man, "The Rhetoric of Temporality," in *Interpretation: Theory and Practice,* ed. Charles S. Singleton (Baltimore: Johns Hopkins, 1969), 195.

50. Ibid., 207.

51. Ibid., 197. De Man waxes hyperbolic about the implications of this: "Irony is unrelieved *vertige,* dizziness to the point of madness. Sanity can exist only because we are willing to function within the conventions of duplicity and dissimulation. . . . When we speak, then, of irony originating at the cost of the empirical self, the statement has to be taken seriously enough to be carried to the extreme: absolute irony is a consciousness of madness, itself the end of all consciousness; it is a consciousness of a non-consciousness, a reflection on madness from the inside of madness itself. . . . [T]he ironist invents a form of him-

self that is 'mad' but that does not know its own madness; he then proceeds to reflect on his madness thus objectified" (198).

52. Ibid., 203.

53. Linda Hutcheon, *Irony's Edge: The Theory and Politics of Irony* (New York: Routledge, 1995), 59–66. Hutcheon considers irony not as binary but instead as "relational, inclusive, and differential" in its semantic functioning. "Ironic meanings . . . are formed through additive oscillations between different said and unsaid meanings" (66).

54. A similar understanding has been proposed by Austin Busch, who uses the notion of Bakhtinian "double voicing" to get at the ways in which irony creates a multivocal space between the ironic text and the reader. See Busch, "Questioning and Conviction: Double-Voiced Discourse in Mark 3:22–30," *Journal of Biblical Literature* 125 (2006): 477–505. Busch finds it hermeneutically significant that the Gospel of Mark "orchestrates a complex dialogue between distinct theological perspectives" (498).

55. Hutcheon, *Irony's Edge,* 63.

56. Muecke, "Irony Markers," 366.

57. Mary Scoggin, "Wine in the Writing, Truth in the Rhetoric: Three Levels of Irony in a Chinese Essay Genre," in *Irony in Action: Anthropology, Practice, and the Moral Imagination,* ed. James W. Fernandez and Mary Taylor Huber (Chicago: University of Chicago Press, 2001), 160.

58. Stephen H. Webb says of hyperbole that its excess explodes the "ordinary and the expected. The nonconformity of the trope of hyperbole can serve as a model for all discourses that seek the meaningful beyond the grammatical rules that limit the reach of meaning" ("Theological Reflections on the Hyperbolic Imagination," in *Rhetorical Invention and Religious Inquiry: New Perspectives,* ed. Walter Jost and Wendy Olmsted [New Haven, Conn.: Yale University Press, 2000], 279). Webb distinguishes between earnest hyperbole and irony, noting that "unlike irony, . . . hyperbole really means what it says" (280), a point that some might debate. The overblown nature of hyperbole could be argued to contain within it the seeds of its own ironizing even in apparently earnest usages. Nevertheless, Webb makes a valuable point about discourse that is "nonconformist" regarding the surface rules and expectations for language use. One may consider the use of irony (and especially ironic hyperbole) as engaging in a similar kind of subversive resistance against the limits of language.

59. Relevant to the operations of irony are the comments of J. Hillis Miller in his "The Critic as Host," in *Deconstruction and Criticism,* ed. Harold Bloom, et al., 217–53 (New York: Seabury Press, 1979). Thinking about the metaphor of "parasite," Miller reflects on ways in which the prefix *para-* implies both sameness and otherness, generating what I would call a tensive irony between host and semantic guest. His observations are worth quoting at some length: "There is no parasite without its host. . . . 'Para' is a double antithetical prefix signifying at once proximity and distance, similarity and difference, interiority and exteriority, something inside a domestic economy and at the same time outside it, something simultaneously this side of a boundary line, threshold, or margin, and also beyond it. . . . A thing in 'para,' moreover, is not only simultaneously on both sides of the boundary line between inside and out. It is also the boundary itself, the screen which is a permeable membrane connecting inside and outside. It confuses them with one another, allowing the outside in, making the inside out. . . . Though a given word in 'para' may seem to choose univocally

one of these possibilities, the other meanings are always there as a shimmering in the word which makes it refuse to stay still in a sentence" (219).

60. Carol A. Newsom, "Bakhtin, the Bible, and Dialogic Truth," *Journal of Religion* 76 (1996): 298. For a fuller exploration of dialogical construction of meaning and implications for hermeneutics, see her *The Book of Job: A Contest of Moral Imaginations* (Oxford: Oxford University Press, 2003).

61. Muecke, "Irony Markers," 367.

62. As Muecke observes, "the very presence of a number of recognized ironies may operate as a signal to look out for others" (ibid., 373).

63. Webb, "Theological Reflections on the Hyperbolic Imagination," 281.

64. Booth, *Rhetoric of Irony*, 23.

65. What Bloomquist says of rhetoric generally is true also, in a more complicated way, regarding ironic rhetorical tropes: "[R]hetoric is about persuasion sometimes, but always about the consent involved in making communication work" ("Role of the Audience," 157). With irony, the consent of the audience requires the further decision to revise and counter one's own understanding as the process of communication is taking place.

66. Discussion of distinctions among real author, implied author, real reader, implied reader, and ideal reader within reader response criticism can be found in Robert M. Fowler, "Who Is 'The Reader' in Reader Response Criticism?" *Semeia* 31 (1985): 5–23. This older essay remains lucid and relevant to ongoing literary debates on these issues.

67. Stephen A. Geller, *Sacred Enigmas: Literary Religion in the Hebrew Bible* (London: Routledge, 1996), 23.

68. Hutcheon, *Irony's Edge*, 44–56. Bloomquist rightly notes the complexity of audience, something that has been noticed piecemeal in redaction-critical and canonical-critical studies of biblical texts but that is often passed over in other kinds of biblical analysis: "[T]here are in fact multiple audiences. Through the incorporation of earlier strands of tradition and texts or the interweaving of discourse modes, authors incorporate multiple audiences, sometimes distant in space and time, in a way that envisions audiences overlapping with other audiences, or future, distant audiences as the goal of the 'movement' of the intended audience. There are also audiences that are in the 'peripheral' vision of the author, audiences that might be the real 'target' of the text, even though the text is 'addressed' to another" ("Role of the Audience," 159).

69. Arlene N. Okerlund, "The Rhetoric of Love: Voice in the *Amoretti* and the *Songs and Sonets*," *Quarterly Journal of Speech* 68 (1982): 37.

70. Significant here is the question of the complexity of the implied audience and the purpose(s) for which that audience is being constructed by the author. L. M. Findlay's critical reading of the rhetoric of Paul de Man ("Paul de Man, Thomas Carlyle, and 'The Rhetoric of Temporality,'" *Dalhousie Review* 65 [1985]: 159–81) makes the point well. Citing the possibility that the reader may be daunted by de Man's facility with multiple languages and European literatures, Findlay writes that de Man's "movement across languages and across historical periods may be guided at least as much by tactical considerations as by the illustrative *copia* of a well-stocked mind. Is de Man making an appeal to an elite readership or effecting a repeal of the rights of less cultivated readers, or both, or neither? Does the allusive fabric of his essay . . . pay tribute via its limited accessibility to that inclusion/exclusion which is a permanent property of discourse, the most incurable of all the diseases of language?" (160).

71. As Thomas Krüger notes, reader participation in constructing meaning

must be negotiated in view of textual dynamics that guide and constrain the reader. Speaking of interpretation of the Book of Qohelet, he writes: "Neben solche Elementen der Argumentation, durch die eine Mehrzahl von Interpretationsmöglichkeiten eröffnet wird, sind aber auch Elemente zu beachten, die die interpretative Mitarbeit des Lesers in eine bestimmte Richtung lenken und so ihren Spielraum begrenzen" (*Kohelet [Prediger]* [Neukirchen-Vluyn, Germany: Neukirchener, 2000], 38).

72. The converse cannot be claimed, namely, that we can know exactly what a text is about because of what it does not say. Yairah Amit strays perilously close to such a formulation when she accords the status of formal criterion to the absence of mention of something as evidence of a "hidden polemic." The fact that Saul is not mentioned in Judges 19–21, per Amit, may fairly be designated as one confirming criterion that a hidden polemic against Saul is being promoted in those chapters. See her "Literature in the Service of Politics: Studies in Judges 19–21," in *Politics and Theopolitics in the Bible and Postbiblical Literature,* ed. Henning Graf Reventlow, Yair Hoffman, and Benjamin Uffenheimer, 28–40 (Sheffield, UK: Sheffield Academic Press, 1994).

73. Speaking of characters in the Book of Jonah, Kenneth M. Craig says: "When characters are quoted in the Jonah narrative, their words are filtered to us through the narrator's own verbal, sociocultural, thematic, aesthetic, and persuasive design. The words spoken, by their very form, entail indirections because the speakers communicate with us through someone else. Characters speak, but their words are of another's devising. Their discourse is speech within speech, a perspectival montage. Any speech event in the book of Jonah entails two levels of communication by two communicators with two perspectives, and one, the narrator's, is always hidden and possibly ironic. Since overt words often hide multiple perspectives, the layers of quotation in Jonah may even manifest themselves as triple talk since a character can always speak something other than his or her own mind." See Kenneth M. Craig, Cynthia L. Miller, and Raymond F. Person, "Conversation Analysis and the Book of Jonah: A Conversation," *Journal of Hebrew Scriptures* (1997): http://www.arts.ualberta.ca/JHS/Articles/article2.htm.

74. Johannes Fabian, "Presence and Representation: The Other and Anthropological Writing," *Critical Inquiry* 16 (1990): 755; emphasis in original. A further observation by Fabian applies, in narratological terms, to those Hebrew Bible stories set in foreign courts (Abraham and Isaac in Egypt and Gerar; Joseph in Egypt; Esther and Daniel in Persia): "[O]ur ways of making the Other are ways of making ourselves. The need to go *there* (to exotic places, be they far away or around the corner) is really our desire to be *here* (to find or defend our position in the world)" (756; emphasis in original).

75. Noteworthy here is the comment of Walter Brueggemann regarding the vulnerability of the employment of broad themes as means of organizing the content of the Old Testament. Brueggemann rightly deconstructs even his own attempts at thematization: ". . . every thematization is bound to fail because the text finally refuses thematization. The text is saturated with disjunctions and contradictions that mark it as an endlessly deconstructive enterprise, and therefore our thematizations are likely to be quite local and provisional" ("Biblical Theology Appropriately Postmodern" [pages 97–108 in *Jews, Christians, and the Theology of the Hebrew Scriptures,* ed. Alice Ogden Bellis and Joel S. Kaminsky; Atlanta: Society of Biblical Literature, 2000], 100). Brueggemann notes that "the text of the Hebrew Scriptures is profoundly plurivocal and does not admit of settled, enforceable larger categories" (98–99).

76. The multiaxial nature of well-wrought criticism is highlighted by Robert L. Ivie in his "Scrutinizing Performances of Rhetorical Criticism," *Quarterly Journal of Speech* 80 (1994): 248. Ivie argues for "locating the intellectual force of criticism in the detailed execution of a scholar's argument along various interconnected dimensions rather than in a singular attraction to progressively abstract and disembodied concepts." For other works demonstrating a multiaxial approach, see Daniel Patte, *Discipleship According to the Sermon on the Mount: Four Legitimate Readings, Four Plausible Views of Discipleship, and Their Relative Values* (Valley Forge: Trinity Press International, 1996), which deploys what Patte calls an "androcritical multidimensional perspective," and Louis C. Jonker, *Exclusivity and Variety: Perspectives on Multidimensional Exegesis* (Kampen: Kok Pharos, 1996), esp. his Chapter 2, "Towards a Multidimensional and/or Integrational Methodology" (39–79).

77. Bloomquist argues for a profoundly context-dependent understanding of all rhetoric: "Rhetoric . . . is about making an argument work locally, not universally" ("Role of the Audience," 158). Further, Hutcheon and others have rightly remarked the engagement of the reader in the construal and construction of context. Hutcheon: ". . . context is not some positivistic entity existing outside the utterance, but rather is itself constructed through interpretive procedures. And these procedures, in turn, have been formed through our prior experience with interpreting other texts and contexts" (*Irony's Edge*, 146).

78. Miscall, "Isaiah: The Labyrinth of Images" (*Semeia* 54 [1991]: 103–21), 106.

79. Mark Cameron Love, *Zechariah 1–8 and the Frustrated Reader* (Sheffield, UK: Sheffield Academic Press, 1999), esp. 40–42.

80. The point has much in common with Hutcheon's idea of the "third meaning" produced by irony and the "thirdspace" notion of geographer and spatial theorist Edward W. Soja. As the "said" and the "unsaid" challenge and deepen each other in the production of irony, so too the material and the ideational recreate and destabilize each other by means of the dynamic relationship between them, creating a "thirdspace" that is not reducible to the binary opposition of material and ideational. See Soja, *Thirdspace: Journeys to Los Angeles and Other Real-and-Imagined Places*, Oxford: Blackwell, 1996, and Matthew Sleeman, "Mark, the Temple and Space: A Geographer's Response," *Biblical Interpretation* 15 (2007): 338–49.

81. On ways in which maps inscribe cultural, political, and social values, see Burke O. Long, "Picturing Biblical Pasts," in *Orientalism, Assyriology and the Bible*, ed. Steven W. Holloway, 297–319 (Sheffield, UK: Sheffield Phoenix, 2006). On ways in which maps can invite imaginative hermeneutical construction and betray what they purport to describe, one might consult the poems of Elizabeth Bishop (see *The Complete Poems, 1927–1979*; New York: Farrar Straus Giroux, 1983). In Bishop's "The Map," the map's surface representation of land and ocean evokes deeper engagement on the part of the interpreter: "Or does the land lean down to lift the sea from under,/ drawing it unperturbed around itself?/ Along the fine tan sandy shelf/ is the land tugging at the sea from under?" (*Complete Poems*, 3). Her "Crusoe in England" ironizes the would-be determinacy of cartography: "But my poor old island's still/ un-rediscovered, un-renamable./ None of the books has ever got it right" (*Complete Poems*, 162).

82. See, for example, Robert Alter's complaint in his Introduction to *Pleasures of Reading*, which he has entitled, "The Disappearance of Reading" (pp. 9–22). Alter objects to jargon (the word "discourse" and the prefix *meta-* come in for special ire) and worries that talk about theory has supplanted actual reading: "What is distressing is that such discussion to the second degree should in many instances come to displace the discussion of literature itself. One can

read article after article, hear lecture after lecture, in which no literary work is ever quoted, and no real reading experience is registered" (11). My own view is that usually in theoretical texts, reading experiences are indeed registered, but simply in a subtle way that does not foreground description.

83. Niditch offers the following discussion of her overlay map technique in *Folklore and the Hebrew Bible* (Minneapolis: Fortress, 1993): "At the generic level, virtually all narrative deals with a problem and its resolution (or perhaps lack of resolution). . . . As one turns over a leaf of the overlay map, one begins to see the contours of narration made more specific, a level I call, (after Propp, Dundes, and Ben-Amos) 'the morphological.' In the morphology of the underdog tales the problem is a 'hero or heroine's lack of status,' its resolution an 'improvement in status.' Motifs between lack of status and improvement are similarly more specific at this level. At a still more specific level called 'the typological' (after Thompson), one paints the pattern with more detail. . . . The problem specified as marginality may be a condition of infertility or one of economic deprivation or political exile; the counterparts of improvement in status would then involve having children or acquiring riches or reassertion of power. At this point, characterizations of heroes and villains become more important as do the relationships between them" (21).

84. The multiaxial quality of the methodology here is shaped as a response to the relatively recent interest in interdisciplinarity, which has implications not only for the "answers" that various disciplines discern but for the kinds of questions they pose and the ways in which meaning is understood. Cooper notes generally of cross-disciplinary work that "the dislocation of disciplinary boundaries . . . and a sense of fragmentation that yet retains a certain ironic coherence are all aspects of a larger problematization of determination and referentiality. . . . The substitution of dynamic, polyvalent models of analysis for static, two-valued ones affects not only the processes of reading and interpretation in literature and the human sciences, but also the ways of conceptualizing the determination of meaning" ("Textualizing Determinacy," 13).

85. Paul H. Fry explores the potential of interpretive error to produce unexpected insight in his "The Distracted Reader," *Criticism* 32 (1990): 295–308. He begins with an anecdote about his having misquoted *The Tempest* and thereby reaching a new understanding about allusive connections between "wrack" and "rack" in Shakespeare's drama. Fry writes, "Hermeneutics is the merger of truth and error by distraction . . . and for this reason a full self-conscious hermeneutics . . . must attend even and especially to the incommensurable vagaries of inattention" (297). Relevant to the interpretation of irony is Fry's conclusion: ". . . what interpretation arising from errors and memory-lapses reveals is the collusion of literature itself with forgetfulness, with the dark backward and abysm of time which leaves not a rack behind. To put it another way, mistakes when we do justice to them trigger the remembrance of something missing, absent" (307). Thus even misreading can matter.

86. The phrase is Wesley D. Avram's, from the Epilogue in his *Where the Light Shines Through: Discerning God in Everyday Life* (Grand Rapids, Mich.: Brazos Press, 2005).

87. Bal, "Dealing/With/Women," 16.

88. Meir Sternberg muses at length on the omniscience of the biblical narrator, and even finds cause for this omniscience in the narrator's transcendence of the dramatic ironies in which all biblical characters and readers are necessarily caught. He writes of the biblical narrator, ". . . [H]is narrative manifests all the privileges of knowledge that transcend the human condition. For one thing, the

narrator has free access to the minds ('hearts') of his dramatis personae, not excluding God himself. . . . For another, he enjoys free movement in time. . . . These two establish . . . a supernatural principle of coherence and intelligibility. . . . [T]he Bible not merely assumes but concretizes the opposition to the human norm throughout, most obviously in the form of dramatic irony that no character (and to rub it in, no reader) escapes" (*The Poetics of Biblical Narrative: Ideological Literature and the Drama of Reading* [Bloomington: Indiana University Press, 1985], 84–85). But Sternberg does not explore the way in which Biblical texts that misdirect serve to inscribe hairline fractures in the narrator's reliability. The Biblical narrator may know all, but the reader can never fully trust that what the narrator says is authentically representative of that knowledge.

89. See Terje Stordalen, *Echoes of Eden: Genesis 2–3 and Symbolism of the Eden Garden in Biblical Hebrew Literature* (Leuven, Belgium: Peeters, 2000), 237–8, 463 and the bibliography he cites.

90. One may read of the demythologizing aspects of Israelite creation stories in many older works of scholarship; for one example, see Nahum M. Sarna, *Understanding Genesis: The Heritage of Biblical Israel* (New York: Schocken, 1966), 26. Far from being reduced to "insignificant, demythologized stature," the serpent is arguably the most powerful character in the story.

91. George Savran, "Beastly Speech: Intertextuality, Balaam's Ass and the Garden of Eden," *Journal for the Study of the Old Testament* 64 (1994): 39.

92. Worthy of note is Stephen Geller's suggestion that the serpent acts as a false prophet (*Sacred Enigmas*, 161). Against that interesting suggestion might be mustered two objections: the fact that what the serpent says is, in fact, not entirely false, and the fact that the serpent never purports to be speaking in the name of this God or another god. Nevertheless, the suggestion remains intriguing.

93. So Jeremy Black and Anthony Green, *Gods, Demons and Symbols of Ancient Mesopotamia: An Illustrated Dictionary* (Austin: University of Texas Press, 1992), 166–67: snakes in ancient Mesopotamia were often associated with deities. This is especially true of the snake god Nirah but may be postulated of others as well.

94. David M. Carr, "The Politics of Textual Subversion: A Diachronic Perspective on the Garden of Eden Story," *Journal of Biblical Literature* 112 (1993): 577–95. Carr notes that the snake was correct about the humans not dying once they had eaten from the tree and says, "It is just this kind of experiential observation of a discrepancy between divine threat and actual consequences that forms the heart of such wisdom texts as Job and Qohelet" (590); the negative consequences that unfold later in the story are attempts to refute that wisdom perspective. Carr also explicates an intertextual relationship between Proverbs 31 and the parts of the Garden narrative that polemicize against wisdom. He writes, ". . . the Garden of Eden story *picks up specific terminology* from Proverbs 31 in the process of contradicting its picture of the wise woman point by point: the woman knows 'good' and 'evil' (Prov 31:12, 17), but this brings disaster (Gen 3:6–23). Rather than 'girding' herself with strength (Prov 31:17), she and her husband now 'gird' themselves with fig leaves (Gen 3:7). Like the good wife in Proverbs (Prov 31:26), the first woman opens her mouth in wisdom (Gen 3:1b–5), but this leads to negative results. Finally, the Proverbs text ends with a call to 'give her of the fruit of her hands' (Prov 31:31), while the Garden of Eden story argues that this 'fruit of [the first woman's] hands' leads to alienation and endless toil" (590–91; emphasis in original).

95. See Mark S. Smith, *The Early History of God: Yahweh and the Other Deities in Ancient Israel* (San Francisco: Harper and Row, 1990), 95.

96. See Sam Dragga, "Genesis 2–3: A Story of Liberation," *Journal for the Study of the Old Testament* 55 (1992): 3–13. For a review of early rabbinic and Christian views regarding whether Adam and Eve did have sex in the Garden (and thus could be said to be fulfilling God's command to procreate), see Gary Anderson, "Celibacy or Consummation in the Garden? Reflections on Early Jewish and Christian Interpretations of the Garden of Eden," *HTR* 82 (1989): 121–48.

97. Reuven Kimelman, "The Seduction of Eve and the Exegetical Politics of Gender" (*Biblical Interpretation* 4 [1996]: 1–39), 30–31.

98. Graham Ward considers aspects of the instability of language and the unreliability of repetition in his "A Postmodern Version of Paradise," *Journal for the Study of the Old Testament* 65 (1995): 3–12. He writes, "The snake imitates God and Adam in its ability to speak. But its representation, and repetition of God's instructions to the earthly creature, distorts them. . . . [R]eiteration, upon which the social construction of language and representation is formed, always brings about a betrayal" (7–8). But where he and other commentators have seen distortion, I would argue for the ironic reversal of meaning in the serpent's revoicing precisely by re-speaking God's truth into a different understanding of context.

99. See among many other commentators Danna Nolan Fewell, "Building Babel," in *Postmodern Interpretations of the Bible—A Reader,* ed. A. K. M. Adam, 1–15 (St. Louis: Chalice, 2001).

100. As Alan Jon Hauser puts it, ". . . their striving to be like God in fact results in their being alienated from him" ("Genesis 2–3: The Theme of Intimacy and Alienation" [pp. 20–36 in *Art and Meaning: Rhetoric in Biblical Literature,* ed. D. J. A. Clines, D. M. Gunn, and A. J. Hauser; Sheffield, UK: JSOT Press, 1982], 34).

101. Marc Vervenne on Genesis 1: "'Creation' is understood here as a continuous transition from disarray to order, from unrest to rest, from chaos to harmony. . . . The dynamics embedded in the structure of the unit lead towards 'the seventh day' in which the divine act of creation reaches its climax. . . . Within this space, Israel escapes from the natural and social 'primal powers' which can throw her back into chaos. To participate in the rest of the seventh day is to participate in the continuous creative activity of Elohim and to ward off the many-sided menace posed by the powers of chaos" ("Genesis 1,1–2,4: The Compositional Texture of the Priestly Overture to the Pentateuch" [pp. 35–79 in *Studies in the Book of Genesis,* ed. A. Wénin; Leuven, Belgium: Leuven University Press, 2001], 53).

102. David M. Carr and many others suggest that Genesis 1, of post-exilic Priestly provenance, was responding to the earlier non-Priestly material in Genesis 2–3. See Carr, *Reading the Fractures of Genesis: Historical and Literary Approaches* (Louisville, Ky.: Westminster John Knox, 1996), 317.

103. Joseph Blenkinsopp, *The Pentateuch: An Introduction to the First Five Books of the Bible* (New York: Doubleday, 1992), 64–65. But Carr has argued that the final shape of Genesis 2–3 counters the wisdom-tradition perspective ("Politics of Textual Subversion," 591).

104. Here one might invite the insights of materialist readings of Genesis 2–3 that focus on political control of the economic means of production in Israelite culture. Two interpretations that explore that question are James M. Kennedy's "Peasants in Revolt: Political Allegory in Genesis 2–3" (*Journal for the Study of the Old Testament* 47 [1990]: 3–14) and Gale A. Yee's "Gender, Class, and the Social-Scientific Study of Genesis 2–3" (*Semeia* 87 [1999]: 177–92).

105. Geller suggests that in Genesis 2–3, the wisdom of the Garden is being ostensibly opposed to the later obedience of Torah in a way that suggests a complex ironic relationship between the two. He writes, ". . . woman in Genesis 3

stands for Old Wisdom itself, based on direct experience rather than the word of God. It must be remembered that she received no direct divine prohibition herself, but only secondhand through Adam, her Moses, so to speak. The elaborate description of her preparation for sin is a perfect representation of the process of empirical observation in Old Wisdom. . . . The result of her sin is the self-awareness that is the presupposition of the individualism of covenantal piety. . . . That in this collocation of ironies sin should eventually banish sin is yet another of those fruitful paradoxes of biblical religion, like blood's purifying of blood guilt" (*Sacred Enigmas*, 161).

2. Foreign Rulers and the Fear of God

1. Lang, *Irony/Humor*, 56.

2. Ibid., 58. In her analysis, she is reading three sections of Barthes's *S/Z* (NewYork: Hill and Wang, 1974): sections 21, 59, and 87.

3. Roland Barthes, *The Semiotic Challenge*, trans. Richard Howard (from *L'aventure sémiologique*, éditions de Seuil, 1985) (NewYork: Hill and Wang, 1988), 7: "The Text . . . is fundamentally to be distinguished from the literary work: it is not an esthetic product, it is a signifying practice; it is not a structure, it is a structuration; it is not an object, it is a work and a game; it is not a group of closed signs, endowed with a meaning to be rediscovered, it is a volume of traces in displacement."

4. The phrase is from Barthes (*Semiotic Challenge*, 259), in his discussion of different ways of understanding the story of Jacob wrestling with a divine being at the Jabbok.

5. Lang, *Irony/Humor*, 59.

6. Hutcheon, *Irony's Edge*, 120.

7. Ted Cohen, "Metaphor and the Cultivation of Intimacy," in *On Metaphor*, ed. Sheldon Sacks (Chicago: University of Chicago Press, 1978), 9–10.

8. Good, *Irony in the Old Testament*, 62–66. Good sums up his view of Saul thus: "The tragic irony of the Saul story, as our narrator wished us to see it, lies in the disparities between the demand on Saul and Saul's capacity to meet it" (79).

9. The text shows how carefully David masks his own culpability in this and other acts of violence, as Baruch Halpern has argued in *David's Secret Demons*. Joab berates David for his naïveté regarding Abner's apparent loyalty (2 Sam 3:24–25), and "when Joab came out from David's presence," he immediately secures Abner and stabs him. The heavily emphasized assertions of the narrative that David knew nothing of this plan may be taken at face value. But there is force to the argument that the hyperbolic grieving of David over Abner and his insistence that he had nothing to do with it amount to "protesting too much." Read within the larger narrative pattern of David's intimidation and outright assassinations of those in his way—and particularly given the reader's familiarity with the murderous treatment of Uriah, whose death was not technically directly at David's hands either—this particular story has the effect of undermining David's purported lack of innocence. Halpern writes of the murders of Abner and Ishbaal, "The narrator's claim . . . is that Abner was the mainstay of northern independence, and that his death led to Israel's collapse into David's bosom. . . . Again, here David is the beneficiary of an assassination, of his chief rival, and again by killers who assume that he will reward their action" (*David's Secret Demons*, 30–31).

10. The shadow of Saul's ephemeral chosenness may fall across an even broader landscape that includes the New Testament. Raymond E. Brown comments on the

way in which some canonical witnesses may be seen implicitly to challenge the triumphalist tone of the Book of Acts. The following observation by Brown could be applied to the ironizing of all covenantal promises by the Saul story: "The O.T. . . . narrates how God's people shrank from twelve tribes to one. . . . Placing the long Deuteronomistic history of the monarchy alongside the brief history of the Christian movement in Acts may warn Bible readers that God's message to his people is not an unconditional promise of increasing numbers to the ends of the earth" (*The Churches the Apostles Left Behind* [New York: Paulist, 1984], 71). My attention was drawn to this irony by Lyons, "The Words of Gamaliel," 39.

11. Walter Brueggemann has reflected on competing representations of David in different Israelite traditions; see his *David's Truth in Israel's Imagination and Memory,* Minneapolis: Fortress, 1985. Brueggemann rightly notes that the complex witness to David's character and significance comes "packaged in ambiguity, inscrutability, polyvalence" (16).

12. Sternberg, *Poetics of Biblical Narrative,* 186–229.

13. Ibid., 191–93.

14. David Gunn, "Reading Right: Reliable and Omniscient Narrator, Omniscient God, and Foolproof Composition in the Hebrew Bible," in *The Bible in Three Dimensions: Essays in Celebration of Forty Years of Biblical Studies in the University of Sheffield,* ed. David J. A. Clines, Stephen E. Fowl, and Stanley E. Porter, 53–64 (Sheffield, UK: Sheffield Academic Press, 1990), 56. He musters the interpretive problem of irony as a foil to Sternberg's notion of "foolproof composition," whereas (ironically enough) Sternberg would cite the narrative use of irony precisely as evidence of same. On ironies in the traditions about Solomon, see further Walter Brueggemann, *Solomon: Israel's Ironic Icon of Human Achievement* (Columbia: University of South Carolina Press, 2005).

15. For more on the possibility of oblique irony in the figuring of "Qohelet" as Solomon or Solomonic, see chapter 5.

16. Rashkow, "Intertextuality, Transference, and the Reader," 60.

17. Herzfeld, "Irony and Power," 64.

18. Jon D. Levenson in his notes to Gen 12:10–20 in *The Jewish Study Bible,* ed. Adele Berlin, and Marc Zvi Brettler, with Michael Fishbane, consulting editor (Oxford: Oxford University Press, 2004), 31.

19. On the pronounced tendency of interpreters to read Abram's character in this story in positive ways, see Robert B. Robinson, "Wife and Sister through the Ages: Textual Determinacy and the History of Interpretation," *Semeia* 62 (1993): 103–28. Robinson analyzes the interpretations of Philo, Augustine, Luther, and E. A. Speiser.

20. Many commentators have seen this, including Rashkow ("Intertextuality, Transference, and the Reader," 67).

21. Sternberg suggests that the "surprise ending" wherein the reader learns that the LORD had closed the wombs of the women in Abimelech's court shows that Abimelech did want to have sex with Sarah but was prevented from doing so by God, an irony that Sternberg reads as "[stripping] his credit down to technical innocence" only (*Poetics of Biblical Narrative,* 316). He speculates that Abimelech kept Sarah for a long time "probably waiting for a respite from impotence." I prefer to read the divine closure of wombs instead as the incentive for Abimelech to return the (unmolested) Sarah, just as 20:6–7 says.

22. Mark E. Biddle, "The 'Endangered Ancestress' and Blessing for the Nations," *Journal of Biblical Literature* 109 (1990): 599–611.

23. In the case of Isaac, it may not even be the promise of progeny as such that

is threatened, but simply covenantal fidelity and the social integrity of the proto-Israelite group. For as David J. A. Clines has pointed out, since Rebekah had already given birth to Esau and Jacob (Genesis 25), the continuity of the patriarchal line would not have been at risk. See Clines, "The Ancestor in Danger: But Not the Same Danger," in *What Does Eve Do to Help? And Other Readerly Questions in the Old Testament* (Sheffield, UK: JSOT Press, 1990), 67–84. George G. Nicol disagrees, arguing that Gen 26:1–33 represents Isaac and Rebekah as childless and constitutes a narratological "flashback." See Nicol, "The Narrative Structure and Interpretation of Genesis XXVI 1–33," *Vetus Testamentum* 46 (1996): 339–60.

24. Van Seters argues, "The second account in chap. 20 (B) gives a fairly consistent revision of the first story, by means of a changed setting, for the purpose of dealing with certain moral and theological issues. . . . The third account in 26:1–11 (C) is yet another composition variant—this time a literary conflation of both of the other stories. It appears to have no interest in the storytelling aspect, nor is it a theological revision," but instead is just an artificial means of creating a parallel between Abraham and Isaac. See his "The Problem of the Beautiful Wife," Chapter 8 in *Abraham in History and Tradition* (New Haven, Conn.: Yale University Press, 1975).

25. Robert Polzin, "'The Ancestress of Israel in Danger' In Danger," *Semeia* 3 (1975): 94. He is aware that an objection might be raised about the reductionism of this equation, stressing that he is speaking only of the chief mode of divine engagement in each of the three Hebrew Bible divisions, not the only mode, and acknowledging much overlap among them.

26. Ken Stone, *Sex, Honor and Power in the Deuteronomistic History* (Sheffield, UK: Sheffield Academic Press, 1996), 43.

27. Ibid., 45.

28. For this line of thought, see the discussion of Susan Niditch in *A Prelude to Biblical Folklore: Underdogs and Tricksters* (San Francisco: Harper and Row, 1987), 23–69.

29. Meir Sternberg, *Hebrews between Cultures: Group Portraits and National Literature* (Bloomington: Indiana University Press, 1998), 118–19.

30. On the role of garments in the Joseph narrative as signals of sociopolitical status, see Victor H. Matthews, "The Anthropology of Clothing in the Joseph Narrative," *Journal for the Study of the Old Testament* 65 (1995): 25–36.

31. Gen 41:45. According to Levenson (annotations to "Genesis," *Jewish Study Bible*), this phrase means "God speaks/he lives" or "creator of life." James M. Weinstein notes that Targumic tradition reads the name has having to do with decoding secrets, and writes: "the Egyptian original behind this particular term is uncertain. Although it has been suggested that it comes from *Djed-pa-netjer-iw.f-ankh* ("The god speaks and he lives"), this name is not attested in Egypt until considerably later than the patriarchal era. It may therefore have been a later addition to the Genesis story" ("Zaphenath-paneah," *Harper's Bible Dictionary* [San Francisco: HarperCollins, 1985], 1155).

32. Sternberg, *Hebrews between Cultures*, 668n18.

33. Jürgen Ebach has explored the ways in which Joseph's rhetorical question may underline the limits to Joseph's authority, particularly regarding Egyptian and Israelite cultural differences concerning the enslavement of peoples to their rulers. See his "'Ja, bin denn *ich* an Gottes Stelle?' (Genesis 50:19): Beobachtungen und Überlegungen zu einem Schlüsselsatz der Josefsgeschichte und den vielfachen Konsequenzen aus einer rhetorischen Frage," *Biblical Interpretation* 11 (2003): 602–16. Ebach argues that the rhetorical question in Gen 50:19 makes

clear that Joseph does not have the power either to judge or to forgive, a power that is appropriate only to the relationship between God and God's worshippers (608). His reading of the question "straight" is certainly intelligent. I would argue, though, that beyond the transparent truth of the expected "no, of course not!" answer to Joseph's rhetorical question is a deeper ironic truth.

34. Even when Joseph weeps in Genesis 45, he has not compromised his power in any substantive way. He makes himself known to his brothers first, then weeps loudly—with bitterness at the trauma he has experienced? with rage that he must now take revenge on his brothers for having sold him into slavery? There is no way to know. But the narrative is clear that the brothers are too terrified to answer him when he addresses them (45:3). The narrative tension becomes almost unbearable when Joseph whispers, "Come closer to me" and "they came closer" (45:4). At that moment, when the brothers must approach their wronged and indescribably powerful brother, the narrative scene throbs with tension. Joseph could have them executed on the spot for their treachery. His power is still fully intact here.

35. Hugh C. White, "The Joseph Story: A Narrative Which 'Consumes' Its Content," *Semeia* 31 (1985): 61.

36. James C. Nohrnberg, "Princely Characters," in *"Not in Heaven": Coherence and Complexity in Biblical Narrative,* ed. Jason P. Rosenblatt and Joseph C. Sitterson Jr., 58–97 (Bloomington: Indiana University Press, 1991), 79.

37. White, "Joseph Story," 60.

38. For a counter-reading to the traditional lionization of Joseph, see Mark A. O'Brien, "The Contribution of Judah's Speech, Genesis 44:18–34, to the Characterization of Joseph," *Catholic Biblical Quarterly* 59 (2006): 429–47. O'Brien argues that Judah's speech in Genesis 44 "provides a subtle but effective exposure of Joseph as a person with a deeply flawed character" (430), one who was "driven, perhaps even obsessed, by the need to have power over his brothers" (440).

39. On this, see Michael V. Fox, "Wisdom in the Joseph Story," *Vetus Testamentum* 51 (2001): 26–41. Many commentators see praise of Joseph's savvy in the biblical text, but Fox argues that while wisdom as a theme is present in the Joseph material, the figure of Joseph and the trajectory of the plot do not, in the main, support traditional wisdom perspectives such as are seen in Proverbs. Indeed, a number of ironies (not named as such by Fox) may be appreciated in the differences between the Joseph material and formal wisdom traditions in the Hebrew Bible. For one example, Fox notes, "Any wise man . . . would have approved of Joseph's rebuff of the advances of Potiphar's wife. Yet this episode does not really reinforce Wisdom literature's ethical teaching, because Joseph's moral stance brings him no lasting benefit. . . . [H]e is thrown into prison for an indefinite term. When he finally prospers it is not because of his sexual virtue but *in spite* of it" (30). Another example: Fox observes, "Joseph exercises *hokmâ* (though not what we usually call 'wisdom') in cleverly exploiting the famine to amass landholdings for the crown and subjugate the Egyptian population. . . . [T]his behavior violates Proverbs' warning, 'He who withholds grain—the nation will curse him' (Prov. xi 26a)" (35).

40. Exod 16:3: "The Israelites said to them [viz., Moses and Aaron], 'If only we had died by the hand of the LORD when we sat by the fleshpots and ate our fill of bread; for you have brought us out into this wilderness to kill this whole assembly with hunger.'" Num 11:4: "The Israelites also wept again, and said, 'If only we had meat to eat! We remember the fish that we used to eat in Egypt for nothing, the cucumbers, the melons, the leeks, the onions, and the garlic; but now our strength is dried up, and there is nothing at all but this manna to look

at.'" These two stories underline the representation of Egypt as a place of flourishing and abundance in the Israelite imagination.

41. Daniel R. Shevitz, "Joseph: A Study in Assimilation and Power," *Tikkun* 8 (1993): 52.

42. Arguments for this position are based on many kinds of evidence, including the lack of narrative coherence between the ending of Genesis and the beginning of Exodus generally, the redactional nature of Gen 50:14, and the redundancy of the Joseph death notices in Gen 50:26 and Exod 1:6. See Konrad Schmid, "The So-Called Yahwist and the Literary Gap between Genesis and Exodus," in *A Farewell to the Yahwist? The Composition of the Pentateuch in Recent European Interpretation,* ed. Thomas B. Dozeman and Konrad Schmid, 29–50 (Leiden, Neth.: Brill, 2006); Jan Christian Gertz, "The Transition between the Books of Genesis and Exodus," in *A Farewell to the Yahwist?* 73–87; Erhard Blum, "The Literary Connection between the Books of Genesis and Exodus and the End of the Book of Joshua," in *A Farewell to the Yahwist?* 89–106; and Christoph Levin, "The Yahwist and the Redactional Link between Genesis and Exodus," in *A Farewell to the Yahwist?* 131–41. David M. Carr argues that thematic and semantic links connecting the Primeval History and the Abraham story to the Exodus story show that non-P material did continue narratively into (some form of) the Moses story. See Carr, "What Is Required to Identify Pre-Priestly Narrative Connections between Genesis and Exodus? Some General Reflections and Specific Cases," in *A Farewell to the Yahwist?* 159–80; "Genesis in Relation to the Moses Story: Diachronic and Synchronic Perspectives," in *Studies in the Book of Genesis: Literature, Redaction and History,* ed. André Wénin, 273–95 (Leuven, Belgium: Leuven University Press; Sterling, Va.: Peeters, 2001); and *Reading the Fractures of Genesis,* 192–218.

43. Shevitz writes, "While Scripture admires Joseph's accomplishments, it also offers a compelling answer to Joseph in the person of Moses. Joseph embraces a life of power in Egypt; Moses disdains it. Joseph wants his brethren to settle in Egypt; Moses routs them out. Joseph creates the circumstances that favor slavery; Moses overturns them" ("Joseph: A Study in Assimilation," 52). Another scholar who reads Joseph as being represented unfavorably—an assimilatory anti-hero in comparison with the valorized Moses—is Aaron Wildavsky in his "Survival Must Not Be Gained through Sin: The Moral of the Joseph Stories Prefigured through Judah and Tamar," *Journal for the Study of the Old Testament* 62 (1994): 37–48. On Wildavsky's reading, Tamar's choice to become impregnated by her father-in-law demonstrates the right way to preserve life, namely, by not mixing with other peoples.

44. Moshe Greenberg: "There is only one way that gives any hope of eliciting the innate conventions and literary formations of a piece of ancient literature, and that is by listening to it patiently and humbly. The critic must curb all temptations to impose his antecedent judgments on the text; he must immerse himself in it again and again, with all his sensors on alert to catch every possible stimulus—mental-ideational, aural, aesthetic, linguistic, visual—until its features begin to stand out and their native shape and patterning emerge" (*Ezekiel 1–20* [New York, Doubleday, 1983], 21).

45. Donald C. Polaski, "*Mene, Mene, Tekel, Parsin*: Writing and Resistance in Daniel 5 and 6," *Journal of Biblical Literature* 123 (2004): 657–58. The irony of this particular means for the message in its Persian setting is even sharper if the Persians are being represented as more invested in coinage than other empires. Daniel L. Smith-Christopher writes, "The Persian 'economy' (if it can be called that) was essentially a system for the hoarding of precious metals. Alexander, so it ap-

pears, was stunned with the amounts of bullion he found stashed at Susa, Ecbatana, and Persepolis" ("Prayers and Dreams: Power and Diaspora Identities in the Social Setting of the Daniel Tales," in *The Book of Daniel: Composition and Reception*, ed. John J. Collins and Peter W. Flint, 266–90 [Leiden, Neth.: Brill, 2001], 278).

46. Polaski writes, "The inscription immediately becomes an 'actor' in imperial politics, exposing the unreality of the power of Belshazzar and his court, while implying the overarching power of the text's mysterious author.... Belshazzar now has an inscription, ironically not from his own propaganda machine but from some other source" ("Mene, Mene, Tekel, Parsin," 651, 653).

47. Mieke Bal, "Lots of Writing," in *Ruth and Esther: A Feminist Companion to the Bible* (second series), ed. Athalya Brenner (Sheffield, UK: Sheffield Academic Press, 1999), 234.

48. His appellation constitutes an aporia, because there was no Darius the Mede historically. Technically, that designation occurs in 5:31, the last verse before chapter 6. But one can argue that there is a reflex of Darius's (impossible) Median ethnicity in the remark of the courtiers in 6:8, "Now, O king, establish the interdict and sign the document, so that it cannot be changed, according to the law of the Medes and the Persians, which cannot be revoked." One may wonder whether he was named Darius "the Mede" because the author simply made a mistake or because it was essential to signal that no such truly good foreign ruler could ever really have existed.

49. Polaski, "Mene, Mene, Tekel, Parsin," 667–68.

50. Ibid., 668–69.

51. Kenneth M. Craig Jr., *Reading Esther: A Case for the Literary Carnivalesque* (Louisville, Ky.: Westminster John Knox, 1995).

52. William T. McBride, "Esther Passes: Chiasm, Lex Talio, and Money in the Book of Esther," in *"Not in Heaven": Coherence and Complexity in Biblical Narrative*, ed. Jason P. Rosenblatt and Joseph C. Sitterson Jr., 211–23 (Bloomington: Indiana University Press, 1991), 213–14.

53. Athalya Brenner has shown the excessiveness of Esther at the levels of semantics and structure: the book is full of duplications, repetitions, multiplications, hendiadys, and inclusios. See her "Looking at Esther through the Looking Glass," in *A Feminist Companion to Esther, Judith, and Susanna*, ed. Athalya Brenner, 71–80 (Sheffield, UK: Sheffield Academic Press, 1995).

54. This excessive celebrating has its satirical edge, too, as regards the power of the king. Alice Bach notes, "Part of the ludic fun in the tale is that the banquet that lasted half a year left no one in charge of the realm" (*Women, Seduction, and Betrayal in Biblical Narrative* [Cambridge: Cambridge University Press, 1997], 189).

55. In the words of Johanna W. H. Van Wijk-Bos, "Death stalks the festivities from beginning to end.... Merriment permeated by conflict is typical" for the Book of Esther (*Ezra, Nehemiah, and Esther* [Louisville, Ky.: Westminster John Knox, 1998], 104, 108). Bach reflects at length on the stories of Jael, Delilah, Esther, Judith, and Salomé and finds deep-level similarities in the cultural codes that produced these stories: "[T]he tropes of beautiful women seducing men with food or wine and killing them instead of soothing them are basically the same, and in my view represent the generalized male fear of the courtesan as killer" (*Women, Seduction, and Betrayal*, 186).

56. On the rabbis' concern about Esther not keeping *kashrut*, see the discussion of the LXX text of Esther, *Midrash Tehillim*, the *Second Targum to Esther*, the *Pirke de Rabbi Eliezer*, and other ancient Jewish sources in Leila Leah Bronner, "Esther Revisited: An Aggadic Approach," in *A Feminist Companion to Esther, Ju-*

dith, and Susanna, ed. Athalya Brenner, 176–97 (Sheffield, UK: Sheffield Academic Press, 1995).

57. Michael V. Fox, here countering Timothy K. Beal: "Nor does the book of Esther show ethnic or gender identity to be unstable or their boundaries porous. Esther may hide her Jewishness tactically, but (as she learns in chapter 4) her identity as a Jew is indissoluble, even in the absence of external markers (such as dietary observances). What is decisive is not the temporary concealment of identity but its ultimate and permanent revelation at the moment of crisis" (*Character and Ideology in the Book of Esther,* 2nd ed. [Grand Rapids, Mich.: Eerdmans, 2001], 296–7).

58. In "Household and Table: Diasporic Boundaries in Daniel and Esther" (*Catholic Biblical Quarterly* 68 [2006]: 408–20), Mary E. Mills suggests that Esther's body serves as a metonymic site of intentional border-crossing. The concern of the article is to probe the implications of the hypothesis that "the implied reader of diasporic novellas is interested in how a person can maintain two social identities and how that process provides either safety or danger for the common social body" (408). Mills writes: "Esther risks her life in order to bring life and pleasure to her community. Paradoxically, she dresses as queen in order to achieve this end. Although she does not avoid external inculturation, her inner role is to do precisely that. Her body represents a type of Trojan horse, bringing Jewish need right to the heart of the kingdom and drawing imperial power to her people. . . . It is Esther's bodily self that links these two extremes of insider/outsider positions. . . . The social body, like the personal body, needs to absorb new influences in order to survive but risks loss of clear identity in the process" (418–20). Mills is intentional in her choice to read the border-crossing in Esther positively. Her excellent insights might be pressed into service as well for a more negative reading of Esther's assimilation, which could be argued to be not simply external (with an emphasis on clothing) but dramatically internal as well (with an emphasis on Esther's having sex with a hyperbolically promiscuous foreign male and eating nonkosher food at numerous feasts). One could draw on Mill's work for a reading that, particularly in view of the hyperbolic slaughter at the end of the book, underlines the irreparable losses of inculturation.

59. The ironic paradox here is wrestled with in various ways in Esther scholarship and can be illustrated from two observations in Mills's article (413). Building on the work of Jon L. Berquist (*Controlling Corporeality: The Body and the Household in Ancient Israel* [New Brunswick, N.J.: Rutgers University Press, 2002]), Mills writes that in Esther, "the body of the heroine acts as a porous boundary that can be used to ensure the survival of an ethnic group." One paragraph later, she observes of Daniel and Esther, "Their function is one of building up the community by sealing its boundaries against cultural erosion, thus resisting inculturation." Does the "porousness" of Esther's cultural body in fact seal the community's boundaries against inculturation? While the books of Daniel and Esther have a great deal in common literarily, a number of crucial differences obtain. The valorization of the heroine in Esther is far more complex and troubled than is the valorization of the hero in Daniel. Jewishness as piety and practice is at stake in Daniel in a way that it clearly is not in Esther. The hero guards his (male) body scrupulously in Daniel and is protected from its defilement or harm by external forces, while the heroine in Esther does not even try to guard her (female) body from exogamic sexual penetration or from defilement by nonkosher food. The way in which Esther readies her body for physical and cultural intercourse with a sexually voracious foreigner contrasts sharply with the way in which Daniel steadfastly composes his own body for prayer in Daniel 6.

60. Jon D. Levenson rightly notes that the complex artistry of the Book of Esther invites multiple readings of many different dimensions of the story. See Levenson, *Esther: A Commentary* (Louisville, Ky.: Westminster John Knox, 1997), 1.

61. An essay by Haim M. I. Gevaryahu illustrates the polarization of opinions on the morality of the Book of Esther. He cites on one end of the spectrum the opinion of L. B. Paton that "'[t]here is not one noble character in this entire book'" and on the other Hans Bardtke's commendation of "the yearning of the Jews for peacefulness and tranquility." See Gevaryahu, "Esther Is a Story of Jewish Defense Not a Story of Jewish Revenge," *Jewish Bible Quarterly* 21 (1993): 3–12, esp. 6–7. For contemporary bifurcation of opinion regarding the slaughter at the end of Esther and the Book of Esther more generally, see the commentaries and A. Kay Fountain, *Literary and Empirical Readings of the Books of Esther* (Frankfurt: Peter Lang, 2002). Fountain is interested in readers' discernment of ethical purpose in biblical narratives. She assesses the reception of Esther in the history of interpretation and collates the responses of 76 contemporary readers: church members from two churches in New Zealand, "the unchurched friends and acquaintances of these church members," and students from Carey Baptist College in Auckland (167). Her study showed that the churched respondents accorded the character of Esther higher marks for justness than did the unchurched respondents. There were also differences between male and female readers regarding various aspects of characterization in the text (for example, regarding assessment of the justness of King Ahasuerus). See Fountain, 167–210.

62. Levenson, *Esther*, 121, citing André LaCocque in *The Feminine Unconventional: Four Subversive Figures in Israel's Tradition* (Minneapolis: Fortress, 1990), 80n64.

63. See Timothy K. Beal, *Esther* (Collegeville, Minn.: Liturgical Press, 1999), 105; Fox, *Character and Ideology*, 105–106. A similar kind of prophylaxis might be seen in Esther's command that all the Jews who can be found in Susa should fast, as she and her servants will. The reason for the fast is to protect Esther when she subsequently goes unbidden into the presence of the king. Now, does this fasting reverse Esther's assimilation? It might be possible to read the fasting of Esther as a practice of Jewishness requiring her renunciation of the nonkosher Persian food. One might even speculate that the fasting implies her becoming sexually unavailable to the king; Fox notes that the fast "could in fact harm the beauty she will have to utilize" in her negotiations with Ahasuerus (*Character and Ideology*, 63). Mills makes an interesting point about Esther's body in this regard: in the fast, "the social body, together with her own body, will be taken out of normal living space to a place in which it can be purified, cleansed of any contamination, in order to be ready to reenter society. Esther's body, emptied of significance, will thus take on new meaning as the conscious crossover point between Jewish and Persian identity" ("Household and Table," 418). This strong reading would be persuasive if the religious nature of the fast had been signaled in the narrative or if Esther had refrained thereafter from the inculturating practices in which she had engaged before. But Esther in fact continues to feast on Persian food and continues to serve as Ahasuerus's queen. The reader may be meant to see incongruity there. Perhaps this fasting is another ironized gesture within the Book of Esther, serving only a pragmatic prophylactic function on behalf of the compromised heroine.

64. Fox, *Character and Ideology*, 226. Many commentators remark on the semantic excess of the several verbs for slaughter here.

65. David J. A. Clines, "Reading Esther from Left to Right: Contemporary

Strategies for Reading a Biblical Text," in *The Bible in Three Dimensions: Essays in Celebration of Forty Years of Biblical Studies in the University of Sheffield;* ed. David J. A. Clines, Stephen E. Fowl, and Stanley E. Porter, 31–52 (Sheffield, UK: Sheffield Academic Press, 1990), 46.

66. Many scholars have noticed that 9:1–19 and 9:20–10:3 do not cohere well in style and language with the preceding chapters; see Beal, *Esther,* 107–108. David Clines suggests that the author of 9:1–19 is a poorer writer than the author of the preceding chapters. He writes, "The narrator of ch. 9 has presented a Jewish massacre of anti-Semites rather than Jewish self-defence against an imperially sponsored pogrom. It cannot have served his purpose either as storyteller or as propagandist to have made this massacre the sequel of the conflicting decrees, and we can only conclude that the author of ch. 9 imperfectly understood the thrust of the plot of chs. 1–8" (*The Esther Scroll: The Story of the Story* [Sheffield, UK: JSOT Press, 1984], 40).

67. André LaCocque argues that the slaughter in Esther is not a revisiting of ancient holy war (although his larger point is that the slaughter was justified, whereas in my view, it is being portrayed as excessive) in his "Haman in the Book of Esther," *Hebrew Annual Review* 11 (1987): 207–22. LaCocque writes, "While Haman is 'Amalek,' the 75,000 slaughtered by the Jews in defending themselves . . . are not. . . . [T]he enemies' goods are of two provenances, they are Haman's (Agag's), and they are Persian. The 'ban' on either one was not recommended. . . . In Persia the property of the Jews' enemies is no spoil of war and is not even 'Amalekite'" (218).

68. Leslie Brisman, "Unequal Affliction: The Scroll of Esther," *Conservative Judaism* 52 (2000): 11.

69. Stan Goldman, "Narrative and Ethical Ironies in Esther," *Journal for the Study of the Old Testament* 47 (1990): 24–25. Brisman, too, reads the story as a "counternormative" voice of Jewish self-critique: "Consider . . . Shakespeare's *Merchant of Venice.* When Antonio, in the end, makes provision that Shylock 'presently becomes a Christian' (IV.i.386), is he demonstrating a quality Shakespeare would have thought a symbol of Christian grace, or a quality closer to cruel revenge, a knife-wound aimed at the heart of Shylock as Shylock aimed at the heart of Bassanio? I myself believe that Antonio's offer here is not grace but cruelty, and that Shakespeare strains the 'quality of mercy' till it is not just questioned but broken. I would similarly like to believe that the Scroll of Esther is critical of the divine providence and Jewish chosenness that others find reaffirmed by the comedic ending" ("Unequal Affliction," 5).

70. Fox, *Character and Ideology,* 115.

71. Athalya Brenner argues for a nuanced reading of Esther in this regard: "[N]o one is wholly evil (Haman) or good (Mordecai) in Esther, although Mordecai is 'ours', and thus superior. A non-simplistic tale of mirrors excludes simplistic morality. Thus, an ideo-moralistic reading of Esther can be rejected in favor of a phenomenological or political reading. . . . What does it take, in a diaspora framework, to survive and succeed as a Jew? The answers given are not altogether comforting: you have to mutate into your former adversary, or nearly that" ("Looking at Esther through the Looking Glass," 79).

72. Beal: "Throughout the history of interpretation [of] MT Esther, many readers have treated this scant notice of Queen Vashti's party as one large gap in the narrative, and have gone about the business of trying to fill it" ("Tracing Esther's Beginnings," in *A Feminist Companion to Esther, Judith, and Susanna,* ed. Athalya Brenner, 87–110 [Sheffield, UK: Sheffield Academic Press, 1995], 93).

73. Beal notes the "utter dependence of this narrative's primary male," that is, Ahasuerus, on Vashti, something that ironically is a sign of the king's weakness and the banished Vashti's power, "since it reveals the male subject's special and highly problematic dependence on her as a fixed object" ("Tracing Esther's Beginnings," 95–96).

74. Fox rightly notes, "Xerxes, as we quickly learn, is weak-willed, fickle, and self-centered. He and his advisers are a twittery, silly-headed, cowardly lot who need to hide behind a law to reinforce their status in their homes. . . . They fabricate a crisis out of nothing and come up with a proposal that throws the spotlight on their own embarrassment. The author makes Vashti shine by the contrast" (*Character and Ideology*, 168). An alternative reading is provided by Susan Niditch in her "Esther: Folklore, Wisdom, Feminism, and Authority," in *A Feminist Companion to Esther, Judith, and Susanna*, ed. Athalya Brenner, 26–46 (Sheffield, UK: Sheffield Academic Press, 1995). Niditch argues that the point of the Book of Esther is to underline the value of the "maintenance of the status quo" and "working from within the system" (39); per Niditch's reading, Vashti is "rash" and her "foolishness is the foil for Esther's wisdom" (33).

75. Fox: "Vashti's fate was not a disaster: one might consider her rewarded by being forbidden to come where she refused to go" (*Character and Ideology*, 170).

76. Timothy K. Beal, *The Book of Hiding: Gender, Ethnicity, Annihilation, and Esther* (London: Routledge, 1997), 25.

77. That this doubling might be due to the existence of two different sources need not reduce the pleasure—or growing discomfort—of the implied audience at this example of "overkill."

78. Jack M. Sasson, "Esther," in *The Literary Guide to the Bible*, ed. Robert Alter and Frank Kermode, 335–42 (Cambridge, Mass.: Harvard University Press, 1987). Niditch suggests that the "just deserts" aspect of the slaughter is simply an expected part of the folktale character of the story ("Esther: Folklore, Wisdom, Feminism, and Authority," 40).

79. Van Wijk-Bos ties the hyperbole at the end of Esther to the unlikeliness of the hope that is being expressed therein for the Jews' salvation: "[T]he narrative aims to empower those who are beaten down with the incredible hope that their day will come. No amount of exaggeration is therefore left out. . . . Nothing is done to modify the bloodthirstiness of those who were destined for destruction. . . . The king, in a final appearance of total silliness, is pleased with the results—the destruction of a large number of his own people!—and asks whether there is anything else Esther wants" (*Ezra, Nehemiah, and Esther*, 142–43).

80. Sasson notes, with his own irony, the "tribulation of a king who must nightly rise to the occasion" ("Esther," 335).

81. Alice Bach writes, "While Esther is seen as a positive literary character for the traditional Jewish reader, an individual less inclined to read with the official line of thought might look at the descriptions of beauty and banquet preparations as metonymic for a seductive woman, using her beauty as power to achieve her ends. . . . The 'magic' contained in Esther's spice jar results in the death of Haman, as well as the reversal of the political enmity toward the Jewish people. . . . the beauty of one woman [affects] an entire populace, not just the man who is the object of the seduction. Read this way, Esther becomes another of those female characters who exert power over men through their seductive wiles" (*Women, Seduction, and Betrayal*, 179).

82. Beal, *Esther*, 117. See Levenson: "The parallel with the Pentateuchal story is striking: dramatic events of deliverance (the exodus and the events of Adar

13) culminate in a solemn affirmation by the redeemed to accept new obligations upon themselves (the commandments of Sinai, the annual observance of Purim)" (*Esther,* 126). He continues, "Esther 9:28 is noteworthy not only for its legal, formulaic style, but also for its twofold invocation of memory. . . . It should not be overlooked that the Hebrew root *zkr,* from which the words 'remembered' and 'memory' here are derived, can have a connotation of ritual observance (e.g., Exod. 13:3; 20:8; cf. Deut. 5:12)" (129).

83. Fox, *Character and Ideology,* 127.

84. Clines, *Esther Scroll,* 22.

85. Joseph's enslavement of the Egyptians in a time of dire national emergency has been read by a number of scholars, correctly in my view, as something that is being represented in Genesis 47 as *not* desirable. Thus my reading moves in a different direction from Fox's interpretation that this literature means earnestly to commend Jews for increasing the money in the coffers of foreign kings (see *Character and Ideology,* 129–30). Especially in the Book of Esther, where the foreign king is portrayed as both contemptible and dangerous, it is hard to see the epilogue as noting with approval that Mordecai helped such a king to become richer at the expense of his own people.

86. Shevitz, "Joseph: A Study in Assimilation," 76.

87. Beal, *Book of Hiding,* 107.

88. Joshua A. Berman has suggested that the character of Esther undergoes a kind of transformation through which she can integrate her Persian and Jewish identities while not subsuming either one under the other. See Berman, "*Hadassah bat Abihail:* The Evolution from Object to Subject in the Character of Esther," *Journal of Biblical Literature* 120 (2001): 647–69. He reads the twofold naming of Esther as "daughter of Abihail" in 2:15 and 9:29 as structuring the space within which Esther works through her cultural hybridity. The beginning of the book saw her "descent into otherness and consequent loss of subjective, essential, Jewish self," but at the end of the book "that identity is redeemed and reclaimed" (668). Acknowledging the power of Berman's reading, I would yet argue that there is very little Jewish about Esther by the close of the book. Berman concedes a final problematization of Esther's Jewish identity, something that I see as, in fact, one of the central points of the ironies of the Book of Esther: "She, unlike Mordecai, can never be labeled 'the Jew.' Even at the close of the scroll, when she emerges as *bat Abihail,* she nonetheless remains—nay, is retained in the palace as—'Esther the king's wife,' a part of her identity forever claimed in the status of otherhood" (668–69). Clines notes that what the Book of Esther "celebrates . . . is a deliverance achieved through *denying* one's Jewishness" ("Reading Esther from Left to Right," 47).

89. Beal, *Esther,* 113.

90. Adding a layer of complexity is the fact that Esth 10:1–3, a key text in the ironic reading of the "Persianization" of Mordecai and Esther, is absent from the Alpha Text tradition. We may consider relevant here the suggestion that the MT redactor removed all references to God in the text. See Clines, *Esther Scroll,* 107–12; Levenson, *Esther,* 33; Fox is more cautious, but he is willing to concede the possibility that "[i]f the references to God in the proto-AT were present in proto-Esther, R-MT pushed God farther into the background" (*Character and Ideology,* 264; cf. his *The Redaction of the Books of Esther: On Reading Composite Texts* [Atlanta, Ga.: Scholars Press, 1991], 120–21). One might suspect that the MT redactor was an ironist who underlined the human provenance of the acts of deliverance in Esther in order to leave room for the ironization of Jewish hybridity at the end of the book.

91. Klara Butting reflects on some of the same issues from a different angle

in her feminist analysis of the Book of Esther as a recreation of the Joseph story that underlines the agency of women ("Esther: A New Interpretation of the Joseph Story in the Fight Against Anti-Semitism and Sexism," in *Ruth and Esther: A Feminist Companion to the Bible* (second series), ed. Athalya Brenner, 239–48 (Sheffield, UK: Sheffield Academic Press, 1999). She notes, "The book of Esther is not another book of Exodus. Therefore, at the closing lines of Esther, the beginning of the book of Exodus is pointed out to us. . . . The exodus from oppression is still missing at the end of the book of Esther. This goes for the whole Jewish diaspora that remains scattered, subjected to an inconstant and unpredictable king. This is the case also with Esther, who remains in the king's harem and is ignored by official historiography" (248).

92. Craig, *Reading Esther*, 151; emphasis in original.

93. Richard Treloar finds Vashti "something of a human palimpsest, whose tell-tale marks of erasure will, ironically, prove indelible" ("The Hermeneutics of Textual Exile: Comparing Rabbinic and Poststructuralist Readings of Esther" [*Pacifica* 14 (2001): 34]). Beal has suggested that while Vashti is officially "exscripted," she is unforgettable (*Book of Hiding*, 23–32).

3. The Prostitute as Icon of the Ironic Gaze

1. Two traditional books often cited are Carol Meyers's historical study, *Discovering Eve: Ancient Israelite Women in Context* (Oxford: Oxford University Press, 1988) and Susan Ackerman's comparativist *Warrior, Dancer, Seductress, Queen: Women in Judges and Biblical Israel* (New York: Doubleday, 1998). The broad scope of her study notwithstanding, Meyers does not treat any of the five biblical characters with which this chapter is concerned (Tamar, Rahab, Jael, Gomer, and Ruth), nor does she address prostitution or levirate marriage. Ackerman's focus on the roles of military hero, cult specialist, queen mother, mother, wife, and daughter precludes her treating prostitution, although she acknowledges the erotic undertones in the story of Jael. Esther Fuchs has criticized analyses of biblical women's roles that emerged in the early days of North American feminist biblical scholarship: "None of these sources discussed the relationship between literary strategies and the ideology of male supremacy. . . . Images of women were discussed in terms of their relationship to the historical context of ancient Israel, as if they reflected a certain ancient reality" (*Sexual Politics in the Biblical Narrative: Reading the Hebrew Bible as a Woman* [Sheffield, UK: Sheffield Academic Press, 2000], 8). For a feminist analysis of semantic and ideological constructions of sexuality and gender in the Hebrew Bible, see Athalya Brenner, *The Intercourse of Knowledge: On Gendering Desire and 'Sexuality' in the Hebrew Bible* (Leiden, Neth.: Brill, 1997).

2. For a review of ways in which Hebrew Bible texts reveal patriarchal biases and implicitly or explicitly support androcentrism and misogyny, see Eryl W. Davies, *The Dissenting Reader: Feminist Approaches to the Hebrew Bible* (Burlington, Vt.: Ashgate, 2003).

3. Elizabeth Grosz, *Volatile Bodies: Toward a Corporeal Feminism* (Bloomington: Indiana University Press, 1994), 23–24.

4. Alice Bach, *Women, Seduction, and Betrayal in Biblical Narrative* (Cambridge: Cambridge University Press, 1997), 128–29.

5. Judith Butler in "Editor's Introduction" to Singer, *Erotic Welfare: Sexual Theory and Politics in the Age of Epidemic*, (New York: Routledge, 1993), 4. A similar point is made by Claudia V. Camp in her treatment of the "strange woman" in biblical literature generally and Proverbs in particular (*Wise, Strange and Holy: The*

Strange Woman and the Making of the Bible [Sheffield, UK: Sheffield Academic Press, 2000]). Camp writes, "The Strange Woman, in spite of her 'foreignness', exists very much within the boundaries of society.... [T]he editor(s) of Proverbs have not excluded strangeness, but, in fact, let it 'in'. In so doing, they have acknowledged (whether consciously or not) the reality that a system of order cannot afford to exclude anomaly without ultimately being overwhelmed by it" (79).

6. Schwartz, "Adultery in the House of David," 343.

7. James Harding pushes further than most on the question of resistance to biblical rhetorics of violence. He considers the intertextual and tradition-historical influence of the marriage metaphor of the Book of Hosea, which conceptualizes the relationship between God and Israel as one between a physically abusive husband and a battered wife. Harding argues that any text of redemption drawing on that metaphor is violent in its underlying cultural and theological assumptions and should be resisted. See his "In the Name of Love: Resisting Reader and Abusive Redeemer in Deutero-Isaiah," *Bible and Critical Theory* 2 (2006): 14.1–14.15, DOI: 10.2104/bc060014.

8. The political power of ironic rhetoric remarked by Booth under the rubric of amiable community-building is flagged in a more cautionary vein by Fuchs, who deplores what she calls the "self-subjugation to the biblical text" of literary-critical readers who do not attend to ideology: "In their attempts to show how artful, how intricate, how ironic, how carefully crafted the biblical narrative is, contemporary critics ignore the prescriptive aspect that is in many ways its most obvious characteristic" (*Sexual Politics in the Biblical Narrative*, 35). J. Cheryl Exum, too, considers the formative powers of offensive literature when she cautions that "prophetic diatribes make claims upon their readers" (*Plotted, Shot, and Painted: Cultural Representations of Biblical Women* [Sheffield, UK: Sheffield Academic Press, 1996], 103).

9. It is important to remember that irony subtly destabilizes the authority of the narrator, at least for readers who read an ironic text "straight" (whether unwittingly or intentionally). What Alice Bach notes about the "blurred" identity of the narrator (whom she presumes to be male) shows precisely the complications that ironic texts pose for their readers. She writes, "The more blurred the portrait of the narrator, the easier it is for the reader to 'forget' the narrator's alliances. Thus, the narrator's anonymity or blurred identity is used as a strategy of manipulation of the reader—to hide narratorial bias.... Faithful readers share the narrator's theological code, male readers the gender code, and those whose political stripe matches that of the narrator the political code. Suspicions arise when the reader does not share the social, political, and gender codes of the narrator. The more codes one does not share with the narrator, the more incongruent the reading" (*Women, Seduction, and Betrayal in Biblical Narrative*, 23).

10. Pertinent here is Schwartz's trenchant observation, "There is no question that owning the sexual rights to a woman (or stealing them, as the case may be) confers power in patriarchy" ("Adultery in the House of David," 343).

11. Phyllis A. Bird, "The Harlot as Heroine: Narrative Art and Social Presupposition in Three Old Testament Texts," *Semeia* 46 (1989): 121.

12. Grosz discerns an anxious ambivalence within (not external to) constructions of masculinity in patriarchal cultures, arguing that male portrayals of women's bodies and women's sexuality articulate that anxiety. Her words are applicable to phallocentric depictions of women prostitutes: "[W]omen's corporeality is inscribed as a mode of seepage.... The metaphorics of uncontrollability, the ambivalence between desperate, fatal attraction and strong revulsion, the deep-seated fear of absorption, the association of femininity with contagion

and disorder, the undecidability of the limits of the female body . . . its powers of cynical seduction and allure are all common themes in literary and cultural representations of women. But these may well be a function of the projection outward of their corporealities, the liquidities that men seem to want to cast out of their own self-representations" (*Volatile Bodies,* 203).

13. Bach, *Women, Seduction, and Betrayal,* 209.

14. Yvonne Sherwood, *The Prostitute and the Prophet: Hosea's Marriage in Literary-Theoretical Perspective* (Sheffield, UK: Sheffield Academic Press, 1996), 320.

15. Bach, *Women, Seduction, and Betrayal in Biblical Narrative,* 3.

16. Throwing off the conceptual constraints of dominant discourses is always difficult. Relevant here are Linda Singer's observations regarding the insistent power of patriarchal discourse: "Male dominance is maintained by a phallocentric organization, founded on a masculine economy which distributes pleasure and entitlement differentially according to gender in a way that disadvantages women, and which inscribes bodies of both genders with a logic of male dominance. This differential economy affects not only sexual practices but also sexual discourse. . . . Women who do not know or are incapable of representing what they want are that much less likely to demand or pursue it. The absence of a female-identified discourse adequate to representing women's sexuality in its difference is both a symptom of and instrumental to the continued subjugation of women within the patriarchal order" ("True Confessions: Cixous and Foucault on Sexuality and Power," in *Erotic Welfare: Sexual Theory and Politics in the Age of Epidemic* (London: Routledge, 1993)], 147).

17. A hermeneutically focused study that addresses competing ancient, medieval, and contemporary readings of Genesis 34 is Robin Parry's *Old Testament Story and Christian Ethics: The Rape of Dinah as a Case Study* (Waynesboro, Ga.: Paternoster, 2004).

18. See Lyn M. Bechtel, "What if Dinah Is Not Raped?" *Journal for the Study of the Old Testament* 62 (1994): 19–36. Also noteworthy in this vein is the novel by Anita Diamant, *The Red Tent* (New York: Picador, 1997), which retells the story as a consensual love affair disrupted by the brothers' misguided patriarchal bloodlust for economic and sexual control of communal boundaries. A feminist retelling that pushes back against both Diamant's version and politicized interpretations may be found in Athalya Brenner's *I Am . . . Biblical Women Tell Their Own Stories* (Minneapolis, Minn.: Fortress, 2005), 25–49. Claudia Camp suggests that disputes over exogamy in Hebrew Bible literature reflect intra-Israelite priestly tensions around identity. See her "The (E)strange(d) Woman in the Land: Sojourning with Dinah," chapter 7 in *Wise, Strange and Holy.*

19. See Sternberg, *Poetics of Biblical Narrative,* 445–75; the critique of Sternberg by Danna Nolan Fewell and David M. Gunn, "Tipping the Balance: Sternberg's Reader and the Rape of Dinah," *Journal of Biblical Literature* 110 (1991): 193–212; and Sternberg's rebuttal, "Biblical Poetics and Sexual Politics: From Reading to Counter-Reading," *Journal of Biblical Literature* 111 (1992): 463–88. Also weighing in with a sharp critique of Sternberg is Fuchs, who speaks of his "obliviousness" in being interested in literary gapping but not seeing beyond his own androcentric assumptions to discern how "female perspectivity" is gapped in biblical texts (*Sexual Politics,* 36–37). An evaluation of the hermeneutical debate between Fewell and Gunn and Sternberg is provided by Paul Noble, "A 'Balanced' Reading of the Rape of Dinah: Some Exegetical and Methodological Observations," *Biblical Interpretation* 4 (1996): 173–204.

20. Jan William Tarlin, "Tamar's Veil: Ideology at the Entrance to Enaim,"

in *Culture, Entertainment and the Bible,* ed. George Aichele, 174–81 (Sheffield, UK: Sheffield Academic Press, 2000), 176–77.

21. Esther Marie Menn, *Judah and Tamar (Genesis 38) in Ancient Jewish Exegesis: Studies in Literary Form and Hermeneutics* (Leiden, Neth.: Brill, 1997), 38.

22. Menn notes that interpretation of this narrative silence about Tamar's ethnicity can be complex: "The absence of any such reference [to Tamar as Canaanite] may actually reflect the narrator or redactor's attempt to shield Tamar and her relations with Judah from the pejorative force of the biblical laws and narratives condemning intermarriage with Canaanites. . . . [H]owever, some later Jewish interpreters view Tamar as an ethnic contrast to the Canaanite daughter of Shua, rather than as her parallel" (*Judah and Tamar,* 54).

23. Diane M. Sharon, "Some Results of a Structural Analysis of the Story of Judah and Tamar," *Journal for the Study of the Old Testament* 29 (2005): 301.

24. Richard J. Clifford, "Genesis 38: Its Contribution to the Jacob Story," *Catholic Biblical Quarterly* 66 (2004): 523–24.

25. On power dynamics in biblical texts generally, see Carol Smith, "Biblical Perspectives on Power," *Journal for the Study of the Old Testament* 93 (2001): 93–110. Smith suggests that the character of Tamar enacts a complex relationship of power and powerlessness simultaneously (105–106). Other narratives explored by Smith that show reversals and ambiguities in power dynamics are Genesis 19, 2 Kings 3, and the relationship between David and Bathsheba throughout the Succession Narrative.

26. Nelly Furman has examined aspects of gender represented in Genesis stories that involve clothing. She argues that where male characters such as Jacob and Joseph use clothing to reinforce male bonds and male authority, female characters (Rebekah, Potiphar's wife, Tamar) use clothing subversively to penetrate the patriarchal semiotic system. See her essay, "His Story Versus Her Story: Male Genealogy and Female Strategy in the Jacob Cycle," *Semeia* 46 (1989): 141–49. Furman writes that "in the Jacob cycle, the women use pieces of attire—which are the symbolic markers of the father-son relationship—to reinscribe themselves in the patriarchal system. . . . For the men, garments are symbolic markers of filial love and recognition, whereas for the women they serve as a means of self-inscription in a system that neglects them" (147). Further on the significance of clothing in Genesis 38 and ways in which that motif links the story of Judah and Tamar to the rest of Genesis 37–50, see John R. Huddlestun, "Divestiture, Deception, and Demotion: The Garment Motif in Genesis 37–39," *Journal for the Study of the Old Testament* 98 (2002): 47–62.

27. Many commentators have noticed these ironies of perception. See, e.g., Johanna W. H. Bos, "Out of the Shadows: Genesis 38; Judges 4:17–22; Ruth 3," *Semeia* 42 (1988): 37–67.

28. Judith Butler in "Editor's Introduction" to Singer, *Erotic Welfare,* 5.

29. On Genesis 38's representation of Judah's alienation from Israelite tradition, see Anthony J. Lambe, "Judah's Development: The Pattern of Departure–Transition–Return," *Journal for the Study of the Old Testament* 83 (1999): 53–68. Lambe writes elsewhere that we can see a contrast being drawn between the "Hebraic" and "pagan" cultures in the deployment of the terms *zōnâ* and *qĕdēšâ* when Judah encounters Tamar veiled as a prostitute and tries to find her again later. He argues that Judah "stands . . . on the threshold between the two" worlds represented by the two terms, and that he "[crosses] over into the pagan one," and "Judah is symbolically re-initiated back into the Hebraic heritage when he recognizes his insignia" as presented to him by Tamar. See Lambe,

"Genesis 38: Structure and Literary Design," in *The World of Genesis: Persons, Places, Perspectives,* ed. Philip R. Davies and David J. A. Clines, 102–20 (Sheffield, UK: Sheffield Academic Press, 1998), esp. 117.

30. See Dvora E. Weisberg, "The Widow of Our Discontent: Levirate Marriage in the Bible and Ancient Israel," *Journal for the Study of the Old Testament* 28 (2004): 403–29. Weisberg underlines a linkage between the passage on levirate marriage in Deut 25:5–10 and the affirmation of Ps 133:1 about the goodness of brothers living together in unity. Speaking of the phrase "when brothers dwell together" in the Deuteronomy passage, she notes that "a reader familiar with the Hebrew Bible can appreciate the irony of the words. . . . What an admirable and altruistic act a man performs for his brother when he marries the latter's widow and provides his deceased brother with a son to inherit his property and preserve his name! . . . At the same time, surely any mention of brothers triggers in the mind of the reader the stories of fraternal conflict that abound in the Hebrew Bible. Nothing about the relationship of brothers in the Hebrew Bible would suggest that a man could expect altruism or affection from his brother" (412).

31. W. Sibley Towner: "The fact that Judah is not criticized for marrying a Canaanite woman suggests that this story is very old. Certainly no narrator who had heard the preaching of the prophets or the injunctions of the Deuteronomist against intermarriage with the local population would tell this story in this way" (*Genesis* [Louisville, Ky.: Westminster John Knox, 2001], 250).

32. J. A. Emerton, "Judah and Tamar," *Vetus Testamentum* 29 (1979): 403–15. The possibility that a "Canaanite" audience might be being constructed in a literarily complex and ideologically freighted fashion, something that cannot be easily determined simply by examining the surface of a biblical narrative, is not considered by Emerton. He remarks with confidence, "If the narrator was a Canaanite, he probably saw nothing wrong in cultic prostitution" (412).

33. Relevant here is Richard Bauckham's exploration of ways in which literary texts suggest decoys for authorial identity, citing a 1985 South African novel as his model in a study of the Book of Ruth as culturally a "woman's text" whether or not it was written by an actual woman. See his "The Book of Ruth and the Possibility of a Feminist Canonical Hermeneutic," *Biblical Interpretation* 5 (1997): 29–45.

34. Towner suggests that Judah is not condemned for his "shortcomings . . . perhaps because the story reflects an earlier stage or even a regional form of the practice" of levirate marriage (*Genesis,* 252). On my reading, the story's condemnation of Judah is sharp indeed, but it is conveyed by means of deft and subtle ironizing.

35. Newsom, *The Book of Job* (see chapter 1, note 58). For more on ironies created by juxtaposition in narrative, see also Lillian R. Klein, *The Triumph of Irony in the Book of Judges* (Sheffield, UK: Almond, 1988).

36. In my view, Judah is portrayed in a consistently negative way throughout Genesis 37–50, contra scholars who maintain that Judah can be shown to have undergone some sort of moral transformation. For that position, see Clifford, "Genesis 38"; Lambe, "Judah's Development"; and the work on which Lambe builds by Meir Sternberg, "Time and Space in Biblical (Hi)Story Telling: The Grand Chronology," in *The Book and the Text: The Bible and Literary Theory,* ed. Regina M. Schwartz, 116–39 (Oxford: Basil Blackwell, 1990). It is quite possible to read Judah's interactions with the powerful Joseph as evasive and calculating throughout. I would argue that, far from embracing noble self-sacrifice and a renewed understanding of patriarchal and filial responsibility, Judah simply musters his characteristic ruthless savvy toward the end of continuing to com-

modify his brothers (by offering Benjamin and continuing to manipulate Joseph). Judah's base instincts and half-truths are ironized throughout Genesis 37–50, something that can be seen most clearly when Judah's speech is considered in contrast to the speech of the compassionate Reuben.

37. See Craig Y. S. Ho, "The Stories of the Family Troubles of Judah and David: A Study of Their Literary Links," *Vetus Testamentum* 49 (1999): 514–31. Ho builds on the work of Gary A. Rendsburg, "David and His Circle in Genesis xxxviii," *Vetus Testamentum* 36 (1986): 438–46, citing semantic and plot parallels of varying degrees of persuasiveness, e.g., speaking of Gen 38:13–14 and 2 Sam 13:23, 28: "[W]e have here a very unique parallel that cannot be found elsewhere in the Hebrew Bible: we do not have a third example in which a sexually wronged woman is vindicated at a sheep-shearing festival" ("Family Troubles of Judah and David," 519). The subsequent critique by Paul R. Noble ("Esau, Tamar, and Joseph: Criteria for Identifying Inner-Biblical Allusions," *Vetus Testamentum* 52 [2002]: 219–52) rightly insists on more rigorous argumentation for biblical intertextuality but does not entirely vitiate the force of parallels adduced by Ho and Rendsburg. Overstated is Noble's contention that because a hermeneutic of intertextuality might yield a number of possible parallels, it is necessarily unlikely and devolves into a *reductio ad absurdum* ("Criteria for Inner-Biblical Allusions," 232). Expecting any biblical text to display full internal coherence and flawless correspondence with only a single set of potential resonances is unrealistic, especially given the lively reuse of material in biblical traditioning processes.

38. Ho disagrees with Rendsburg's assessment of the mocking overtones of the story, arguing instead that "for an important person such as David his Judahite identity must be proved and thus we have this narrative 'evidence'. It was probably composed to silence those who looked upon him as one of them who 'could not prove their fathers' houses for their descent, whether they belonged to Israel' (Neh. vii 61 // Ezra ii 59)" ("Family Troubles of Judah and David," 529).

39. Alter, *The Art of Biblical Narrative*, 10.

40. Heroism and horror may be the most obvious features of the narrative, but some have discerned hilarity here as well. See Yair Zakovitch, "Humor and Theology or the Successful Failure of Israelite Intelligence: A Literary-Folkloric Approach to Joshua 2," in *Text and Tradition: The Hebrew Bible and Folklore*, ed. Susan Niditch, 75–98 (Atlanta, Ga.: Scholars Press, 1990) and the rebuttal by Frank Moore Cross, "A Response to Zakovitch's 'Successful Failure of Israelite Intelligence,'" in the same volume, 99–104. I do not detect in Joshua 2 textual signals of the comic adequate for me to read this story as a mocking treatment of the Israelite spies, a point that is crucial to Zakovitch's creative (per Cross, speculative and calumnious) argument. Another of Zakovitch's points, that "a woman rescuing a man" may be considered a formally recognizable "story-type," is debatable as well. Where Zakovitch is most helpful is in his implicit flagging of the gender and sexual issues in the text as potential sites of irony. The discussion that follows here incorporates some material from my article, "The Formation of Godly Community: Old Testament Hermeneutics in the Presence of the Other," *Anglican Theological Review* 86 (2004): 623–36.

41. Aaron Sherwood, "A Leader's Misleading and a Prostitute's Profession: A Re-examination of Joshua 2," *Journal for the Study of the Old Testament* 31 (2006): 53–54.

42. See in this regard L. Daniel Hawk, "Strange Houseguests: Rahab, Lot, and the Dynamics of Deliverance," in *Reading between Texts: Intertextuality and the Hebrew Bible*, ed. Danna Nolan Fewell, 89–97 (Louisville, Ky.: Westminster John Knox,

1992). Hawk argues that narratological and semantic parallels between Joshua 2 and the story of Lot (Genesis 19) freight the Rahab story with intertextual resonances of danger: "By evoking the story of Lot at every point in the story of Rahab, the narrator elicits the mood of wickedness and impropriety that characterizes the former episode: 'hardly an auspicious beginning for a campaign of conquest. The allusions to Lot's story increase the sense that something very wrong is happening at Jericho, despite Israel's subsequent success'" (96).

43. Others usually mentioned in this discussion are Jethro, Naaman the Syrian, and Ruth. On this, see among others Frank Moore Cross, "A Response to Zakovitch," 100. The earliest Christian tradents of this reading are well known: Matthew 1 names a "Rahab" in the genealogy of Jesus, Hebrews 11:31 acclaims Rahab for her faith, and James 2:25 offers that epistle's highest praise when it lauds Rahab as "justified by works." Clement of Alexandria reads the scarlet cord tied by Rahab outside her window as prefiguring the saving blood of Christ (Alexander Roberts and James Donaldson, eds., *The First Epistle of Clement to the Corinthians*, XII, in *The Ante-Nicene Fathers*, vol. 1 [Edinburgh: T and T Clark/ Grand Rapids: Eerdmans, 1996], 8). Justin Martyr sees this redemption specifically for outsiders, the means "by which those who were at one time harlots and unrighteous persons out of all nations are saved" (*Dialogue with Trypho*, CXI, in *Ante-Nicene Fathers*, vol. 1, 254).

44. See Bernard H. Mehlman, "Rahab as a Model of Human Redemption," in *"Open Thou Mine Eyes . . .": Essays on Aggadah and Judaica Presented to Rabbi William G. Braude on His Eightieth Birthday and Dedicated to His Memory*, ed. Herman J. Blumberg et al., 193–207 (Hoboken, N.J.: KTAV, 1992).

45. Tikva Frymer-Kensky, "Reading Rahab," in *Tehillah le-Moshe: Biblical and Judaic Studies in Honor of Moshe Greenberg*, ed. Mordechai Cogan, Barry L. Eichler, and Jeffrey H. Tigay, 57–67 (Winona Lake, Ind.: Eisenbrauns, 1997), 61, 66.

46. Susanne Gillmayr-Bucher, "'She Came to Test Him with Hard Questions': Foreign Women and Their View on Israel" (*Biblical Interpretation* 15 [2007]: 135–50), 145.

47. The term "outside the camp" mapped a place of shame and defilement in ancient Israelite understandings of holy and profane spaces. It is where Israelites who were temporarily unclean waited to be allowed back into the community and where those afflicted with "leprosy" had their dwellings (Lev 13:46; Num 5:2–3, 12:14–15). It is where the unusable parts of sacrificed animals were burned (Lev 4:12) and where the latrines were dug (Deut 23:11–15; English vv 10–14). Sin offerings were made there, and those who offered them were cleansed there before reentering the camp (Exod 29:14; Lev 4:21, 17:27–28). Those guilty of major infractions of community rules were stoned to death "outside the camp" (Num 15:32–36, Lev 24:14) or buried there after execution (Lev 10:4). Holy-war booty was kept outside the camp until it was purified (Num 31:19). The suggestion that the Rahab group's time outside the camp was simply a kind of temporary detention would run counter to Deuteronomic legislation regarding Canaanites and is unlikely, Num 31:13 notwithstanding (note there that only virgins could be spared in the Israelite raid on Midian) and *pace* M. A. Beek, "Rahab in the Light of Jewish Exegesis," in *Von Kanaan bis Kerala*, ed. W. C. Delsman, et al., 27–44 (Neukirchen-Vluyn, Germany: Neukirchener/Kevalaer: Verlag Butzon and Bercker, 1982), and Jerome F. D. Creach, *Joshua* (Louisville, Ky.: John Knox, 2003), 66. A sexually viable, autonomous foreign woman represented the greatest temptation to apostasy that the Deuteronomistic imagination could construct, and the defiled status of a Canaanite prostitute could

not have been remedied. As Jonathan Klawans argues regarding ancient Israelite conceptions of sexual sins and idolatry, moral impurity (a category entirely different from ritual impurity) "does not refer to a temporary contagion, but to a permanent debasement. . . . Ablutions . . . are not efficacious here. . . . Such [morally defiled] sinners either live out their lives in a degraded state (like the guilty adulteress) or suffer capital punishment (like apprehended murderers). The land, it appears, likewise suffers a permanent degradation" (*Impurity and Sin in Ancient Judaism* [Oxford: Oxford University Press, 2000], 27–30).

48. On the ongoing threat to the Rahabites, see Murray L. Newman's speculative but intriguing proposal that the story of Rahab was in fact told by the Rahab group "to ensure the status and safety of the clan from overzealous Yahweh worshippers . . . as a reminder to the Israelites of their debt to this particular group of non-royal Canaanites" ("Rahab and the Conquest," in *Understanding the Word: Essays in Honor of Bernhard W. Anderson,* ed. James T. Butler, Edgar W. Conrad, and Ben C. Ollenburger, 167–81 [Sheffield, UK: JSOT Press, 1985], esp. 174).

49. Scholars have argued about whether Jeroboam's golden calves are to be understood as syncretistic in nature or as traditionalist attempts to return to an earlier iconic Yahwism; see Gary N. Knoppers, "Aaron's Calf and Jeroboam's Calves," in *Fortunate the Eyes that See: Essays in Honor of David Noel Freedman in Honor of His Seventieth Birthday;* ed. Astrid B. Beck, et al., 92–104 (Grand Rapids, Mich.: Eerdmans, 1995). Whatever the case, it is clear that the cultic practices of Jeroboam were represented in biblical tradition as an occasion of crisis in communal religious identity and were represented by some (Deuteronomists) as paradigmatic for monarchical malfeasance throughout the remaining history of kingship in ancient Israel.

50. See Lori L. Rowlett, "Disney's Pocahontas and Joshua's Rahab in Postcolonial Perspective," in *Culture, Entertainment and the Bible,* ed. George Aichele, 66–75 (Sheffield, UK: Sheffield Academic Press, 2000). Rowlett observes that Rahab "represents the 'good native' who acquiesces almost immediately to the conquerors, as though she recognizes from the start an innate superiority in them and in the colonizing culture" (66). See also Judith E. McKinlay, "Rahab: A Hero/ine?" *Biblical Interpretation* 7 (1999): 44–57. McKinlay's postcolonial reading problematizes Deuteronomistic notions of Canaanite ethnic distinctiveness in the Rahab story and in the rhetoric of the Conquest writ larger.

51. Danna Nolan Fewell, "Joshua," in *The Women's Bible Commentary,* ed. Sharon H. Ringe and Carol A. Newsom, 63–66 (Louisville, Ky.: Westminster/John Knox, 1992), 63.

52. Lori Rowlett, "Inclusion, Exclusion and Marginality in the Book of Joshua," *Journal for the Study of the Old Testament* 55 (1992): 22–23.

53. See Beek, "Rahab in the Light of Jewish Exegesis"; Larry L. Lyke, "What Does Ruth Have to Do With Rahab? Midrash *Ruth Rabbah* and the Matthean Genealogy of Jesus," in *The Function of Scripture in Early Jewish and Christian Tradition,* ed. Craig A. Evans and James A. Sanders, 262–84 (Sheffield, UK: Sheffield Academic Press, 1998); Phyllis Silverman Kramer, "Rahab: From Peshat to Pedagogy, or, The Many Faces of a Heroine," in *Culture, Entertainment, and the Bible,* ed. George Aichele, 156–72 (Sheffield, UK: Sheffield Academic Press, 2000); Frymer-Kensky, "Reading Rahab," 67; Mehlman, "Rahab as a Model of Redemption," 196–97. Rowlett notes that this later rabbinic elaboration on Rahab's marriage and parturition fits well with the trope of colonized women giving "their bodies willingly to the colonizer for reproduction. When children were born, they belonged to the conquering culture of the father. Therefore the

woman not only lost much of her personal and ethnic heritage, but she had to watch her children lose their ancestral heritage. In a sense the women's bodies, their wombs, were colonized" ("Disney's Pocahontas and Joshua's Rahab," 74).

54. On ambivalence about Jael in the history of interpretation, see David M. Gunn, *Judges* (Oxford: Blackwell, 2005), 71–92.

55. Baruch Margalit, "Observations on the Jael-Sisera Story (Judges 4–5)," in *Pomegranates and Golden Bells: Studies in Biblical, Jewish, and Near Eastern Ritual, Law, and Literature in Honor of Jacob Milgrom*, ed. David P. Wright, David Noel Freedman, and Avi Hurvitz, 629–41 (Winona Lake, Ind.: Eisenbrauns, 1995).

56. The complexity of kinship relations here may also be being ironized by the subtle suggestion that Jael acts as a (death-dealing) mother to Sisera. Building on the work of Fewell and Frymer-Kensky, Brittany E. Wilson argues that Jael's covering of Sisera and giving him milk are quintessential mothering acts ("Pugnacious Precursors and the Bearer of Peace: Jael, Judith, and Mary in Luke 1:42," *Catholic Biblical Quarterly* 68 [2006]: 436–56, esp. 443–45). Wilson writes of the climactic moment in Judges 5, "This evocative image of Sisera sinking 'between her feet' . . . projects Jael as a grim caricature of a mother. Sisera lies between Jael's feet in a twisted parody of birth" (444–45). Here, then, we may see ironizing of the theme of mothering: Deborah arises as a "mother in Israel" who leads into battle; Jael "mothers" Sisera with fatal consequences; and Sisera's own mother waits in vain for the return of her boy.

57. This view has obtained for many centuries, with commentators differing mostly on whether or not actual sexual activity is represented as having taken place. See, among many others, Danna Nolan Fewell and David M. Gunn, "Controlling Perspectives: Women, Men, and the Authority of Violence in Judges 4 and 5," *Journal of the American Academy of Religion* 58 (1990): 389–411; Lillian R. Klein, *From Deborah to Esther: Sexual Politics in the Hebrew Bible* (Minneapolis, Minn.: Fortress, 2003), 38. Pseudo-Philo's retelling of this story heightens the sexual elements, adding roses strewn on the bed and Sisera's explicit hope to make Jael his wife. On this, see the analysis of Pseudo-Philo's *Liber Antiquitatum Biblicarum* by Rhonda Burnette-Bletsch, "At the Hands of a Woman: Rewriting Jael in Pseudo-Philo," *Journal for the Study of the Pseudepigrapha* 17 (1998): 53–64. Some conservative scholars (although not all) object to the proposal that sexual imagery tints the story of the heroic Jael. See, e.g., the objection of Daniel I. Block concerning Judges 5:26–27, "Recent interpretations . . . have ascribed to these verses strong sexual content, but such approaches detract from the author's intention to glorify God whose mysterious but providential hand produces the victory" (*Judges, Ruth* [Nashville, Tenn.: Broadman and Holman, 2002], 241n446).

58. See Susan Niditch, "Eroticism and Death in the Tale of Jael," in *Gender and Difference in Ancient Israel*, ed. Peggy L. Day, 43–57 (Minneapolis, Minn.: Fortress, 1989). Mieke Bal interprets the penetration of Sisera's temple by the tent peg as an ironic figure of emasculating rape. See her *Death and Dissymmetry: The Politics of Coherence in the Book of Judges* (Chicago: University of Chicago Press, 1988), 215. Similarly, J. Clinton McCann Jr. observes that "the potential rapist is subdued by the potential victim" in what amounts to "the 'womanization' of Sisera" (*Judges* [Louisville, Ky.: John Knox, 2002], 57). Susan Niditch analyzes the interweaving of "motifs of sex, violence, and trickery" in broader terms in her *War in the Hebrew Bible: A Study in the Ethics of Violence* (New York: Oxford University Press, 1993), esp. 106–119.

59. Danna Nolan Fewell and David M. Gunn see an ironic emasculation in several details of the story: "[T]he narrator constructs a symbolic picture in

which the tent and its opening become uterine and vaginal images respectively. Sisera, like a man penetrating his lover, has entered, upon invitation, a woman's sphere. Now, like a child in a womb, Sisera lies sleeping in Jael's tent. On this reading, one might even hear the narrator's humor dancing behind Sisera's order to the woman, 'Stand at the opening . . . and if anyone comes and asks you, "Is there a man here?" say, "No."' For Sisera, the answer 'No, there is no man here' is intended to be a lie, but for the reader attentive to irony, the answer 'no' reflects the truth. The mighty man has become a vulnerable child; the virile man lies impotent" ("Controlling Perspectives," 393).

60. Gale A. Yee, "By the Hand of a Woman: The Metaphor of the Woman Warrior in Judges 4," *Semeia* 61 (1993): 105. Further on the woman warrior (in an argument that Esther should be considered such), see Timothy S. Laniak, *Shame and Honor in the Book of Esther* (Atlanta, Ga.: Scholars Press, 1998), 154–57.

61. Interesting if not fully persuasive is Victor H. Matthews's theory that because Sisera repeatedly violated the protocols demanded by the ancient Near Eastern hospitality ethic, Jael is presented as fully within her rights to have murdered him and her action cannot, therefore, be taken as undermining her husband's political standing with King Jabin. See Matthews, "Hospitality and Hostility in Judges 4," *Biblical Theology Bulletin* 21 (1991): 13–21. That normal social rules of hospitality would be expected to obtain in life-and-death battle situations does not go without saying. Further, the sexual politics shaping the narrative require more ideological-critical scrutiny than Matthews affords them.

62. The argument that the contradiction is only apparent, that "Sisera" can mean either the armies of Sisera or the soldier himself, would seem to be an unwarranted harmonizing of a clear signal of tension in the text. Among those who hold that too much is made of the contradiction is Klein, *From Deborah to Esther*, 36.

63. See Baruch Halpern, "Sisera and Old Lace: The Case of Deborah and Yael," chapter 4 in his *The First Historians: The Hebrew Bible and History* (University Park: Pennsylvania State University Press, 1988). Halpern argues that Judges 4 is an "organic reconstruction" of the tradition told in lyric style in Judges 5.

64. Mieke Bal, *Murder and Difference: Gender, Genre, and Scholarship on Sisera's Death* (Bloomington: Indiana University Press, 1988), 131–32.

65. Adrien Janis Bledstein, "Is Judges a Woman's Satire of Men Who Play God?" in *A Feminist Companion to Judges*, ed. Athalya Brenner, 34–54 (Sheffield, UK: JSOT Press, 1993), 54.

66. J. Cheryl Exum, "Feminist Criticism: Whose Interests Are Being Served?" in *Judges and Method: New Approaches in Biblical Studies*, ed. Gale A. Yee, 65–90 (Minneapolis, Minn.: Fortress, 1995), 74.

67. Bledstein, "Is Judges a Woman's Satire?" 35.

68. Klein, *The Triumph of Irony in the Book of Judges*, 20.

69. Among many commentators on this, see Alice A. Keefe, *Woman's Body and the Social Body in Hosea* (Sheffield, UK: Sheffield Academic Press, 2001); Renita Weems, "Gomer: Victim of Violence or Victim of Metaphor?" *Semeia* 47 (1989): 87–104.

70. On the many readings of Gomer through the centuries that have reinforced patriarchal constructions of women's agency and sexuality, see Yvonne Sherwood, "Boxing Gomer: Controlling the Deviant Woman in Hosea 1–3," in *The Feminist Companion to the Latter Prophets*, ed. Athalya Brenner, 101–25 (Sheffield, UK: Sheffield Academic Press, 1995).

71. Scholarly speculation about the mental state of Hosea (and Ezekiel, the prophet whose book has drawn the most attention in psychoanalytic circles) has

tended to rely on simplistic assumptions about literature transparently reflecting deep emotions. Biblical scholars interested in psychological dimensions of prophetic discourse surely need to take far more nuanced and sophisticated account of theories of rhetoric, study of genre conventions, and the social and semantic effects of scribal activity before assuming that the turbulent diction of the Book of Hosea gives us access to the psyche of the prophet.

72. In a section on semiotic analysis, Yvonne Sherwood teases out the implications of the textualization of characters in Hosea 1–3, speaking of little Jezreel, Lo-Ruhamah, and Lo-Ammi as "infant signifiers" (*The Prostitute and the Prophet*, 86). Sherwood writes, "The metaphor of 'conceiving meaning' is acted out in the eighth-century text: Hosea makes (fathers) the signifiers and crafts significance from members of his own family. . . . Gomer-bat-Diblayim . . . gives birth to three children, who are then appropriated as a kind of text" (115).

73. Francis Landy, *Hosea* (Sheffield, UK: Sheffield Academic Press, 1995), 34.

74. Renita Weems claims that we see "the versatility of the (marriage) metaphor as a model for shedding light on the capriciousness of the divine-human relationship" ("Gomer: Victim of Violence," 99). Indeed, the discourse of Hosea is capricious beyond the power of its metaphors to contain it. On deconstruction in the Book of Hosea, see Sherwood, *The Prostitute and the Prophet*. An earlier resistant reading has been offered by Helgard Balz-Cochois, who rereads the Gomer story as the tale of a powerful and blessed woman active in the Baal cult who leaves Hosea because she can no longer bear his narrow-minded, obsessive ranting. See her "Gomer oder die Macht der Astarte: Versuch einer feministischen Interpretation von Hos 1–4," *Evangelische Theologie* 42 (1982): 37–65, and *Gomer: Der Höhenkult Israels im Selbstverständnis der Volksfrömmigkeit: Untersuchungen zu Hosea 4, 1–5, 7* (Frankfurt: Lang, 1982). There are moments of hilarity in Balz-Cochois's feminist rereading: "Sie verläßt Hosea, und keiner verdenkt es ihr; denn, 'Ein Narr ist der Prophet, verrückt der Geistesmann' (Hos 9,7). Keiner verdenkt es ihr, außer einem: Hosea selbst" ("Gomer oder die Macht der Astarte," 53). Her ironizing of the perspective trumpeted throughout the Book of Hosea draws both on the voice of opposition articulated in 9:7 and on the instability of the hyperbolically rageful tone of Hosea's discourse.

Another rereading of the narrative politics in Hosea may be seen in Teresa J. Hornsby, "'Israel Has Become a Worthless Thing': Re-Reading Gomer in Hosea 1–3," *Journal for the Study of the Old Testament* 82 (1999): 115–28. Hornsby argues that Hosea 1–3 preserves the voice of Persian-period natives of Judah/Yehud polemicizing against the returned elite. Her suggestion that Hosea represents a corrupting influence on a once-proud, powerful, and autonomous Israel (Gomer) has the merit of raising important questions about the assumptions commentators bring to the text.

75. Tarlin, "Utopia and Pornography in Ezekiel: Violence, Hope, and the Shattered Male Subject," in *Reading Bodies, Writing Bodies: Identity and The Book*, ed. Timothy K. Beal and David M. Gunn, 175–83 (New York: Routledge, 1997).

76. Ibid., 181–82.

77. Landy, *Hosea*, 32–3. See also Athalya Brenner, "Pornoprophetics Revisited: Some Additional Reflections," *Journal for the Study of the Old Testament* 70 (1996): 77, and Tarlin, "Utopia and Pornography in Ezekiel," 175.

78. Landy, *Hosea*, 38.

79. The appropriateness of the term "pornographic" as a descriptor of the rhetorics of sexual violence in Hosea, Jeremiah, and Ezekiel has been vigorously debated. Especially visible contributions to this debate have been: Fokke-

lien van Dijk-Hemmes, "The Metaphorization of Woman in Prophetic Speech: An Analysis of Ezekiel 23," in *On Gendering Texts: Female and Male Voices in the Hebrew Bible,* ed. Athalya Brenner and Fokkelien van Dijk-Hemmes, 167–76 (Leiden, Neth.: Brill, 1993); Athalya Brenner, "On 'Jeremiah' and the Poetics of (Prophetic?) Pornography," in *On Gendering Texts,* 177–93, and "Pornoprophetics Revisited"; Robert P. Carroll, "Desire under the Terebinths: On Pornographic Representation in the Prophets—A Response," in *A Feminist Companion to the Latter Prophets,* ed. Athalya Brenner, 275–307 (Sheffield, UK: Sheffield Academic Press, 1995), and "Whorusalamin: A Tale of Three Cities as Three Sisters," in *On Reading Prophetic Texts: Gender-Specific and Related Studies in Memory of Fokkelien van Dijk-Hemmes,* ed. Bob Becking and Meindert Dijkstra, 67–82 (Leiden, Neth.: Brill, 1996); and Exum, "Prophetic Pornography," chapter 4 in her *Plotted, Shot, and Painted.* An early definition of pornography by T. Drorah Setel was influential in the study of Hosea. She writes, "The distinguishing *features* of pornography can be characterized as follows: (1) Female sexuality is depicted as negative in relationship to a positive and neutral male standard; (2) women are degraded and publicly humiliated; and (3) female sexuality is portrayed as an object of male possession and control, which includes the depiction of women as analogous to nature in general and the land in particular, especially with regard to imagery of conquest and domination. The *function* of pornography can be summarized as a maintenance of male domination through the denial, or misnaming, of female experience" ("Prophets and Pornography: Female Sexual Imagery in Hosea," in *Feminist Interpretation of the Bible,* ed. Letty M. Russell, 86–95 [Philadelphia: Westminster, 1985], 87; emphasis in original). Brenner further emphasizes the coercive nature of pornography in terms of its characteristically objectifying representation: "[T]he lack of gender differentiation in attributing or creating a sexual fantasy may mutate that fantasy into a pornographic fantasy through lack of knowledge about the other's desire"; and she stresses the element of woman's "bodily exposure (in language or vision) to public view within a shaming framework" ("Pornoprophetics Revisited," 77).

80. Francis I. Andersen and David Noel Freedman note the more benign possibility that the story implies "Hosea took over the management of a prostitute, but did not put her to work"; alternatively, they cite as a possible "parallel situation" David's incarceration of Absalom's concubines (2 Sam 20:3). See Andersen and Freedman, *Hosea* (New York: Doubleday, 1980), 299, 304.

81. Andersen and Freedman find the syntax of that translation to be so strained as to produce "a grammatical monstrosity" (*Hosea,* 490). They prefer instead to emend "My God," *'ĕlōhay,* to "God" in construct (*'ĕlōhê*), yielding the still-awkward "God of Israel" with a verb interposed in the construct chain. A.A. Macintosh notes, "The absence of the word 'Israel' in the LXX and Peshiṭta has led some scholars to suppose that in the MT it is an early gloss explaining the identity of 'we', the subject of the verb, or else it is a dittograph of Israel in v. 3" (*Hosea* [Edinburgh: T & T Clark, 1997], 294).

82. Here, Deborah Krause's analysis of a local irony in Hos 9:14 and 14:9 is relevant. Citing Gen 49:25, Krause argues that the "intercessory curse" in Hos 9:14, "give them a miscarrying womb and dry breasts," constitutes an ironic reversal of an ancient fertility blessing, and that the key to understanding the unspoken here is given in Hos 14:9: true fruit comes from God—a God of healing and blessing, I would stress, not the idolatrous God of destruction known in the earlier chapters of Hosea and rendered untenable through metadiscursive irony. See Krause, "A Blessing Cursed: The Prophet's Prayer for Barren Womb and Dry

Breasts in Hosea 9," in *Reading between Texts: Intertextuality and the Hebrew Bible,* ed. Danna Nolan Fewell, 191–202 (Louisville, Ky.: Westminster John Knox, 1992).

83. See Choon-Leong Seow, "Hosea 14:10 and the Foolish People Motif," *Catholic Biblical Quarterly* 44 (1982): 212–24. Seow argues that Hos 14:10 is not redactional but rather an integral part of a larger discourse within Hosea that incisively characterizes the people and their leaders as fools—that is, that caustically ironizes their erroneous self-understanding and missteps.

84. Kierkegaard, *Concept of Irony,* 85.

85. That question is freighted here just as it was in the story of Rahab. An instructive tracing of the interpretive poles between dramatic earnestness and dramatic irony can be found in Bonnie Honig's juxtaposition of the readings of Cynthia Ozick and Julie Kristeva ("Ruth, the Model Emigrée: Mourning and the Symbolic Politics of Immigration," in *Ruth and Esther: A Feminist Companion to the Bible* (second series), ed. Athalya Brenner, 50–74 [Sheffield, UK: Sheffield Academic Press, 1999]). Honig writes that according to Ozick, "Ruth's conversion to Judaic monotheism from Moabite idolatry testifies to the worthiness of the Jewish God. Ruth's devotion to Naomi exemplifies Ruth's virtue, which is an example for everyone and a ground for the rule of David. Ruth, the model immigrant and convert, supplements the Israelite order and saves it from its wayward rule by judges by founding a new sovereign monarchy. For Kristeva, by contrast, Ruth unsettles the order she joins. Israelite sovereignty is secured by Ruth, but it is also riven by her, by the moment of otherness she personifies as a Moabite. While Ozick's Ruth completes the Israelite order, Kristeva's Ruth makes it impossible for the order ever to attain completeness" ("Ruth, the Model Emigrée," 54). For a reading of Ruth that focuses not on the effect on Israel of her immigration but on the potential cultural loss experienced by the one assimilating, see Laura E. Donaldson, "The Sign of Orpah: Reading Ruth Through Native Eyes," in *Ruth and Esther,* 130–44.

86. For a sophisticated reading that celebrates Ruth's autonomy and moral vision, see Mira Morgenstern, "*Ruth* and the Sense of Self: Midrash and Difference," *Judaism* 48 (1999): 131–45. See also the lyrical feminist characterization of the Book of Ruth offered by Alicia Ostriker in her "The Book of Ruth and the Love of the Land," *Biblical Interpretation* 10 (2002): 343–59. Ostriker writes, "[T]he book of Ruth is an exquisite and transformative countertext within the overwhelmingly patriarchal design of the Bible. . . . It is pastoral and idyllic, where the dominant narrative mode is epic. It is erotic and woman-centered rather than heroic or legalistic. . . . Ruth stretches our notion of community and nation, quietly endorsing the acceptance of the Other, the outsider. Here, for once, we learn how to make love not war, how to love and accept those who are conventionally supposed to be our enemies" (357).

87. Jon L. Berquist, "Role Dedifferentiation in the Book of Ruth," in *Social-Scientific Old Testament Criticism,* ed. David J. Chalcraft, 358–71 (Sheffield, UK: Sheffield Academic Press, 1997); originally printed in *Journal for the Study of the Old Testament* 57 (1993): 23–37. Berquist argues that Ruth takes on a traditionally male role, acting as surrogate husband in the way that she provides for Naomi. The story could be read by a queer theorist as a proto-lesbian narrative of redemption: Berquist characterizes the plot as "a disadvantaged foreigner's deconstruction of gender boundaries in order to save herself and her woman" (371). I would stress, further, the importance of the semantic subtext of forbidden exogamy in three of the four other occurrences of *dbq* that occur outside of Ruth (Gen 34:3, in the story of Shechem and Dinah; Josh 23:12, in a prohibition

on intermarrying with foreign women; and 1 Kgs 11:2, narrating Solomon's illicit attachment to foreign women).

88. See Berquist, "Role Dedifferentiation," 364–67. Tod Linafelt observes that Ruth here is actively taking on the traditional role of the male in type-scenes involving finding mates at watering holes, as some of the Israelite patriarchs do. Of 2:9b, where Boaz instructs Ruth to procure water from the young men if she gets thirsty, Linafelt observes that "what is most interesting about the scene is the fact of its reversal of narrative expectations with regard to gender. For all her deference (or mock deference) and for all the inequality with regard to power and wealth between her and Boaz, Ruth is nevertheless cast in the role that, in the other well scenes, is played by Isaac, Jacob, and Moses. In that sense, perhaps the allusion is a signal that Ruth is more of an actor in the narrative than traditional gender roles would suggest" (*Ruth* [Collegeville, Minn.: Liturgical Press, 1999], 35).

89. Honig, "Ruth, the Model Emigrée," 72.

90. Irmtraud Fischer suggests that Ruth "exegetes" three Torah texts and re-reads them in ways that are sympathetic to foreign women: a text that mandates exclusion of Moabites from the Israelite assembly (Deut 23:4–5), a text that discusses levirate marriage (Deut 25:5–10), and a text regarding redemption of land (Lev 25:23–24). See her "The Book of Ruth: A 'Feminist' Companion to the Torah?" in *Ruth and Esther: A Feminist Companion to the Bible* (second series), ed. Athalya Brenner, 24–49 (Sheffield, UK: Sheffield Academic Press, 1999).

91. Roland Boer, *Marxist Criticism of the Bible* (London: T & T Clark, 2003), 85–86.

92. Bauckham considers the genealogy to be pointing up the androcentric and only partial nature of the form itself: "The male voice of the genealogy . . . is quoted . . . in order to be exposed by the female voice of the narrative as pitifully inadequate in its androcentric selectivity. . . . [T]he book of Ruth, its conclusion tells us, is the kind of story which official, masculine history leaves out" ("The Book of Ruth," 40).

93. Judith E. McKinlay writes trenchantly of the "final erasure of Moabite maternity" effected by the genealogy at the end of Ruth ("A Son Is Born to Naomi: A Harvest for Israel," in *Ruth and Esther: A Feminist Companion to the Bible* (second series), ed. Athalya Brenner, 151–57 [Sheffield, UK: Sheffield Academic Press, 1999], 156). She is concerned with the political implications of colonizing history and the risks to women in such histories: "Mothers, and Moabite mothers even more so, know of daughters taken off by the powerful and the consequences of that. Young women creeping among the gleanings, in danger of rape, promised rewards by older power-holding men who may or may not deliver; who if they do, will make sure the deed is done secretly at night, with all that that implies—this is not a story, this is known experience" (156).

94. André LaCocque, *Ruth* (Minneapolis, Minn.: Fortress, 2004), 12. LaCocque's reading of the meaning of the Book of Ruth diverges, though, from the emphasis on polemics that I see in the book. He suggests that the Book of Ruth is subversive in that it urges a "creative and flexible" reading of the Torah, suggests that "Moab can also have a place in Israel," and hints that the "sexual audacity of Tamar and Rahab the Canaanites; of Ruth the Moabite; and, through incest, of Lot's daughters, mothers of Moab and Ammon, must be judged leniently" (21). While such a vision of inclusivity would be a welcome counterpoint to xenophobic biblical texts, it is unlikely that Israelites even in the post-exilic period would be inclined either to make a place for Moab at the

Israelite table or to look leniently on the sexual transgressions of women from ethnic groups that Israel had loathed for centuries.

95. Menn writes: "[I]t is important to note that David himself has no birth narrative whatsoever in the Bible. . . . This silence is curious, given that David is one of the most important heroes of the Hebrew Bible. Narratively, the lack of a birth story corresponds to David's sudden entrance on the scene as a young man in the middle of Saul's reign. His appearance out of nowhere emphasizes his intrusion into Israelite history and his upsetting its apparent course. . . . [T]he shrewdness and resourcefulness of David's ancestresses, their opportunism and daring, their effective control of history through unorthodox means, also correspond more generally to the character of David's reign. A usurper and empire builder, David . . . succeeds magnificently through the unconventional" (*Judah and Tamar*, 100–102).

96. Among those who similarly read Ruth as commenting with ironic critique on the Davidide monarchy is Linafelt, *Ruth*, 80–81. Halpern's argument runs as follows. The "we have no share in the son of Jesse!" objection in 1 Kgs 12:16 and similar derogatory mentions of David's patronym suggest that David was seen by his political opponents as a usurper. The tribe of Judah did not emerge as a coherent ethno-political entity until well after David's birth. 1 Sam 22:3–4 (in which David sends his parents to stay with the King of Moab) indicates that David had a long-standing amicable connection to Moab. Halpern concludes, "[T]here is every reason to question whether David's ancestral affiliation was Israelite. . . . David's opponents may well have claimed he was a foreigner" (*David's Secret Demons*, 270–75).

97. As chapter 2 has discussed, the anxiety visible in patriarchal narratives about the reverse possibility—that foreign rulers might disrupt Israelite identity through their sexual access to Israelite women—is repeatedly named and suppressed in the three matriarch-in-danger stories in Genesis.

98. See Halpern, *David's Secret Demons*, for persuasive arguments that David's administrative polity, martial practices, and diplomatic ties all suggest that his alliance with the Philistines was an enduring one.

4. The Irony of Prophetic Performance

1. So we may say, given that God's primal speaking in Genesis 1 utters language itself for the first time in the biblical cosmogony. But with the first speech come the first possibility for misunderstanding and the first instance of indeterminacy. George Aichele writes of the Garden of Eden, which he reads in light of the story of the Tower of Babel, that "God's Word/Law brings with it *of necessity* its own inevitable misunderstanding and transgression. . . . [J]ust as humankind has been created in the 'likeness' or 'image' of God, so also the linguistic corruption that taints the entire human world already in the Garden of Eden must itself arise in the divine realm and infect God's own language. Even the perfect language demands the play of metaphor and connotation" (*The Control of Biblical Meaning: Canon as Semiotic Mechanism* [Harrisburg, Pa.: Trinity Press International, 2001], 116; emphasis in original). Thus the prophetic word may be deemed problematic even prior to the translation issue that arises in the prophet's mimetic speech.

2. James C. Scott has studied veiled means of dissent in his *Domination and the Arts of Resistance: Hidden Transcripts* (New Haven, Conn.: Yale University Press, 1990). What he says of the politics of spirit possession, drawing on the work of I. M. Lewis, may be considered with regard to biblical prophecy as well: that dispossessed or marginalized groups (such as Israelites under Babylonian hegemony)

may press their political demands more safely under cover of prophetic intermediation. Scott writes, "[S]pirit possession in many societies represents a quasi-co-
vert form of social protest for women and for marginal, oppressed groups of men
for whom any open protest would be exceptionally dangerous. . . . [T]he humilia-
tions of domination produce a critique that, if it cannot be ventured openly and at
the site at which it arises, will find a veiled, safe outlet" (141).

3. Holland writes, "Those whose violation of accepted standards the ironist
has implicitly brought to light, if they accept his message, feel shame. The shame
thus elicited may provoke anger, but it may also provoke a desire to return to the
common normative standards the rhetor implicitly supports. . . . If the rhetor,
through irony, is able to bring about such a change of heart among the members
of his audience, shame has its desired result: repentance" ("Paul's Use of Irony,"
239). James G. Williams has expressed well the paradox of prophetic irony: "The
images of Presence, which inform Israel's life and consciousness, are preserved
through royal and cultic institutions, but they are reinterpreted, even turned on
their head, by the prophetic word. What was once life to Israel has now become
death, but the prophetic word of death is nonetheless the prelude to life" ("Irony
and Lament: Clues to Prophetic Consciousness," *Semeia* 8 [1977]: 63).

4. Mark Brummitt, "Of Secretaries, Secrets, and Scrolls: Jeremiah 36 and
the Irritating Word of God" in *Derrida's Bible (Reading a Page of Scripture with a
Little Help from Derrida)*, ed. Yvonne Sherwood, 39–48 (New York: Palgrave Macmillan, 2004), 45.

5. Gary J. Handwerk, *Irony and Ethics in Narrative: From Schlegel to Lacan*
(New Haven, Conn.: Yale University Press, 1985), 2.

6. Handwerk, *Irony and Ethics in Narrative*, 2.

7. Relevant along this line is the argument of Jerry Lynn Ray about irony in
the Gospel of Luke, in her *Narrative Irony in Luke–Acts: The Paradoxical Interaction
of Prophetic Fulfillment and Jewish Rejection* (Lewiston, N.Y.: Mellen, 1996). Ray
finds the elaboration in Luke of "two major ironic paradoxes—the Jewish rejection of Jesus as Messiah demonstrates his messiahship, and the Jewish rejection
of the gospel engenders its worldwide acceptance" (8).

8. Thomas Jemielity, *Satire and the Hebrew Prophets* (Louisville, Ky.: Westmin-
ster/John Knox, 1992), 112.

9. Jones, *Howling over Moab*, 128.

10. Martin Kessler, *Battle of the Gods: The God of Israel Versus Marduk of Babylon:
A Literary/Theological Interpretation of Jeremiah 50–51* (Assen, Neth.: Van Gorcum,
2003).

11. David Fishelov, "The Prophet as Satirist," *Prooftexts* 9 (1989): 195–211.

12. Fishelov, "Prophet as Satirist," 209.

13. Jemielity, *Satire and the Hebrew Prophets*, 193.

14. Marcus, *From Balaam to Jonah: Anti-prophetic Satire in the Hebrew Bible* (Atlanta, Ga.: Scholars Press, 1995), 43–65. Marcus notes an element of the gro-
tesque in the bears' horrendous mangling of 42 children for their relatively
minor offense of rudeness to an elder. He notes also the irony of this being dramatically out of character for Elisha, given that he performs five other miracu-
lous acts that help people rather than harming them. Finally, he underlines the
potential parody involved in the children's taunt that Elisha should "go up" (i.e.,
ascend to heaven) as Elijah had done.

15. See ibid., 67–91; quotation at 73.

16. David Marcus says, "[T]he message of the book is not any of the standard ones usually advanced (universalism, repentance, prophecy, God's mercy,

tension between God's justice and God's mercy, or some combination of these). . . . [T]he book is not advocating any particular philosophy or point of view. The purpose of the book is to satirize the prophet for behavior thought to be unbecoming to a prophet" (*From Balaam to Jonah*, viii).

17. In the view of David C. Mitchell, this reference in Ezekiel is (earnestly) underlining the connection between Temple musicians and prophesying. See Mitchell, *The Message of the Psalter: An Eschatological Programme in the Book of Psalms* (Sheffield, UK: Sheffield Academic Press, 1997), 92.

18. John Haiman, *Talk Is Cheap: Sarcasm, Alienation, and the Evolution of Language* (Oxford: Oxford University Press, 1998).

19. Haiman, *Talk Is Cheap*, 30–39.

20. So, e.g., John Van Seters, in "From Faithful Prophet to Villain: Observations on the Tradition History of the Balaam Story," in *A Biblical Itinerary: In Search of Method, Form and Content: Essays in Honor of George W. Coats*, ed. Eugene E. Carpenter, 126–32 (Sheffield, UK: Sheffield Academic Press, 1997). Van Seters suggests that "the talking ass story is a final degradation of the faithful prophet into a buffoon who must be instructed by his own humble donkey" (132). That the story serves chiefly to denigrate Balaam is the view of David Marcus (*From Balaam to Jonah*) and many others, as well.

21. Baruch A. Levine, *Numbers 21–36* (New York: Doubleday, 2000). Levine provides a clear articulation of the consensus view regarding the relationship between the donkey story and the rest of the Balaam narrative: "[T]he author of this picaresque tale effectively integrated his pejorative characterization of Balaam into the primary historiography of the Balaam Pericope, where Balaam is depicted positively as a gifted magical practitioner who became a devotee of the God of Israel" (155). My analysis will suggest that there is substantial ambiguity in the other Balaam material as well and that Balaam's primary allegiance, from beginning to end, is to himself.

22. John William Wevers, "The Balaam Narrative According to the Septuagint," in *Lectures et Relectures de la Bible: Festschrift P.-M. Bogaert*, ed. J.-M. Auwers and A. Wénin, 133–44 (Leuven, Belgium: Leuven University Press, 1999), 144.

23. See John T. Greene, *Balaam and His Interpreters: A Hermeneutical History of the Balaam Traditions* (Atlanta, Ga.: Scholars Press, 1992), 95. The three passages quoted are Num 24:17 ("a star shall come forth out of Jacob, and a scepter shall rise out of Israel; it shall crush . . . Moab"), 24:18 ("Edom shall be dispossessed"), and 24:8 (the metaphor comparing Israel to a wild ox that shall devour its adversaries).

24. Martin Rösel, "Wie einer vom Propheten zum Verführer wurde: Tradition und Rezeption der Bileamgestalt," *Biblica* 80 (1999): 519. 4Q339 is "palaeographically Herodian in date," per Géza Vermès, ed. and trans., *The Complete Dead Sea Scrolls in English* (New York: Allen Lane/Penguin Press, 1997), 590.

25. Greene, *Balaam and His Interpreters*, 136. Greene may be overreading to suggest that the representation of Enoch is as "a Balaam type" (139). He bases this assessment in part on two more allusions (as he finds them) later in 1 Enoch, in chap. 93, of which he says "From Balaam is also borrowed the practice of entering the world of dreams" (140). More evidence would be needed to demonstrate that the reflex of this mantic practice was traceable to literary or traditio-historical dependence on Numbers 22–24.

26. Josephus, *Antiquities of the Jews*, 4.6.2.ff: Balaam was "the greatest of the prophets at that time" (line 104) and "God had raised him to great reputation on account of the truth of his predictions" (105). But after the cursing does not

work, Balaam does counsel Balak to send the most beautiful Moabite women to the Israelites to be a snare to them to "leave off obedience to their own laws and the worship of that God who established them, and to worship the gods of the Midianites and Moabites; for by this means God will be angry at them" (130).

27. Additional sources on the ambivalence inscribed in the early rabbinic and Christian reception of Balaam are Judith R. Baskin, *Pharaoh's Counsellors: Job, Jethro, and Balaam in Rabbinic and Patristic Tradition* (Chico, Calif.: Scholars Press, 1983); Kevin J. Cathcart, "Numbers 24:17 in Ancient Translations and Interpretations," in *The Interpretation of the Bible: The International Symposium in Slovenia,* ed. Jože Krašovec, 511–20 (Sheffield, UK: Sheffield Academic Press, 1998); and C. T. R. Hayward, "Balaam's Prophecies as Interpreted by Philo and the Aramaic Targums of the Pentateuch," in *New Heaven and New Earth: Prophecy and the Millennium: Essays in Honour of Anthony Gelston,* ed. P. J. Harland and C. T. R. Hayward, 19–36 (Leiden, Neth.: Brill, 1999*).*

28. *Numbers Rabbah* XIV.1. See Greene, *Balaam and His Interpreters,* 151.

29. See e.g. Horst Seebass, "Zur literarischen Gestalt der Bileam-Perikope," *Zeitschrift für die alttestamentliche Wissenschaft* 107 (1995): 409–19. Seebass argues on the basis of the divine name criterion that the Elohist, responsible for 22:2, 5–6, 7b-21, 36–41; 23:2b, 3, 4a, 5b-15, 18–26, represents Balaam as sincerely faithful: "Der Erzähler E kann den Ausländer Bileam im Namen des Gottes Israels ebenso ehrwürdig und gottesfurchtig schildern wie den Kanaanäer Abimelech v. Gerar in Gen 20,1–17; 22,22–31a, 33 oder den Pharao in Gen 41,37–39" (416).

30. See Rösel, "Wie einer vom Propheten zum Verführer wurde," 510.

31. Robert Alter, "Biblical Imperatives and Literary Play," in *"Not in Heaven": Coherence and Complexity in Biblical Narrative,* ed. Jason P. Rosenblatt and Joseph C. Sitterson Jr., 13–27 (Bloomington: Indiana University Press, 1991), 19.

32. On the extortionist machinations of Ephron, see Alter's incisive analysis, ibid., 46–51.

33. See *Numbers Rabbah* XX.10. Balaam is convicted of the vice of love of money by Ambrose of Milan (c. 339–97) (*De Officiis Ministrorum* 2.26.130); see Joseph T. Lienhard, ed., *Ancient Christian Commentary on Scripture: Old Testament* III (Downers Grove, Ill.: InterVarsity, 2001), 243.

34. The mention of the deity in Balak's indignant remark is best understood, I would suggest, in ironic scare quotes.

35. Note, for example, the position of John Van Seters that Numbers 22–24 (apart from the donkey story and some editorial glosses) is the work of the Yahwist, who represents Balaam as a "completely faithful prophet of Yahweh" ("From Faithful Prophet to Villain," 126). Van Seters offers source-critical and literary arguments in more detail in chapter 16, "The Story of Balaam: Numbers 22–24," in *The Life of Moses: The Yahwist as Historian in Exodus—Numbers* (Louisville, Ky.: Westminster/John Knox, 1994), 405–35.

36. James S. Ackerman, "Numbers," in *The Literary Guide to the Bible,* ed. Robert Alter and Frank Kermode, 78–91 (Cambridge, Mass.: Belknap, 1987), 86.

37. Robert Alter, *The Art of Biblical Narrative* (New York: Basic Books, 1981), 106.

38. See Marcus, *From Balaam to Jonah,* 29–41. Marcus notes a number of other ironies and parodic elements as well, including the overarching irony that Balaam as seer misinterprets virtually everything that happens and possible ironic parallels with the story of the call of Samuel and the story of the binding of Isaac.

39. R. W. L. Moberly, "On Learning to Be a True Prophet: Balaam and His Ass," in *New Heaven and New Earth: Prophecy and the Millennium: Essays in Honour*

of Anthony Gelston, ed. P. J. Harland and C. T. R. Hayward, 1–17 (Leiden, Neth.: Brill, 1999), 11. Moberly's reading overall is an attempt to salvage the thoroughly ironized Balaam as a paradigm for repentance. For him, "the angel with the deadly sword represents the moral and spiritual responsiveness of God to Balaam's self-seeking" (16).

40. Michael S. Moore, *The Balaam Traditions: Their Character and Development* (Atlanta, Ga.: Scholars Press, 1990), 102–3.

41. Savran, "Beastly Speech," 51.

42. See Marcus: "The tradition that Balaam conversed with God and ultimately blessed Israel was too strong to deny, but they [viz., editors who inserted the donkey story] tried to diminish Balaam's stature by emphasizing the fact that he was essentially incompetent, able to operate only with God's help. . . . If Balaam were to represent a type of non-Israelite seer, then the satire could have been used to demonstrate that all 'Balaams', all non-Israelite seers, were equally incompetent and thus illegitimate sources of the divine word" (*From Balaam to Jonah*, 166).

43. Geert Van Oyen, "Intercalation and Irony in the Gospel of Mark," in *The Four Gospels: Festschrift Frans Neirynck*, ed. F. Van Segbroeck, et al., 2:949–74 (Leuven, Belgium: Leuven University Press, 1992).

44. The examples Van Oyen and others list are Mark 3:20–21 (22–30) 31–35; 5:21–24 (25–34) 35–43; 6:7–13 (14–29) 30–31; 11:12–14 (15–19) 20–25; 14:1–2 (3–9) 10–11; and 14:53 (54) 55–65 (66–72).

45. Van Oyen had access to Tom Shepherd's Andrews University dissertation, "The Definition and Function of Markan Intercalation as Illustrated in a Narrative Analysis of Six Passages" (1991), which has since been published as *Markan Sandwich Stories: Narration, Definition, and Function* (Berrien Springs, Mich.: Andrews University Press, 1993). Shepherd argues that Mark's technique of intercalation involves the reader in a kind of implicit community-building. He writes, "Intercalation is a reader-elevating storytelling method. It places the reader with the narrator above the ironic situations of the story characters. As such, the reader is drawn subtly to the narrator's norms" (*Markan Sandwich Stories*, 386). Shepherd argues in a subsequent article that the dramatized ironies produced by intercalation also highlight the paradoxes that lie at the heart of Mark's sense of Jesus's ministry and Markan Christology. See Shepherd, "The Narrative Function of Markan Intercalation," *New Testament Studies* 41 (1995): 522–40.

46. Robert M. Fowler, *Let the Reader Understand: Reader-Response Criticism and the Gospel of Mark* (Minneapolis, Minn.: Fortress, 1991), 142–44. A related argument is offered by Scott G. Brown, "Mark 11:1–12:12: A Triple Intercalation?," *Catholic Biblical Quarterly* 64 (2002): 78–89. Brown suggests that the depth and complexity of symbolic meanings in the Markan frame stories are illuminated by the intercalary stories.

47. See Jacob Milgrom, *Numbers* (Philadelphia: Jewish Publication Society, 1990), 331n31, citing Targum Onkelos.

48. Levine, *Numbers 21–36*, 175.

49. Levine argues that *yĕšārîm* here should be translated within the semantic range of "heroic, valiant," as depicting military strength rather than with its more usual sense of moral integrity (*Numbers 21–36*, 177–8).

50. Levine cites William Albright for this reading, in Albright's "The Oracles of Balaam," *Journal of Biblical Literature* 63 (1944): 207–33.

51. Compare the overt suggestion of violence in the usage of the "horns of a wild ox" in Deut 33:17: Moses' blessing of Joseph notes that "his horns are the horns of a wild ox; with them he gores peoples."

52. Job 22:25: "If the Almighty is your gold and your *precious* silver." Ps 95:4, "In His hand are the depths of the earth; the *heights* of the mountains are His also."

53. Robert R. Wilson points this out regarding Deut 18:9–14's designation of diviners as "abominations" in Israel (*Prophecy and Society in Ancient Israel* [Philadelphia: Fortress, 1980], 150).

54. Many read the oracle this way. Thomas B. Dozeman finds irony in the use of this animal imagery as countering the ox simile expressed by the king of Moab in 22:4: "Balak has underestimated the threat of Israel. They are a lion and not an ox. They will lick up not only the grass of the fields of Moab, but also its people" ("Numbers," in *New Interpreter's Bible*, vol. 2, 3–268 [Nashville, Tenn.: Abingdon, 1998], 188).

55. Levine, *Numbers 21–36,* 165; Milgrom, *Numbers,* 200.

56. See Levine's discussion (*Numbers 21–36,* 192) of Albright's argument for šetummāh ʿên[ô], "whose eye is pure/clairvoyant," with defective orthography so that the suffixed pronoun was not indicated orthographically. He says "Albright's interpretation has gained wide acceptance" and finds it reasonable himself, while yet preferring to read "whose eye is opened" according to Aramaic and Mishnaic Hebrew usage for štm.

57. So, for example, Jo Ann Hackett, "Balaam," in *Anchor Bible Dictionary,* vol. 1 (New York: Doubleday, 1992), 569–72; Robert R. Wilson, *Prophecy and Society in Ancient Israel,* 148.

58. See David Marcus, "Some Antiphrastic Euphemisms for a Blind Person in Akkadian and Other Semitic Languages," *Journal of the American Oriental Society* 100 (1980): 307–10.

59. Ibid., 307 and 310.

60. Milgrom, *Numbers,* 203.

61. Levine, *Numbers 21–36,* 193.

62. Ibid.

63. Per Joshua 3–4, Shittim was the location of the last Israelite camp on the east side of the Jordan and Gilgal was the site of the first camp on the west side. Regarding the larger point of the Micah passage, Andersen and Freedman read Mic 6:5 as reflecting on the "historic and exemplary case of prophet-king confrontation" that they see in Numbers 22–24, although they admit that the parallels of this with Israelite tradition "are skewed" because in Numbers, both parties are foreigners. See their *Micah* (New York: Doubleday, 2000), 531. They write, "Just as Balaam neutralized and reversed the king more than once in a contest of wills, so here is a prophet who is proclaiming the truth against a king who is trying to subvert the country and destroy it in the process" [viz., Micah versus Ahaz] (532).

64. Michael L. Barré, "The Portrait of Balaam in Numbers 22–24," *Interpretation* 51 (1997): 264.

65. Shubert Spero, "Multiplicity of Meaning as a Device in Biblical Narrative," *Judaism* 34 (1985): 472.

66. Dennis T. Olson, "Numbers," in *Harper's Bible Commentary,* 182–208 (San Francisco: HarperCollins, 1988), 200.

67. The thesis of Savran ("Beastly Speech") is that the Balaam story carefully and precisely reworks the complex of blessings and curses from the Garden of Eden story. He cites parallels with talking animals (snake and donkey respectively) more intelligent than the humans with whom they converse, the important function of the root nḥš, the concept of dust, the significance of cursing, and the presence of an angel armed with a sword in both stories. I do not read every potential correspondence as Savran does, but his arguments under-

line, with regard to Numbers 25, the way in which ironic reversals affect the fate of blessed humans who do not understand their own responsibility.

68. Dennis T. Olson, *Numbers* (Louisville, Ky.: John Knox, 1996), 151. My own reading would emphasize the importance of the Balaam cycle in highlighting the irony that the old generation caused its own demise. I do not see much connection of the Balaam material with the hopeful new generation that begins in Numbers 26. Olson, though, has a more positive view, and his perspective may be commended for taking account of the "spoken" in Balaam's prophecies, which cannot be erased even as the "unspoken" presses in another direction. He writes: "In the midst of the dismal end of the old desert generation, a new generation of hope is about to rise up. These children of the wilderness will be propelled into a more hopeful future by the powerful words of blessing that God has resolved to speak through Balaam in the face of all outside pressures to the contrary" (151).

69. In addition to the commentaries, numerous essays show an appreciation of the subversive uses of form and rhetoric in the Book of Amos. See, e.g., Katharine J. Dell, "The Misuse of Forms in Amos," *Vetus Testamentum* 45 (1995): 45–61, and Joyce Rilett Wood, "Tragic and Comic Forms in Amos," *Biblical Interpretation* 6 (1998): 20–48.

70. Alter uses this term in discussing Isa 1:2–9 and other examples of what he calls the prophetic "poetry of reproof," which functions rhetorically in ways not dissimilar to the entrapment enacted by Nathan's parable to King David about the ewe lamb. See Alter, *The Art of Biblical Poetry* (New York: Basic Books, 1985), 142–44. As Wood comments, by the time Israel becomes the focus of the indictment, "it is too late to withhold assent" ("Tragic and Comic Forms in Amos," 27). See also the discussion in Dell, "Misuse of Forms," 54–55. Andersen and Freedman concede that "placing Judah or Israel at the end of the list [in Amos 1–2] reflects a literary and dramatic interest on the part of the speaker or author" (*Amos* [New York: Doubleday, 1989], 209). But they object, "It is a mistaken theory that Amos, in chaps. 1–2, is only interested in Israel, the last of the eight nations, and that his long analysis of the crimes of every state in the region is just a rhetorical buildup, a feint to put Israel off guard before delivering the knockout punch, a trick to secure their moral consent to the verdicts on all of the neighbors before surprising them by adding their name to the list, on analogy of Nathan's parable to David" (137–38). Their objection represents the ironizing in Amos 1–2 in exaggeratedly simplistic terms. As is always the case with irony, there is indeed truth on some level to the overt "said"—they are correct that the list of indictments against other nations is not "just" rhetorical—but that truth is relativized and a more important truth is emphasized through its indication in the negative. John Barton's comments in his *Amos's Oracles against the Nations* (Cambridge: Cambridge University Press, 1980) are helpful here: "The prophet begins by condemning the surrounding nations for atrocities committed during military campaigns, and by mentioning well-known incidents he ensures that his hearers will experience a sense of moral outrage—which indeed he fully shares himself: the condemnations are meant with full seriousness. . . . [Then] he rounds on them by proclaiming judgment on Israel, too. This technique has two obvious advantages. First, it ensures that the prophet's word of doom will be heard, since he has gained his audience's attention by flattering their feelings of superiority and their natural xenophobia. Secondly, it makes it much harder for them to exculpate themselves . . . since they have implicitly conceded that sin and judgment are rightly linked, by their approval of what has gone before" (3–4).

71. Francis Landy interprets the irony of Amos 3:8 differently: "Prophecy . . . involves a loss of self, dramatizing the prophet as God's prey; at the same time it affirms the prophet as the only one who is truly and courageously conscious. The rhetorical question, 'My Lord YHWH has spoken; who can but prophesy?' ironically evokes the unexpected answer: no one prophesies except Amos, the deportee, who alone fulfills Israel's prophetic purpose" ("Vision and Poetic Speech in Amos," *Hebrew Annual Review* 11 [1987]: 241).

72. Paul R. Noble suggests that Amos here parodies the people's busyness doing legitimate activities without concern for ethics; he sees this passage as corresponding to 5:21–27 in a chiastic structure. See his "The Literary Structure of Amos: A Thematic Analysis," *Journal of Biblical Literature* 114 (1995): 211–12.

73. Landy, "Vision and Poetic Speech in Amos," 225–35.

74. Alan Cooper names as ironic the following three aspects of Amos 7: that Amaziah's charge of conspiracy against Amos "ignores Amos's co-conspirator, God"; that Amos's prophesying has so far "actually saved Israel from destruction"; and that in expelling Amos, Amaziah expels the very "word of God in Israel's midst" from Bethel, a place-name meaning "House of God." See his "The Meaning of Amos's Third Vision (Amos 7:7–9)," in *Tehillah le-Moshe: Biblical and Judaic Studies in Honor of Moshe Greenberg*, ed. Mordechai Cogan, Barry L. Eichler, and Jeffrey H. Tigay, 13–21 (Winona Lake, Ind.: Eisenbrauns, 1997), esp. 15 and 20.

75. Paul R. Noble, "Amos and Amaziah in Context: Synchronic and Diachronic Approaches to Amos 7–8," *Catholic Biblical Quarterly* 60 (1998): 429. Also important is Landy's discussion of dramatic irony in the Amaziah episode; see Landy, "Vision and Poetic Speech," 234–37.

76. So Linville, who finds in Amos 8 as a "significant theme" "the contrast between speech, divine and human, and silence" and suggests that the "interjection may be YHWH's ironic comment to the dead themselves; they would certainly obey this command" ("Visions and Voices," 35). Put a slightly different way, we may see 8:3 representing a tension between the ostensible meaning that the living are to be silent in the presence of the dead (from terror, shock, or reverence?) and an unspoken meaning that because the audience themselves are as good as dead already, they themselves can no longer viably give utterance.

77. See the discussion in Jörg Jeremias, *The Book of Amos* (Louisville, Ky.: Westminster John Knox, 1998), 70–72. Andersen and Freedman refer to plague language shared in Amos 4:6–11, Leviticus 26, Deuteronomy 28, and 1 Kings 8, but they are not sanguine about the possibility of analyzing this literary datum: "[A]ll are clearly drawn from a common tradition; even so, literary connections or interdependence among them cannot be demonstrated" (*Amos,* 436).

78. Jeremias sees the theology of Amos here to be in line with Deuteronomistic theology: "Because even this most extreme act of God did not attain its pedagogical goal, the coming encounter with God (v. 12) is portrayed as one, final chance for Israel's survival. In preparation for this final chance, the exilic community is presented with the book of Amos itself, with its harsh reproofs and demonstrations of culpability" (*Amos,* 72).

79. Shalom M. Paul, *Amos* (Hermeneia; Minneapolis: Fortress, 1991), 143.

80. On the intensifying effect of the three doxologies read progressively, see among others Karl Möller, "'Hear This Word against You': A Fresh Look at the Arrangement and the Rhetorical Strategy of the Book of Amos," *Vetus Testamentum* 50 (2000): 499–518, p. 514. Andersen and Freedman note that these hymnic fragments "celebrate his [viz., God's] limitless, terrifying power, his control of all the elements and forces in his creation, and his continued supervision and deploy-

ment of these agencies and forces. The most ominous threat of all is that every act of creation can be canceled, the work reversed and undone" (*Amos*, 490).

81. M. Daniel Carroll R., "The Prophetic Text and the Literature of Dissent in Latin America: Amos, García Márquez, and Cabrera Infante Dismantle Militarism," *Biblical Interpretation* 4 (1996), 92.

82. Many interpreters have noticed this. In addition to the commentaries generally, see Yair Hoffman, "A North Israelite Typological Myth and a Judaean Historical Tradition: The Exodus in Hosea and Amos," *Vetus Testamentum* 39 (1989): 169–82.

83. The syntax of the phrase in 8:2 is strange. The Hebrew preposition there is not the prefixed *bêt* or the *ʿal* that one might expect for the sense of "to pass them by." It is instead a prefixed *lāmed*, a preposition that can express the semantic idea of "advantage," the so-called *lāmed* of interest, indicating the *dativus commodi* or "benefactive dative." If one reads the preposition in this way, the sense of contrast with that first "passing over" in the Exodus is made explicit: destruction is coming, just as in ancient days, but this time Israel will not be spared.

84. Hans Walter Wolff, *Joel and Amos* (Philadelphia: Fortress, 1977), 330. The verb *šûṭ* comes up only 13 times in the Hebrew Bible, and all other instances are in contexts unrelated to food-gathering. Wolff ties this allusion in Amos to the reinterpretation of the manna we find in Deut 8:3: "He humbled you by letting you hunger, then by feeding you with manna, . . . in order to make you understand that one does not live by bread alone, but by every word that comes from the mouth of the LORD." Andersen and Freedman agree, "The contrast with Moses and Sinai seems deliberate: at that time Moses fasted while receiving the words and the people listened and promised to obey. Now or in the future there will be no famine of food or drink, rather of listening and obeying, and that dearth will bring judgment" (*Amos*, 825).

85. Walter Brueggemann rightly notes the impossibility of Israel's responding to this last rhetorical question of Amos: for Amos's audience: "Israel does not answer 'no,' because it will not give up its positive claim upon the God of the Exodus. It will not answer 'yes,' because that answer will . . . open Yahweh up to a plurality of exoduses beyond Israel, which Israel cannot countenance" (*Texts That Linger, Words That Explode: Listening to Prophetic Voices* [Minneapolis, Minn.: Fortress, 2000], 95).

86. Those who would emend "Ashdod" to "Assyria" sometimes apply the argument for the existence of a fixed word-pair in prophetic rhetoric (Assyria // Egypt), but it is precisely the variation from the more usual word-pair that may make this oracle effective. Further, see Noble's arguments that 3:9–11 and 6:2, 8 are corresponding pairs in his overarching chiastic structure of Amos 3–6 (and not only for reasons having to do with mention of Philistine territories; "Literary Structure of Amos," 215). Such a macro-structural equivalence would support the reading of "Ashdod" here as well.

87. Jeremias, who does not emend "Ashdod" to "Assyria" in 3:9, supplies three different pragmatic explanations for this unusual summons: "That specifically Ashdod . . . and Egypt are summoned as the two witnesses probably derives from their own status as countries with especially splendid palaces, perhaps also ironically from their familiarity with oppression (so Rudolph), but in any case from their competence in judgment (Ashdod as the representative of a neighboring nation, Egypt as the representative of a high power?)," *Amos*, 58. S. D. Snyman suggests, on the basis of three references to Ashdod in Joshua, that Ashdod represents the conquest tradition as yet another tradition that Amos is

attempting to subvert ("A Note on Ashdod and Egypt in Amos III 9," *Vetus Testamentum* 44 [1994]: 559–62).

88. Following the superior translation of Andersen and Freedman (*Amos*, 401) with the exception of their emendation of "Ashdod" to "Assyria." There are no substantive grounds for emendation other than reader perplexity when the larger function of the Philistines in the Book of Amos is not fully appreciated.

89. Möller sees the irony here, calling it "poetic justice" that "even heathen peoples, such as the Philistines and the Egyptians, would confirm the need for divine judgement" ("'Hear This Word,'" 505).

90. This contra Andersen and Freedman, who show a fine appreciation for Amos's ironies elsewhere but here can think of no reason why the rhetoric of Amos might want to employ these enemies in ironically privileged positions: "It is not sensible to threaten a nation with destruction and then invite it to be a witness or observer. If 'Egypt' is correct, and it must be, then Ashdod is wrong" (*Amos*, 406).

91. Jeremias: "[I]t can hardly be an accident that with the Philistines and Arameans it is precisely Israel's archenemies from the past and from Amos' own present . . . who are adduced" (*Amos*, 163).

92. Andersen and Freedman, Amos, 138 and 233. They also argue that whenever the term "Israel" is used in the Book of Amos with a modifier of any kind, it refers to the whole people of Israel and Judah as under the reign of David and Solomon (136).

93. Jon L. Berquist is certainly correct to understand Amos 5:24 in this way. See his "Dangerous Waters of Justice and Righteousness: Amos 5:18–27," *Biblical Theology Bulletin* 23 (1993): 54–63.

94. Wood perceives a kind of doubled audience in the Book of Amos: "Amos's poetic cycle leads us to believe that the audience is Northern Israel. . . . But then with the sudden shift in audience perspective at the mid-point of the cycle, it gradually dawns on the Judean spectators listening to the drama that they are the ones being addressed" ("Tragic and Comic Forms in Amos," 33). I would argue that the thoroughgoing irony suffusing the Book of Amos sets up a "doubleness" of audience that goes beyond the north/south distinction. Wood uses classical dramaturgical categories to argue for a redactional layer in Amos that updates its originally tragic cast and creates a comic plot. In my view, some of the comedic upturns she cites are subordinate elements of a coherent ironizing that merely feints toward the comic in its inexorable movement toward tragic doom, with the exception of the last three verses of the book.

95. Möller acknowledges the critiques of Wolff's original proposal regarding Hosea, but he wisely sidesteps some of the problems by focusing on rhetorical presentation in the Book of Amos rather than a diachronic reconstruction of actual settings in which the historical prophet may have debated. Möller on Amos: "Reading the book consecutively . . . one gets the impression of a prophet struggling, and indeed failing, to persuade his addressees that they stand condemned in the eyes of [the LORD]. . . . [T]he portrayal of the debating prophet is. . . . best understood as an attempt to persuade its hearers or readers to learn from the failure of the prophet's audience to respond appropriately to his message" ("Hear This Word," 510–11). For a related approach to Amos modeled on Bakhtinian dialogism, see Barbara Green, "How the Lion Roars: Contextualizing the Nine Riddles in Amos 3:3–8," in *Theology and the New Histories,* ed. Gary Macy, 112–32 (Maryknoll, N.Y.: Orbis, 1998).

96. Thus Jer 1:2, Hos 1:1, Joel 1:1, Jon 1:1, Mic 1:1, Zeph 1:1, Hagg 1:1, Zech 1:1, and Mal 1:1.

97. As in Isa 1:1, Ezek 1:1, Obad 1, Nah 1:1, and Hab 1:1.

98. The discussion of the term *nōqēd* is substantial in the scholarship. Andersen and Freedman concede that the term theoretically could signify that Amos was a "wealthy pastoralist" but argue on the basis of 7:14 that it is more likely that he was a modest herdsman. See Andersen and Freedman, *Amos,* 187–88 and 778.

99. Lyle Eslinger argues that Amos undergoes a process of education (or better, formation in the discernment of God's will) and that the prophet's earnest intercession eventually yields to his acknowledgement of the rightness of the divine judgment on Israel. See his "The Education of Amos," *Hebrew Annual Review* 11 (1987): 35–57. Eslinger's intriguing and original argument does not address the objection that the persona of Amos is presented from the beginning of the book as a judge speaking uncompromising words of doom, and he does not entertain the possibility that Amos's two earlier intercessions themselves may constitute an ironic feint in line with Amos's numerous other sarcastic (mis)uses of ancient Israelite forms and traditions. Also emphasizing the kindness of Amos is Paul House: "In Amos 7–9 the prophet's personality and his humanity become evident. He is shocked into interceding for his hearers when he realizes the enormity of the judgment he and Yahweh proclaim (7:1–6)." See House, "Amos and Literary Criticism," *Review and Expositor* 92 (1995): 185.

100. Following Alan Cooper's argument that the word *'anak* in 7:7–8, often rendered "a plumb line" and thought by many scholars now to be the word for "tin," may also be generating wordplay as a shortened form of the first-person pronoun, here being used as a divine epithet. See his "The Meaning of Amos's Third Vision (Amos 7:7–9)."

101. Dennis T. Olson, "Dialogues of Life and Monologues of Death: Jephthah and Jephthah's Daughter in Judges 10:6–12:7," in *Postmodern Interpretations of the Bible—A Reader,* ed. A. K. M. Adam, 43–54 (St. Louis: Chalice, 2001), 43.

102. As Linville has recognized regarding Amos 7, this incongruence and "lack of closure" creates "an aura of strangeness and suspense" that leaves the audience in a state of heightened vulnerability regarding Amos's oracles of judgment ("Visions and Voices," 33–34).

103. Eslinger speaks of a "Samsonian demolition of the Temple roof" ("Education of Amos," 53), and Wood argues, in service of her larger thesis about the comic plot of the redacted Book of Amos, that Amos was modeled on the figure of Samson and that "the shaking of the temple is the comic catharsis or resolution of the whole story" ("Tragic and Comic Forms in Amos," 43).

104. Given that Amos has been the recipient of all of the other visions in the book, the masculine singular imperative in 9:1 is best read as addressing Amos himself. Scholars who emend the text to make it God who is to destroy the Temple do so usually out of interpretive discomfort that such a powerful act of destruction would be beyond the strength of a single human being. This argument is flawed in that it holds the text of Amos to a realism that this often hyperbolic text nowhere claims for itself. It assumes that the divine command should be understood as being capable of being fulfilled realistically, when the rhetoric of judgment may just as well be directed toward catalyzing repentance so that the threat need not actually be fulfilled (cf. Ezek 18:32).

105. Ehud Ben Zvi has argued this in a number of works, including his commentary *Micah* (Grand Rapids, Mich.: Eerdmans, 2000).

106. Booth, *Rhetoric of Irony,* 24.

107. So, e.g., Landy: "[T]he controlling metaphor of the book is the lion roaring in 1:2, one that all the words attempt to interpret, to accommodate in a human,

beautiful language, in the perennial poetic task of articulating the inarticulate, crossing the threshold of horror and wonder" ("Vision and Poetic Speech," 240).

108. Scholars who have argued that the summer fruit should be understood as desiccated, rotting, or otherwise unappetizing are speculating about its undesirable character in the absence of textual cues that the fruit is unappealing. The traditionists who added politicized prose interpolations to the Book of Jeremiah allowed for no such ambiguity in Jeremiah's vision of rotting figs: these fruits are explicitly and excessively "bad, so bad that they could not be eaten," as the text says three times (Jer 24:2, 3, 8).

109. Yvonne Sherwood, "Of Fruit and Corpses and Wordplay Visions: Picturing Amos 8.1–3," *Journal for the Study of the Old Testament* 92 (2001): 7.

110. Sherwood writes that in Amos 1–3, God "throws a monkey-wrench into the mechanisms of perception and plays with a fruit—death conjunction that he toyed with once before in Eden" (ibid., 9).

111. Jeremias's comments on Amos 8:1–2 limn in clearer perspective the deeper resonances between Samson's wedding feast and the feast of the harvest that may be being evoked in Amos: "[T]he basket of fruit is a symbol of the year's foremost time of joy, the time in which Israel celebrated its main festival, the festival of wine and oil, of figs and pomegranates, the festival of thanksgiving for the precious gifts of the land, the festival of free-flowing jubilation and dancing" (*Amos*, 134).

112. Linville finds irony too in the doxology that follows in 9:5–6. He writes that it "ironically inverts the destruction of v. 1's temple, by asserting that the destroying god is no other than YHWH: 'Who built his chamber in the heavens, and founded his vault upon the earth' (v. 6). . . . Although the earthly counterpart may, perhaps, be here thought of as Bethel, its destruction only serves to maintain the integrity and sacrality of the heavenly ideal" ("Visions and Voices," 38). I would nuance this only by saying that it is more likely not a local shrine whose destruction is in view in Amos 9 but rather the Temple as an ancient and enduring cultural construct.

113. It is worth noting that the LXX takes something like this compound noun as the subject of the sentence. The Greek, presumably translating or correcting toward *'ādām* instead of the MT's *'ĕdôm*, renders the relevant phrase in 9:12, *hoi kataloipoi ton anthropon kai panta ta ethne eph' hous epikekletai to onoma mou*. This subject, "the remnant of humans and all the nations that are called by my name," is the group that is to seek the LORD. This reading is reflected, then, in the allusion to Amos 9:11–12 in Acts 15:16–18: "I will rebuild the dwelling of David . . . so that all other peoples may seek the Lord—even all the Gentiles over whom my name has been called." See the discussion in Aaron W. Park, *The Book of Amos as Composed and Read in Antiquity* (New York: Peter Lang, 2001), 191–98.

114. Linville, "Visions and Voices," 25. See his fuller exploration of the ambiguity here in his "What Does 'It' Mean? Interpretation at the Point of No Return in Amos 1–2," *Biblical Interpretation* 8 (2000): 400–24.

115. Carroll R., "Prophetic Text and the Literature of Dissent," 95–96.

116. Here, James R. Linville's perspicacious reading of Amos 3:7–8 is worth quoting at length: "If one reads the text with the understanding that Amos is addressing Israel, then Amos is implying that they should begin to prophesy as he has done. But of course, none of them truly understand that they are threatened themselves, even if they do agree with Amos' point in v. 6, that threatening situations are the work of YHWH. But the actual audience of the passage, the readers, must supply for the textual audience the answers to Amos' questions. They too are caught in the logic of v. 8. But can the readers fulfil their prophetic obligation by reading and proclaiming the message of the book itself? Or are new revelations

demanded? The trap here forces the readers to judge their own relationships *vis-à-vis* the word of YHWH" (Linville, "Visions and Voices: Amos 7–9," *Biblica* 80 [1999]: 25–26). Linville also perceives an irony in Amos 8:11 that relates to 3:3–8: "The text [viz., 3:8] speaks of a time in the reader's future, and so by reading, the prophecy is delivered once again. This is all the more ironic in view of the prediction of the silence of YHWH on that terrible day [8:11]" (ibid., 37).

117. This has been noticed by a number of commentators, among them Linville, who writes, "The writers [of the Book of Amos] confront their readers with God's direct speech, which draws them into its own implied narrative. It is done subtly and brilliantly, with the final syllable, a final possessive" ("Visions and Voices," 42).

118. This section is a revised version of a presentation I delivered at the Israelite Prophetic Literature section for the 2006 annual meeting of the Society of Biblical Literature.

119. See Mignon R. Jacobs, *The Conceptual Coherence of the Book of Micah,* Sheffield, UK: Sheffield Academic Press, 2001; David G. Hagstrom, *The Coherence of the Book of Micah: A Literary Analysis* (Atlanta, Ga.: Scholars Press, 1988).

120. Erin Runions, "Playing It Again: Utopia, Contradiction, Hybrid Space and the Bright Future in Micah," in *The Labour of Reading: Desire, Alienation, and Biblical Interpretation,* ed. Fiona C. Black, Roland Boer, and Erin Runions, 285–300 (Atlanta, Ga.: Society of Biblical Literature, 1999).

121. See Homi K. Bhabha, "Representation and the Colonial Text: A Critical Exploration of Some Forms of Mimeticism," in *The Theory of Reading,* ed. Frank Gloversmith, 93–122 (Sussex, UK: Harvester, 1984), and *The Location of Culture* (London: Routledge, 1994), among other works.

122. Runions, "Playing It Again," 286.

123. For a scholarly defense of the judgment reading, see Gershon Brin, "Micah 2,12–13: A Textual and Ideological Study," *Zeitschrift für die Alttestamentliche Wissenschaft* 101 (1989): 118–24. On the history of interpretation of the passage more generally, see William McKane, *Micah: Introduction and Commentary* (Edinburgh: T and T Clark, 1998), 87–94; Andersen and Freedman, *Micah,* 332–34; Bruce K. Waltke, *A Commentary on Micah* (Grand Rapids, Mich.: Eerdmans, 2007), 138–43.

124. So, e.g., McKane, *Micah,* 89.

125. Andersen and Freedman, *Micah,* 339.

126. Delbert R. Hillers, *A Commentary on the Book of the Prophet Micah* (Philadelphia: Fortress, 1984), 39.

127. Brian Britt, "Death, Social Conflict, and the Barley Harvest in the Hebrew Bible," *Journal of Hebrew Scriptures* 5 (2005): 21.

128. Note also that drunkenness and death are associated with two of the four sheep-shearing allusions in the Hebrew Bible. Jeffrey C. Geoghegan notes, in his article, "Israelite Sheepshearing and David's Rise to Power" (*Biblica* 87 [2006]: 55–63), that "both sheepshearing incidents in Samuel involve the demise of drunken participants" (Nabal in 1 Samuel 25 and Amnon at the hand of Absalom in 2 Samuel 13). The other two mentions of sheep-shearing festivals are in Genesis 31 and 38.

129. Andersen and Freedman (*Hosea*) identify Adam as "the town at the Jordan crossing on the main road linking Shechem to the Israelite centers in Transjordan, notably Succoth and Mahanaim." They translate 6:7, "They, as at Adam, broke the covenant," and point out, "Adam was the scene of terrible crime" (436), which would increase the intensity of the reference in Micah. A couple of

verses later, in Hos 6:9b, is, "they committed murder on the way to Shechem"; it is worth noting that Shechem was also a sheep-shearing center.

130. Erin Runions, *Changing Subjects: Gender, Nation, and Future in Micah* (New York: Sheffield Academic Press, 2001), 220; emphasis in original.

131. Andersen and Freedman object that the false *šālôm* prophets always prophesied that no harm would come, not that restoration was imminent; therefore Mic 2:12 cannot qualify as a false *šālôm* prophecy. But their objection does not take into account the story of Hananiah in Jeremiah 28, whose false prophecy is precisely that God will restore Judah and bring the Temple vessels back from exile soon, within two years. That this is taken as a false *šālôm* prophecy is made clear by Jeremiah's rejoinder, "The prophets who preceded you and me from ancient times prophesied war, famine, and pestilence. . . . As for the prophet who prophesies *šālôm*, when the word of that prophet comes true, then it will be known that the LORD has truly sent the prophet" (Jer 29:8).

132. *Pāraṣ* occurs with God as subject in a negative sense in 2 Sam 5:20 = 1 Chron 4:11 (David, versus the Philistines, is successful at Baal-perazim, and David says, "The LORD has burst forth against my enemies before me, like a bursting flood") and Ps 60:3 (a communal lament that opens, "O God, you have rejected us, broken our defenses," and goes on in vv 9–10 English/11–12 Hebrew to say, "Who will bring me to the fortified city? Who will lead me to Edom? Have you not rejected us, O God? You do not go out with our armies"). It is interesting that Edom is mentioned there too.

133. *Wā'ōmar* occurs also in Isaiah 40:6, not in the Masoretic text, which has the 3rd masculine singular *wĕ'āmar*, but in the Septuagint (*kai eipa*).

134. John D. Caputo, *More Radical Hermeneutics: On Not Knowing Who We Are* (Bloomington: Indiana University Press, 2000).

135. Ibid., 221.

136. Ibid., 237. His full sentence is "Undecidability is a condition of choice, not an excuse for staying on the sidelines."

137. Catherine Keller on November 18, 2006 at the Society of Biblical Literature annual meeting in Washington, D.C., presenting on a panel responding to Caputo's book, *The Weakness of God: A Theology of the Event* (Bloomington: Indiana University Press, 2006).

138. Caputo, *More Radical Hermeneutics*, 221.

139. A comprehensive summation of the various ironies in the Book of Jonah is provided by David Marcus, *From Balaam to Jonah*, 93–159. Marcus discusses elements of the absurd, the fantastical, the ridiculous, the distorted, and the parodic, identifying numerous ironies that range from the subtly incongruous to the ridiculously problematic.

140. See the overview of Kenneth M. Craig Jr., "Jonah in Recent Research," *Critical Review: Biblical Studies* 7 (1999): 97–118.

141. Michael E. W. Thompson, "The Mission of Jonah," *Expository Times* 105 (1994): 233–36. Thompson's reading reclaims a "straight" reading of the message of Jonah on the far side of the irony that he sees as operative in the book. He argues that the intention of the author of Jonah 1, 3, and 4 was to indict Israel for its "failure to engage in . . . a preaching mission to Nineveh" (234). Jonah 2 was added later because it "breathes a spirit of hope and optimism" (235). Thompson reads 2:9 as an earnest "exclamation of faith and confidence" (236) meant to encourage the audience to understand that they would have survived any dangers attendant upon their evangelistic mission to Assyria.

142. Uriel Simon: "[T]he moral grandeur of a man who could say, 'Lift me

and cast me into the sea' (1:12), should warn us against condescending scorn. The fundamental seriousness of the fugitive prophet and his utter fidelity to himself are meant to arouse the reader's sympathy rather than derision: Jonah is a genuinely pathetic figure in his hopeless struggle with his God" (*Jonah* [Philadelphia: Jewish Publication Society, 1999], xxi).

143. Simon sees a "compassionate irony" of a pedagogical sort as characterizing the plot of Jonah, "set[ting] the hero in his proper place without humiliating him" (*Jonah*, xxii). How Jonah's obliviousness in the storm, petulance regarding his mission, and pettiness concerning the plant are not supposed to be seen as humiliating in the eyes of the implied audience is hard to imagine. Nevertheless, Simon argues for a gently didactic function to the ironizing that goes on in the book, and says that "the irony actually intensifies the pathos" of the protagonist's experience: Jonah "suffers from self-righteousness and conceit; these are the traits of which the divine irony comes to wean him. . . . The merciful irony that undercuts his conceit and righteousness leads Jonah to recognize the heavy but loving hand of the Lord, who wishes to return him, too, to His bosom" (xxii).

144. The dating of the Book of Jonah is generally considered to be late, although many interpreters would not go so far as to locate the composition of the book in the Hellenistic period. Scholars who do see a Hellenistic literary-cultural background here include Thomas M. Bolin, "Should I Not Also Pity Nineveh? Divine Freedom in the Book of Jonah," *Journal for the Study of the Old Testament* 67 (1995): 109–20, and Gildas Hamel, "Taking the Argo to Nineveh: Jonah and Jason in a Mediterranean Context," *Judaism* 44 (1995): 341–59.

145. A number of scholars provide cogent summaries of the differing interpretations of Jonah that have emerged throughout the history of interpretation. See Yvonne Sherwood: *A Biblical Text and Its Afterlives: The Survival of Jonah in Western Culture* (Cambridge: Cambridge University Press, 2000); David Marcus, "Implications of a Satirical Reading of Jonah," in *From Balaam to Jonah*, 143–59; Jack M. Sasson, *Jonah* (New York: Doubleday, 1990), 323–51; and John Day, "Problems in the Interpretation of the Book of Jonah," in *In Quest of the Past: Studies on Israelite Religion, Literature and Prophetism*, ed. A. S. van der Woude, 32–47 (Leiden, Neth.: Brill, 1990).

146. Sandor Goodhart notes an "ironic conjunction of cause and effect" in the plot, that "the very efforts Jonah makes to avoid undertaking the mission God requires of him are the efforts which bring it about" ("Prophecy, Sacrifice and Repentance in the Story of Jonah," *Semeia* 33 [1985]: 45–46). David Marcus draws attention to the many parallels between Jonah's journey and the flight of Elijah in 1 Kings 19, writing that many "parodic elements" serve to "highlight and magnify the difference between the two prophets" and noting that whereas Elijah's complaint that his life is in danger is viable, by contrast, "Jonah's complaints are not credible, and are parodic" (*From Balaam to Jonah*, 131–33).

147. Interpreters have noticed that God ruthlessly pursues and brutally handles Jonah himself. See, e.g., Serge Frolov, "Returning the Ticket: God and His Prophet in the Book of Jonah," *Journal for the Study of the Old Testament* 86 (1999): 85–105. Frolov writes, "Applied to Jonah's relentless persecutor and torturer, such epithets as 'gracious', 'merciful' and 'abounding in steadfast love' sound sarcastically" (101). Yvonne Sherwood argues that irony in Jonah points to the fragility and powerlessness of the human protagonists at the hands of an "uncompromisingly all-appointing and all-controlling" God (*Biblical Text and Its Afterlives*, 283). Against the idea that God is unmerciful in the book of Jonah, see Meir Sternberg: "Of the two, Jonah has been the ruthless one all along and God the merci-

ful. . . . [H]e [God] has pursued (and will continue to pursue) his prophet so relentlessly not in order to break but to temper his spirit: to teach him a much-needed lesson in love as opposed to self-love" (*Poetics of Biblical Narrative*, 320).

148. See the discussion in Thomas M. Bolin, *Freedom beyond Forgiveness: The Book of Jonah Re-Examined* (Sheffield, UK: Sheffield Academic Press, 1997), 98–105.

149. I find unpersuasive the objection that one does see poetic thanksgivings in prose accounts before the promised deliverance has happened (such as Hezekiah's prayer in Isaiah 38, Daniel's prayer in Daniel 2, and Hannah's song in 1 Samuel 2; see Bolin, *Freedom beyond Forgiveness*, 102, citing the work of John D. W. Watts). Hezekiah's prayer comes after he is given a prophetic assurance that he will recover and indeed, after he has recovered; the mystery is revealed to Daniel before he thanks God for the illumination; and Hannah in fact does bear a son before singing her song of thanksgiving.

150. Jack A. Miles has made this point well in his "Laughing at the Bible: Jonah as Parody," *Jewish Quarterly Review* 65 (1975): 168–81. See also Jonathan Magonet, *Form and Meaning: Studies in Literary Techniques in the Book of Jonah*, Sheffield, UK: Almond Press, 1983. Athalya Brenner suggests that the cluster of figures from psalmody is so dense that even the allusiveness of Jonah 2 itself is parodic. See Brenner, "Jonah's Poem Out of and Within Its Context," in *Among the Prophets: Language, Image and Structure in the Prophetic Writings*, ed. Philip R. Davies and David J. A. Clines, 183–92 (Sheffield, UK: Sheffield Academic Press, 1993), 189.

151. See the comment of Paul Kahn: "The midrash describes Jonah's entering the fish's mouth as one entering a great synagogue. . . . This [viz., 2:3] suggests that Jonah perceives a more positive image than one would have expected in this strange dungeon. It becomes a kind of holy enclave in the midst of terror" ("An Analysis of the Book of Jonah," *Judaism* 43 [1994]: 91).

152. Kenneth M. Craig, Jr., *A Poetics of Jonah: Art in the Service of Ideology* (Columbia: University of South Carolina Press, 1993), 87.

153. Whether we are meant to perceive narcissism in the very offering of the prayer at all is an open question. John C. Holbert suggests that we might read here an emphasis on Jonah's undue concern for self over against his utter lack of concern for others (the sailors, the Ninevites), because he is using the prophetic action of "crying out" (Hebrew *qārā'*) on behalf of himself rather than for others, as a prophet should ("'Deliverance Belongs to Yahweh!': Satire in the Book of Jonah," *Journal for the Study of the Old Testament* 21 [1981]: 71).

154. Magonet observes that "the extent and quality of Jonah's knowledge is also questioned. . . . He <u>knows</u> his tradition, and recites it at three significant points (in answering the sailors, in his prayer from the belly of the fish, and in his self-justification before God in chapter 4). Yet . . . the irony lies in the fact that what he quotes has a paradoxical relationship to what he actually does, his very disobedience illustrating the distance between his <u>formal</u> knowledge of tradition and his <u>experienced</u> knowledge" (*Form and Meaning*, 91–92; emphasis in original). The psalm fragments that Magonet finds Jonah to quote or to which he alludes in the belly of the fish are Pss 3:9; 31:7, 23; 42:8b; 69:2; 103:4; 116:17a;120:1; 142:4; and 143:4. See the discussion of Magonet, *Form and Meaning*, 44–49. Other scholars of Jonah have even longer lists of the psalmic quotations and allusions in Jonah.

155. Marcus, *From Balaam to Jonah*, 128–30. In view of this point, Jonah's misuse or misunderstanding of psalmic tropes is rendered all the more ludicrous.

156. Many commentators find irony in the way in which animals in this story are apparently more obedient to God than is God's own prophet. Marcus argues that a common theme in anti-prophetic satires is the employment of talk-

ing or otherwise intelligent animals to shame disobedient humans. Marcus finds, "from the donkey of Balaam, to the she-bears in the tale of boys and the bald prophet, and to the great fish that swallows Jonah," that "all are illustrations of the contrast between the faithful behavior of animals as contrasted with [humans'] rejection of God's directives" (*From Balaam to Jonah*, 75–76).

157. Magonet observes, "[T]he speaker undergoes an inner development through the course of the 'psalm,' but now we can recognise the irony even of this. Jonah sees his prayer as an appropriate, dutiful thanksgiving one. . . . Yet, precisely because no mention is made of the mission he failed to fulfil, the reader can see through the inadequacy of his confession, the spitefulness of the 'lying vanities' remark as it must apply to Nineveh . . . and the careful assumption that the arrival of his prayer at 'Thy holy temple' and the offering of a sacrifice is the end of the whole matter. . . . Naturally, Jonah cannot see, as can the reader throughout the book, the inadequacy of his responses (what they really are in comparison with what he thinks they are) up to the very last question of the book" (*Form and Meaning*, 52–53).

158. Sasson comments: "When God calls Jonah a second time, the story, in fact, is renewing itself, and our hero has a new chance by which to fill the prophet's role better. I therefore advise against following current commentators . . . who run 2:11 into 3:1, thus effortlessly transporting Jonah from dry land to Nineveh's outskirts" (*Jonah*, 225). Jonah was deposited back home, indeed, but the narrative elides the journey; this allows for the narratological portrayal of all of Jonah's efforts as being in vain while yet showing that no complications or delays occur in his journeying to Nineveh. My own interpretation would depart from Sasson's, of course, in that I would render the "our hero has a new chance" sentiment with heavy irony. Jonah shows no signs of a change of temperament for the better when he arrives in Nineveh.

159. Here, one might nuance Simon's assertion, "The paradoxical tension between the Lord's inordinate severity with Jonah and His extraordinary leniency with Nineveh teaches us about the absolute sovereignty of the divine will" (*Jonah*, xxiv). In view of the multiple ironies suffusing the Book of Jonah, this paradoxical tension—which indeed exists and is significant—does teach us, but perhaps not (only) in the earnest sense in which Simon means it. Rather, it teaches us by ironizing both the divine sovereignty and the divine mercy.

160. The verb *ḥûs* comes up nine times in Ezekiel (5:11; 7:4, 9; 8:18; 9:5, 10; 16:5; 20:17, 24:14). In the rest of the prophetic corpus apart from Jonah, it comes up only twice in Jeremiah (13:14, 21:7) and once in Isaiah (13:18). There are only scattered occurrences in the Pentateuch, Psalms, and Writings. While one might theoretically privilege any occurrence of the verb, the density of usages in the prophet Ezekiel may be taken to be noteworthy when considering the construction of prophetic views of God's mercy.

161. See Walter B. Crouch, "To Question an End, to End a Question: Opening the Closure of the Book of Jonah," *Journal for the Study of the Old Testament* 62 (1994): 101–12.

162. See Kahn, "Analysis of the Book of Jonah." Kahn emphasizes that the verb used when the fish "vomits" Jonah out onto dry land is a verb used elsewhere only in Leviticus 18 and 20, there to characterize the people of Israel being vomited out of their land due to their committing sexual and cultic abominations (92). While Kahn reads Jonah's acclamation of God's mercy straight ("Does he deny the validity of God's attributes of mercy and compassion? Obviously not. The graciousness and mercy of God are among the most

wonderful and beautiful of Judaism's teachings. Jonah himself seems to say it with love and affection," 94), he nevertheless sees that the narrator of the Book of Jonah may have in mind the expulsion of the Israelites from their land when representing Jonah as unhappy about God's exercising mercy (91–92).

163. Simon, *Jonah*, xxxi.

5. "How Long Will You Love Being Simple?"

1. Bruce K. Waltke, *The Book of Proverbs, Chapters 1–15* (Grand Rapids, Mich.: Eerdmans, 2004), 40–41.

2. Ibid., 41.

3. Dianne Bergant suggests, with many others, that this juxtaposition is intended to underline the importance of discernment on a case-by-case basis. See Bergant, *Israel's Wisdom Literature: A Liberation-Critical Reading* (Minneapolis: Fortress, 1997), 89–90. Kenneth G. Hoglund sees here a reflection of the dilemma facing the wise person, who is morally bound to enter into dialogue with the fool (so as to try to teach), but who faces risk in that endeavor because it is a burdensome and possibly futile exercise that might cause the wise person inadvertently to become foolish. See Hoglund, "The Fool and the Wise in Dialogue: Proverbs 26:4–5," in *Learning from the Sages: Selected Studies on the Book of Proverbs,* ed. Roy B. Zuck, 339–52 (Grand Rapids, Mich.: Baker, 1994). Pertinent here is the observation of James L. Crenshaw that an "ever-present ambiguity" underlies many aspects of Israelite wisdom teaching. See his *Old Testament Wisdom: An Introduction,* rev. and enlarged ed. (Louisville, Ky.: Westminster John Knox, 1998), 71.

4. T. A. Perry, *Dialogues with Kohelet: The Book of Ecclesiastes* (University Park: Pennsylvania State University Press, 1993).

5. Carol A. Newsom, "Woman and the Discourse of Patriarchal Wisdom: A Study of Proverbs 1–9," in *Gender and Difference in Ancient Israel,* ed. Peggy L. Day, 142–60 (Minneapolis, Minn.: Fortress, 1989), 159.

6. Bergant argues that the quotidian images used in proverbs as metaphors may be seen to have a beneficial subversive quality in that they authorize hearers/readers to discern paradigmatic truths in their daily lives. She writes, "[T]he regular use of metaphor provides a figurative quality that, while more implied than explicit, is, nonetheless, quite provocative. The descriptions themselves derive from what is commonplace in life. It is their clever artistic use that enables one to discern the exceptional in the familiar. In this way, the flexible quality of proverbs really does argue against rigid conformity to the structures of society" (*Israel's Wisdom Literature,* 79).

7. See Sternberg, *Poetics of Biblical Narrative,* 131–52.

8. As Gerald Wilson has argued, the "preknowledge" that the readers are given in Job 1 about the impeccable character of Job renders other understandings of what is happening to him—notably, the friends' understandings—impossible. See Wilson, "Preknowledge, Anticipation, and the Poetics of Job," *Journal for the Study of the Old Testament* 30 (2005): 243–56.

9. Athalya Brenner, "Job the Pious? The Characterization of Job in the Narrative Framework of the Book," *Journal for the Study of the Old Testament* 43 (1989): 37–52; reprinted in *The Poetical Books,* ed. David J. A. Clines, 298–313 (Sheffield, UK: Sheffield Academic Press, 1997), 298. Two of Brenner's points are particularly telling. Discussing Job 1, she notes of the four adjectival phrases of commendation for Job ("blameless," "upright," "God-fearing," and "avoiding wrongdoing"), "Such a cluster of superlatives attributed to the moral and reli-

gious character of a single person is to be found nowhere else in the Old Testament. The unqualified praise of Job . . . looks too good to be true" (302). She also finds extreme "the notation that Job habitually protects his offspring by offering sacrifices on their behalf, on the off-chance that they have accidentally sinned in their hearts. There is no other Old Testament passage that recommends a habitual (as distinguished from occasional) practice of pre-emptive sacrifice on behalf of individuals. . . . The religiosity of Job the pious is almost a parody of faith rather than a climactic manifestation of it" (306).

10. So Dirk Geeraerts, "Caught in a Web of Irony: Job and His Embarrassed God," in *Job 28: Cognition in Context*, ed. Ellen van Wolde, 37–55 (Leiden, Neth.: Brill, 2003). Geeraerts writes of the divine speech at the end of the book, "The inaptness of God's words with regard to Job's question turns the text as a whole into an ironic statement. All along, the text seems to work its laborious way towards an answer, but when the answer finally comes, it is way off the mark" (44).

11. Good, *Irony in the Old Testament*, 197–98.

12. Ibid., 212.

13. Ibid., 240. Good's later commentary on Job touches on a number of ironies in the biblical text as well. See his *In Turns of Tempest: A Reading of Job* (Stanford, Calif.: Stanford University Press, 1990).

14. Crenshaw, *Old Testament Wisdom*, 93. He also points to the conflicting irony that Job would much prefer not to be attended to by God either: "Job dares to parody familiar assertions of the faithful. The comforting thought that God watches over men and women (Psalm 8) fails to console Job, who longs for a moment's relaxation of that watchful eye" (97).

15. Ibid., 94.

16. Ibid., 95.

17. The literature on Job is vast, and other volumes could have been chosen as well. Other recent treatments of Job that address irony, paradox, and parody in that book are: Bruce Zuckerman, *Job the Silent: A Study in Historical Counterpoint* (New York: Oxford, 1991); Yair Hoffman, *A Blemished Perfection: The Book of Job in Context* (Sheffield, UK: Sheffield Academic Press, 1996); and Edward Greenstein, "In Job's Face/Facing Job," in *The Labour of Reading: Desire, Alienation, and Biblical Interpretation*, ed. Fiona C. Black, Roland Boer, and Erin Runions, 301–17 (Atlanta, Ga.: Society of Biblical Literature, 1999).

18. See full bibliographical information in chapter 1, note 60. The brief discussion of Newsom that follows is taken, in revised and condensed form, from my 2004 review of her *Book of Job* in the *Review of Biblical Literature*, accessible at http://www.bookreviews.org/pdf/3404_3715.pdf.

19. Catherine Keller, "'Recesses of the Deep': Job's Comi-Cosmic Epiphany," in *Face of the Deep: A Theology of Becoming* (London: Routledge, 2003), 124–40.

20. Newsom, *Book of Job*, 46.

21. Ibid., 71.

22. Ibid., 183.

23. Marvin H. Pope writes of this clause, "What Job now despises, refuses, rejects is his former attitude and utterances. The verb *m's* is not used of self-loathing" (*Job* [Garden City, N.Y.: Doubleday, 1965], 348).

24. William Whedbee argues that Job should be read as comedic. See his "The Comedy of Job," *Semeia* 7 (1977): 1–39; reprinted in *On Humour and the Comic in the Hebrew Bible*, ed. Yehuda T. Radday and Athalya Brenner, 217–49 (Sheffield, UK: Almond Press, 1990). He makes a number of interesting points, for example that "the friends resort more and more to stereotyping as they in-

dulge in long, lurid portrayals of the grim destiny of the wicked. . . . In so be-having, the friends become increasingly ludicrous" (227). But I am not con-vinced of his reading of the ending of Job, that "it is comedy—rich, full, celebrative of life despite its contradictions and riddles—that emerges as the final and dominant note in the Joban chorus of dissonant voices" (247). Job had a rich and full life back in Job 1, and the reader has seen how fragile that was.

25. Keller, *Face of the Deep,* 128.

26. Ibid., 132.

27. Ibid., 136; emphasis in original.

28. Ernest W. Nicholson, "The Limits of Theodicy as a Theme of the Book of Job," in *Wisdom in Ancient Israel: Essays in Honour of J. A. Emerton,* ed. John Day, Rob-ert P. Gordon, and H. G. M. Williamson, 71–82 (Cambridge: Cambridge University Press, 1995), 81–82. Nicholson's passage is worth quoting in full: "Job exposed the yawning chasm between the harsh reality of life and what orthodox piety, as repre-sented by his companions, declared to be the automatic harvest of the righteous. For this truthfulness he is commended by God. . . . But disjunction is pressed by Job at the expense of the conjunction of realism and faith. Present experience is allowed to eclipse faith, and lament and plea grounded in hope and trust are re-placed by the bitter accusation that God is unjust and his creation a travesty. It is for this that Job is rebuked and censured, and it is against this that God rouses himself to speak from the whirlwind—not to assert himself like a bully against Job, coerc-ing him into humiliating submission, but to declare his mastery in and over cre-ation, and so to renew his ancient pledge and in this way reawaken faith."

29. Colebrook, *Irony,* 165.

30. This section is a revised and expanded version of an article that ap-peared in *Biblical Interpretation* 12 (2004): 37–68.

31. E.g., James L. Crenshaw, *Ecclesiastes* (Philadelphia: Westminster, 1987); Roland Murphy, *Ecclesiastes* (Dallas, Tex.: Word, 1992); R. N. Whybray, *Ecclesias-tes,* New Century Bible Commentary (Grand Rapids, Mich.: Eerdmans, 1989); Alexander A. Fischer, *Skepsis Oder Furcht Gottes? Studien zur Komposition und The-ologie des Buches Kohelet,* BZAW 247 (Berlin: de Gruyter, 1997); Otto Kaiser, "Die Botschaft des Buches Kohelet," *Ephemerides Theologicae Lovaniensis* 71 (1995): 48–70; and many others. Eric S. Christianson's nuanced discussion of narrative framing techniques resolves into a traditional conclusion: "I cannot refute any-one's belief that Qoheleth (i.e. an author) achieved a subversive literary sophis-tication by creating the whole, but I suggest rather that someone chose the frame for him. . . . to present Qoheleth's largely pre-formed story in his own garish, 'establishment-issue' frame" (*A Time to Tell: Narrative Strategies in Ecclesi-astes* [Sheffield, UK: Sheffield Academic Press, 1998], 125).

32. Perry, *Dialogues with Kohelet;* Tremper Longman III, *The Book of Ecclesias-tes* (Grand Rapids, Mich.: Eerdmans, 1998). Michael V. Fox takes "Qohelet" as a constructed persona but avoids committing himself definitively on the composi-tional issue, asserting that the framing device seen in the superscription and epilogue "likely belongs to the original creative stage of the work" but then re-treating to a more tentative position: "Whether he is best described as an au-thor or as an editor, the author of the epilogue basically supports Qohelet's teachings. Otherwise he could have refrained from writing, editing, or trans-mitting the book" (*A Time to Tear Down and A Time to Build Up: A Rereading of Ec-clesiastes* [Grand Rapids, Mich.: Eerdmans, 1999], 370–71). Murphy, who main-tains that the Epilogue comes from a different hand than the material in the body of the book (*Ecclesiastes,* xxxiv), does concede that Fox's position as articu-

lated in Fox's earlier *Qohelet and His Contradictions* (Sheffield, UK: Almond, 1989) is "attractive and well thought out," but decides with Fox that "since it is virtually impossible to distinguish between the meaning of one voice and the other, the distinction between the author and persona makes little, if any, contribution to the exegesis of the book" (130). Choon-Leong Seow maintains a formally agnostic stance on whether the frame narrator and the speaker "Qohelet" have been created by the same author or by different authors/editors, contenting himself to note strengths and weakness of the relevant lines of argument (*Ecclesiastes* [New York: Doubleday, 1997], 38, 392).

33. David J. A. Clines, "The Postmodern Adventure in Biblical Studies," in *Auguries: The Jubilee Volume of the Sheffield Department of Biblical Studies,* ed. David J. A. Clines and Stephen D. Moore, 276–91 (Sheffield, UK: Sheffield Academic Press, 1998), 290.

34. So A. K. M. Adam in his *What Is Postmodern Biblical Criticism?* (Minneapolis, Minn.: Fortress, 1995): "Interpreters cannot 'make the Bible mean whatever they want it to mean' unless there are audiences that find those interpretations convincing. And thereby hangs the hermeneutical dilemma: No interpretation is self-authenticating, but the validity of any interpretation depends on the assent of some audience" (68).

35. George Aichele, *Sign, Text, Scripture: Semiotics and the Bible* (Sheffield, UK: Sheffield Academic Press, 1997), 14. This position shifts the evaluative problem from text proper to the arena of context but still manages to avoid specifying criteria for how such determinations of "reasonableness" might be made.

36. Stephen D. Moore, *Mark and Luke in Poststructuralist Perspectives: Jesus Begins to Write* (New Haven, Conn.: Yale University Press, 1992), xv. Scholars oriented toward more traditional (pre-poststructuralist) exegesis might happily embrace Moore's metaphor of deconstructionists as beach bullies kicking sand in the faces of those who simply want to read quietly.

37. Consider the following perfectly intelligent criteria suggested by Dale Patrick and Allen Scult (*Rhetoric and Biblical Interpretation* [Sheffield, UK: Almond Press, 1990], 85–87): comprehensiveness ("an interpretation must take the whole work into account"), consistency ("an interpretation of a work must avoid internal contradictions, shifting premises, arbitrary thematic changes . . . [and] it should endeavor to find the work itself consistent"), cogency (an interpretation "should, other things being equal, be the most natural or public way of construing" the text), plenitude (i.e., interpretation should not be reductive and should not focus in unwarranted fashion on certain moments in the text's interpretive history at the expense of others), and profundity (interpretation should make "the text the most profound understanding of its subject that the interpreter can envisage"). All of these criteria assume that the text can support them, that is, that a text itself is consistent, meaningful, and profound in more or less the same way throughout. Such an assumption must be judged suspect, and not just by the postmodernist who balks at the idea of imposing a "master narrative" or dominant interpretive rule, but also by the historical critic who takes seriously the vagaries of accident and creativity that affect human production and reception of texts. Why should an interpretation of, say, a highly stylized or idiosyncratic text be "natural" or "public"? We cannot expect consistency in a text's language or larger rhetorical structures if markers of inconsistency or disjuncture prove themselves to be significant, as is so often the case with ironic texts.

38. Ogden, *Qoheleth* (Sheffield, UK: JSOT Press, 1987), 9–10; emphasis in original.

39. Benjamin Lyle Berger, "Qohelet and the Exigencies of the Absurd," *Biblical Interpretation* 9 (2001): 141–79.

40. A comprehensive listing of the contradictions and ironies that have been perceived in Qohelet's thought is not possible here, but see the commentaries and the article of Franz Josef Backhaus, "Kohelet und die Ironie: Vom Umgang mit Widersprüchen durch die Kunst der Ironie," *Biblische Notizen* 101 (2000): 29–55. One might point to two representative examples. First, the elliptical poem and commentary in 3:1–15 seem to be subtly at odds with each other. Joseph Blenkinsopp thinks that 3:1–8 is a Stoic poem with which Qohelet disagrees, in the following verses of commentary, as regards human ability to perceive the right time to act ("Ecclesiastes 3.1–15: Another Interpretation," *Journal for the Study of the Old Testament* 66 [1995]: 55–64). Second, Douglas B. Miller and others have argued that 6:12, "Who knows what is good?" ironizes the series of *ṭôb*-sayings (comparisons) that follows in 7:1–12 (see his *Symbol and Rhetoric in Ecclesiastes: The Place of Hebel in Qohelet's Work* [Leiden, Neth.: Brill, 2002], 175). Perry has noted the "ironic distancing" that must be presumed often when Qohelet cites traditional wisdom teaching in order to subvert it (*Dialogues with Kohelet*, 187). For Perry, repetition can be an indication that "one speaker takes up the words of another for ironic or sarcastic purposes. . . . Repetitions are thus an important element of refutation and emphasis. In Kohelet this frequently takes the form of irony and wordplay" (195). C. Robert Harrison Jr., offers that the discussion of contradiction in Qohelet should take account of sociological factors as well. See his "Qoheleth among the Sociologists," *Biblical Interpretation* 5 (1997): 160–80. Harrison suggests that Qohelet combined elements from Judaism and Hellenistic philosophy idiosyncratically as a way of responding to the strain under which traditional belief systems were placed by rapid Hellenization. Harrison writes, "Here lies one key to the vexing problem of many inconsistencies which plague Qoheleth's world view. Rather than looking to rhetoric and redaction to explain Qoheleth's contradictions, it may be possible to understand much of the sage's erratic belief system as a sociological response" (171).

41. Good's chapter on Qohelet (*Irony in the Old Testament*, 168–95) focuses on Qohelet's resistance to commercial valuation of life's meaning. For Good, Qohelet's insistence that there is no reliable "profit" in any human behavior lies at the heart of the book's ironic suggestion that humans must simply accept what God gives. Timothy Polk musters a list of incongruities in the book of Qohelet that point to the limitations of human existence, arguing that these ironies serve to undergird Qohelet's commendation of joy and of fear of God ("The Wisdom of Irony: A Study of *Hebel* and Its Relation to Joy and the Fear of God in Ecclesiastes," *Studia Biblica et Theologica* 6 [1976]: 3–17). Izak J. J. Spangenberg makes some useful observations about the pervasive ironic tone of Qohelet and about Qohelet's use of rhetorical questions and the "better-than" aphoristic form to ironic ends ("Irony in the Book of Qohelet," *Journal for the Study of the Old Testament* 72 [1996]: 57–69). Thomas Krüger, who is sympathetic to Fox's claim that a single author is behind both authorial voices in Qohelet, hopes that the coherence of the book may be rescued once one reckons with an ironic manipulation of known genres and themes (*Kohelet*, 35).

42. Fox, *Time to Tear Down*, 3.

43. Seow, *Ecclesiastes*, 41.

44. Harold Fisch, "Qohelet: A Hebrew Ironist," chapter 9 in his *Poetry with a Purpose: Biblical Poetics and Interpretation* (Bloomington: Indiana University Press, 1988), 158–78.

45. Fisch, *Poetry with a Purpose*, 175.

46. Perry, *Dialogues with Kohelet,* xii.
47. Ibid., 6.
48. See ibid., 190–96.
49. Longman, *Ecclesiastes,* 9.
50. Longman: "Qohelet's speech is a foil, a teaching device, used by the second wise man in order to instruct his son (12:12) concerning the dangers of speculative, doubting wisdom in Israel" (ibid., 38).
51. Fox, *A Time to Tear Down,* 365.
52. Ibid., 363–75.
53. Gary D. Salyer writes, "By choosing to base the rhetoric of the book essentially on the strengths and weaknesses of Qoheleth's 'I', the implied author spurned the aura of 'omnisciency' which surrounds so many of the Canon's third-person narrators" (*Vain Rhetoric: Private Insight and Public Debate in Ecclesiastes* (Sheffield, UK: Sheffield Academic Press, 2001), 13). Here I read otherwise: in my view, Qohelet is the most God-like of any human narrator in the Bible by far, and the point of his hyperbolic truth claims is indeed to generate an aura of omniscience—but one that the audience is invited to see as deceptive and limited.
54. Ibid., 15.
55. See Salyer's review of scholarly literature dealing with masking and fictive autobiography in Qohelet in his chapter 4, "The Epistemological Spiral: The Ironic Use of Public and Private Knowledge in the Narrative Presentation of Qoheleth" (167–238).
56. Stuart Weeks, "Whose Words? Qoheleth, Hosea and Attribution in Biblical Literature," in *New Heaven and New Earth: Prophecy and the Millennium,* ed. P. J. Harland and C. T. R. Hayward, 151–70 (Leiden, Neth.: Brill, 1999), 164. On the idea of Qohelet "openly disguising himself as another character," see the argument of Rüdiger Lux that the quasi-Solomonic identification in Qohelet was always meant to be understood as a fiction ("'Ich, Kohelet, bin König . . .': Die Fiktion als Schlüssel zur Wirklichkeit in Kohelet 1,12–2,26," *Evangelische Theologie* 50 [1990]: 331–42). Lux suggests that the arena in which the pronouncements and epistemological explorations of "Qohelet" are true is not the arena of historical reality but the realm of the heart: "Das Herz is offensichtlich die Ebene der Realität, aus der ein fiktiver Text hervorsprießt. . . . Wohl ist die Realität des Herzens von anderer Art als die eines geschichtlichen Datums oder einer materiellen Größe" (339).
57. Brueggemann, *Solomon,* 203.
58. Tremper Longman III, *Fictional Akkadian Autobiography: A Generic and Comparative Study* (Winona Lake, Ind.: Eisenbrauns, 1991), 69: "A fictional autobiography may contain many statements that are historically true, and a nonfictional royal inscription may distort or even ignore historical accuracy for political purposes."
59. See Longman's treatment of Qohelet, *Fictional Akkadian Autobiography,* 120–23.
60. James L. Crenshaw, "Qoheleth's Understanding of Intellectual Inquiry," in *Qohelet in the Context of Wisdom,* ed. A. Schoors, 205–24 (Leuven, Belgium: Leuven University Press, 1998,), 213.
61. Crenshaw, "Qoheleth's Understanding of Intellectual Inquiry," 224. Similarly, Weeks writes: "[T]he author has created a wise man in whom the conventional characteristics of didactic writers are emphasised and exaggerated, perhaps almost to the point of satire; this character's speech is filled with the sort of poetic and verbal gymnastics in which ancient writers so often took great pride, but is more than a little rambling and inconsistent" ("Whose Words?"

165). I would need only to excise the word "almost" from Weeks's observation in order to subscribe to it fully: in my view, this is certainly satire.

62. Thomas Krüger, *Qoheleth,* trans. O. C. Dean Jr. (Minneapolis, Minn.: Fortress, 2004), 11.

63. Donna G. Fricke notes that in the "Verses on the Death of Dr. Swift," Swift "makes clear how he had hoped to be received in his own time and how he hopes to be remembered, and how he knows human blindness has and probably will distort his motivation and intentions" ("The A-mazing Mirror of 'Verses on the Death of Dr. Swift,'" in *Critical Approaches to Teaching Swift,* ed. Peter J. Schakel, 281–89 [New York: AMS Press, 1992], 288–89).

64. The English translation Zuckerman uses is based on an 1893 edition of the story, with interpolated variants from a 1901 edition. See Zuckerman, *Job the Silent,* 181–95.

65. Ibid., 41.

66. Ibid., 193.

67. See ibid., 16–24.

68. The *yōd* in *bôrĕ'ēkā* may be a marker of the plural (presumably then the plural of majesty, per older commentaries and some modern interpreters, e.g., Perry, *Dialogues with Kohelet,* 166) or a morphological peculiarity of vocalic representation (see Fox, *Time to Tear Down,* 321; Seow, *Ecclesiastes,* 351–52). The governing sense of the word "Creator" is clearly preferable to textual emendation and to imaginative midrashic elaborations based on homophones, even if aural polyvalence may have been intended, as Seow suggests.

69. In addition to the commentaries, see John Jarick, "An 'Allegory of Age' as Apocalypse," *Colloquium* 22 (1990): 19–27, and Timothy K. Beal, "C(ha)osmopolis: Qohelet's Last Words," in *God in the Fray: A Tribute to Walter Brueggemann,* ed. Tod Linafelt and Timothy K. Beal, 290–304 (Minneapolis, Minn.: Fortress, 1998).

70. Salyer, *Vain Rhetoric,* 17–18. Jennifer L. Koosed makes a similar point. Koosed theorizes the body of Qohelet (in the sense of the written textual corpus and in the sense of figurings of the human body within the book) in her *(Per)mutations of Qohelet: Reading the Body in the Book* (London: T & T Clark, 2006). She writes of 12:1–8, "The text is resisting interpretation because meaning itself is subject to death. As a result, the meanings imposed on the text by interpreters multiply as if the text in its own death throes spews forth an excess of signification. At one moment the text is perhaps speaking about the body, the next a storm, house, scene of mourning, then the universe, social world, cosmos. . . . The interpreter moves back and forth among allegory, symbol, literal meaning, metaphor, never able to secure the text to any one interpretation. Re-enacting in a radical manner the condition of all language and the fate of all bodies, Qohelet decomposes" (100).

71. One is put in mind of Jonathan Swift once again. Ronald Paulson reflects on the ironized death of the writer in his essay, "'Suppose Me Dead': Swift's *Verses on the Death of Dr. Swift* (in *Critical Essays on Jonathan Swift,* ed. Frank Palmeri, 240–44 [New York: G. K. Hall, 1993]). Paulson writes, "Two of Swift's most powerful symbols are the political hack writer who claims that he is unrewarded and shabby, his body battered with poxes and beatings, and the writer whose work is unread, unpreserved, and simply absent—whose own identity and existence themselves are therefore in jeopardy. . . . [I]n the *Verses on the Death of Dr. Swift* . . . both body and writings deteriorate to the point of demise. . . . [Swift] can be seen, having broken all the other idols, to have iconoclasted himself. He has proved himself the iconoclast . . . who first destroys external idols and at last the internal idol that may have served as point of origin for all the others" (240–41).

72. Michael Carasik offers an imaginative metaphor for the way in which this process has been enacted literarily by the author of the Book of Qohelet: "The frame narrator is not a later writer who has neutralized the dangerous teachings of Qohelet. He is, rather, a writer who has imagined himself into the persona of the sage, 'Qohelet son of David, king in Jerusalem' (1:1) and then transcended that persona, casting it aside like a costume that no longer has an actor inside it, for one higher and wiser still" ("Transcending the Boundary of Death: Ecclesiastes through a Nabokovian Lens," *Biblical Interpretation* 14 [2006]: 438–39). His metaphor beautifully evokes the maneuver made by an ironist who has been dissembling toward the goal of persuading the audience of a higher truth. I would disagree only with Carasik's suggestion that the epilogist is not neutralizing "Qohelet."

73. Paulson, "'Suppose Me Dead,'" 243.

74. Fox, *A Time to Tear Down,* 349.

75. Midrashic connections between Qohelet and the Garden of Eden suggest the context of Law as that which, paradoxically, can make sense of death. Twice in the midrash on Qohelet, the rabbis collocate the glory of primordial wisdom with dust/ashes and death, each time pointing obliquely to fulfillment of halakhic obligation as a hermeneutical key. In the midrash on Qoh 7:13, the sin of Adam is linked to the death of the paradigmatic lawgiver, Moses. Gen 3:22 and Deut 31:14 are drawn into a probing of the importance of Law in the face of not only human mortality generally but the seemingly unfair death of the righteous. In answer to Qohelet's rhetorical question, "Who can make straight what God has made crooked?" (Qoh 7:13), the rabbis subtly interpret Moses's impending death by means of the Deuteronomic future-looking hortatory instruction regarding halakhic obedience (Deut 31:9–32:47). Also noteworthy is the midrash on Qoh 8:1, which ponders the resplendent glory of Adam's wisdom and its subsequent transmogrification into dust (Gen 3:9). Engaged here is Ezekiel's sarcastic paean to the king of Tyre, "You were in Eden, the Garden of God" (Ezek 28:13). This foreign ruler had been "full of wisdom and perfect in beauty" (28:12) but "corrupted [his] wisdom for the sake of [his] splendor" (28:17) and was turned to ashes by God (28:18). Ezekiel's indictment of Tyre for unrighteousness and profanation of (presumably already apostate) sanctuaries is perplexing until one recognizes the veiled reference to the Israelite high priesthood in the list of gems studding Tyre's garments (28:13; cf. Exod 28:17–20, 39:10–13; for the argument, see Robert R. Wilson, "The Death of the King of Tyre: The Editorial History of Ezekiel 28," in *Love and Death in the Ancient Near East: Essays in Honor of Marvin H. Pope,* ed. J. H. Marks and R. M. Good, 211–18 [Guilford, Conn.: Four Quarters, 1987]). If Tyre is a figure of the abdication of priestly halakhic responsibility in the rhetoric of Ezekiel, then the rabbis' citing of Tyre as an illustration of Qoh 8:1, "Who is like the wise man?" shows that disobedience to the Law leaves Israel as ashes, despite its primordial, preeminent glory in the Garden of Eden.

76. Adrian Verheij has argued that the narration of Qohelet about planting vineyards, gardens, and so forth (Qohelet 2) describes what amounts to a failed attempt to recreate something like the Garden of Eden. Where God's primal creative work was "very good," the creative work of Qohelet yields only vanity and a chasing after wind (2:11). See Verheij, "Paradise Retried: On Qohelet 2.4–6," *Journal for the Study of the Old Testament* 50 (1991): 113–15.

77. See the nuanced discussion of methodological issues involved in determining inner-biblical allusion and influence in Sommer, *A Prophet Reads Scripture,* 6–31.

78. Against R. N. Whybray ("Qoheleth as a Theologian," in *Qohelet in the*

Context of Wisdom, ed. A. Schoors, 239–65 [Leuven, Belgium: Leuven University Press, 1998], 251), I would argue that oppression of the weak does not arouse "Qohelet's" fierce indignation for ethical reasons so much as vex his sense of how things should operate.

79. The contention of Whybray and others that 7:16 means something like, "Do not pretend to be righteous" or "do not be self-righteous" would not adequately explain how one might then "go forth with both of them" (7:18, Seow, *Ecclesiastes*, 255) or "escape from all dangers" (Perry, *Dialogues with Kohelet*, 125) or "fulfill them both"/"do his duty by them both" (per rabbinic Hebrew; so Fox, *Time to Tear Down*, 259, 262). That choosing both righteousness and wickedness is intended here to plot out some sort of *via media* (so Longman, *Ecclesiastes*, 196, and many others) is a logically impossible proposition. 7:16–18 is surely best read as ironic.

80. Eric Gans, *Signs of Paradox: Irony, Resentment, and Other Mimetic Structures* (Stanford, Calif.: Stanford University Press, 1997), 69.

81. What Hutcheon says of parody can readily be applied to the Book of Qohelet: it is "a perfect postmodernist form in some senses, for it paradoxically both incorporates and challenges that which it parodies" ("Beginning to Theorize Postmodernism," in *A Postmodern Reader*, ed. Joseph Natoli and Linda Hutcheon, 243–72 [Albany: State University of New York Press, 1993], 251).

82. Leo G. Perdue, "The Death of the Sage and Moral Exhortation: From Ancient Near Eastern Instructions to Graeco-Roman Paraenesis," *Semeia* 50 (1990): 81–109.

83. Ibid., 99.

84. Ibid., 82.

85. Zuckerman, *Job the Silent*, 81. Zuckerman sees the epilogist as concerned to highlight the worthiness of "Qohelet's" message while nevertheless placing it squarely under the aegis of the authorized pietistic tradition that "Qohelet" so clearly criticizes. See *Job the Silent*, 81–84.

86. Perdue, "Death of the Sage," 99.

87. Zuckerman (*Job the Silent*, 83) suggests that the epilogist "is affirming the worthiness of Qoheleth's message, a worthiness that makes the book well worth both celebration and preservation."

88. Krüger, *Qoheleth*, 211.

89. Paulson, "'Suppose Me Dead,'" 243.

90. Connop Thirlwall, "On the Irony of Sophocles," *Philological Museum* 1–2 (1833): 484; quoted in Joseph A. Dane, *The Critical Mythology of Irony* (Athens: University of Georgia Press, 1991), 127. One might compare here Zuckerman's conclusions regarding interpretation of "Bontsye Shvayg" and the Book of Job, wherein he suggests that a change of historical context rendered readers less able to discern the irony. In each case, a folk legend and "the pietistic ideals it portrayed provoked the anger of a great literary artist who determined to counterattack its message, utilizing the literary weapon of parody. But then the forces of history played a trick upon the parodist. The very extremes he so subtly wrote into his text to illustrate the absurdity of the traditional premises themselves became realities as history itself took a turn toward the extreme. Then his parody had to be reread and its interpretations reshaped. What I have called the 'Ozymandias effect' worked on the perceptions of the story's audience and caused them to strip from it all hint of parody and irony. Instead, the story that began as an attack upon tradition became the very embodiment of tradition" (*Job the Silent*, 175).

91. De Man, "Rhetoric of Temporality," 198.

92. Booth, *Rhetoric of Irony*, 36.

93. Brueggemann makes an interesting suggestion regarding the juxtaposition of the obliquely Solomonic Ecclesiastes and Proverbs within the wisdom corpus: "The interface of good Solomon and failed Solomon and the interface of Solomonic wisdom in Proverbs and Ecclesiastes, each and both together, offer a double read of life in the world under God. That double read . . . is perhaps the truth of Israel's wisdom. Either account, read by itself in buoyancy or in resignation, is inadequate" (*Solomon,* 205). I agree that the reader of the Book of Qohelet is invited into a "double read"—one the dialogical tensions of which are then intensified if one considers the Book of Proverbs too. But in my view, the "doubleness" is flagging the inadequacy of one position more insistently than the inadequacy of the other. To be sure, a simplistic Torah piety can never stand again for the reader who has taken "Qohelet" seriously. But I think that halakhic obedience was intended to be the site of final authority in this shifting and unstable book.

94. The absence in Qohelet of any reference to traditions about Israel's deliverance and covenant have long been noticed by commentators. Fisch asserts that the absence of concern for covenant and the God of Israel in Qohelet is a telling absence. Covenant here "defines itself, paradoxically, through the bleakness and emptiness of an existence in which it is never affirmed" ("Qohelet: A Hebrew Ironist," 162), and the God of Israel is "half concealed and half revealed" through elusive intertextual references that constitute a "dialectic of presence and absence" (165). Berger notes that the book of Qohelet mimetically represents one of its central themes, forgetfulness: "It is as though the kingship, and with it Israel's history, are invoked only to be erased by silence. Covenant, exodus, exile, and strife—all are conspicuous in their absence from the book. These topics of central concern to the rest of the Tanach exist only as shadows—absences—in the book of Qohelet" ("Qohelet and the Exigencies of the Absurd," 149).

95. Berger, "Qohelet and the Exigencies of the Absurd," 141.

96. The point here about the still-powerful presence of what has been ironized finds resonance in Gans's recognition of the paradoxical vulnerability of ironic deconstruction: "Deconstruction inhabits structure from the beginning; irony continually knits up what it has undone. . . . Irony removes the security of the sign and returns us to originary chaos, but this chaos is accessible only through a system of representation that remains intact" (*Signs of Paradox,* 73).

97. Fisch finds covenant—the particular covenant of Israel with Israel's God—to be present via its ostensible absence: Qohelet's death-obsessed anthropology serves up "human destiny, viewed without the aspect of covenant. Nothing is said directly of covenant in Ecclesiastes. That bond of relation which gives meaning to a world, purpose to human life, and shape to history, is implied by a kind of pointed silence, by an absence that seems to cry out and draw attention to itself. It defines itself, paradoxically, through the bleakness and emptiness of an existence in which it is never affirmed" (*Poetry with a Purpose,* 162).

98. Hutcheon, *Irony's Edge,* 59.

99. Berger ably evokes the fractures of the text and the woundedness of those who read it straight: "Even the final verses of the book are like a bandage applied to a broken leg. 'Fear God and keep His commandments; for this concerns every man' (12:13). The wound may be covered, may appear more attractive, but beneath the surface, and not far beneath, the trauma remains" ("Qohelet and the Exigencies of the Absurd," 154).

100. Malcolm Bowie, review of *The Book of Lieder: The Original Text of Over 1000 Songs* by Richard Stokes (Faber and Faber, 2005), *Times Literary Supplement,* December 1, 2006, 3.

101. This phrase reflects the consensus view as that is expressed in the article by Leslie C. Allen, "Psalm 73: Pilgrimage from Doubt to Faith," *Bulletin for Biblical Research* 7 (1997): 1–10. An influential earlier treatment along these lines was Martin Buber's "The Heart Determines: Psalm 73," reprinted in *Theodicy in the Old Testament*, ed. James L. Crenshaw, 109–18 (Philadelphia: Fortress, 1983), from a 1968 original.

102. J. Luyten, "Psalm 73 and Wisdom," pp. 59–81 in *La Sagesse de l'Ancien Testament: Nouvelle édition mise à jour* (Leuven, Belgium: Leuven University Press, 1990). Luyten reviews the history of scholarship on relevant issues with special attention to the important work of Kenneth Kuntz, Leo G. Perdue, and James L. Crenshaw. He notes stylistic features that are "typical" of wisdom literature— even if not restricted to it—such as the frequent use of particles such as *'ak* and *lākēn*, employment of a relatively high number of abstract nouns (*harṣubbôt, maśkiyyôt, halāqôt, maṣṣu'ôt,* and *ballāhôt*), and independent use of demonstratives, and he notes that "summarizing references, found here in v. 12 (for vv. 3–12) and vv. 27–28 (for vv. 18–20 and 23–26), are a favourite technique used in Job to close a particular theme or a whole speech" (66). Luyten also cites the "partiality to rare words" and a density of vocabulary of "wisdom words" having to do with the heart, understanding, and so on. He notes that "the psalmist and *Qoheleth* mention first, in autobiographical style, how they have expended great effort to obtain insight," and he notes the use in Ps 73:16 of *'āmāl*, "one of *Qoheleth's* favourite terms" (72). A useful older review of arguments for and against the sapiential nature of Psalm 73 can be found in Leslie C. Allen, "Psalm 73: An Analysis," *Tyndale Bulletin* 33 (1982): 93–118. For a consideration of constraints and possibilities in determining wisdom influence on the Psalms more generally, see Avi Hurvitz, "Wisdom Vocabulary in the Hebrew Psalter: A Contribution to the Study of 'Wisdom Psalms,'" *Vetus Testamentum* 38 (1988): 41–51.

103. James L. Crenshaw, "Standing Near the Flame: Psalm 73," in his *The Psalms: An Introduction* (Grand Rapids, Mich.: Eerdmans, 2001), 125. In Crenshaw's view, the psalmist's self-critique here is suggesting that "whoever dares to challenge God would do well to possess Behemoth's attributes." He also proposes that the image of God seizing the hand of the psalmist in verse 23 is intended to evoke "a domestic scene of a child and parent walking hand in hand" (126). He is followed in both of these readings by William Brown, who writes, "In Job, the creature [Behemoth] bears mythic stature and is portrayed as a formidable, lumbering beast (40:15–24). Such imagery serves to capture the psalmist's former self, one who was intransigent and defiant toward God. . . . [T]he ignorant beast is transformed into enlightened witness, not by dint of intellectual power but by means of God's sustaining guidance" (*Seeing the Psalms: A Theology of Metaphor* [Louisville, Ky.: Westminster John Knox, 2002], 148–49). These readings are engaging and powerful, but my own reading goes in a different direction. I am not persuaded that the psalmist is imaging his own rebellion in the terms in which Behemoth is being represented in Job 40:15–24 (as strong, fearless, confident). Further, I do not think the psalm is easily read as postulating a nurturing relationship between God and the psalmist.

104. The word *'āmal* comes up in Qoh 1:3; 2:11, 18, 19, 20, 22, 24; 3:13; 4:4, 6, 8; 5:14, 17, 18; 6:7; 8:15; 9:9; 10:15. It occurs also in Job 3:10; 4:8; 5:6, 7; 7:3; 11:16; 15:35; 16:2; but in the Joban corpus it seems more often to mean "trouble" or "misery" than laborious work.

105. J. Clinton McCann, Jr., "Psalm 73: A Microcosm of Old Testament Theology," in *The Listening Heart: Essays in Wisdom and the Psalms in Honor of Roland E.*

Murphy, ed. Kenneth G. Hoglund and Roland E. Murphy, 247–57 (Sheffield, UK: JSOT Press, 1987); Walter Brueggemann, "Bounded by Obedience and Praise: The Psalms as Canon," *Journal for the Study of the Old Testament* 50 (1991): 63–92.

106. McCann, "Psalm 73," 252–53.

107. Brueggemann, "Bounded by Obedience and Praise," 80.

108. Ibid., 83. He reads the overall tenor of the psalm in a way that honors the disruptive complaint of the psalmist while moving beyond it: "The old troublesome issues of 'conduct and consequence' . . . are not resolved. These issues are rather left behind for a greater good. No judgment is finally made whether the world is morally coherent or not, whether Psalm 1 is true or not, whether Ps. 73.1 is sustainable or not. It is enough that the God of long-term fidelity is present, caring, powerful and attentive" (86). My reading differs from Brueggemann's proposal only in that I find subtle but important ambiguities and tensions still to inhere even in verses 23–26.

109. Ibid., 89.

110. Boadt, "The Use of 'Panels' in the Structure of Psalms 73–78," *Catholic Biblical Quarterly* 66 (2004): 539.

111. Allen, "Psalm 73," 105–106.

112. Mitchell, *Message of the Psalter,* 106.

113. McCann notes that there have been seven distinct suggestions regarding the genre of the psalm: "wisdom psalm, song of thanksgiving, song of lament, song of confidence, royal psalm, pronouncement of a sanctuary charge, and psalm of the guest of Yahweh" ("Psalm 73," 247). Frank-Lothar Hossfeld and Erich Zenger suggest that Psalm 73 reflects an innovative development of Israelite literature: "[H]ere a new form of Wisdom theology makes itself known, one that can be profiled in the context of postexilic Wisdom theology as a specific form of 'theologized wisdom,' or even as 'revelation wisdom' or 'mystical experience wisdom'" (*Psalms 2: A Commentary on Psalms 51–100* [Minneapolis, Minn.: Fortress, 2005], 224).

114. Newsom, *The Book of Job,* 12.

115. Ibid., 13.

116. Walter Brueggemann, "'Until' . . . Endlessly Enacted, Now Urgent," *Journal for Preachers* 27 (2003): 17.

117. Literally "sanctuaries," perhaps indicating the temple precincts.

118. Hossfeld and Zenger, *Psalms 2,* 233.

119. Many interpreters find this plausible, despite the anomalous nature of such an experience in psalmic narration. Among those who postulate a theophanic or other revelatory experience for the psalmist are Hans-Joachim Kraus, *Psalms 60–150: A Commentary* (Minneapolis, Minn.: Augsburg, 1989), 89.

120. The sense of the cohortative is rendered by Mitchell Dahood as follows: "At present too difficult for his understanding, the glaring inconsistencies of this life will become intelligible to the psalmist in the hereafter" (*Psalms II: 51–100* [Garden City, N.Y.: Doubleday, 1968], 192). One may certainly suggest that the temporal marker of the past at the beginning of verse 17, *ʿad* (usually translated "until" in English versions), ensures that the imperfect verbs that follow do signal activity in the past. But this is necessarily true only of the first verb in verse 17, and the absence of a connective *wāw* before *'ābînâ* gives the interpreter freedom to suggest that that clause begins something new. Further worth noting on this is Gesenius's point that imperfect verbs following *ʿad* may sometimes signal the future tense (*Gesenius' Hebrew Grammar,* 2nd ed. [Oxford: Clarendon, 1910], para. 107c). Paul Joüon and T. Muraoka suggest that this occurrence of the cohortative

might not bear optative valence: "In some cases the [cohortative] form is perh. only due to emphasis, e.g. Jer 4.19; Ps 73:17" (*A Grammar of Biblical Hebrew, Part Three: Syntax*, third reprint [Rome: Pontifical Biblical Institute, 2000], para. 114c, note 2). But optative valence makes eminent sense in this psalm and, as the primary sense of the cohortative, should be taken seriously here.

121. I find generally persuasive Goulder's explanation of that troubled clause. He draws on Tiglath-pileser's boast of his defeat of Gath, in which the Assyrian monarch describes having set up images of himself and his gods in the Philistine palace (Goulder suggests the temple, instead, as the more likely locale for this performance of cultural superiority). See Goulder, *The Psalms of Asaph and the Pentateuch: Studies in the Psalter, III* (Sheffield, UK: Sheffield Academic Press, 1996), 52–61. I disagree with only two points in Goulder's analysis. The phrase "as a dream [is completely swept away—gapped verb *sāpû* serving from the preceding clause] upon waking," should be applied to the preceding verse as an example of enjambment. Goulder reads it as a sort of protasis for verse 20b, but the sense would more readily suggest that verse 20a goes with what precedes. The second point on which I would depart from Goulder's cogent analysis is in his assumption that the unexpressed referent for all of verses 18–19 is the Assyrian enemies; it is better taken, in my alternative reading, as referring to the destroyed Israelites.

122. In the Psalms: Ps 11:1, "How can you say to me, flee?" and Ps 137:4, "How can we sing the LORD's song in a foreign land?" The other occurrences in the wisdom literature are as follows: Prov 5:12 (the only exclamative), "How I hated discipline!"; Qoh 2:16, "How can the wise die along with fools?"; Qoh 4:11, "How can one keep warm alone?"; and Job 21:34, "How then will you comfort me?"

123. Hossfeld and Zenger translate, "I was like a dumb ox, a brute beast— and yet, I was with you" (*Psalms 2*, 222). But there is no conjunctive signal of any kind in the last clause, whether disjunctive or other, so "and yet" is unmerited by the Hebrew.

124. The "and yet" in this translation is of course represented in the Hebrew of verse 23 by the emphatic *wĕ'ănî*. Hossfeld and Zenger translate, "Yes, truly, I am always with you."

125. Hossfeld and Zenger, *Psalms 2*, 232–5. Per Kraus, Hugo Gressman was the first to argue this.

126. Goulder, *Psalms of Asaph*, 61.

127. Kraus, *Psalms 60–150*, 90.

128. Emendation of *lĕyiśrā'ēl* to *layyāšār 'ēl*, so that the full clause reads, "Surely God is good to the upright," is thus unnecessary. See the nuanced discussion of Hossfeld and Zenger (*Psalms 2*, 222). They suggest that in diachronic terms, the graceful parallelism of an emended "Truly God is good to the upright // to the pure in heart" was likely original, as was the contrast between righteous and wicked rather than a focus on the nation of Israel. The reading "to Israel" likely then came in when Psalm 73 was placed as the first of the collection of Asaph psalms (Psalm 50 being displaced). At that point in the psalm's transmission history, the psalm becomes "about 'Israel' in contrast to the wicked foreign nations who have destroyed the Temple and oppress Israel, and on the other hand it is about the mass of 'pure' poor and guiltless suffering people in Israel" (237). This developmental conjecture may be accurate. But interest in Israel is also expressed, albeit obliquely, in the formulation "the generation of your children" in verse 15, something that is integral to the psalm and cannot be considered a later addition or emendation. Hossfeld and Zenger interpret that verse: "The petitioner's temptation to adopt the life-maxims and the practical atheism of

the wicked would have meant saying farewell to 'Israel' and its history" (*Psalms* 2, 229–30).

129. Hossfeld and Zenger, *Psalms 2*, 226.

130. Note also in this regard Amos 9:2–3.

131. Martin Buber's reading of this verse stays close to the Hebrew and thus approaches the proposed interpretation, although Buber represents the meaning of those cries as positive. Buber writes, "This sense of *being taken* is now expressed by the Psalmist in the unsurpassably clear cry, 'Whom have I in heaven!'" He does not aspire to enter heaven after death, for God's home is not in heaven, so that heaven is empty. But he knows that in death he will cherish no desire to remain on earth, for now he will soon be wholly 'with Thee'" ("The Heart Determines," 116). My own reading does not accord with Buber's in the interpretation of God's presence as uncomplicated and congenial for the psalmist; Psalm 139 and Amos 9 are too near to hand for that, in my view. But Buber does see that these exclamations are indicating the impoverishment of the heavens and earth in the psalmist's experience. I simply propose that the coercive presence and ubiquity of an inscrutable God are key factors in the psalmist's experience of impoverishment.

132. The two words occurring only in Isaiah 58 and Psalm 73 are *ḥarṣubbôt* (Ps 73:4, Isa 58:6) and *qirăbat* (Ps 73:28, Isa 58:2). Sommer notes a connection between Psalm 72 and Isaiah 51 (*dôrîm* in Ps 72:5 and Isa 51:8), and writes of Deutero-Isaiah's use of psalmody more generally, "In Isa 51.6–8, Deutero-Isaiah reuses the imagery and language of Ps 102.25–27. . . . In both Isaiah 51 and Psalm 102 an author contrasts the figure of the worn-out earth with God and His eternal promises, which never wear thin. The allusion displays the typical Deutero-Isaianic tendency to extend a figure" (*A Prophet Reads Scripture*, 269n44).

133. Luyten, "Psalm 73 and Wisdom," 70.

134. Harry P. Nasuti, *Tradition History and the Psalms of Asaph* (Atlanta, Ga.: Scholars Press, 1988), 65.

135. Ibid., 151.

136. Walter Brueggemann and Patrick D. Miller have made a case for the pivotal positioning of Psalm 73 within the canonical form of the Psalter. See Brueggemann and Miller, "Psalm 73 as a Canonical Marker," *Journal for the Study of the Old Testament* 72 (1996): 45–56. They write, "Psalm 89 reflects a judgment, if we are to accept the premise of 73.1, in which the king did not 'stay near' God and so experienced the disastrous consequence of God's departing *hesed*" (52).

137. Given that the "I" in Psalm 73 might be said to stand for the community via construction of a royal identity, it is perhaps not necessary to bracket Psalm 73 when studying the communal voice of the Asaph psalms, as Klaus Seybold has done in his article, "Das 'Wir' in den Asaph-Psalmen: Spezifische Probleme einer Psalmgruppe" (in *Neue Wege der Psalmenforschung: Für Walter Beyerlin*, ed. Klaus Seybold and Erich Zenger, 143–55 [Freiburg, Germany: Herder, 1994]). Seybold argues for an exilic provenance for the Asaph psalms, while acknowledging that the psalms were shaped and edited later as well.

138. The function of Psalm 73 as a royal psalm is noteworthy also because, as Gerald Wilson has argued, it is exegetically meaningful that royal psalms are situated at the literary seams between Books I and II and Books II and III in the Psalter. See Wilson, "The Use of Royal Psalms at the 'Seams' of the Hebrew Psalter," *Journal for the Study of the Old Testament* 35 (1986): 85–94, as well as his later works on the redaction of the Psalter.

139. Nasuti notes that "the psalm's complaint is not so much a personal misfortune affecting the speaker as a general dissatisfaction with the working of

divine justice. Indeed, even this theological dissatisfaction is dismissed from the start as unacceptable, even by the speaker, and it is seen instead as a source of temptation to the speaker's faith. [This] clearly removes the psalm from the setting of the individual lament, where the complaints are very real throughout" (*Tradition History and the Psalms of Asaph*, 149).

140. That this psalm is about kingship generally rather than about the particular situation of an unnamed king seems likely, given the absence of specific details. Scott R. A. Starbuck has argued that royal psalms in the Hebrew Scriptures are notable in their ancient Near Eastern literary context for not preserving names of monarchs in the psalmody, and that one reason has to do with the intention of the royal psalms to reflect on the institution of kingship more generally. See Starbuck, *Court Oracles in the Psalms: The So-Called Royal Psalms in Their Ancient Near Eastern Context* (Atlanta, Ga.: Scholars Press, 1999). Psalm 73 is not identified by Starbuck as a royal psalm.

141. Liturgically performed coherence across individual psalms should not be ruled out. Hans Ulrich Steymans has argued, on the basis of comparative work on Mesopotamian prayers for the New Year festival at Asshur, that a number of the Psalms of Asaph were likely intended to be performed in order as part of a single liturgical festival. This theory, unprovable because of its speculative nature, nevertheless expresses a reader response that underlines narratological coherence in the Asaph psalms' liturgical representation of Israel's history. See Steymans, "Traces of Liturgies in the Psalter: The Communal Laments, Psalms 79, 80, 83, and 89 in Context," in *Psalms and Liturgy*, ed. Dirk J. Human and Cas J. A. Vos, 168–234 (London: T & T Clark, 2005).

142. Mitchell, *Message of the Psalter*, 98. The so-called Deutero-Asaph psalms are Psalms 96, 105, and 106, attributed to the Asaphites by the Chronicler in the psalmic "medley" of 1 Chron 16:7–36.

143. Among the evidences cited by Michael Goulder: "Joseph" as a designation for the people of Israel comes up in Pss 77, 80, and 81 but nowhere else in the Psalter; the divine epithets *'Elohim*, *'El*, and *'Elyon* are more frequent in this collection than elsewhere in the Psalter; language and imagery for God's covenant with Israel are featured. See Goulder, "Asaph's *History of Israel* (Elohist Press, Bethel, 725 BCE)," *Journal for the Study of the Old Testament* 65 (1995): 71–81. Goulder argues that the historical representations reflected in the Asaph psalms constitute strong evidence of the Elohist "source" for Pentateuchal traditions in Exodus, Numbers, and Deuteronomy. See on thematic cohesion among small Psalms collections Walter J. Houston, "David, Asaph, and the Mighty Works of God: Theme and Genre in the Psalm Collections," *Journal for the Study of the Old Testament* 68 (1995): 93–111. Houston underlines the strong communal character of the Psalms of Asaph.

144. Boadt, "The Use of 'Panels,'" 548.

145. Brueggemann and Miller, "Psalm 73 as a Canonical Marker," 56.

6. Conclusion

1. Webb, "Theological Reflections on the Hyperbolic Imagination," 281.

2. The list of prize-winning titles appears in an essay by Ben Schott, "The Bibliognost's Handbook," in the *New York Times Book Review*, December 7, 2006, 87. Online reviews at the site of the Internet vendor Amazon.com show that these books may be taken seriously or viewed ironically depending on the temperament of the reader. Of *The Joy of Chickens*, a serious reviewer offered this encomium: "Over 2 dozen varieties of chickens described and illustrated, including a frizzle,

a silkie, a chicken with a 30 ft. tail, and one with no tail at all. Chickens with top-knots, stripes, and spots. A dazzling array of chickens with histories dating back over thousands of years." But for *How to Avoid Huge Ships,* most of the eight reviewers had ironic comments such as the following: "This book lacks criteria for discerning between huge ships and merely really big ships. Some well-designed lists, charts or colorful pop-up sections would have been nice for readers who were unsure what size of ship they were avoiding," and, "I never leave the house without this indispensible [*sic*] little book. It has literally saved my life many times while walking down Peckham High Street and Ealing Broadway."

3. David Quammen, "A Drink of Death," review of Steven Johnson, *The Ghost Map: The Story of London's Most Terrifying Epidemic—and How It Changed Science, Cities, and the Modern World* (London: Riverhead, 2006), in the *New York Times Book Review,* November 12, 2006, 16.

4. Ze'ev Weisman, *Political Satire in the Bible* (Atlanta, Ga.: Scholars Press, 1998).

5. Deeanne Westbrook, "Paradise and Paradox," in *Mappings of the Biblical Terrain: The Bible as Text,* ed. Vincent L. Tollers and John Maier, 121–33 (Lewisburg, Pa.: Bucknell University Press, 1990), 123–24.

6. Jemielity, *Satire and the Hebrew Prophets,* 61 and 111.

7. Holland, *Divine Irony,* 74.

8. Levine, *Numbers 21–36,* 226. Weisman has an entire chapter on ironic and satirical elements in biblical appellations (*Political Satire in the Bible,* 9–23). He discusses the use of animal images in human names as a means of communicating opprobrium, the formulation of names as satirical political comments (such as the name of King Cushan-rishathaim—Weisman translates as "twofold evil"; others have suggested "double trouble"—in Judges 3), pejorative derivations of names (Nabal in 1 Samuel 25 means "fool," Gaal in Judges 9 means "beetle"), and the use of double entendre in naming.

9. Camp, *Wise, Strange and Holy,* 141–42. The work to which she refers in the quotation is Howard Eilberg-Schwartz's *The Savage in Judaism: An Anthropology of Israelite Religion and Ancient Judaism* (Bloomington: Indiana University Press, 1990).

10. Brueggemann, *Solomon,* 51.

11. Ibid., 62.

12. Shimon Bar-Efrat, *Narrative Art in the Bible* (Sheffield, UK: Almond, 1989), 126–27.

13. See ibid., 127–29.

14. See Christine Mitchell, "The Ironic Death of Josiah in 2 Chronicles," *Catholic Biblical Quarterly* 68 (2006): 421–35. Josiah survives his wounds until he reaches Jerusalem in 2 Chron 35:24; in 2 Kgs 23:29–30, the king is already dead at Megiddo.

15. Francis Landy, "The Song of Songs" (pp. 305–19 in *The Literary Guide to the Bible,* ed. Robert Alter and Frank Kermode; Cambridge: Belknap, 1987), 316.

16. Landy, "Song of Songs," 318.

17. A. R. Pete Diamond, "Deceiving Hope: The Ironies of Metaphorical Beauty and Ideological Terror in Jeremiah," *Scandinavian Journal of the Old Testament* 17 (2003): 34–48.

18. In Diamond's words, "The composition exploits traditions about the prophetic mission between the deportations and within a splintered 'Israel' as the place to anchor hope for its restoration subtext. Here one must ask for whom is the prophet instructed to write (30.2)!" (ibid., 40).

19. Ibid., 39.

20. Ibid., 42.

21. Ibid., 45–46.

22. Here may be spotted a difference of degree between irony and satire. Satire's main purpose is to mock, to render untenable something that is inadequate. As Feinberg has it, "Satire entertains—that is its basic appeal. Its business, as [H. L.] Mencken says, is diagnostic, not therapeutic. It is not responsible for alternatives, nor should it be" (*Introduction to Satire,* 273). Irony has those diagnostic and deconstructive purposes at heart as well, but sheer mockery and parody per se are usually not the ultimate goal of irony. Rather, because irony operates in the space created by the interaction between the said and the unsaid, it characteristically impels the audience to help create the new understanding that is (being portrayed as) better than what was being ironized.

23. Geller, *Sacred Enigmas,* 136–37.

24. Brueggemann, *Solomon,* 243.

25. Jerry Camery-Hoggatt, *Irony in Mark's Gospel: Text and Subtext* (Cambridge, Mass.: Cambridge University Press, 1992), 32–33.

26. Webb, "Theological Reflections on the Hyperbolic Imagination," 282.

BIBLIOGRAPHY

Ackerman, James S. "Numbers." In *The Literary Guide to the Bible,* ed. Robert Alter and Frank Kermode, 78–91. Cambridge, Mass.: Belknap, 1987.

———. "Satire and Symbolism in the Book of Jonah." In *Traditions in Transformation: Turning Points in Biblical Faith,* ed. Baruch Halpern and Jon Levenson, 213–46. Winona Lake, Ind.: Eisenbrauns, 1981.

Ackerman, Susan. *Warrior, Dancer, Seductress, Queen: Women in Judges and Biblical Israel.* New York: Doubleday, 1998.

Adam, A. K. M. *What Is Postmodern Biblical Criticism?* Minneapolis, Minn.: Fortress, 1995.

Aichele, George. *The Control of Biblical Meaning: Canon as Semiotic Mechanism.* Harrisburg, Pa.: Trinity Press International, 2001.

———. *Sign, Text, Scripture: Semiotics and the Bible.* Sheffield, UK: Sheffield Academic Press, 1997.

Albright, William. "The Oracles of Balaam." *Journal of Biblical Literature* 63 (1944): 207–33.

Allen, Leslie C. "Psalm 73: An Analysis." *Tyndale Bulletin* 33 (1982): 93–118.

———. "Psalm 73: Pilgrimage from Doubt to Faith." *Bulletin for Biblical Research* 7 (1997): 1–10.

Alter, Robert. "Anteriority, Authority, and Secrecy: A General Comment." *Semeia* 43 (1988): 155–67.

———. *The Art of Biblical Narrative.* New York: Basic Books, 1981.

———. *The Art of Biblical Poetry.* New York: Basic Books, 1985.

———. "Biblical Imperatives and Literary Play." In *"Not in Heaven": Coherence and Complexity in Biblical Narrative,* ed. Jason P. Rosenblatt and Joseph C. Sitterson Jr., 13–27. Bloomington: Indiana University Press, 1991.

———. *The Pleasures of Reading in an Ideological Age.* New York: Simon and Schuster, 1989.

Amit, Yairah. "Literature in the Service of Politics: Studies in Judges 19–21." In *Politics and Theopolitics in the Bible and Postbiblical Literature,* ed. Henning Graf Reventlow, Yair Hoffman, and Benjamin Uffenheimer, 28–40. Journal for the Study of the Old Testament Supplement Series 171. Sheffield, UK: Sheffield Academic Press, 1994.

Andersen, Francis I., and David Noel Freedman. *Amos.* Anchor Bible 24A. New York: Doubleday, 1989.

———. *Hosea.* Anchor Bible 24. New York: Doubleday, 1980.

———. *Micah.* Anchor Bible 24E. New York: Doubleday, 2000.

Anderson, Gary. "Celibacy or Consummation in the Garden? Reflections on Early Jewish and Christian Interpretations of the Garden of Eden." *Harvard Theological Review* 82 (1989): 121–48.

Arnold, Bill T. "Wordplay and Narrative Technique in Daniel 5 and 6." *Journal of Biblical Literature* 112 (1993): 479–85.

Asbury, Herbert. *Carry Nation.* New York: Knopf, 1929.

Auerbach, Erich. *Mimesis: The Representation of Reality in Western Literature.* Trans. Willard R. Trask. Princeton, N.J.: Princeton University Press, 1953; reprint, 1968.

Avram, Wesley D. *Where the Light Shines Through: Discerning God in Everyday Life.* Grand Rapids, Mich.: Brazos, 2005.

Bach, Alice. *Women, Seduction, and Betrayal in Biblical Narrative.* Cambridge: Cambridge University Press, 1997.

Backhaus, Franz Josef. "Kohelet und die Ironie: Vom Umgang mit Widersprüchen durch die Kunst der Ironie." *Biblische Notizen* 101 (2000): 29–55.

Bahti, Timothy. "Ambiguity and Indeterminacy: The Juncture." *Comparative Literature* 38 (1986): 209–23.

Bal, Mieke. "Dealing/With/Women: Daughters in the Book of Judges." In *The Book and the Text: The Bible and Literary Theory,* ed. Regina M. Schwartz, 16–39. Oxford: Basil Blackwell, 1990.

———. *Death and Dissymmetry: The Politics of Coherence in the Book of Judges.* Chicago: University of Chicago Press, 1988.

———. "Lots of Writing." In *Ruth and Esther: A Feminist Companion to the Bible* (second series), ed. Athalya Brenner, 212–38. Sheffield, UK: Sheffield Academic Press, 1999.

———. "Metaphors He Lives By." *Semeia* 61 (1993): 185–207.

———. *Murder and Difference: Gender, Genre, and Scholarship on Sisera's Death.* Trans. Matthew Gumpert. Bloomington: Indiana University Press, 1988.

Balz-Cochois, Helgard. *Gomer: Der Höhenkult Israels im Selbstverständnis der Volksfrömmigkeit: Untersuchungen zu Hosea 4, 1–5, 7.* Frankfurt: Lang, 1982.

———. "Gomer oder die Macht der Astarte: Versuch einer feministischen Interpretation von Hos 1–4." *Evangelische Theologie* 42 (1982): 37–65.

Bar-Efrat, Shimon. *Narrative Art in the Bible.* Sheffield, UK: Almond, 1989. First published in Hebrew by Sifriat Poalim (Tel Aviv), 1979.

Barré, Michael L. "The Portrait of Balaam in Numbers 22–24." *Interpretation* 51 (1997): 254–66.

Barthes, Roland. *The Semiotic Challenge.* Trans. Richard Howard from *L'aventure sémiologique* (Éditions du Seuil, 1985). New York: Hill and Wang, 1988.

———. *S/Z.* Trans. Richard Miller. New York: Hill and Wang, 1974.

Barton, John. *Amos's Oracles against the Nations.* Cambridge: Cambridge University, 1980.

Baskin, Judith R. *Pharaoh's Counsellors: Job, Jethro, and Balaam in Rabbinic and Patristic Tradition.* Chico, Calif.: Scholars Press, 1983.

Bauckham, Richard. "The Book of Ruth and the Possibility of a Feminist Canonical Hermeneutic." *Biblical Interpretation* 5 (1997): 29–45.

Bauman, Zygmunt. *Postmodern Ethics.* Oxford: Blackwell, 1993.

Beal, Timothy K. *The Book of Hiding: Gender, Ethnicity, Annihilation, and Esther.* London: Routledge, 1997.

———. "C(ha)osmopolis: Qohelet's Last Words." In *God in the Fray: A Tribute to Walter Brueggemann,* ed. Tod Linafelt and Timothy K. Beal, 290–304. Minneapolis, Minn.: Fortress, 1998.

———. *Esther.* Berit Olam. Collegeville, Minn.: Liturgical Press, 1999.

———. "Ideology and Intertextuality: Surplus of Meaning and Controlling the Means of Production." In *Reading Between Texts: Intertextuality and the Hebrew Bible,* ed. Danna Nolan Fewell, 27–39. Louisville, Ky.: Westminster/John Knox, 1992.

———. "Tracing Esther's Beginnings." In *A Feminist Companion to Esther, Judith, and Susanna,* ed. Athalya Brenner, 87–110. Sheffield, UK: Sheffield Academic Press, 1995.

Bechtel, Lyn M. "Shame as a Sanction of Social Control in Biblical Israel: Judicial, Political, and Social Shaming." *Journal for the Study of the Old Testament* 49 (1991): 47–76.

———. "What if Dinah Is Not Raped?" *Journal for the Study of the Old Testament* 62 (1994): 19–36.

Beecher, Catharine E. *Miss Beecher's Domestic Receipt Book, Designed as a Supplement to Her Treatise on Domestic Economy.* New York: Harper and Brothers, 1857.

Beecher, Catharine E., and Harriet Beecher Stowe. *The American Woman's Home.* Ed. and with introduction by Nicole Tonkovich. Reprint, New Brunswick, N.J.: Rutgers University Press, 2002. Orig. published in 1869.

Beek, M. A. "Rahab in the Light of Jewish Exegesis." In *Von Kanaan bis Kerala: Festschrift für Prof. Mag. Dr. Dr. J. P. M. van der Ploeg O.P. zur Vollendung des siebzigsten Lebensjahres am 4. Juli 1979,* ed. W. C. Delsman et al., 37–44. Neukirchen-Vluyn, Germany: Neukirchener/Kevalaer: Verlag Butzon and Bercker, 1982.

Ben Zvi, Ehud. *Micah.* Forms of Old Testament Literature 21B. Grand Rapids, Mich.: Eerdmans, 2000.

Bergant, Dianne. *Israel's Wisdom Literature: A Liberation-Critical Reading.* Minneapolis, Minn.: Fortress, 1997.

Berger, Benjamin Lyle. "Qohelet and the Exigencies of the Absurd." *Biblical Interpretation* 9 (2001): 141–79.

Berlin, Adele. "The Role of the Text in the Reading Process." *Semeia* 62 (1993): 143–47.

Berman, Joshua A. "*Hadassah bat Abihail:* The Evolution from Object to Subject in the Character of Esther." *Journal of Biblical Literature* 120 (2001): 647–69.

Berquist, Jon L. *Controlling Corporeality: The Body and the Household in Ancient Israel.* New Brunswick, N.J.: Rutgers University Press, 2002.

———. "Dangerous Waters of Justice and Righteousness: Amos 5:18–27." *Biblical Theology Bulletin* 23 (1993): 54–63.

———. "Role Dedifferentiation in the Book of Ruth." *Journal for the Study of the Old Testament* 57 (1993): 23–37. Reprinted in *Social Scientific Old Testament Criticism,* ed. David J. Chalcraft, 358–71. Sheffield, UK: Sheffield Academic Press, 1997.

Bhabha, Homi K. *The Location of Culture.* London: Routledge, 1994.

———. "Representation and the Colonial Text: A Critical Exploration of Some Forms of Mimeticism." In *The Theory of Reading,* ed. Frank Gloversmith, 93–122. Sussex, UK: Harvester, 1984.

Biddle, Mark E. "The 'Endangered Ancestress' and Blessing for the Nations." *Journal of Biblical Literature* 109 (1990): 599–611.

Bird, Phyllis A. "The Harlot as Heroine: Narrative Art and Social Presupposition in Three Old Testament Texts." *Semeia* 46 (1989): 119–39.

———. "'To Play the Harlot': An Inquiry into an Old Testament Metaphor." In *Gender and Difference in Ancient Israel,* ed. Peggy L. Day, 75–94. Minneapolis, Minn.: Fortress, 1989.

Bishop, Elizabeth. *The Complete Poems, 1929–1979.* New York: Farrar Straus Giroux, 1983.

Black, Jeremy, and Anthony Green. *Gods, Demons and Symbols of Ancient Mesopotamia: An Illustrated Dictionary.* Austin: University of Texas Press, 1992.

Bledstein, Adrien Janis. "Is Judges a Woman's Satire of Men Who Play God?" In *A Feminist Companion to Judges,* ed. Athalya Brenner, 34–54. Sheffield, UK: JSOT Press, 1993.

Blenkinsopp, Joseph. "Ecclesiastes 3.1–15: Another Interpretation." *Journal for the Study of the Old Testament* 66 (1995): 55–64.

Block, Daniel I. *Judges, Ruth.* New American Commentary 6. Nashville, Tenn.: Broadman and Holman, 2002.

Bloomquist, L. Gregory. "The Role of the Audience in the Determination of Argumentation: The Gospel of Luke and the Acts of the Apostles." In *Rhetorical Argumentation in Biblical Texts,* ed. Anders Eriksson, Thomas H. Olbricht, and Walter Übelacker, 157–73. Emory Studies in Early Christianity 8. Harrisburg, Pa.: Trinity Press International, 2002.

Blum, Erhard. "The Literary Connection between the Books of Genesis and Exodus and the End of the Book of Joshua." In *A Farewell to the Yahwist? The Composition of the Pentateuch in Recent European Interpretation,* ed. Thomas B. Dozeman and Konrad Schmid, 89–106. Leiden, Neth.: Brill, 2006.

Boadt, Lawrence. "The Use of 'Panels' in the Structure of Psalms 73–78." *Catholic Biblical Quarterly* 66 (2004): 533–50.

Boer, Roland. *Marxist Criticism of the Bible.* London: T & T Clark, 2003.

Bolin, Thomas M. *Freedom beyond Forgiveness: The Book of Jonah Re-Examined.* Journal for the Study of the Old Testament Supplement Series 236/ Copenhagen International Seminar 3. Sheffield, UK: Sheffield Academic Press, 1997.

———. "'Should I Not Also Pity Nineveh?' Divine Freedom in the Book of Jonah." *Journal for the Study of the Old Testament* 67 (1995): 109–20.

Booth, Wayne C. *A Rhetoric of Irony.* Chicago: University of Chicago Press, 1974.

Bos, Johanna W. H. "Out of the Shadows: Genesis 38; Judges 4:17–22; Ruth 3." *Semeia* 42 (1988): 37–67.

Bowie, Malcolm. Review of *The Book of Lieder: The Original Text of Over 1000 Songs* by Richard Stokes (Faber and Faber, 2005). *Times Literary Supplement,* December 1, 2006, 3–4.

Bowman, Richard G., and Richard W. Swanson. "Samson and the Son of God or Dead Heroes and Dead Goats: Ethical Readings of Narrative Violence in Judges and Matthew." *Semeia* 77 (1997): 59–73.

Brenneman, James E. *Canons in Conflict: Negotiating Texts in True and False Prophecy.* New York: Oxford University Press, 1997.

Brenner, Athalya. "Afterword." In *A Feminist Companion to Judges,* ed. Athalya Brenner, 231–35. Sheffield, UK: JSOT Press, 1993.

———. *I Am . . . Biblical Women Tell Their Own Stories.* Minneapolis, Minn.: Fortress, 2005.

———. *The Intercourse of Knowledge: On Gendering Desire and "Sexuality" in the Hebrew Bible.* Biblical Interpretation 26. Leiden, Neth.: Brill, 1997.

———. "Job the Pious? The Characterization of Job in the Narrative Framework of the Book." *Journal for the Study of the Old Testament* 43 (1989): 37–52. Reprinted in *The Poetical Books,* ed. David J. A. Clines, 298–313. Sheffield, UK: Sheffield Academic Press, 1997.

———. "Jonah's Poem Out of and Within Its Context." In *Among the Prophets: Language, Image and Structure in the Prophetic Writings,* ed. Philip R. Davies and David J. A. Clines, 183–92. Journal for the Study of the Old Testament Supplement Series 144. Sheffield, UK: Sheffield Academic Press, 1993.

———. "Looking at Esther through the Looking Glass." In *A Feminist Companion to Esther, Judith, and Susanna,* ed. Athalya Brenner, 71–80. Sheffield, UK: Sheffield Academic Press, 1995.

———. "On 'Jeremiah' and the Poetics of (Prophetic) Pornography." In *On Gendering Texts: Female and Male Voices in the Hebrew Bible,* ed. Athalya Brenner and Fokkelien van Dijk-Hemmes, 177–93. Leiden, Neth.: Brill, 1993.

———. "Pornoprophetics Revisited: Some Additional Reflections." *Journal for the Study of the Old Testament* 70 (1996): 63–86.

———. "Who's Afraid of Feminist Criticism? Who's Afraid of Biblical Humour? The Case of the Obtuse Foreign Ruler in the Hebrew Bible." *Journal for the Study of the Old Testament* 63 (1994): 38–55.

Brenner, Athalya, and Yehuda T. Radday, eds. *On Humour and the Comic in the Hebrew Bible.* Journal for the Study of the Old Testament Supplement Series 92. Sheffield, UK: Almond, 1990.

Brett, Mark G. "Reading the Bible in the Context of Methodological Pluralism: The Undermining of Ethnic Exclusivism in Genesis." In *Rethinking Contexts, Rereading Texts: Contributions from the Social Sciences to Biblical Interpretation,* ed. M. Daniel Carroll R., 48–74. Journal for the Study of the Old Testament Supplement Series 299. Sheffield, UK: Sheffield Academic Press, 2000.

Brettler, Marc Zvi. *The Book of Judges.* Old Testament Readings. London: Routledge, 2001.

Brin, Gershon. "Micah 2,12–13: A Textual and Ideological Study." *Zeitschrift für die Alttestamentliche Wissenschaft* 101 (1989): 118–24.

Brisman, Leslie. "Unequal Affliction: The Scroll of Esther." *Conservative Judaism* 52 (2000): 3–13.

Britt, Brian. "Death, Social Conflict, and the Barley Harvest in the Hebrew Bible." *Journal of Hebrew Scriptures* 5 (2005): 1–29.

Bronner, Leila Leah. "Esther Revisited: An Aggadic Approach." In *A Feminist Companion to Esther, Judith, and Susanna,* ed. Athalya Brenner, 176–97. Sheffield, UK: Sheffield Academic Press, 1995.

Brooke-Rose, Christine. "Whatever Happened to Narratology?" *Poetics Today* 11 (1990): 283–93.

Brown, Raymond E. *The Churches the Apostles Left Behind.* New York: Paulist, 1984.

Brown, Scott G. "Mark 11:1–12:12: A Triple Intercalation?" *Catholic Biblical Quarterly* 64 (2002): 78–89.

Brown, William P. *Seeing the Psalms: A Theology of Metaphor.* Louisville, Ky.: Westminster John Knox, 2002.

Brueggemann, Walter. "Biblical Theology Appropriately Postmodern." In *Jews, Christians, and the Theology of the Hebrew Scriptures,* ed. Alice Ogden Bellis and Joel S. Kaminsky, 97–108. SBL Symposium Series 8. Atlanta, Ga.: Society of Biblical Literature, 2000.

———. "Bounded by Obedience and Praise: The Psalms as Canon." *Journal for the Study of the Old Testament* 50 (1991): 63–92.

———. *David's Truth in Israel's Imagination and Memory.* Minneapolis, Minn.: Fortress, 1985.

———. *Solomon: Israel's Ironic Icon of Human Achievement.* Columbia: University of South Carolina Press, 2005.

———. *Texts That Linger, Words That Explode: Listening to Prophetic Voices.* Minneapolis, Minn.: Fortress, 2000.

———. *Texts under Negotiation: The Bible and Postmodern Imagination.* Minneapolis, Minn.: Fortress, 1993.

———. "'Until' . . . Endlessly Enacted, Now Urgent." *Journal for Preachers* 27 (2003): 16–21.

Brueggemann, Walter, and Patrick D. Miller. "Psalm 73 as a Canonical Marker." *Journal for the Study of the Old Testament* 72 (1996): 45–56.

Brummitt, Mark. "Of Secretaries, Secrets, and Scrolls: Jeremiah 36 and the Irritating Word of God." In *Derrida's Bible (Reading a Page of Scripture with a Little*

Help from Derrida), ed. Yvonne Sherwood, 39–48. New York: Palgrave Macmillan, 2004.

Buber, Martin. "The Heart Determines: Psalm 73." Reprinted in *Theodicy in the Old Testament*, ed. James L. Crenshaw, 109–18. Philadelphia: Fortress, 1983. Orig. English version in Martin Buber, *On the Bible: Eighteen Studies*. Ed. Nahum N. Glatzer, 199–210. New York: Schocken, 1968.

Burnette-Bletsch, Rhonda. "At the Hands of a Woman: Rewriting Jael in Pseudo-Philo." *Journal for the Study of the Pseudepigrapha* 17 (1998): 53–64.

Busch, Austin. "Questioning and Conviction: Double-Voiced Discourse in Mark 3:22–30." *Journal of Biblical Literature* 125 (2006): 477–505.

Butler, Judith. Editor's Introduction in Linda Singer, *Erotic Welfare: Sexual Theory and Politics in the Age of Epidemic*. New York: Routledge, 1993.

Buttigieg, Joseph A. "The Interest of Irony." *Notre Dame English Journal* 15 (1983): 29–47.

Butting, Klara. "Esther: A New Interpretation of the Joseph Story in the Fight against Anti-Semitism and Sexism." In *Ruth and Esther: A Feminist Companion to the Bible* (second series), ed. Athalya Brenner, 239–48. Sheffield, UK: Sheffield Academic Press, 1999.

Caird, George Bradford. *The Language and Imagery of the Bible*. Philadelphia: Westminster, 1980.

Camery-Hoggatt, Jerry. *Irony in Mark's Gospel: Text and Subtext*. Society for New Testament Studies Monograph Series 72. Cambridge: Cambridge University Press, 1992.

Camp, Claudia V. *Wise, Strange and Holy: The Strange Woman and the Making of the Bible*. Journal for the Study of the Old Testament Supplement Series 320/Gender, Culture, Theory 9. Sheffield, UK: Sheffield Academic Press, 2000.

Caputo, John D. *More Radical Hermeneutics: On Not Knowing Who We Are*. Bloomington: Indiana University Press, 2000.

———. *The Weakness of God: A Theology of the Event*. Indiana Series in the Philosophy of Religion. Bloomington: Indiana University Press, 2006.

Carasik, Michael. "Transcending the Boundary of Death: Ecclesiastes through a Nabokovian Lens." *Biblical Interpretation* 14 (2006): 425–43.

Carr, David M. "Genesis in Relation to the Moses Story: Diachronic and Synchronic Perspectives." In *Studies in the Book of Genesis: Literature, Redaction and History*, ed. André Wénin, 273–95. Bibliotheca ephemeridum theologicarum lovaniensium 155. Leuven, Belgium: Leuven University Press; Sterling, Va.: Peeters, 2001.

———. "The Politics of Textual Subversion: A Diachronic Perspective on the Garden of Eden Story." *Journal of Biblical Literature* 112 (1993): 577–95.

———. *Reading the Fractures of Genesis: Historical and Literary Approaches*. Louisville, Ky.: Westminster John Knox: 1996.

———. "What Is Required to Identify Pre-Priestly Narrative Connections between Genesis and Exodus? Some General Reflections and Specific Cases." In *A Farewell to the Yahwist? The Composition of the Pentateuch in Recent European Interpretation*, ed. Thomas B. Dozeman and Konrad Schmid, 159–80. Leiden, Neth.: Brill, 2006.

Carroll, Robert P. "Desire under the Terebinths: On Pornographic Representation in the Prophets—A Response." In *A Feminist Companion to the Latter Prophets*, ed. Athalya Brenner, 275–307. Sheffield, UK: Sheffield Academic Press, 1995.

———. "Whorusalamin: A Tale of Three Cities as Three Sisters." In *On Reading Prophetic Texts: Gender-Specific and Related Studies in Memory of Fokkelien van Dijk-Hemmes*, ed. Bob Becking and Meindert Dijkstra, 67–82. Leiden, Neth.: Brill, 1996.

Carroll R., M. Daniel. "The Prophetic Text and the Literature of Dissent in Latin America: Amos, García Márquez, and Cabrera Infante Dismantle Militarism." *Biblical Interpretation* 4 (1996): 76–100.

Cathcart, Kevin J. "Numbers 24:17 in Ancient Translations and Interpretations." In *The Interpretation of the Bible: The International Symposium in Slovenia,* ed. Jože Krašovec, 511–20. Journal for the Study of the Old Testament Supplement Series 289. Sheffield, UK: Sheffield Academic Press, 1998.

Christianson, Eric S. *A Time to Tell: Narrative Strategies in Ecclesiastes.* Journal for the Study of the Old Testament Supplement Series 280. Sheffield, UK: Sheffield Academic Press, 1998.

Clifford, Richard J. "Genesis 38: Its Contribution to the Jacob Story." *Catholic Biblical Quarterly* 66 (2004): 519–32.

Clines, David J. A. "The Ancestor in Danger: But Not the Same Danger." In *What Does Eve Do to Help? And Other Readerly Questions in the Old Testament,* 67–84. Journal for the Study of the Old Testament Supplement Series 94. Sheffield, UK: JSOT Press, 1990.

———. "Deconstructing the Book of Job." In *What Does Eve Do to Help? And Other Readerly Questions in the Old Testament,* 106–23. Journal for the Study of the Old Testament Supplement Series 94. Sheffield, UK: JSOT Press, 1990.

———. *The Esther Scroll: The Story of the Story.* Journal for the Study of the Old Testament Supplement Series 30. Sheffield, UK: JSOT Press, 1984.

———. "The Postmodern Adventure in Biblical Studies." In *Auguries: The Jubilee Volume of the Sheffield Department of Biblical Studies,* ed. David J. A. Clines and Stephen D. Moore, 276–91. Journal for the Study of the Old Testament Supplement Series 269. Sheffield, UK: Sheffield Academic Press, 1998.

———. "Reading Esther From Left to Right: Contemporary Strategies for Reading a Biblical Text." In *The Bible in Three Dimensions: Essays in Celebration of Forty Years of Biblical Studies in the University of Sheffield,* ed. David J. A. Clines, Stephen E. Fowl, and Stanley E. Porter, 31–52. Journal for the Study of the Old Testament Supplement Series 87. Sheffield, UK: Sheffield Academic Press, 1990.

Cohen, Ted. "Metaphor and the Cultivation of Intimacy." In *On Metaphor,* ed. Sheldon Sacks, 1–10. Chicago: University of Chicago Press, 1978.

Colebrook, Claire. *Irony.* The New Critical Idiom. New York: Routledge, 2004.

Collins, John J. *The Bible after Babel: Historical Criticism in a Postmodern Age.* Grand Rapids, Mich.: Eerdmans, 2005.

———. *Daniel: A Commentary on the Book of Daniel.* Hermeneia. Minneapolis, Minn.: Fortress, 1993.

Cooper, Alan. "In Praise of Divine Caprice: The Significance of the Book of Jonah." In *Among the Prophets: Language, Image and Structure in the Prophetic Writings,* ed. Philip R. Davies and David J. A. Clines, 144–63. Journal for the Study of the Old Testament Supplement Series 144. Sheffield, UK: JSOT Press, 1993.

———. "The Meaning of Amos's Third Vision (Amos 7:7–9)." In *Tehillah le-Moshe: Biblical and Judaic Studies in Honor of Moshe Greenberg,* ed. Mordechai Cogan, Barry L. Eichler, and Jeffrey H. Tigay, 13–21. Winona Lake, Ind.: Eisenbrauns, 1997.

Cooper, Richard. "Textualizing Determinacy/Determining Textuality." *Semeia* 62 (1993): 3–18.

Cosgrove, Charles H. "Toward a Postmodern *Hermeneutica Sacra:* Guiding Considerations in Choosing between Competing Plausible Interpretations of Scripture." In *The Meanings We Choose: Hermeneutical Ethics, Indeterminacy and the Conflict of Interpretations,* ed. Charles H. Cosgrove, 39–61. New York: T & T Clark, 2004.

Craig, Kenneth M., Jr. "Jonah in Recent Research." *Critical Review: Biblical Studies* 7 (1999): 97–118.

———. *A Poetics of Jonah: Art in the Service of Ideology.* Columbia: University of South Carolina Press, 1993.

———. *Reading Esther: A Case for the Literary Carnivalesque.* Louisville, Ky.: Westminster John Knox, 1995.

Craig, Kenneth M., Cynthia L. Miller, and Raymond F. Person. "Conversation Analysis and the Book of Jonah: A Conversation." *Journal of Hebrew Scriptures* (1997). http://www.arts.ualberta.ca/JHS/Articles/article2.htm.

Creach, Jerome F. D. *Joshua.* Louisville, Ky.: John Knox, 2003.

Crenshaw, James L. *Ecclesiastes.* Old Testament Library. Philadelphia: Westminster, 1987.

———. *Old Testament Wisdom: An Introduction.* Rev. and enlarged ed. Louisville, Ky.: Westminster John Knox, 1998.

———. "Qoheleth's Understanding of Intellectual Inquiry." In *Qohelet in the Context of Wisdom,* ed. A. Schoors, 205–24. Leuven, Belgium: Leuven University Press, 1998.

———. "Standing Near the Flame: Psalm 73." In *The Psalms: An Introduction,* 109–27. Grand Rapids, Mich.: Eerdmans, 2001.

Crook, Zeba A. "Methods and Models in New Testament Interpretation: A Critical Engagement with Louise Lawrence's Literary Ethnography." *Religious Studies Review* 32 (2006): 87–97.

Cross, Andrew. "Neither Either Nor Or: The Perils of Reflexive Irony." In *The Cambridge Companion to Kierkegaard,* ed. Alastair Hannay and Gordon D. Marino, 125–53. Cambridge: Cambridge University Press, 1998.

Cross, Frank Moore. "A Response to Zakovitch's 'Successful Failure of Israelite Intelligence.'" In *Text and Tradition: The Hebrew Bible and Folklore,* ed. Susan Niditch, 99–104. Atlanta, Ga.: Scholars Press, 1990.

Crouch, Walter B. "To Question an End, To End a Question: Opening the Closure of the Book of Jonah." *Journal for the Study of the Old Testament* 62 (1994): 101–12.

Crüsemann, Frank. "The Unchangeable World: The 'Crisis of Wisdom' in Koheleth." In *God of the Lowly: Socio-Historical Interpretations of the Bible,* ed. Willy Schottroff and Wolfgang Stegemann, trans. Matthew J. O'Connell, 57–77. Maryknoll, N.Y.: Orbis, 1984. Orig. German edition, 1979.

Culler, Jonathan. "The Literary in Theory." In *What's Left of Theory? New Work on the Politics of Literary Theory,* ed. Judith Butler, John Guillory, and Kendall Thomas, 273–92. New York: Routledge, 2000.

———. *On Deconstruction: Theory and Criticism after Structuralism.* Ithaca, N.Y.: Cornell University Press, 1982.

Dahood, Mitchell. *Psalms II: 51–100.* Anchor Bible 17. Garden City, N.Y.: Doubleday, 1968.

Dane, Joseph A. *The Critical Mythology of Irony.* Athens: University of Georgia Press, 1991.

Davies, Eryl W. *The Dissenting Reader: Feminist Approaches to the Hebrew Bible.* Burlington, Vt.: Ashgate, 2003.

Day, John. "Problems in the Interpretation of the Book of Jonah." In *In Quest of the Past: Studies on Israelite Religion, Literature and Prophetism,* ed. A. S. van der Woude, 32–47. Leiden, Neth.: Brill, 1990.

De Man, Paul. "The Concept of Irony." Lecture given at Ohio State University, 1977. Transcribed in *Aesthetic Ideology,* ed. with introd. by Andrzej Warminski, 163–84. Theory and History of Literature 65. Minneapolis: University of Minnesota Press, 1996.

———. "The Rhetoric of Temporality." In *Interpretation: Theory and Practice,* ed. Charles S. Singleton, 173–209. Baltimore: Johns Hopkins, 1969.

De Pury, Alfred. "The Jacob Story and the Beginning of the Formation of the Pentateuch." In *A Farewell to the Yahwist? The Composition of the Pentateuch in Recent European Interpretation,* ed. Thomas B. Dozeman and Konrad Schmid, 51–72. Leiden, Neth.: Brill, 2006.

Dell, Katharine J. "The Misuse of Forms in Amos." *Vetus Testamentum* 45 (1995): 45–61.

Diamant, Anita. *The Red Tent.* New York: Picador, 1997.

Diamond, A. R. Pete. "Deceiving Hope: The Ironies of Metaphorical Beauty and Ideological Terror in Jeremiah." *Scandinavian Journal of the Old Testament* 17 (2003): 34–48.

Dobbs-Allsopp, F. W. "Rethinking Historical Criticism." *Biblical Interpretation* 7 (1999): 235–71.

Dokka, Trond Skard. "Irony and Sectarianism in the Gospel of John." In *New Readings in John: Literary and Theological Perspectives. Essays from the Scandinavian Conference on the Fourth Gospel, Århus 1997,* ed. Johannes Nissen and Sigfred Pedersen, 83–107. Journal for the Study of the New Testament Supplement Series 182. Sheffield, UK: Sheffield Academic Press, 1999.

Donaldson, Laura E. "The Sign of Orpah: Reading Ruth through Native Eyes." In *Ruth and Esther: A Feminist Companion to the Bible* (second series), ed. Athalya Brenner, 130–44. Sheffield, UK: Sheffield Academic Press, 1999.

Dozeman, Thomas B. "Numbers." In the *New Interpreter's Bible,* 2:3–268. Nashville, Tenn.: Abingdon, 1998.

Dragga, Sam. "Genesis 2–3: A Story of Liberation." *Journal for the Study of the Old Testament* 55 (1992): 3–13.

Duke, Paul D. *Irony in the Fourth Gospel.* Atlanta, Ga.: John Knox, 1985.

Eagleton, Terry. *The Illusions of Postmodernism.* Oxford: Blackwell, 1996.

———. "J. L. Austin and the Book of Jonah." In *The Book and the Text: The Bible and Literary Theory,* ed. Regina M. Schwartz, 231–36. Oxford: Basil Blackwell, 1990.

Ebach, Jürgen. "'Ja, bin denn *ich* an Gottes Stelle?' (Genesis 50:19): Beobachtungen und Überlegungen zu einem Schlüsselsatz der Josefsgeschichte und den vielfachen Konsequenzen aus einer rhetorischen Frage." *Biblical Interpretation* 11 (2003): 602–16.

Eilberg-Schwartz, Howard. *The Savage in Judaism: An Anthropology of Israelite Religion and Ancient Judaism.* Bloomington: Indiana University Press, 1990.

Emerton, J. A. "Judah and Tamar." *Vetus Testamentum* 29 (1979): 403–15.

Eslinger, Lyle. "The Education of Amos." *Hebrew Annual Review* 11 (1987): 35–57.

———. "Inner-Biblical Exegesis and Inner-Biblical Allusion: The Question of Category." *Vetus Testamentum* 42 (1992): 47–58.

Exum, J. Cheryl. "Feminist Criticism: Whose Interests Are Being Served?" In *Judges and Method: New Approaches in Biblical Studies,* ed. Gale A. Yee, 65–90. Minneapolis, Minn.: Fortress, 1995.

———. *Plotted, Shot, and Painted: Cultural Representations of Biblical Women.* Journal for the Study of the Old Testament Supplement Series 215/Gender, Culture, Theory 3. Sheffield, UK: Sheffield Academic Press, 1996.

Fabian, Johannes. "Presence and Representation: The Other and Anthropological Writing." *Critical Inquiry* 16 (1990): 753–72.

Feinberg, Leonard. *Introduction to Satire.* Ames: Iowa State University Press, 1967.

Fernandez, James W. "The Irony of Complicity and the Complicity of Irony in Development Discourse." In *Irony in Action: Anthropology, Practice, and the Moral Imagination,* ed. James W. Fernandez and Mary Taylor Huber, 84–102. Chicago: University of Chicago Press, 2001.

Fernandez, James W., and Mary Taylor Huber. "The Anthropology of Irony." In *Irony in Action: Anthropology, Practice, and the Moral Imagination,* ed. James W. Fernandez and Mary Taylor Huber, 1–37. Chicago: University of Chicago Press, 2001.

Fewell, Danna Nolan. "Building Babel." In *Postmodern Interpretations of the Bible—A Reader,* ed. A. K. M. Adam, 1–15. St. Louis: Chalice, 2001.

———. "Deconstructive Criticism: Achsah and the (E)razed City of Writing." In *Judges and Method: New Approaches in Biblical Studies,* ed. Gale A. Yee, 119–45. Minneapolis, Minn.: Fortress, 1995.

———. "Joshua." In *The Women's Bible Commentary,* ed. Sharon H. Ringe and Carol A. Newsom, 63–66. Louisville, Ky.: Westminster/John Knox, 1992.

Fewell, Danna Nolan and David M. Gunn. "Controlling Perspectives: Women, Men, and the Authority of Violence in Judges 4 and 5." *Journal of the American Academy of Religion* 58 (1990): 389–411.

———. "Shifting the Blame: God in the Garden." In *Reading Bibles, Writing Bodies: Identity and The Book,* ed. Timothy K. Beal and David M. Gunn, 16–33. New York: Routledge, 1997.

———. "Tipping the Balance: Sternberg's Reader and the Rape of Dinah." *Journal of Biblical Literature* 110 (1991): 193–211.

Findlay, L. M. "Paul de Man, Thomas Carlyle, and 'The Rhetoric of Temporality.'" *Dalhousie Review* 65 (1985): 159–81.

Fisch, Harold. *Poetry with a Purpose: Biblical Poetics and Interpretation.* Bloomington: Indiana University Press, 1988.

Fischer, Alexander A. *Skepsis Oder Furcht Gottes? Studien zur Komposition und Theologie des Buches Kohelet.* BZAW 247. Berlin: de Gruyter, 1997.

Fischer, Irmtraud. "The Book of Ruth: A 'Feminist' Commentary to the Torah?" In *Ruth and Esther: A Feminist Companion to the Bible* (second series), ed. Athalya Brenner, 24–49. Sheffield, UK: Sheffield Academic Press, 1999.

Fish, Stanley. *Is There a Text in This Class? The Authority of Interpretive Communities.* Cambridge, Mass.: Harvard University Press, 1980.

———. "Short People Got No Reason to Live: Reading Irony." In *Doing What Comes Naturally: Change, Rhetoric, and the Practice of Theory in Literary and Legal Studies,* 180–96. Durham, N.C.: Duke University Press, 1989.

Fishbane, Michael. "The Book of Job and Inner-Biblical Discourse." In *The Voice from the Whirlwind: Interpreting the Book of Job,* ed. Leo G. Perdue and W. Clark Gilpin, 86–98. Nashville, Tenn.: Abingdon, 1992.

Fishelov, David. "The Prophet as Satirist." *Prooftexts* 9 (1989): 195–211.

Fountain, A. Kay. *Literary and Empirical Readings of the Books of Esther.* Studies in Biblical Literature 43. Frankfurt: Peter Lang, 2002.

Fowler, Robert M. *Let the Reader Understand: Reader-Response Criticism and the Gospel of Mark.* Minneapolis, Minn.: Fortress, 1991.

———. "Who Is 'The Reader' in Reader Response Criticism?" *Semeia* 31 (1985): 5–23. Reprinted in *Beyond Form Criticism: Essays in Old Testament Literary Criticism,* ed. Paul R. House, 376–94. Winona Lake, Ind.: Eisenbrauns, 1992.

Fox, Michael V. *Character and Ideology in the Book of Esther.* 2nd ed. Grand Rapids, Mich.: Eerdmans, 2001.

——. *JPS Torah Commentary: Ecclesiastes.* Philadelphia: Jewish Publication Society, 2004.

——. *Qohelet and His Contradictions.* Bible and Literature Series 18. Sheffield, UK: Almond, 1989.

——. *The Redaction of the Books of Esther: On Reading Composite Texts.* Society of Biblical Literature Monograph Series 40. Atlanta, Ga.: Scholars Press, 1991.

——. *A Time to Tear Down and A Time to Build Up: A Rereading of Ecclesiastes.* Grand Rapids, Mich.: Eerdmans, 1999.

——. "Wisdom in the Joseph Story." *Vetus Testamentum* 51 (2001): 26–41.

Fricke, Donna G. "The A-mazing Mirror of 'Verses on the Death of Dr. Swift'." In *Critical Approaches to Teaching Swift,* ed. Peter J. Schakel, 281–89. New York: AMS Press, 1992.

Frolov, Serge. "Returning the Ticket: God and His Prophet in the Book of Jonah." *Journal for the Study of the Old Testament* 86 (1999): 85–105.

Fry, Paul H. "The Distracted Reader." *Criticism* 32 (1990): 295–308.

Frymer-Kensky, Tikva. "Reading Rahab." In *Tehillah le-Moshe: Biblical and Judaic Studies in Honor of Moshe Greenberg,* ed. Mordechai Cogan, Barry L. Eichler, and Jeffrey H. Tigay, 57–67. Winona Lake, Ind.: Eisenbrauns, 1997.

Fuchs, Esther. *Sexual Politics in the Biblical Narrative: Reading the Hebrew Bible as a Woman.* Journal for the Study of the Old Testament Supplement Series 310. Sheffield, UK: Sheffield Academic Press, 2000.

Furman, Nelly. "His Story Versus Her Story: Male Genealogy and Female Strategy in the Jacob Cycle." *Semeia* 46 (1989): 141–49.

Gans, Eric. *Signs of Paradox: Irony, Resentment, and Other Mimetic Structures.* Stanford, Calif.: Stanford University Press, 1997.

Geeraerts, Dirk. "Caught in a Web of Irony: Job and His Embarrassed God." In *Job 28: Cognition in Context,* ed. Ellen van Wolde, 37–55. Leiden, Neth.: Brill, 2003.

Geller, Stephen A. *Sacred Enigmas: Literary Religion in the Hebrew Bible.* London: Routledge, 1996.

Geoghegan, Jeffrey C. "Israelite Sheepshearing and David's Rise to Power." *Biblica* 87 (2006): 55–63.

Gertz, Jan Christian. "The Transition between the Books of Genesis and Exodus." In *A Farewell to the Yahwist? The Composition of the Pentateuch in Recent European Interpretation,* ed. Thomas B. Dozeman and Konrad Schmid, 73–87. Leiden, Neth.: Brill, 2006.

Gevaryahu, Haim M. I. "Esther Is a Story of Jewish Defense Not a Story of Jewish Revenge." *Jewish Bible Quarterly* 21 (1993): 3–12.

Gillmayr-Bucher, Susanne. "'She Came to Test Him with Hard Questions': Foreign Women and Their View on Israel." *Biblical Interpretation* 15 (2007): 135–50.

Goldman, Stan. "Narrative and Ethical Ironies in Esther." *Journal for the Study of the Old Testament* 47 (1990): 15–31.

Good, Edwin M. *In Turns of Tempest: A Reading of Job.* Stanford, Calif.: Stanford University Press, 1990.

——. *Irony in the Old Testament.* 1st ed., Philadelphia: Westminster, 1965. 2nd ed., Sheffield, UK: Almond, 1981.

Goodhart, Sandor. "Prophecy, Sacrifice and Repentance in the Story of Jonah." *Semeia* 33 (1985): 43–63.

Goulder, Michael D. "Asaph's *History of Israel* (Elohist Press, Bethel, 725 BCE)." *Journal for the Study of the Old Testament* 65 (1995): 71–81.
———. *The Psalms of Asaph and the Pentateuch: Studies in the Psalter, III.* Journal for the Study of the Old Testament Supplement Series 233. Sheffield, UK: Sheffield Academic Press, 1996.
Green, Barbara. "How the Lion Roars: Contextualizing the Nine Riddles in Amos 3:3–8." In *Theology and the New Histories,* ed. Gary Macy, 112–32. Annual Publication of the College Theology Society, vol. 4. Maryknoll, N.Y.: Orbis, 1998.
Greenberg, Moshe. *Ezekiel 1–20.* Anchor Bible 22. New York: Doubleday, 1983.
Greene, John T. *Balaam and His Interpreters: A Hermeneutical History of the Balaam Traditions.* Brown Judaic Studies 244. Atlanta, Ga.: Scholars Press, 1992.
Greenstein, Edward L. "In Job's Face/Facing Job." In *The Labour of Reading: Desire, Alienation, and Biblical Interpretation,* ed. Fiona C. Black, Roland Boer, and Erin Runions, 301–17. Society of Biblical Literature Semeia Studies 36. Atlanta, Ga.: Society of Biblical Literature, 1999.
Grosz, Elizabeth. *Volatile Bodies: Toward a Corporeal Feminism.* Bloomington: Indiana University Press, 1994.
Grunwald, Lisa, and Stephen J. Adler. *Letters of the Century: America 1900–1999.* New York: Dial Press, 1999.
Gunn, David M. *Judges.* Blackwell Bible Commentaries. Oxford: Blackwell, 2005.
———. "Reading Right: Reliable and Omniscient Narrator, Omniscient God, and Foolproof Composition in the Hebrew Bible." In *The Bible in Three Dimensions: Essays in Celebration of Forty Years of Biblical Studies in the University of Sheffield,* ed. David J. A. Clines, Stephen E. Fowl, and Stanley E. Porter, 53–64. Journal for the Study of the Old Testament Supplement Series 87. Sheffield, UK: Sheffield Academic Press, 1990.
Hackett, Jo Ann. "Balaam." In *Anchor Bible Dictionary,* 1:569–72. New York: Doubleday, 1992.
Hagstrom, David G. *The Coherence of the Book of Micah: A Literary Analysis.* Society of Biblical Literature Dissertation Series 89. Atlanta, Ga.: Scholars Press, 1988.
Haiman, John. *Talk Is Cheap: Sarcasm, Alienation, and the Evolution of Language.* Oxford: Oxford University Press, 1998.
Halpern, Baruch. *David's Secret Demons: Messiah, Murderer, Traitor, King.* Grand Rapids, Mich.: Eerdmans, 2001.
———. *The First Historians: The Hebrew Bible and History.* University Park: Pennsylvania State University Press, 1988.
Hamel, Gildas. "Taking the Argo to Nineveh: Jonah and Jason in a Mediterranean Context." *Judaism* 44 (1995): 341–59.
Handwerk, Gary J. *Irony and Ethics in Narrative: From Schlegel to Lacan.* New Haven, Conn.: Yale University Press, 1985.
Harding, James. "In the Name of Love: Resisting Reader and Abusive Redeemer in Deutero-Isaiah." *Bible and Critical Theory* 2 (2006): 14.1–14.15, DOI: 10.2104/bc060014.
Harrison, C. Robert, Jr. "Qoheleth among the Sociologists." *Biblical Interpretation* 5 (1997): 160–80.
Hauser, Alan Jon. "Genesis 2–3: The Theme of Intimacy and Alienation." In *Art and Meaning: Rhetoric in Biblical Literature,* ed. David J. A. Clines, David M. Gunn, and Alan J. Hauser, 20–36. Sheffield, UK: JSOT Press, 1982.
———. "Should Ahab Go to Battle or Not? Ambiguity as a Rhetorical Device in 1 Kings 22." In *Rhetorical Argumentation in Biblical Texts: Essays from the Lund 2000 Conference,* ed. Anders Eriksson, Thomas H. Olbricht, and Walter Übelacker,

141–54. Emory Studies in Early Christianity. Harrisburg, Pa: Trinity Press International, 2002.

Hawk, L. Daniel. "Strange Houseguests: Rahab, Lot, and the Dynamics of Deliverance." In *Reading between Texts: Intertextuality and the Hebrew Bible,* ed. Danna Nolan Fewell, 89–97. Louisville, Ky.: Westminster/John Knox, 1992.

Hayward, C. T. R. "Balaam's Prophecies as Interpreted by Philo and the Aramaic Targums of the Pentateuch." In *New Heaven and New Earth: Prophecy and the Millennium: Essays in Honour of Anthony Gelston,* ed. P. J. Harland and C. T. R. Hayward, 19–36. Leiden, Neth.: Brill, 1999.

Hens-Piazza, Gina. *The New Historicism.* Minneapolis, Minn.: Fortress, 2002.

Herzfeld, Michael. "Irony and Power: Toward a Politics of Mockery in Greece." In *Irony in Action: Anthropology, Practice, and the Moral Imagination,* ed. James W. Fernandez and Mary Taylor Huber, 63–83. Chicago: University of Chicago Press, 2001.

Hillers, Delbert R. *A Commentary on the Book of the Prophet Micah.* Hermeneia. Philadelphia: Fortress, 1984.

Ho, Craig Y. S. "The Stories of the Family Troubles of Judah and David: A Study of Their Literary Links." *Vetus Testamentum* 49 (1999): 514–31.

Hoffman, Yair. *A Blemished Perfection: The Book of Job in Context.* Journal for the Study of the Old Testament Supplement Series 213. Sheffield, UK: Sheffield Academic Press, 1996.

———. "A North Israelite Typological Myth and a Judaean Historical Tradition: The Exodus in Hosea and Amos." *Vetus Testamentum* 39 (1989): 169–82.

Hoglund, Kenneth G. "The Fool and the Wise in Dialogue: Proverbs 26:4–5." In *Learning from the Sages: Selected Studies on the Book of Proverbs,* ed. Roy B. Zuck, 339–52. Grand Rapids, Mich.: Baker, 1994.

Holbert, John C. "'Deliverance Belongs to Yahweh!' Satire in the Book of Jonah." *Journal for the Study of the Old Testament* 21 (1981): 59–81.

Holland, Glenn S. *Divine Irony.* Selinsgrove, Pa.: Susquehanna University Press, 2000.

———. "Paul's Use of Irony as a Rhetorical Technique." In *The Rhetorical Analysis of Scripture: Essays from the 1995 London Conference,* ed. Stanley E. Porter and Thomas E. Olbricht, 234–48. Journal for the Study of the New Testament Supplement Series 146. Sheffield, UK: Sheffield Academic Press, 1997.

Honig, Bonnie. "Ruth, the Model Emigrée: Mourning and the Symbolic Politics of Immigration." In *Ruth and Esther: A Feminist Companion to the Bible* (second series), ed. Athalya Brenner, 50–74. Sheffield, UK: Sheffield Academic Press, 1999.

Hornsby, Teresa J. "'Israel Has Become a Worthless Thing': Re-Reading Gomer in Hosea 1–3." *Journal for the Study of the Old Testament* 82 (1999): 115–28.

Hossfeld, Frank-Lothar, and Erich Zenger. *Psalms 2: A Commentary on Psalms 51–100.* Hermeneia. Minneapolis, Minn.: Fortress, 2005.

House, Paul R. "Amos and Literary Criticism." *Review and Expositor* 92 (1995): 175–87.

Houston, Walter J. "David, Asaph, and the Mighty Works of God: Theme and Genre in the Psalm Collections." *Journal for the Study of the Old Testament* 68 (1995): 93–111.

Huddlestun, John R. "Divestiture, Deception, and Demotion: The Garment Motif in Genesis 37–39." *Journal for the Study of the Old Testament* 98 (2002): 47–62.

Hurvitz, Avi. "Wisdom Vocabulary in the Hebrew Psalter: A Contribution to the Study of 'Wisdom Psalms.'" *Vetus Testamentum* 38 (1988): 41–51.

Hutcheon, Linda. "Beginning to Theorize Postmodernism." In *A Postmodern Reader*, ed. Joseph Natoli and Linda Hutcheon, 243–72. Albany: State University of New York Press, 1993.

———. *Irony's Edge: The Theory and Politics of Irony*. New York: Routledge, 1995.

Ivie, Robert L. "Scrutinizing Performances of Rhetorical Criticism." *Quarterly Journal of Speech* 80 (1994): 248.

Jacobs, Mignon. *The Conceptual Coherence of the Book of Micah*. Journal for the Study of the Old Testament Supplement Series 322. Sheffield, UK: Sheffield Academic Press, 2001.

Jarick, John. "An 'Allegory of Age' as Apocalypse." *Colloquium* 22 (1990): 19–27.

Jasper, David. *Rhetoric, Power and Community: An Exercise in Reserve*. Louisville, Ky.: Westminster/John Knox, 1993.

Jemielity, Thomas. *Satire and the Hebrew Prophets*. Louisville, Ky.: Westminster/John Knox, 1992.

Jeremias, Jörg. *The Book of Amos*. Trans. Douglas W. Stott. Old Testament Library. Louisville, Ky.: Westminster John Knox, 1998. Orig. *Der Prophet Amos*. Göttingen, Germany: Vandenhoeck and Ruprecht, 1995.

Jones, Brian C. *Howling over Moab: Irony and Rhetoric in Isaiah 15–16*. SBL Dissertation Series 157. Atlanta, Ga.: Scholars Press, 1996.

Jonker, Louis C. *Exclusivity and Variety: Perspectives on Multidimensional Exegesis*. Kampen, Neth.: Kok Pharos, 1996.

Joüon, Paul, and T. Muraoka. *A Grammar of Biblical Hebrew*. 2 vols. Third reprint. Rome: Pontifical Biblical Institute, 2000.

Kahn, Paul. "An Analysis of the Book of Jonah." *Judaism* 43 (1994): 87–100.

Kaiser, Otto. "Die Botschaft des Buches Kohelet." *Ephemerides Theologicae Lovaniensis* 71 (1995): 48–70.

Kaufer, David S., and Christine M. Neuwirth. "Foregrounding Norms and Ironic Communication." *Quarterly Journal of Speech* 68 (1982): 28–36.

Keefe, Alice A. *Woman's Body and the Social Body in Hosea*. Journal for the Study of the Old Testament Supplement Series 338/Gender, Culture, Theory 10. Sheffield, UK: Sheffield Academic Press, 2001.

Keegan, Terence J. "Biblical Criticism and the Challenge of Postmodernism." *Biblical Interpretation* 3 (1995): 1–14.

Keller, Catherine. *Face of the Deep: A Theology of Becoming*. London: Routledge, 2003.

Kennedy, James M. "Peasants in Revolt: Political Allegory in Genesis 2–3." *Journal for the Study of the Old Testament* 47 (1990): 3–14.

Kermode, Frank. "Anteriority, Authority, and Secrecy: A General Comment." *Semeia* 43 (1988): 155–67.

Kessler, Martin. *Battle of the Gods: The God of Israel Versus Marduk of Babylon: A Literary/Theological Interpretation of Jeremiah 50–51*. Studia Semitica Neerlandica 42. Assen, Neth.: Van Gorcum, 2003.

Kierkegaard, Søren. *The Concept of Irony, With Constant Reference to Socrates*. Trans. Lee M. Capel. Bloomington: Indiana University Press, 1965.

Kimelman, Reuven. "The Seduction of Eve and the Exegetical Politics of Gender." *Biblical Interpretation* 4 (1996): 1–39.

Klawans, Jonathan. *Impurity and Sin in Ancient Judaism*. Oxford: Oxford University Press, 2000.

Klein, Lillian R. *From Deborah to Esther: Sexual Politics in the Hebrew Bible*. Minneapolis, Minn.: Fortress, 2003.

———. "Structure, Irony and Meaning in the Book of Judges." In *Proceedings of the Tenth World Congress of Jewish Studies, Jerusalem, August 16–24, 1989*, ed. David Assaf, 83–90. Jerusalem: Magnes Press, 1990.

———. *The Triumph of Irony in the Book of Judges.* Journal for the Study of the Old Testament: Supplement Series 68/Bible and Literature Series 14. Sheffield, UK: Almond, 1988.

Kleven, Terence. "The Cows of Bashan: A Single Metaphor at Amos 4:1–3." *Catholic Biblical Quarterly* 58 (1996): 215–27.

Knoppers, Gary N. "Aaron's Calf and Jeroboam's Calves." In *Fortunate the Eyes that See: Essays in Honor of David Noel Freedman in Honor of His Seventieth Birthday*, ed. Astrid B. Beck, et al., 92–104. Grand Rapids, Mich.: Eerdmans, 1995.

Koh, Y. V. *Royal Autobiography in the Book of Qoheleth.* Berlin: De Gruyter, 2006.

Koosed, Jennifer L. *(Per)Mutations of Qohelet: Reading the Body in the Book.* London: T & T Clark, 2006.

Kramer, Phyllis Silverman. "Rahab: From Peshat to Pedagogy, Or: The Many Faces of a Heroine." In *Culture, Entertainment and the Bible*, ed. George Aichele, 156–72. Journal for the Study of the Old Testament Supplement Series 309. Sheffield, UK: Sheffield Academic Press, 2000.

Kraus, Hans-Joachim. *Psalms 60–150: A Commentary.* Trans. Hilton C. Oswald. Continental Commentary Series. Minneapolis, Minn.: Augsburg, 1989.

Krause, Deborah. "A Blessing Cursed: The Prophet's Prayer for Barren Womb and Dry Breasts in Hosea 9." In *Reading between Texts: Intertextuality and the Hebrew Bible*, ed. Danna Nolan Fewell, 191–202. Louisville, Ky.: Westminster/John Knox, 1992.

Krüger, Thomas. *Kohelet [Prediger].* Biblischer Kommentar, Altes Testament 19. Neukirchen-Vluyn, Germany: Neukirchener, 2000.

———. *Qoheleth.* Trans. O. C. Dean Jr. Hermeneia. Minneapolis, Minn.: Fortress, 2004.

Kwok Pui-Lan. "Postcolonialism, Feminism and Biblical Interpretation." In *Scripture, Community, and Mission: Essays in Honor of D. Preman Miles*, ed. Philip L. Wickeri, 269–84. Hong Kong: Clear-Cut Publishing, 2002.

LaCocque, André. *The Feminine Unconventional: Four Subversive Figures in Israel's Tradition.* Minneapolis: Fortress, 1990.

———. "Haman in the Book of Esther." *Hebrew Annual Review* 11 (1987): 207–22.

———. *Ruth.* Trans. K. C. Hanson. Continental Commentaries. Minneapolis, Minn.: Fortress, 2004.

Lambe, Anthony J. "Genesis 38: Structure and Literary Design." In *The World of Genesis: Persons, Places, Perspectives*, ed. Philip R. Davies and David J. A. Clines, 102–20. Journal for the Study of the Old Testament Supplement Series 257. Sheffield, UK: Sheffield Academic Press, 1998.

———. "Judah's Development: The Pattern of Departure–Transition–Return." *Journal for the Study of the Old Testament* (1999): 53–68.

Landy, Francis. *Hosea.* Sheffield, UK: Sheffield Academic Press, 1995.

———. "The Song of Songs." In *The Literary Guide to the Bible*, ed. Robert Alter and Frank Kermode, 305–19. Cambridge, Mass.: Belknap, 1987.

———. "Vision and Poetic Speech in Amos." *Hebrew Annual Review* 11 (1987): 223–46.

Lang, Candace D. *Irony/Humor: Critical Paradigms.* Baltimore: Johns Hopkins University Press, 1988.

Laniak, Timothy S. *Shame and Honor in the Book of Esther.* SBL Dissertation Series. Atlanta, Ga.: Scholars Press, 1998.

Levenson, Jon D. *Esther: A Commentary.* Old Testament Library. Louisville, Ky.: Westminster John Knox, 1997.

———. "Genesis." Introduction and annotations. In *The Jewish Study Bible,* ed. Adele Berlin and Marc Zvi Brettler, with Michael Fishbane, consulting editor. Oxford: Oxford University Press, 2004.

Levin, Christoph. "The Yahwist and the Redactional Link between Genesis and Exodus." In *A Farewell to the Yahwist? The Composition of the Pentateuch in Recent European Interpretation,* ed. Thomas B. Dozeman and Konrad Schmid, 131–41. Leiden, Neth.: Brill, 2006.

Levine, Baruch A. *Numbers 21–36.* Anchor Bible 4A. New York: Doubleday, 2000.

Levinson, Joshua. "An-Other Woman: Joseph and Potiphar's Wife: Staging the Body Politic." *Jewish Quarterly Review* 87 (1997): 269–301.

Lienhard, Joseph T., ed. *Ancient Christian Commentary on Scripture: Old Testament III.* Downers Grove, Ill.: InterVarsity, 2001.

Linafelt, Tod. *Ruth.* Berit Olam. Collegeville, Minn.: Liturgical Press, 1999.

Linville, James R. "Visions and Voices: Amos 7–9." *Biblica* 80 (1999): 22–42.

———. "What Does 'It' Mean? Interpretation at the Point of No Return in Amos 1–2." *Biblical Interpretation* 8 (2000): 400–24.

Long, Burke O. "Picturing Biblical Pasts." In *Orientalism, Assyriology and the Bible,* ed. Steven W. Holloway, 297–319. Sheffield, UK: Sheffield Phoenix, 2006.

Longman, Tremper, III. *The Book of Ecclesiastes.* New International Commentary on the Old Testament. Grand Rapids, Mich.: Eerdmans, 1998.

———. *Fictional Akkadian Autobiography: A Generic and Comparative Study.* Winona Lake, Ind.: Eisenbrauns, 1991.

Love, Mark Cameron. *The Evasive Text: Zechariah 1–8 and the Frustrated Reader.* Journal for the Study of the Old Testament Supplement Series 296. Sheffield, UK: Sheffield Academic Press, 1999.

Lux, Rüdiger. "'Ich, Kohelet, bin König . . .': Die Fiktion als Schlüssel zur Wirklichkeit in Kohelet 1,12–2,26." *Evangelische Theologie* 50 (1990): 331–42.

Luyten, J. "Psalm 73 and Wisdom." In *La Sagesse de l'Ancien Testament: Nouvelle édition mise à jour,* 59–81. Leuven, Belgium: Leuven University Press, 1990.

Lyke, Larry L. "What Does Ruth Have to do with Rahab? Midrash *Ruth Rabbah* and the Matthean Genealogy of Jesus." In *The Function of Scripture in Early Jewish and Christian Tradition,* ed. Craig A. Evans and James A. Sanders, 262–84. Journal for the Study of the New Testament Supplement Series 154/ Studies in Scripture in Early Judaism and Christianity 6. Sheffield, UK: Sheffield Academic Press, 1998.

Lyons, William John. "The Words of Gamaliel (Acts 5.38–39) and the Irony of Indeterminacy." *Journal for the Study of the New Testament* 68 (1997): 23–29

Machinist, Peter. "Fate, *miqreh,* and Reason: Some Reflections on Qohelet and Biblical Thought." In *Solving Riddles and Untying Knots: Biblical, Epigraphic, and Semitic Studies in Honor of Jonas C. Greenfield,* ed. Ziony Zevit, Seymour Gitin, and Michael Sokoloff, 159–75. Winona Lake, Ind.: Eisenbrauns, 1995.

Macintosh, A. A. *Hosea.* International Critical Commentary. Edinburgh: T & T Clark, 1997.

Magonet, Jonathan. *Form and Meaning: Studies in Literary Techniques in the Book of Jonah.* Bible and Literature Series 8. Sheffield, UK: Almond, 1983.

Mandt, A. J. "The Domain of Silence in Humanistic Discourse." *Soundings* 65 (1982): 31–40.

Marcus, David. *From Balaam to Jonah: Anti-prophetic Satire in the Hebrew Bible.* Brown Judaic Studies 301. Atlanta, Ga.: Scholars Press, 1995.

———. "Some Antiphrastic Euphemisms for a Blind Person in Akkadian and

Other Semitic Languages." *Journal of the American Oriental Society* 100 (1980): 307–10.

Margalit, Baruch. "Observations on the Jael-Sisera Story (Judges 4–5)." In *Pomegranates and Golden Bells: Studies in Biblical, Jewish, and Near Eastern Ritual, Law, and Literature in Honor of Jacob Milgrom*, ed. David P. Wright, David Noel Freedman, and Avi Hurvitz, 629–41. Winona Lake, Ind.: Eisenbrauns, 1995.

Matthews, Victor H. "The Anthropology of Clothing in the Joseph Narrative." *Journal for the Study of the Old Testament* 65 (1995): 25–36.

———. "Hospitality and Hostility in Judges 4." *Biblical Theology Bulletin* 21 (1991): 13–21.

McBride, William T. "Esther Passes: Chiasm, Lex Talio, and Money in the Book of Esther." In *"Not in Heaven": Coherence and Complexity in Biblical Narrative*, ed. Jason P. Rosenblatt and Joseph C. Sitterson Jr., 211–23. Bloomington: Indiana University Press, 1991.

McCann, J. Clinton, Jr. *Judges*. Interpretation. Louisville, Ky.: John Knox, 2002.

———. "Psalm 73: A Microcosm of Old Testament Theology." In *The Listening Heart: Essays in Wisdom and the Psalms in Honor of Roland E. Murphy*, ed. Kenneth G. Hoglund and Roland E. Murphy, 247–57. Journal for the Study of the Old Testament Supplement Series 58. Sheffield, UK: JSOT Press, 1987.

McKane, William. *Micah: Introduction and Commentary*. Edinburgh: T & T Clark, 1998.

McKinlay, Judith E. "Rahab: A Hero/ine?" *Biblical Interpretation* 7 (1999): 44–57.

———. "A Son Is Born to Naomi: A Harvest for Israel." In *Ruth and Esther: A Feminist Companion to the Bible* (second series), ed. Athalya Brenner, 151–57. Sheffield, UK: Sheffield Academic Press, 1999.

Mehlman, Bernard H. "Rahab as a Model of Human Redemption." In *"Open Thou Mine Eyes . . . ": Essays on Aggadah and Judaica Presented to Rabbi William G. Braude on His Eightieth Birthday and Dedicated to His Memory*, ed. Herman J. Blumberg et al., 193–207. Hoboken, N.J.: KTAV, 1992.

Melugin, Roy F. "Amos in Recent Research." *Currents in Research: Biblical Studies* 6 (1998): 65–101.

Mendecki, Norbert. "Die Sammlung und der Neue Exodus in Mich 2,12–13." *Kairos* 23 (1981): 96–99.

Menn, Esther Marie. *Judah and Tamar (Genesis 38) in Ancient Jewish Exegesis: Studies in Literary Form and Hermeneutics*. Leiden, Neth.: Brill, 1997.

Meyers, Carol. *Discovering Eve: Ancient Israelite Women in Context*. Oxford: Oxford University Press, 1988.

Miles, Jack A. "Laughing at the Bible: Jonah as Parody." *Jewish Quarterly Review* 65 (1975): 168–81. Reprinted in *On Humour and the Comic in the Hebrew Bible*, ed. Yehuda T. Radday and Athalya Brenner, 203–15. Bible and Literature Series 23. Sheffield, UK: Almond Press, 1990.

Milgrom, Jacob. *Numbers*. JPS Torah Commentary. Philadelphia: Jewish Publication Society, 1990.

Miller, Douglas B. *Symbol and Rhetoric in Ecclesiastes: The Place of Hebel in Qohelet's Work*. Leiden, Neth.: Brill, 2002.

Miller, J. Hillis. "The Critic as Host." In *Deconstruction and Criticism*, ed. Harold Bloom, et al., 217–53. New York: Seabury Press, 1979.

Mills, Mary E. "Household and Table: Diasporic Boundaries in Daniel and Esther." *Catholic Biblical Quarterly* 68 (2006): 408–20.

Miscall, Peter D. "Isaiah: The Labyrinth of Images." *Semeia* 54 (1991): 103–21.

Mitchell, Christine. "The Ironic Death of Josiah in 2 Chronicles." *Catholic Biblical Quarterly* 68 (2006): 421–35.

Mitchell, David C. *The Message of the Psalter: An Eschatological Programme in the Book of Psalms.* Journal for the Study of the Old Testament Supplement Series 252. Sheffield, UK: Sheffield Academic Press, 1997.

Moberly, R. W. L. "On Learning To Be a True Prophet: The Story of Balaam and His Ass." In *New Heaven and New Earth: Prophecy and the Millennium: Essays in Honour of Anthony Gelston,* ed. P. J. Harland and C. T. R. Hayward, 1–17. Leiden, Neth.: Brill, 1999.

Möller, Karl. "'Hear This Word against You': A Fresh Look at the Arrangement and the Rhetorical Strategy of the Book of Amos." *Vetus Testamentum* 50 (2000): 499–518.

Moore, Michael S. *The Balaam Traditions: Their Character and Development.* Atlanta, Ga.: Scholars Press, 1990.

Moore, Stephen D. *Mark and Luke in Poststructuralist Perspectives: Jesus Begins to Write.* New Haven, Conn.: Yale University Press, 1992.

Morgenstern, Mira. "*Ruth* and the Sense of Self: Midrash and Difference." *Judaism* 48 (1999): 131–45.

Muecke, D. C. *The Compass of Irony.* London: Methuen, 1969.

———. *Irony.* The Critical Idiom. London: Methuen, 1970.

———. "Irony Markers." *Poetics* 7 (1978): 363–75.

Murphy, Roland. *Ecclesiastes.* Word Biblical Commentary 23A. Dallas, Tex.: Word, 1992.

Nasuti, Harry P. *Defining the Sacred Songs: Genre, Tradition and the Post-Critical Interpretation of the Psalms.* Journal for the Study of the Old Testament Supplement Series 218. Sheffield, UK: Sheffield Academic Press, 1999.

———. *Tradition History and the Psalms of Asaph.* Atlanta, Ga.: Scholars Press, 1988.

Nation, Carry A. *The Use and Need of the Life of Carry A. Nation.* Topeka, Kans.: F. M. Steves and Sons, 1905.

Newman, Murray L. "Rahab and the Conquest." In *Understanding the Word: Essays in Honor of Bernhard W. Anderson,* ed. James T. Butler, Edgar W. Conrad, and Ben C. Ollenburger, 167–81. Journal for the Study of the Old Testament Supplement Series 37. Sheffield, UK: JSOT Press, 1985.

Newsom, Carol A. "Bakhtin, the Bible, and Dialogic Truth." *Journal of Religion* 76 (1996): 290–306.

———. *The Book of Job: A Contest of Moral Imaginations.* Oxford: Oxford University Press, 2003.

———. "Woman and the Discourse of Patriarchal Wisdom: A Study of Proverbs 1–9." In *Gender and Difference in Ancient Israel,* ed. Peggy L. Day, 142–60. Minneapolis, Minn.: Fortress, 1989.

Nicholson, Ernest W. "The Limits of Theodicy as a Theme of the Book of Job." In *Wisdom in Ancient Israel: Essays in Honour of J. A. Emerton,* ed. John Day, Robert P. Gordon, and H. G. M. Williamson, 71–82. Cambridge: Cambridge University Press, 1995.

Nicol, George G. "The Narrative Structure and Interpretation of Genesis XXVI 1–33." *Vetus Testamentum* 46 (1996): 339–60.

Niditch, Susan. "Eroticism and Death in the Tale of Jael." In *Gender and Difference in Ancient Israel,* ed. Peggy L. Day, 43–57. Minneapolis, Minn.: Fortress, 1989.

———. "Esther: Folklore, Wisdom, Feminism, and Authority." In *A Feminist Companion to Esther, Judith, and Susanna,* ed. Athalya Brenner, 26–46. Sheffield, UK: Sheffield Academic Press, 1995.

———. *Folklore and the Hebrew Bible.* Minneapolis, Minn.: Fortress, 1993.

———. *A Prelude to Biblical Folklore: Underdogs and Tricksters.* San Francisco: Harper and Row, 1987.

———. *War in the Hebrew Bible: A Study in the Ethics of Violence.* New York: Oxford, 1993.

Nielsen, Eduard. "Psalm 73: Scandinavian Contributions." In *Understanding Poets and Prophets: Essays in Honour of George Wishart Anderson,* ed. A. Graeme Auld, 273–83. Journal for the Study of the Old Testament Supplement Series 152. Sheffield, UK: JSOT Press, 1993.

Noble, Paul R. "Amos and Amaziah in Context: Synchronic and Diachronic Approaches to Amos 7–8." *Catholic Biblical Quarterly* 60 (1998): 423–39.

———. "A 'Balanced' Reading of the Rape of Dinah: Some Exegetical and Methodological Observations." *Biblical Interpretation* 4 (1996): 173–204.

———. "Esau, Tamar, and Joseph: Criteria for Identifying Inner-Biblical Allusions." *Vetus Testamentum* 52 (2002): 219–52.

———. "'I Will Not Bring 'It' Back' (Amos 1:3): A Deliberately Ambiguous Oracle?" *Expository Times* 106 (1994–95): 105–109.

———. "The Literary Structure of Amos: A Thematic Analysis." *Journal of Biblical Literature* 114 (1995): 209–26.

Nohrnberg, James C. "Princely Characters." In *"Not in Heaven": Coherence and Complexity in Biblical Narrative,* ed. Jason P. Rosenblatt and Joseph C. Sitterson Jr., 58–97. Bloomington: Indiana University Press, 1991.

Noort, Ed. "Joshua: The History of Reception and Hermeneutics." In *Past, Present, Future: The Deuteronomistic History and the Prophets,* ed. Johannes C. de Moor and Harry F. van Rooy, 199–215. Leiden, Neth.: Brill: 2000.

O'Brien, Mark A. "The Contribution of Judah's Speech, Genesis 44:18–34, to the Characterization of Joseph." *Catholic Biblical Quarterly* 59 (2006): 429–47.

O'Day, Gail R. *Revelation in the Fourth Gospel: Narrative Mode and Theological Claim.* Philadelphia: Fortress, 1986.

Ogden, Graham S. *Qoheleth.* Sheffield, UK: JSOT Press, 1987.

———. "'Vanity' It Certainly Is Not." *Bible Translator* 38 (1987): 301–306.

Okerlund, Arlene N. "The Rhetoric of Love: Voice in the *Amoretti* and the *Songs and Sonets.*" *Quarterly Journal of Speech* 68 (1982): 37–46.

Olbricht, Erika Mae. "Constructing the Dead Author: Postmodernism's Rhetoric of Death." In *The Rhetorical Analysis of Scripture: Essays from the 1995 London Conference,* ed. Stanley E. Porter and Thomas E. Olbricht, 66–78. Journal for the Study of the New Testament Supplement Series 146. Sheffield, UK: Sheffield Academic Press, 1997.

Olson, Dennis T. "Dialogues of Life and Monologues of Death: Jephthah and Jephthah's Daughter in Judges 10:6–12:7." In *Postmodern Interpretations of the Bible—A Reader,* ed. A. K. M. Adam, 43–54. St. Louis: Chalice, 2001.

———. *Numbers.* Interpretation. Louisville, Ky.: John Knox, 1996.

———. "Numbers." In *Harper's Bible Commentary,* 182–208. San Francisco: HarperCollins, 1988.

Ostriker, Alicia. "The Book of Ruth and the Love of the Land." *Biblical Interpretation* 10 (2002): 343–59.

Park, Aaron W. *The Book of Amos as Composed and Read in Antiquity.* Studies in Biblical Literature 37. New York: Peter Lang, 2001.

Parry, Robin. *Old Testament Story and Christian Ethics: The Rape of Dinah as a Case Study.* Paternoster Biblical Monographs. Waynesboro, Ga.: Paternoster, 2004.

Patrick, Dale, and Allen Scult. *Rhetoric and Biblical Interpretation.* Journal for the

Study of the Old Testament Supplement Series 82/Bible and Literature Series 26. Sheffield, UK: Almond, 1990.

Patte, Daniel. *Discipleship according to the Sermon on the Mount: Four Legitimate Readings, Four Plausible Views of Discipleship, and Their Relative Values.* Valley Forge, Pa.: Trinity Press International, 1996.

Paul, Shalom M. *Amos.* Hermeneia. Minneapolis, Minn.: Fortress, 1991.

Paulson, Ronald. "'Suppose Me Dead': Swift's *Verses on the Death of Dr. Swift.*" In *Critical Essays on Jonathan Swift,* ed. Frank Palmeri, 240–44. New York: G. K. Hall, 1993.

Penchansky, David. *The Politics of Biblical Theology: A Postmodern Reading.* Studies in American Biblical Hermeneutics 10. Macon, Ga.: Mercer University Press, 1995.

Perdue, Leo G. "The Death of the Sage and Moral Exhortation: From Ancient Near Eastern Instructions to Graeco-Roman Paraenesis." *Semeia* 50 (1990): 81–109.

Perry, T. A. *Dialogues with Kohelet: The Book of Ecclesiastes.* University Park: Pennsylvania State University Press, 1993.

Polaski, Donald C. "*Mene, Mene, Tekel, Parsin:* Writing and Resistance in Daniel 5 and 6." *Journal of Biblical Literature* 123 (2004): 649–69.

Polk, Timothy. "The Wisdom of Irony: A Study of *Hebel* and Its Relation to Joy and the Fear of God in Ecclesiastes." *Studia Biblica et Theologica* 6 (1976): 3–17.

Polzin, Robert. "'The Ancestress of Israel in Danger' In Danger." *Semeia* 3 (1975): 78–95.

Pope, Marvin H. *Job.* Anchor Bible 15. Garden City, N.Y.: Doubleday, 1965.

Quammen, David. "A Drink of Death." Review of Steven Johnson, *The Ghost Map: The Story of London's Most Terrifying Epidemic—and How It Changed Science, Cities, and the Modern World* (London: Riverhead, 2006). *New York Times Book Review,* November 12, 2006, 16.

Radday, Yehuda T. "Esther with Humour." In *On Humour and the Comic in the Hebrew Bible,* ed. Yehuda T. Radday and Athalya Brenner, 295–313. Sheffield, UK: Almond Press, 1990.

Rakel, Claudia. "'I Will Sing a New Song to My God': Some Remarks on the Intertextuality of Judith 16.1–17." In *Judges: A Feminist Companion to the Bible* (second series), ed. Athalya Brenner, 27–47. Sheffield, UK: Sheffield Academic Press, 1999.

Raschke, Carl. "Fire and Roses, or the Problem of Postmodern Religious Thinking." In *Shadow of Spirit: Postmodernism and Religion,* ed. Philippa Berry and Andrew Wernick, 93–108. London: Routledge, 1992.

Rashkow, Ilona N. "Intertextuality, Transference, and the Reader In/Of Genesis 12 and 20." In *Reading between Texts: Intertextuality and the Hebrew Bible,* ed. Danna Nolan Fewell, 57–73. Louisville, Ky.: Westminster/John Knox, 1992.

Ray, Jerry Lynn. *Narrative Irony in Luke–Acts: The Paradoxical Interaction of Prophetic Fulfillment and Jewish Rejection.* Lewiston, N.Y.: Mellen, 1996.

Rendsburg, Gary A. "David and His Circle in Genesis xxxviii." *Vetus Testamentum* 36 (1986): 438–46.

Roberts, Alexander, and James Donaldson, eds. *The Ante-Nicene Fathers: Translations of the Writings of the Fathers down to A.D. 325.* Vol. 1. American reprint of the Edinburgh edition. Edinburgh: T & T Clark; Grand Rapids, Mich.: Eerdmans, 1996.

Robinson, Robert B. "Wife and Sister through the Ages: Textual Determinacy and the History of Interpretation." *Semeia* 62 (1993): 103–28.

Rösel, Martin. "Wie einer vom Propheten zum Verführer wurde: Tradition und Rezeption der Bileamgestalt." *Biblica* 80 (1999): 404–15.

Rosenblatt, Louise M. "On the Aesthetic as the Basic Model of the Reading Process." In *Theories of Reading, Looking, and Listening,* ed. Harry R. Garvin, 17–32. Lewisburg, Pa.: Bucknell University Press; London and Toronto: Associated University Presses, 1981.

Ross, James F. "Psalm 73." In *Israelite Wisdom: Theological and Literary Essays in Honor of Samuel Terrien,* ed. John G. Gammie, et al., 161–75. New York: Scholars Press, 1978.

Rowlett, Lori. "Disney's Pocahontas and Joshua's Rahab in Postcolonial Perspective." In *Culture, Entertainment and the Bible,* ed. George Aichele, 66–75. Journal for the Study of the Old Testament Supplement Series 309. Sheffield, UK: Sheffield Academic Press, 2000.

———. "Inclusion, Exclusion, and Marginality in the Book of Joshua." *Journal for the Study of the Old Testament* 55 (1992): 15–23.

Runions, Erin. *Changing Subjects: Gender, Nation, and Future in Micah.* New York: Sheffield Academic Press, 2001.

———. "Playing It Again: Utopia, Contradiction, Hybrid Space and the Bright Future in Micah." In *The Labour of Reading: Desire, Alienation, and Biblical Interpretation,* ed. Fiona C. Black, Roland Boer, and Erin Runions, 285–300. Atlanta, Ga.: Society of Biblical Literature, 1999.

Rutledge, David. "Faithful Reading: Poststructuralism and the Sacred." *Biblical Interpretation* 4 (1996): 270–87.

Salyer, Gary D. *Vain Rhetoric: Private Insight and Public Debate in Ecclesiastes.* Journal for the Study of the Old Testament Supplement Series 327. Sheffield, UK: Sheffield Academic Press, 2001.

Sarna, Nahum M. *Understanding Genesis: The Heritage of Biblical Israel.* New York: Schocken, 1966.

Sasson, Jack M. "Esther." In *The Literary Guide to the Bible,* ed. Robert Alter and Frank Kermode, 335–42. Cambridge, Mass.: Harvard University Press, 1987.

———. *Jonah.* Anchor Bible 24B. New York: Doubleday, 1990.

———. "Ruth." In *The Literary Guide to the Bible,* ed. Robert Alter and Frank Kermode, 320–28. Cambridge, Mass.: Harvard University Press, 1987.

Savran, George. "Beastly Speech: Intertextuality, Balaam's Ass and the Garden of Eden." *Journal for the Study of the Old Testament* 64 (1994): 33–55.

Schlegel, Friedrich. *Philosophical Fragments.* Trans. Peter Firchow. Minneapolis: University of Minnesota Press, 1991.

Schmid, Konrad. "The So-Called Yahwist and the Literary Gap between Genesis and Exodus." In *A Farewell to the Yahwist? The Composition of the Pentateuch in Recent European Interpretation,* ed. Thomas B. Dozeman and Konrad Schmid, 29–50. Leiden, Neth.: Brill, 2006.

Schott, Ben. "The Bibliognost's Handbook." *New York Times Book Review,* December 7, 2006, 87.

Schwartz, Regina M. "Adultery in the House of David: The Metanarrative of Biblical Scholarship and the Narratives of the Bible." In *Women in the Hebrew Bible: A Reader,* ed. Alice Bach, 335–50. New York: Routledge, 1999.

Scoggin, Mary. "Wine in the Writing, Truth in the Rhetoric: Three Levels of Irony in a Chinese Essay Genre." In *Irony in Action: Anthropology, Practice, and the Moral Imagination,* ed. James W. Fernandez and Mary Taylor Huber, 145–71. Chicago: University of Chicago Press, 2001.

Scott, James C. *Domination and the Arts of Resistance: Hidden Transcripts.* New Haven, Conn.: Yale University Press, 1990.

Seebass, Horst. "Zur literarischen Gestalt der Bileam-Perikope." *Zeitschrift für die alttestamentliche Wissenschaft* 107 (1995): 409–19.

Seow, Choon-Leong. *Ecclesiastes.* Anchor Bible 18C. New York: Doubleday, 1997.

———. "Hosea 14:10 and the Foolish People Motif." *Catholic Biblical Quarterly* 44 (1982): 212–24.

Setel, T. Drorah. "Prophets and Pornography: Female Sexual Imagery in Hosea." In *Feminist Interpretation of the Bible,* ed. Letty M. Russell, 86–95. Philadelphia: Westminster, 1985.

Seybold, Klaus. "Das 'Wir' in den Asaph-Psalmen: Spezifische Probleme einer Psalmgruppe." In *Neue Wege der Psalmenforschung: Für Walter Beyerlin,* ed. Klaus Seybold and Erich Zenger, 143–55. Freiburg, Germany: Herder, 1994.

Sharon, Diane M. "Some Results of a Structural Analysis of the Story of Judah and Tamar." *Journal for the Study of the Old Testament* 29 (2005): 289–318.

Shepherd, Tom. *Markan Sandwich Stories: Narration, Definition, and Function.* Berrien Springs, Mich.: Andrews University Press, 1993.

———. "The Narrative Function of Markan Intercalation." *New Testament Studies* 41 (1995): 522–40.

Sherwood, Aaron. "A Leader's Misleading and a Prostitute's Profession: A Re-examination of Joshua 2." *Journal of the Study of the Old Testament* 31 (2006): 43–61.

Sherwood, Yvonne. *A Biblical Text and Its Afterlives: The Survival of Jonah in Western Culture.* Cambridge: Cambridge University Press, 2000.

———. "Boxing Gomer: Controlling the Deviant Woman in Hosea 1–3." In *The Feminist Companion to the Latter Prophets,* ed. Athalya Brenner, 101–25. Sheffield, UK: Sheffield Academic Press, 1995.

———. "Of Fruit and Corpses and Wordplay Visions: Picturing Amos 8.1–3." *Journal for the Study of the Old Testament* 92 (2001): 5–27.

———. *The Prostitute and the Prophet: Hosea's Marriage in Literary-Theoretical Perspective.* Journal for the Study of the Old Testament Supplement Series 212/Gender, Culture, Theory 2. Sheffield, UK: Sheffield Academic Press, 1996.

Shevitz, Daniel R. "Joseph: A Study in Assimilation and Power." *Tikkun* 8 (1993): 51–73.

Simon, Uriel. *Jonah.* JPS Bible Commentary. Philadelphia: Jewish Publication Society, 1999.

Singer, Linda. *Erotic Warfare: Sexual Theory and Politics in the Age of Epidemic.* Ed. and introd. Judith Butler and Maureen MacGrogan. New York: Routledge, 1993.

Sleeman, Matthew. "Mark, the Temple and Space: A Geographer's Response." *Biblical Interpretation* 15 (2007): 338–49.

Smith, Carol. "Biblical Perspectives on Power." *Journal for the Study of the Old Testament* 93 (2001): 93–110.

Smith, Mark S. *The Early History of God: Yahweh and the Other Deities in Ancient Israel.* San Francisco: Harper and Row, 1990.

Smith, Ruth L. "Morals and Their Ironies." *Journal of Religious Ethics* 26 (1998): 367–88.

Smith-Christopher, Daniel. "Prayers and Dreams: Power and Diaspora Identities in the Social Setting of the Daniel Tales." In *The Book of Daniel: Composition and Reception,* ed. John J. Collins and Peter W. Flint, 266–90. Leiden, Neth.: Brill, 2001.

Snyman, S. D. "A Note on Ashdod and Egypt in Amos III 9." *Vetus Testamentum* 44 (1994): 559–62.

Soja, Edward W. *Thirdspace: Journeys to Los Angeles and Other Real-and-Imagined Places.* Oxford: Blackwell, 1996.

Sommer, Benjamin D. *A Prophet Reads Scripture: Allusion in Isaiah 40–66.* Stanford, Calif.: Stanford University Press, 1998.

Spangenberg, Izak J. J. "A Century of Wrestling with Qohelet: The Research History of the Book Illustrated with a Discussion of Qoh 4,17–5,6." In *Qohelet in the Context of Wisdom,* ed. A. Schoors, 61–91. Leuven, Belgium: Leuven University Press, 1998.

———. "Irony in the Book of Qohelet." *Journal for the Study of the Old Testament* 72 (1996): 57–69.

Spero, Shubert. "Multiplicity of Meaning as a Device in Biblical Narrative." *Judaism* 34 (1985): 462–73.

Starbuck, Scott R. A. *Court Oracles in the Psalms: The So-Called Royal Psalms in Their Ancient Near Eastern Context.* Atlanta, Ga.: Scholars Press, 1999.

Sternberg, Meir. "Biblical Poetics and Sexual Politics: From Reading to Counter-Reading." *Journal of Biblical Literature* 111 (1992): 463–88.

———. *Hebrews between Cultures: Group Portraits and National Literature.* Bloomington: Indiana University Press, 1998.

———. *The Poetics of Biblical Narrative: Ideological Literature and the Drama of Reading.* Bloomington: Indiana University Press, 1985.

———. "Time and Space in Biblical (Hi)story Telling: The Grand Chronology." In *The Book and the Text: The Bible and Literary Theory,* ed. Regina M. Schwartz, 81–145. Oxford: Basil Blackwell, 1990.

Steymans, Hans Ulrich. "Traces of Liturgies in the Psalter: The Communal Laments, Psalms 79, 80, 83, and 89 in Context." In *Psalms and Liturgy,* ed. Dirk J. Human and Cas J. A. Vos, 168–234. Journal for the Study of the Old Testament Supplement Series 410. London: T & T Clark, 2005.

Stone, Ken. *Sex, Honor and Power in the Deuteronomistic History.* Journal for the Study of the Old Testament Supplement Series 234. Sheffield, UK: Sheffield Academic Press, 1996.

Stordalen, Terje. *Echoes of Eden: Genesis 2–3 and Symbolism of the Eden Garden in Biblical Hebrew Literature.* Leuven, Belgium: Peeters, 2000.

Stringfellow, Frank. "Irony and Ideals in *Gulliver's Travels.*" In *Critical Essays on Jonathan Swift,* ed. Frank Palmeri, 91–103. New York: G. K. Hall, 1992.

Tarlin, Jan William. "Tamar's Veil: Ideology at the Entrance to Enaim." In *Culture, Entertainment and the Bible,* ed. George Aichele, 174–81. Journal for the Study of the Old Testament Supplement Series 309. Sheffield, UK: Sheffield Academic Press, 2000.

———. "Utopia and Pornography in Ezekiel: Violence, Hope, and the Shattered Male Subject." In *Reading Bibles, Writing Bodies: Identity and The Book,* ed. Timothy K. Beal and David M. Gunn, 175–83. New York: Routledge, 1997.

Thirlwall, Connop. "On the Irony of Sophocles." *Philological Museum* 1–2 (1833): 483–537.

Thompson, Michael E. W. "The Mission of Jonah." *Expository Times* 105 (1994): 233–36.

Thomson, J. A. K. *Irony: An Historical Introduction.* Cambridge, Mass.: Harvard University Press, 1927.

Towner, W. Sibley. *Genesis.* Westminster Bible Companion. Louisville, Ky.: Westminster John Knox, 2001.

Treloar, Richard. "The Hermeneutics of Textual Exile: Comparing Rabbinic and Poststructuralist Readings of Esther." *Pacifica* 14 (2001): 31–54.

Trible, Phyllis. *Rhetorical Criticism: Context, Method, and the Book of Jonah.* Minneapolis, Minn.: Fortress, 1994.

Van Dijk-Hemmes, Fokkelien. "The Metaphorization of Woman in Prophetic Speech: An Analysis of Ezekiel 23." In *On Gendering Texts: Female and Male Voices in the Hebrew Bible,* ed. Athalya Brenner and van Dijk-Hemmes, 167–76. Leiden, Neth.: Brill, 1993.

Van Oyen, Geert. "Intercalation and Irony in the Gospel of Mark." In *The Four Gospels 1992: Festschrift Frans Neirynck,* ed. F. Van Segbroeck, et al., 2:949–74. Leuven, Belgium: Leuven University Press, 1992.

Van Seters, John. *Abraham in History and Tradition.* New Haven, Conn.: Yale University Press, 1975.

———. "From Faithful Prophet to Villain: Observations on the Tradition History of the Balaam Story." In *A Biblical Itinerary: In Search of Method, Form and Content: Essays in Honor of George W. Coats,* ed. Eugene E. Carpenter, 126–32. Journal for the Study of the Old Testament Supplement Series 240. Sheffield, UK: Sheffield Academic Press, 1997.

———. *The Life of Moses: The Yahwist as Historian in Exodus—Numbers.* Louisville, Ky.: Westminster/John Knox, 1994.

Van Wijk-Bos, Johanna W. H. *Ezra, Nehemiah, and Esther.* Westminster Bible Companion. Louisville, Ky.: Westminster John Knox, 1998.

Van Wolde, Ellen. "Texts in Dialogue with Texts: Intertextuality in the Ruth and Tamar Narratives." *Biblical Interpretation* 5 (1997): 1–28.

Verheij, Adrian. "Paradise Retried: On Qohelet 2.4–6." *Journal for the Study of the Old Testament* 50 (1991): 113–15.

Vermès, Géza, ed. and trans. *The Complete Dead Sea Scrolls in English.* New York: Allen Lane/Penguin Press, 1997.

Vervenne, Marc. "Genesis 1,1–2,4: The Compositional Texture of the Priestly Overture to the Pentateuch." In *Studies in the Book of Genesis,* ed. A. Wénin, 35–79. Leuven, Belgium: Leuven University Press, 2001.

Waltke, Bruce K. *The Book of Proverbs, Chapter 1–15.* New International Commentary on the Old Testament. Grand Rapids, Mich.: Eerdmans, 2004.

———. *A Commentary on Micah.* Grand Rapids, Mich.: Eerdmans, 2007.

Ward, Graham. "A Postmodern Version of Paradise." *Journal for the Study of the Old Testament* 65 (1995): 3–12.

Webb, Stephen H. "Theological Reflections on the Hyperbolic Imagination." In *Rhetorical Invention and Religious Inquiry: New Perspectives,* ed. Walter Jost and Wendy Olmsted, 279–99. New Haven, Conn.: Yale University Press, 2000.

Weeks, Stuart. "Whose Words? Qoheleth, Hosea and Attribution in Biblical Literature." In *New Heaven and New Earth: Prophecy and the Millennium,* ed. P. J. Harland and C. T. R. Hayward, 151–70. Leiden, Neth.: Brill, 1999.

Weems, Renita J. "Gomer: Victim of Violence or Victim of Metaphor?" *Semeia* 47 (1989): 87–104.

Weinstein, James M. "Zaphenath-paneah." In *Harper's Bible Dictionary.* San Francisco: HarperCollins, 1985.

Weisberg, Dvora E. "The Widow of Our Discontent: Levirate Marriage in the Bible and Ancient Israel." *Journal for the Study of the Old Testament* 28 (2004): 403–29.

Weisman, Ze'ev. *Political Satire in the Bible.* Atlanta, Ga.: Scholars Press, 1998.

Westbrook, Deeanne. "Paradise and Paradox." In *Mappings of the Biblical Terrain: The Bible as Text,* ed. Vincent L. Tollers and John Maier, 121–33. Lewisburg, Pa.: Bucknell University Press, 1990.

Wevers, John William. "The Balaam Narrative according to the Septuagint." In

Lectures et Relectures de la Bible: Festschrift P.-M. Bogaert, ed. J.-M. Auwers and A. Wénin, 133–44. Leuven, Belgium: Leuven University Press, 1999.

Whedbee, William. "The Comedy of Job." *Semeia* 7 (1977): 1–39. Reprinted in *On Humour and the Comic in the Hebrew Bible,* ed. Yehuda T. Radday and Athalya Brenner, 217–49. Sheffield, UK: Almond Press, 1990.

White, Hugh C. "The Joseph Story: A Narrative Which 'Consumes' Its Content." *Semeia* 31 (1985): 49–69.

Whybray, R. N. *Ecclesiastes.* New Century Bible Commentary. Grand Rapids, Mich.: Eerdmans, 1989.

———. "Qoheleth as a Theologian." In *Qohelet in the Context of Wisdom,* ed. A. Schoors, 239–65. Leuven, Belgium: Leuven University Press, 1998.

Wildavsky, Aaron. "Survival Must Not Be Gained through Sin: The Moral of the Joseph Stories Prefigured through Judah and Tamar." *Journal for the Study of the Old Testament* 62 (1994): 37–48.

Williams, James G. "Irony and Lament: Clues to Prophetic Consciousness." *Semeia* 8 (1977): 51–74.

Williamson, H. G. M. "The Prophet and the Plumb-Line: A Redaction-Critical Study of Amos vii." In *In Quest of the Past: Studies on Israelite Religion, Literature, and Prophetism,* ed. A. S. van der Woude, 101–21. Old Testament Studies 26. Leiden, Neth.: Brill, 1990.

Wills, Lawrence M. *The Jew in the Court of the Foreign King: Ancient Jewish Court Legends.* Harvard Dissertations in Religion 26. Minneapolis, Minn.: Fortress, 1990.

Wilson, Brittany E. "Pugnacious Precursors and the Bearer of Peace: Jael, Judith, and Mary in Luke 1:42." *Catholic Biblical Quarterly* 68 (2006): 436–56.

Wilson, Gerald. "Preknowledge, Anticipation, and the Poetics of Job." *Journal for the Study of the Old Testament* 30 (2005): 243–56.

———. "The Use of Royal Psalms at the 'Seams' of the Hebrew Psalter." *Journal for the Study of the Old Testament* 35 (1986): 85–94.

Wilson, Robert R. "The Death of the King of Tyre: The Editorial History of Ezekiel 28." In *Love and Death in the Ancient Near East: Essays in Honor of Marvin H. Pope,* ed. John H. Marks and Robert M. Good, 211–18. Guilford, Conn.: Four Quarters, 1987.

———. *Prophecy and Society in Ancient Israel.* Philadelphia: Fortress, 1980.

Wolff, Hans Walter. *Joel and Amos.* Trans. Waldemar Janzen, S. Dean McBride Jr., and Charles Muenchow. Hermeneia. Philadelphia: Fortress, 1977.

Wood, Joyce Rilett. "Tragic and Comic Forms in Amos." *Biblical Interpretation* 6 (1998): 20–48.

Yee, Gale A. "By the Hand of a Woman: The Metaphor of the Woman Warrior in Judges 4." *Semeia* 61 (1993): 99–132.

———. "Gender, Class, and the Social-Scientific Study of Genesis 2–3." *Semeia* 87 (1999): 177–92.

———. *Poor Banished Children of Eve: Woman as Evil in the Hebrew Bible.* Minneapolis, Minn.: Fortress, 2003.

Zakovitch, Yair. "Humor and Theology or the Successful Failure of Israelite Intelligence: A Literary-Folkloric Approach to Joshua 2." In *Text and Tradition: The Hebrew Bible and Folklore,* ed. Susan Niditch, 75–98. Atlanta, Ga.: Scholars Press, 1990.

Zuckerman, Bruce. *Job the Silent: A Study in Historical Counterpoint.* New York: Oxford, 1991.

INDEX

CAROLYN J. SHARP's research explores the composition, redaction, and rhetoric of Hebrew Scripture texts. She has examined the representation of Hebrew Bible traditions in the Septuagint and the Dead Sea Scrolls, urged the creation of an Old Testament theology shaped by the notion of diaspora identity, and explored the potential of biblical hermeneutics to address contemporary ecclesial debates. Sharp's first book, *Prophecy and Ideology in Jeremiah,* analyzes theological and political debates that animate the prose of the Book of Jeremiah.